INDIAN POLITICAL PARTIES ANNUAL, 2006

INDIAN POLITIAL PARTIES ANNUAL, 2006

PART III

CHRONOLOGY OF EVENTS

(1 DECEMBER 2005 to 31 MARCH 2006)

Dr. Mahendra Gaur

Publications

KALPAZ PUBLICATIONS

Delhi - 110052

Indian Political Parties Annual, 2006

ISBN : 81-7835-539-6 (Set)
ISBN : 81-7835-542-6 (Part III)

Published in 2006 in India by
Kalpaz Publications
C-30, Satyawati Nagar,
Delhi - 110052
e-mail : kalpaz@hotmail.com

Printed at : Salasar Imaging System, Delhi

INDIAN POLITICAL PARTIES ANNUAL, 2006

PART III

01-12-2005

(4616) Hyderabad : Telugu Desam President, N. Chandrababu Naidu has lamented declining public investment in agriculture since mid-nineties.

(4617) Devarapalli (Vizag Dt.) : Houses constructed for poor tribals in Devarapalli are in a dilapidated condition and when the beneficiaries approached the MRO, he 'advised' them to sleep in the open. The tribals poured out their woes to the CPI (M) leaders who visited them on Wednesday as part of the ongoing 'Sadhana Yatra' seeking integrated development of Visakhapatnam district.

(4618) New Delhi : Under intense pressure from his party colleagues, Telangana Rashtra Samithi president and Union Minister K. Chandrasekhara Rao on Wednesday made a public appeal to dissidents that differences could be sorted through discussions.

(4619) Hyderabad : Telugu Desam Party leaders from Telangana have criticised the Andhra Pradesh Government for seeking Central funds for irrigation projects in the region while taking up projects in other regions with State funds.

(4620) Mumbai : The Shiv Sena is making efforts to placate Raj Thackeray who resigned from his posts in the party last Sunday. Several MLAs led by Leader of the Opposition Ramdas Kadam met Raj at his residence on Wednesday morning. Mr. Kadam said he would meet Raj again on Thursday evening.

(4621) New Delhi : The Bharatiya Janata Party on Wednesday got ready to expel its recently appointed general secretary, Uma Bharti.

(4622) Varanasi: BJP workers on Wednesday set ablaze three railway stations, a power sub-station and several houses in eastern Uttar Pradesh in protest against the killing of BJP legislator Krishnanand Rai.

(4623) Karur : Work on repairing the damaged portion of the new bridge across the Amaravathy river here has come to a grinding halt, following the Chief Minister, Jayalalithaa, ordering a probe into the issue. Meanwhile, the Dravida Munnetra Kazhagam has joined issue with the Chief Minister over charges of corruption.

(4624) Hyderabad : Summons were issued to Telugu Desam Party president and former Chief Minister N. Chandrababu Naidu to appear before the designated court on December 15 in connection with the allotment of land to a sports management committee.

(4625) Bhopal : Suspended Bharatiya Janata Party leader Uma Bharti said on Wednesday that the former Prime Minister, Atal Bihari Vajpayee, party president L.K. Advani and senior leader Jaswant Singh were like her parents.

(4626) New Delhi : The killing of Bharatiya Janata Party MLA Krishnand Rai and his security guards in Ghazipur district in Uttar Pradesh rocked Parliament on Wednesday.

(4627) Bangalore: The Congress on Wednesday released an election manifesto for the coming panchayat elections which promises a host of schemes and facilities for people in rural areas.

(4628) New Delhi: The Maharashtra-Karnataka boundary dispute had its echo in the Lok Sabha for the second day on Wednesday with Shiv Sena members making a strong demand for Central intervention in the wake of the supersession of the Belgaum City Corporation by the Karnataka Government.

(4629) Kochi : Kerala Pradesh Congress Committee (KPCC) general secretary M.I. Shanavaz, reiterating on Wednesday the Congress allegation that K. Karunakaran facilitated a 'vote purchase' from the Bharatiya Janata Party (BJP) in the Thiruvananthapuram byelection, said that the Democratic Indira Congress (Karunakaran) leader was a veteran at this.

(4630) Thiruvananthapuram : State secretary of the CPI(M) Pinarayi Vijayan has given sufficient hints that his party is favourably disposed towards taking the Democratic Indira Congress (Karunakaran) on board the Opposition Left Democratic Front (LDF) either as a constituent or an ally.

(4631) Thiruvananthapuram : Kerala secretary of the CPI(M) Pinarayi Vijayan has given sufficient hints that his party is favourably disposed towards taking the Democratic Indira Congress (Karunakaran) on board the Opposition Left Democratic Front (LDF) either as a constituent or an ally.

(4632) Bhopal : The former Madhya Pradesh Chief Minister, Uma Bharti, said on Wednesday that she would "live and die" for the Bharatiya Janata Party.

(4633) New Delhi : Amid a walkout by Bharatiya Janata Party members, Union Minister for Petroleum and Natural Gas Mani Shankar Aiyar assured the Lok Sabha on Wednesday that new liquefied petroleum gas (LPG) connections would be released from December 1, and the gas supply would stabilise soon.

(4634) New Delhi : The Capital's private power distribution companies will be brought under the Right to Information Act and people will be able to seek all information about their working after filing an application. This assurance was given by the Chief Information Commissioner, Wajahat Habibullah, to a delegation led by former Union Minister Vijay Goel on Wednesday.

(4635) Guwahati : The Assam Assembly on Wednesday witnessed uproarious scenes over the continued violence in Karbi Anglong with the Opposition Asom Gana Parishad (AGP) and its breakaway faction AGP (Progressive) demanding a clarification on a senior Minister's statement.

(4636) Chennai : Marumalarchi Dravida Munnetra Kazhagam general secretary Vaiko met Union Textiles Minister Shankarsinh Vaghela on Tuesday and requested him not to privatise two NTC-owned Mills in Coimbatore - Sharada Mills and Coimbatore Spinning and Weaving Mills. A press note said Mr. Vaiko pointed out that most of the workers were aged between 40 and 50. Their future was at stake.

02-12-2005

(4637) Hyderabad : Telugu Desam president N. Chandrababu Naidu on Thursday said the Government was not doing enough to raise awareness and prevent HIV/AIDS, as indicated by the rising incidence in the State.

(4638) Hyderabad : Telugu Desam Party President N. Chandrababu Naidu has received a notice from the Anti-Corruption Bureau's designated court in the case relating to the allotment of land to IMG Sports Academy. The party spokesman has criticised the way the notice was served at 8.30 p.m.

(4639) Hyderabad : The Telangana Rashtra Samithi has decided to boycott the golden jubilee celebrations of the AP Legislative Assembly on December 3. It will observe it as protest day on the grounds that the Telangana region had suffered on all fronts in the last five decades after the formation of a separate Andhra Pradesh State.

(4640) Kadapa : CPI(M) State Secretariat member and Kurnool MLA M.A. Gafoor on Thursday demanded that the State Government keep G.O. 170 in abeyance and convene an all-party meeting to infuse confidence among leaders and people of other regions that their ayacut interests would be safeguarded.

(4641) Palakkad : Communist Party of India (Marxist) general secretary Prakash Karat on Thursday warned the Manmohan Singh Government that the Left parties would vote against the Banking Act Amendment Bill and the Pension Bill in Parliament.

(4642) Mangalore : The Janata Dal (Secular), which is attempting to establish a base in Dakshina Kannada, is making all efforts to bag the maximum number of seats in the coming elections to the taluk and zilla panchayats. In some places it has made seat adjustments with the Communist Party of India (Marxist) and the Communist Party of India.

(4643) Chikmagalur : The former Prime Minister and President of the Janata Dal (Secular) H.D. Deve Gowda has reiterated that the internal reservation system will be introduced if his party is elected to power in the elections to zilla and taluk panchayats.

(4644) Kozhikode : Leader of the Opposition V.S. Achuthanandan has said it will not be fair for the State Government to treat the association formed by policemen as a threat to discipline in the force even when it is viewed in the context of the row that has broken out between it and the Inspector-General of Police T.P. Senkumar over the recent police action at M.G. College in Thiruvananthapuram.

(4645) Thiruvananthapuram : It is not just the CPI(M) that is putting on its collective thinking cap to evolve a new development paradigm for the State. The CPI too is planning to do so through a major three-day brainstorming exercise on governance and development.

(4646) Thiruvananthapuram: The Democratic Indira Congress (Karunakaran) has started the process of conducting its organisational elections. In the first round, the party has announced the appointments of District Returning Officers, who would, in consultation with the respective district committee, appoint the returning officers for the election of booth, mandalam and block committees and office-bearers, DIC(K) State Election Authority K.R. Kurup said here in a statement. DIC(K) president K. Muraleedharan and K. Karunakaran had promised that their party would conduct organisational polls.

(4647) Thiruvananthapuram : Communist Party of India (Marxist) State secretary Pinarayi Vijayan has alleged that the Inspector-General of Police T.P. Senkumar's intervention during a police action at M.G. College here and his decision to suspend a police constable on the spot were part of the Government's bid to appease the Rashtriya Swayamsevak Sangh (RSS).

(4648) New Delhi : The Opposition on Friday attacked the Government for its "soft attitude" towards terrorists and the repeal of the Prevention of Terrorism Act (POTA). This had triggered recent incidents of violence including the pre-Diwali blasts in Delhi, terrorist attacks in Jammu and Kashmir and naxalite attacks in Jehanabad and Giridih.

(4649) Palakkad : CPI(M) general secretary Prakash Karat said on Thursday that if tax arrears were collected from the rich that would be enough to meet the funds for the development of infrastructure, roads, investment in agriculture, rural employment generation etc.

(4650) Guwahati : The Congress Government in Assam on Thursday defeated by voice vote an Opposition sponsored no-confidence motion alleging breakdown of law and order situation in the State and the State Government's failure to control the ethnic violence in Karbi Anglong.

(4651) New Delhi : The Congress on Thursday said that some parties were trying to make political capital out of the killing of Border Roads Organisation (BRO) employee Ramankutty Maniappan in Afghanistan and said that the Governments of both countries did their best to secure his release.

(4652) New Delhi : The Samajwadi Party on Thursday protested in the Rajya Sabha the withdrawal of an invitation to film actor Amitabh Bachchan-who is recuperating after a surgery in a Mumbai hospital-to be the Chief Guest at the ongoing International Film Festival of India (IFFI) in Goa.

(4653) Panaji : Goa Pradesh Congress Committee president Ravi Naik has decided to lead a delegation to New Delhi to meet the Central leaders, including Prime Minister Manmohan Singh, to resolve the controversy regarding the likely closure of Dabolim airport for civilian traffic once the proposed Mopa airport was commissioned.

(4654) Lucknow : One of the 10 accused in the sensational killing of BJP legislator Krishnanand Rai on Thursday surrendered in a Ghazipur court.

(4655) Villupuram : Pattali Makkal Katchi founder S. Ramadoss has urged the Jayalalithaa Government not to act in isolation, but to constitute district and State-level committees headed by Members of Parliament for distributing relief to the flood-affected.

03-12-2005

(4656) Hyderabad : Unfazed by a court notice served on the party president N. Chandrababu Naidu in the allotment of land to IMG Academies Bharata, the Telugu Desam has dared the Government to go ahead with the enquiry.

(4657) Hyderabad : The Congress Legislature Party (CLP) has refuted the Telugu Desam Party's claim that the Government was burdening people with taxes.

(4658) Palakkad : General secretary of the Communist Party of India (Marxist) Prakash Karat said on Friday that the party Polit Bureau would take a final decision on the issue of an alliance between the Left Democratic Front (LDF) and the Democratic Indira Congress (Karunakaran) before the next Assembly elections in Kerala.

(4659) New Delhi : The Left parties on Friday joined the government in dismissing the Opposition demand for the resignation of Congress president Sonia Gandhi as Chairperson of the National Advisory Council (NAC), even as fresh claims on the Volcker Report added to the controversy just days after it quietened following discussions in both Houses of Parliament.

(4660) Mangalore : Dakshina Kannada will prove to be the litmus test for the Congress in the zilla and taluk panchayat elections. If its archrival BJP were going to have its way in the elections, it would be the result of complete neglect of the rural sector especially in Dakshina Kannada by the Government.

(4661) Panaji : A meeting of the State Executive Committee of the Bharatiya Janata Party (BJP) on Friday lambasted the Congress-led coalition Government in the State as "inefficient, directionless and beset with too many contradictions and confusion for it to deliver goods to the people."

(4662) Thiruvananthapuram : KPCC media cell convener M. M. Hassan on Friday alleged that the RSS had transferred its votes to the LDF candidate in the recent Thiruvananthapuram Lok Sabha byelection in order to weaken the Congress prior to the Assembly elections due in a few months time.

(4663) Thiruvananthapuram : The storm in the State unit of the BJP following the steep reduction in its vote share in the Thiruvananthapuram byelection appears to be blowing over.

(4664) Kozhikode : BJP Kerala State unit president P. S. Sreedharan Pillai on Friday announced withdrawal of his resignation from the party post.

(4665) New Delhi : The National Campaign for People's Right to Information (NCPRI) has condemned the Government's effort to limit the scope of the Right to Information (RTI) Act. In a press statement issued on Friday, Aruna Roy and Shekhar Singh on behalf of NCPRI have opposed the Government's attempt "to further restrict access to various types of file notings."

(4666) Bhopal : After initially softening her stand, suspended Bharatiya Janata Party leader Uma Bharti has once again adopted a tough posture alleging that she has been betrayed and exploited by some within the party.

(4667) Kolkata: The Left parties will oppose any move towards centralisation of power, senior member of the Polit Bureau of the Communist Party of India (Marxist), Jyoti Basu, said here on Friday.

(4668) New Delhi: The Supreme Court on Friday issued notice to the Central Bureau of Investigation on two special leave petitions (SLPs) filed by Railway Minister Lalu Prasad and his wife Rabri Devi challenging the validity of the Bihar Governor's order according it sanction to prosecute them in disproportionate assets cases.

(4669) New Delhi : Parliament was paralysed on Friday on the Volcker issue following fresh disclosures with the Opposition demanding the resignation of Sonia Gandhi as chairperson of the National Advisory Council, and the arrest of Union Minister Natwar Singh.

(4670) Patna : The Bihar Assembly was adjourned twice on Friday amid commotion, with the Rashtriya Janata Dal demanding the dismissal of two Ministers for their alleged involvement in criminal cases.

(4671) Varanasi : Bharatiya Janata Party president L. K. Advani will launch a Statewide 'Nyay Yatra' from here on December 6, seeking justice to the family of party MLA from Uttar Pradesh Krishnanand Rai who was murdered last Tuesday along with seven others in Ghazipur district.

(4672) Bhubaneswar : Opposition members walked out of the Orissa Assembly on Friday afternoon after Chief Minister Naveen Patnaik refused to hand over the tender fixing scam probe to the Central Bureau of Investigation.

04-12-2005

(4673) Hyderabad : The loyal and rebel MLAs of TRS avoided seeing eye to eye in a protest demonstration at the Telangana Martyrs Memorial after boycotting the golden jubilee celebrations of the Assembly . The demonstration was also marked by exchange of words . Rebel MLA B. Shara Rani even threw away a letter containing a party whip asking the legislators not to attend the golden jubilee seminar where Lok Sabha Speaker Somnath Chatterjee was the chief guest. Earlier, the loyal and rebel MLAs went separately to the memorial although they took a pledge there to fight for separate Telangana collectively. Union Minister of State for Rural Development A. Narendra led the first group.

(4674) Hyderabad : The special session of the Andhra Pradesh Legislative Assembly to commemorate its golden jubilee on Saturday saw Chief Minister Y.S. Rajasekhara Reddy renewing his call to naxalites to return to the negotiating table.

(4675) New Delhi : Senior BJP leaders on Saturday made light of the charge by the former Madhya Pradesh Chief Minister, Uma Bharati, that the party did not give adequate representation to backward classes, Scheduled Castes and Dalits.

(4676) Mysore : Echoing public resentment against the increase in power tariff, described as inevitable by Karnataka Power Transmission Corporation Ltd. (KPTCL), the city unit of the Bharatiya Janata Party (BJP) has demanded that the Government bring out a White Paper on the performance of the power sector.

(4677) Thiruvananthapuram : Leader of the Opposition V.S. Achuthanandan has accused the Revenue Minister K.M. Mani of trying to alienate large tracts of forest land in the State to favour encroachers and big estate owners.

(4678) New Delhi : P. Shiv Shankar, who along with Natwar Singh was part of the Congress delegation which visited Iraq in January 2001, said the Minister's son, Jagat Singh, and businessman Andaleeb Sehgal travelled with them up to Jordan.

(4679) Kolkata : With the Assembly elections due next year, the Congress leadership in West Bengal, riven by factionalism, appears determined to make last month's arrest of party MP Adhir Chowdhury, charged with double murder, a rallying issue for closing ranks.

(4680) New Delhi : The Communist Party of India (Marxist) on Saturday reiterated its demand that the Government should ensure that all relevant material and information in regard to the oil-for-food contracts was made available to Justice R.S. Pathak Inquiry Authority and that investigation was "expanded to cover all the beneficiaries."

(4681) Jaipur : Bharatiya Janata Party president L.K. Advani on Saturday accused "some political parties" in the country of doing politics with money from foreign countries. The `revelations' of the Volcker Committee were no ordinary corruption charges, he said.

(4682) Raisen (Madhya Pradesh) : Suspended BJP leader Uma Bharti has decided to reply to the party's show cause notice at a public meeting here on Sunday, her loyalist and former Madhya Pradesh Minister Sunil Nayak said on Saturday.

(4683) Jaipur : The Bharatiya Janata Party's national women's convention, titled "matrushakti sammelan" here on Saturday harped on the pending Women's Reservation Bill and blamed the ruling United Progressive Alliance Government at the Centre for the delay in its passage.

(4684) New Delhi : In a move to step up pressure on the Government ahead of the crucial World Trade Organisational meeting at Hong Kong this month, the Left and other parties have asserted that they would demand a discussion in Parliament.

(4685) Pondicherry : Secretary of the Pondicherry State committee of the Communist Party of India (CPI) N.Kalainathan MLA has expressed strong protest against what he said "dubious stand the ruling Congress is adopting" on the matter of delimitation of Assembly constituencies for the forthcoming polls. (Assembly polls are due here in 2006).

(4686) Lucknow : Brother of slain BJP MLA Krishnanand Rai, Brijesh Rai, on Friday met Uttar Pradesh Chief Minister Mulayam Singh Yadav and demanded a CBI probe into the daylight killing.

(4687) Chennai : Marumalarchi Dravida Munnetra Kazagam general secretary Vaiko has charged that the Chief Minister had "failed in her responsibility" in executing speedy flood relief works in the State.

05-12-2005

(4688) Hyderabad : The Congress Legislature Party has decided to adopt a two-pronged strategy to counter the Opposition onslaught during the ongoing winter session of the Assembly. An executive meeting of the CLP, presided over by Chief Minister Y.S. Rajasekhara Reddy here on Sunday, planned to ensure proper conduct of the House while asking members to be fully geared to meet any challenge thrown by the main Opposition - Telugu Desam Party.

(4689) Hyderabad : A protest meeting organised by the MIM on Sunday wanted reconstruction of Babri masjid at the same place where it was demolished in Ayodhya. A large number of people attended the public meeting held at Hashim grounds, Mallepally. Majlis president Sultan Salahuddin Owaisi blamed former Prime Minister P.V. Narasimha Rao for the tragedy.

(4690) Karimnagar : BJP senior leader and former Union Minister Ch. Vidyasagar Rao has alleged that the Congress had once again betrayed the Telangana region by not fulfilling its election promise of formation of separate Telangana State.

(4691) New Delhi : Minister without portfolio Natwar Singh was dropped from the Congress Working Committee (now being called Congress Steering Committee). This decision was taken after midnight on Sunday. Congress general secretary Ambika Soni made the announcement here.

(4692) Thiruvananthapuram : Leader of the Opposition V.S. Achuthanandan on Sunday said that the 2006-07 annual Plan, finalised by the Cabinet on Saturday, will retard development in crucial sectors of the State economy.

(4693) London : Janata Party president Subramanian Swamy has called for "new forms of Hindu consolidation," saying that Hinduism is "under siege."

(4694) Belgaum : The Congress as well as Janata Dal (Secular) have become unpopular in the district because of their own actions, and yet the Congress is our main rival in the panchayat elections, BJP district unit President Eranna Kadadi and party's Lok Sabha member Suresh C. Angadi have said.

(4695) Kozhikode : Democratic Indira Congress-Karunakaran (DIC-K) State president K. Muraleedharan, on Sunday, expressed the aspiration of the fledgling party to join the Left Democratic Front (LDF), led by the Communist Party of India-Marxist (CPI-M).

(4696) New Delhi : Even as the Minister without portfolio, Natwar Singh, on Sunday refused to quit the Union Council of Ministers as it would look like an "admission of guilt" over the Volcker controversy, Communist Party of India (CPI) leader A. B. Bardhan said the BJP's demand for UPA chairperson Sonia Gandhi's resignation was "funny."

(4697) New Delhi : A parting of ways between the Bharatiya Janata Party and the former Madhya Pradesh Chief Minister Uma Bharti was strongly indicated here on Sunday, with Ms. Bharti replying to the party's notice and launching a direct attack on the central leadership "for straying away from the ideological path laid down by the BJP's "guru" Deendayal Upadhyaya.

(4698) Jaipur : All-India Congress Committee spokesman Abhishek Singhvi on Sunday said the fresh allegations against Union Minister Natwar Singh had not "in principle" changed the substance of the Volcker controversy, which was being probed by a Commission of Inquiry.

(4699) Jammu : The Jammu and Kashmir National Panthers Party chief Bhim Singh alleged on Sunday that in the garb of the Volcker issue foreign forces were out to destabilise the United Progressive Alliance Government. Mr. Bhim Singh was named a 'non-contractual beneficiary' in Volcker Committee Report on Iraq's Oil-for-Food programme.He said the game was clear, first to oust Natwar Singh and then target Congress president Sonia Gandhi.People should see through this, he told The Hindu .

(4700) Nedumbassery : Congress MP Vayalar Ravi on Sunday sought an investigation on whether the former Petroleum Minister, Ram Naik, had accepted commission from business groups for securing oil coupons from the Iraqi regime.

(4701) Hyderabad : The former Union Minister, P. Shiv Shankar, who was a member of the delegation which visited Iraq in 2001, on Sunday denied the reported attribution to him that Natwar Singh's son Jagat Singh and his cousin Andaleeb Sehgal were present during the official meeting with the Iraqi authorities.

(4702) Amethi : Congress president Sonia Gandhi on Sunday said she was concerned about the state of affairs in Uttar Pradesh and sought people's support for a change.

(4703) Raisen (Madhya Pradesh) : Suspended Bharatiya Janata Party leader Uma Bharti announced at a public rally here on Sunday that she would not tender an apology in response to the notice served on her. She wanted party president L.K. Advani and the former Prime Minister, Atal Bihari Vajpayee, to break their silence and purge the party of those who are "far removed from the grass-root level party workers and have hijacked the BJP."

(4704) New Delhi : The BJP Delhi Pradesh president, Harsh Vardhan, has demanded that the Delhi Government and the Municipal Corporation of Delhi recover arrears of Rs 4,500 crore in property tax from various Government departments and spend the amount on improvement of infrastructure in Delhi.

(4705) New Delhi : A delegation of Bharatiya Janata Party's Delhi Assembly office-bearers led by the Leader of Opposition, Jagdish Mukhi, met the Union Urban Development Minister, Jaipal Reddy, at his residence on Sunday and submitted a memorandum demanding the immediate notification of Delhi Master Plan 2021 so that six lakh shops being run in residential areas are not demolished or sealed as per the recent decision of the Supreme Court.

(4706) Lucknow : The BJP will take up the issue of the killing of party MLA Krishnanad Rai in Ghazipur last week in the State Legislature and confront the Mulayam Singh Yadav Government on the poor law and order situation in Uttar Pradesh.

(4707) Chennai : Dravida Munnetra Kazhagam president M. Karunanidhi and senior party functionaries visited the flood affected areas in the city and assured the people all help that the party could render.

(4708) Chennai : The guidelines governing the Calamity Relief Fund (CRF) and National Calamity Contingency Fund (NCCF) should be relaxed for Tamil Nadu, which has been battered by a series of floods, Bharatiya Janata Party demanded on Sunday.

06-12-2005

(4709) Hyderabad : The Communist Party of India (Marxist) Polit Bureau member and MP, Sitaram Yechury, on Monday dismissed the Opposition charge that the party was soft on the Congress in the Volcker issue. It was because of the CPI (M)'s pressure Natwar Singh was relieved of the External Affairs portfolio and investigation ordered into the oil-for-food scam, Mr. Yechury told reporters here.

(4710) Hyderabad : Congress MLAs from Telangana have criticised the Telugu Desam Party's decision to undertake a padayatra from Pranahitha to Chevella from January 20 next and said the decision smacked of hypocrisy.

(4711) Hyderabad : The Congress Legislature Party has decided to back Assembly Speaker, K. R. Suresh Reddy since there was no way the House could deviate from traditions and conventions in conducting its business.

(4712) Hyderabad : In an unprecedented move, the entire Opposition stayed away from the Business Advisory Committee (BAC) meeting convened by Speaker K. R. Suresh Reddy on Monday.

(4713) Hyderabad : CPI(M) Polit Bureau member and MP Sitaram Yechury, has asked the party cadre to be cautious about the designs of the communal elements and forces trying to perpetrate the imperialist policies of the United States.

(4714) Bhopal : After her dismissal from the Bharatiya Janata Party, the former Madhya Pradesh Chief Minister, Uma Bharti, demanded that BJP president L.K. Advani immediately resign as he "disgraced" the party by going to Pakistan and praising its founder Mohammad Ali Jinnah.

(4715) Thiruvananthapuram : The United Democratic Front (UDF) liaison committee on Monday endorsed the Congress party's recommendations to reduce electricity tariff, besides deciding to implement programmes beneficial for the poor and weaker sections of society.

(4716) New Delhi : The Bharatiya Janata Party's Parliamentary Board on Monday expelled Uma Bharti from primary membership on charges of indiscipline and anti-party activities.

(4717) Bidar : The Janata Dal (Secular) has alleged that some well-to-do Congress leaders are trying to contest from constituencies reserved for the economically weaker sections by producing false certificates.

(4718) Mangalore : Mangalore MP and vice-president of the State unit of the Bharatiya Janata Party D.V. Sadananda Gowda has said his party will ask the Election Commission to direct the district administration in the State to ensure fair and free elections in the panchayat elections.

(4719) Udupi : The former Chief Minister M. Veerappa Moily on Monday said that the former Prime Minister and Janata Dal (S) H.D. Deve Gowda was indulging in "blackmail politics" and the people would give him a fitting reply in the zilla and taluk panchayat elections.

(4720) Shiroor (Udupi district) : Union Minister of State for Statistics and Programme Implementation Oscar Fernandes said on Monday that the Bharatiya Janata Party (BJP) is unnecessarily dragging the name of Congress President Sonia Gandhi into the Volcker report controversy.

(4721) Kannur : Leader of the Opposition V. S. Achuthanandan said here on Monday that the Communist Party of India (Marxist) would take an appropriate decision ahead of the next Assembly elections on whether to include the Democratic Indira Congress (Karunakaran) in the Left Democratic Front (LDF).

(4722) New Delhi : The Samajwadi Party on Monday criticised the Congress, named in the Volcker Report in relation to the oil-for-food scam and said Union Minister Natwar Singh should not be made a "scapegoat."

(4723) Guwahati : The former Andhra Pradesh Chief Minister, N. Chandrababu Naidu, on Monday led leaders of regional parties in issuing a call to the people of Assam to dethrone the Congress Government and vote the Asom Gana Parishad (AGP) to power in the May 2006 Assembly elections.

(4724) New Delhi : The Opposition came under attack from the Congress and the Communist Party of India (Marxist) for stalling Parliament on Monday. They charged the Bharatiya Janata Party-led Opposition with "lowering the dignity of and prestige of the institution" and unwillingness to discuss issues of importance.

(4725) New Delhi : The Congress Legislature Party (CLP) will meet on Tuesday to discuss the issue of holding marriages and other functions in farmhouses across the Capital and misuse of residential properties for commercial purposes, issues that are at present before the courts. Interestingly, Delhi Mayor Satbir Singh, MCD House leader Jitendra Jeetu and MCD Standing Committee Chairman Mukesh Goyal will also attend the CLP.

(4726) Raipur : Keeping a distance from BJP's intra-party squabbles and controversies, Chhattisgarh Chief Minister Raman Singh has had a smooth sailing tenure so far as he completes two years in office on December 7. Unlike neighbouring Madhya Pradesh, which saw three BJP Chief Ministers in 24 months, the Raman Singh Government remained stable without even facing any major onslaught from the opposition Congress.

(4727) Pondicherry : The executive committee of the Pradesh Congress Committee has called upon the Pondicherry Government to conduct a proper assessment of the damage caused by the heavy rain in the Union Territory in the last few weeks.

(4728) Pondicherry : Volunteers of the Pondicherry unit of Janata Dal (Secular) led by its president E. Ganesan staged on Monday an eight-hour fast here to urge the Administration to release a white paper containing details of the total contributions mobilised for tsunami relief works in the Union Territory. Mr. Ganesan said that the fast was also aimed at urging the Administration to distribute Rs. 5000 for an acre of land lost in the recent floods in Pondicherry and Karaikal regions, compensation of Rs. 10,000 for each of the houses lost and assistance for the daily wage earners and members of the unorganised sector.

(4729) Lucknow : The ruling Samajwadi Party in Uttar Pradesh on Monday received a setback in Assembly by-polls when the Opposition BSP won both the seats - wresting one and retaining the other.

(4730) Lucknow : Disowning controversial Independent MLA Mukhtar Ansari, the ruling Samajwadi Party in Uttar Pradesh on Monday charged the previous Mayawati and Rajnath Singh governments of having more proximity with criminals.

(4731) Dehra Dun : Forty-one Block Pramukhs belonging to the ruling Congress and 11 of the Bharatiya Janata Party have decided to resign from the primary membership of their respective parties as the present Congress-run government and the erstwhile BJP government had been a mute spectator to the dilution of the 73rd Constitutional Amendment that provides for empowerment of the local bodies.

(4732) Kolkata : The Trinamool Congress and its allies, including the Bharatiya Janata Party, staged a rally here on Monday demanding that the coming Assembly elections in West Bengal be conducted in a "free and fair" manner.

(4733) Chennai : Tamil Nadu Congress committee president G.K. Vasan has appealed to party workers in flood-affected districts in the State to undertake relief works as part of 59th birthday celebrations of party president Sonia Gandhi on December 9.

(4734) Chennai : Pattali Makkal Katchi founder S. Ramadoss on Monday joined issue with Chief Minister Jayalalithaa on Central assistance.

(4735) Tiruchi : The Marumalarchi Dravida Munnetra Kazhagam, which has received petitions from flood-hit people across the State, will forward a statement to the Collectors concerned and the Chief Secretary, drawing their attention to the plight of the affected and for ensuring relief, party general secretary Vaiko said on Monday.

(4736) Tirunelveli : Considering the colossal destruction triggered by the unprecedented torrential rain and consequent floods in 22 districts, including Chennai, Chief Minister Jayalalithaa should meet the Prime Minister Manmohan Singh immediately and explain the extent of damage caused to men and material by the natural calamity, the Communist Party of India (Marxist), has urged.

07-12-2005

(4737) Hyderabad : BJP Vice-President M. Venkaiah Naidu has said there would have been no need for the party to disturb the proceedings of Parliament if Natwar Singh, who was in the eye of a stormcreated by the Volcker report, had resigned from the Union Cabinet earlier.

(4738) Hyderabad : Telugu Desam Party president N. Chandrababu Naidu has favoured strong networking of regional parties in the country.

(4739) Hyderabad : The Telugu Desam Party president N. Chandrababu Naidu has strongly opposed pre-marital sex.

(4740) Hyderabad : A meeting of the Chief Ministers of BJP-ruled States would be held at New Delhi on December 12 to take a final decision on implementation of Value Added Tax (VAT) in these States.

(4741) New Delhi : Accusing the Bhartiya Janata Party-led Opposition of indulging in "parliamentary terrorism," the Communist Party of India on Tuesday criticised the disruption of both Houses for the third consecutive day.

(4742) New Delhi : Union Minister Natwar Singh announced on Tuesday night that he had resigned from the Council of Ministers.

(4743) Nagpur : Shiv Sena MLA Gulabrao Gawande on Tuesday attempted suicide on the floor of the Maharashtra Assembly to express solidarity with debt-ridden farmers. Shocked members and ministers overpowered him. Later, the House suspended him for the rest of the winter session. Also, his entry into the legislature campus was banned.

(4744) Madikeri : The Dharam Singh-led coalition Government is remote-controlled by Congress President Sonia Gandhi and Janata Dal (Secular) President H.D. Deve Gowda, said Bharatiya Janata Party (BJP) State unit President Jagdish Shettar.

(4745) Panaji : At a stormy meeting of the Congress Legislative Party (CLP) held in the presence of the party High Command observer B.K. Hari

Prasad on Tuesday, the party decided to seek the continuation of the Dabolim airport for civilian traffic even after the proposed Mopa airport is commissioned.

(4746) Kottayam : The two splinter groups of Kerala Congress (Secular) should be kept out of the LDF meetings in future.

(4747) Varanasi : On the 13th anniversary day of the demolition of Babri Masjid, Bharatiya Janata Party (BJP) president L.K. Advani launched yet another Hindutva oriented political yatra in the eastern Uttar Pradesh districts of Varanasi and Ghazipur. The initiative titled 'Nyay Yatra' has the stated objectives of getting justice to the family of slain party MLA Krishnanand Rai and highlighting the "rampant criminalisation of politics" in Uttar Pradesh.

(4748) New Delhi : The Samajwadi Party and the Kaifi Azmi Foundation observed Tuesday as 'Black Day', to mark the 13th anniversary of the demolition of the Babri Masjid by holding public rallies in the capital.

(4749) New Delhi : Terming the demolition of the disputed structure at Ayodhya as a "tragic incident", the former Prime Minister, Atal Bihari Vajpayee, on Tuesday expressed hope that the temple would be built at the Ram Janmasthan (disputed site) with everyone's cooperation.

(4750) Ahmedabad : The Gujarat Congress has complained to the State Election Commission against the Bharatiya Janata Party and Chief Minister Narendra Modi for allegedly violating the model code of conduct. The model code is in force in view of the elections to five Municipal Corporations and four Municipalities in the State.

(4751) New Delhi : The Opposition on Tuesday made it clear that it would not allow Parliament to function till the resignation of Natwar Singh came through. This was decided at a meeting of the National Democratic Alliance leaders on Tuesday morning.

(4752) New Delhi : Faced with a barrage of uncomfortable queries from her own party MLAs on failure of her Government to implement its promises to end the power and water crises in the Capital, Chief Minister Sheila Dikshit on Tuesday announced convening of a Congress Legislature Party meeting on December 17 to discuss these issues.

(4753) New Delhi : Former Union Minister and Bharatiya Janata Party leader Vijay Goel has accused the Delhi Development Authority of flouting all norms of the much talked about Right to Information Act.

(4754) New Delhi : Indicating mounting resentment in the party against her style of functioning, Delhi Chief Minister Sheila Dikshit on Tuesday came under attack from her party MLAs at the Congress Legislature Party meeting that witnessed heated exchanges, allegations of working at the behest of the farmhouse lobby and accusations of deviating from the agenda set by Congress president Sonia Gandhi.

(4755) New Delhi : It is a classic case of public money going down the drain with no one being held accountable. The Rs. 880-crore 140-million-gallons-a-day (MGD) Sonia Vihar water treatment plant seems yet another scandal waiting to happen with even Ministers in the Sheila Dikshit Cabinet now asking questions about the future of the plant.

(4756) New Delhi : The Communist Party of India (Marxist) on Monday demanded that the Government immediately stop the privatisation exercise of the Delhi and Mumbai airports and examine the report by an Airport Authority of India committee suggesting modernisation on a fast-track route.

(4757) Pondicherry : The AICC secretary K B Krishnamoorthy MP who is in charge of the affairs of the Congress in the Union Territory of Pondicherry has called upon the rank and file to face the future challenges united.

(4758) Dehra Dun : A general feeling of despair among the masses in the Garhwal region due to lack of adequate development works over the past four years of Congress rule has sent the party MLAs into a panic.

(4759) Tirunelveli : The workers of Communist Party of India (Marxist) staged a demonstration at Jawahar Grounds in Palayamkottai on Monday against the setting up of a soft drink unit at the SIPCOT Industrial Estate in Gangaikondan near here.

(4760) New Delhi : With their third attempt to raise the flood situation in the State in the Lok Sabha coming to naught, members of the Democratic Progressive Alliance (DPA) in Tamil Nadu staged dharna at Parliament House on Tuesday to protest the disruption of proceedings by the Bharatiya Janata Party-led National Democratic Alliance.

08-12-2005

(4761) Hyderabad : APCC official spokesperson N. Tulasi Reddy has asked the Telugu Desam Party to stop casting aspersions on the CBI for giving a clean chit to Y. S. Jagan Mohan Reddy and J. C. Diwakar Reddy in the murder case of former MLA, Paritala Ravindra.

(4762) Bangalore : Senior leaders of the All-India Progressive Janata Dal (AIPJD), including former Deputy Chief Minister Siddaramaiah and former Union Minister C.M. Ibrahim, have said that their newly revived party will fight the panchayat elections independently although, at the local level, some of its candidates have arrived at an understanding with the Congress.

(4763) Bangalore : The election manifesto of the Janata Dal (Secular) for panchayat elections focusses on measures for farmers and unemployed youth in villages.

(4764) Mangalore : The Dakshina Kannada district committee of Indian Union Muslim League (IUML) has requested President A.P.J. Abdul Kalam to ask the Centre rebuild the Babri Masjid in Ayodhya. It termed the demolition of the mosque on December 6, 1992 a 'black day.'

(4765) Mysore : Even though the Congress enjoyed a mutual understanding with the All-India Progressive Janata Dal (AIPJD) of the former Deputy Chief Minister Siddaramaiah, the two parties had not clinched any seat-sharing arrangement for the zilla and taluk panchayat elections either in Mysore district or elsewhere in the State, claimed the former Minister and Congress leader H. Vishwanath.

(4766) Malappuram : Democratic Indira Congress (Karunakaran) State president K. Muraleedharan has said that his party will accept Bharatiya Janata Party (BJP) leader C.K. Padmanabhan into its fold if the latter gives up the communal policies of the BJP.

(4767) Mumbai : Bharatiya Janata Party general secretary Pramod Mahajan has said that the "impending resignation" of party president L. K. Advani will not be discussed at the BJP's silver jubilee convention in Mumbai later this month.

(4768) New Delhi : Addressing a meeting of the Bharatiya Janata Party's parliamentary wing here on Wednesday, Leader of the Opposition

L.K. Advani claimed "victory" for the Opposition in the matter related to the former External Affairs Minister, Natwar Singh's resignation.

(4769) New Delhi : The Congress on Wednesday demanded a public apology from BJP president L.K. Advani for reportedly terming Prime Minister Manmohan Singh "useless [nikamma]."

(4770) Nagpur : Shiv Sena executive president Uddhav Thackeray on Wednesday said doors of his house are still open for his cousin and dissident party leader Raj Thackeray who quit all the party posts.

(4771) New Delhi : The Communist Party of India (Marxist) on Wednesday reiterated its opposition to allowing foreign direct investment (FDI) in the retail sector as it could jeopardise the livelihood of nearly four crore people.

(4772) New Delhi : Even as business resumed in Parliament on Wednesday after three days of disruption, the Opposition staged a walkout in both Houses demanding the resignation of Congress president Sonia Gandhi as National Advisory Council chairperson over the Volcker Report disclosures.

(4773) New Delhi : "From tomorrow, I shall be writing a book and having a damn good time," said the former External Affairs Minister, Natwar Singh, in his first comments after meeting Prime Minister Manmohan Singh on Wednesday evening.

(4774) New Delhi : Delhi Bharatiya Janata Partry president Harsh Vardhan has called upon the Delhi Government to frame a strict and categorical trade, commerce and housing policy and implement it within a fixed time frame to save the Capital from becoming a slum.

(4775) Varanasi (UP) : Aiming to counter the Congress' bid to project first time MP Rahul Gandhi as a young dynamic leader and a crowd-puller in Uttar Pradesh, the BJP has sought to project his cousin, Varun Gandhi, in a similar light hoping to infuse fresh blood into party leadership and enthuse its rank and file in the State.

(4776) Dehra Dun : The doling out of ministerial privileges to over 200 Congressmen enjoying the jobs of heads of various boards and corporations has become more than an embarrassment for the Uttaranchal Chief Minister, Narayan Dutt Tiwari, with his own party men and the

Bharatiya Janata Party leaders staging protest marches led by bullock carts complete with a red beacon and siren.

(4777) Chennai : The Communist Party of India (Marxist) has urged Chief Minister, Jayalalithaa to convene an all-party meeting to discuss the current flood situation in the State and to apprise Opposition leaders of steps taken by the Government towards relief and rehabilitation of flood-hit people.

(4778) Chennai : The Opposition's demand for resignation of Congress president Sonia Gandhi from the post of chairperson of the National Advisory Council "smacked of political opportunism."

(4779) Tiruchi : Present day youths should come forward to address various evils plaguing the society, particularly issues such as corruption, economic imbalances and other inequalities, said Vaiko, General Secretary, Marumalarchi Dravida Munnetra Kazhagam.

09-12-2005

(4780) Hyderabad : Proceedings in the Assembly were disrupted for about 20 minutes by Telugu Desam Party members who demanded that Home Minister K. Jana Reddy give a reply on the action initiated against those responsible for the murder of a party activist, Anjibabu, in Narasaraopet last month.

(4781) Visakhapatnam : The district committee of the Communist Party of India (Marxist) on Thursday demanded that the Government include 260 Girijan-majority villages, located on the fringe of the agency area in the V Schedule so that Girijans of those villages received the benefits due to them.

(4782) Visakhapatnam : The Telugu Desam Party has deplored the abnormal rise in the prices of essential commodities and vegetables and blamed lack of sincerity on the part of the State Government and administrative failure leading to black-marketing and middlemen for the situation.

(4783) Arakur (Khammam dt.) : The CPI(M) has decided to intensify its anti-Polavaram project struggle significantly taking support of all political parties, including the Telugu Desam and the TRS, beginning with a huge rall · at the dam site.

(4784) Hyderabad : Members of the Communist Party of India-Marxist staged a walkout from the Assembly in protest against the passage of the Industrial Disputes (Andhra Pradesh Amendment) Bill, 2005, an enactment, they said, would strangle the rights of the working classes.

(4785) Mahabubnagar : Andhra Pradesh Congress Committee President K. Keshava Rao has said that he does not attach much importance to the issue of giving Deputy Chief Minister's post to a person belonging to the Telangana region.

(4786) Thiruvananthapuram : A gang of about 25 persons, claiming allegiance to the RSS, attacked the BJP State headquarters here on Thursday in an apparent escalation of faction fight in the State unit of the party.

(4787) Hyderabad : Members of the Communist Party of India-Marxist staged a walkout from the Assembly in protest against the passage of the Industrial Disputes (Andhra Pradesh Amendment) Bill, 2005, an enactment, they said, would strangle the rights of the working classes.

(4788) New Delhi : The Left on Thursday delivered a "friendly warning" to the Government over the proposed reduction of interest on Employees' Provident Fund deposits but told the Opposition that if it was waiting for its "bite" to bring it back to power, the wait would last five years.

(4789) Raisen (M.P.) : Warning the BJP that it would perish if it ignored grassroots workers, expelled BJP leader Uma Bharti on Thursday claimed that her contribution could not be overlooked and would have to be highlighted during the party's coming silver jubilee convention in Mumbai. "My name will have to be taken during the Mumbai convention, while commemorating 25 years of achievements of BJP... or [BJP president] Advaniji will have to carry a blank paper in his hand to the meet," Ms. Bharti said, addressing a public meet." - PTI

(4790) New Delhi : Prime Minister Manmohan Singh will on Thursday next provide clarifications sought by members in Parliament on the statement he made on the Volcker issue before he left for Moscow last week.

(4791) Mangalore : The former Karnataka Pradesh Congress Committee President and Rajya Sabha Member Janardhana Poojary on

Thursday launched the Congress campaign for the zilla and taluk panchayat elections in his own inimitable style.

(4792) Mysore : The former Deputy Chief Minister Siddaramaiah on Thursday launched the All India Progressive Janata Dal's (AIPJD) campaign for the elections to zilla and taluk panchayats, atop the Chamundi Hills here.

(4793) Shimoga : The former Prime Minister and President of the Janata Dal (S) H.D. Deve Gowda here on Thursday took strong exception to the "paltry" sanction of Rs. 360 crores by the Centre towards flood and rain relief and alleged that different yardsticks were being applied to different States by the Congress-led UPA Government.

(4794) Shimoga : "It is my ambition to see that my party should come to power in the State on its own," said the former Prime Minister and President of the Janata Dal (S), H.D. Deve Gowda.

(4795) Udupi : Tourism Minister D.T. Jayakumar has said that the Congress and the Janata Dal (Secular) will part ways and fresh Assembly elections will be held if either of them gets a majority of zilla panchayat seats.

(4796) Kolkata : Marxist leader and West Bengal Chief Minister Buddhadeb Bhattacharjee on Thursday said he preferred the word 'worker' to 'labour,' as the latter smacked of slavery.

(4797) New Delhi : The Congress leadership was not aware of the presence of Jagat Singh [Natwar Singh's son] and his friend Andaleeb Sehgal in Baghdad when a four-member party delegation led by him [Natwar Singh] visited Iraq in January 2001 and the news was received with "indignation" when it came to light, Aneil Mathrani, a member of the group, said here on Thursday.

(4798) New Delhi : It was the Prime Minister Manmohan Singh who enacted a political drama on the Volcker issue, not the Bharatiya Janata Party, deputy leader of the party in the Lok Sabha, V.K. Malhotra, alleged on Thursday.

(4799) New Delhi : The Congress on Thursday demanded that the terms of reference of the Justice R.S. Pathak inquiry authority be expanded to go into the latest accusation that an unnamed close associate of the former Prime Minister, Atal Bihar Vajpayee, was involved in the Iraqi oil-for-food contracts.

(4800) New Delhi : In a letter to Chief Minister Sheila Dikshit, the president of the Delhi unit of the Bharatiya Janata Party, Harsh Vardhan, has demanded that for issuing caste certificates to persons belonging to Other Backward Classes the recommendations of any Member of Parliament, Legislator or Councillor be treated as sufficient.

(4801) New Delhi : After having drawn flak from her party MLAs for convening a Congress Legislature Party (CLP) meeting to discuss the future of farmhouses and commercial properties in residential areas, Delhi Chief Minister Sheila Dikshit has now put the ball in thc United Progressive Alliance Government's court, stating that the Delhi Development Authority and the Urban Development Ministry have to take a decision on the issue.

(4802) Bhopal : Two years after coming to power and with two Chief Ministers - Uma Bharti and Babulal Gaur - already sidelined, the mood remains upbeat in the ruling Bharatiya Janata Party circles and this was amply reflected by the new Chief Minister, Shivraj Singh Chauhan, who asserted soon after taking the oath of office that he has inherited a healthy fiscal legacy and now it is for him to carry forward the State on the fast track of development.

(4803) Lucknow : Uttar Pradesh Assembly on Thursday witnessed another day of bedlam as BJP members forced adjournment for the entire day over the killing of party legislator Krishnanand Rai on November 29.

(4804) Chennai : The Bharatiya Janata Party will launch agitation if the Centre fails to enhance the flood relief assistance to Tamil Nadu in a week, party State president C.P.Radhakrishnan said on Thursday.

(4805) Chennai : Dravida Munnetra Kazhagam president M. Karunanidhi on Thursday endorsed the call for an all-party meeting to discuss the flood situation in Tamil Nadu.

(4806) Villupuram : The Tamil Nadu Government should create a separate Ministry for the maintenance of irrigation systems and adopt better water management practices, S. Ramadoss, founder leader of the Pattali Makkal Katchi, said.

10-12-2005

(4807) New Delhi : The Government on Friday ruled out a Joint Parliamentary Committee (JPC) probe into the findings of the Volcker Report but assured the Lok Sabha that Parliament would be taken into confidence on the Justice Pathak Inquiry Authority's findings. Dissatisfied with the Government's response, the Opposition staged a walkout.

(4808) Panaji : The Leader of the Opposition and former BJP Chief Minister, Manohar Parrikar, on Thursday reiterated his party stand that Goa has to have an additional airport even while simultaneously emphasising that the Dabolim airport has to continued for civilian use.

(4809) Chikmagalur : The former Prime Minister, H.D. Deve Gowda, said here on Friday that the Janata Dal (S) intends to provide protection to those adversely affected by globalisation and privatisation.

(4810) Thiruvananthapuram : CPI national secretary D. Raja has called for forging a common platform of various interest groups to fight globalisation.

(4811) Thiruvananthapuram : The three-day second International Congress on Kerala Studies got under way here on Friday with West Bengal Chief Minister and CPI(M) Polit Bureau member Buddhadeb Bhattacharjee calling for countrywide land reforms to make rural development programmes sustainable.

(4812) Poonch : It was a touching moment for Congress president Sonia Gandhi when girl students wished her a happy birthday on her arrival in a quake-affected belt, which adjoins Pakistan-occupied Kashmir, on Friday.

(4813) Bhubaneswar : Bharatiya Janata Party president L.K. Advani on Friday reiterated the Opposition demand for a Joint Parliamentary Committee probe into the Volcker Report findings even as the Centre turned down the demand in the Lok Sabha earlier in the day.

(4814) New Delhi : Minister of State for Parliamentary Affairs Suresh Pachouri told the Rajya Sabha on Friday that "The report of the Justice Pathak Inquiry Authority [probing into the Volcker Report disclosures] will be tabled in Parliament along with the action taken report. We will do whatever is possible as the Government is keen on going into the entire matter." He was responding to Leader of the Opposition Jaswant Singh who demanded a Joint Parliamentary Committee (JPC) probe into the issue.

(4815) New Delhi : Stepping up its pressure, the Communist Party of India (Marxist) cautioned against an "imminent confrontation" building up with the United Progressive Alliance Government over slashing of interest rate on the Employees Provident Fund.

(4816) New Delhi : It was a big birthday bash without the 'guest of honour' at 10 Janpath here on Friday. With flags, posters and drums, a large number of folk dancers gathered outside the residence of United Progressive Alliance (UPA) chairperson Sonia Gandhi early in the morning hoping to wish her on her birthday. But they were all disappointed when they learnt that she was away in Kashmir spending time with the quake victims.

(4817) Nagpur : The suicide bid of Shiv Sena MLA, Gulabrao Gawande, on the floor of the Maharashtra Assembly was the result of the State Government's negative reply to his question about a case of a money-lender grabbing the lands of indebted farmers in Vidarbha.

(4818) Pondicherry : Pondicherry Assembly Speaker M. D. R. Ramachandran has greeted the All India Congress Committee president and Chairperson of the National Coordination Council Sonia Gandhi on the occasion of her birthday on Friday.

(4819) Jaipur : The Communist Party of India (Marxist) has described the two years of the Bharatiya Janata Party Government in Rajasthan as a period of oppression of the working class, the farmers and the common people.

(4820) Lucknow : The Uttar Pradesh Chief Minister, Mulayam Singh Yadav, slammed the Opposition on Friday for demanding a CBI inquiry into the killing of BJP MLA Krishnanad Rai and said that State police was capable of working out the murder.

11-12-2005

(4821) Hyderabad : The Congress Legislature Party has lashed out at TDP president N. Chandrababu Naidu, accusing him of harbouring criminals in his party. In a statement here on Saturday, CLP secretaries - E. Pratap Reddy and S. Ganga Ram - and its executive member V. Vasanth Kumar, criticised Mr. Naidu's visit to Narasaraopet to pay tributes Anjibabu since the latter was named in several criminal cases.

(4822) Hyderabad : The veiled warning issued by Andhra Pradesh Congress Committee president K. Keshava Rao to his party MLA P. Janardhan Reddy on Friday found takers in in-charge Minister of the city Mohd. Ali Shabbir.

(4823) Vipparla (Guntur Dist) : Telugu Desam Party president N. Chandrababu Naidu has warned the Congress against continuing political murders and has said otherwise it will have to pay a heavy price for it.

(4824) Thiruvananthapuram : Polit Bureau member of the CPI(M) S. Ramachandran Pillai has said that the Left must occupy a greater space in the polity if it is to intervene decisively in national policies.

(4825) New Delhi : The controversy over Pramod Mahajan's alleged anti-Bihar remarks found its echo here on Saturday with people from the State holding a protest demonstration and demanding an apology from the BJP leader.

(4826) London : Janata Party president Subramanian Swamy has urged Congress president Sonia Gandhi to resign as chairperson of the UPA Government's National Advisory Council, pending investigations into the Volcker Committee's report on the Iraqi food-for-oil issue.

(4827) Bangalore : The State unit of the Bharatiya Janata Party (BJP) proposes to set up district planning committees to formulate policies and programmes for zilla panchayats and a panchayat development council to ensure the speedy implementation of programmes approved by the zilla panchayats.

(4828) Bangalore : All India Progressive Janata Dal (AIPJD) President C.M. Ibrahim on Saturday said his party has rejected an offer by the Congress for an alliance in the zilla and taluk panchayat elections. Instead, the party has an understanding with the Samajwadi Party of the former Chief Minister S. Bangarappa in Shimoga, Dakshina Kannada, Uttara Kannada, Mangalore and Udupi districts.

(4829) Hubli : There is no secret alliance between the Congress and Janata Dal(Secular) for elections to zilla and taluk panchayats, the former Prime Minister H.D. Deve Gowda has said.

(4830) Mangalore : The former President of the Karnataka Pradesh Congress Committee and Rajya Sabha Member B. Janardhana Poojary has said he is confident that the Congress will win in the elections to the zilla and taluk panchayats in the State.

(4831) Davangere : Bharatiya Janata Party leader and Leader of the Opposition in the Legislative Assembly B.S. Yediyurappa has challenged Chief Minister N. Dharam Singh and Janata Dal (Secular) President H.D. Deve Gowda to hold an open discussion on the performance of the coalition Government in the last 18 months if they had the moral satisfaction of doing any thing for the poor, downtrodden and farmers.

(4832) Alappuzha : The CPI(M)'s action of accepting advertisement from Cochin Minerals and Rutile Ltd (CMRL) for the second volume of compiled articles published in connection with the International Congress on Kerala Studies (ICKS)organised by the AKG Centre for Research and Studies has exposed the double standards being followed by the party in the issue of mineral sand-mining, the KPCC secretary Johnson Abraham has said.

(4833) Kolkata : "One has the right to trade union [activity], one has the right to strike," A.B. Bardhan, general secretary, Communist Party of India, said here on Saturday. "There can be a strike" on the lines of the one called by Left trade unions on September 29 if the Centre failed to restore the Employees Provident Fund rate to 9.5 per cent, he said.

(4834) Srinagar : The Congress president and UPA chairperson Sonia Gandhi on Saturday concluded her two-day visit to the quake hit areas of Jammu and Kashmir. She pledged support for complete rehabilitation of thousands of earthquake victims saying that whole nation was behind them.

(4835) New Delhi : Expressing outrage at alleged remarks by Bharatiya Janata Party general secretary Pramod Mahajan about people of Bihar living in Mumbai and other parts of Maharasthra, Congress MLA and Poorvanchal leader Mahabal Mishra on Saturday warned that Mr. Mahajan would not be allowed to speak from any forum in Delhi till he apologises for his 'derogatory' outpourings.

(4836) Pondicherry : P. Shanmugham, president of the Pondicherry Pradesh Congress Committee, has said that with the enforcement of the

Right to Information Act, 2005, there could be no room for any section of people to make charges against the government.

(4837) Chennai : The Rising Sun, an English weekly being published by the Murasoli Trust, was re-launched here on Saturday.

(4838) New Delhi : All-India Anna Dravida Munnetra Kazhagam on Friday asked the Government to take up the Chennai Metro Rail Project for its immediate inclusion in the list of projects to be funded by the Japanese Bank.

(4839) Chennai : At a function to mark the 127the birth anniversary of Rajaji on Saturday, speakers, including Dravida Munnetra Kazhagam (DMK) president M. Karunanidhi, Union Minister for Urban Development and Culture Jaipal Reddy, and National Advisory Council Member Jairam Ramesh, recalled his contribution to the country as freedom fighter, politician, statesman and administrator.

12-12-2005

(4840) Hyderabad : The Congress Legislature Party on Sunday questioned TDP president N. Chandrababu Naidu whether he would own up the murders of Congress activists during the party's nine-year rule.

(4841) Hyderabad : The Telugu Desam Party has objected to Finance Minister K. Rosaiah tending to find fault with the Opposition in general and TDP President N. Chandrababu Naidu in every issue and asked him to set "his house in order before criticising others".

(4842) Hyderabad : CPI (M) Polit Bureau member Brinda Karat has expressed serious concern over the State Government's moves to go ahead with construction of the Polavaram project despite the adverse impact it will have on the lives of tribals in the agency areas of Khammam and West Godavari districts.

(4843) New Delhi : Monday's conclave of the Chief Ministers of Bharatiya Janata Party-ruled States is expected to clear a roadmap for their joining the Value Added Tax regime.

(4844) Thiruvananthapuram : CPI(M) general secretary Prakash Karat has called for a Left agenda for Kerala's development, one that will protect the gains of the past in the social sectors and show a viable path for the future, particularly in enhancing material production.

(4845) Gulbarga : Chief Minister N. Dharam Singh on Sunday ruled out extending the coalition arrangement with the Janata Dal (Secular) at the State level to the taluk and zilla panchayats for which elections are due in December.

(4846) Hubli : "We have not received any invitation from Chief Minister N. Dharam Singh to join him in the delegation to be taken to New Delhi to meet the Prime Minister in connection with the funds for the relief and rehabilitation work in flood affected areas," Bharatiya Janata Party (BJP) State unit president Jagadish Shettar said here on Sunday.

(4847) Hubli : Karnataka Pradesh Youth Congress Committee President Dinesh Gundu Rao has alleged that in the districts where the presence of Janata Dal (Secular) is prominent, the Congress activists are being ill-treated and exploited.

(4848) Hubli : H.N. Ananth Kumar, BJP General Secretary and MP, has said that Sonia Gandhi, Congress President, should resign as chairperson of the National Advisory Council in the light of the revelations in the Volcker report.

(4849) Kadaganchi (Gulbarga Dist.) : Chief Minister N. Dharam Singh on Sunday warned the rebel candidates of the Congress in the fray to withdraw or retire from the zilla and taluk panchayat elections or face disciplinary action.

(4850) Davangere : B.S. Yediurappa, Leader of the Opposition in the Legislative Assembly and Bharatiya Janata Party leader, alleged that the coalition Government has failed to utilise the released funds for taking up flood relief works.

(4851) Thiruvananthapuram : Congress leader and former Member of Parliament V.M. Sudheeran on Sunday criticised the CPI (M) leadership for carrying a sponsorship advertisement of a controversial mineral sand-mining company in the party's document prepared for its ongoing Kerala Study Congress.

(4852) Thiruvananthapuram : The leader of the Opposition V.S. Achuthanandan has urged Prime Minister Manmohan Singh to intervene in the case of Noushad, a Keralite, languishing in a Saudi jail for nearly two-and-a-half years.

(4853) Thiruvananthapuram : Communist Party of India (Marxist) Polit Bureau member Sitaram Yechury has said that the Left will strive hard to make foreign direct investment subject to conditions that will be in the best interests of the country.

(4854) Hyderabad : Communist Party of India (Marxist) Polit Bureau member and MP Brinda Karat on Sunday emphasised the need for the urban poor to wage a united struggle.

(4855) New Delhi : Ranjan Bhattacharya, foster son-in-law of the former Prime Minister, Atal Bihari Vajpayee, on Sunday issued a legal notice to the former Governor, Romesh Bhandari, for accusing a "very close" associate of Mr. Vajpayee of involvement in the Iraqi oil scam and said he had neither met nor had any dealings with the former Iraqi President, Saddam Hussein's son, Uday, as alleged.

(4856) Jaipur : Former Bharatiya Janata Party president Murli Manohar Joshi accused the Congress party of ''escaping" a discussion on the World Trade Organization (WTO) related aspects. "The Congress Governments always escaped discussions on the matter.

(4857) Jaipur : Senior Bharatiya Janata Party leader and former Union Minister Murli Manohar Joshi has denied any leadership crisis in the party on the eve of stepping down of L.K.Advani as the party president.

(4858) Lucknow : A day after announcing several developmental schemes in Congress president Sonia Gandhi's parliamentary constituency Rai Bareli, Uttar Pradesh Chief Minister Mulayam Singh Yadav on Sunday gave another set of incentives worth Rs 268 crores to people of Farrukhabad and Kannauj districts.

(4859) Lucknow : Taking exception to the reported remarks of BJP general secretary Pramod Mahajan against the people from Bihar, the Rashtriya Janata Dal said on Sunday it would launch a countrywide agitation on the issue and demanded that Chief Minister Nitish Kumar sever all ties with the BJP in protest against Mr. Mahajan's statement.

(4860) Chennai : Former Andhra Pradesh Chief Minister and Telugu Desam Party leader, N. Chandrababu Naidu, on Sunday stressed the need for providing more subsidy and budgetary support to the farm sector.

(4861) Karur : Under the pretext of seeking Central relief, Chief Minister Jayalalithaa is trying to secure funds to fund the populist schemes she announced recently, Pattali Makkal Katchi founder president S. Ramadoss has alleged.

13-12-2005

(4862) Hyderabad : The Congress Legislature Party (CLP) has flayed the campaign of the TDP that the Congress Government was getting its political rivals eliminated with a vengeance.

(4863) Hyderabad : Union Statistics and Programme Implementation Ministry Additional Secretary R.C. Panda has asked State Governments to prepare Panchayat Raj (PR) Yearbook with statistical data of 'panchayats' on the lines of the municipalities.

(4864) Hyderabad : The ambitious Integrated Novel Development in Rural Areas and Model Municipal Areas (Indiramma) programme to build model villages and towns at a cost of Rs. 23,000 crores drew heavy flak from the Opposition parties in the Assembly on Monday, pushing the Government into defensive.

(4865) Thiruvananthapuram : Communist Party of India (CPI) State secretary Veliyam Bhargavan has said that his party has not foresworn the Democratic Indira Congress (Karunakaran) and only wished to make it clear that the DIC(K)'s role in the Left Democratic Front's victory in the Thiruvananthapuram Lok Sabha byelection must not be exaggerated.

(4866) Bangalore : The Janata Dal (Secular) did not enter into an alliance with the Congress because it is confident of emerging victorious on its own in the zilla and taluk panchayat elections, Finance Minister P.G.R Sindhia has asserted.

(4867) Bangalore : The All India Progressive Janata Dal (AIPJD) has criticised the Government's decision to amend the Karnataka State Universities Act, 2000, on the grounds that it will politicise higher education.

(4868) Bangalore : The All-India Progressive Janata Dal (AIPJD) has alleged that the former Prime Minister and Janata Dal (S) President H.D. Deve Gowda is indulging in opportunistic politics by raising the issue of internal reservation for backward classes during the campaigning for zilla and taluk panchayat elections.

(4869) Mangalore : The State is likely to face Assembly elections in March-April 2006, according to the former Chief Minister S. Bangarappa, who heads the State unit of the Samajwadi Party.

(4870) New Delhi : BJP General Secretary in charge of Karnataka affairs Ananth Kumar on Monday alleged that the Reserve Bank of India has asked the State Government to return Rs. 158 crores out of the Rs. 357 crores provided by the Centre as ad hoc interim relief for the flood affected areas in the State from the National Calamity Contingency Fund.

(4871) Thiruvananthapuram : CPI(M) State secretariat members M. A. Baby and T. M. Thomas Isaac have said that the development agenda being chalked out on the basis of the deliberations at the second International Congress on Kerala Studies, which concluded here on Sunday, would impact Government policies regardless of whether the LDF or the UDF won the next Assembly election.

(4872) New Delhi : The Bharatiya Janata Party decided on Monday to reverse its earlier directive to State Governments ruled by it not to join the Value Added Tax regime. A statement issued after a one-day meeting of Chief Ministers of BJP-ruled States declared, "In principle BJP-ruled States will adopt VAT."

(4873) New Delhi : Political parties have initiated disciplinary proceedings against their party MPs who were caught on camera accepting cash for the favour of asking specific questions in Parliament. The indication is that they could face expulsion from their parties and lose their seats in Parliament if parliamentary committees looking into the matter find them guilty.

(4874) New Delhi : Accusing the Sheila Dikshit Government of having failed to fulfil its promise to regularise hundreds of unauthorised colonies in the Capital and using the residents of these colonies as vote banks, the Bharatiya Janata Party MLA from Saket, Vijay Jolly, on Monday demanded regularisation of these colonies with immediate effect and without any development charges being levied.

(4875) Ludhiana : Claiming that Chief Minister Amarinder Singh has failed to bring any foreign investment to Punjab, Shiromani Akali Dal on Monday said his proposed visit to Dubai should be banned.

(4876) Lucknow : Samajwadi Party supremo and Uttar Pradesh Chief Minister Mulayam Singh Yadav on Monday apprehended "misuse" of the Central Bureau of Investigation (CBI) against him and other party leaders at the behest of the Centre.

14-12-2005

(4877) Hyderabad : Chief Minister Y. S. Rajasekhara Reddy has discounted the oft-repeated claim of the Telugu Desam that it is the champion of backward classes and said that it was the Congress Government, which had first provided political reservation for these sections in 1969.

(4878) Hyderabad : Bharatiya Janata Party has accused Chief Minister Y.S. Rajasekhara Reddy and APCC president K. Keshava Rao of belittling the Gentlemen's Agreement by their utterances on the demand for appointing a person from Telangana as Deputy Chief Minister.

(4879) Hyderabad : Power purchase agreements (PPAs) signed by the TDP Government rocked the Andhra Pradesh Assembly on Tuesday, with Chief Minister Y. S. Rajasekhara Reddy and Leader of the Opposition N. Chandababu Naidu trading charges.

(4880) Srikakulam : F ormer Minister and senior TDP leader Gunda Appala Suryanarayana on Tuesday described the MP's demand for money for raising questions in Parliament as 'most heinous', and said that political corruption in a democratic set-up could not be controlled unless reforms were introduced in the election process.

(4881) Nagpur : Three BJP MLAs were suspended for six months for allegedly using certain "derogatory" remarks against the Speaker and Deputy Speaker in their chambers. The House had been adjourned over the Treasury benches' insistence on condemning the graft charges against State BJP MPs. - PTI

(4882) Mahabubnagar : The Congress retained with ease the Makthal Assembly seat in the byelection caused by the gunning down of party's senior MLA C. Narsi Reddy along with ten others by Maoists on Independence Day this year.

(4883) New Delhi : The Rajya Sabha on Tuesday suspended BJP member Chhattrapal Singh Lodha on the recommendation of the House

Ethics Committee that observed that the sting operation showing him allegedly accepting money on camera had damaged the image of Parliament.

(4884) Gandhinagar : The Gujarat Chief Minister, Narendra Modi, led his BJP to a sweeping victory in the civic elections capturing all the five municipal corporations and all the four municipalities where the elections were held on Sunday.

(4885) Mangalore : The Communist Party of India (Marxist) on Tuesday urged the Union Government to reserve the rights to imposing quantitative restrictions on import particularly in the agriculture sector.

(4886) Davangere : C.M. Ibrahim, All-India Progressive Janata Dal (AIPJD) leader, said that it is unfortunate that former Prime Minister and Janata Dal (Secular) President H.D. Deve Gowda has been trying to create disharmony among the backward classes by raising the internal reservation issue and using it for his election campaign.

(4887) Kochi : The Communist Party of India (Marxist) should apologise to the people for its anti-development activities before making public its report on the International Congress on Kerala Studies, said Congress leader M.M. Hassan on Tuesday.

(4888) New Delhi : Amid reports that the Congress-led Government in Kerala will be expanded, Chief Minister Oommen Chandy on Tuesday met party president Sonia Gandhi and held discussions.

(4889) New Delhi : Bharatiya Janata Party president L.K. Advani on Tuesday deplored the incidents of MPs allegedly taking money for asking questions in Parliament as "sad and shameful." Of the 11 MPs allegedly involved, and `caught on camera' in a sting operation by a television channel, six were from the BJP.

(4890) New Delhi : The Constitution Amendment Bill seeking to provide reservation to the Scheduled Castes and the Scheduled Tribes and other socially and educationally deprived groups in unaided private, professional institutions seems to have run into hurdles.

(4891) New Delhi : Rajya Sabha member Vijay Darda (Congress) on Monday urged the government to take note of the issue of female foeticide and adopt a multiple strategy.

(4892) New Delhi : The Janata Dal (Secular) has opposed the reported statement of the Prime Minister, Manmohan Singh that the Government would go ahead and allow foreign direct investment in retail marketing, despite strong opposition from parties supporting the Government.

(4893) New Delhi : Calling for national crusade against corruption and installing a foolproof monitoring system to look into complaints of and malpractices by Members of Parliament, the Communist Party of India on Tuesday offered suggestions, including the 'right to recall' by the voters.

(4894) Mumbai : Shiv Sena chief Bal Thackeray feels that Union Agriculture Minister and Nationalist Congress Party (NCP) president Sharad Pawar can become the Prime Minister even though his party does not have the number of MPs to see him reach the top post.

(4895) New Delhi : At a time when lakhs of rupees are being spent by the Municipal Corporation of Delhi on foreign tours of the Mayor and the Chairman of the MCD Standing Committee, the Leader of the Opposition in the Corporation, Subhash Arya, has accused the Congress-ruled MCD of not distributing blankets to the poor, jerseys to the students and setting up temporary night shelters for the lakhs who spend their nights in the biting cold outside.

(4896) Chennai : Tamil Nadu Congress Committee president G.K. Vasan on Tuesday accused Chief Minister Jayalalithaa of adopting a "confrontationist course" towards the Centre on relief and rehabilitation for the flood-hit.

15-12-2005

(4897) Hyderabad : The remarks reportedly made by State BJP president N. Indrasena Reddy that it was a common practice for members in the State Assembly to accept money to raise questions evoked sharp criticism.

(4898) Hyderabad : Expressing concern over the raw deal meted out to Backward Classes by successive Governments, members of various parties on Wednesday favoured reservation for BCs in the legislature.

(4899) Hyderabad : Members of the Telugu Desam Party stormed out of the Assembly on Wednesday after the Speaker disallowed their attempt to raise the findings of the Ramachenna Reddy Commission report on farmers' suicide.

(4900) Devarakonda (Nalgonda) : Vice-president of the Telugu Desam Gutta Sukhender Reddy has warned of undertaking padayatra from Devarakonda to Narayanpur, if the Government fails to begin work to supply potable water for the fluoride-affected villages in the district by January.

(4901) New Delhi : The Government on Wednesday postponed the introduction of the Bill to provide for reservation to the socially and educationally backward classes in unaided educational institutions after the Parliamentary Forum of OBC MPs sought clarifications. Added to this were reservations expressed by the Bharatiya Janata Party (BJP) and the Communist Party of India (Marxist).

(4902) New Delhi : While voicing concern over the "collapse" and "inefficiency" of the Public Distribution System (PDS) in the country, members, cutting across party lines, in the Rajya Sabha on Wednesday demanded strengthening of the PDS to provide food security for all citizens.

(4903) New Delhi : The Rajya Sabha members on Wednesday expressed concern at the continuation of manual scavenging in the country.

(4904) New Delhi : As the Bharatiya Janata Party prepares to hold its national council session in Mumbai from December 26, the countdown has begun for the end of L.K. Advani's innings as party president.

(4905) New Delhi : Reasserting its opposition to privatise pension fund or investing it in the stock market, the Polit Bureau of the Communist Party of India (Marxist) on Tuesday discussed issues of concern such as modernisation of airport and reviewed political developments during the last three months ahead of its central committee meeting.

(4906) New Delhi : The Janata Dal (Secular) has opposed the reported statement of the Prime Minister, Manmohan Singh that the Government would go ahead and allow foreign direct investment in retail marketing, despite strong opposition from parties supporting the Government.

(4907) Shimla : The State Committee of the CPI (M) has expressed deep shock and anguish over the sting operation in which Himachal BJP Member of Parliament Suresh Chandel was shown allegedly taking bribe for asking questions in the House. The party has demanded his immediate arrest

(4908) Jaipur : The country's negotiators at the ongoing World Trade Organisation's ministerial level meeting in Hong Kong have been asked to seek greater flexibility for India and other developing countries in retaining high tariffs lines to protect their producers and local markets. The right of farmers over use of land, water and seeds should be protected along with the indigenous knowledge and the sovereignty to decide the crop pattern and production, a consultation held at the Institute of Development Studies said.

(4909) Lucknow : Bahujan Samaj Party (BSP) supremo and former chief minister Mayawati on Wednesday alleged that the hand of Uttar Pradesh CM Mulayam Singh Yadav and his aide Amar Singh could not be ruled out in the sensational cash-on-camera MPs' bribery case.

(4910) Chennai : The Tamil Nadu Pollution Control Board (TNPCB) is working on ways to tackle e-waste generated by information technology companies, Environment and Forests Secretary Surjit K. Chaudhary said here on Wednesday.

(4911) Madurai : The Dalit Panthers of India has urged the Centre to declare Tamil Nadu as affected by natural calamity considering the intensity of the situation where 22 out of 30 districts have been hit due to floods.

16-12-2005

(4912) Hyderabad : Irregularities allegedly committed in the execution of Kalwakurthy irrigation project in Mahabubnagar district rocked the Assembly on Thursday, leading to an acrimonious debate that forced the Speaker to end it by using the closure-motion for the first time in the recent times.

(4913) New Delhi : The Andhra Pradesh Legislative Council Bill - aimed at reviving the Upper House in the State - was passed by the Lok Sabha on Thursday. The Communist Party of India (Marxist) along with the Telugu Desam Party (TDP) voted against the Bill while the CPI abstained.

(4914) Mumbai : Raj Thackeray, who quit his party posts on November 27, met his uncle, Shiv Sena leader Bal Thackeray, on Thursday after a rapprochement bid effected by former Lok Sabha speaker Manohar Joshi.

(4915) Bijapur : Janata Dal (Secular) is strictly adhering to the code of conduct with regard to the coming zilla and taluk panchayat elections, party leader H.D. Deve Gowda has said.

(4916) Gulbarga : The Communist Party of India (Marxist) on Wednesday accused the Congress of misusing its official status and violating the model code of conduct prescribed by the State Election Commission for the zilla and taluk panchayat elections.

(4917) Shimoga : The general secretary and spokesperson of the Janata Dal(S), Y.S.V. Datta, said here on Thursday that the party would not invite the leader of AHINDA and All India Progressive Janata Dal (AIPJD) Siddaramaiah to join it. "But if he comes on his own he will be accorded the same importance that he had enjoyed before quitting Janata Dal (S)," he added.

(4918) Thiruvananthapuram : Democratic Indira Congress (Karunakaran) leader T.M. Jacob alleged on Thursday that Revenue Minister K.M. Mani was hoodwinking small farmers in the Cardamom Hill Reserves issue.

(4919) Thiruvananthapuram : United Democratic Front (UDF) convener P. P. Thankachan on Thursday said that it was grossly improper on the part of CPI(M) State secretary Pinarayi Vijayan to have used the recent International Congress on Kerala Studies organised by the AKG Study Centre to "score political points against Chief Minister Oommen Chandy."

(4920) Bhopal : The former Madhya Pradesh Chief Minister, Uma Bharati, on Thursday lashed out at Bharatiya Janata Party president L.K. Advani and demanded his resignation. She said he was pursuing "politics devoid of any ideology or principles."

(4921) New Delhi : L.K. Advani will not resign as Bharatiya Janata Party president till December 30, when the Mumbai national council session ends, general secretary Pramod Mahajan said on Thursday.

(4922) New Delhi : Terming the government move to introduce labour market flexibility under the garb of reforms as an attack on the working conditions of workers, veteran Marxist Jyoti Basu on Thursday said the working class would end up being "absolutely worse off."

(4923) New Delhi : The Centre of Indian Trade Unions (CITU) has expressed concern over the observation made recently by the Supreme Court suggesting that "casual worker" was not covered within the definition of a "workman" as per the Workmen Compensation Act.

(4924) New Delhi : Mounting a scathing attack against the Government's move to restructure and privatise Delhi and Mumbai airports, the Communist Party of India (Marxist) on Thursday raised questions on the "transparency" of the process, dubbed it as "dubious" and cautioned that a scam was in the making.

(4925) Pondicherry : Pattali Makkal Katchi parliamentary party leader M. Ramadoss has called upon Chief Minister N. Rangasamy to intervene and ensure that the demands of the ministerial staff of the Union Territory are settled amicably and without room for the staff to continue their strike any further.

(4926) Chennai : Volunteers of the Dalit Panthers party staged a demonstration near Memorial Hall here on Thursday demanding that the Centre release adequate funds to Tamil Nadu for flood relief work.

(4927) Kanyakumari : Tamil Nadu Congress Committee president G.K. Vasan said on Thursday that the Centre was ready to extend all kinds of assistance, including allocation of adequate funds, for relief and rehabilitation measures in flood-affected areas of Tamil Nadu. But the State Government should list out the demands as per the guidelines governing the Calamity Relief Fund and the National Calamity Contingency Fund.

(4928) Tirupur : The Marumalarchi Dravida Munnetra Kazhagam, a United Progressive Alliance partner, has cautioned the Centre against helping Sri Lanka in re-laying the Palaly airstrip.

17-12-2005

(4929) Anantapur : The district units of the Communist Party of India (CPI) and Andhra Pradesh Rythu Sangham (APRS) have alleged that the two Ministers from the district had forgotten the promises made to the farmers in the district, after coming to power.

(4930) Hyderabad : The Assembly was adjourned for 15 minutes during question hour when Telangana Rashtra Samithi members rushed to the well waving placards after their adjournment motion on violation of six-point formula was rejected by Speaker K.R. Suresh Reddy.

(4931) New Delhi : As part of the preparations for the Congress plenary to be held next month in Hyderabad, the organising committee of the All India Congress Committee held a meeting to review the preparations for the event and decided to send a team to the State during the last week.

(4932) Nagarjunasagar (Nalgonda) : BJP national secretary K. Haribabu has said there is no scope for the formation of a third front as is being dreamt by TDP president N. Chandrababu Naidu.

(4933) New Delhi : The Communist Party of India (Marxist) on Friday urged the Centre to intervene and ask the Andhra Pradesh Government to stop the construction activity of Indira Sagar (Polavaram) multi-purpose irrigation project stating it would jeopardise interests of tribals.

(4934) Hyderabad : Notices were ordered to be issued to former Chief Minister N. Chandrababu Naidu and three others on Monday by the High Court in a criminal case pertaining to alleged diversion of funds to the Right to Sight Society.

(4935) New Delhi : Jagat Singh, son of the former Foreign Minister K. Natwar Singh, questioned for the second day by the Enforcement Directorate in connection with the Volcker controversy, on Friday furnished proof of his having been part of the Indian Youth Congress delegation to Iraq in 2001, and not as a tag-along of his father.

(4936) Mysore : The Congress's stand on the continuity of the coalition set up with the Janata Dal (Secular) in the State will be announced after the outcome of the ensuing elections to the zilla and taluk panchayats, former Minister and senior Congress leader D.K. Shivakumar said.

(4937) Davangere : The Bharatiya Janata Party (BJP) leader H.N. Ananth Kumar, said that just like in Bihar where people had rejected Lalu Prasad and voted in favour of the National Democratic Alliance (NDA) constituents such as the BJP and the Janata Dal (U), there will be change in government in the State soon.

(4938) Kittur (Belgaum) : Leaders of the Congress and the Janata Dal (S) seem to be making contradictory statements on panchayat elections if their statements quoting Chief Minister N. Dharam Singh and Finance Minister P.G.R. Sindhia are any indication.

(4939) Thiruvananthapuram : KPCC president Ramesh Chennithala said here on Friday that the CPI(M) still held a "distorted" view of development.

(4940) New Delhi : The Communist Party of India (Marxist) on Friday said the Pension Fund Regulatory Authority Bill was not acceptable to it in the present form and suggested that the United Progressive Alliance Government rework some major provisions.

(4941) New Delhi : That the fate of the Women's Reservation Bill was uncertain became obvious on Friday when Brinda Karat (CPI-M) raised the issue in the Rajya Sabha during the post-lunch session.

(4942) New Delhi : Accusing the Delhi Government of overlooking the interests of the people of Delhi and selling them out to multinational and private companies, the Delhi Bharatiya Janata Party on Friday said completion of the seventh year in office by Chief Minister Sheila Dikshit was marked by mis-governance, stalling of development works and resentment among the public at large.

(4943) Raipur : The Chhattisgarh Vidhan Sabha was adjourned on Friday without transacting any business as the Opposition Congress members raised slogans demanding an inquiry by the CBI into the disappearance of rice stocks meant for distribution under the food for work programme.

(4944) Chandigarh : The Indian National Lok Dal (INLD) has strongly condemned the "brutal cane-charge" by the Chandigarh police on employees protesting against the Haryana Government here on Thursday.

(4945) Rae Bareli : Congress President Sonia Gandhi today made light of Uttar Pradesh Chief Minister Mulayam Singh Yadav announcing a development package for her constituency and said people in power are ruffled whenever the development of Amethi and Rae Bareli is mentioned.

(4946) Chennai : The Dravida Munnetra Kazhagam has moved the Madras High Court to restrain Revenue and police authorities of various districts from interfering with the public screening of the party's propaganda film, 'Vetri Namadhae.'

(4947) Chennai : Janata Party president Subramanian Swamy has criticised the All-India Anna Dravida Munnetra Kazhagam Government and the previous Dravida Munnetra Kazhagam regime, for "unplanned and unauthorised illegal construction" in many waterways, which led to flooding of may areas in Chennai and other towns.

(4948) Villupuram : The Pattali Makkal Katchi founder S. Ramadoss has urged the AIADMK Government to convene an emergency Assembly session to resolve making Tamil the language of the Madras High Court.

18-12-2005

(4949) Hyderabad : In the light of efforts to convert education into a "commercial commodity," the Communist Party of India (Marxist) has favoured measures for imposing social control over private educational institutions.

(4950) Hyderabad : The Communist Party of India (Marxist) has decided to wait for the response of Prime Minister Manmohan Singh before finalising the future course of action on the construction of the Polavaram (Indirasagar) project.

(4951) Hyderabad : Telugu Desam president N.Chandrababu Naidu has expressed concern that the benefits of economic reforms were not reaching the poor and asked the party's trade union wing, TNTUC, to fight for ensuring justice to workers.

(4952) Tirupati : In a significant development in the Uma Bharti episode, a section of the Tirupati city unit of the Bharatiya Janata Party (BJP) have not only condemned her expulsion from the party but also threw their lot behind her.

(4953) Vijayawada : Communist Party of India (Marxist) leader Ch. Babu Rao has expressed concern over the conditions imposed by the Centre for giving funds to urban local bodies under the Jawaharlal Lal Nehru National Urban Renewal Mission (JNNURM).

(4954) Hyderabad : The Congress Government is considering a move to postpone the actual constitution of the Andhra Pradesh Legislative Council till the completion of elections to the panchayat bodies.

(4955) Gulbarga : Chief Minister N. Dharam Singh said on Saturday that the Government will go ahead with its idea of holding a Legislative Assembly session in northern Karnataka.

(4956) Hassan : Dismissing the claims of a few Janata Dal (Secular) leaders, including Minister for Tourism D.T. Jayakumar recently that, the coalition Government would collapse after the election to zilla and taluk panchayats, party President H.D. Deve Gowda, said here on Saturday that the longevity of the coalition Government depended on the decisions of national presidents of both parties and statements by others need not be taken seriously.

(4957) Mangalore : The former President of the Karnataka Pradesh Congress Committee and Rajya Sabha MP Janardhana Poojary has appealed to voters to give a clear verdict to the Congress in the panchayat elections.

(4958) Haveri : After receiving a major setback in the Haveri district in the last general elections, the Congress is now facing stiff competition from the BJP in the panchayat polls, along with the Janata Dal (Secular) and the Samajwadi Party, which are making every effort to wrest seats.

(4959) Thrissur : President of the Democratic Indira Congress (Karunakaran) K. Muraleedharan has said that State secretary of the Communist Party of India (Marxist) Pinarayi Vijayan and Pannian Ravindran, CPI MP, have accepted the contributions of his party in the victory of Mr. Ravindran in the recent Lok Sabha byelection in Thiruvananthapuram.

(4960) Malappuram : Kerala Pradesh Congress Committee (KPCC) president Ramesh Chennithala said here on Saturday that the United Democratic Front (UDF) was trying hard for a consensus on implementation of the Narendran Commission report. The UDF will consider the concerns aired by organisations such as the Nair Service Society and Sree Narayana Dharma Paripalana Yogam before taking a decision, the KPCC president said.

(4961) Bhubaneswar : The vice-president of the All India Democratic Women's Association and Rajya Sabha MP, Brinda Karat, on Saturday criticised both the Centre and State Governments for the failure of the public distribution system that led to the denial of foodgrain to innumerable poor families.

(4962) Kolkata : Defence Minister and West Bengal Pradesh Congress chief Pranab Mukherjee has declined Trinamool Congress leader Mamata Banerjee's invitation to attend her party's youth convention, to be inaugurated by Bharatiya Janata Party president L K Advani here on Sunday.

(4963) New Delhi : All-India Congress Committee secretary Jai Kishan has said that all those political parties and leaders who are today talking about the right of reservation for scheduled castes and scheduled tribes and backward classes in the private sector had kept mum during the time of previous National Democratic Alliance Government at the Centre.

(4964) New Delhi : The Congress Legislature Party (CLP) stood sharply divided on Saturday as a section of dissident MLAs created a flutter demanding resignation of Chief Minister Sheila Dikshit expressing "lack of confidence" in her leadership. On her part, Ms. Dikshit successfully managed to retrieve the situation by ensuring that the controversial power and water issues were pushed into the background and demolitions by the Municipal Corporation of Delhi dominated the proceedings.

19-12-2005

(4965) Hyderabad : The Congress Legislature Party has derided the "vindictive" attitude of TDP president N. Chandrababu Naidu against Congress leaders particularly Chief Minister Y.S. Rajasekhara Reddy.

(4966) Hyderabad : Andhra Pradesh Congress Committee president K. Keshava Rao has asserted that the proposed Legislative Council will not be a rehabilitation centre for party leaders.

(4967) Khammam : The loss of CPI (ML New Demoracy) has turned out to be a gain for CPI(M) in Khammam. Three important leaders - Nunna Nageswara Rao, Bandi Ramesh and Jeevan - and some 40 village secretaries who have deserted the New democracy joined the CPI(M) here on Sunday. Some 400 partymen, including sarpanches, chairmen of agriculture cooperative societies and some MPTCs, sifted loyalties, thus giving a severe blow to the New Democracy.

(4968) Hyderabad : The Communist Party of India (Marxist) will strongly oppose any move by the Government to allow the entry of foreign universities at the expense of the existing institutions of higher learning in the country.

(4969) Hyderabad : Union Minister of State for Rural Development A. Narendra has said the Telangana Rashtra Samithi (TRS) will serve an ultimatum on the United Progressive Alliance (UPA) Government at the Centre asking the latter to make its stand clear on the demand for separate Telangana.

(4970) Bhubaneswar : POSCO, the world's fifth-largest steel maker, said on Sunday that its proposed 12-million-tonne integrated steel plant in Orissa's Jagatsinghpur district would be constructed in three phases of four million tonnes.

(4971) Mysore : Predicting the collapse of the coalition Government in the State after the elections to zilla and taluk panchayats, the former Deputy Chief Minister Siddaramaiah has said that his All India Progressive Janata Dal (AIPJD) is geared up to face midterm elections to the Assembly.

(4972) Malur (Kolar) : Though the State Government has implemented many welfare programmes, the credit has not gone in favour of the Congress because of the coalition set up, Chief Minister N. Dharam Singh said here on Sunday.

(4973) Sugatur (Kolar Dt.) : It was AICC President Sonia Gandhi who first mooted the idea of forming a coalition government in the State to prevent the BJP from coming to power, said the former Prime Minister and Janata Dal (S) President H.D. Deve Gowda.

(4974) Panaji : The Bharatiya Janata Party (BJP) has reiterated that it is not interested in destabilising the Congress-led coalition Government in the State despite its "lackadaisical performance", but is confident that it will collapse on its own. BJP Goa State unit President Rajendra Arlekar on Saturday accused the Congress spokesman Jitendra Deshprabhu of misguiding the people blaming the BJP for rumour mongering about the instability of the Government. Taking a swipe at the Congress Legislature Party's observations on Friday that bureaucracy was instrumental in holding up files and consequently halting the development works, Mr. Arlekar ridiculed the ruling Congress for blaming the bureaucracy instead of owning the responsibility for bad governance. The BJP leader said the truth is that the administration is paralysed and there is no governance in the State.

(4975) Kozhikode : Kerala Pradesh Congress Committee (KPCC) president Ramesh Chennithala has urged the Centre to create an exclusive railway zone for the State in view of the move of the Railways to bifurcate the Palakkad division and form the Salem division in Tamil Nadu.

(4976) Palakkad : Leader of the Opposition V.S. Achuthanandan will file a Special Leave Petition (SLP) in the Supreme Court "against the attempts by the State Government and the Public Prosecutor to protect the accused in the Kozhikode ice-cream parlour sex scandal case."

(4977) Thiruvananthapuram : Revolutionary Socialist Party (RSP) general secretary K. Pankajakshan on Sunday said his party was against any move to "water down" the basic character of the Left Democratic Front (LDF) by including in it political parties that did not conform to that character.

(4978) Thiruvananthapuram : The Union Minister for Power Padannatha Mohammed Sayeed who passed away at Seoul on Sunday was a veteran parliamentarian who represented the Lakshadweep islands in the Lok Sabha for about four decades. He had the unique distinction of winning from the same constituency 10 times consecutively.

(4979) Thiruvananthapuram : Kerala Chief Minister Oommen Chandy on Sunday night condoled the death of Union Power Minister P.M. Sayeed.

(4980) Thrissur : Communist Party of India (Marxist) (CPI-M) State Secretary Pinarayi Vijayan has challenged the leadership of the ruling United Democratic Front (UDF) to specifically state which development project of the State was scuttled by his party.

(4981) Bhubaneswar : Communist Party of India (Marxist) MP Brinda Karat on Sunday welcomed the introduction of the Scheduled Tribe (Recognition of Rights) Bill, 2005 but said there were many infirmities in it that would hamper the interests of the tribals living in reserved forests.

(4982) New Delhi : President A.P.J. Abdul Kalam condoled the loss of lives in the stampede at a flood relief distribution centre in Chennai on Sunday.

(4983) Kolkata : Trinamool Congress leader Mamata Banerjee's hopes of the Congress party's endorsement of her call for a "mahajot" (grand alliance) to fight the Left Front in next year's Assembly elections have received a setback. On Sunday Defence Minister and president of the West Bengal Pradesh Congress Committee Pranab Mukherjee declined to share the dais with BJP president L.K. Advani at a special convention of the Trinamool Youth Congress here.

(4984) Srinagar : Notwithstanding its "unconditional" support to the coalition Government headed by Ghulam Nabi Azad, the National Conference (NC) is under tremendous pressure to oppose a Bill that proposes to reduce the term of the Assembly from six to five years.

(4985) Mumbai : Raj Thackeray quit the Shiv Sena on Sunday, saying he had done his best to stay but could not. Making the announcement at a press conference, he said he would form a political party soon.

(4986) New Delhi : A Telugu Desam Party MP on Sunday suggested that the MPs' Local Area Development Scheme be restructured to prevent misuse of funds.

(4987) New Delhi : Following the major demolition drive against illegal constructions by the Municipal Corporation of Delhi on High Court orders, the Delhi Congress on Sunday has sought changes in building bye-laws to legalise such constructions and decided to meet Union Urban Development Minister S. Jaipal Reddy to seek early implementation of Delhi Master Plan 2021 and V.K. Malhotra Committee report that allowed 'mix land use' of properties in the Capital.

(4988) Pondicherry : P. Shanmugham the president of the reconstituted Pradesh Committee of the ruling Congress here left for Delhi on Sunday to have a meeting with the AICC president Sonia Gandhi and the Secretaries of the high command and to apprise them of the current political situation in the Union Territory hich would have its next Assembly polls in the next few months.

(4989) Chandigarh : With a little more than a year left for the elections to the State Assembly, the Punjab Chief Minister, Amarinder Singh chose the backwaters of Muktsar district to blow the conch for the campaign of his Congress party, by organising a rally in Lambi constituency, which is represented by his predecessor and President of the Shiromani Akali Dal, Parkash Singh Badal.

(4990) Jaipur : The Communist Party of India will celebrate the 58th anniversary of its foundation in Rajasthan on Monday even as the party at the national level is making preparations to observe its 80th birthday a week later on December 26. The tiny village Bhava in Rajsamand district's Kankroli tehsil, where an underground meeting on December 19, 1948, marked the beginning of the party in Rajasthan with the formation of the POC (Provincial Organising Committee), will be the venue for an Adivasi-Kisan convention on Monday.

(4991) Lucknow : Janata Dal (United) on Sunday announced to hold State-wide agitation on January 23 next year in Uttar Pradesh to protest the alleged lawlessness, corruption and misrule of the Mulayam Singh Yadav Government.

(4992) Lucknow : The BJP on Sunday joined the Congress in demanding public disclosure of assets allegedly accumulated by Uttar Pradesh Chief Minister Mulayam Singh Yadav and his kin.

(4993) Chennai : Tamil Nadu Governor Surjit Singh Barnala on Sunday expressed shock and grief over the deaths due to stampede at a flood relief token distribution centre at MGR Nagar here.

(4994) Chennai : Expressing shock and concern over the tragedy at a flood relief centre at MGR Nagar here, MDMK general secretary Vaiko on Sunday said the Chief Minister alone should take responsibility for the administrative lapses.

(4995) Coimbatore : Close to 100 Dravida Munnetra Kazhagam members led by the party deputy general secretary, M.K. Stalin, attempted to take out a rally here on Sunday alleging that flaws in flood relief distribution caused the stampede in Chennai.

(4996) Madurai : Bharatiya Janata Party vice-president Venkaiah Naidu on Sunday urged the State Government to initiate measures for distributing relief tokens to the affected families at their doorstep to ensure that only the flood-hit benefited.

(4997) Chennai : Dravida Munnetra Kazhagam president M. Karunanidhi on Sunday criticised the State Government for the stampede, which claimed 42 lives.

20-12-2005

(4998) Hyderabad : Deputy leader of the Congress in Lok Sabha G. Venkat Swamy reminded the Telangana Rashtra Samithi leadership on

Monday that the Congress high command would take the decision on separate Statehood for Telangana at an appropriate time.

(4999) Hyderabad : Chief Minister Y. S. Rajasekhara Reddy, APCC president K. Keshav Rao and former Chief Minister N. Janardhana Reddy expressed grief over the death of Union Power Minister P. M. Sayeed.

(5000) Vijayawada : The Communist Party of India (CPI) has retained its identity and has not compromised on people's issues even while supporting the United Progressive Alliance (UPA) Government at the Centre from outside, CPI State secretary K. Narayana said here on Monday.

(5001) Mahabubnagar : Andhra Pradesh Congress Committee OBC Cell Chairperson-designate J. Chittaranjan Das on Sunday hoped that the backward class communities would get their due share in the Legislative Council that would be revived soon.

(5002) Hyderabad : Members belonging to the Telangana Rashtra Samithi (TRS) pinned down the Andhra Pradesh Government in the Assembly on Monday over GO No: 610, forcing it to announce that it would spell out measures for its implementation on December 28 after consultations with a Cabinet sub-committee.

(5003) New Delhi : Bharatiya Janata Party president L.K. Advani will exit his post on December 31, a day after the party's Mumbai conclave comes to en end.

(5004) New Delhi : The National Democratic Alliance decided at a meeting here on Monday that it would oppose the Constitution Amendment Bill proposed by the Government to provide for reservation in unaided private professional colleges.

(5005) Jammu : Reiterating that the restoration of greater autonomy to Jammu and Kashmir was the best possible solution, National Conference (NC) president Omar Abdullah on Monday asked both New Delhi and Islamabad to take "away their guns from the soil of Kashmir" to facilitate peaceful resolution of the 58-year problem.

(5006) Gulbarga : Akhila Bharata Banjara Sangha President Baburao Chavan, a former Minister who was expelled from the Congress, on Monday accused the Chief Minister N. Dharam Singh of sidelining the Lambada community members in the Assembly by not giving them representation in his Ministry.

(5007) Davangere : Chief Minister N. Dharam Singh said that the Congress President Sonia Gandhi has to take a decision whether to continue the coalition Government in the State or not after the elections and no one within the party or outside can take a decision in this regard.

(5008) Davangere : Chief Minister N. Dharam Singh said he referred to a feedback from the "intelligence wing" of the Congress when he said there was a wave of support for the party in most districts in the panchayat elections and he did not mean any report from the Intelligence Bureau.

(5009) New Delhi : Describing the death of 42 persons in the Chennai stampede as a heartbreaking tragedy, Congress president Sonia Gandhi on Monday said she shared the grief and pain of the families of all victims.

(5010) New Delhi : Charging the Manmohan Singh Government with failing to stand up firmly for a "more equitable agreement" for India and the developing countries, the Communist Party of India (Marxist) and the anti-World Trade Organisation front demanded that it explain how the Hong Kong declaration would benefit Indian farmers.

(5011) Mumbai : A day after the resignation of party leader Raj Thackeray, most members of the Shiv Sena's Solapur district unit joined the Congress.

(5012) New Delhi : Lok Sabha Speaker Somnath Chatterjee has expressed shock over an expose highlighting corruption in selecting projects for the Member of Parliament Local Area Development Scheme (MPLADS).

(5013) New Delhi : Warning of a "full-fledged scam" in the privatisation of the Delhi and Mumbai airports, the Communist Party of India (Marxist) on Monday demanded that the process be scrapped and asked the government to adopt a transparent system.

(5014) New Delhi : Even as political parties cutting across political affiliations joined hands to find a way out to stop demolition of illegal structures in the Capital, the Delhi Government and the Delhi Pradesh Congress Committee seemed to be pulling in different directions over the issue.

(5015) New Delhi : Blaming the policies of the Congress-led Delhi Government and the Municipal Corporation of Delhi (MCD) for the ongoing demolition exercise in the Capital, the Leader of the Opposition in the MCD, Subhash Arya, on Monday demanded immediate implementation of the Amnesty Scheme as per the Malhotra Committee Report so that some relief could been given to people. Asking the Delhi Government and the civic body to file a plea in the Delhi High Court requesting some relief to citizens, Mr. Arya alleged that the MCD and the Govt. had failed to apprise the Court of the facts in the entire case that has led to such a massive demolition drive.

(5016) Chandigarh : All the eight Indian National Lok Dal MLAs present in the Haryana Assembly were suspended for the day on Monday by the Speaker, H.S.Chatha, after they created a ruckus and occupied the well of the House demanding dismissal of Haryana Parliamentary Affairs Minister Randeep Singh Surjewala over la affaire Volcker.

(5017) Pondicherry : Volunteers of the Pondicherry unit of the Bharatiya Janata party on Monday held a demonstration in front of Collector's office at Saram near here urging the Administration to sanction immediately Rs. 5 crores for restoration of roads and other infrastructure in Reddiarpalayam Assembly constituency which bore the brunt of recent torrential rain. The president of Pondicherry State Committee of the party R. Kesavalu and the party's lone legislator in Pondicherry Assembly, A. M. Krishnamoorthy were among those who addressed the agitators despite inclement weather.

(5018) Lucknow : The Samajwadi Party on Monday slammed media reports about acquisition of properties by Uttar Pradesh Chief Minister Mulayam Singh Yadav and his family members, describing them as a "political conspiracy".

(5019) Chennai : Political parties and trade unions have expressed grave concern over the death of 42 persons in a stampede at a relief distribution centre in Chennai on Sunday.

21-12-2005

(5020) Eluru : Tribals backed by the CPI(M) on Tuesday resorted to a fresh bout of violence at Bhuttayagudem as a follow-up to the violent incidents reported in Jangareddygudem in connection with removal of encroachments, leaving three policemen and a Deputy Mandal Revenue Officer seriously injured.

(5021) Hyderabad : The 17-day-long winter session of the Assembly, which began on a positive note, coinciding with its golden jubilee celebrations, ended amid bitter accusations with the Congress and TDP blaming each other for wasting the time of the House. The Left and Telangana Rashtra Samithi held the ruling party and TDP responsible for failure to discuss important issues.

(5022) Hyderabad : The non-TDP Opposition has blamed the ruling Congress and the Telugu Desam Party for preventing debates on important public issues by making the Assembly a platform to trade allegations.

(5023) Vijayawada : The observation by Kankipadu Congress MLA Devineni Rajasekhar (Nehru) that an "efficient leader like Tadi Sakuntala should continue in the post of city mayor at least for three years" stirred the proverbial hornet's nest in the Congress on Tuesday.

(5024) Tirupati : As predicted the increasing interference of the State Government even in the day-to-day administration of the Tirumala Tirupati Devasthamans (TTD) is assuming political dimensions. Predictably, again it was the Bharatiya Janata Party (BJP) which has taken the cudgels against the Government in this regard on two major issues - thrusting the Tirumala rope-way project into its lap ignoring protests from the pundits and secondly the reported move to siphon off crores of rupees from the TTD coffers for use on 'non-religious' projects, like the setting up of Sri Venkateswara Veterinary University and the Sri Padmavathi Medical University at Tirupati.

(5025) Chandigarh : The Constitution Amendment Bill to reserve seats for socially and educationally backward classes, besides the Scheduled Castes and the Scheduled Tribes, in private unaided educational institutions other than those run by minorities was introduced in the Lok Sabha on Tuesday amid protests from the Bharatiya Janata Party and reservations expressed by some allies of the government.

(5026) Bangalore : The Bharatiya Janata Party (BJP) has accused Chief Minister N. Dharam Singh of misusing official machinery during the campaign for the zilla and taluk panchayat elections and urged Governor T.N. Chaturvedi to "dismiss him from the post."

(5027) Mysore : Irked by Chief Minister N. Dharam Singh's disclosure that former Union Minister and veteran Dalit leader V. Srinivas Prasad has written to him seeking re-entry into the Congress, Mr. Prasad clarified that he has neither written nor decided on joining the Congress.

(5028) Davangere : Chief Minister N. Dharam Singh has ruled out the possibility of Assembly elections being called soon after the panchayat polls and said the coalition government is strong and stable and there is no immediate threat to it.

(5029) Kannur : Communist Party of India (Marxist) State secretary Pinarayi Vijayan has accused the United Democratic Front (UDF) Government of having 'ruined' the State on all fronts.

(5030) Thiruvananthapuram : RSP State Secretary T. J. Chandrachoodan said here on Tuesday an effective investigation into the ice-cream parlour sex racket case would take place if the Left Democratic Front (LDF) comes to power.

(5031) Kolkata : Senior CPI(M) Polit Bureau member Jyoti Basu on Tuesday said the Congress was likely to go in for tacit electoral understanding with the Trinamool Congress-BJP combine during the West Bengal Assembly elections due next year. The Congress has, however, denied it.

(5032) New Delhi : The former Lok Sabha Speaker, Purno A. Sangma, on Tuesday returned to the Nationalist Congress Party, which he floated along with Sharad Pawar six years ago. Mr. Sangma, who resigned his Tura Lok Sabha seat earlier this year, contested the 2004 general elections on the Trinamool Congress ticket.

(5033) New Delhi : Lok Sabha Speaker Somnath Chatterjee has taken the initiative to bring the Member of Parliament Local Area Development Scheme (MPLADS) under the scrutiny of political parties. He is hosting a dinner meeting on Wednesday to broach the subject with leaders of the Congress and the Bharatiya Janata Party.

(5034) New Delhi : Unnerved by the current demolition drive at the instance of the Delhi High Court and worried about the possible political fallout, MLAs cutting across party lines on Tuesday demanded an end to the ongoing demolition drive by the Municipal Corporation of Delhi. A number of Congress MLAs even suggested that Chief Minister Sheila Dikshit should lead the legislators in facing the bulldozers to express solidarity with the people of Delhi.

(5035) Raipur : Opposition Congress members in the Chhattisgarh Assembly today resorted to slogan shouting throughout the day barring the question hour demanding an inquiry by the Central Bureau of Investigation (CBI) into the "rice scam" in the state.

(5036) Chandigarh : The Opposition parties in Haryana, including the Bharatiya Janata Party and the Indian National Lok Dal (INLD), have separately demanded that the State Parliamentary Affairs Minister and former Youth Congress president Randeep Singh Surjewala resign over his "involvement" in Volcker issue.

(5037) Lucknow : Claiming that the party's 'Nyay Yatra' against criminalisation of politics was a huge success, the BJP in Uttar Pradesh on Tuesday announced that the programme would be intensified from January next year.

(5038) Chennai : The State unit secretariat of the Communist Party of India (Marxist) on Tuesday urged the State Government to arrange long-term relief, rehabilitation and reconstruction measures in flood-affected areas "without shirking its responsibility." It also asked the Government not to attempt to divert people's attention by blaming Opposition parties for the tragedy.

(5039) Chennai : The Dravida Munnetra Kazhagam (DMK) is to apply to District Collectors, specifying venue and time, for permission to screen its propaganda film, Vetri Namadhae, the Madras High Court has said.

(5040) New Delhi : Members from Tamil Nadu staged a walkout in the Lok Sabha on Tuesday in protest against Speaker Somnath Chatterjee's refusal to allow all of them to make brief interventions on the issue of the stampede at a flood relief camp in Chennai on Sunday.

22-12-2005

(5041) Hyderabad : Having attracted flak for plans to spend heavily on arrangements for the plenary of All-India Congress Committee (AICC) at the swank G.M.C. Balayogi stadium at Gachibowli here, the Congress on Wednesday announced that the meeting would be a simple and unostentatious affair.

(5042) Hyderabad : Telugu Desam Party on Wednesday justified its walkout from the all- party meeting on Government Order 170 raising the capacity of the Pothireddypadu head regulator, saying it had no other option.

(5043) Hyderabad : Telugu Desam will not hesitate to stage a dharna, if necessary, to seek more Central funds to the State during the All-India Congress Committee president Sonia Gandhi's visit to the city for attending the AICC plenary next month.

(5044) New Delhi : The Lok Sabha on Wednesday passed the Bill providing reservation for the socially and educationally backward classes, besides the Scheduled Castes and the Scheduled Tribes, in private unaided educational institutions.

(5045) Hyderabad : An all-party meeting to resolve the controversy over the Pothireddypadu head-regulator of the Srisailam project ended on a sour note here on Wednesday but the Government announced that it would go ahead with its earlier plan to increase its discharge capacity to 40,000 cusecs.

(5046) Gulbarga : Chief Minister N. Dharam Singh, who has completed a State-wide tour, campaigning for Congress candidates in the zilla and taluk panchayat elections, said on Wednesday that the party's prospects are bright. Although it will be a close contest in a few districts, the Congress will win a majority in all zilla and taluk panchayats, according to him.

(5047) Kochi : The Democratic Indira Congress (Karunakaran) president K. Muraleedharan has said the welfare schemes and other governmental programmes being announced by the Oommen Chandy Government are just an eyewash.

(5048) New Delhi : The Constitution Amendment (104th) Bill to reserve seats for socially and educationally backward classes, besides the Scheduled Castes and the Scheduled Tribes, in private unaided educational institutions drew all-round support in the Lok Sabha despite apprehension over the exclusion of minority institutions.

(5049) New Delhi : Ahead of Speaker Somnath Chatterjee's dinner meeting with party leaders on the MP Local Area Development Scheme on Wednesday, a BJP member made a plea in the Lok Sabha against scrapping the programme.

(5050) New Delhi : The issue of demolitions once again rocked the Delhi Assembly on Wednesday with the Bharatiya Janata Party stalling the proceedings, forcing five adjournments demanding an immediate end to the ongoing demolition drive by the Municipal Corporation of Delhi. It also charged the Delhi Government with having failed to protect the interests of the people. The Speaker finally adjourned the House for the day at 4-45 p.m. after efforts to restore order failed.

(5051) Shimla : There have been claims and counter claims over the election results of the first two phases of panchayat polls in Himachal Pradesh with the Congress Party and the BJP claiming that a majority of the winners belong to their party.

(5052) Bhopal : The main Opposition Congress is determined to corner the ruling Bharatiya Janata Party in the winter session of the Madhya Pradesh Assembly beginning here on Friday by raising issues like deteriorating law and order, electricity crisis, corruption, growing atrocities on SC/ST communities and women, shortage of seeds and fertilizers and malnutrition.

(5053) Pondicherry : The secretary of the Pondicherry State unit of the All India Anna Dravida Munetra Kazhagam (AIADMK) A.Anbalagan, MLA, has said that President A. P. J. Abdul Kalam, Prime Minister Manmohan Singh and the Central Relief Committee complimented Tamil Nadu Chief Minister Jayalalithaa for the good work sh e and her Government had done in relieving the people of the agony of havoc caused by the floods.

(5054) Jaipur : The Rajasthan Pradesh Congress Committee leaders on Wednesday met Chief Minister Vasundhara Raje to submit a 15-point memorandum, which among other things demanded immediate commencement of drought relief operations in the State and eight hours power supply to farmers. The delegation, led by PCC (I) president B.D.Kalla, protested against the said move to convert the diary cooperative in the State to milk production companies after entering into a loan agreement with the National Diary Development Board(NDDB).

(5055) Kolkata : Senior CPI(M) Polit Bureau member Jyoti Basu on Tuesday said the Congress was likely to go in for tacit electoral understanding with the Trinamool Congress-BJP combine during the West

Bengal Assembly elections due next year. The Congress has, however, denied it.

(5056) Chennai : The Dravida Munnetra Kazhagam and its allies will hold a public meeting on December 25, to protest the arrest of a party councillor in connection with the stampede at a relief token distribution centre on Sunday.

(5057) Chennai : The Madras High Court on Wednesday dismissed a writ petition by the AIADMK seeking to restrain the Election Commission from initiating legal action against party functionaries who had submitted voters' applications for inclusion in electoral rolls in bulk.

(5058) Chennai : The State unit secretariat of the Communist Party of India (Marxist) on Tuesday urged the State Government to arrange long-term relief, rehabilitation and reconstruction measures in flood-affected areas "without shirking its responsibility." It also asked the Government not to attempt to divert people's attention by blaming Opposition parties for the tragedy.

23-12-2005

(5059) Hyderabad : The Bharatiya Janata Party (BJP) has faulted the Telugu Desam and the Telangana Rashtra Samithi for walking out of yesterday's all-party meet which was meant to put forth respective party's stand on the Pothyreddypadu head regulator and not make demands.

(5060) Hyderabad : Telugu Desam on Thursday contended that there was no clarity in the Government's stand on enhancing the capacity of Pothireddypadu head regulator as indicated by the number of orders it had issued and modified them following criticism.

(5061) Ongole : CPI(M) State secretary B.V. Raghavulu has asked the Congress Government to give up its anti-people policies, lest the CPI(M) should launch agitations.

(5062) Rajahmundry : Telugu Desam Party leader and former Finance Minister Yanamala Ramakrishnudu has alleged that the State Government intends to do real estate business in the name of establishing another Special Economic Zone in Kakinada.

(5063) Bangalore : In an interesting political development on the eve of the final phase of elections to the zilla and taluk panchayats, Chief

Minister N. Dharam Singh is facing opposition from his party leaders to his proposal to extend the Congress's alliance with the Janata Dal (Secular) to panchayats if the party falls short of a majority in any of them.

(5064) Kollam : The keys of the 43 houses constructed by the CPI(M) for the tsunami victims of Alapad were handed over by CPI(M) general secretary Prakash Karat to the Fisheries Minister Dominic Presentation here today. These houses form the first batch of 69 units being constructed by the party for the tsunami victims of Alapad. Speaking at the function, Mr. Karat said that since the past couple of years the country was being hit by natural calamities and this warranted a mechanism in the form of an institution to deal with such disasters. He wanted sufficient infrastructure and funds to be allocated for the purpose. But the institution could succeed only with popular support and cooperation, he said.

(5065) Thiruvananthapuram : The CPI(M) State committee, which met here on Thursday, expressed its concern over the circumstances that had led to the key witnesses in the ice-cream parlour sex scandal case turning hostile en masse.

(5066) New Delhi : Party leaders at the meeting convened by Lok Sabha Speaker Somnath Chatterjeehere on Thursday by and large felt that some corrections were necessary to the Member of Parliament Local Area Development Scheme (MPLADS), but the scheme itself should not be scrapped, as suggested by some.

(5067) New Delhi : Members of the Left parties walked out of the Lok Sabha on Thursday in protest unable to secure a commitment from the Government on restoring the interest rate of the Employees' Provident Fund (EPF). The Left members - who warned that the United Progressive Alliance (UPA) could meet the same fate as the National Democratic Alliance if it pursued "anti-people" policies - found support from the Samajwadi Party, the Bahujan Samaj Party and the Shiv Sena as they walked out.

(5068) New Delhi : Uttar Pradesh Chief Minister Mulayam Singh Yadav on Thursday ruled out the possibility of early elections in the State and said Assembly polls would be held on schedule in 2007. He was addressing a press conference here after meeting Planning Commission Deputy Chairman Montek Singh Ahluwalia to finalise the State's annual plan,

(5069) Guwahati : Former Lok Sabha Speaker P.A. Sangma on Wednesday demanded that the Member of Parliament Local Area Development Scheme (MPLADS) be scrapped and insisted that the MPs should not be dragged into implementation of any such development scheme.

(5070) New Delhi : Congress president Sonia Gandhi and Prime Minister Manmohan Singh, at a meeting of party MPs here on Thursday, underlined the need for dispelling wrong impressions about parliamentarians.

(5071) Chandigarh : Haryana Congress MLA, Karan Singh Dalal, who single-handedly criticized the Om Parkash Chautala regime during its six - year tenure in the State and played a key role in the formulation of the Congress party's ''charge-sheet' against the Chautala clan, said that his stand had been vindicated as the CBI had taken "cognisance" of the "charge-sheet" in its probe against the former Chief Minister.

(5072) Chandigarh : Shiromani Akali Dal president Parkash Singh Badal has said that by agreeing to the "subsidy reduction clause" in the recent Hong Kong round of WTO negotiations India had virtually signed on the death warrants of millions of beleaguered farmers of the country.

(5073) Chennai : Welcoming the State Government's announcement that the flood relief package will be distributed to the affected with no final date set, the Bharatiya Janata Party on Thursday criticised the attempts at politicising the stampede.

24-12-2005

(5074) Hyderabad : Telugu Desam president N. Chandrababu Naidu on Friday accused the Government of wreaking vengeance on Backward Classes for being solidly behind his party.

(5075) Hyderabad : Accusing the Government with misuse of official machinery for the All India Congress Committee plenary scheduled here next month, Telugu Desam party on Friday demanded a white paper on the expenditure incurred and mobilisation of funds.

(5076) Visakhapatnam : The first death anniversary of former Prime Minister P.V. Narasimha Rao was observed at the City Congress party office here on Friday.

(5077) New Delhi : Parliament on Friday expelled 11 members - 10 from the Lok Sabha and one from the Rajya Sabha - whose conduct was found to be "unethical and unbecoming" of Members of Parliament.

(5078) Mahabubnagar : The Bhoomi puja programme for the construction of the second lift irrigation project took a violent turn at Kalwakurthy on Friday when activists of the Congress and the Telugu Desam clashed by pelting stones at each other.

(5079) Thiruvananthapuram : The CPI(M) State secretariat has denied reports that there were schisms in the party State secretariat on organisational issues.

(5080) New Delhi : Friday's vote in Parliament for expelling the 11 members found guilty of misconduct represented the "collective will of MPs" and not of political parties. None of the constituents of the United Progressive Alliance and their supporting parties had issued a whip, asking its MPs to vote in favour of the expulsion resolutions in the two Houses.

(5081) New Delhi : Though unanimous on the need for action against the 10 MPs involved in the cash-for-questions scam, political parties differed on their expulsion from the Lok Sabha without a thorough investigation. While the ruling benches pressed for their immediate expulsion to redeem the dignity of Parliament, the principal Opposition Bharatiya Janata Party maintained that the matter be referred to the Privileges Committee as the MPs were entitled to the natural course of justice.

(5082) Chennai : Janata Party president Subramanian Swamy has asked the Union Government to make clear to Sri Lankan President Mahinda Rajapakse that India would offer help to Sri Lanka only if it unilaterally announced adoption of a federal Constitution to replace the present unitary one.

(5083) Kolkata : The Congress is keeping open its options of an electoral tie-up with the Trinamool Congress, but unlike the latter "has a different set of compulsions as a national party." Therefore, it was not in a position to go in for any "direct or indirect" seat adjustment with the Trinamool as long as it "maintains its relationship" with the Bharatiya Janata Party, senior party leaders told The Hindu here on Friday.

(5084) New Delhi : In the Rajya Sabha, the process of expulsion of Chatrapal Singh Lodha of the Bharatiya Janata Party, who was found guilty in the "cash for questions" scam, was devoid of rancour with Leader of the Opposition Jaswant Singh setting the tone for the near-unanimity with which the motion was adopted on Friday.

(5085) New Delhi : The former Uttar Pradesh Chief Minister has emerged a frontrunner to succeed L. K. Advani as Bharatiya Janata Party president. The former party chief, M. Venkaiah Naidu, who claims to have bowed out of the race, and the BJP deputy leader in the Rajya Sabha, Sushma Swaraj, are said to be the other contenders.

(5086) New Delhi : The general secretary of Marumalarchi Dravida Munnetra Kazhagam, Vaiko, met Prime Minister Manmohan Singh on Friday and apprised him of the escalating situation in Sri Lanka and the plight of Tamils in the island.

(5087) New Delhi : Charging the Delhi Government with having failed to fulfil the promises made in its party manifesto, the Nationalist Congress Party (NCP) legislator, Ramvir Singh Bidhuri on Friday alleged in the Delhi Assembly that the promise to extend the Lal Dora, waive off house tax for the villages, increase in land compensation for the farmers still remain unfulfilled even two years after the Congress Government got elected for the second consecutive time.

(5088) New Delhi : Demanding immediate suspension of the ongoing citywide demolition drive, former Delhi Chief Minister and senior Bharatiya Janata Party leader Madan Lal Khurana on Friday said grant of full Statehood to Delhi was the only way to solve the city's civic problems. He lambasted the Congress for not clearing the Statehood proposal despite being in power at the Centre and Delhi.

(5089) Ranchi : Almost all the opposition parties have decided to boycott the all party meeting convened by Jharkhand Chief Minister Arjun Munda tomorrow to discuss industrialisation and development issues of the State.

(5090) Vadodara : The Vishwa Hindu Parishad on Friday declared a 14-point "Hindu charter of demands" and its desire to create a "Hindu vote-bank." "We will support any political party or candidate who supports our Hindu charter," international general secretary Pravin Togadia said at the end of a three-day conclave of the VHP board of trustees at Sokhada near here.

(5091) Pondicherry : Leader of the Opposition in the Pondicherry Assembly R. V. Janakiraman (Dravida Munnetra Kazhagam) has said that there was need for the authorities to clarify whether or not the order of the Delimitation Commission redrawing the territorial limits of Assembly constituencies in the Union Territory would come into force for the Assembly polls due in 2006.

(5092) Pondicherry : Secretary of the Pondicherry State unit of the all India Anna Dravida Munnetra Kazhagam (AIADMK) A. Anbalagan MLA has urged that the civic polls due for more than three decades in the Union Territory of Pondicherry be held along with the Assembly polls (due here in next few months).

(5093) Chandigarh : The contest among Congressmen for three Mayoral posts in the Chandigarh Municipal Corporation is hotting up with councillors owing allegiance to the local MP, Pawan Kumar Bansal, and the president of the Chandigarh unit of the party, B.B. Bahl, staking their claim before party high command. The last date for filing nominations for the post of Mayor, Senior Deputy Mayor and Deputy Mayor is December 26 and the election is to be held on January 1.

(5094) Lucknow : Bharatiya Janata Party wound up the first leg of its Rajnath Singh-led 'Nyaya Yatra' enthusing confidence that the success of the Yatra was a censure on the present 'criminal regime' of Mr Mulayam Singh Yadav in the State and was a beginning of the end of his governance.

(5095) Chennai : Blaming the State Government for not carrying out the tsunami rehabilitation work upto the desired level, Tamil Nadu Congress Committee president and MP, G.K. Vasan, said the initiatives of non-governmental organisations for the affected fishing community were more effective.

(5096) Villupuram : Pattali Makkal Katchi has termed as "Second Independence" the passage of the Bill on reservation in self-financing colleges. If such an effort were to come, as a corollary, the reservation concept should be extended to the Central educational institutions and the private sector too, said S. Ramadoss, party founder.

25-12-2005

(5097) Anantapur : Congress legislator from Singanamala S. Sailajanath has asked his Telugu Desam Party (TDP) counterparts from the district to exert pressure on their party leadership to change its stand regarding opposition to increasing the capacity of Pothireddypadu head regulator or be held guilty for working against the district's interests in future.

(5098) New Delhi : Bharatiya Janata Party general secretary and former Chief Minister of Uttar Pradesh Rajnath Singh is tipped to take over as BJP president next week when L.K. Advani quits the post immediately after the five-day Mumbai conclave starting December 26.

(5099) Gulbarga : The Congress decided to form a coalition government with the Janata Dal (Secular) to keep the Bharatiya Janata Party (BJP), which emerged as the single largest party in the Legislative Assembly after the last elections, from forming the government and gaining a foothold in the South.

(5100) Panaji : Leader of the Opposition in the Goa Assembly Manohar Parrikar on Saturday called for investing the authority of deciding the disqualification of members with an autonomous constitutional body instead of presiding officers of legislatures.

(5101) Panaji : Manohar Parrikar, Leader of the Opposition in the Goa Assembly, on Saturday called for modifications in the norms to implement the MP's Local Area Development scheme to stop "gross misuse and irregularities." Replying to a question at his press briefing whether he favours scrapping of the scheme on account of its alleged misuse, Mr. Parrikar said that he will support its continuation.

(5102) Panaji : Shantaram Naik, Congress MP, on Friday moved a Private Member's Bill in the Rajya Sabha seeking introduction of an Article 40A in the Constitution to make it obligatory on the State to take legal and other administrative steps to develop scientific temper, humanism and spirit of inquiry and reform among the people. He told The Hindu that in his Statement of Objects and Reasons, he has stated that superstitious beliefs have taken strong roots in society and have done irreparable harm to it.

(5103) Kochi : Kerala Congress (Secular) leader P.C. George has urged Chief Minister Oommen Chandy to take steps to expose those political parties which allegedly have links with the Pakistan intelligence agency ISI.

(5104) Kozhikode : Indian National League (INL) will hold talks with like-minded parties to forge an alliance with them in view of the coming Assembly elections in Kerala, Tamil Nadu, West Bengal and Pondicherry.

(5105) Thiruvananthapuram : CPI State secretary Veliyam Bhargavan has sought a CBI investigation into how most of the witnesses in the Kozhikode ice-cream parlour sex racket case turned hostile at the trial stage.

(5106) Thiruvananthapuram : Democratic Indira Congress (Karunakaran) leader T. M. Jacob has urged the Government to take away the task of providing relief to tsunami victims from the State Government.

(5107) Thiruvananthapuram : The Youth Congress is compiling a comprehensive list of bureaucrats who have made corruption an integral part of their functioning style, organisation's State president K. P. Anil Kumar said here on Saturday. He said a list was already with the Youth Congress, but it would be made all-inclusive during the 43-day 'padayatra' (tour on foot) he is undertaking from Kasaragode to Parassala from December 28. No bureaucrat who deserved to be included in the list would be left out, Mr. Anil Kumar said at a press conference.

(5108) Ballia (UP) : Widening the family divide, Samajwadi Party general secretary Amar Singh's brother Arvind Singh has decided to join the Congress.

(5109) New Delhi : Expelled BJP Members of Parliament are considering moving the Delhi High Court against the decision.

(5110) Salem : All India Secretary of the Communist Party of India (CPI) D. Raja has urged the Centre to "explain the follow-up action" it would initiate against those Members of Parliament (MP) who were expelled for involvement in the cash-for-questions scam, as they were "no longer MPs."

(5111) New Delhi : The Bharatiya Janata Party chief L.K. Advani said the scenario of Indian agriculture, small scale industry and the informal sector did not give him much cheer, though he felt the country was fast becoming a key player.

(5112) Srinagar : The Communist Party of India (M) state secretary Mohammad Yusuf Tarigami said on Saturday that India and Pakistan should open more transit points along the Line of Control.

(5113) Hyderabad : The Telugu Desam Party president, N. Chandrababu Naidu, has fully backed the expulsion of 11 Members of Parliament who were at the centre of a sting operation by a television channel while accepting money for tabling questions. Parliament's decision would go a long way in strengthening value-based politics, he said.

(5114) New Delhi : In June this year, after the face-off with the RSS, it had become clear that the countdown had begun for senior BJP leaders like L.K. Advani. Almost a year ago, the RSS chief K.S. Sudarshan fired the first salvo when he said in a televised interview that it was time for the aged BJP leadership to make room for the next generation.

(5115) New Delhi : The ongoing demolition drive in the Capital against unauthorised constructions remained a low-key affair on Saturday as only 20 properties were targeted by demolition squads during the day, the lowest so far since the drive began on Monday. Though the drive remained peaceful, Bharatiya Janata Party leaders and workers including former Chief Minister Madan Lal Khurana courted arrest demanding immediate suspension of the exercise.

(5116) Chennai : The All India Anna Dravida Munnetra Kazhagam (AIADMK) on Saturday called upon its activists to be prepared for any sacrifice while carrying out all the instructions of party general secretary and Chief Minister Jayalalithaa to ensure that the party returned to power after the Assembly elections.

26-12-2005

(5117) Hyderabad : The State council of the Communist Party of India has threatened to occupy the vast stretches of land being allotted by the Government to industrialists in the name of industrial promotion if the latter indulged in 'real estate' development instead of industries.

(5118) Hyderabad : Rashtriya Swayamsevak Sangh chief K.S. Sudarshan has lashed out at Maoists for indulging in 'mindless' violence and dared them to choose the path of development instead of destruction.

(5119) Hyderabad : Deputy Floor Leader of the Telugu Desam Party and Nagarkurnool MLA Nagam Janardhan Reddy on Sunday said he was prepared for any punishment if he was proved wrong in his allegations on irregularities in the Kalwakurthy Lift Irrigation Scheme-II in Mahabubnagar district.

(5120) Thiruvananthapuram : Communist Party of India (CPI) State secretary Veliyam Bhargavan has said that 'subjective factors' rather than ideological differences are hampering Communist unity in the country.

(5121) Bangalore : The recent defections from the Janata Dal (Secular) to the AIPJD of the former Deputy Chief Minister Siddaramaiah in the Ramanagaram town municipality which resulted in the election of one of the deserters as the president of the municipality has been termed as inconsequential by the Working President of the State unit of the Janata Dal (S) H.D. Kumaraswamy.

(5122) Mysore : Former Deputy Chief Minister and All-India Progressive Janata Dal (AIPJD) leader Siddaramaiah has reiterated that the Krishna Temple is public property and that the Ashta Mutts have no right over the historical shrine.

(5123) Bangalore : Vice-president of the Bharatiya Janata Party M. Venkaiah Naidu said here on Sunday that the top leaders had not finalised the successor to party president L.K. Advani, though the name of the former Uttar Pradesh Chief Minister, Rajnath Singh, was under consideration.

(5124) New Delhi : The former Prime Minister, Atal Bihari Vajpayee, turned 81 on Sunday and was greeted by a number of party leaders and activists at his residence here.

(5125) Bhubaneswar : The Left parties in the country should form a confederation to work together on a common minimum programme, Secretary of the Communist Party of India (ML-Liberation) Dipankar Bhattacharya said here on Sunday.

(5126) Patna : The completion of one month in power of the NDA in Bihar has been described by Chief Minister Nitish Kumar as "a good beginning" during which the government has reached a stage of take off, but the opposition RJD and Congress disagreed and hoped little from them.

(5127) Raisen (M.P.) : Expelled Bharatiya Janata Party leader Uma Bharti's loyalist and former State minister Gaurishankar Shejwar has expressed annoyance against the administration for the 'adverse' law and order situation in his native district.

(5128) Chennai : Democratic Progressive Alliance (DPA) leaders demanded the "immediate" and "unconditional" release of the Chennai Corporation councillor and local Dravida Munnetra Kazhagam (DMK) functionary, K. Dhanasekaran, who was arrested in connection with the stampede in a MGR Nagar school.

(5129) Chennai : Railway Minister Lalu Prasad met Dravida Munnetra Kazhagam president M. Karunanidhi at his Gopalapuram residence here on Sunday. It was described as a courtesy call.

(5130) Chennai : Be it in the massive tsunami relief and rehabilitation programme, or even in the more recent flood relief activities, politics appears to be playing a major role. Following Chief Minister Jayalalithaa's regret that Central assistance under the tsunami rehabilitation programme has been just over Rs. 600 crore, Finance Minister Chidambaram issued a detailed statement outlining a Rs. 5,025 crore package for Tamil Nadu. But Ms. Jayalalithaa's point was that the money has not been received.

(5131) Nagapattinam : The Communist Party of India (Marxist) on Sunday demanded the Government to provide flood relief and adequate compensation to farmers for crop loss.

27-12-2005

(5132) Hyderabad : Accepting the gauntlet thrown by the Telugu Desam Party (TDP) MLA, N. Janardhan Reddy, the Congress Legislature Party (CLP) on Monday asked if he would step down from his post if works on Phase I of Kalwakurthy lift irrigation projects were completed before December 2007.

(5133) Hyderabad : The Communist Party of India has asked Prime Minister Manmohan Singh to consult the Left and other parties supporting the UPA coalition at the Centre before taking any decision on reforms in the labour laws.

(5134) Tirupati : Communist Party of India (Marxist) Rajya Sabha member P. Madhu appears to have spoken his heart out when he listed the privileges being extended by the Government to the MPs and MLAs even as it was dragging its feet in meeting the housing needs of the poor and the deprived classes.

(5135) Rajahmundry : Akhil Bharatiya Vidyarthi Parishad (ABVP) southern region secretary P. Chandrasekhar has alleged that the State Government is hand-in-glove with the managements of corporate colleges, which are minting money through commercialisation of education.

(5136) Mumbai : Bharatiya Janata Party president L.K. Advani was all praise for the achievements of his party in his opening remarks at the National Executive Meeting on Monday, but did not touch the "cash-for-query" episode or his own controversial remarks on M.A. Jinnah or the not so cordial relations with the Rashtriya Swayamsevak Sangh.

(5137) New Delhi : The Communist Party of India on Monday re-emphasised its concern over the direction of the Manmohan Singh Government while standing by the commitment to support the United Progressive Alliance for the full term.

(5138) Mumbai : The change of guard in the Bharatiya Janata Party has yet to take place, but already rumblings are being heard about the party president, L.K. Advani's handling of some recent major issues.

(5139) Thrissur : State Secretary of the Communist Party of India (CPI) Veliyam Bhargavan has said that the conditionalities set by the Asian Development Bank (ADB) for extending loan to five Corporations of the State are harmful to the people.

(5140) Nedumbassery : The Bharatiya Janata Party (BJP) will set its house in order and will come out as a rejuvenated group from its silver jubilee celebrations in Mumbai, O. Rajagopal, senior party leader from the State, said here on Monday.

(5141) Mumbai : Differences between the Rashtriya Swayamsevak Sangh (RSS) and the Bharatiya Janata Party (BJP) came to the fore during a book release function, shortly before the BJP national executive met here on Monday.

(5142) Coimbatore : The United Progressive Alliance (UPA) Government at the Centre should tread cautiously on the Sri Lankan issue at a time when a fresh assassination threatens to end the ceasefire pact between the island nation's Government and the Liberation Tigers of Tamil

Eelam (LTTE), the Communist Party of India (CPI) national secretary, D. Raja, said on Monday.

(5143) Lucknow : Former Uttar Pradesh Chief Minister and Bahujan Samaj Party (BSP) national president Mayawati on Monday announced the expulsion of four party MPs, including three who were caught on camera in the cash-for-query scam.

(5144) Srinagar : The former Jammu and Kashmir Chief Minister, Mufti Mohammad Sayeed, has "politely" declined the Congress invitation to join the Union Cabinet. Sources close to the Mufti told The Hindu on Monday that the People's Democratic Party founder was not interested in leaving the home turf at this juncture. They dismissed media reports that he had been "eyeing" the Power Ministry after the death of P.M. Sayeed, as "mere speculation."

(5145) Patna : The RJD hit the roads for the first time as an opposition party with the Leader of the Opposition in the Bihar Assembly, Rabri Devi, staging a dharna in the Gandhi Maidan protesting against the police lathicharge on shiksha mitras (temporary teachers) here on Monday.

(5146) New Delhi : The decision of the Bharatiya Janata Party leaders to come out on the streets over the issue of demolition of illegal structures could not have come at a worse time. The saffron outfit is being seen as patronising the builder-official nexus alienating the party from the masses, especially the Capital's middle class, who feel that this initiative should have come on the issue of fast running electricity meters, inflated bills and the poor power and water situation in the city.

(5147) New Delhi : Delhi Bharatiya Janata Party president Harsh Vardhan has demanded that registration of all builders, property dealers and those associated with the trade in the Capital be made mandatory to prevent illegal constructions.

(5148) Bhopal : Leader of the Opposition in the Madhya Pradesh Assembly Jamuna Devi today submitted a memorandum to Governor Balram Jakhar against withdrawal of a criminal case, from Raisen district's Gohargunj court, against Chief Minister Shivraj Singh Chauhan.

(5149) Kanpur : With political parties accusing each other of supporting criminals, it was the turn of Uttar Pradesh Chief Minister

Mulayam Singh Yadav on Monday to attack BJP on its 'Nyaya Yatra' (march for justice) against the murder of party MLA Krishna Nand Rai.

(5150) Chennai : Tamil Nadu Congress Committee president G.K. Vasan on Monday criticised the ruling AIADMK for its alleged attempt to create a rift in the State Congress unit. Mr. Vasan, while speaking to newsmen here, told Congress workers not to fall prey to the "evil designs" of the ruling party. He asked them not to discuss inner party matters in public or give interviews to electronic media supported by the ruling party. He directed them not to organise public meetings for expressing their views against the party leadership.

28-12-2005

(5151) Hyderabad : The State Council of the Communist Party of India (CPI) has demanded that police and labour departments take steps to conduct the verification elections for the recognised trade union of APSRTC in a non-partisan manner.

(5152) Hyderabad : Telugu Desam Legislature Party deputy leader N. Janardhan Reddy has accepted the Congress challenge and agreed to place before the media the documents to prove "irregularities" in Kalwakurthy lift irrigation scheme work, in Mahabubnagar district in Andhra Pradesh.

(5153) Thiruvananthapuram : Leader of the Opposition V. S. Achuthanandan has urged the National Human Rights Commission (NHRC) to intervene in the ice-cream parlour sex scandal case to ensure that the human rights of the girls sexually exploited by those involved in the racket are protected.

(5154) Mumbai : The Bharatiya Janata Party on Tuesday charged the United Progressive Alliance Government with failure in the management of India's foreign policy resulting in a "drift," but differences appeared to have surfaced between Mr. Vajpayee and the party's resolution on foreign policy.

(5155) Bangalore : The Congress has emerged the clear victor in the medley that the zilla and taluk panchayat elections in rural Karnataka turned out to be. The Congress stands far ahead of its coalition partner, the Janata Dal (Secular), and dashed its hopes of gaining control over the panchayat raj bodies. The Bharatiya Janata Party (BJP), the largest group in the Legislative Assembly, will have to be content with the third place.

(5156) Mumbai : Bharatiya Janata Party general secretary in-charge of organisation Sanjay Joshi resigned on Tuesday following allegations of his involvement in a sex scandal.

(5157) Bangalore The Siddaramaiah-led All India Progressive Janata Dal (AIPJD) played the spoilsport for the Janata Dal (Secular) and put paid to its ambition of securing the first place in the zilla and taluk panchayat elections.

(5158) Mangalore : The BJP has made a huge turnaround by winning 15 seats in the Dakshina Kannada Zilla Panchayat even as the third round of counting was under progress in all the five taluks. The Congress has won 12 seats as against its previous tally of 31 seats in the body.

(5159) Mysore : The Janata Dal (Secular) has suffered a setback in Mysore district with the Congress and the All India Progressive Janata Dal (AIPJD) sharing the spoils of a mixed electoral verdict in the Mysore Zilla Panchayat.

(5160) Kozhikode : KPCC president Ramesh Chennithala on Tuesday demanded early completion of the ongoing probe into the SLC-Lavalin deal in which the Accountant General (AG) had, in its preliminary report, found irregularities.

(5161) Thiruvananthapuram : The Democratic Indira Congress (K) Leader M. P. Gangadharan, ex-MLA, on Tuesday demanded a white paper on tsunami funds, focussing on the amount received and its utilisation.

(5162) New Delhi : The Communist Party of India (Marxist) said on Tuesday that it was for the Election Commission to explain the irregularities it had pointed out in the issue of photo identity cards in West Bengal.

(5163) Mumbai : The controversy over L.K. Advani continuing as the Leader of the Opposition after giving up the post of party president continued to trouble the Bharatiya Janata Party on the second day of its national executive committee session here on Tuesday.

(5164) New Delhi : The Left parties have suggested that the Government work on alternative methods to raise resources to fund social security schemes, including raising the tax-GDP ratio, and use a portion of the surplus in public enterprises.

(5165) New Delhi : Responding to local sentiments and demands by local leaders, Congress president Sonia Gandhi on Tuesday cleared the name of former Member of Parliament J.P. Aggarwal for nomination to the Rajya Sabha from Delhi for the third vacant seat. Sitting members Karan Singh and Janardhan Diwedi are being re-nominated for the second tenure by the party.

(5166) Chandigarh : The nine-month-old Congress regime in Haryana headed by Bhupinder Singh Hooda has achieved remarkable success in improving the lot of the weaker and under-privileged sections of society besides ushering in rapid industrial and social development.

(5167) Dharamsala : Pandemonium prevailed in the Himachal Assembly on Tuesday after BJP members started shouting slogans over the proposed ski-village project in Manali. Deputy Speaker Dharam Pal later adjourned the House. Intervening during a heated discussion on the issue between Tourism Minister G.S. Bali and opposition leader Prem Kumar Dhumal, Chief Minister Virbhadra Singh said that the recent Memorandum of Understanding for the $135- million mega project with the Henry Ford Company would be cancelled and global tenders re-floated if any discrepancies were found in the detailed project report.

(5168) Chennai : The Dravida Munnetra Kazhagam has strongly protested the delay in grant of permission by District Collectors for screening a publicity videocassette brought out by the party.

(5169) Dharmapuri : The Communist Party of India (CPI) is opposed to Foreign Direct Investment in the retail sector, D. Raja, CPI all India secretary told reporters here on Tuesday. Appreciated the UPA Government for bringing out the Right to Information Act and Rural Employment Guarantee Scheme, he appealed to the Union Government to protect Public Sector Undertakings and not to do anything in violation of the Common Minimum Programme.

29-12-2005

(5170) Hyderabad : A delegation of Telangana Rashtra Samithi (TRS) MLAs and senior leaders on Wednesday appealed to Chief Minister Y.S. Rajasekhara Reddy, to implement the Government Order (GO) which seeks to check the release of water to K-C canal from the Rajolibanda dam and reopen a vent in the Sunkesula barrage to meet the drinking water requirements of Mahabubnagar. TRS MLA, G. Vijayarama Rao, told reporters later that Dr. Reddy assured closure of sluices in Rajolibanda anicut which carry water "illegally" to K-Canal within two months.

(5171) Hyderabad : The APCC celebrated the Congress Party foundation day at its headquarters, Gandhi Bhavan, on Wednesday with a call to its workers to rededicate themselves for the development of the country.

(5172) Hyderabad : The Telugu Desam Party is willing to join hands with the Left to secure best relief and rehabilitation package for people to be displaced by new irrigation projects.

(5173) Hyderabad : Taking a cue from the functioning of the overseas affairs cell of the Congress and the Bharatiya Janata Party (BJP), the Telugu Desam Party has decided to constitute a similar cell to cater to the needs of NRI Telugus.

(5174) Kurnool : CPI State Secretariat member K. Ramakrishna said the party was bringing pressure on the Government to complete irrigation projects early and stop migration of farm workers from backward areas.

(5175) Nellore : State secretary of the Communist Party of India (CPI), K. Narayana, has lashed out at Director-General of Police Swaranjit Sen for his reported comments on Home Minister K. Jana Reddy that the latter should wear uniform.

(5176) Mumbai : Bharatiya Janata Party president L.K. Advani is optimistic of an "impending return" of the National Democratic Alliance to the "nation's helm" after early Lok Sabha elections. He brushed aside his party's recent "troubles" and held the Congress responsible for all corruption in the country, including in the BJP.

(5177) Bangalore : The Congress has gained a majority in 14 of the 27 zilla panchayats, and its coalition partner, the Janata Dal (Secular), has emerged the leader in two zilla panchayats. The main Opposition party, Bharatiya Janata Party, has not been able to secure a majority in any zilla panchayat in the elections held on December 19 and 23.

(5178) Bangalore : The Congress is against forcing mid-term elections in the State despite its good performance in the zilla and taluk panchayat elections.

(5179) Bangalore : The Janata Dal (Secular) will convene its legislature party meeting shortly to analyse the results of the zilla and taluk panchayat elections and related issues, Deputy Chief Minister M.P. Prakash has said.

(5180) Bangalore : The Bharatiya Janata Party is happy over its performance in the panchayat elections, wresting 105 zilla panchayat and more than 360 taluk panchayat seats from the ruling Congress-led coalition.

(5181) Mangalore : The district unit of the Bharatiya Janata Party (BJP) has urged the Centre to bring two stations as well as railway areas of Mangalore under the South Western Railway Zone, Hubli.

(5182) Mangalore : The former Chief Minister and Chairman of the Central Administrative Reforms Commission M. Veerappa Moily has been appointed by the AICC President Sonia Gandhi the convener of the elite group of financial experts.

(5183) Mysore : Even though the Congress emerged as the single largest party in the 46-member Mysore Zilla Panchayat, it is the former Deputy Chief Minister Siddaramaiah's AIPJD which is basking in the glory of the mixed results thrown up in the elections to the Mysore Zilla Panchayat and seven taluk panchayats.

(5184) Kozhikode : Indian Union Muslim League (IUML) State Committee member and Calicut Development Authority (CDA) chairman M.C. Mayin Haji on Wednesday testified before the Marad Special Court that the first accused in the massacre case of May 2, 2003, Thekkapurathu Muhammed Ali had told him that he wanted to avenge the killing of his brother T. Aboobaker, who was killed in the communal conflagration at Marad in January 2002.

(5185) New Delhi : The Congress on Wednesday described the finding of a mass grave in Panchmahals district of Gujarat as a "gross violation of human rights and unfortunate."

(5186) Mumbai : Gujarat and Jharkhand Chief Ministers Narendra Modi and Arjun Munda on Wednesday complained that the United Progressive Alliance Government was discriminating against the Bharatiya Janata Party-ruled States.

(5187) Mumbai : Bharatiya Janata Party president L.K. Advani on Wednesday dared Congress chief Sonia Gandhi to come clean on the Volcker

Committee revelations on Iraq's 'Oil-for-Food' programme or resign as the head of the National Advisory Council.

(5188) Mumbai : Organising the logistics for several thousand delegates attending the Bharatiya Janata Party's national council session here would not have been an easy task. But to the credit of the party's Maharashtra unit that hosted the three-day event, the arrangements were perfect.

(5189) New Delhi : Janata Dal (United) president Sharad Yadav on Wednesday termed the recovery of mass graves in Gujarat "inhuman" and said steps should be taken to ensure that riot-affected get justice.

(5190) Bhopal : The Madhya Pradesh police are investigating anonymous calls and extortion threats received by Sanjay Joshi before he submitted his resignation as Bharatiya Janata Party general secretary.

(5191) Kolkata : Barely six months before the Assembly elections in West Bengal, veteran Communist Party of India (Marxist) leader and former Chief Minister Jyoti Basu on Wednesday said the State Government would start fresh recruitment.

(5192) New Delhi : Sharp differences within the ruling Congress over the issue of ongoing demolitions in the Capital came out into the open on Wednesday when Congress leaders in the Municipal Corporation of Delhi led by the Mayor, Satbir Singh, had a "verbal clash" with Chief Minister Sheila Dikshit over the issue of putting the names of over 18,000 illegal buildings and their owners who are facing the hammer on the MCD website.

(5193) New Delhi : Amid drumbeats, trumpets and showering of flower petals former Union Minister Karan Singh, three-time Member of Parliament J.P. Aggarwal and senior Congress leader Janardhan Diwedi filed their nominations for the three Rajya Sabha seats from Delhi at the Old Secretariat Complex housing the Delhi Assembly on Wednesday. With the Bharatiya Janata Party not fielding any candidate for the Upper House polls, all the three Congress candidates are set to get elected unopposed.

(5194) Lucknow : Dubbing the Samajwadi Party as "casteist," Amar Singh's disowned younger brother Arvind Singh on Tuesday joined the Congress saying it is the only party that sought social harmony and secularism.

(5195) Lucknow : The Congress on Wednesday gave a clarion call for waging a "final battle" against the Mulayam Singh Yadav government and reviving the party in the politically crucial State of Uttar Pradesh.

(5196) Chennai : The State Congress unit on Wednesday celebrated the party's 120th anniversary.

(5197) Chennai : Shedding its post-tsunami hesitation to force the formation of all party relief distribution panels, the Democratic Progressive Alliance (DPA) is stepping up pressure on the government to form such committees, at least for flood relief.

(5198) Chennai : Any agreement to find a lasting solution to the ethnic crisis in Sri Lanka should be between the Island Government and the Liberation Tigers of Tamil Eelam (LTTE) said the Pattali Makkal Katchi (PMK) leader S. Ramadoss here on Wednesday.

30-12-2005

(5199) Hyderabad : The Telugu Desam has sought to take credit for the success of the free power scheme of the Congress Government on the ground that the infrastructure created by the former during its rule has paved the way for its implementation.

(5200) Hyderabad : Rich tributes were paid to veteran Congress leader Dronamraju Satyanarayana who died here late on Wednesday night at Care Hospital.

(5201) Tirupati : Chief Minister Y.S. Rajasekhar Reddy on Thursday showered eulogies on, "Visalandhra", the official organ of the Communist Party of India (CPI) on the eve of the Telugu daily launching its Tirupati edition- third in Andhra Pradesh after Hyderabad and Vijayawada.

(5202) Mumbai : The former Prime Minister, Atal Bihari Vajpayee, told the Bharatiya Janata Party's silver jubilee public rally here on Thursday that he would not contest any election now and virtually nominated 'Ram and Lakshman' of the party, L.K. Advani and Pramod Mahajan, to lead the BJP.

(5203) Madikeri : The Congress has established its hold in the just-concluded elections to the zilla and taluk panchayats in the State because of the Siddaramaiah factor, not due to the charisma of Chief Minister N.

Dharam Singh or Karnataka Pradesh Congress Committee President M. Mallikarjun Kharge, former MLC A.K. Subbaiah told presspersons here on Thursday.

(5204) Mysore : Leaders of the All India Progressive Janata Dal (AIPJD) will tour the State in January to strengthen the party.

(5205) Mysore : Former Deputy Chief Minister and All-India Progressive Janata Dal (AIPJD) leader Siddaramaiah has claimed that the former Prime Minister and Janata Dal (Secular) supremo H.D. Deve Gowda's "caste politics" has come a cropper during the recent elections to the zilla and taluk panchayats in the State.

(5206) Thiruvananthapuram : Congress MLA A. Sujanapal will be inducted as a Minister in the Oommen Chandy Government in Kerala on January 4.

(5207) New Delhi : Congress president Sonia Gandhi has expressed shock over the Bangalore shoot-out on Wednesday. Extending her condolences to the family of Prof. M.C. Puri, who was killed, she said it was "a sombre moment."

(5208) Mumbai : For the first time since the expulsion of 11 MPs following the cash-for-questions scandal, the Bharatiya Janata Party here on Thursday "unreservedly" expressed "regret" over the involvement of some of its representatives, with party leader Sushma Swaraj adding that the matter "made the BJP hang its head in shame."

(5209) Chennai : Supporters of Sri Lankan Tamils, including two constituents of the United Progressive Alliance (UPA) at the Centre - the Pattali Makkal Katchi (PMK) and the Marumalarchi Dravida Munnetra Kazhagam (MDMK), on Thursday urged the Manmohan Singh Government not to extend any military assistance to the island Government.

(5210) New Delhi : The Rashtriya Janata Dal and the Nationalist Congress Party on Thursday denied news reports that suggested attempts were underway to create a pressure group within the United Progressive Alliance.

(5211) New Delhi : Defining her relationship with Prime Minister Manmohan Singh as "perfect" and denying the existence of two power centres in the Government, Congress president Sonia Gandhi on Thursday said the only complaint she had with him was that he did not highlight his achievements enough.

(5212) Mumbai : The United Progressive Alliance Government is suffering from "policy paralysis" leading to a serious deterioration of the economic situation, the Bharatiya Janata Party alleged in its economic resolution adopted here on Thursday.

(5213) New Delhi : Ruling out the possibility of issuing an Ordinance on the lines of what the Maharashtra Government did to regularise illegal buildings in Ulhasnagar township, the Congress party on Thursday decided to form another committee to coordinate with the Municipal Corporation of Delhi and the Delhi Government to look into the widespread public hue and cry over the issue of demolitions of illegal buildings in the Capital.

(5214) Chennai : The Pattali Makkal Katchi on Thursday demanded a special session of the Assembly to decide the issue of reservation in self-financing professional colleges.

31-12-2005

(5215) Guntur : The Communist Party India has expressed concern over the ever reducing number of days of transaction in a year in either the State Assembly or Parliament and its national secretary Suravaram Sudhakar Reddy has given a call to all political parties to ensure that more people's issues are debated.

(5216) Hyderabad : Telugu Desam MLA Nagam Janardhan Reddy has requested Chief Secretary T.K. Dewan to get complaints of irregularities in the implementation of Kalwakurthy lift-irrigation scheme enquired by the Vigilance and Enforcement Department.

(5217) Kadapa : Kamalapuram MLA G. Veerasiva Reddy, who was suspended from the TDP and Proddatur MLA N. Varadarajulu Reddy on Friday separately lambasted TDP president N. Chandrababu Naidu for trying to take credit for the free power scheme of the Rajasekhara Reddy Government.

(5218) Mumbai : The Bharatiya Janata Party's political "message" from its silver jubilee National Council session was "back to basics," not forgetting that it was part of a larger Parivar with the aim of not just catapulting itself into power, but to change India.

(5219) New Delhi : The Samajwadi Party chief and Uttar Pradesh Chief Minister, Mulayam Singh Yadav, on Friday charged that telephones of three party leaders including his son Akhilesh Singh were being tapped, an accusation rubbished by the Congress as "baseless."

(5220) Mumbai : At the closing session of the Bharatiya Janata Party's silver jubilee National Council session here on Friday, leaders reminded the delegates and the cadre that the BJP was founded "to change the very character and culture of Indian politics" and not to emulate the prevailing political culture.

(5221) Bangalore : The former Chief Minister and State Samajwadi Party President S. Bangarappa has alleged that the coalition partners, Congress and Janata Dal (Secular), and the Opposition party, Bharatiya Janata Party (BJP) indulged in corruption in the recent elections to zilla and taluk panchayats. They distributed money, liquor and jewellery among voters and resorted to muscle power, he said.

(5222) Mangalore : The Janata Dal (Secular) could have done better in the zilla and taluk panchayat elections, Deputy Chief Minister M.P. Prakash has said. "We have not done as well as we could have, but there were several factors that gave the Bharatiya Janata Party an upper hand," he told The Hindu here on Friday.

(5223) Kottayam : The Democratic Indira Congress - Karunakaran (DIC-K) will announce its future course of action, including the issue of relationship with the LDF, by the second week of January, party president K. Muraleedharan said here on Friday.

(5224) Thiruvananthapuram : Leader of the Opposition V. S. Achuthanandan has urged President A.P.J. Abdul Kalam to issue necessary orders under Article 170 (2) of the Constitution to give effect to the delimitation of Assembly constituencies carried out seven months ago.

(5225) Mumbai : D elegates at the closing session of the five-day BJP conclave here on Friday were warned by leaders to stay away from the media, desist from appearing on television shows or giving interviews to the print media. Only the official spokespersons should speak to the press, they were told.

(5226) Chennai : At a demonstration here, leaders of parties in the Democratic Progressive Alliance on Friday deplored the State Government's decision to detain Dravida Munnetra Kazhagam functionary K. Dhanasekaran under the Goondas Act. They wanted the Chief Minister to accept responsibility for the December 18 stampede at MGR Nagar in the city.

01-01-2006

(5227) Anantapur : The extensive 1,500-km 'padayatra' taken up by the district unit of Communist Party of India (Marxist) in the name of 'Anantha Prasthanam' wishing the comprehensive development of the district completed 500 km on Friday, after 20 days of its launch.

(5228) Hyderabad : The BJP has demanded the resignation of Home Minister, K. Jana Reddy for granting remission of sentence and releasing from jail, Muzeeb Ahmed, who was recently arrested in a fresh case related to terrorist activities.

(5229) Mumbai : Lal Krishna Advani resigned as Bharatiya Janata Party president on Saturday and formally declared that his successor would be Rajnath Singh. The new chief would take charge at the BJP headquarters in New Delhi on January 2. With this the controversy that started in June this year in the Sangh Parivar, after Mr. Advani made the controversial remark that Pakistan founder Mohammad Ali Jinnah was secular, has ended. Mr. Advani denied that he was forced to resign under the pressure of the Rashtriya Swayamsevak Sangh. He said he had acted on his declaration at the Chennai national executive session in September. Mr. Advani announced his resignation at a press conference here, a day after the party's silver jubilee National Council session concluded. The resignation letter had been given to vice-president M. Venkaiah Naidu, he said. Several senior leaders including Rajnath Singh, Jaswant Singh, Pramod Mahajan, Venkaiah Naidu, Ananth Kumar, Gopinath Munde, Prakash Javadekar and Atul Shah were present.

(5230) Thiruvananthapuram : Kerala Pradesh Congress Committee president Ramesh Chennithala has dismissed with contempt the BJP call for a joint movement against the CPI (M) in the State.

(5231) Bangalore : Chief Minister N. Dharam Singh on Saturday hit back at his detractors in the Congress and said it is only the Congress

High Command that can take a decision on a leadership change in the State.

(5232) Bangalore : Encouraged by its improved performance in the elections to zilla and taluk panchayats compared with last year's poor show in the Assembly and Lok Sabha polls, the Congress is confident of winning 140 of the 224 seats in the Assembly if snap polls are to be announced.

(5233) Bijapur : The outcome of zilla and taluk panchayat elections has come as an eye opener for major parties, especially the Congress, the Bharatiya Janata Party (BJP) and the Janata Dal (Secular). It has provided them an opportunity to redraw their political strategies. With 20 seats, the Congress is far ahead of its two main rivals. But this is a poor show by the Congress compared to its performance in the previous elections, in which it won 31 seats in the 32-member House. The Congress has some reasons to be elated over the result in the wake of its poor show in the last general elections in which it can win only three of eight Assembly seats.

(5234) Hassan : The landslide victory of the Janata Dal (Secular) in Hassan district where it won 36 of the 40 zilla panchayat seats is a repeat of its 1995 performance. The party had secured 34 of 37 zilla panchayat seats when H.D. Deve Gowda was the Chief Minister.

(5235) Mangalore : The Karnataka State Council of the Communist Party of India (CPI) will strive to forge unity among various pro-people movements to "cleanse the polluted political system" in the State, Siddana Gouda Patil, Secretary of State unit of the CPI, has said.

(5236) Chikmagalur : C.T. Ravi, MLA and BJP Yuva Morcha State unit President, said here on Saturday that a resolution to launch a Statewide campaign against terrorists and naxalites will be adopted at the office-bearers' meeting of the morcha in Bangalore on January 6.

(5237) Alappuzha : The Nava Kerala Yatra lead by DIC(K) president KMuraleedharan reached Alappuzha on Saturday evening. DIC(K) district president M.J. Job and party workers accorded a rousing reception to the yatra at Parumala, from where the yatra entered the district. Later, a public meeting was held at Store Junction in Mannar. The yatra would cover Chengannur and Mavelikkara on Sunday and end at Kayamkulam in the evening.

(5238) Kochi : Revolutionary Socialist Party (RSP) State general secretary T.J. Chandrachoodan has urged Chief Minister Oommen Chandy to desist from the move to induct a new Minister into the State Cabinet.He told a press conference here on Saturday that Mr. Chandy had no moral right to induct a new Minister into his Cabinet as there was hardly five months left for the Government to bow out. He urged the Chief Minister not to take any policy decision during this period.

(5239) Kozhikode : Leader of the Opposition V. S. Achuthananadan on Saturday remarked that Agriculture Minister K. R. Gouri was defying orders of even Chief Minister Oommen Chandy.Addressing mediapersons here, Mr. Achuthanandan said: " Ms. Gouri has accused me of speaking as if I am the Chief Minister. But the fact is that I am only saying what I should as Leader of the Opposition," he said when the journalists sought his reaction to the statement reported to have been made by the Agriculture Minister.

(5240) Kozhikode : Leader of the Opposition V.S. Achuthanandan, on Saturday, demanded a judicial investigation into complaints about large-scale looting alleged to have taken place after the massacre of nine persons at Marad village on May 2, 2003.

(5241) Thodupuzha : Kerala Congress (Joseph) leader and chairman of the Gandhiji Study Centre P.J. Joseph has stressed the need to harness the possibilities of frontier technologies to enhance productivity and income from agriculture.

(5242) Mumbai : L.K. Advani held the top job of president for 11 years in the 25-year old Bharatiya Janata Party. Other presidents came and went, never to return as the head of the party, but Mr. Advani always did. He was president of the Jan Sangh for nearly seven years from 1970 to 1977 with a break in-between. He first took over as BJP president in 1986 after two consecutive tenures were given to Atal Bihari Vajpayee; after six years in that position till 1986, he returned to the top job in 1993 and kept it till 1998, when he became part of the Vajpayee Government. From 1989 to 1993, Mr. Advani was Leader of the Opposition in the Lok Sabha when Murli Manohar Joshi took over the reins of the party. He once again took over as party head after the BJP lost the 2004 Lok Sabha elections and M. Venkaiah Naidu quit the post. Since then he had held both positions of party chief and Leader of the Opposition.

(5243) Purulia (West Bengal) : Rabindranath Kar, CPI(M) leader and former zilla president, and his wife were killed when Maoists attacked and set their residence on fire at Bhomragrah in Purulia district on the Bengal-Jharkhand border on Saturday.

(5244) New Delhi : With the UPA suggesting disinvestment in profit-making non-navratna public sector undertakings, the Left parties would meet here on Monday to take a view on their alternative proposals to raise funds for social sector schemes. Having heard the Finance Minister P. Chidamabaram on his proposal to carry out disinvestment, the CPI (M) general secretary Prakash Karat said on Saturday that alternative methods to raise resources would be submitted by the Left parties in due course. The broad understanding was that the Government could raise the tax-GDP ratio, which the Left feel was brought downThe central committee of the CPI (M)at its recent meeting had said that the overall direction of the UPA Government was not in favour of working people and the poor and called for a change in the direction of economic policiesSuggesting that the Government taxes luxury consumption, the party said corporate profits have risen sharply in the recent period and the super-rich in the country were indulging in obscene levels of conspicuous consumptionIt also asked the Government to take steps to increase the tax-GDP ratio, which alone could generate resources for rural development and social sector spending The CPI (M) said categorically that this should be the path to follow rather than disinvestment of shares in profitable public sector enterprises.The Monday meeting could lead to finalisation of the alternative set of proposals by the Left parties.

(5245) New Delhi : Uttar Pradesh Chief Minister and Samajwadi Party supremo Mulayam Singh Yadav on Saturday reiterated his allegation that the Congress was behind the phone tapping of senior leaders of his party including Amar Singh, despite denial by the Union Home Ministry.

(5246) Chennai : Janata Party president Subramanian-Swamy has welcomed the joint statement issued by the Governments of India and Sri Lankaat the conclusion of President Mahinda Rajapakse's visit to New Delhi.

(5247) Mumbai : The ascendancy of Rajnath Singh has taken place against the backdrop of strong signals from the Rashtriya Swayamsevak

Sangh that the Bharatiya Janata Party must go back to its ideological roots and a view in the parent organisation that the BJP, especially during the years in power from 1998 to 2004, drifted from the course laid out by the RSS 'gurus.'

(5248) New Delhi: Disgruntled BJP leader Madan Lal Khurana, who was briefly suspended from the organisation for his outbursts against L K Advani in July, on Saturday described new party chief Rajnath Singh as a "committed Swayamsevak."

(5249) Varanasi : Despite the denial by the Union Home Ministry, Uttar Pradesh Chief Minister and Samajwadi Party supremo Mulayam Singh Yadav on Saturday reiterated his allegation that Congress president Sonia Gandhi was behind the phone tapping of senior leaders of his party including Amar Singh.

(5250) Ramanathapuram : The Democratic Progressive Alliance will remain in tact, and the "efforts" to create rupture among the allies will not succeed, Tamil Nadu Congress Committee president G.K. Vasan said on Saturday.

02-01-2006

(5251) Hyderabad : The Congress Legislature Party (CLP) has advised TDP President N. Chandrababu Naidu to stop opposing irrigation projects and refrain from 'dividing' people on the basis of region.

(5252) Hyderabad : The Bharatiya Janata Party has demanded that Chief Minister Y. S. Rajasekhara Reddy apologise in the wake of the recent arrest of Mujib Ahmed, who was released in August following remission of his prison term.Addressing a press conference here on Sunday, BJP national secretary B. Dattatreya also sought an explanation from the Government for the basis on which Mujib was released after being sentenced in connection with the killing of an IPS officer. Normally the country's security, the law and order situation and person's antecedents are considered before granting remission, he added.

(5253) Thrissur : The United Democratic Front (UDF) Government will try to implement the recommendations of the Narendran Commission, Kerala Pradesh Congress Committee (KPCC) president Ramesh Chennithala said here on Sunday.At a press conference, Mr. Chennithala said the ruling front was trying to bring about a consensus among different communities on the recommendations of the commission.

(5254) Manjeswaram : A 'Kerala March' being led by Communist Party of India (Marxist) State secretary Pinarayi Vijayan, highlighting the slogan 'Comprehensive development and social justice,' was flagged off by party Polit Bureau member and Leader of the Opposition V.S. Achuthanandan at a function here on Sunday in the presence of a huge turnout of party workers.

(5255) Chennai : The Marumalarchi Dravida Munnetra Kazhagam will approach the Assembly election taking into consideration lessons from the past and the future of the party. "Our steps will be measured," said the MDMK general secretary Vaiko at a press conference here on Sunday. The party was looking for a "respectable" representation in the Assembly and would work towards this goal, he said in response to a question. However, Mr. Vaiko refused to elaborate on how many seats constituted a respectable representation.

(5256) Bangalore : The party which performed the worst in the zilla and taluk panchayat elections is the Janata Dal (United) comprising hardcore followers of Ramakrishna Hegde. The party, which has five members in the State Assembly, could not win any seat in any of the 27 zilla panchayats. Its performance was dismal even in the elections to the 175 taluk panchayats, and it had to be content with a mere 18 seats. The party, which was ally of the Bharatiya Janata Party in the Assembly and parliamentary elections last year, severed its ties with that party and contested the elections on its own this time.

(5257) Shimoga : Shimoga MP and State President of the Samajwadi Party S. Bangarappa said here on Sunday that he had asked local leaders of his party to decide on aligning with parties, except the Bharatiya Janata Party, in sharing power in the zilla panchayats where no party is in a position to come to power on its own.

(5258) Thiruvananthapuram : Bharatiya Janata Party (BJP) State president P.S. Sreedharan Pillai said here on Sunday that he would enforce strict discipline in the party.At a press conference here, he said the party had permitted internal democracy, but recent developments called for stricter discipline.

(5259) Kolkata : The ruling Left Front in West Bengal on Sunday observed a "protest day" across the State, condemning the killing of a senior district leader of the Communist Party of India (Marxist) and his wife by Maoists at Bandwan in Purulia district early on Saturday.

(5260) Chandigarh : The Congress managed to retain the three posts of Mayor, Senior Deputy Mayor and Deputy Mayor in the 30-member Chandigarh Municipal Corporation in the annual election held here on Sunday. However, 28 members, including the local MP, Pawan Kumar Bansal, cast their votes in the absence of two nominated members.While Surender Singh was declared elected as the Mayor in the first round of the triangular contest, Shyama Negi was elected Senior Deputy Mayor after she defeated Rajesh Gupta of the BJP. The President of the local unit of the Youth Congress, H.S.Lucky, was elected Deputy Mayor after a tough contest.

(5261) Villupuram : Pattali Makkal Katchi founder S. Ramadoss has set the agenda for the party for the Assembly elections: to oust the All-India Anna Dravida Munnetra Kazhagam from power. Only the Democratic Progressive Alliance (DPA) has the capability to do so, and the PMK has a vital role to play in it, he said at the end of the executive committee and general body meeting, held at Thailapuram near here, on Saturday.

03-01-2006

(5262) Guntur : The State Government is lacking clarity on levying of user charges at Government hospitals as Chief Minister Y.S. Rajasekhara Reddy himself was constantly changing his statements, said former Minister and Telugu Desam Party official representative Kodela Siva Prasada Rao. Speaking to reporters here on Monday, he said the Congress had gone back on its pre-poll promise of abolishing user charges. "The Congress, which made a hue and cry on the user charges during the TDP rule, is now going back on its word and trying to levy user charges," he said.

(5263) V. R. Puram (Khammam) : The State cannot deprive the tribals of their special status in violation of the Fifth Schedule for the sake of the Polavaram project, according to BJP leader Ch. Vidyasagar Rao. Addressing a massive rally of the tribals and the tribal students organised under the aegis of the Adivasi Vidyarthi Samkshema Parishad, he said the project would cost the very existence of the primitive tribal groups in the area. In all 240 villages would be submerged.

(5264) Pathanamthitta : RSP State secretary T. J. Chandrachoodan said the LDF, if elected to power in the ensuing Assembly polls, should ensure that the key portfolios of Education, Revenue, Health, Finance and Home were allotted only to national parties "devoid of any sectional, communal or parochial interests."

(5265) Bangalore : Chief Minister N. Dharam Singh on Monday downplayed Saturday's meeting between Karnataka Pradesh Congress Committee President M. Mallikarjun Kharge and Maharashtra Governor S.M. Krishna, and said the success of the Congress in 14 of 27 zilla panchayats in the elections has proved that he has consolidated his position.

(5266) Mysore : The Congress party's local leadership has opposed any tie-up with Janata Dal(S) in the hung zilla panchayats of Mysore and Mandya districts.The Congress leadership in the two districts favour an alliance with All India Progressive Janata Dal (AIPJD) led by the former Deputy Chief Minister Siddaramaiah. All the 18 newly elected Congress members of Mysore Zilla Panchayat met at the party office here on Monday and decided against any truck with Janata Dal(S), which has eleven members in the 46-member House. The Congress, which has emerged as the single largest party in Mysore Zilla Panchayat, chose to align with the AIPJD, which has 15 members.

(5267) Kannur : Youth Congress State president K. P. Anilkumar has said that the Communist Party of India (Marxist) is seeking to extend its 'Kannur style politics' to the entire State.Mr. Anilkumar, who was leading the Youth March of the Youth Congress, was addressing a public function held at Taliparamba here to receive the foot march. He said the CPI(M)'s practice of finishing off or physically assaulting its political rivals should not be allowed to be extended to the entire State.

(5268) Kozhikode : Communist Marxist Party (CMP) leader and Minister for Co-operation M.V. Raghavan has asked CPI(M) leadership to clarify if Democratic Indira Congress (Karunakaran) (DIC-K) led by K. Karunakaran would be inducted into the Left Democratic Front (LDF).Inaugurating the seventh State convention of CMP women's wing in Kozhikode on Monday, Kerala Mahila Federation, here, Mr. Raghavan also demanded that the matter be clarified before the Assembly elections.

(5269) Kanhangad : Communist Party of India-Marxist (CPI-M) State secretary Pinarayi Vijayan has called upon the State Government to end its evasive stand on Narendran Commission recommendations in the backdrop of the conflicting stances on the issues by the Indian Union Muslim League (IUML) and the Nair Service Society (NSS).

(5270) New Delhi : The Left parties on Monday decided to oppose the United Progressive Alliance Government's proposal to disinvest shares in profitable public sector undertakings as also privatisation of pension funds. These decisions were among the five taken at the Coordination Committee meeting the four Left parties - the CPI, CPI (M), RSP and AIFB - held here. Addressing a news conference, CPI (M) general secretary Prakash Karat said the Left parties also discussed alternative proposals for resource mobilisation that would be sent to the Government shortly. The Left parties decided to organise a widespread campaign against the U.S. policies to coincide with the visit of American President George Bush next month; take up plans to modernise Delhi and Mumbai airports; and put forward positions to be taken by India and the developing countries in the forthcoming negotiations of the WTO.

(5271) Bhubaneswar : The Opposition has condemned Monday's police firing on tribals at Kalinga Nagar in Jajpur district and demanded the resignation of Chief Minister Naveen Patnaik, who holds the Home portfolio. Six tribals and one policeman were killed in a clash at Kalinga Nagar, police said. Unconfirmed reports put the toll at 13. The incident took place around 11 a.m. when nearly 800 tribals from nearby villages reached the spot to protest against the construction of a boundary wall for a proposed six-million tonne Tata Steel plant.

(5272) New Delhi : Rajnath Singh took over as Bharatiya Janata Party president here on Monday, signalling the end of the Advani era in the party. In about 10 days, he is expected to put in place a new team of office-bearers. Until a final decision is taken, senior vice-president Bal Apte, close to the Rashtriya Swayamsevak Sangh, will be given the key responsibility related to the party organisation, it is expected. Mr. Singh said he would make "no compromise on the issues of corruption and indiscipline." It is expected that the six BJP MPs indicted by Parliament in the cash-for-questions scandal will be expelled from the party also. This would be different from Mr. Advani's stand - he walked out of the Lok

Sabha and dissociated himself and the party with the expulsion of the MPs on December 23. Mr. Singh took charge amid scenes of great celebration. There were drumbeaters, 'shehnai' players, firecrackers and the mandatory ladoos. A hoarding displaying a smiling picture of Mr. Singh was put up at the entrance of the party headquarters here. Almost the entire BJP top brass, including the former Prime Minister, Atal Bihari Vajpayee, were present to see him take charge from Mr. Advani. Both senior leaders expressed the confidence that under Mr. Singh the party would reach greater heights. Mr. Vajpayee went a step further, saying the "bed of spikes and the crown of thorns" that came with the party president's post would become the "crown of power." This was a clear signal that Mr. Singh would remain president till 2010. In short, the BJP could well fight the next Lok Sabha elections under his leadership. Sending the "right" message to the RSS, Mr. Singh said he would remain focussed on "cultural nationalism" and "integral humanism," phrases often used by the BJP as a synonym for Hindutva. "These will serve as the basis for all our future programmes." Mr. Singh spelt out four priorities: keeping the party's image clean, expanding its base, strengthening the National Democratic Alliance and "struggling" on the streets to expose the "anti-people policies of the United Progressive Alliance." He wanted the party "to always honour Mother India, the people, the farmers who give us our daily food and the ordinary party worker who helps to take the party forward."

(5273) New Delhi : Will Rajnath Singh's entry as Bharatiya Janata Party president lead to the return of expelled former Madhya Pradesh Chief Minister Uma Bharti to the Bharatiya Janata Party? Neither the supporters of the new party president nor those of Ms. Bharti ruled out that possibility. Mr. Singh said in response to a question that the BJP's parliamentary board had decided to expel Ms. Bharti. As for Mr. Bharti, her supporter Prahlad Patel said "she cannot and will not return to the nakli [fake] BJP."

(5274) Lucknow : Uttar Pradesh Legislative Council today passed a censure motion against alleged phone tapping of Chief Minister Mulayam Singh Yadav and Samajwadi Party General Secretary Amar Singh, terming it as infringement on right to privacy. Raising the matter in the Zero Hour, Yagya Dutt Sharma of BJP termed phone tapping a conspiracy to create hurdles in the democratic process. "Ironically it is a conspiracy between the two political parties extending support to each other at the Centre and State," Sharma said.

(5275) Chennai : The Democratic Progressive Alliance will launch a campaign from January 18 to oust the "anti-people" and "anti-democratic" Jayalalithaa Government. Asked if it would mark the beginning of the DPA's preparations for the Assembly elections, Dravida Munnetra Kazhagam president M.Karunanidhi said the poll work began on Monday.

(5276) Tiruchi : "The Communist Party of India will not be a silent spectator, if the ruling United Progressive Alliance at the Centre deviates from the Common Minimum Programme," the National Executive Member of the CPI, R. Nallakannu, has said here. Speaking after honouring 80 veteran cadres of the party from Tiruchi and neighbouring districts as part of the party's 80th anniversary here on Monday, Mr. Nallakannu said the CPI and other left parties supported the Congress only with the sole aim of unseating the BJP from power.

04-01-2006

(5277) Hyderabad : All-India Congress Committee general secretary Digvijay Singh has said all Congressmen across the country will be happy if Amethi MP Rahul Gandhi is nominated to the Central Steering Committee (CSC), earlier known as the Congress Working Committee (CWC). Replying to a question on whether Mr. Rahul Gandhi would be included in the CSC, Mr. Singh told reporters that the Congress had always encouraged young people to come up. "If that happens, the popular demand of all Congressmen will be fulfilled and all of them will be elated and happy," he remarked.

(5278) Hyderabad : The Congress has reacted sharply to Telugu Desam president N. Chandrababu Naidu's letter to Chief Minister Y.S. Rajasekhara Reddy complaining that the Government is neglecting the NTR memorial film award. It has blamed the previous TDP Government for discontinuing the practice of presenting the prestigious award. G. Muddukrishnama Naidu, Congress MLA, and PCC spokesperson N. Tulasi Reddy told a press conference here on Tuesday that the TDP Government failed to announce the award for 2003 and 2004. The award had been given away only thrice since its institution in 1996. Mr. Naidu said the TDP leaders, who unceremoniously dethroned the late leader as Chief Minister and removed him as party president, were "shedding crocodile tears for NTR."

(5279) Hyderabad : CPI (M) state committee secretary B.V. Raghavulu has written to Chief Minister Y.S. Rajasekhara Reddy urging the Government to bring in a law for providing reservation for weaker sections in private professional colleges.

(5280) Hyderabad : The Telugu Desam Party has expressed doubts about the planned completion of irrigation projects in the next two years.

(5281) Tirupati : The Bharatiya Janata Party is of the view that the Government's approval for the Tirumala ropeway project, despite mounting pressure from the public and the various religious heads, would amount to "hurting the Hindu sentiments." The party seems to be unable to digest the decision that closely followed an assurance from the Chief Minister himself to its delegation that a final nod would be given only after consulting all the people concerned. BJP secretary Bandaru Dattatreya has taken serious exception to Y.S. Rajasekhara Reddy announcing the decision by keeping everyone, including the saints and pontiffs, in the dark.

(5282) Visakhapatnam : The Congress Government was allowing the Special Economic Zone (SEZ) here to be shifted to Haldia in West Bengal, Telugu Desam Party's rural unit president Bandaru Satyanarayana Murthy said here on Tuesday.

(5283) Mahabubnagar : The Communist Party of India (Marxist) State secretary B.V.Raghavulu has asked the State Government to announce a special package of Rs.100 crores for the development of Mahabubnagar, one of the most backward districts in the country.

(5284) New Delhi : Uttar Pradesh Chief Minister Mulayam Singh Yadav on Tuesday demanded that allegations of phone tapping of certain Samajwadi Party leaders by the Centre be looked into by any non-Congress Chief Minister, including West Bengal Chief Minister Buddhadev Bhattacharya, Tamil Nadu Chief Miniser J. Jayalalithaa or Bihar Chief Minister Nitish Kumar.Addressing a press conference here, Mr. Yadav said Congress president Sonia Gandhi was behind the tapping of party general secretary Amar Singh's phone and alleged a conspiracy against his Government.

(5285) Kochi : The KPCC executive meeting held here on Tuesday decided to ask the UDF Government to find a 'unanimous view' on the Narendran Commission report after consulting 'all parties concerned' and to implement the recommendations 'without much delay.' This was necessary to keep the UDF's commitment to social justice.

(5286) Gulbarga : The nine Janata Dal (S) legislators, who have sided with former Deputy Chief Minister Siddaramaiah and claim to be part of the AIPJD, are for all practical purposes still official Janata Dal (S) members in the Assembly. Senior AIPJD leader B.R. Patil, who was elected to the Assembly from the Aland Assembly constituency in Gulbarga district, told presspersons here on Tuesday that although legislators, who had sided with Mr. Siddaramaiah, including himself, have been expelled from the JD(S), the party leadership has not submitted any letter in this regard to the Speaker of the Legislative Assembly landing the position of the expelled legislators in a piquant situation.

(5287) Shravanabelagola : Dismissing the media reports that the Janata Dal (Secular) is planning to have an alliance with the Bharatiya Janata Party (BJP) in the zilla and taluk panchayats, Deputy Chief Minister M.P. Prakash on Tuesday said there is no question of joining hands with BJP for the sake of power.

(5288) Kochi : KPCC president Ramesh Chennithala on Wednesday met senior Church leaders here, apparently in an effort to help find a compromise on the thorny Narendran Commission recommendations.However, Mr. Chennithala later claimed at a news conference that his meeting with the bishops had nothing to do with the issue. He had met them as part of a circulation drive of the Congress newspaper 'Veekshanam,' he said.

(5289) Thiruvananthapuram : The BJP on Monday demanded that the Government publish a white paper on the extremist activities and the security situation in the State.

(5290) Thiruvananthapuram : The Opposition Left Democratic Front (LDF) has called off the dawn-to-dusk hartal it had proposed to organise on Wednesday to register its protest against the rise in thefts in the city and suburbs.

(5291) Iritty (Kannur) : Communist Party of India-Marxist (CPI-M) State secretary Pinarayi Vijayan has said that the State Government has failed to check activities of religious extremists and fundamentalist outfits.At a press conference here on Tuesday, after a public reception to the Kerala March, led by him, Mr. Vijayan said the Government had not taken seriously intelligence warnings about such activities in some parts of the State.

(5292) New Delhi : Having rejected the Government's proposal to disinvest shares in profitable non-Navratna public sector undertakings, the Left parties have come out with suggestions for alternative resource mobilisation. This includes payroll tax, mopping up of tax arrears, crackdown on tax evasion and recovery of non-performing assets of banks.These are among measures considered by the CPI, the CPI(M), the RSP and the AIFB that would be finetuned and submitted to the Government shortly. Payroll tax on employers was being suggested as a measure to fund the schemes the Government has for social security, especially for the unemployed and unorganised workers. A new inheritance tax with suitable exemption limit could also be imposed, sources in the Left parties said. The major thrust is the Rs. 2.21 lakh crore cash reserves available with the 50 odd public sector undertakings as per the Public Enterprises Survey. Only a small number of companies have invested more than a third of such reserves while the rest made no effort, the sources said. A part of these reserves are lent to the Government by holding securities.

(5293) Ahmedabad : The controversy over the Sanjay Joshi sex CD episode deepened further on Tuesday with the Vadodara-based school teacher suspected to be the woman in the filmdenying her involvement in the case. "The woman in the CD with the person supposed to be Sanjay Joshi is not me," Bhubaneswari Chitte said in a written statement in Vadodara. Leader of the Opposition in the State Assembly and State Congress president Arjun Modhvadia demanded a judicial inquiry into the episode. Ms. Chitte and her family returned to their home in Swati Society after being reported "missing" since the episode came to light.

(5294) New Delhi : The Delhi High Court on Tuesday ordered the former Union Minister and Janata Party leader Subramanian Swamy to pay a compensation of Rs. five lakh to criminal lawyer Ram Jethmalani for defaming the latter by charging him with having links with the LTTE in the wake of the Rajiv Gandhi assassination case. Noting that the defendant (Swamy) refused to apologise or withdraw his offending statements, Justice Pradeep Nandrajog, observed that "a statement against a person that he has been receiving money from LTTE is ex-facie defamatory." During the inquiry by the M.C. Jain Commission of Inquiry to probe the circumstances leading to the assassination of the former Prime Minister Rajiv Gandhi, Dr. Swamy made certain statements before the panel that Mr. Ram Jethmalani, had received money from the LTTE for taking up cases on behalf of the banned organisation.At that time Mr. Jethmalani was defending the Tamil Nadu Chief Minister Jayalalithaa, who was also accused by Dr. Swamy of having prior information about the impending killing of Rajiv Gandhi. - PTI

(5295) New Delhi : Rajya Sabha member Brinda Karat on Tuesday said she had recently received a letter from the Health and Family Welfare Ministry confirming the presence of animal products and human skulls in the Ayurvedic preparations of Divya Yog Pharmacy. The pharmacy is owned by yoga guru Ramdev. "I had sent medicines that I had got from the pharmacy in Uttaranchal to the Ministry in July. I had requested that these medicines be tested for animal matter and powder made from human skulls. I received a letter from them on December 29 that confirmed my apprehensions," she said at a press conference here.Ms. Karat has also written to Uttaranchal Chief Minister N.D. Tiwari asking him to take legal action against Mr. Ramdev "for his blatant violation of the labelling procedure of the Drugs and Cosmetics Act."

(5296) New Delhi : Accusing the Congress of failure to safeguard the interests of Delhiites with regard to the ongoing demolition drive, the Leader of the Opposition in the Municipal Corporation of Delhi, Subhash Arya, on Tuesday alleged that the current tussle between the Congress leadership in the State Government and the civic body had led to undue delay in implementation of Master Plan 2021 resulting in the present crisis.

(5297) Raipur : A controversy is raging in Chhattisgarh after a BJP MP demanded 'disenfranchisement' of non-tribals, alleging that there was an alarming increase in their population in the tribal areas of the State. As representatives of various organisations and opposition Congress workers came out on the streets in Kanker and burnt effigies of BJP MP Sohan Potai and others, the State BJP distanced itself from the controversy saying the party did not approve his reported remarks on non-tribals. Semi-urban areas like Pakhanjor,. Bande, Badgaon, Antagarh and Bhanupratapur in Bastar region witnessed agitation on the issue on Monday, markets remained closed on Tuesday at many places to protest the tribal MP's comments against non-tribals. The Youth Congress called for a bandh in Bhanupratappur on Tuesday.

(5298) Bhubaneswar : The Opposition has condemned Monday's police firing on tribals at Kalinga Nagar in Jajpur district and demanded the resignation of Chief Minister Naveen Patnaik, who holds the Home portfolio. Six tribals and one policeman were killed in a clash at Kalinga Nagar, police said. Unconfirmed reports put the toll at 13. The incident took place around 11 a.m. when nearly 800 tribals from nearby villages reached the spot to protest against the construction of a boundary wall for a proposed six-million tonne Tata Steel plant. Leaders of Opposition parties will visit Kalinga Nagar on Tuesday and announce their course of action on their return here. Pradesh Congress Committee chief Jayadev Jena, who reached there late in theevening, said the police had brutally killed innocent people in the name of industrialisation. "The Chief Minister should resign. He cannot wash his hands of the issue by announcing an ex gratia of Rs. 1 lakh each for the families of those killed," Mr. Jena said over phone.

(5299) Pondicherry : The Congress MP V. Narayanasamy has said that the enforcement of the order of the Delimitation Commission refixing the Assembly constituencies for the forthcoming polls, was a matter to be decided by the Election Commission (EC) and President of India.

(5300) Lucknow : Yoga guru Swami Ramdev today demanded a high-level probe into allegations by CPI(M) Polit Bureau member Brinda Karat that his Pharmacy, which produces ayurvedic medicines, was selling drugs containing animal residue and said there was a conspiracy by multi national companies against him. Earlier, Ms Karat accused Swami Ramdev-owned Pharmacy, which produces ayurvedic medicines, of selling drugs containing animal residue, saying the Union Health Ministry had confirmed the medicines were adulterated. Ms Karat told a news conference at New Delhi that the Union Health Ministry, in a letter addressed to her, had confirmed prima facie evidence of animal residue in the medicines of Uttaranchal-based Divya Yog Pharmacy. Ms Karat claimed even Labour laws were being violated at the Hardwar manufacturing unit of the pharmacy.

05-01-2006

(5301) Anantapur : State president of Andhra Pradesh Rythu Sangham affiliated to CPI, K. Nageswara Rao, has suggested the State Government to accord priority in completion of the irrigation projects meant for backward areas.

(5302) Hyderabad : The Congress Legislature Party (CLP) ridiculed the claim of the Telugu Desam that the Congress Government was inaugurating the projects completed by the TDP regime.Listing the allocations made to the irrigation sector under the previous regime, CLP spokesperson G.Muddukrishnama Naidu said here on Wednesday that the CAG report of 2005 had criticised the TDP Government for its apathy.

(5303) Hyderabad : The Telugu Desam Party has sought the resignation of five MLAs from Mahabubnagar, who it alleged, happened to be the bane of Kalwakurthy lift irrigation scheme in the district. The TDP deputy leader in the Assembly, Nagam Janardhan Reddy, shot off a letter to these legislators — J. Krishna Rao, G. Chinna Reddy, Y. Kista Reddy, Ch. Vamshi Krishna and Swarna Sudhakar — appealing to them not to bring down the capacity of the project for their selfish interests.

(5304) Ongole : BJP State general secretary K. Lakshman has criticised the Government for what he called the display of regional discrimination in irrigation development.

(5305) Bangalore : The Janata Dal (Secular) has decided to await the decision of the Congress on forging alliances in the districts where none of the political parties has gained a majority in the zilla and taluk panchayats. The reports that the Janata Dal (S) is talking to senior BJP leaders on an alliance in the panchayats were on Wednesday spiked as "utter nonsense" and an effort aimed at misleading the people. As a matter of principle, the Janata Dal (S) is waiting to know the stand of the Congress before deciding on a course of action. The "wait and watch" decision was taken at the meeting of the Janata Dal (S) Legislature Party here on Wednesday to ascertain the views of the party legislators on the steps to be taken on the coalition arrangement and what the party has to do if the Congress decides to join hands with others, including the All India Progressive Janata Dal (AIPJD) of Siddaramaiah, in some of the zilla and taluk panchayats. The meeting was more of a stocktaking nature. It was also to convey to the party legislators the views of the senior leaders and the discussions that party President H.D. Deve Gowda has been having with them.

(5306) New Delhi : The Samajwadi Party on Wednesday sought to mobilise political support for its case against the Congress and the Centre in the phone-tapping issue, with its leader Amar Singh calling on Communist Party of India (Marxist) general secretary Prakash Karat here. Soon after the meeting, Mr. Karat told the media that the issue was "serious" and demanded an investigation. "It has been established that through a private telephone company tapping has been done illegally. There should be a proper investigation to uncover the conspiracy behind it."

(5307) Bangalore : The Government will appoint chairpersons to only 75 boards and corporations, which have been considered viable. The Congress, which had secured the posts when it was in power with S.M. Krishna as Chief Minister, is now forced to share the 75 boards and corporations with its coalition partner, the Janata Dal (Secular). Disclosing this to presspersons on Wednesday, N.S. Boseraju, Political Secretary to Chief Minister N. Dharam Singh, said the Chief Minister and KPCC President M. Mallikarjun Kharge would meet leaders of the Congress High Command in New Delhi armed with the report of the discussion they had with party leaders and workers about the election of presidents and vice-presidents of zilla and taluk panchayats. Mr. Boseraju assured that his party (Congress) workers would not be neglected while appointing them as chairmen. But they would have to content with sharing the posts. Both Mr. Singh and Mr. Kharge have made it clear that the Congress was ready to share power with other parties in the panchayat bodies.

(5308) Koothuparamba : CPI(M) State secretary Pinarayi Vijayan has said that Health Minister K.K. Ramachandran's tendering his resignation to Chief Minister Oommen Chandy has exposed the severity of the problems in the United Democratic Front (UDF) Government.

(5309) New Delhi : The Congress on Wednesday joined issue with the Samajwadi Party, which has accused that Congress president Sonia Gandhi has had a hand in the telephone-tapping incident, and sought to know what was it that makes the SP so apprehensive. Taking exception to the manner in which SP chief Mulayam Singh Yadav and Mr. Amar Singh have been attacking the Congress president, AICC general secretary Ambika Soni said that while the issue raised was of serious nature, the SP's approach could not be understoodMs. Soni posed a set of questions and said the Congress expected the SP leaders to respond to it. Why was it that the Uttar Pradesh Chief Minister did not think it necessary to file an FIR or what action he wants to take against the [telecom] company whose employee had been arrested by Delhi police? She said the suggestion by Mr. Yadav to set up a Committee of Chief Ministers of Tamil Nadu, West Bengal and Bihar to inquire into the episode was "laughable." Why Mr.

Yadav did not think it proper to appoint a similar committee to go into the murder or BJP MLA Krishnanand Rai?

(5310) Dehra Dun : The Bharatiya Janata Party says it is fully with yoga guru Swami Ram Dev, who has come under attack from CPI (M) Polit Bureau member Brinda Karat. "Ms. Karat's allegations that the medicines manufactured and sold by Swami Ram Dev contain animal residues have been made at the instance of certain multinationals that fear losses if the traditional Indian system of medicines and yoga become popular," the BJP leader in charge of Uttaranchal, Sheshadrichari, told presspersons here on Wednesday. People would not tolerate any attack on Hindu holy men or the traditional medicine system, he said.

(5311) Panaji : As the "Saleli landlord murder" controversy continued to hot up, Goa Chief Minister Pratapsing Rane on Wednesday alleged that BJP is behind the episode and asked Leader of the Opposition Manohar Parrikar to desist from politicising the issue and instigating the people for political mileage.

(5312) Fatehpur : Expelled BJP leader and former Madhya Pradesh Chief Minister Uma Bharti on Wednesday claimed that Uttar Pradesh had become a virtual stronghold of criminals.Addressing a news conference here, Ms Bharti said U.P. politicians felt elated and blessed in standing next to mafias. "Former UP Chief Minister and Congress leader late Veer Bahadur Singh had started the trend of harbouring criminals. Now the baton has been held by present incumbent and Samajwadi Party supremo Mulayam Singh Yadav," she alleged.

(5313) Chennai : DMK president M. Karunanidhi denigrated the Bhagvad Gita in a letter published in Murasoli, the prosecution submitted on Wednesday in its counter to a petition filed by the daily's Editor, S. Selvam, seeking discharge from a case in which he and Mr. Karunanidhi been cited as accused.

(5314) Cuddalore : Factionalism in the Congress came to the fore here on Wednesday when party leaders and cadres belonging to two groups clashed in the presence of Tamil Nadu Congress Committee president G.K. Vasan. The partymen manhandled photographers and damaged their cameras. AICC member A.S. Alagiri and Cuddalore north district president Nedunchezhian exchanged blows on the dais. Mr. Nedunchezhian's shirt was torn.

(5315) Madurai : The Central Committee of the All India Foward Bloc (AIFB) will decide on the party post to be given to actor Karthik. He has recently joined the party. Accepting his entry into the party, the State Committee of the AIFB, which met here on Tuesday, left the issue of the post to be offered to Karthik to the Central Committee, its general secretary L. Santhanam said in a statement.

06-01-2006

(5316) Hyderabad : CPI(M) general secretary Prakash Karat has denied reports that the party is coming closer to the Telugu Desam, saying it should not be perceived that way just because two parties have somewhat similar views on certain issues. He was responding to a question on the CPI(M) and the TDP making similar allegations of corruption in irrigation project tenders.

(5317) Hyderabad : Telugu Desam leaders from Telangana will undertake a padayatra for 24 days from near the confluence of Pranahita with the Godavari in Adilabad district on January 28 to mount pressure on the State Government to take up the Yellampally - Pranahita - Chevella link project. The 450-km long padayatra by a large group of leaders and party activists will culminate in a public meeting, most likely on February 20, at Nizam College grounds here. It will be addressed by the TDP president, N. Chandrababu Naidu. The decision to take up the padayatra followed a meeting of the Telangana leaders of TDP at the party office on Thursday.

(5318) Karimnagar : "There is no permanent agreement with the Congress on the continuation of alliance in the State or at the Centre," according to CPI State secretary K. Narayana.Talking to newsmen here on Thursday, he said that there was no question of forging an alliance with the TDP. To a query about the TDP's plans to forge an alliance with Left parties, he said: "We cannot jump and a take a decision independently."

(5319) Vijayawada : TDP urban president Gadde Rammohan on Thursday demanded that the Government revive the awards instituted in the name of former Chief Minister N.T. Rama Rao.

(5320) Sangareddy : TRS dissident legislator Toorpu Jayaprakash Reddy has said that he will support any decision of party leader K. Chandrasekhar Rao to bridge the gap between workers and leaders sitting in New Delhi.

(5321) Chennai : Just hours after Samajwadi Party general secretary Amar Singh called on her and claimed "100 per cent support" in the alleged telephone tapping controversy, Chief Minister Jayalalithaa on Thursday urged the United Progressive Alliance Government to take responsibility for "this shocking act of infringing the basic rights guaranteed by the Constitution."

(5322) New Delhi : The Congress on Thursday announced that it will not like to interfere in the formation of zilla panchayats in Karnataka, and left the decision to the local units to chart the future course. The party also made it clear that it is for the continuation of the present arrangement in the State where it runs a coalition government with the Janata Dal (Secular) of H.D. Deve Gowda. Yet, by giving a free hand to the local units, the party appears to have kept the options open of aligning either with the Janata Dal (S) or its rival the All-India Progressive Janata Dal of the former Deputy Chief Minister Siddaramaiah. The decision was taken after a meeting the Congress President Sonia Gandhi had with Chief Minister N. Dharam Singh, President of the Karnataka Pradesh Congress Committee M. Mallikarjun Kharge, AICC leader A.K. Antony and Ahmed Patel, Political Secretary to the Congress President.

(5323) Kollam : Kerala Pradesh Congress Committee (KPCC) president Ramesh Chennithala said here on Thursday that certain major political developments would take place in the State during the next three months. Inaugurating the golden jubilee block of the Congress Bhavan in the city, he said these developments would cause the Left Democratic Front (LDF), particularly the Communist Party of India-Marxist (CPI-M), major setbacks. The front would face serious internal problems.

(5324) Kollam : Democratic Indira Congress (Karunakaran) president K. Muraleedharan has said that Health Minister K.K. Ramachandran should have been expelled from the Cabinet following Wednesday's developments that rocked the ruling United Democratic Front (UDF).

(5325) Kozhikode : Rousing receptions were accorded to the Kerala March, led by Communist Party of India (Marxist) State secretary Pinarayi Vijayan, at various places in Kozhikode district on Thursday.

(5326) Thiruvananthapuram : The West Bengal Bharatiya Janata Party (BJP) will use unemployment and 'infiltration from Bangladesh' and the resulting demographic transformations as the major campaign issues in the Assembly elections to be held this year in the State, said president of the West Bengal unit of the BJP Tathagatha Roy at a meeting organised by the party's district unit here on Thursday to discuss the political situation in West Bengal.

(5327) Chennai : Samajwadi Party general secretary Amar Singh on Thursday thanked Prime Minister Manmohan Singh for taking a "good and reasonable" stand on the telephone tapping issue. He also urged the United Progressive Alliance (UPA) Government to ask West Bengal Chief Minister Buddhadeb Bhattacharjee to probe the case.

(5328) New Delhi : The Bharatiya Janata Party said on Thursday that the Allahabad High Court verdict in the Aligarh Muslim University case was a "double blow to the appeasement politics" of the Congress in less than 24 hours.BJP spokesman Prakash Javdekar said that close on the heels of the Supreme Court refusing to stay the Andhra High Court decision to quash five per cent reservation for Muslims in the State, the Allahabad High Court upheld the order of its single-judge Bench quashing minority status to AMU. According to the BJP, the Congress is pursuing a "totally communal agenda" by introducing reservation for Muslims on the basis of religion at AMU and in Andhra Pradesh.

(5329) New Delhi : Railway Minister and RJD supremo Lalu Prasad on Thursday added a new twist to the ongoing phone tapping controversy by demanding that the recorded conversations of Samajwadi Party leaders, including Amar Singh, be made public. r. Prasad told media persons that the nation should know what was in the tapes. Congress president Sonia Gandhi was "wrongly being blamed" for the phone tapping, he said.

(5330) Hyderabad : CPI(M) general secretary Prakash Karat on Thursday made light of the protests against the party in New Delhi for its stand on Swamy Ramdev's herbal medicine and rubbished the campaign that it had acted at the behest of the multinational corporations. Mr. Karat told presspersons that it was ridiculous for anyone to hurl such accusations against a party that had been in the forefront of opposing MNCs. Everyone knew its stand and contribution to the fields of patents and Intellectual Property Rights.

(5331) New Delhi : Supporters of yoga guru Swamy Ramdev clashed with Communist Party of India (Marxist) members outside the party headquarters near Gole Market here on Thursday before the police dispersed them. Twenty supporters of Swamy Ramdev were arrested on charges of rioting, while one person was injured in the clash. The Delhi State Committee of the CPI (M) said the protest demonstration was the work of a handful of hoodlums belonging to the Vishwa Hindu Parishad and the Rashtriya Sewak Sangh, who attempted to forcibly enter the central party office.

(5332) New Delhi : Condemning the killing of 12 tribals in police firing at Kalinga Nagar in Orissa, the Communist Party of India (Marxist-Leninist)-New Democracy staged a demonstration at Jantar Mantar here on Thursday demanding arrest of the District Collector and the Superintendent of Police. The tribals were killed on January 2 during a demonstration against the construction of a boundary wall by Tata Steel, allegedly resulting in usurping of their land.

(5333) Pondicherry : The Pattali Makkal Katchi on Thursday expressed concern over the "administrative inefficiency" and lack of appropriate measures to ensure the smooth working of the Jayaprakash Narayan Cooperative spinning mill in Karaikal. In a release, parliamentary party leader M. Ramadoss said while speedy steps were taken to cater to the requirements of SPINCO [a cooperative spinning corporation] at Tirubuvanai, near here, nothing was done to protect the mill, set up in 1995. The Central funds were being squandered . The mill reportedly suffered a loss to the extent of Rs. 27 crore.

(5334) Chandigarh : Punjab Pradesh Congress Committee (PPCC) president Shamsher Singh Dullo has sent a three-member committee under Member of Parliament (MP) from Jalandhar, Rana Gurjit Singh to Uttaranchal for making an on-the-spot assessment of the situation in Kashipur where the crops and property of the farmers mostly Sikhs is reported to have been destroyed on the orders of the government. Meanwhile, Shiromani Akali Dal general secretary Sukhbir Singh Badal has asked Prime Minister Manmohan Singh and Congress President Sonia Gandhi to break their silence over what he described as "unspeakable atrocities being committed against the Sikhs in Kashipur". He questioned Chief Minister's silence on the happenings in Kashipur. — UNI

(5335) Lucknow : Former Uttar Pradesh Chief Minister and senior BJP leader Kalyan Singh on Thursday came out in defence of Congress president Sonia Gandhi on the phone-tapping issue and said she was "too mature" a leader to indulge in such activities. Rejecting the allegation of Chief Minister Mulayam Singh Yadav and Samajwadi Party general secretary Amar Singh that the phone of the latter was tapped at behest of Ms Gandhi, the BJP leader maintained: "Sonia Gandhi cannot do this."Over the years, "She (Sonia) has matured as a politician and given all her maturity, this was not expected of her," he told reporters in a chat on the occasion of his 78th birthday.

(5336) Dharmapuri : Members of the Pattali Makkal Katchi (PMK) staged a demonstration in front of the Collectorate here on Thursday requesting the State Government to provide flood relief to all affected persons without disparity. PMK State Leader and Pennagaram MLA, G.K. Mani led the demonstration.

(5337) Villupuram : The Pattali Makkal Katchi on Thursday expressed its opposition to the Andhra Pradesh Government's proposal to construct a mega dam across the PalarOnce the dam - under the Rs. 100-crore Kuppam project - is built, the river basin for a distance of 200 km coursing through Chennai, Kancheepuram and Vellore districts will turn into a desert. Many municipalities and hundreds of panchayats will face acute water shortage. Above all, the ground water table will drastically dip further, Dr. S. Ramadoss told presspersons at Thailapuram, near here.

07-01-2006

(5338) Kadapa : CPI State Secretariat member T. Lakshminarayana on Friday advocated merger of Leftist trade unions like AITUC and CITU or their unity, as they were waging struggles on common issues and had similar ideologies. Scope for forging unity among trade unions of Left parties at the State and national-levels was being seriously explored, he told a delegates meeting as part of 10th CITU State mahasabha here.

(5339) New Delhi : Congress president Sonia Gandhi on Friday announced her new team of Working Committee and party office-bearers. There are four new faces in the highest policy-making body but the most conspicuous omission is that of her son Rahul Gandhi. Utilising the party "authorisation," Ms. Gandhi nominated 20 members to the CWC including B.K. Hari Prasad, MP from Karnataka, V. Narayanswamy, MP from Pondicherry, the former Madhya Pradesh Congress chief, Urmila Singh, and Saifuddin Soz from Jammu and Kashmir. There are still five vacancies and it is understood that Ms. Gandhi could fill them after the Hyderabad AICC plenary to be held from January 21 to 23. The former External Affairs Minister, K. Natwar Singh, who was removed from the Steering Committee after the Volcker Committee report named him in the food-for-oil scam, does not figure in the recast team. The names of the Uttar Pradesh Congress chief, Salman Khursheed, and the former Karnataka Minister, Motamma, are also not in the list. M.L. Fotedar and Satyavrat Chaturvedi have been shifted to the 14-member permanent invitee category that has new faces in Noor Bano (former MP from Rampur in Uttar Pradesh), the former Arunachal Pradesh Chief Minister, Mukut Mithi, C.K. Jaffer Sharief and the former Karnataka Chief Minister, Veerappa Moily. Among the new entrants in the 13-member special invitees category are Dr. Ashok Ram from Bihar, Jagmeet Singh Brar from Punjab, Dr. Parmeshwar and the former Pondicherry Chief Minister, V. Vaithilingam.

(5340) Bangalore : Chief Minister N. Dharam Singh said here on Friday that the Congress is going to forge alliances with the Janata Dal (Secular) or the All India Progressive Janata Dal (AIPJD) in the zilla and taluk panchayats where no party has gained a majority. Mr. Dharam Singh, who returned to Bangalore from New Delhi, told presspersons that the party High Command has left it to the State leadership to decide on the formation of zilla and taluk panchayats. After holding discussions with district leaders, the party will enter into alliance with either of the two parties. He said there is no difference of opinion between him and Mr. Kharge on the issue of alliance with Janata Dal (S) in the zilla panchayats.

(5341) Narikkuni (Kozhikode district) : CPI(M) State secretary Pinarayi Vijayan has alleged that the investigations being ordered by the UDF Government in sexual harassment cases have been conducted in such a way so as to allow culprits to go scot-free. Talking to presspersons at Narikkunni during his ongoing Kerala Yatra in Kozhikode district on Friday, Mr.Vijayan said that attempts were being made to help the accused in all these cases. "Such things are happening in a lot of cases. An investigation is needed in this regard. No accused should be allowed to escape (from the clutches of law) in these cases," he said.

(5342) Kolkata : Anil Biswas, State Secretary of the Communist Party of India (Marxist) in West Bengal, has sought Rs. 45 crore in damages from

Congress MP Adhir Chowdhury in a defamation suit filed against the latter in the Calcutta High Court on Friday.

(5343) New Delhi : Terming the Government's decision to cut food subsidy a "very retrograde move" the Communist Party of India (Marxist) on Friday demanded that the "anti-poor measure" be reversed.In a statement, the party Polit Bureau said the move to cut the food subsidy by Rs. 4524 crores by reducing the quantity of wheat and rice issued through the PDS and Antyodaya Anna Yojana was "a betrayal of the UPA Government's commitment to the people." The move will adversely affect millions of people at a time when calorie consumption was declining and nutritional deficiencies were on the increase, it said. Further, the move would limit the turnover of the Food Corporation of India and affect its ability to undertake procurement at minimum support prices. At a time when farmers were facing an agrarian crisis, the attempt should be to ensure stable prices, the statement said.

(5344) New Delhi : The Bharatiya Janata Party on Friday said "there was no threat to the Naveen Patnaik Government in Orissa." While it could suggest the setting up of a mechanism for resolving problems in the coalition, there was no question of the BJP withdrawing support.Party spokesperson Prakash Javadekar was responding to questions here on a statement made by senior leader and MP from Orissa Jual Oram that the BJP should withdraw support to the Patnaik Government to protest against the death of 12 tribals in police firing at Kalinga Nagar. Mr. Javadekar said continuous efforts had to be made to keep a coalition government running. Some problems could arise and "there should be a mechanism to sort out all issues."

(5345) New Delhi : Samajwadi Party general secretary Amar Singh on Friday alleged that his phones were tapped at the behest of a journalist-turned-Congress MP and industrialist, whose name he had divulged to Prime Minister Manmohan Singh. "I met the Prime Minister at a function this morning and used the opportunity to tell him the name of the industrialist who was behind the nefarious tapping incident," Mr. Singh told a hurriedly-called press conference here.

(5346) New Delhi : The Prime Minister's Office (PMO) on Friday night said none of its officials was involved in the tapping of phones of Samajwadi Party leaders. The allegations levelled by Samajwadi Party leader Amar

Singh were "utterly baseless and mischievous," Sanjaya Baru, Media Adviser to Prime Minister Manmohan Singh, said. "No official in the PMO is involved in any way in the phone tapping episode."

(5347) New Delhi : Janata Dal (United) leader Sharad Yadav on Friday described telephone tapping as a violation of human rights and suggested the setting up of a mechanism to redress such complaints. These should be referred to the National Human Rights Commission or a separate commission headed by a serving High Court or Supreme Court judge constituted for the purpose, he told a press conference here. The Centre should consider enacting a law to prevent such incidents in future. Cyber crime should also be brought under the purview of this law. "We have more and more people complaining of phone tapping, including the Tamil Nadu Chief Minister, and morphed obscene pictures of well-known women in field of art and culture are also being circulated freely," Mr. Yadav said.

(5348) Kolkata : Communist Party of India (Marxist) in West Bengal is not unduly concerned over any step the Election Commission might be contemplating for the State in the run up to the coming Assembly elections, senior Polit Bureau member Jyoti Basu said on Friday. "West Bengal is not Bihar," Mr. Basu said when asked to comment on the decision of the Commission to depute 19 observers including K. J. Rao (who had overseen elections in Bihar) to oversee the on-going revision of electoral rolls in the State. "I do not know K. J. Rao... , But West Bengal is not Bihar and people here will vote for us," he added. "Till now none has criticised us and every election has been held in a free and fair manner," he said adding that even the former Chief Election Commissioner, T. N. Seshan, had said after voting (during a previous Assembly election) "that polling was peaceful."

(5349) New Delhi : Delhi is among the six States which have got new Youth Congress presidents in a reshuffle carried out by Congress president Sonia Gandhi. Student leader Amit Malik has been appointed president of the Delhi Pradesh Congress Committee replacing sitting party MLA Rajesh Lilothia. According to Indian Youth Congress president Ashok Tanwar, the appointments were announced by AICC general secretary Ashok Gehlot with the aim of providing a new direction to the units in these States, some of which are likely to go to the polls during the next one year. Zenith M Sangma has been appointed president of the Meghalaya Youth Congress unit, Sunil Ahire of the Mumbai Youth Congress, Rohit Pujari of the Orissa

Youth Congress, Sukhamay Saha of the Tripura Youth Congress and Rajpal Singh Khairola of the Uttarnachal Youth Congress.

(5350) New Delhi : A delegation of Delhi Bharatiya Janata Party legislators led by the Leader of the Opposition in the Delhi Assembly, Jagdish Mukhi, on Friday lodged a formal complaint with the Chief Vigilance Commissioner against gross irregularities allegedly committed by officials of the State Transport Department in implementing the smart card scheme for registration of new vehicles in the Capital.

(5351) Chennai : Tamil Nadu Congress Committee president G.K. Vasan has criticised the State Government for foisting cases against the Dravida Munnetra Kazhagam president M. Karunanidhi and a few others for alleged irregularities in the construction of a bridge across river Amaravathi near Karur.In a statement here on Friday, Mr. Vasan said the bridge was constructed by a private agency under the "Build, operate and transfer" scheme at a cost of Rs 14 crore. The selection of contractor, the plan and design of the bridge were approved by the previous All-India Anna Dravida Munnetra Kazhagam Government and only the construction was executed during the successive DMK Government. So, Mr. Karunanidhi had no role in it.

08-01-2006

(5352) Hyderabad : The Congress legislature Party (CLP) has asked the Opposition parties to come out with a transparent and consistent policy on irrigation projects. Referring to the objections raised by the TDP, the CPI(M) and the TRS to Polavaram project works undertaken by the Government, the CLP members on Saturday asked whether those parties were not harming the interests of the State in opposing the project.

(5353) Hyderabad : The national council meeting of the BJP in New Delhi on January 20 will chalk out a strategy to mount pressure on the UPA Government to withdraw its decision to reduce the food subsidy by Rs. 4,500 crores. The decision to reduce the quantum of rice and wheat supplied under the public distribution system and the interest rate reduction under the employees' provident fund will also be discussed before the finalisation of the programme, M. Venkaiah Naidu said at a news conference here.He said the measures were 'anti-people' and a cruel act of the Government to cheat common public after giving them an assurance to the contrary before elections. Mr. Naidu demanded a high-level inquiry to probe allegations and counter allegations of phone tapping.

(5354) Hyderabad : Gujarat Chief Minister Narendra Modi has launched a sharp attack on the Congress Government in Andhra Pradesh accusing it of "lacking guts to meet the challenge of Maoists and Pakistan-sponsored terrorism." Addressing a public meeting of BJP here on Saturday, Mr. Modi said a strong political will was required to face the twin threats which was lacking in the Government. While the Maoists were going ahead with their corridor from Pasupathi in Nepal to Tirupati, the Pakistani terrorist organisations had established their base in the State.The Government had turned a blind eye to the terrorist activities as it was pursuing vote bank politics to appease minorities, he alleged. "The entire country will be a loser if this policy is continued. The Government has failed to see the point", he remarked.

(5355) Hyderabad : Former BJP president M. Venkaiah Naidu has said he had conveyed to the incumbent, Rajnath Singh, not to consider him for any post when he reconstitutes the party's national executive. Mr. Naidu told reporters here on Saturday that he wanted to work for the party without holding any post. He said Mr. Singh would constitute his team after the national council meeting of the BJP on January 20.He dismissed reports that he was unwilling to work under Mr. Singh as he was junior to him. There was no need for speculation as the question of a junior or a senior did not arise in the party. All of them were equals. The former BJP chief complimented Mr. Singh as an able and experienced party leader and a good administrator.Insisting that he had never hankered for posts, he said he had refused accepting the presidentship on the last occasion for four months when Mr. Advani asked him to take over the reins. It was only after much persuasion by Mr. Advani, who was reluctant to assume the office himself as he was already holding two responsibilities, that he accepted.

(5356) Sangareddy : Four Telangana Rashtra Samithi (TRS) dissident legislators, who met here on Saturday, declared that lobbying for separate Telangana by TRS chief K. Chandrasekhar Rao in New Delhi had failed, and called for a new strategy to achieve the goal. Addressing a press conference following closed door confabulations MLAs - Mandadi Satyanarayana Reddy, Toorpu Jayaprakash Reddy, Dugyala Srinivasa Rao and Mukunda Reddy - said they would step up pressure on the party leadership to work for the development of the region till a new State was carved out. The four legislators ridiculed that none of them had heard anything from UPA Chairperson Sonia Gandhi that remotely sounded like statehood for Telangana. Trading their guns on the Telugu Desam Party (TDP) and the Communist Party of India (Marxist) they pointed out that both the TDP and the CPI (M) were the main enemies of Telangana region. However, they claimed that a majority of the legislators in the Congress and the BJP were for a separate State. The dissidents still seem to be unhappy with the party president saying he had not changed his autocratic way of functioning. The MLAs, however, said that they would attend the forthcoming TRSLP meeting to voice their demands.

(5357) Adilabad : The Telangana Rashtra Samiti (TRS) would hold a series of meetings of its elected representatives and cadres in the second half of January and early February to build up pressure on the Union Government seeking a commitment on the separate Telangana issue. Resignations by TRS president K. Chandrasekhara Rao and A. Narendra from the Union Cabinet will also be considered, according to Adilabad MP T. Madhusudan Reddy.Giving details of the 'pressure building' activities at a press conference here on Saturday, the MP said the TRS was seeking a firm commitment from UPA Chairperson Sonia Gandhi on the issue before the start of the Budget session in February. Answering questions, Mr. Reddy said the resignations were on the agenda since some time. However, the option was not used because of the failed tactics of resignations by six TRS Minister from the State Government.

(5358) Barasat (West Bengal) : The Kolkata police were on Saturday directed by a district court here to arrest Trinamool Congress chief Mamata Banerjee and some others by February 27 in a case of violence during a political meeting here in 1994. The Chief Judicial Magistrate, Barasat, Siddharta Roy Chowdhury, took umbrage at a report by the Deputy Commissioner (HQ), Kolkata police, expressing his inability to arrest Ms. Banerjee and directed that the warrant of arrest be forwarded to the Kolkata police again for execution. The warrant of arrest against Mamata Banerjee, Saugata Roy and some other political leaders was issued on November 11, 2005 and the same was forwarded for execution.The counsel for the accused informed the CJM that out of 202 accused, 194 were on bail and two of the eight remaining, Ratan Dey and Biman Dutta, had died.

(5359) Chennai : Chief Minister Jayalalithaa on Saturday criticised the Centre's decision to increase the issue price of foodgrains under the Public Distribution System, saying this had come at a time when there was "compelling need to protect the poor and needy with an effective social safety net."

(5360) Kottayam : Chief Minister Oommen Chandy and Kerala Pradesh Congress Committee (KPCC) president Ramesh Chennithala on Saturday held a closed-door discussion with Nair Service Society (NSS) general secretary P.K. Narayana Panicker and assistant secretary G. Sukumaran Nair on the Narendran Commission recommendations. While both the parties were tight-lipped about the details of the discussion, Congress circles appeared to be optimistic and expressed confidence that they would be able to reach a consensus on the issue by mid-January. According to Mr. Sukumaran Nair, the talks centred on the situation arising out of the recommendations and Friday's talks were only part of the ongoing parleys with the parties concerned. Divulging details of the talks at this juncture will upset its progress, he said. According to Congress sources, the discussions are progressing satisfactorily. A consensus could be reached by next week..

(5361) Bangalore : The All-India Progressive Janata Dal (AIPJD), led by former Deputy Chief Minister Siddaramaiah, is ready for an alliance with the Congress in zilla and taluk panchayats where no party has gained a majority of seats. This was announced by Mr. Siddaramaiah at a programme to felicitate new members of panchayats from the AIPJD here.

(5362) Bangalore : Public Works and Power Minister H.D. Revanna on Saturday said the Janata Dal (Secular) increased its vote share in the zilla panchayat elections to 38 per cent from 25 per cent in the Legislative Assembly elections. Addressing presspersons here, he said neither the Janata Dal (S) nor party President H.D. Deve Gowda "will surrender to anyone". He said the Congress should realise that its base has shrunk since the Assembly polls.

(5363) Mangalore : The Bharatiya Janata Party (BJP) has said the results of the zilla and taluk panchayat elections in the State are a clear verdict for change considering the number of seats won by the BJP. Addressing presspersons, State spokesperson of the party Suresh Kumar who was here to train the newly elected zilla and taluk panchayat members of the BJP said that all over the State the BJP has made a resounding victory by improving its total number of seats by three times in some districts and has doubled it in some others when compared to the elections results of 2000. Mr. Kumar said the Congress has lost its base in Karnataka.

(5364) Davangere : Senior BJP leader and MLC D.H. Shankaramurthy said that the BJP will not ally with Janata Dal (Secular) to form a new Government if the coalition breaks up. Mid-term poll is the only alternative, he said. He said that the fall of the coalition Government in the State was imminent and uncertainty and anxiety are bothering coalition partners - the Congress and the Janata Dal (Secular). Talking to reporters here on Saturday, Mr. Shankaramurthy said joining hands with the Congress did not arise at all as both the BJP and the Congress are different ideologically and in all other aspects.

(5365) Kollam : The question whether the Democratic Indira Congress(Karunakaran) (DIC(K) should be included in the Left Democratic Front (LDF) is not at all a live issue at present, RSP State secretary T.J. Chandrachoodan said here on Saturday.

(5366) Kottayam : The KPCC will take up the issue of curtailment of ration subsidy and slash in the quantity of rice and wheat distributed through the ration shops with the Centre, KPCC president Ramesh Chennithala has said.

(5367) Thiruvananthapuram : The CPI is of the considered opinion that the LDF will spoil its good image among the people if K. Karunakaran's Democratic Indira Congress (DIC-K) is allowed to join it as a coalition partner, CPI State secretary Veliyam Bharghavan has said. At a press conference here on Saturday, Mr. Bharghavan said the State council of his party had discussed in detail the issue of allowing the DIC(K)'s entry into the LDF.The unanimous opinion was that Mr. Karunakaran's party would damage the reputation of the LDF, he said.

(5368) Malappuram : Communist Party of India (Marxist) State secretary Pinarayi Vijayan has criticised the Central Government for increasing the ration price for those above poverty line (APL). Addressing the media at Tanur on Saturday, Mr. Vijayan said that the policies of both the Centre and the State Government would destroy the public distribution system (PDS) in the country.

(5369) Chennai : The Chennai police on Saturday registered a case against DMK president M. Karunanidhi on charges that he hurt the sentiments of Hindus while addressing a rally three years ago. Police sources said the Madras High Court had directed the Mambalam police to register the case and dispose it on merit based on a public interest litigation. B.R. Gautaman, director of the Vedic Sciences Research Institute based in Valasarawakkam, had moved the court in October 2002 stating that Mr. Karunanidhi had hurt the sentiments of Hindus. Sources said the case had been registered under Sections 295 A (deliberate act intended to outrage religious feeling) and 298 (Insulting religious sentiments by speech) of the Indian Penal Code. This is the second police case against the DMK chief this week. Earlier, the State Crime Branch filed a criminal complaint against Mr. Karunanidhi over alleged irregularities in the construction of the Amaravathi bridge in Karur.

(5370) New Delhi : The Bharatiya Janata Party on Saturday launched an attack on the United Progressive Alliance (UPA) for the decision to further cut back food subsidies and said "it is the beginning of the dismantling of the public distribution system (PDS)." The party spokesperson, Prakash Javadekar, said that the decision to increase the offtake price of foodgrains under the PDS for those above the poverty line and the reduction in the quantity each person could take from fair price shops would save the Government more than Rs. 4000 crore but at the cost of the poorest strata of society. He recalled that it was the Vajpayee Government that increased the quota of foodgrains made available through the ration shops. That was now being reversed. His charge was that since the UPA came power in May 2004, it had already cut back on food subsidies to the tune of 60 per cent. "The BJP demands a rollback of this decision to cut food subsidies," Mr. Javadekar said. The farmers were also hit by the UPA Government's policies, the party said. "The mid-term economic review stated that there would be no increase in the minimum support price offered to farmers for wheat and rice," the BJP claimed. On the issue of a commission being set up to identify minority educational institutions, the BJP said that it seemed the Congress was bent upon undoing court decisions, which quashed the minority status given to Aligarh Muslim University. The effect of this, the spokesperson warned, would be as disastrous as was the overturning of the Shah Bano case judgment during the Rajiv Gandhi Government's tenure.The BJP blamed the Congress for playing "cheap political tricks to further its vote bank politics." Mr. Javadekar's charge was that the Congress wanted to desperately get the Muslim vote back and was trying every means, including unconstitutional decisions, to do this.

(5371) New Delhi : The Communist Party of India (CPI) and the All-India Forward Bloc have condemned the Government's decision to cut down food subsidy. Both parties have decided to oppose the Cabinet's decision to reduce the allocation of foodgrains through the Targeted Public Distribution System with the latter also demanding a public debate on the food policy. In a statement, the CPI said though the price of foodgrains released through TPDS for Below Poverty Line (BPL) families remained the same, it would impact the poor since the quantum of foodgrains allocated per family had been reduced. "Rather than improving and streamlining the public distribution system (PDS), the Government is out to dismantle it. The Government seems to be bent upon imposing burden and misery on the poor and reducing whatever meagre benefits they have while merrily handing out concessions to the affluent and corporate houses." The Forward Bloc said food security was the fundamental right of the people and there should be universalisation of PDS.

(5372) New Delhi : Bharatiya Janata Party president Rajnath Singh on Saturday told a delegation from Orissa that there was no question of withdrawing support to the Naveen Patnaik Government, but matters that have soured the relationship between the Biju Janata Dal and the BJP's State unit would be sorted out. Mr. Singh apparently spoke to Mr. Patnaik, who has reportedly agreed to improve the relief and rehabilitation package being offered to relatives of those killed in the police firing at Kalinga Nagar recently.

(5373) New Delhi : Rajya Sabha member Brinda Karat on Saturday sought to clarify that Communists were not against any form of traditional system of medicine or any individual. Referring to the controversy over the issue of alleged use of human and animal matter in Ayurvedic medicines prepared in Baba Ramdev's Divya Pharmacy, Ms. Karat said her objection was only to violation of labour laws and the Drugs and Cosmetics Act, 1940 by the management. "I myself practise yoga and Ayurveda is flourishing in Kerala, while West Bengal is considered the hub of homoeopathy," she said at a press conference organised by the Centre of

Indian Trade Unions (CITU) here to highlight the issues of the striking workers of Divya Pharmacy in Haridwar. "It is a war for ideology, principles and transparency. Please don't personalise it." She said the entire issue had been given a different connotation to divert the attention of people from gross violation of laws of the land by the management. "If any medicine helps a patient, we support it but the people have a right to know about its contents. In this case, Divya Pharmacy claims that its preparations are purely herbal, whereas the laboratory tests conducted by the Health and Family Welfare Ministry have shown ingredients of human and animal origin which is a clear violation of the Drugs and Cosmetics Act, 1940," she said, hoping that the Ministry would take action against the pharmacy.

(5374) Chennai : Janata Party president Subramanian Swamy on Saturday urged the Union Government to withdraw the decision to cut the subsidy for the Public Distribution System.In a statement, he said the decision had been made to obtain Rs. 4,524 crore as revenue. Finance Minister P. Chidambaram was directly responsible for the trend towards bankruptcy, he alleged. "He has allowed the fiscal deficit to rise above the danger mark of nine per cent of the GDP to 13 per cent," he said.

(5375) Patna : Just a few months after power slipped from the hands of the Lalu-Rabri duo, senior RJD leader Ramai Ram on Saturday revolted against his party leadership for allegedly denying him an important position in the party, charging it with 'ignoring dalits and leaders enjoying significant mass support.' Apparently peeved at denial of an important position in the party, Mr. Ram, a senior Minister in the erstwhile Rabri Devi Cabinet, alleged here that leaders like Union Ministers Raghuvansh Prasad Singh, Akhilesh Prasad Singh, Prem Gupta and Kanti Singh who have "no significant mass support" have blessings of Lalu Prasad. "But a person like me enjoying people's support has virtually become unimportant and irrelevant. The dalits are being ignored and the leaders who played a vital role in the establishment of RJD have become unimportant," Mr. Ram said. He said while Rabri Devi herself has become Opposition Leader in the State Assembly, Shakeel Ahmed Khan is the party's deputy leader in the House. "Another man close to Lalu Prasad has been nominated chief whip of the RJD legislature party," Mr. Ram said without naming former Bihar Minister Ramchandra Purve.

(5376) Pondicherry : The Secretary of the Pondicherry State Communist Party of India (CPI), N. Kalainathan, MLA, has mounted scathing attack on the Congress Government headed by N. Rangasamy. Addressing newsmen on Saturday he said that the Administrative Committee of the State unit of the party held earlier under the chairmanship of A.M.Saleem had resolved to mobilise the support of all like-minded parties to launch a sustained movement and agitation against the government.

(5377) Tiruchi : Tripura Chief Minister Manic Sarcar on Saturday alleged that the Congress was conniving with militants backed by the Pakistan Inter-Services Intelligence and the CIA to destabilise the Left Front Government in the North-eastern State. At a function organised by the CPI(M) here, he said the Congress had "joined hands" with secessionist groups that had no faith in the Constitution and were intent on "weakening" the party's base in Tripura.

09-01-2006

(5378) Hyderabad : If the nation is to move forward on the path of progress Bihar has to be developed and the JD-BJP Government will strive to achieve it, Nitish Kumar, Chief Minister of Bihar, has said. At a felicitation function organised by the State BJP here on Sunday, he described as "national duty" the Government's task to usher in development, opening a new chapter in the troubled State's chequered history. "Development is possible if the ruling dispensation resolves to improve the lot of the poor. We are committed to this and `dharmapalan' (rule of justice)", he said.

(5379) Hyderabad : The Andhra Pradesh Congress Committee president K. Kesava Rao has sought to put an end to the ongoing war of words between the CPI(M) State secretary B.V. Raghavulu and the Congress leadership saying the two parties can sit together and sort out any contentious issues.

(5380) Hyderabad : Chief Minister Y.S. Rajasekhara Reddy received support from unexpected quarters against the criticism he is facing on the formation of Telangana. A meeting organised by the Telangana Employees' Association for release of its diary turned out to be a platform for the Congress and TRS leaders to vent their ire against each other. Even as the TRS leaders criticised Dr. Reddy, Congress MLA P. Janardhan Reddy warned them against criticising the Chief Minister since the Telangana issue was not in his hands. He wanted the TRS leaders to make public the agreement they entered into with the Congress leadership before the elections. "There is no point in criticising Congress president Sonia Gandhi or the Chief Minister," he said. Union Minister A. Narendra who was the chief guest said the party had tried several ways to achieve separate Telangana democratically. "We are prepared to launch an intensive struggle and give sleepless nights to the Chief Minister. The Congress will have no future if it cheats the people of Telangana one more time," he said. As Mr. Narendra was about to leave the stage, Mr. Reddy stopped him objecting to the way the former was criticising the Congress. "How can you say the Congress will not have a future in the State. Is it because the TRS realised the fact that the continued dissidence had already posed questions on the party's survival?" Mr. Narendra, on his part, wanted to know why the Congress MLAs from Telangana remained silent after coming to power. "How long does the Congress want us to wait? Is it till the next elections? There is a limit to everything," he said.

(5381) Kurnool : The Communist Party of India (CPI) is likely to deviate from the stand taken by its cousin CPI(M) on the Polavaram project issue and press for its speedy completion. The Andhra Pradesh Raithu Sangham, affiliated to the CPI, is going to take up a lengthy debate on the Polavaram project at its three-day 15th State meet beginning here on Monday.

(5382) Visakhapatnam : Congress MP and former Chief Minister N. Janardhan Reddy on Sunday called for immediate steps to plug loopholes to make cooperative movement a grand success. "At present, the cooperative institutions are faced with a plethora of problems. The Centre is seized of the matter and Union Finance Minister P. Chidambaram has launched an exercise to bring about drastic changes in the cooperative laws," he told the 10th annual conference of AP Urban and Town Co-operative Banks' Association (APUTCBA) here.

(5383) Manjeri : The CPI(M) has demanded that the Centre chalk out a comprehensive policy on migration for the benefit of thousands of Indians working abroadMany Indian labourers who migrate to countries in the Gulf face inhuman treatment there, and their protection can be ensured only through formulation of a comprehensive migration policy by the Centre, said CPI(M) State Secretary Pinarayi Vijayan here on Sunday.

(5384) Kolkata : The ruling Left Front kicked off its campaign for the coming Assembly elections in West Bengal with a massive rally here on Sunday. At the meeting, organised by the Communist Party of India (Marxist), party leaders called on the people to return the Front to power for the seventh successive time. Industrialisation would be the top priority if the Government was voted back to power. The struggle to improve the lot of the economically weak would continue along with efforts for greater development. The CPI(M) dismissed the Opposition's attempt to forge an alliance as "an unprincipled exercise, lacking an agenda of any substance that the disparate parties engage in prior to any election."Polit Bureau member Jyoti Basu said: "Nowhere in India, nowhere in the world where there is a parliamentary democracy, has a government been returned to power six times in a row as had the Left Front in the last Assembly polls. This is a historic achievement. I urge you to ensure that we come to power for the seventh time this time around and with more than the two-thirds of the total seats we had won the last time.

(5385) Agartala : CPI(M) general secretary Prakash Karat on Sunday said party MP Brinda Karat's allegations against Swamy Ramdev has the full support of the party and CITU, its trade union wing. He said the questions she had raised about the formulation of Ayurvedic medicine sold by Swamy Ramdev and the labour relations in the factory, where the medicines are made, are not her individual opinion. They are as much those of the CPI(M) as the CITU.Asked if he was aware that Prime Minister Manmohan Singh had offered to resign in the wake of the party's strong opposition to the India-U.S. joint military exercise at Kalaikunda airbase in West Bengal in November, Mr. Karat said: "This is the first time I am hearing such news that the Prime Minister had offered to quit." The Left parties will soon submit alternative proposals, before the unveiling of the Union budget, to the Government and the UPA-Left Coordination Committee, Mr. Karat said. "There are so many sectors and ways of mobilising resources without taking measures which are harmful for the country and the people. We are surprised at the decision of the Government to cut subsidy and quantity of foodgrains for people Below Poverty Line," he said. He said the Centre took the decision to reduce food subsidy of Rs. 4,000 crores, but this logic was not acceptable. "We want more expansion of the PDS and include more people under the scheme and we are asking the government to reconsider the anti-people decision because the PDS is essential for millions of people," he said. Asked whether the Government was ignoring the Left on important policy matters, Mr. Karat said there was no question of ignoring it but there were differences of policies between the Congress and the Left parties. The Left parties were intervening in each and every policy matter of the Government. "We are supporting the pro-people decisions and opposing the anti-people steps. "We shall intensify our mass movement if the Congress led government does not work for the labour, farmers, small businessmen, working class and general people," he said. - UNI

(5386) Nashik : Nationalist Congress Party (NCP) president and Union Agriculture Minister Sharad Pawar ruled out here on Sunday the possibility of a third front taking shape in the country in view of growing bipolarism in national politics.Asked about political grapevine that he could form a third front with other centrist parties, Mr. Pawar told presspersons that his party had just seven MPs, which was too few to consider the option. Mr. Pawar said governments would now be formed either by the Congress-led or Bharatiya Janata Party-led fronts. Earlier, he opened the inaugural session of the Maharashtra NCP's convention. He denied reports that the NCP and other small parties were forming a pressure group within the ruling UPA. Such talk had started after his meeting with Telangana leader Chandrasekhar Rao. Mr. Pawar said he met Dr. Rao only to enquire about his health. The latter had asked about the progress on the formation of the Telangana state - a promise made in the UPA agenda. Mr. Pawar said the NCP would not contest elections on its own but in alliance with other parties, particularly the Congress, to avoid division of secular votes and would strictly adhere to coalition norms.

(5387) Bangalore : Four State Bharatiya Janata Party (BJP) leaders have opposed any alliance with the Janata Dal (Secular) in the State and alleged that it is trying to form an alternative coalition with their party to remain in power. The four leaders, R. Ashok, MLA and State General Secretary, Aravind Limbavali MLC, Katta Subramanya Naidu, MLA and President of Slum Morcha, and P.C. Mohan, MLA and State Treasurer, have said the Janata Dal (S), which has been rejected in the zilla and taluk panchayat elections, is now looking to the BJP.

(5388) Bangalore : The Karnataka Pradesh Congress Committee (KPCC) President, M. Mallikarjun Kharge, on Saturday ruled out the possibility of midterm elections and declared that the coalition Government will complete its term.

(5389) Bangalore : It has turned out that the "voyage" of the former Prime Minister H.D. Deve Gowda to New Delhi is to meet two Vajpayees and not the former Prime Minister A.B. Vajpayee alone, which has in the last few days been speculated upon, denied and challenged.The meeting between the two former Prime Ministers did take place in New Delhi on Sunday evening.

(5390) Davangere : The former Minister B.K. Chandrashekar said that it is wrong for the Janata Dal (Secular) to ask the Congress not to hold any truck with the All India Progressive Janata Dal (AIPJD) in zilla and taluk panchayats. The Congress leader told presspersons here on Sunday that his party had not given any commitment to the Janata Dal (S) before the elections in this regard.

(5391) Kannur : Minister for Co-operation and Communist Marxist Party (CMP) general secretary M.V. Raghavan has said that Communist Party of India (Marxist) is favouring an alliance with the Democratic Indira Congress (Karunakaran) because of its apprehension about the outcome of the next Assembly elections. Inaugurating the State conference of the Kerala Socialist Youth Federation (KSYF) here on Sunday, Mr. Raghavan said that DIC(K) leader K. Karunakaran should say whether he would allow his party to have only seat adjustments with the Left Democratic Front (LDF) as some LDF constituents, including the Communist Party of India (CPI), was strongly opposed to the idea of bringing in the DIC(K) in the front. CPI(M) State secretary Pinarayi Vijayan, on his part, should say whether DIC(K) would ever be included in the LDF, Mr. Raghavan said.

(5392) Thiruvananthapuram : The CPI and the RSP have criticised the Union Government's decision to slash food subsidy.

(5393) Thiruvananthapuram : DIC(K) president K. Muraleedharan's 47-day-long padayatra will conclude on Monday, with the party looking forward to a new set of developments that would find it on the winning side of Kerala politics. As Mr. Muraleedharan entered the last day of his padayatra, he was received by a debate on whether the DIC(K) should be included in the LDF, with the CPI, the second largest partner in the Opposition coalition, making it clear that it was opposed to the move. Mr.

Muraleedharan and the veteran, K Karunakaran, strongly reacted to the CPI stand. Mr. Muraleedharan stated that his party had not submitted an application for entry, but was only trying to forge a larger Left secular platform. He said his party had supported the LDF in the Assembly and Lok Sabha byelections only to strengthen this platform. The DIC(K)'s entry into the LDF was a matter to be discussed later, he added. Mr. Karunakaran, in an interview to a private television channel, said the voices of dissent were isolated ones. CPI (M) State secretary Pinarayi Vijayan said a final decision would be taken after discussions in the LDF. Mr. Muraleedharan's padayatra named 'Navakerala Yatra' completed 843 km. covering 13 districts. According to a DIC (K) statement, Mr. Muraleedharan attended more than 122 major public meetings, and thousands of other smaller functions during the padayatra, which was flagged off on November 24. The yatra was undertaken to explain to the people the reasons for forming a new party as well as to get sanction of the party workers for the Left democratic secular alliance and mobilise party funds.

(5394) Manjeri : The people of Kerala have welcomed and accepted the Left Democratic Front (LDF)'s cooperation with the Democratic Indira Congress (DIC-K) of K. Karunakaran in the recent elections, CPI(M) State Secretary Pinarayi Vijayan has said.At a news conference here on Sunday, the CPI(M) leader said that the LDF's image had not suffered by associating with the DIC(K). Rather, he said, the DIC(K) had played a major role in the LDF victories, especially in Thiruvananthapuram Lok Sabha byelection.

(5395) Hyderabad : Samajwadi Party leader Amar Singh told presspersons here on Sunday that even Prime Minister Manmohan Singh's phone was being tapped. "My source surprised me by saying that I had spoken to the Prime Minister. Asked how he knew, he replied that Dr. Singh's phone was also being tapped". He said he was receiving threats. If anything were to happen to him and his family, the UPA Government would be held responsible. Mr. Singh briefed Telugu Desam president N. Chandrababu Naidu about the phone-tapping issue.Demanding a high-level, impartial probe, they said Chief Ministers Jayalalithaa, Buddhadeb Bhattacharjee and Nitish Kumar could monitor the probe. Mr. Naidu said it was time the Opposition came together to fight the menace.

(5396) Guwahati : Defence Minister Pranab Mukherjee and other All India Congress Committee leaders on Sunday kick-started the Congress campaign for the 2006 Assembly polls in Assam. They joined Chief Minister Tarun Gogoi and PCC leaders in showcasing the achievements of the Congress Government in the State.Addressing a rally chaired by PCC president Bhubaneswar Kalita here, Mr. Mukherjee said the Tarun Gogoi-led Congress Government had fulfilled all its promises made to the people of Assam. He said the Congress-led Government rebuilt the State by bringing back peace, improving the economy and by maintaining unity among various ethnic communities.Mr. Mukherjee said the Government also protected minorities. He urged both linguistic and religious minorities to be unafraid, now that the Illegal Migrants (Determination by Tribunals) Act was struck down by the Supreme Court. He said the Government accepted the verdict and would abide by it.

(5397) Nashik : Nationalist Congress Party (NCP) president and Union Agriculture Minister Sharad Pawar on Sunday rejected the recently passed Maharashtra law that gave voters the right to recall a village sarpanch. It was uncalled for and not envisaged by the Constitution makers, he said. Mr. Pawar was speaking at the inaugural session of the convention of the State unit of the party. Mr. Pawar, who heads the committee on job reservation for the Scheduled Castes and Scheduled Tribes in the private sector, said the committee had prepared its scheme and sent it to the Attorney-General for his opinion about its constitutional validity. He said most suicides were among cotton growers of the State and the Agriculture Ministry was considering a change in the crop pattern to improve the farmers' lot.

(5398) Nashik : Baba Ramdev, involved in a controversy following an allegation by CPI (M) leader Brinda Karat, on Sunday received support from Nationalist Congress Party chief Sharad Pawar. He said: "I appreciate the work done [by Baba Ramdev] to propagate yoga in a scientific way." On the allegation that Baba Ramdev's medicines contained animal remains, Mr. Pawar said: "I have been reading from childhood that some Ayurvedic medicines contained such things, say for example deer horns." Baba Ramdev, who is conducting yoga classes here for the last couple of days, said on Sunday that a Hyderabad-based laboratory had found nothing wrong with samples of his medicines. - PTI

(5399) Bhubaneswar : Communist Party of India (Marxist) Polit Bureau member Sitaram Yechury on Sunday condemned the killing of 12 tribals in a police firing at Kalinga Nagar, and demanded that the Orissa Government take immediate steps to solve the problems of the tribals facing displacement. Addressing a press conference here after his return from Kalinga Nagar, Mr. Yechury blamed the BJD-BJP Government for the police firing. The injured tribals had bullet marks on their back, he said. The CPI (M) leader said the State Government should not go ahead with its unilateral policy of evicting tribals by use of force in the name of industrialisation and development. "The Government should finalise the compensation and rehabilitation package after consulting the tribals who were to be displaced to make space for industries. The problems pertaining to displacement should be settled by involving the tribals in the development process." Observing that there were a lot of ambiguities over the tribals' right to land and use of forest resources, Mr. Yechury said the Government should not take any measure that would be in contrary to the Tribal Rights Bill pending in Parliament. Mr. Yechury also underlined the need for a complete ban on export of iron ore and other minerals.

(5400) Jaipur : Congress general secretary Ashok Gehlot has held the partnerships the party had in the past with other political parties in Uttar Pradesh responsible for the poor condition of the Congress in that State. "Alliances, especially the ones in which the Congress played the role of the junior partner, caused maximum damage," Mr. Gehlot, who has been made in charge of Uttar Pradesh, said. "It has been 15 years of wilderness for the Congress in Uttar Pradesh," Mr. Gehlot, who was on his first visit to the Rajasthan Capital after the party leadership bestowing on him the new assignment, said talking to a group of media persons here on Sunday. "During the period many permutations and combinations were tried out and all proved futile. The Congress should have never entered into any partnership. It should have had tried to stand on its own," Mr. Gehlot, who is scheduled to visit Lucknow on January 15, said. "The alliances, especially with the Bahujan Samaj Party did the maximum damage. It upset the Congress party's support base. The morale of the workers went down," Mr. Gehlot, who had been always against the Congress aligning with other political parties in Rajasthan as well, said. "My efforts would be to bring back the lost glory to the Congress in U.P. The people still look up to the Congress as a reliable political party. I am confident that its glorious past, the sacrifices made by its leaders and the leadership of the party president, Sonia Gandhi would help Congress to return to power in U.P. one day," Mr. Gehlot said. "My attempt will be to bring together the Congress family. I am making an appeal to all Congressmen to return to the party. We want to take all 36 communities with us," he said. "It is going to be a big challenge," Mr. Gehlot said conceding that the party presently stood at a poor fourth in U.P. "We will keep away from both caste and religion and try to strengthen the social fabric presently torn into pieces due to the reckless politics. "Ram Mandir issue is no more. The Bharatiya Janata Party too has taken the stand that the court would decide on the disputed site. As for caste politics is concerned the political parties are to blame for the present situation. The politics of caste in U.P. and Bihar has weakened the communities involved as well as the whole country," he said. Talking about Rajasthan Mr. Gehlot said the State Government failed to perform in the past two years, despite the "wholehearted support" from the Centre. The drought situation was grim in various parts. The drought affected people in Banswara and Dungarpur district had started migrating to other States in large numbers. The State Government's announcement of employment to 1.25 lakh persons under drought relief was a cruel joke on the people, he charged. Congress General Secretary Ashok Mr. Gehlot on Sunday denounced the charges of telephone tapping levelled by the Samajwadi Party leader Amar Singh against the Congress president Sonia Gandhi as an "attention catching gimmick". "There are some people who always want to be in the headlines. They can go to any level to accomplish this," Mr. Gehlot said. "The utterances speak volumes about their personality," Mr. Gehlot said referring to the comments from Amar Singh and the U.P. Chief Minister Mulayam Singh Yadav on Ms. Gandhi. "Levelling such allegations against a leader of Ms. Gandhi's stature and reputation is an act of desperation on their part," he charged. "The Congress leadership can never stoop to their levels," he said. Mr. Gehlot said the people of Uttar Pradesh disliked both Mr. Yadav and Mr. Singh. "As such both should be suffering from certain guilt feeling to make such observations," he noted. Mr. Gehlot also challenged the stand of Mr. Singh that he was free to do things the way he wanted in private life. "Public figures do no have personal life. They are public property. They have to remain transparent and accountable to the people," he asserted.

(5401) Lucknow : The Uttar Pradesh Chief Minister Mulayam Singh Yadav on Sunday once again accused the Congress of hatching a conspiracy against the ruling Samajwadi Party, by tapping the phones of one of its prominent leaders and said the struggle on the issue would continue till the end. Addressing the youth wings of party here, Mr. Yadav said the phone tapping issue was not only against party MP Amar Singh, but the entire party. "The conspiracy hatched by Congress is against the party and not any individual leader," he added. Calling upon youths to be wary of campaign launched by political opponents, particularly the Congress, he said the Opposition aimed at hitting the party hardest. Commenting on the law and order issue raked up by the opposition parties against the state government, the Chief Minister claimed that the situation in U.P. was far more conducive than several other States. "It was part of their (Opposition's) effort to defame the SP Government in the State for gaining public sympathy," he added. Mr. Yadav, criticising the Centre's warm-hearted welcome to the Multi National Companies (MNCs) stated that these alien companies will endanger the country's economic interests by engulfing the domestic industry. On the initiatives taken by his government in the development arena, he said several States including Rajasthan and Punjab have been "inspired" by U.P.'s recipe for development. "In Bihar too, the new government wants to replicate the U.P. formula for attaining development," he quipped. – UNI

(5402) Lucknow : Samajwadi party supremo and Uttar Pradesh Chief Minister Mulayam Singh Yadav announced holding of a youth rally and a "cycle" campaign to prepare for Assembly polls after his party's stupendous success in Zila Panchayat Chairmen polls. Addressing the four youth wings of the party here, Mr Yadav said that a massive youth rally would be held in the state capital on January 29 and a cycle campaign would be kicked off from Februrary 21 as part of preparations for the Assembly polls in 2007. Claiming that the opposition parties have been wiped out in the Zila Panchayat chairmen elections in which SP and its ally Rashtriya Lok Dal bagged 53 out of the total 69 seats, he said it was high time the party went for a 'kill' against the opponents.

(5403) Lucknow : Flaying the ruling Samajwadi Party leaders for using objectionable language over the phone tapping issue, the Uttar Pradesh Congress today demanded that the conversation between SP MP Amar Singh and others that was allegedly tapped, should be made public. "People have all the right to know the activities, private or public about their representatives," claimed U.P. Congress president Salman Khurshid here. Addressing a press conference, Mr. Khurshid slammed the SP leaders including U.P. CM Mulayam Singh Yadav and Rajya Sabha MP Amar Singh for using "abusive" language to defend themselves in the phone tapping case. He also made it clear that the UPA Government at the Centre had nothing to do with the case. "A probe was already underway and some people have been arrested in this connection," he further added. The Congress leader said like the candidates in the elections who have to give all details pertaining to their properties or criminal history, nothing is private in the life of political leaders. "In the U.S. also the political leaders have to face several charges which are extremely private," he added. Quoting that "Parde ke peeche kutch to hai," he said Mr. Singh himself was putting on questions and then giving their answers in the case, subsequently making more mockery of himself. Commenting on the Zila Panchayat chairmen elections held yesterday in which the ruling SP supported candidates won the maximum posts, the U.P. Congress president said everyone knew about the results beforehand as all norms were broken to win the elections. "Now we have to see, how the SP wins the Assembly polls with the help of the officials," he said. "I am of the firm opinion that Mulayam has always rigged the poll which forced him to change his constituency frequently," the Congress leader alleged. The bubble will burst once the Assembly polls are announced as people do not want the elections to be held under the present regime, Mr Khurshid said. — UNI

(5404) Chennai : Dravida Munnetra Kazhagam president M. Karunanidhi has written to Prime Minister Manmohan Singh and Congress president Sonia Gandhi, requesting them to withdraw the decision to effect a cut in allotment of foodgrains through the PDS and increase the issue price. In separate fax messages, Mr. Karunanidhi said: "Poor people, who are solely dependent on the foodgrains distributed through fair price shops run by the Government, are upset over the revision in price and quantum."The situation in Tamil Nadu was particularly bad since people "have been put to a lot of suffering and hardship continuously for the past few years due to drought, tsunami and floods. Therefore, any revision in price will adversely affect their interests and economic condition." He wanted the decision withdrawn "immediately." Pattali Makkal Katchi founder S. Ramadoss said his party would insist that the Centre reconsider its decision. The Centre's announcement was not final.

(5405) Chennai : DMKpresident M. Karunanidhi on Sunday contested the CB-CID claim that it was his government that shifted the concept of construction to the Build-Operate-Transfer basis.Handing over copies of a letter written by the Commissioner of Municipal Administration in early 1996, an extract of a resolution of the Karur municipal council and an order of the Municipal Administration and Water Supply Department, Mr. Karunanidhi said that the BOT concept—which forms the thrust of the CB-CID FIR—was mooted by the earlier AIADMK government, and not by him.

(5406) Thanjavur : Tripura Chief Minister Manic Sarcar on Saturday said that the Communist Party of India (Marxist) was, for years, urging the Centre to undertake radical land reforms. Addressing a public meeting here as part of the 26th State-level conference of the Tamil Nadu Vivasayigal Sangam, affiliated to the CPI (M), Mr. Sarcar said no government at the Centre had taken steps for radical land reforms. His party had been insisting that land should belong to the tillers, the poorest of the poor. He also said that his party was unhappy with the implementation of the Common Minimum Programme by the UPA Government. The Left parties, with a view to keeping the "communal" BJP away from power, were supporting the Congress-led Government on the condition that it would stick to the CMP.

10-01-2006

(5407) Hyderabad : The CPI (Maoist) Central Committee has condemned the killing of 12 tribals at Kalinganara in Orissa, terming it as a "pre-hatched" conspiracy of the BJD-BJP Government and Tata Steel. In a statement, Azad, spokesperson of the committee (provisional) hit out at various political parties for "shedding crocodile tears and showing mock opposition" to killing of tribals even while carrying out the same policies where they were in power. He blamed them for massive deployment of paramilitary and armed forces in seven States including Andhra Pradesh.

(5408) Hyderabad : A fresh wordy duel between the Telangana Rashtra Samithi leadership and the Congress over separate Statehood for Telangana has begun with the former seeking a resolution on it in the forthcoming Congress plenary. Provoked by the TRS leadership claim that there was no mention of the second SRC in the pre-election understanding between the two parties, the PCC president K. Keshava Rao on Monday reminded the

TRS leaders that the issue would be decided by the AICC president Sonia Gandhi. Khairatabad MLA P. Janardhan Reddy was the first to hit back at the Union Minister A. Narendra on Sunday over the latter's observation that the TRS could mess up things for the Congress if it continued to dilly dally on the issue. It was at a meeting of the employees where both of them were present.The APSRTC chairman Gone Prakasa Rao joined the chorus and went a step further and said that separate Telangana would not materialise under the present political scenario. He was echoing similar sentiment of another senior leader G. Venkat Swamy.

(5409) Kurnool : CPI State secretary K. Narayana said the party would oppose any move to stall the irrigation projects in the name of corruption.Talking to reporters at the 15th State conference of the Andhra Pradesh Raithu Sangham here on Monday, he said irrigation projects were the only answer for addressing the agriculture crisis in the State.

(5410) New Delhi : Samajwadi Party general secretary and spokesman Amar Singh on Monday offered an apology to Prime Minister Manmohan Singh for his remarks that some people in the Prime Minister's Office (PMO) were also involved in the phone tapping case. Mr. Singh, who filed a petition in the Supreme Court seeking a judicial probe into the incident, said he was mindful of "causing hurt to the Prime Minister," as expressed by the latter's press adviser Sanjay Baru. He tried to express his regrets to Dr. Singh over the phone, but was unable to get through to him. Meanwhile, the Bharatiya Janata Party claimed that it had credible information that the telephone of its former president, L.K. Advani, was tapped during the Volcker controversy, and sought an all-party meeting to discuss the "serious issue." Party president Rajnath Singh said the Government should immediately inquire into the matter.Mr. Advani said he was surprised when he was told that his telephone too was tapped. "In the six years we were in government, we did not order tapping of anyone's telephone," he said.

(5411) New Delhi : The differences between the Congress and the Janata Dal (Secular) in Karnataka deepened on Monday, with the former Prime Minister, H.D. Deve Gowda, announcing that his party's national executive would decide on February 8 whether to continue in or withdraw from the coalition government in the State.Mr. Gowda told reporters here that the coalition came under "severe stress" after the Congress decided to explore the possibility of aligning with "JD (S) rebels" led by the former

Deputy Chief Minister, Siddaramaiah, in zilla panchayats following the recent elections. "The JD (S) joined with the Congress to form the government after the last Assembly elections to check the growth of communal forces in the State. We came to some understanding. Now, the Congress has decided to deviate from it. We will assess the situation at various levels and take a decision at the national executive meeting. I will meet Congress president Sonia Gandhi after the meeting and convey the party's decision." Mr. Gowda said he had remained silent though he was "attacked and humiliated" by some Congress leaders for over a year. He was reacting now because the Congress was attempting to align with the very persons against whom the JD (S) had taken action for trying to break the party. Mr. Gowda stressed that neither any Congress leader in the party headquarters here, including Ms. Gandhi, nor Chief Minister Dharam Singh was to blame. He, however, declined to name those who he thought were responsible. The JD (S) president denied any move to tie up with the Bharatiya Janata Party. Describing his meeting with the former Prime Minister, Atal Bihari Vajpayee, on Sunday night as a "courtesy call," Mr. Gowda said he rejected the BJP's offer of support when he was on the verge of losing his post as Prime Minister. Reacting to Mr. Gowda's remarks,Congress spokesperson Jayanti Natarajan said the issue would be sorted out. "In a coalition arrangement, problems can crop up. They will be sorted out. The government in Karnataka is stable and will complete its term." Mr. Dharam Singh, who was here on an official visit, said he would convey Mr. Gowda's views to the Congress high command and request it to resolve the issue.

(5412) New Delhi : Chief Minister Oommen Chandy and Pradesh Congress Committee (PCC) president Ramesh Chennithala on Tuesday demanded rollback of the Cabinet decision to reduce the quantum of foodgrains allocated per household through the Targeted Public Distribution System (TPDS). The two leaders met Prime Minister Manmohan Singh, United Progressive Alliance chairperson Sonia Gandhi and Union Agriculture Minister Sharad Pawar on Monday in this regard.

(5413) Kanpur : Uttar Pradesh Chief Minister Mulayam Singh Yadav alleged here on Monday that a conspiracy to assassinate him and party MP Amar Singh had been hatched by the Congress in collusion with a prominent industrialist.Addressing a public rally at Bithoor, near here, the

Samajwadi Party chief said that "it has been brought to my notice that the Congress, along with a leading industrialist, was conspiring to kill me and Mr. Amar Singh. The details of the entire conspiracy will be disclosed at an appropriate time."On the notice issued by the Supreme Court to him and his family members on a PIL petition pertaining to property held by them, Mr. Yadav said he always respected the judiciary and would submit a reply within the stipulated time. Earlier, at another rally in Hathras in Aligarh, Mr. Yadav said tapping phones of senior party leaders like Mr. Amar Singh not only amounted to intrusion into privacy but was also an onslaught on the entire socialist ideology. Those alleging lawlessness in the State were only trying to defame his Government, out of fear of its rising popularity, he said. Mr. Amar Singh said in New Delhi that phones of the former External Affairs Minister, Natwar Singh, and some judges of the Supreme Court were also being tapped. This indicated an "undeclared emergency." Mr. Singh told reporters that he had been informed by reliable sources that Mr. Natwar Singh's "phone is being tapped and his entire house has been bugged by intelligence agencies." He said, "Mr. Natwar Singh is under strict surveillance; he can't even talk to his son." About the alleged tapping of phones of some Supreme Court judges, he said, "I am not the first person to reveal this. A prominent national daily has even carried out the transcript of the tapped conversation of a judge."

(5414) Shimoga : The Leader of Opposition in the State Legislative Assembly and senior leader of the BJP, B.S. Yediyurappa, said on Sunday that his party will not join hands with the Janata Dal (S) in sharing power in some zilla and taluk panchayats where no party has been able to secure a clear majority. Talking to presspersons at Sri Ramachandrapur Mutt where he participated in a valedictory function of the 68-day Bharatiya Go Yatra, he described the meeting of the former Prime Minister and President of the Janata Dal (S), H.D. Deve Gowda, with the former Prime Minister, A.B. Vajapayee, in New Delhi as a "courtesy call". He said it had nothing to do with the sharing of power of the Janata Dal (S) with the BJP. He dismissed the rumours in this connection as false and baseless. He said the differences between the Congress and the Janata Dal (S) had indicated that the coalition Government will not last long. Stating that the midterm Assembly elections were round the corner, he said they are likely to be held in May.

(5415) Kozhikode : Member of the CPI(M) Polit Bureau V. S. Achuthanandan on Monday once again made it clear that he was averse to admitting the Democratic Indira Congress (Karunakaran) into the Left Democratic Front. Mr. Achuthanandan made his stand very clear while inaugurating the State-level silver jubilee celebrations of the LDF organised by the Congress (S) led by Ramachandran Kadannappally at Town Hall in Kozhikode even though his own party is yet to make a clear and official statement on the issue.

(5416) Palakkad : Communist Party of India (Marxist) State secretary Pinarayi Vijayan has said his party is against all environmentally harmful industries, including the Coca-Cola unit at Plachimada. Replying to questions on the proposal to shift the Coke plant to some other place, at a press conference at Ottappalam near here on Monday, the CPI(M) leader said his party was against the exploitation of groundwater by such companies, depriving the local people of their drinking water sources. The CPI(M) will stand by the people on such issues. The Coca-Cola bottling plant has remained closed for nearly two years because of an agitation by the local people against exploitation of groundwater by the firm.

(5417) Thiruvananthapuram : The Democratic Indira Congress (Karunakaran) leader K. Karunakaran on Monday announced that his party would discuss with the CPI(M), the major party in the Opposition coalition, on its entry into the LDF. He said the discussions would be between DIC (K) president K. Muraleedharan and CPI (M) State secretary Pinarayi Vijayan. Addressing a public meeting marking the conclusion of Mr. Muraleedharan's 47-day padayatra, Mr. Karunakaran said there was only one party, the CPI (M), and one leader, Mr. Vijayan, that his party proposed to hold talks on the question of its alliance with the LDF. On the DIC (K)'s side, Mr. Muraleedharan would lead the talks, he said. Mr. Karunakaran also took a confrontationist position vis-a-vis the CPI and the RSP, both coalition partners opposed to his party's entry into the LDF. He said the DIC (K) had already proved its political relevance in Kerala, besides establishing its State-wide presence. However, he refused to divulge the details of the proposed structure of the alliance within the Left coalition. "We are ready to have ties with any force, except communal outfits," he said. In his address, Mr. Muraleedharan said his party was not in a hurry to gain entry into the LDF. Its position was to strengthen the Left, secular and democratic forces and it had performed its task well. He said there was no question of going back to the Congress because of fundamental differences. The DIC (K) was born in protest against the lack of inner party democracy in the Congress. The `nomination raj' had found even `sweepers' being accommodated in key positions, he remarked.Both Mr. Karunakaran and Mr. Muraleedharan did not spare the UDF Government, making personal attacks against the Chief Minister. Both of them referred to corruption in the Chandy Government. Mr. Muraleedharan questioned the rationale of inducting a Minister with just 65 days of effective rule possible.

(5418) New Delhi : Samajwadi Party leader Amar Singh on Monday moved the Supreme Court seeking a judicial inquiry into the alleged tapping of his telephone by the Delhi police. Mr. Singh, in an application filed on a PUCL petition disposed of by the court in 1996, sought a direction to the Central and State governments to strictly enforce its guidelines as well as Rule 419 A of the Indian Telegraph Rules.Mr. Singh cited eight respondents - the Union Telecommunications and Home Ministries, the Chief Secretary and the Home Secretary of Delhi, the Delhi Police Commissioner, the Additional Commissioner (crime), the Congress through its president and Reliance Infocomm. Mr. Singh alleged that the personal telephones of Uttar Pradesh Chief Minister Mulayam Singh Yadav and his son Akhilesh Yadav, a member of Parliament, were also being tapped.

(5419) Kolkata : Trinamool Congress leader Mamata Banerjee and the Congress leadership in West Bengal will soon discuss the latter's invitation to her to lead a "secular" anti-Left alliance for the Assembly polls provided she dissociates herself from the National Democratic Alliance.The Congress' decision was taken at a recent meeting of the West Bengal Pradesh Congress Committee (WBPCC) presided over by its president, Defence Minister Pranab Mukherjee. "We [the Congress] will be sitting for talks with Ms. Banerjee with the offer shortly," party working president Pradip Bhattacharya told The Hindu here on Monday. Mr. Mukherjee and Ms. Banerjee had earlier discussed the possibility of forging an alliance days ahead of the WBPCC meeting.

(5420) New Delhi : The Congress on Monday urged the Manmohan Singh Government to reconsider the decision to hike issue prices of foodgrains under the public distribution system stating that the move caused hardship to people including those above poverty line. The party said while it understands the compulsions of the Government and fiscal prudence, it believes that the decision to hike the price for above poverty line was "harsh." Party spokesperson Jayanti Natarajan told presspersons that women belonging to families above poverty line were already burdened with increase in the cost of living, the hike in prices of foodgrains would make it difficult to make both ends meet. "We urge the Government to reconsider and review the decision and take a new look..."

(5421) Pondicherry : Newly appointed AICC general secretary and Member of Parliament V. Narayanasamy said here on Monday that he would undertake an extensive campaign to strengthen the Democratic Progressive Alliance in Pondicherry.

(5422) Pondicherry : The Congress leader, V. Narayanasamy MP, has urged the Pondicherry Administration to form a corporation or a society to enable women Self-Help Groups (SHGs) to market their products using loans from banks and also subsidies from the Government.

(5423) Lucknow : Holding HRD Minister Arjun Singh responsible for the Allahabad High Court verdict scrapping minority status of Aligarh Muslim University (AMU), the ruling Samajwadi Party on Monday charged the Congress with drawing political mileage from the tangle. SP general secretary and State Urban Development Minister Mohammad Azam Khan said here that Congress and the HRD Minister should be held responsible for the AMU episode. "When everyone knows that without amending the Constitution the minority status of the university would be struck down, then why did the Centre not do the needful," he questioned. "The Congress was only trying to derive political mileage from the issue and they are waiting for the right time to go for the amendment to the Constitution," he alleged. Accusing Mr Singh of backstabbing the minorities, Mr Khan said the HRD Minister was also responsible for issues like imposition of emergency in 1975 and Ayodhya demolition in 1992, as on both occasions, the then prime ministers had acted on his advice. Demanding that the UPA Government at Centre immediately convene a special session of Parliament to amend Articles 25, 29 and 30 of the Constitution, the SP leader said the HRD Ministry should quickly work upon it. UNI

(5424) Chennai : The Communist Party of India (Marxist) on Monday reiterated its opposition to any attempt to make the labour laws flexible. Addressing the inaugural session of an all-India conference of the Income

Tax Employees Federation, CPI(M) floor leader in the Lok Sabha Basudeb Acharia said of the total workforce of 40 crore, only 2.5 crore was in the organised sector governed by the labour laws. Most of the workers were in the unorganised sector, which did not have any laws. There was no adequate social security system for them either.

(5425) Chennai : District secretaries of the Dravida Munnetra Kazhagam, who met here to discuss the party's state conference, have condemned the "false case" against party president M. Karunanidhi on the Karur bridge construction issue.

(5426) Chennai : Chief Minister Jayalalithaa on Monday accused Dravida Munnetra Kazhagam president M. Karunanidhi of indulging in "double talk" on the Centre's decision to increase the price and reduce the quantum of rice allocated for the public distribution system (PDS).

(5427) Thanjavur : Factionalism in the Congress came to the fore on Monday, when supporters of party leader Tindivanam Ramamurthy and TNCC president G.K. Vasan clashed at a meeting organised here to celebrate the 121st anniversary of the party. When the meeting, organised by supporters of Mr. Ramamurthy, started, Satyaraj, son of Nanji K.Varadarajan, district president, was allegedly beaten up by supporters of Mr. Ramamurthy. He was whisked away by the police. Mr. Vasan's supporters staged a demonstration in front of the marriage hall where the meeting was held. When they tried to enter the hall, they were arrested. Fortyfive supporters of Mr. Vasan, led by Vayalur Ramanathan, were held.

11-01-2006

(5428) Hyderabad : The State BJP has alleged that the much-hyped 'Jalayagnam' launched to complete pending irrigation projects by 2009 became a 'farce' with the Government unable to cross any of the milestones it fixed for itself. Addressing a press conference, BJP State secretary N.V.S.S. Prabhakar said the fact that the Government could not spend Rs. 2,800 crores of the Rs. 6,734 crores allotted for irrigation in the budget ending March 2006 reflects its own poor performance.

(5429) Kurnool : Telugu Desam district president K.E. Krishna Murthy has said Backward Classes are were under-represented in the State. Addressing a meeting of the BC cell of the party here on Tuesday, he said though Backward Classes constitute 56 per cent of the population, they were subservient to minority upper classes in society. The Congress always promises cattle and sheep before elections but was reluctant to share power with BCs. In the last four decades of its rule, the Congress suppressed BCs, he alleged.

(5430) Ongole : Telugu Desam Party leaders have blamed the Congress-I Government for neglecting the welfare of Backward Classes.Addressing a meeting of Backward Classes held here on Tuesday, the district TDP leaders opposed the attempts of the Government to delete seven castes from the list of Backward Classes. They demanded that the Government pay scholarships to BC students immediately.

(5431) Kadiri (Anantapur Dt.) : Floor leader of CPI (M) in the Assembly N. Narasimhaiah has observed that lack of sincerity among successive rulers is the main cause for the backwardness of Anantapur district. He called upon the people to question the rulers to drive away their problemsSpeaking at a public meeting organised here on Tuesday on the occasion of completion of 1,000 km of the 1,800-km padayatra, Anantha Prasthanam, taken up by the district unit of the party he stated that nature had bestowed the district with every resource except water. There were no sincere efforts since Independence to improve irrigation facilities in the district, he alleged.

(5432) Vizianagaram : CPI(M) State secretary B.V. Raghavulu has asked Chief Minister Y.S. Rajasekhara Reddy to bring pressure on the Centre to withdraw its decision to reduce foodgrains quota to households.At a public meeting here on Tuesday, Mr. Raghavulu said the UPA Government's decision would burden people to the tune of Rs. 600 crores. If the State Government failed to pursue the Centre to withdraw the decision, it must shoulder the burden and continue the present supply position, he said. Though Tripura, Kerala and West Bengal opposed the Centre's decision, the Chief Minister chose to remain silent on the issue. Instead, he complained against CPI(M) leaders for raising the Polavaram issue.

(5433) Karimnagar : Senior leader of the BJP and former Union Minister Ch. Vidyasagar Rao has demanded that the AICC president and UPA chairperson Sonia Gandhi disclose her stand on Telangana statehood as she has raised expectations on the issue after her speech during electioneering in Karimnagar district.

(5434) Palakkad : State secretary of the Communist Party of India (Marxist) Pinarayi Vijayan has said that it is the Left Democratic Front (LDF) which has to decide on the entry of the Democratic Indira Congress (Karunakaran) into the Front. Reacting to a statement made by the DIC(K) leader K. Karunakaran in Thiruvananthapuram on Monday that talks [on the proposed entry of the DIC(K) into the LDF] would be held only between DIC(K) president K. Muraleedharan and Mr. Vijayan, the CPI(M) leader told presspersons during his Kerala Yatra at Kolllengode on Tuesday that the issue had to be decided by the CPI(M) Polit Bureau first. Then it would be discussed at the CPI(M) State committee meeting.

(5435) Sultanpur (U.P.) : The expelled Bharatiya Janata Party leader, Uma Bharti, on Tuesday accused senior party leaders Atal Bihari Vajpayee and L.K. Advani of having "betrayed the nation." "While Mr. Vajpayee compromised with foreign business organisations, Mr. Advani showered praise on Mohammad Ali Jinnah who was responsible for the massacre of lakhs of people during Partition," she told a public meeting at Jagadishpur near hereShe alleged that Mr. Advani "betrayed the nation by praising Mohammad Ali Jinnah" and both of them had "forgotten (Lord) Ram after assuming power." - PTI

(5436) Bangalore : Ministers legislators, advocates, writers, academics and others on Tuesday expressed reservations over some of the contents of the Communal Violence (Prevention, Control, and Rehabilitation of Victims) Bill, 2005, though they welcomed it in generalThey were participating in an interaction on the Bill (which has been introduced in the Rajya Sabha) organised by the Union Ministry of Home and the State Government. After initial remarks on the Bill by Union Home Minister Shivaraj Patil, Leader of the Opposition in the Legislative Assembly B.S. Yediyurappa said the proposed Bill is not appropriate at the moment. There already exist provisions in the law to deal with communal violence and prevent it. Effective enforcement of laws and a strong administrative machinery are required to eliminate social and caste discrimination, he said.

(5437) Davanagere : As the rift between the Congress and the Janata Dal (S) on the issue of forging ties in zilla and taluk panchayats continued, Janata Dal (S) President H.D. Deve Gowda said on Tuesday he will begin consulting party members from Wednesday to decide whether to continue the coalition. Heads of district units of the party will be invited to Bangalore from Wednesday to elicit their views, he told presspersons here. He said he will also consult Ministers from the Janata Dal (S). Mr. Deve Gowda is concerned by the stand adopted by the Congress to allow its State units to decide on forging alliance with other parties in panchayats and has said he might review ties with the Congress. He said a decision will be announced in this regard on February 9, after the party's national executive meeting to be held in Bangalore. Karnataka Pradesh Congress President M. Mallikarjun Kharge has said the party has not issued any "specific" direction to its district units on the issue of forging an alliance with other parties.

(5438) New Delhi : Samajwadi Party leader Amar Singh on Tuesday lodged a complaint with the Delhi Police, saying that some miscreants, purportedly belonging to the Youth Congress, forcibly tried to enter his Lodhi Estate accommodation on Tuesday. However, the police denied that there was any such attempt.

(5439) New Delhi : Union Food and Agriculture Minister Sharad Pawar on Tuesday said the Government was not involved in the tapping of the telephone of Samajwadi Party leader Amar Singh. Speaking to media persons on the sidelines of the launching of a Dairy and Poultry Venture Capital Fund, Mr. Pawar said he had definite information from the Home Ministry that allegations on involvement about phone tapping were not correct and were unfair.

(5440) Guwahati : Bharatiya Janata Party general secretary Pramod Mahajan on Monday said that liberalisation of the telecom sector had nothing to do with phone tapping. Talking to the media, he rejected the argument that phone tapping cases had increased because of liberalisation of the telecom sector and demanded that the Centre amend the Indian Telegraph Act to ensure that the privacy of citizens were not invaded under the garb of "public interest.Mr. Mahajan said the BJP would put pressure on the Centre both inside and outside Parliament to amend the Act in the budget session. He said telephone tapping without a real and substantial reason was unauthorised or illegal. Asked to comment on Samajwadi Party leader Amar Singh's claim that Mr. Mahajan's phone was being tapped, the BJP leader said that he would "hardly mind." He, however, said that the arrest of three people in connection with the tapping of Mr.

Amar Singh's phone had shown that "there is a lot of strength in his [Amar Singh's] allegation. He is not talking nonsense. Already three persons have been arrested and half-a-dozen CDs of his phone recordings are with the police."He said the telephones of militants and anti-national elements could be tapped in the national interest but it was illegal to tap those of political or business rivals. He said the party's objective was to ``defeat and dislodge the corrupt and communal Congress'' in the Assembly polls in Assam. To achieve this, the BJP was ready to cooperate with any political party, he added. The position was firmed up after a two-day meeting of State leaders. Asked if this was an open invitation to the Asom Gana Parishad, Mr. Mahajan said it was for the other political parties to decide. He said the BJP had not talked to the AGP or any other party so far. On whether it would field candidates in all the 126 constituencies if the AGP did not cooperate, he said while deciding the poll strategy it had decided to adopt Savarkar's mantra: ``If you come with us, with you, if not, without you. If you oppose, in spite of your opposition we will defeat the Congress." The BJP had a pre-poll tie-up with the AGP in the 2001 Assembly polls.

(5441) New Delhi : Following the adoption of the Public Accounts Committee report by the Delhi Assembly on alleged bungling in privatisation of power distribution in the Capital, the Delhi Bharatiya Janata Party has written a letter to the Chief Justice of India calling for a judicial probe into the matter or an enquiry by the Central Bureau of Investigation or the Chief Vigilance Commissioner.

(5442) Pondicherry : A new political alignment is on the anvil for the coming elections to the State Assembly, with the AIADMK and the Pudhucherry Munnetra Congress (PMC) on Tuesday signalling a possible alliance between the two parties. The State secretary of the AIADMK, A. Anbalagan, MLA, told a press conference that his party was likely to join hands with the PMC during the coming polls. "The AIADMK chief, Jayalalithaa, will be the deciding authority", he said and added that both the parties had been jointly holding agitations on various issues.

(5443) Chennai : The proposed dam across the Palar in Andhra Pradesh and the furore it has caused in Tamil Nadu may turn out to be much ado about nothing." At least this is the impression gathered by Tamil Nadu officials who visited the neighbouring State last week to study the situation, according to an official. The team's interaction with Andhra Pradesh officials indicated that the neighbouring State may not be pursuing any such proposal seriously.Reports about Andhra Pradesh's plan to build a dam in the Kuppam area had prompted a strong reaction from political parties in Tamil Nadu. Chief Minister Jayalalithaa shot off a letter to her counterpart Y.S. Rajasekhara Reddy, urging him to give up the project The Pattali Makkal Katchi, with its vote bank in the northern parts of the State, was among the first to oppose the proposal. It has also planned an agitation. The Pattali Makkal Katchi organised a demonstration at Kancheepuram to protest the Andhra Pradesh Government's proposal to construct the a dam and to urge the State Government to convene an all-party meeting to discuss the issue. Party president G.K. Mani said the proposal would not only affect agricultural operations and drinking water needs of Vellore, Kancheepuram, Tiruvannamalai districts but also industrial activity in Kancheepuram district.

(5444) Chennai : The State Government has filed a defamation complaint against Dravida Munnetra Kazhagam president M. Karunanidhi, for his reported statements against Chief Minister Jayalalithaa in October 2005. The complaint, lodged in the Principal Sessions Court here, assailed Mr. Karunanidhi's reported remarks at an Iftar party hosted by the Tamil Maanila National League at Ashoka Hotel on October 16, 2005.

12-01-2006

(5445) Hyderabad : The forthcoming 82nd plenary of the AICC will be dealing with four resolutions deviating from the usual practice of discussing only three, to lay emphasis on rural development in order to sustain the economic growth rate of 7 per cent. The AICC normally discusses only three resolutions — political, economic and foreign policy. But, this time, a fourth resolution had been included at the instance of Prime Minister Manmohan Singh who wanted a techno-rural model to ensure that the GDP growth rate is not only sustained but also increased. APCC president K. Keshav Rao said the State Congress leaders would make the most of this opportunity to showcase the State's economic model based on development of irrigation potential.

(5446) Hyderabad : The Telugu Desam has lashed out at the Centre for notifying the PF rate at 8.5 per cent, saying that lakhs of workers would lose Rs.360 crores following the decision. At a press conference here on

Wednesday, TDP leaders E. Peddi reddy, M. Narasimhulu and P. Chandrashekhar demanded the Centre to restore the interest rate at 9.5 per cent. They said the party would organise struggles in support of its demand, besides raising the issue in Parliament and the Assembly.

(5447) Khammam : The Bharatiya Janata Party State president N. Indrasena Reddy wanted the Congress leadership to spell out its stand clearly on the demand for separate Telangana State. Addressing a news conference, he said the Congress party owed an explanation to the people on the kind of understanding it had with the Telangana Rashtra Samiti (TRS) before going for the last general election. There could be no better occasion than the AICC plenary session to be held in Hyderabad for the Congress president, Sonia Gandhi to end her silence on the issue, he added. He said if the statements made by the Congress leaders G. Vekataswamy were of any indication, separate Telangana seems to be not on the agenda of the party. The TRS leadership, which still continued to share power with the Congress at the Centre should speak out. He said the Congress Government continued to mete out a raw deal for Telangana region.

(5448) Hyderabad : The 82nd AICC plenary will not discuss the Telangana statehood issue at all as it is not even listed on its agenda. Any reference to Telangana could at best be made by the State's leaders vis-a-vis its development, as distinct from statehood for the region, a demand raised by the Telangana Rashtra Samithi (TRS). Making this clear in an interview to The Hindu here on Wednesday, APCC president K.Keshava Rao said Defence Minister Pranab Mukherji who heads the UPA sub-committee on Telangana had indicated that the party would express its views on the issue at the plenary. But, beyond Mr. Mukherji's statement, little could be expected in the form of a resolution.

(5449) Bangalore : The Bharatiya Janata Party (BJP) is preparing to face the midterm elections and it will not join hands with the Janata Dal (Secular) to form a government if the coalition breaks up. Leader of the Opposition in the Assembly B.S. Yediyurappa made the BJP's stand clear on Wednesday at a meeting of party legislators. The meeting was attended by the State unit office-bearers. It went into the rift between the coalition partners, Congress and the Janata Dal (Secular), over tie-up in the zilla and taluk panchayats.Prominent among the leaders who attended the meeting were party General Secretary H.N. Ananth Kumar, State unit President

Jagadish Shettar, BJP group leader in the Legislative Council D.H. Shankaramurthy, Deputy Leader in the Assembly Govind Karjol and Chairman of the Public Accounts Committee K.S. Eshwarappa.

(5450) Bangalore : There is no danger to the Government as seen by some vested interests, Minister for Finance and Industry P.G.R. Sindhia, who belongs to the Janata Dal (S), has asserted. The political situation will ease by the time his party announces its decision by February 8. He told presspersons here on Tuesday that the Janata Dal (S) would not take any hasty decision.

(5451) Bangalore : The Janata Dal (Secular) leadership on Wednesday took the first decisive step towards continuing the coalition arrangement or opting for mid-term elections to the Legislative Assembly by interacting with the party's district-level leaders on the twin issues. The former Prime Minister H.D. Deve Gowda and the State President of Janata Dal (S) N. Thippanna will meet the leaders, including legislators and Ministers concerned at the rate of two districts every day. This exercise will continue until February 1, and the former Prime Minister would thereafter place the findings before the other senior leaders of the party. The Janata Dal (S) has called for a meeting of the national executive here on February 8 and the final decision of the party pertaining to either continuing with the understanding with the Congress or withdrawing from the Government, will be arrived at thereafter.

(5452) Bijapur : Bijapur MP and Bharatiya Janata Party State unit Vice-President Basanagouda R. Patil Yatnal has opined that the party should opt for elections if the coalition Government in the State falls apart.

(5453) Madikeri : Mangalore MP D.V.Sadananda Gowda on Wednesday blamed the Congress and the Janata Dal (Secular) coalition for the poor state of finances in the State.Addressing presspersons after a meeting organised by the district unit of the Bharatiya Janata Party to felicitate newly-elected zilla panchayat members of the party, Mr. Gowda alleged that the rumblings between the collation partners has pushed the State to the brink of crises on all fronts.

(5454) Panaji : Margaret Alva, All-India Congress Committee (AICC) General Secretary, said on Friday that the party is prepared for any political development in Karnataka. "We are prepared for any eventuality," she said to a question about the Congress's position over the possibility of early elections in Karnataka.At her press briefing on Goa affairs, Ms. Alva, who heads a coalition coordination committee, said the coalition government in Goa had fewer problems compared with "some other coalitions". Asked whether she meant the Congress-NCP coalition in Maharashtra of which she is in charge, Ms. Alva said: " I did not mean Maharashtra, but Karnataka." Asked whether Karnataka would have mid-term elections, after recent hints of review of support to the Congress by Janata Dal (S) President H.D. Deve Gowda, Ms. Alva declined to comment and said she was not in charge of the party affairs in Karnataka. However, she added that the party was prepared to face any eventuality and it was preparing for elections.

(5455) Panaji : Ostensibly with an eye on the Assembly elections slated for 2007, the Congress, which heads the coalition Government in the State, decided to shelve the ticklish issue of airports, by declaring on Wednesday that the Dabolim airport will continue, while an expert group will be set up to study the infrastructure needs and feasibility of supporting another airport - proposed Mopa airport - in Goa. All-India Congress Committee general secretary in-charge of Goa Margaret Alva, who had a series of meetings, including that of the coordination committee of the coalition Government, during her two-day visit to the State, said that the Civil Aviation Ministry will help Goa expand, and upgrade the Dabolim airport under Naval jurisdiction by enhancing its proposed allocation from Rs. 300 crores to Rs. 500 crores. The Dabolim upgradation and expansion would be undertaken on a fast track basis, she said. Ms. Alva said that the year 2006 will be "Election preparation year" for the Congress in the State. All party Ministers and MLAs have been told to shun their internal differences.

(5456) Alappuzha : Leader of the Opposition V. S. Achuthanandan has demanded that Chief Minister Oommen Chandy take immediate steps to oust Health Minister K. K. Ramachandran from the Cabinet. At a press conference here on Wednesday, Mr. Achuthanandan said the Chief Minister was delaying action against the Health Minister. The reluctance to take action against Mr. Ramachandran should be viewed in the backdrop of the general policy of the UDF defending the corrupt, said Mr. Achuthanandan.

(5457) Alappuzha : Leader of the Opposition V.S. Achuthanandan has defended the right of Left Democratic Front (LDF) constituents to express their opinion on the entry of the Democratic Indira Congress (Karunakaran) into the Front. Addressing a press conference here on Wednesday, Mr. Achuthanandan said such attempts in public were not right. "No leader has the right to ridicule LDF constituents in public." He said the opinion expressed by DIC(K) leader K. Karunakaran in Thiruvananthapuram that the Revolutionary Socialist Party (RSP) had had few members was unbecoming of a political leader like Mr. Karunakaran. The RSP has opposed the inclusion of the DIC(K) in the LDF and that is the political stand of the party. Mr. Karunakaran should have opposed the RSP's stance politically and should not have mocked it. The CPI(M) Polit Bureau member said Mr. Karunakaran who ridiculed the RSP as a small party had gone out of the way to help the M.V. Raghavan-led Communist Marxist Party (CMP) when he was Chief Minister.

(5458) Thiruvananthapuram : Activists of two Left Democratic Front (LDF) youth organisations staged black flag protests demanding the resignation of Health Minister K.K. Ramachandran at a public function attended by the Minister in the city on Thursday.

(5459) Kozhikiode : A rousing reception greeted Democratic Indira Congress (Karunakaran) president K. Muraleedharan on his first visit to his hometown in Kozhikode on Wednesday after successfully completing his "Nava Kerala Yatra" from Kasaragod to ThiruvananthapuramA large number of DIC(K) loyalists turned up at the railway station to greet him and later at the Town Hall where he made a speech narrating his experiences during the Nava Kerala Yatra. Mr. Muraleedharan said DIC(K) had proved beyond doubt that it was a political force to reckon with.He said it would not be fair for Leader of the Opposition V.S. Achuthanandan to dub all Congress men as "cheats" on the basis of what the Antony group did to the LDF in 1980. (Mr. Achuthanandan had said so at a meeting in Kozhikode, making it clear that he is against admitting breakaway Congress groups like DIC(K) into the LDF. The Antony group which was accommodated in the LDF later left the front and went back to the Congress much to the chagrin of LDF leader CPI-M).

(5460) Thiruvananthapuram : P. C. Thomas, MP, on Wednesday said that he and his colleagues in the Indian Federal Democratic Party (IFDP) had decided to leave the NDA, dissolve the party and merge with the Kerala Congress (Joseph) when they sensed that the BJP would adopt a hardline communal stance after its debacle in the last Lok Sabha election causing untold damage to the secular fabric of the nation. In a statement here, Mr. Thomas said the IFDP had no illusions about the secular credentials of the BJP when it joined the NDA and that it had done so very much like the other secular parties who were also partners in the NDA dispensation. All the secular parties had done so on the basis of a common minimum programme. However, after the Lok Sabha election debacle, a feeling began to gain strength in the BJP that the party could retain its electoral base only if it adopted an even harder communal stance. Precisely at this time, KC(J) chairman P. J. Joseph came up with the call for reunification of all Kerala Congress groups and the IFDP decided to respond to the call positively.

(5461) Chavakkad : Communist Party of India (Marxist) (CPI-M) State secretary Pinarayi Vijayan has vehemently countered the arguments put forward by Communist Party of India (CPI) leader Veliyam Bhargavan and Leader of the Opposition V.S. Achuthanandan against the entry of the Democratic Indira Congress (Karunakaran) (DIC-K) into the Left Democratic Front (LDF).

(5462) New Delhi : Issues relating to MPs caught in the two sting operations were discussed by Bharatiya Janata Party leaders at a meeting at the former Prime Minister, Atal Bihari Vajpayee's residence here.After the meeting, the party's deputy leader in the Lok Sabha, V.K. Malhotra, described as "inappropriate" the all-party meeting of leaders called by Lok Sabha Speaker Somnath Chatterjee on January 20 to discuss issues arising out of the expulsion of 11 MPs involved in the cash-for-query scam and the court decision to hear the petitions of some MPs who had challenged the Parliament decision. Mr. Malhotra said: "The BJP believes this meeting [called by the Speaker] could amount to generating a clash between the judiciary and the legislature. Such a meeting is inappropriate."However, earlier in the afternoon while talking informally to reporters, party president Rajnath Singh had indicated that the BJP would participate in the meeting.Parliamentary committee reports on the second sting operation, relating to MPs caught on camera asking for commission for implementation of projects under the Member of Parliament Local Area Development Scheme, are to be submitted by January 31. Some BJP MPs would like the

MPLAD scheme to continue while others are for discontinuing it.The party is also divided on the issue of expulsion of MPs. Six BJP MPs were expelled after the cash-for-questions scam. Mr. Rajnath Singh has said he would tolerate "no compromise with corruption" suggesting that he would like the BJP to adopt a hard stance on the MPs caught on camera.

(5463) Srinagar : Maintaining that the Congress and the People's Democratic Party (PDP) were "natural allies" in Jammu and Kashmir, senior Congress leader Saifuddin Soz said on Wednesday that all efforts should be made to strengthen the coalition which "has been working well" during the past three years. Talking to The Hindu here, Prof Soz said: "only the Congress and PDP coalition can answer the political concerns in Kashmir." He said "Mufti Saheb did a good job and now Azad Saheb is leading the coalition in an effective manner." "He [Mr. Azad] has taken some good steps and we are here to extend full support to him." Stating that this was the best combination for ensuring "good governance" in the State, the former Minister said "the coalition culture in which both national and regional parties are joining hands is becoming a reality now."Without naming the opposition National Conference (NC), Prof. Soz said, "any other coalition in Jammu and Kashmir will prove disastrous for the State." He ruled out Congress allying with the NC in the near future and said, "it will not be in consonance with value-based politics." The Congress leader said "the NC's overtures towards Chief Minister Ghulam Nabi Azad had no meaning. They [NC leaders] are doing it just as part of their petty politics."

(5464) Kalinga Nagar : Congress president Sonia Gandhi on Wednesday assured the agitating tribals of Kalinga Nagar in Orissa's Jajpur district that justice would be done to the families of those killed in the police firing on January 2. The law and order situation needs to be looked into, she said"I am here to share the grief of the families of those who were brutally killed. I feel their anguish. They are heartbroken. We will see to it that justice is done to them," Ms. Gandhi told presspersons after interacting with the family members of the victims. Union Home Minister Shivraj Patil and Union Home Secretary V.K. Duggal accompanied her. Mr. Patil said the Centre would pay an ex-gratia of Rs. 5 lakh each to the families of the tribals killed in the police firing 10 days ago. The demands of the tribals would be considered sympathetically. Ms. Gandhi said the Congress would also give relief to the bereaved families. She, however, did not mention the amount. On reaching the ground, she paid floral tributes to those killed and then talked to the bereaved families by entering a barricaded enclosure. She spent more than 10 minutes interacting with them before going around and talking to the tribal men and women.

(5465) New Delhi : The Left parties on Wednesday urged the Government to reconsider its decision and retain the Employees Provident Fund interest rate at 9.5 per centThe Communist Party of India (Marxist) said the decision to have the rate of interest at 8.5 per cent this year would affect four crore workers and employees. A majority of them were employed in small and medium industries and the EPF was their only social security or old-age benefit. The CPI (M) said it had demanded that the Government increase the rate of interest on the Special Deposit Scheme (SDS). The Government had benefited greatly from the scheme. It had secured over one lakh crore rupees from the EPF deposits. A marginal increase in the rate of interest could ensure 9.5 per cent interest, the CPI (M) Polit Bureau said in a statement.

(5466) New Delhi : Delhi Bharatiya Janata Party president Harsh Vardhan has charged that corrupt councillors and senior Municipal Corporation of Delhi officials have taken bribes from the accused senior engineers and officers who were behind the illegal constructions and were now trying to protect them. "Therefore, instead of punishing all the 933 people found guilty, they are targeting only 94."

(5467) Jaipur : Former national treasurer of the Bharatiya Janata Party, Ramdas Agarwal, has accused the United Progressive Alliance Government of functioning under the pressure of the Left parties. "This is a dangerous situation in which the political parties in the Government are dictated by those outside," Mr. Agarwal said."The Congress proposes and the CPI (M) disposes is the current situation in the UPA," Mr. Agarwal said participating in a "Meet the Press" Programme at the Pink City Press Club here on Wednesday. "The Congress party is a weak leading partner in the coalition Government. It appears as if the Communists are ruling the country now. The people have to be alerted on the situation," Mr. Agarwal said.

(5468) Vellore : Bharatiya Janata Party State president C.P. Radhakrishnan on Wednesday urged the Centre to intervene and force Andhra Pradesh to drop its move to build a dam across the Palar.

13-01-2006

(5469) Hyderabad : A pressure group within the Congress is being created by senior Congress leaders of Telangana in an attempt to dent the credibility of the Telangana Rashtra Samithi (TRS) during the AICC plenary.

(5470) Chennai : Pattali Makkal Katchi MLA R. Krishnan on Thursday resigned his seat and joined the All-India Anna Dravida Munnetra Kazhagam (AIADMK). His resignation came a day before the commencement of the Assembly session. With Mr. Krishnan's resignation, the PMK's strength in the House came down to 18.

(5471) Bangalore : Members of the Legislative Assembly from all parties, with a few exceptions, fear that the coalition government is doomed and the Legislative Assembly will be dissolved. They feel that the government may fall before the legislature session which is scheduled to start on January 19. Their apprehensions have heightened after the firm stand taken by the Congress High Command to allow district units to seek the support of any group, barring the Bharatiya Janata Party, to come to power in zilla and taluk panchayats where no party has a majority. The Congress's district units have been told not to heed the request of the Janata Dal (Secular) to extend the coalition arrangement to zilla panchayats. To counter the Congress, Janata Dal (S) President H.D. Deve Gowda has convened a meeting of the party's national executive here on February 8 to decide whether to withdraw from the coalition. The MLAs' full term ends in April 2009 and they are wary of the prospect of early elections. Leader of Opposition in the Legislative Assembly B.S. Yediyurappa told presspersons after a meeting of the BJP's legislature party that the State unit favours midterm elections if the coalition collapses. The party MLAs have been told to begin their election campaign.

(5472) PANAJI : The Leader of the Opposition in the Goa Assembly, Manohar Parrikar, on Thursday alleged that law and order situation in the State has collapsed, and said the Rane Government has no right to rule. He claimed that Goa witnessed 45 murder, 19 rape and 18 abduction cases last year.

(5473) Chennai : The Bharatiya Janata Party (BJP) on Thursday demanded fresh elections to the Karnataka Assembly. "There is an open fighting between the Congress and the Janata Dal (Secular), constituents of the ruling alliance in the State. As there is no scope for any alternative government, we want fresh polls," BJP vice-president Venkaiah Naidu said. Asked about the infighting in the Karnataka BJP unit , Mr. Naidu said the problems had been sorted out. As for the party's performance in the recent local body elections, he said that compared to the previous elections, the party increased its strength three times.

(5474) Kozhikode : The Kerala Congress (Secular) (KC-S) alleged on Thursday that the Oommen Chandy Government was a failure on all fronts. At a press conference here, the Kerala Congress (Secular) office-bearers said the State Government has ceased to be a force and was equivalent to a caretaker Government. They added that the Government was not justified in announcing projects estimated at crores of rupees, when it had only a short term in office.

(5475) Thiruvananthapuram : Leader of the Opposition V.S. Achuthanandan on Thursday said the Sessions Court verdict acquitting all the accused in the Kozhikode ice-cream parlour case was expected and added that he would move the Supreme Court against the High Court's order dismissing his plea seeking a CBI inquiry into the circumstances under which the witnesses in the ice-cream parlour sex scandal case had turned hostile.

(5476) Chalakudy : Communist Party of India (Marxist) State secretary Pinarayi Vijayan has warned against 'unnecessary confrontations' between the constituents of the Left Democratic Front (LDF) in the State.

(5477) Ahmedabad : The Pradesh Congress Committee has taken exception to Chief Minister Narendra Modi "violating" all norms of protocol in sending a junior Minister to deputise for him at an official function in Porbandar on Thursday in which President A.P.J. Abdul Kalam took part. As the `International kite festival' was to be opened in Ahmedabad on Thursday, Mr. Modi authorised Minister of State for Labour and Employment Mulu Bera to represent the Cabinet at the inauguration of the Sandipani Science Gallery in Porbandar. Most Cabinet Ministers were asked to be present at the kite festival, being held as part of the `Vibrant Gujarat' celebrations. However, Mr. Modi sent senior Minister Anandiben Patel for Mr. Kalam's lecture on "21st century's higher education in India" at Saurashtra University in Rajkot. Governor Nawal Kishore Sharma, however, accompanied the President at both functions. Pradesh Congress spokesman

Hasmukh Patel said the presidential protocol demanded that the Chief Minister remain present. In case he was pre-occupied, he should deputise a senior Cabinet Minister to represent him. But Mr. Modi had flouted "all norms of protocol and decent behaviour" by deputing Mr. Bera, a junior Minister. This only demonstrated his "arrogance."

(5478) New Delhi : The Bharatiya Janata Party on Thursday denounced the Government for its attempt to give a clean certificate to Bofors payoff case accused Ottavio Quattrocchi, saying what the Law Officer conveyed to the British courts was "astonishing and unprecedented in legal history."At a press conference here, senior BJP leader Arun Jaitley wanted to know whether the Prime Minister Manmohan Singh approved of what the Law Officer said about Mr. Quattrocchi. The Government had no business to convey anything to the British Government or its courts. If at all anything had to be conveyed, it should have been done by the Central Bureau of Investigation. "It was a clear attempt by the political executive to help a primary accused in a corruption case." He was commenting on the report that Additional Solicitor-General B. Dutta had on December 22 last informed the United Kingdom's Crown Prosecution Service that it had no evidence to link the money held by the Italian businessman in two accounts to the Bofors payoff funds.

(5479) New Delhi : The Communist Party of India (Marxist) on Thursday questioned the United Progressive Alliance Government's action conveying to the Crown Prosecution Service in Britain that the Central Bureau of Investigation had no evidence to link the two frozen bank accounts of Italian businessman Ottavio Quattrocchi with the Bofors case. While the Delhi High Court had quashed the case against the Hindujas and some others, Mr. Quattrocchi was still charge sheeted in the case. He neither cooperated nor appeared in the court for the framing of charges. Further, the CBI had stated that efforts to bring him to court would continue and that the Interpol red corner notices had not been revoked, the CPI(M) Polit Bureau said in a statement here. "In such a situation, it is questionable why such a legal opinion about the bank accounts has been conveyed to the British authorities. The Government has to explain why and how this has happened." The Samajwadi Party also questioned the "clean chit" given to Mr. Quattrochhi. "The Central Bureau of Investigation is a sound agency. But why has it given a clean chit to Mr. Quattrocchi in the Bofors case? Now, the Government has decided to unseal his bank accounts in London," party vice-president Janeshwar Mishra told mediapersons here. He was responding to questions why the phone tapping matter should not be handed over to the CBI, as suggested by CPI leader A.B. Bardhan to party general secretary Amar Singh, when the latter met him on Wednesday. Earlier, Mr. Amar Singh also questioned the CBI decision. The Congress said the Additional Solicitor-General's communication was in response to a query from the Crown Prosecution Service. "The response has to be based on the material, has to be correct that there was no proof," party spokesperson Abhishek Singhvi said.

(5480) Kolkata : By announcing a common "agenda" of the Paschimbanga Ganatantrik Front (PGF) led by the Trinamool Congress, its chief Mamata Banerjee has virtually turned down the Congress offer of her leading an anti-Left alliance in the West Bengal Assembly elections. Just as the Congress has been insisting that "the doors are open" to her joining it and leading the secular alliance provided she disassociates herself from the Bharatiya Janata Party, Ms. Banerjee said the 12-party PGF's "doors are open" to the Congress to fight the Left Front as part of a mahajot (grand alliance). The Trinamool leader described the PGF as a "secular" combine as opposed to a "pseudo secular" front.On the Congress' stand that it cannot be part of any alliance which includes the BJP and that Ms. Banerjee will be acceptable only if she leaves the National Democratic Alliance, Subrata Bakshi, Trinamool State unit president, asked: "Why should the Congress make this insistence when we are not making an issue of its being the main constituent of the Untied Progressive Alliance?" "The PGF, which was set up in October 2005, on the basis of a common programme, has now become a political front with an eye on the Assembly elections", Pankaj Banerjee, Trinamool leader and leader of the Opposition in the Assembly, told The Hindu here on Thursday.

(5481) New Delhi : The Samajwadi Party on Wednesday fielded one of its most respectable faces, socialist leader Janeshwar Mishra, to tone down its tirade against the Congress party in the phone tapping case and deny rumours of the party withdrawing its outside support to the United Progressive Alliance government on the issue. "I would not make allegations against Prime Minister Manmohan Singh or Congress President Sonia Gandhi unless there is definite evidence. But I would expect the

Congress to control its workers. It does not behove of the party to have Youth Congress workers shout slogans outside party general secretary Amar Singh's house. But we are not withdrawing support. These ups and downs are part of politics," the party vice-president said here. Speculation was rife about withdrawal of support after party president and Uttar Pradesh Chief Minister, Mulayam Singh Yadav, and Mr. Amar Singh called on Mr. Mishra, who is recuperating from a knee surgery. The party has 38 members in the Lok Sabha but their support or withdrawal is not crucial to the Central Government's survival.

(5482) Jaipur : A decision on the next president of the Bharatiya Janata Party in Rajasthan will be taken after consultations with the national president of the party Rajnath Singh. However, the choice of the next State president, hanging fire for sometime, is not likely before January 20, when the party's national council is scheduled to meet. The proposed changes in the State Cabinet led by Vasundhara Raje, are also likely only thereafter, it is being hinted. BJP general secretary in charge for Rajasthan Kalraj Misra talking to mediapersons here on Thursday said the choice of the president and the mode of his selection would be decided after the State leaders' meeting with the new national president of the party. As such the minimum pre-requisite for holding the election of the president — that is elections in more than 50 per cent of the total districts- has already been met, he noted. "Prior to the Cabinet reshuffle the Chief Minister would meet the party president. Basically any change in the Cabinet is her prerogative," Mr.Misra said.

(5483) Chennai : The Congress Legislature Party will also boycott the opening day of the Assembly Session, beginning on January 13. This means the entire Opposition, barring the BJP, will boycott the Assembly during the Governor's address. In a statement, CLP leader S.R. Balasubramoniyan said the Government's decision to begin the session on the day of Boghi was an attempt to wound the feelings of Tamils.

(5484) Chennai : Dravida Munnetra Kazhagam president M. Karunanidhi will lead the 'oust Jayalalithaa' campaign in Chennai on January 18. The DMK-led Democratic Progressive Alliance had announced that it would launch the campaign all over the State.TNCC president G.K. Vasan will lead the campaign in Tiruchi, Pattali Makkal Katchi founder S. Ramadoss in Kancheepuram, Marumalarchi Dravida Munnetra Kazhagam general secretary Vaiko in Virudhunagar, Communist Party of India (Marxist) State secretary N.Varadarajan in Dindigul and DMK deputy general secretary M.K. Stalin, in Vellore.

14-01-2006

(5485) Hyderabad : AICC secretaries — V. Arun Kumar and P. Sudhakar Reddy — lashed out at the Telugu Desam Party on Friday accusing its leaders of making baseless charges about official machinery misuse.They said the TDP was getting increasingly restless in playing its role as the main opposition party and was unable to distinguish between the party and the Government.Talking to reporters, they said it was pitiable that they had taken objection to the display of the colours of the national flag on the poles in the city hosting the 82nd AICC plenary. The TDP had, for that matter, never displayed any nationalistic fervour nor had it any commitment towards the national causes, they added. It was ridiculous that someone objected to the colours of the national flag being painted, they said.

(5486) Hyderabad : The Telugu Desam Parliamentary Party (TDPP) on Friday demanded Prime Minister Manmohan Singh to come out with a white paper on the entire issue of Bofors. At a press conference, TDPP leader K. Yerran Naidu and MPs K. Ramamohan Rao and S. Ramamuni Reddy described the clean chit given to Italian businessman Ottavio Quattrochi as anti-constitutional and a blow to Indian pride. They alleged that it was clearly aimed at protecting former Prime Minister, Rajiv Gandhi's friends and relatives.Mr. Naidu regretted that while on one hand the investigating agencies had always been hinting at Quattrochi's involvement in the Bofors deal, the Government had given a clean chit to him. He said it was shameful that Quattrochi's frozen assets in the UK were being released. Meanwhile, BJP national secretary B. Dattatreya while criticising the clean chit given to Quattrochi, demanded a clarification by Dr. Singh on the issue.

(5487) Hyderabad : The AICC delegation consisting of Ambika Soni, Digvijay Singh and Motilal Vora has ruled out any official discussion on Telangana statehood at the coming plenary. Addressing a press conference here on Friday, Ms. Ambika Soni said: "Telangana will not be discussed in the manner others want us to. If any individual wants to raise it, one may as well do it. But whatever will be said will be treated as someone's personal opinion alone." Ms. Soni termed the allegations of misuse of official machinery "silly" and asked the political rivals to get involved in some constructive activity, instead. TDP president N. Chandrababu Naidu's allegations of phone tapping were also rubbished as `childish.' The AICC was not planning to invite delegates from friendly parties or coalition partners as it did not want to crowd it. "We already have more than 10,000 delegates attending it. There is no point in overdoing it. We prefer to retain it as a family affair," Ms. Ambika Soni said. The plenary would be a simple affair reminding the delegates the contribution of the past presidents and eminent leaders.

(5488) New Delhi : Samajwadi Party leader Amar Singh was on Friday questioned by the Delhi Police special cell in connection with the illegal tapping of his telephone.His friend, an Uttar Pradesh-based industrialist, who had purportedly tipped him off about the tapping, will be summoned later as he expressed his inability to appear due to "health reasons."

(5489) Madikeri : The Bharatiya Janata Party (BJP) will not allow Janata Dal (Secular) President H.D. Deve Gowda to blackmail the BJP in the State in the garb of forging a coalition, party spokesperson S. Suresh Kumar said here on Friday.

(5490) Alappuzha : Kerala Pradesh Congress Committee (KPCC) president Ramesh Chennithala held an in-camera discussion with Communist Party of India (CPI) State secretary Veliyam Bhargavan in Alappuzha on Friday. The discussion assumes significance in the context of the criticism aired by Communist Party of India (Marxist) State secretary Pinarayi Vijayan against the late Chief minister C. Achutha Menon and the opposition of the CPI towards the entry of the Democratic Indira Congress (Karunakaran) into the Left Democratic Front (LDF).

(5491) Alappuzha : KPCC president Ramesh Chennithala has demanded that CPI State secretary Veliyam Bhargavan clarify his stand on the criticism levelled by CPI(M) State secretary Pinarayi Vijayan against the former Chief Minister and CPI leader C. Achutha Menon.

(5492) Kozhikode : Indian Union Muslim League (IUML) !eader P.K. Kunhalikutty has that people close to the social activists spearheading the ice-cream parlour sex racket case have approached him for favours when he was Minister, But he was not able to meet their demand as it was beyond the resources at his command. The IUML leader said at a news conference on Friday that he would not disclose the names of those who had demanded favours from him. "I am not going to reveal even their gender," he added. But he said he had documentary evidence to prove his charge. However, he was all remorse over the attack on mediapersons at the airport in Kozhikode. It had happened when he had reached the airport from abroad (soon after the scandal was revived by revelations of a witness, Rejina).

(5493) New Delhi : The Bharatiya Janata Party and the Janata Dal (United) on Friday demanded the resignation of Law Minister H.R. Bhardwaj, alleging that he had interfered with the Central Bureau of Investigation's independent functioning and decision-making. BJP leader Arun Jaitley and the former JD (U) president, George Fernandes, questioned the "extraordinary step" taken by Additional Solicitor-General B. Dutta, at the behest of the Law Minister, of informing the Crown Prosecution that the CBI had no evidence to link the funds in two British accounts held by Ottavio Quattrocchi to the kickbacks in the Bofors deal. Both leaders alleged that the Government had done this to help Mr. Quattrocchi. Mr. Fernandes also demanded Mr. Dutta's resignation.

(5494) Kolkata : Allegations over the existence of a large number of "bogus" voters in the electoral rolls in West Bengal are highly exaggerated, Jyoti Basu, senior Polit Bureau member of the Communist Party of India (Marxist), said here on Friday.

(5495) Faizabad : Former Madhya Pradesh Chief Minister and expelled party leader Uma Bharti on Friday dared the party leadership to remove Leader of the Opposition L.K. Advani from the party for "his acts of gross indiscipline".Launching an attack on the BJP leadership on the culmination of her over a month long Bhopal-to-Ayodhya "Ram-Roti Yatra", Ms. Bharti said if the BJP leadership had guts, it should take action against Mr. Advani for openly appreciating founder of Pakistan Mohd. Ali Jinnah.

(5496) Kolkata : West Bengal CPI (M) secretary Anil Biswas alleged on Friday that the weaker sections in the National Democratic Alliance-ruled States were being victimised at the behest of the Rashtriya Swayamsevak Sangh.Speaking at a party rally to protestagainstthe killing of Kalinga Nagar tribals, Mr. Biswas charged that "wherever the NDA is in power, tribals, peasantry and workers are being attacked with impunity, irrespective of which constituent is leading the NDA in the respective States."

(5497) Cuddalore : Chief Minister Jayalalithaa can never ever dream of causing a split in the Pattali Makkal Katchi. Rather, the days of the All India Anna Dravida Munnetra Kazhagam's rule are numbered, said E.Ponnuswami, PMK MP.In a statement released here on Friday, Mr. Ponnuswami alleged that Ms. Jayalaltihaa had adopted many ploys to cause a division in the PMK, but her designs have failed miserably.

16-01-2006

(5498) Hyderabad : The Bharatiya Janata Party on Sunday extended support to the agitation launched by the Madiga Reservation Porata Samithi (MRPS) demanding categorisation of Scheduled Castes. At a meeting to express solidarity with MRPS, party President N. Indrasena Reddy demanded that the Government allow the Samithi to hold a public meeting here on January 21, coinciding with the AICC plenary.

(5499) New Delhi : The Bharatiya Janata Party (BJP) on Sunday sought Prime Minister Manmohan Singh's intervention to ensure that the two accounts of Mr. Quattrocchi remain frozen. In a letter to the Prime Minister, senior BJP leader and former Union Law Minister, Arun Jaitley, said the moneys would fly out of "these accounts to unknown destinations and this needs to be prevented immediately." The issue of concern to the entire country, he said, was with regard to preventing the damage caused by the action of the Law Minister and Additional Solicitor-General of India B. Dutta. Taking exception to the visit of Mr. Dutta to London last month to inform the Crown Prosecutor that moneys lying deposited in the two British accounts be paid to Mr. Quattrocchi after de-freezing the accounts, Mr. Jaitley termed it as "an extraordinary concession volunteered by the Government of India." Mr. Jaitley pointed out that the Law Ministry has no locus standi in the matter. "Under the allocation of business rules, the CBI comes under the Department of Personnel of which you are the Cabinet Minister. The job of the Law Ministry is merely to tender legal advice and to provide for lawyers to represent different departments of the Government. Who authorised the Law Ministry to deal with this matter? Who authorised the visit of the Additional Solicitor-General to Britain? Who prevented the CBI officer from accompanying the ASG?" he asked in the letter to Dr. Singh. The BJP leader said that "fairness requires that since Mr. Quattrocchi has close connections in high places, the role of the Government and the investigative agencies in dealing with him must confirm to the highest standards of fair play, transparency and impartiality." .

(5500) Kochi : Veerappa Moily, Congress Working Committee member in charge of Kerala affairs, has denied any attempts to bring back the former Congress leader K. Karunakaran to the party fold. Talking to presspersons here on Sunday, Mr. Moily, a long-time friend of Mr. Karunakaran, said that though they were good friends they were now in different parties.

(5501) Kochi : Putting out feelers to Mr. Karunakaran and his supporters to come back to the Congress fold, Congress Working Committee (CWC) member A.K. Antony asked them to make a self-retrospection and realise that it would be 'better late than never.' "To come back to the Congress family can be the only political option they have now to put an end to the suffering, inflicted by those who lured them out of the Congress," Mr. Antony said while inaugurating a meeting in connection with the merger of Kerala Vikas Party with the CongressSending a covert invitation, senior leader Vayalar Ravi, MP, said the splinter groups could never feel at home outside while Mr. Chennithala said all those who split away should come back to the 'one Congress family.' Mr. Chennithala made the merger declaration with Kerala Vikas Party headed by K. Sankaranarayana Pillai, one-time colleague of Mr. Antony.

(5502) Hyderabad : Three dissident legislators — D. Srinivas Rao, T. Jayaprakash Reddy and Shara Rani — kept away from a meeting of the TRS legislature party convened by party president K. Chandrasekhar Rao here on Sunday. Earlier, eight dissident MLAs met at the residence of former Minister S. Santosh Reddy to discuss their strategy at the meeting. Of them, five proceeded to the TRS party officeAfter a marathon meeting that lasted over six hours, one of the rebel MLAs, G. Mukund Reddy, walked out in a huff but refused to speak to the media. S. Bapu Rao and Narayan Rao Patel also left.

(5503) Hyderabad : In a new turn to the internal squabbles of the TRS, a meeting of the legislature and parliamentary wings of the party asked its three dissident MLAs to resign and face fresh elections.The MLAs, D. Srinivas Rao, T. Jayaprakash Reddy and B. Shara Rani, had abstained from the meeting which was specifically held to discuss issues raised by the dissidents in the last few months. The absentees felt no purpose would be served by going to the meeting. A resolution to initiate action against the three was moved by T. Padma Rao.

(5504) Davangere : H.D. Deve Gowda, Janata Dal (S) President and former Prime Minister, has said that he will meet Congress President Sonia Gandhi on February 9 in Delhi after a meeting of Janata Dal (S) office-bearers and presidents of the district units on February 8. Mr. Deve Gowda, who did not give a direct reply to many of the questions posed to him, said he would not like to say anything now on the continuance of the Janata Dal (S) in the coalition government. He also refused to say what exactly caused the differences between the two parties. "Let the Congress tie up with the AIPJD in zilla and taluk panchayats; it does not bother me," he said. The Janata Dal (S) supremo pleaded ignorance about reports that a Union Cabinet Minister had been mediating between leaders of the Congress and the Janata Dal (S) to sort out their differences. No one had approached him so far, was all Mr. Deve Gowda could say. He said the strained relations between the two parties would not affect the administration.

(5505) Kochi : Former Chief Minister and Congress Working Committee member A.K. Antony has said that the United Democratic Front (UDF) will be able to come into power in the coming Assembly elections if the Congress leadership is ready to go ahead after correcting the mistakes committed earlier.

(5506) Kochi : KPCC president Ramesh Chennithala has asked the State Government to inquire into the tapping of phones of public persons. Talking to media persons at Kochi on Sunday, Mr. Chennithala said that the tapping of phones posed a serious situation in the State where the phones of private individuals were illegally tapped. Health Minister K.K. Ramachandran had to put in his papers following the airing of taped version of one of his telephonic conservations.

(5507) Nedumbassery : The Bharatiya Janata Party leader and former Union Minister, Yashwant Sinha, expressed confidence that his party would open its account in the coming Assembly elections. Talking to The Hindu at the Nedumbassery airport here on Sunday, he claimed that the BJP had recovered from the factional feuds witnessed following the Thiruvananthapuram byelection. He said that the party would project a united face in the Assembly elections. Mr. Sinha called for a Joint Parliamentary Committee probe the Amar Singh phone tapping episode stating that this alone would ensure an independent and unbiased inquiry. He said that it should be found out whether the central intelligence agencies had any role in the phone tapping.

(5508) New Delhi : Even as the Centre declared on Saturday that the Amar Singh phone tapping issue was a "sting operation for monetary gains in which no political party or political personality nor the Delhi Government, including the Delhi Police, were involved," Uttar Pradesh Chief Minister Mulayam Singh Yadav ordered a parallel probe at the State level. Mr. Yadav and Mr. Amar Singh on Saturday rejected the Government statement saying it was a "cover-up."According to Mr. Yadav, when he learnt that "those behind phone tapping were now probing it," he ordered an inquiry by the Government's Special Task Force. The Chief Minister dismissed suggestions that this was aimed at confronting the Centre.Samajwadi Party leaders had been saying they had no faith in either the Central Bureau of Investigation or the Delhi Government, which is now probing the case.

(5509) Lucknow : Congress president Sonia Gandhi and Amethi MP Rahul Gandhi have been elected AICC members from Uttar Pradesh. The list, cleared by Ms. Gandhi, was issued at the Congress headquarters here.But against expectations, the name of Priyanka Gandhi Vadra was not in the list of 141 elected and 90 co-opted members. While the inclusion of Ms Gandhi and her son Rahul was a mere formality, this is the second time Mr. Rahul has been included in the AICC list. The last time, he was included as a co-opted member. Other Congress leaders in the list are UPCC president Salman Khurshid, his MLA wife Louis Khurshid, Congress Legislature Party leader Pramod Tiwari, Minister of State for Home Sri Prakash Jaiswal, Shahjahanpur MP, Jitin Prasad, son of Jitendra Prasada, and UPCC chief spokesperson A.P. Singh. - UNI

(5510) Lucknow : The Congress in Uttar Pradesh on Sunday urged the Centre to take "appropriate measures" to rid the State of the current dispensation so that there could be an end to the "prevailing mafia and jungle raj". In a resolution adopted at the party state unit meeting here, it claimed the Samajwadi Party-led Government in the State had lost the "trust of the people".

(5511) New Delhi : Bahujan Samaj Party supremo Mayawati turned 50 on Sunday and was greeted by party leaders and workers from across the country. Party MPs, MLAs and workers thronged Ms. Mayawati's residence at Humayun Road here and greeted her with sweets and flowers in the presence of party founder Kanshi Ram. Mr. Ram offered the customary cake to Ms. Mayawati on her birthday. Mr. Kanshi Ram also released two volumes of a book "Mere Sangharshmay Jeevan yewam Bahujan Movement ka Safarnama" written by Ms. Mayawati. The two volumes comprise 2,200 pages in which Ms. Mayawati had narrated her political struggle along with the movement for empowerment of Bahujan Samaj, party sources told PTI.Later, the BSP chief announced formation of Bahujan Prerna Trust for the downtrodden. Festivities marked the occasion with party workers singing songs in praise of Ms. Mayawati and the party founder. - PTI

(5512) Chennai : The Dravida Munnetra Kazhagam and the Pattali Makkal Katchi have raised serious concern over the proposed monorail project and said they were keenly watching its progress.In a statement on Sunday, DMK president M. Karunanidhi alleged that even before tenders were invited, a firm in Malaysia had been approached. He had been informed that the project would cost Rs. 20,000 crore. His party would keep a close watch on the developments to sensitise people to the manner in which the Government went about such projects. In a statement, PMK founder S. Ramadoss said the project left many questions unanswered. This was a result of the "contradictory" announcements.

17-01-2006

(5513) Anantapur : State president of Bharatiya Janata Party (BJP) N. Indrasena Reddy has likened the row between State secretary of CPI (M) B.V. Raghavulu and Chief Minister Y.S. Rajasekhara Reddy to a match-fixing episode.

(5514) Hyderabad : The CPI (M) received support from BJP, on Monday with senior leader and former Union Minister B. Dattatreya criticising the Government for filing a defamation case against the party's Polit Bureau member B.V. Raghavulu, for the latter's remarks on the ongoing irrigation projects.

(5515) Ongole : CPI(M) State secretary B.V. Raghavulu has found fault with the Government for serving defamation notice on him for alleging corruption in irrigation projects. Speaking to newspersons at Podili on Monday, Mr. Raghavulu said it was not politically correct for the Government to issue legal notices to political leaders. He asserted that the CPI(M) would fight it out.

(5516) Warangal : Telangana Rasthra Samithi (TRS) president K. Chandrasekhar Rao has said the party will settle the Telangana issue with the Congress in the next two or three months, and exhorted people to be prepared for another bout of mass movement. Addressing a meeting of partymen here on Monday, Mr. Rao urged youth to join the Telangana Jagarana Sena in a big way as the party planned to organise a public meeting 'Maha Sainik Sammelan' with one lakh members in Hyderabad soon. The TRS leader apprised the party cadre of the important developments of the movement since emergence of the party. He asked them not to believe in contradictory statements being issued by Congress leaders in the State. "There is no Congress Government at the Centre. It is a coalition of different parties. We are in touch with Prime Minister Manmohan Singh and Sonia Gandhi. The issue is included in the Common Minimum Programme and we will achieve our goal in a democratic way," Mr. Rao explained. He asked people to pressure 'betrayers' to resign from the Assembly. The response to the meeting was tremendous with over 10,000 partymen from Khammam, Warangal and Karimnagar attending it. It was described as a success by party leaders. Senior leader A. Narendra too tried to explain the 'game plan' of Congress leaders, and urged people to rally behind KCR till the goal was achieved. "The movement has reached a crucial stage." Meanwhile in Sangareddy, dissident MLA Toorpu Jayaprakash Reddy, accepting Mr. Chandrasekhar Rao's challenge, offered to resign and face elections in a couple of months.

(5517) Boodhan Pochampally(Nalgonda dist) : The UPA sub-committee on Telangana is still consulting leaders of different political parties and trying to reach a consensus about carving out a separate State.Speaking to presspersons here on Monday, Union Minister for Rural Development Raghuvansh Prasad Singh said though the sub-committee had asked for consultative meetings to be held on the issue once a month, only two such meetings had taken place until now. "While some parties are in support and some are opposed to the idea of a separate Telangana State, others are silent. I will leave it to you to draw your own conclusions," said Mr. Singh, who is a member of the sub-committee.Elaborating, he said while the RJD, NCP, BSP and RPI were in favour of Telangana, the Left parties and TDP were strongly against the formation of a separate State. The Congress, BJP, DMK and BJD were keeping mum on the issue.

(5518) Thiruvananthapuram : The KPCC has deferred its move to drop some of the presidents of District Congress Committees on grounds of expediency. The final decision was taken at the end of a meeting of KPCC office-bearers, Ministers, and Congress legislators here on Monday. The Congress Working Committee member Veerappa Moily, who is in charge of Kerala, attended the meeting. KPCC president Ramesh Chennithala, at a press conference later, confirmed that the existing DCC presidents would continue to hold their post.

(5519) Bangalore : President of the State unit of the Samajwadi Party S. Bangarappa, MP, has spoken of a "looting spree" by those in authority and in the administration even as the coalition partners are threatening that mid-term elections to the Assembly are around the corner.Speaking to presspersons on Monday, the former Chief Minister alleged that the Congress and the Janata Dal (Secular) had spent heavily in the panchayat elections and now they wanted to recover the money. The elections were likely to be held by April. Though the Janata Dal (S) leader H.D. Deve Gowda was threatening to pull out of the Government, he might not precipitate matters now, he said.

(5520) Belgaum : The Indian Union Muslim League (IUML) is the sole representative of Muslims in the country, the party's President Alhaz G.M. Banatwala said here on Sunday. Muslims can either tread the path shown by former IUML President Mohammed Ismail and get socially, economically and politically empowered or "perish" like those who followed Abdul Kalam Azad, according to him. Addressing a public meeting here, he preferred not to comment on the reasons that prompted Abdul Kalam Azad to advise Muslims to wind up the IUML after independence and join the political mainstream by voting for parties of their choice. However, he said all those who heeded the advice perished or were left without an "identity" while those who continued to work with the IUML achieved political power. He noted that Kerala had seen an IUML Chief Minister while the party was a coalition partner with the Congress in West Bengal in the past. An IUML member was a Minister of State in the UPA Government at the Centre.

(5521) Bellary : Deputy Chief Minister M.P. Prakash has said that Congress's efforts to share power with the All India Progressive Janata Dal (AIPJD) in some zilla and taluk panchayats is illogical and unwarranted. Mr. Prakash told presspersons here on Monday that when the coalition government is going on smoothly, there is no need for the Congress to join hands with others. Even Chief Minister N. Dharam Singh had openly admitted this. Mr. Prakash accused some of the disgruntled Congressmen of raking up such issues. He said the State's finances were sound and stable and there will not be any hindrance for the implementation of the common minimum programme.

(5522) Bellary : Janata Dal (Secular) State unit President N. Thippanna has categorically said his party will continue in the coalition as long as the Congress does not join hands with the "enemies" of the Janata Dal (S) in zilla and taluk panchayats. "We have made it clear to the Congress that if the coalition Government has to continue then it should share power with the Janata Dal (S) in zilla and taluk panchayats and should not have any ties with our enemies at any cost," Mr. Thippanna said.

(5523) Panaji : The ruling Congress continues to be divided over the Mopa airport issue with former Union Law Minister Ramakant Khalap, who is a member of the All India Congress Committee, opposing the decision of the Government to put the Mopa airport proposal on hold.He said a delegation of Congress leaders from North Goa will be taken to Prime Minister Manmohan Singh and Congress President Sonia Gandhi to persuade them to instruct the Goa Government not to stop the ongoing process of land acquisition and other works for the proposed airport.

(5524) Kollam : Congress Working Committee member A.K. Antony has said that anyone prepared to return by recognising the policies of Congress president Sonia Gandhi need not be kept away from the party.Inaugurating the C.M. Stephen commemoration organised by the Kollam DCC on Monday, he said that such persons should in fact be welcomed into the party.

(5525) Kozhikode : The Indian Union Muslim League (IUML) has said that it would not remain a mute witness to the character assassination of party State general secretary P.K. Kunhalikutty by some political leaders and organisations in the name of the Kozhikode ice-cream parlour sex scandal case. Addressing a news conference here on Monday, IUML district general secretary M.C. Mayin Haji said that Mr. Kunhalikutty had been exonerated in the case during the rule of the last Left Democratic Front Government. No court in the country had said that he was guilty. The Communist Party of India (Marxist) was picking on the IUML to divert the attention on the factional war led by the State secretary Pinarayi Vijayan and the Leader of the Opposition V.S. Achuthanandan within the CPI(M), Mr. Mayin Haji said.

(5526) Thiruvananthapuram : Leader of the Opposition V.S. Achuthanandan has urged the Union Agriculture Minister Sharad Pawar to drop the "move" to shift the marine aquarium and allied research institutions from Vizhinjam.In a letter to Mr. Pawar, he said the aquarium had been functioning in a commendable manner since 1951. Last year, the centre had won the Jawaharlal Nehru Award for research in biotechnology.

(5527) New Delhi : Communist Party of India (Marxist) General Secretary Prakash Karat called on Janata Dal (Secular) president and former Prime Minister H.D. Deve Gowda on Monday at his residence and reportedly discussed the current political situation in Karnataka.The meeting lasted for about an hour. The two reportedly focussed on the differences between Congress and JD (S) in Karnataka, which has grown following the recent Zila Panchayat election.

(5528) New Delhi : The Congress on Monday said its president Sonia Gandhi always maintained that the law must take its course in the Bofors caseThe party was responding to questions on the controversy over defreeezing of the London bank accounts of Italian businessman Ottavio Quattrocchi and whether she was aware of the move by the Law Ministry.Party spokesman Anand Sharma said that even earlier Ms. Gandhi asked the National Democratic Alliance Government to act and bring to book anybody who was allegedly involved in the Bofors payoffs caseIn 1998, when she campaigned for the Congress in the general elections, Ms. Gandhi made her position clear on Bofors As for the recent developments, Mr. Sharma said neither the Congress president nor the party interfered with the functioning of any Ministry or any government agency such as the Central Bureau of Investigation.Mr. Sharma wondered how the Bharatiya Janata Party arrived at definitive conclusions before the Government clarified its position.He said there were certain questions and suggested that the party await an official response to its charge.

(5529) New Delhi : Seeking to turn the heat on Chief Minister Sheila Dikshit over the issue of ongoing demolitions in the Capital, Delhi Pradesh Congress Committee president Ram Babu Sharma on Monday asked for immediate identification and dismissal of all corrupt officials. Also, he demanded putting the lists of all illegal constructions in Delhi since 1954 on the website and intensification of the ongoing demolition drive in the Capital.

(5530) Lucknow : Holding former Uttar Pradesh Chief Minister Rajnath Singh responsible for the BJP's debacle in the State, expelled party leader Uma Bharti on Monday dubbed him as "the architect of corruption-criminal nexus in U.P." "I do not know how far Mr Kalyan Singh consented, but Mr. Rajnath Singh is solely responsible for the poor state of the BJP in Hindi heartland," she told newspersons at 'Meet the Press' programme at U.P. Press Club here.BJP would have to first begin from U.P. if it wanted a facelift to the party, she said adding Mr Rajnath Singh had an onerous task of undoing his past follies towards the party. "No party can hope to improve its prospects before it make amends in states like U.P. and Bihar," she said.

(5531) Chennai : Chief Minister and AIADMK general secretary Jayalalithaa on Monday appealed to party workers to strive for the success of the organisation in the coming Assembly elections by exposing those who were trying to belittle the AIADMK Government's achievements in the last five years. In a statement on the eve of the birth anniversary of party founder M.G. Ramachandran, she said unity, cooperation and effort on the part of the cadre were essential to exposing those who were claiming that no development had taken place in Tamil Nadu in the last five years.

(5532) Chennai : The Pattali Makkal Katchi on Monday suffered another jolt with two more dalit party MLAs resigning from the Assembly and joining the All-India Anna Dravida Munnetra Kazhagam. With this, the PMK strength in the Assembly is down to 16. Even as the Assembly was in session, V. Sivakami, representing Dharapuram (Reserved), and K. Murugavel Rajan from Vandavasi (Reserved), called on AIADMK general secretary and Chief Minister Jayalalithaa at her residence and enrolled themselves as primary members of the ruling party. Only four days ago, PMK MLA R. Krishnan, who represented Anthiyur (Reserved), joined the AIADMK in the presence of Ms. Jayalalithaa, after resigning his Assembly seat. In a joint statement, Ms. Sivakami and Mr. Rajan said though they, as representatives of the Scheduled Castes, had once occupied important positions in the PMK, they were "sidelined by party founder S. Ramadoss and his son R. Anbumani." They claimed they were harassed and deprived of their rights. They also accused Dr. Ramadoss and Dr. Anbumani of running "family politics."

18-01-2006

(5533) Nizamabad : Former Minister and Telugu Desam Party State secretary P. Babu Mohan has accused the Government for of failing to take any action with regard to the implementation of the G.O Ms No. 610 during its 20-month rule.Addressing 'Gram Chaitanya Yatra' launched by the TDP seeking diversion of Godavari water to upland areas of the district at Khanapur in Nizamabad mandal on Tuesday, he said the Congress and the Telangana Rashtra Samithi had come to power by making a plethora of promises to people but after coming to power, went back on their promises.

(5534) Visakhapatnam : The pro-Congress wave or climate witnessed during the 2004 elections did not exist now and by working hard, the Bharatiya Janata Party could regain the Visakha-I Assembly seat in the February 16 by-election, BJP State president N. Indrasena Reddy said here on Monday.

(5535) New Delhi : The Bharatiya Janata Party indicated here on Tuesday that it would support any move by the Government to bring forward legislation to create a quota for the sub-caste Madiga within the overall reservation quota for Scheduled Castes in Andhra Pradesh Krishna Madiga, who had been struggling for a separate quota of reservations for Madigas through an organisation, met Leader of Opposition L.K. Advani here on Tuesday to seek his support. Party leader Venkaiah Naidu told reporters that several senior BJP leaders were present and they assured him that if the Centre were to legislate on the issue, the BJP would support it.According to Mr. Naidu, it was the Telugu Desam that has first taken up the Madiga cause and now the Congress Government in State wants to do justice to the Madigas. The BJP will support any move on this, Mr. Naidu added.

(5536) Hyderabad : AICC in charge of Andhra Pradesh Affairs Digvijay Singh has asked leaders of Madiga Reservation Porata Samithi (MRPS) to exercise restraint in seeking solution to the SC reservations classification problem.Talking to the presspersons here on Tuesday evening, Mr. Singh said that there was no point in adopting a confrontationist attitude on any issue as long the doors for negotiations were open. The MRPS leaders, however, had not approached him, he said referring to their demand for an audience with Ms. Sonia Gandhi.

(5537) Kakinada : Holding of the stir in the name of 'Kurukshetra' proposed by MRPS was not in the interests of the Dalits and aimed at disrupting the AICC plenary session, said Patri Siddardhi, chairman of District Congress SC Cell here on Tuesday.

(5538) Ramayampet (Medak) : Telangana Rashtra Samithi (TRS) president K. Chandrasekhar Rao on Tuesday gave a call for social boycott of the 'traitors' of Telangana. Addressing party cadre of the Western Telangana region here, without naming the three rebels, Mr. Rao asked his followers to get tough with them till they offered resignation. He said that party would not suspend them, as it would bring them close to the Congress. Mr. Rao also announced that he would soon arrange for a meeting of non-Left and non-Congress political affiliates of the UPA as a last ditch effort to solve the Telangana issue. He said that he did not want to break ties with the UPA at this juncture, as Congress had not yet announced its final decision on formation of a separate state. Mr. Rao asked Telugu Desam president N. Chandrababu Naidu to first declare the share of Telangana in Godavari water before launching the Godavari Jala Sadhana programme. He, however, invited TDP leaders from the region to join the struggle. He said that he would step down and hand over the steering wheel if they joined hands with TRS.

(5539) New Delhi : Bharatiya Janata Party activists held a demonstration here on Tuesday, charging the ruling Congress with colluding with Italian businessman Ottavio Quattrocchi, an accused in the Bofors case, in getting his London bank accounts defreezed. Led by senior leaders, the protesters - who raised slogans against the Congress and its leaders - symbolically pulled down police barricades on Parliament Street before courting arrest.Addressing the gathering, party spokesperson Arun Jaitley charged the Congress with letting Mr. Quattrocchi off the hook through its action, which led to the defreezing of the accounts in which the kickbacks money had allegedly been stashed away. The Congress misused constitutional institutions while in power. "First it attacked the Supreme Court and the Election Commission. Now, it is misusing the Central Bureau of Investigation. If the dignity of the Constitution continues to be eroded, the people will lose their trust in democracy," he said.

(5540) Kottayam : The invitation to DIC(K) activists by KPCC president Ramesh Chennithala and former Chief Minister A. K. Antony to rejoin the Congress reflects the sense of defeat that has set in Congress circles, according to CPI(M) secretary Pinarayi Vijayan. Speaking to reporters at Pampady during his Kerala Yatra through the Chief Minister's home turf, Puthupally Assembly segment, the CPI(M) leader said the Congress leadership was fully aware of the isolation of the party from the masses.

(5541) Bangalore : On a day of rapid political developments, moves towards the formation of an alternative government in the State, with the Bharatiya Janata Party and the Janata Dal (Secular) as partners, were made. The developments come two days before the commencement of the session of the State Legislature. Among the top BJP leaders who rushed to New Delhi for talks with party President Rajnath Singh and others were State unit President Jagadish Shettar, Leader of the Opposition in the Legislative Assembly B.S. Yediyurappa, and former State unit President K.S. Eshwarappa. According to reports reaching here, Mr. Rajnath Singh is quoted as having said that political developments in Karnataka have been taken note of and a final decision will be taken. Janata Dal (S) President H.D. Deve Gowda returned from New Delhi this evening. There is no change in the public stand of the two parties. For the Janata Dal (S), the BJP is still a communal party and its tie-up with the Congress in the State is to uphold secularism. For public consumption, the BJP is saying that it sees no difference between the Congress and the Janata Dal (S).

(5542) New Delhi : Janata Dal (Secular) President and former Prime Minister H.D. Deve Gowda on Tuesday denied any move by his party to align with the Bharatiya Janata Party in Karnataka. "No, there is no question of any such move," Mr. Deve Gowda told The Hindu on telephone on Tuesday soon after his two-day visit to the capital. "There is not even an idea in my mind on going with the BJP. At the fag end of my life, I do not want to make such a mistake." BJP President Rajnath Singh has deputed senior party leader in charge of southern States Venkaiah Naidu to visit

Karnataka. Senior BJP leaders said on Tuesday that the recent "courtesy call" by Mr. Deve Gowda on former Prime Minister Atal Bihari Vajpayee may have been a warning signal to the Congress. "Mr. Deve Gowda did say that he was unhappy with the situation in Bangalore," a senior BJP leader said.

(5543) Chennai : Blaming Union Health Minister Anbumani Ramadoss of the Pattali Makkal Katchi for inaction in the Common Entrance Test issue, Chief Minister Jayalalithaa on Tuesday said the PMK, which resorted to "double talk and duplicity" on the CET, had no locus standi to raise the issue. Intervening in the debate on the motion of thanks to the Governor's address, she said the Government would give effect to the new scheme of making Plus Two marks of the State Board as the common platform for evaluation, besides ensuring a quota system, by bringing a legislation in the current session itself.

(5544) Thiruvananthapuram : There exists no unholy alliance between the Congress and BJP, but on the contrary, it is the LDF that allied with the BJP during the last Thiruvananthapuram Lok Sabha byelection, KPCC president Ramesh Chennithala has said. He was responding to CPI(M) State secretary Pinarayi Vijayan's allegation that there was an electoral understanding between the Congress and the RSS to contest in five seats in the next Assembly elections.

(5545) New Delhi : The Bharatiya Janata Party on Tuesday continued its tirade on the Bofors issue, charging the CBI with making a u-turn. The agency, it said, maintained that the Italian businessman Ottavio Quattrocchi was still an accused in the Bofors case and yet justified its decision to inform the British prosecution that there was no clinching evidence to link the money held by Mr. Quattrocchi in two British bank accounts to the Bofors payoffs. "The CBI's credibility has been a casualty," said party spokesperson Prakash Javadekar, adding that "a question mark has been put on the trustworthiness of this agency." The party also wanted to know why the CBI did not inform the country about the Bofors-related developments and why it hid the fact that it had information about the de-freezing of Mr. Quattrocchi's accounts. It said the Government must now "find out" where Mr. Quattrocchi had transferred the funds held by him in the two accounts. BJP president Rajnath Singh met Rashtriya Swayamsevak Sangh general secretary Mohan Rao Bhagwat at the RSS headquarters in

Jhandewalan here to discuss several important issues, including the ideological direction to be given to the party. Mr. Singh has reportedly finalised the party's central office bearers.

(5546) Chennai : Janata Party president Subramanian Swamy has described as "pathetic and ridiculous," the "attempt" by the CBI to "cover up for Law Minister H.R. Bhardwaj in the Quattrocchi fiasco."In a statement here on Tuesday, Dr. Swamy said: "The CBI has owned responsibility for the decision to allow de-freezing of the Rs. 20 crore deposits in two U.K. banks of Ottavio Quattrocchi, and also claimed that the agency had decided sending the Additional Solicitor General B. Dutta to U.K. to inform that country's official prosecutors."

(5547) New Delhi : The former Human Resource Development (HRD) Minister, Murli Manohar Joshi, on Tuesday held his successor Arjun Singh responsible for the "minorityism" of the United Progressive Alliance (UPA) Government. Addressing a press conference here, Dr. Joshi said: "A weak Government, unable to understand the games being played by its own ambitious Minister can never be expected to see reason and checkmate the impending disasters in education." He was critical of the decision to keep minority institutions out of the ambit of the Constitutional Amendment to provide reservation in all unaided educational institutions and the HRD Ministry's position on the "minority" status of the Aligarh Muslim University (AMU). From the platform of Shiksha Bachao Aandolan Samiti, Dr. Joshi said "the policy of creating permanent divisions and dissensions in Indian society in the name of minorities and their so-called welfare are blatantly against the national interests and communal harmony." Accusing the Government of pursuing a single-point agenda in education on how to convert minorities into a committed vote-bank, he questioned the setting up of the National Commission for Minority Educational Institutions (NCMEI). According to him, the Commission had eroded the credibility of institutions like the All India Council for Technical Education (AICTE) and University Grants Commission (UGC). "Are UGC and AICTE not trustworthy enough to deal with minority institutions?" Stating that it was "majority-minority" politics that had partitioned the country in the first place, he said "this jaundiced view of education" would create mutual distrust among the youth of the country. The Constitutional Amendment, he said, was not only flawed but also injurious to the rights of a large section of the population as it denied reservation to Scheduled Castes,

Scheduled Tribes and other backward classes of citizens in minority educational institutions. On AMU's minority status, he said: "Those who argue in terms of Article 29 (protection of the interest of minorities) and Article 30 (rights of minorities to establish and administer educational institutions) of the Constitution must also read Section 29(2) which says, 'No citizen shall be denied admission into any educational institution maintained by the State or receiving aid out of State funds only on grounds of religion, race, caste, language or any of them."

(5548) New Delhi : The Bharatiya Janata Party councillor and member of the Standing Committee of the Municipal Corporation of Delhi, Vijender Gupta, on Tuesday alleged that Chief Sheila Dikshit and her MP son, Sandeep Dikshit, had committed major violations in their houses at Nizamuddin in South Delhi by flouting building bylaws."Ms. Dikshit moved in the Delhi Assembly a controversial resolution to regularise their unauthorised constructions that was later notified," he said, adding that her house in Nizamuddin East violated the provisions of the Delhi Municipal Corporation Act as well as the Preservation of Historical Monuments and Heritage Buildings Act.

(5549) New Delhi : The stage is set for another confrontation between the party and the Government in Delhi with the Delhi Pradesh Congress Committee president Ram Babu convening a meeting of the executive committee on January 19. Mr. Sharma has also written to Chief Minister Sheila Dikshit to be present at the meeting that will "debate all issues" pertaining to Delhi and its citizens.

(5550) New Delhi : Janata Dal (Secular) president and former Prime Minister H.D. Deve Gowda on Tuesday denied any move by his party to align with the Bharatiya Janata Party in Karnataka. "No, there is no question of any such move," Mr. Deve Gowda told The Hindu on telephone on Tuesday soon after his two-day visit to the capital. "There is not even an idea in my mind on going with the BJP. At the fag end of my life, I do not want to make such a mistake." In the BJP, the Karnataka question was clearly very much on the agenda of senior leaders. A number of party leaders from Karnataka, including general secretary H.N. Ananth Kumar, met BJP president Rajnath Singh, Leader of Opposition L.K. Advani and senior party leader in-charge of southern States Venkaiah Naidu to discuss the fluid political situation in Karnataka. While the BJP, the single largest party in the Legislative Assembly, seems anxious to see the end of what it describes as "misrule" by the Dharam Singh Government, it is also wary of being "used" by the Janata Dal (S) to send warning signals to its coalition partner, the Congress. Senior BJP leaders said on Tuesday that the recent "courtesy call" by Mr. Deve Gowda on former Prime Minister Atal Bihari Vajpayee might have been one of those signals. "Nothing significant was discussed at the meeting. It was a general meeting. However, Mr. Deve Gowda did say that he was unhappy with the situation in Bangalore," a senior BJP leader said. But, he insisted that the BJP is not willing to see anything more in this, at this juncture. "There have been no contacts at any level between the BJP and the Janata Dal (S) and no feelers to the BJP from the Janata Dal (S)," Mr. Naidu said when asked whether there was a possibility of the two parties coming together if the coalition in the State breaks up.

(5551) New Delhi : In a move that is likely to bring out infighting within the Congress into the open, four legislators owing allegiance to Chief Minister Sheila Dikshit have resigned from the Public Accounts Committee (PAC) of the Delhi Assembly in protest against the adoption of the report on privatisation of power on Monday. In their resignation letters addressed to Delhi Assembly Speaker Chaudhary Prem Singh, the four MLAs — Narendra Nath, Baljore Singh, Vir Singh Dhingan and Ramesh Lamba — have protested against the functioning of the PAC chairman and Congress MLA, S.C. Vats, and have expressed their lack of confidence in his leadership. Surprisingly, these MLAs did not resign the day the report was adopted by the PAC and waited for more than a week to express their feelings. It is learnt that these MLAs met the Speaker on Tuesday afternoon and submitted their resignations. All the MLAs are considered close to the Chief Minister and their move is being seen as an attempt to block the adoption of the report in the budget session of the Vidhan Sabha.

(5552) Chennai : Led by their deputy leader, members of the DMK walked out of the Assembly protesting against the Speaker's decision to expunge certain remarks made by party MLA J. Anbazhagan during the debate on the motion of thanks to the Governor's address. The trouble started when Mr. Anbazhagan referred to certain measures of the State Government during the past four years. Speaker K. Kalimuthu, who expunged those remarks, asked the member to adhere to the Assembly Rules.

(5553) Chennai : All India Anna Dravida Munnetra Kazhagam general secretary and Chief Minister Jayalalithaa on Tuesday paid floral tributes to the statue of her political mentor and former Chief Minister M.G. Ramachandran on his 89th birth anniversary. Ms. Jayalalithaa arrived at the AIADMK headquarters here around 9.15 a.m. and garlanded the statue. She released a souvenir brought out by the party. Ministers, legislators and functionaries of the party also paid floral tributes.

(5554) Chennai : Chief Minister Jayalalithaa on Tuesday alleged that Union Ministers from Tamil Nadu had asked the Centre not to sanction Rs. 13,000 crore sought by the State for flood relief work. Intervening in the motion of thanks to the Governor's address in the Assembly, she said the Ministers would have told the Centre that the elections were near and that she would "get a good name" if the amount was released. The Democratic Progressive Alliance was capable of getting anything that it wanted from the Centre. When this was the situation, should it be inferred that the Centre did not accord due respect and consideration to the DPA resolution (it had urged the Prime Minister to release the amount sought by the Chief Minister), she asked. Or did the Centre throw the resolution into the wastebasket? The resolution was "an eyewash." DMK leader Arcot N. Veerasamy said the Centre did not give the money because the State had not given a detailed expenditure plan. The Chief Minister contested this and said the detailed heads were given long back.

(5555) Cuddalore : The Congress should get a fair deal when the Democratic Progressive Alliance finalises seat-sharing arrangement for the Assembly elections, former president of the Tamil Nadu Congress Committee, Tindivanam K. Ramamurthi, has said. Addressing a press conference here on Tuesday, Mr. Ramamurthi said, "What counts more is fair representation for the Congress, than the number of seats to be shared." The general view among party workers was that the party should share power in a future government. He laid the onus of preserving the identity of the Congress without compromising its rights, on its State leadership. After the Lok Sabha elections, the party was facing a decline in Tamil Nadu. He cautioned that if the party did not assert itself, it faced the risk of being reduced to a regional party.

19-01-2006

(5556) Hyderabad : The Bharatiya Janata Party, while lambasting the Government for the proposed Outer Ring Road (ORR), has also taunted the Telugu Desam Party for keeping 'mum' over the project which it alleged was about to displace many small farmers and the poor. It accused the Government of turning a deaf ear to the protest launched taken up by the affected people. "Both TDP and Congress are protecting the interests of big realtors without bothering rehabilitation for those facing eviction," charged former Union Minister Bandaru Datta

(5557) Hyderabad : The Government on Wednesday evening announced that the NTR National Award for the years 2003, 2004 and 2005, would be given away on Andhra Pradesh Formation Day on November 1.It has asked the Commisioner of Information and Public Relations, K.V.Ramanachary to take action in this regard.Earlier, the Telugu Desam Party threatened to take on the Government on the issue of the award carrying a cash prize of Rs. 5 lakhs. The party president N. Chandrababu Naidu had on Wednesday made it clear that the party and NTR's family would give away the award, if the Government did not respond soon. Addressing party workers at a meeting convened to observe the tenth death anniversary of NTRMr. Naidu said,"It smacks of petty politics and intolerance for political adversaries. They even removed the name of NTR from the international airport though the TDP Government did all the groundwork. But a day is not far off when we will be able to rename it," he said. Mr. Naidu and party leaders, K. Yerran Naidu, Y. Ramakrishnudu, R. Chandrasekhara Reddy, B. V. Mohan Reddy, K. Pratibha Bharathi, Ch. Rajeswara Rao, Vanga Geetha and Mohd Yousuf Ali, paid tributes to NTR and recalled the role he played in bringing a fledgling party to power within nine months.

(5558) Hyderabad : CPI(M) Polit Bureau member B.V. Raghavulu has said that the defamation notice served on him by the Irrigation Department has exposed the Government's weakness in countering the struggles launched against its anti-people measures.

(5559) Hyderabad : The ST Cell of the Telugu Desam Party has demanded stringent action against the Excise personnel of Saroornagar Excise Station in whose custody a tribal woman, Nanavath Bujji, allegedly died three days ago.

(5560) Hyderabad : A section of Congress leaders from Telangana held a demonstration in front of the PCC headquarters here protesting against the TRS demand for separate statehood for Telangana at this juncture. Cautioning the PCC against entertaining the TRS leadership any longer, they said any division of the State now would lead to further disintegration. They held aloft banners with the slogan "stop bifurcation of the State into five smaller ones". They justified the slogan by arguing that separate Statehood for the Telangana region would give rise to similar demands in Rayalaseema, North Coastal Andhra and South Coastal Andhra.Led by DCC presidents of Warangal and Karimnagar, G. Venkataramana Reddy and S. Santosh Kumar respectively, the group later submitted a memorandum to the PCC president, K. Keshava Rao, complaining against the TRS leadership. They said the TRS leaders had deceived both the people and the Congress by projecting a false strength during the last general elections, they said. Later addressing a press conference, Gone Prakasa Rao, Chairman of the APSRTC, asked the TRS to stick to its deadline of February 28 for parting ways with the Congress.

(5561) Visakhapatnam : The State unit of the Bharatiya Janata Party has criticised the Government for not taking steps to alleviate the difficulties of farmers."More farmers had resorted to suicide during the Congress Government's rule than during the Telugu Desam Party regime," BJP State president N. Indrasena Reddy told a press conference here on Wednesday.

(5562) Visakhapatnam : Hyderabad has become the base for terrorists, but the State Government is not bothered to control and eliminate such activities, according to Bharatiya Janata Party State president N. Indrasena Reddy.Attacks on Akshardham, attack on IISc in Bangalore, Haren Pandya's murder and several other incidents in the country had been planned in Hyderabad. "There was no surveillance on the terrorist activities and the police were not being given a free hand," he alleged at a press conference here on Wednesday. He said that the Congress Government was trying to play down the whole issue. "The police say that there are 55 human bombs lurking in the city but the fact is that there are some hundreds of them are ready to strike. There is no surveillance on the thousands of Pakistanis who are overstaying," the BJP leader said.

(5563) Hyderabad : Not many of the delegates seeking passes for attending the Congress plenary are aware of the fact that their requests are being subjected to a police scan in all the States. Heightened security concerns have forced the AICC to route the clearance of many delegates through the Intelligence Bureau (IB) network for checking their antecedents. Though the IB did not enter the scene in the case of known entities like Ministers, MPs, MLAs and Pradesh Congress Committee presidents, the requests of many others for issue of identity cards were referred to the bureau.Applications from Jammu & Kashmir and Assam are being subjected to the maximum scrutiny as these States have been receiving the highest attention of terrorist outfits. Party sources said Chief Minister of Jammu & Kashmir Ghulam Nabi Azad personally verified every application before forwarding it to the AICC. It took more than a week for these names to be finally cleared by intelligence agencies. When it came to the host State - Andhra Pradesh— 72 names of Seva Dal volunteers had to be dropped at the instance of the State police. The AP contingent in the, 1,500-strong Seva Dal was expected to be 1,000 but this number has now come down.

(5564) Bangalore : The former Prime Minister, H.D. Deve Gowda, upset over the political crisis in the Janata Dal (Secular) arising out of his son and working president of the State JD (S) H.D. Kumaraswamy and his supporters withdrawing support to the coalition Government, has said "today is the saddest day in my political career spanning 54 years." A visibly upset Mr. Gowda told The Hindu: "Even when I relinquished the office of the Prime Minister I was not at all sad. But today, the commitment with which I had all along fought has been shattered by a group of legislators of the party. It is a very sad day in my life. I feel betrayed." Members of the Gowda family had interacted with Mr. Kumaraswamy and pleaded with him not to align himself with the BJP.

(5565) Chennai : Chief Minister Jayalalithaa on Wednesday accused the Dravida Munentra Kazhagam, a constituent of the United Progressive Alliance Government at the Centre, of exerting pressure on income tax officials to conduct raids on her family doctor and chartered accountant.Since Wednesday morning, the Income Tax department had been carrying out raids on the house of her family doctor and office and residence of her chartered accountant in Chennai. Raids were also being conducted on the residences and workplaces of those who were close to her, she told the Assembly, intervening in a debate on the motion of thanks to the Governor for his address.Despite "pressure exerted repeatedly" by the DMK president, M. Karunanidhi, and Union Minister of State for

Finance S.S. Palanimanickam, the department's officers refused to carry out raids on her house, on the ground that there was no precedent for conducting a raid on the house of an incumbent Chief Minister.

(5566) Bangalore : The end of the 19-month-old Dharam Singh Government in Karnataka appeared imminent on Wednesday night with the dominant group in the Janata Dal (Secular) informing Governor T.N. Chaturvedi about its decision to withdraw from the coalition with the Congress and staking claim, along with the Bharatiya Janata Party, to form an alternative government.The JD (S) group, which comprises 44 members out of its total of 59, announced its decision to align itself with the BJP, the largest group in the 224-member Assembly with 79 members. The group is led by H.D. Kumaraswamy, State JD(S) working president and third son of H.D. Deve Gowda, the former Prime Minister. The undivided JD(S) had until now shunned the BJP as being communal. Later in the night, Chief Minister Dharam Singh called on the Governor and claimed that his Government still enjoyed a majority in the Assembly and requested him not to take cognisance of a letter submitted by Mr. Kumaraswamy withdrawing support to the coalitionMr. Dharam Singh was accompanied by Deputy Chief Minister M.P. Prakash, KPCC president and Water Resources Minister Mallikarjuna Kharge, Law Minister H.K. Patil and Finance and Industries Minister P.G.R. Sindhia. They told the Governor that any test of strength should be on the floor of the legislature. Mr. Prakash said Mr. Kumaraswamy's letter was illegal. Being the duly elected the leader of the Janata Dal Legislature Party, only he could write to the Governor on any such withdrawal, Mr. Prakash said. Leader of the Opposition in the Assembly B.S. Yediyurappa, of the BJP, announced on Wednesday night that Mr. Kumaraswamy was elected leader of the joint BJP-JD(S) Legislature Party. He was addressing the press along with Mr. Kumaraswamy in front of the Raj Bhavan. BJP vice-president M. Venkaiah Naidu earlier announced here that Mr. Kumaraswamy would be the Chief Minister with Mr. Yediyurappa as Deputy Chief Minister. Under an arrangement agreed upon by the two parties, the JD (S) will lead the government in the first 20 months; a government on the Jammu and Kashmir model. The 12th Karnataka Assembly has still 40 months to complete its term. Putting an end to day-long speculation, Mr. Kumaraswamy drove to the Raj Bhavan around 6-30 p.m. to inform the Governor that he had been elected leader of the JD (S) and submit in writing that his group was withdrawing support to the Dharam Singh-led Government. Mr. Kumaraswamy met the Governor for a second time along with Mr.Yediyurappa to stake claim to form a government. Another letter was submitted stating that the party had entered into an understanding with the BJP and seeking an invitation to form the next government. The decisive action taken by Mr. Kumaraswamy does not have the blessings of his father, Mr. Deve Gowda. The veteran has distanced himself from the developments. He told The Hindu that he had written to the Governor asking him to ignore the claims made by the group of legislators of the JD(S) about withdrawal of support to the Government. Mr. Prakash and five other Ministers - P.G.R. Sindhia, H.D. Revanna (the second son of Mr. Deve Gowda), D. Manjunath, Amaregowda Bayyapur and Mahadeva Prasad - have not joined the Kumaraswamy group. Two MLAs - Mahima Patel and Parimala Nagappa - are also not a part of the group. Earlier in the day, in a neatly executed move, JD(S) MLAs elected Mr. Kumaraswamy the new Legislature Party leader in the place of Mr. Prakash. Mr. Kumaraswamy met the Governor accompanied by 43 MLAs, some of them Ministers.In the Assembly, the BJP is the largest group, of which two have rebelled. The Congress has 64 members. The Janata Dal (Secular) has 59 members, of which about eight are supporting the former Deputy Chief Minister, Siddaramaiah. The JD (U) has five members. The CPI(M), the Kannada Chaluvaligars and the Republican Party have one each. There are 14 independents.

(5567) Bangalore : The State Cabinet met late Wednesday to discuss the day's political developments, and Deputy Chief Minister M.P. Prakash and Finance Minister P.G.R. Sindhia said Janata Dal (S) President H.D. Deve Gowda is with the coalition, and he has not "blessed" the withdrawal of support by JD(S) State unit Working President H.D. Kumaraswamy. Chief Minister N. Dharam Singh said the legislature session will begin as scheduled on Thursday, and the Government is willing to prove its majority in the House if the need arises. However, Mr. Prakash pointed out that the Janata Dal (S) legislators who spurred the developments have not said they have no trust in the Government. Although only Mr. Prakash, Mr. Sindhia and Mahadeva Prasad among the Janata Dal (S) Ministers attended the meeting of the Cabinet,Mr. Prakash told presspersons that the Cabinet has expressed support to the Chief Minister. The other Ministers, he said, are not in the city. Mr. Dharam Singh said only some junior members of the

Janata Dal (S) are with Mr. Kumaraswamy. H.D. Revanna, Minister for Public Works and Energy and Mr. Deve Gowda's son, said he will not support Mr. Kumaraswamy. "I would rather prefer to retire from politics than join the unholy coalition government (the new government that Mr. Kumaraswamy is making efforts to form)," he said.

(5568) Bangalore : A feeling of betrayal enveloped the Congress camp on Wednesday evening as it expected the worst for the Government led by it: withdrawal of support by the Janata Dal (Secular). Chief Minister N. Dharam Singh was closeted with some Ministers, legislators and party leaders at his official residence before leaving for a meeting of the Cabinet held at his home office, "Krishna", which is next door.According to sources, the Congress leaders were not prepared to buy the claim that Working President of the State unit of the Janata Dal (S) H.D. Kumaraswamy rebelled against his father and former Prime Minister H.D. Deve Gowda in deciding on breaking the coalition.

(5569) Palakkad : Leader of the Opposition V.S. Achuthanandan has demanded the resignation of Chief Minister Oommen Chandy in the wake of the Lok Ayukta's adverse comments against him.

(5570) Alappuzha : Communist Party of India-Marxist (CPI-M) State secretary Pinarayi Vijayan has called for a reorientation of the policies of the State Government in agriculture, industries and education to protect the interests of the poor and marginalised sections of society.

(5571) Thiruvananthapuram : State secretary of the Communist Party of India Veliyam Bhargavan too has questioned Chief Minister Oommen Chandy's right to continue in office in the light of the characterisation of the step taken by him in the K.K. Ramachandran case as wrong and unjust by the Lok Ayukta.

(5572) Thiruvananthapuram : The Democratic Indira Congress (Karunakaran) on Monday made it clear that it was angling for seat adjustments with the LDF in the State, envisaging primarily a tie-up that would have the character of a coalition. The party authorised its president K. Muraleedharan and the veteran leader K. Karunakaran to carry forward its search for a slot in the Left coalition that would include further bilateral discussions with the LDF major CPI(M) and if necessary, with other LDF constituents.

(5573) New Delhi : The Bharatiya Janata Party on Wednesday said the Government made no sincere effort to implement the January 16 Supreme Court directive that status quo be maintained on the two London bank accounts of Ottavio Quattrocchi, Italian businessman accused in the Bofors payoffs case. Party leader Arun Jaitley pointed out that within hours of the court's order that efforts be made to prevent withdrawals from the unfrozen accounts, the Central Bureau of Investigation said it had no evidence to link the money in these accounts to the Bofors payoffs.

(5574) Pondicherry : The leader of the Pondicherry State unit of the Tamil Maanila Congress (Moopanar) C. Jayakumar MLA, called upon the Congress Government to ensure that farmers and the poor who were affected by the recent rain in Pondicherry were paid adequate compensation.

(5575) Lucknow : An application seeking registration of an FIR against Congress president Sonia Gandhi in connection with the tapping of telephones of U.P. Chief Minister Mulayam Singh Yadav and Samajwadi Party general secretary Amar Singh was filed in Chief Judicial Magistrate's court here on Wednesday. In his application, city lawyer Ashok Pandey alleged that Mrs. Gandhi and her associates were involved in the tapping of phones, a charge already denied by the Congress and the Government.

(5576) Chennai : Leaders of the Democratic Progressive Alliance on Wednesday took part in public meetings across the State, kicking off its campaign to "prepare people to oppose the anti-people and autocratic AIADMK Government." Dravida Munnetra Kazhagam president M. Karunanidhi inaugurated a meeting in the city, and asked people to remain vigilant against rumour-mongers trying to create an illusion of the DPA breaking up.

(5577) Chennai : The Pattali Makkal Katchi (PMK) has charged that it was Chief Minister Jayalalithaa who was adopting double standards on various issues, including on common entrance test, and not the PMK. Reacting to the Chief Minister's accusation that the PMK was adopting double standards on the abolition of CET for admission to professional colleges, party leader S. Ramadoss in a statement here on Wednesday said from the beginning the party had been insisting on enacting a legislation for abolition of the CET.

(5578) Chennai : Tamil Nadu Congress Committee president G.K. Vasan has warned that the party will not tolerate those who indulge in activities detrimental to the interests of the party.Any grievance against the leadership should be discussed in party forum and not in the public, Mr. Vasan said, addressing party workers on the occasion of the 66th birth anniversary of the former TNCC president late Vazhapadi K. Ramamurthi here on Wednesday.

(5579) Chennai : Chief Minister Jayalalithaa on Wednesday alleged that the DMK had threatened to withdraw support to the United Progressive Alliance Government at the Centre if more flood relief aid was given to the State without discussing with the party.Intervening in the motion of thanks to the Governor's address, Ms. Jayalalithaa said that the Centre had no intention of releasing more than the initial Rs. 500 crore. But after she met Prime Minister Manmohan Singh, he announced the additional Rs. 500 crore in relief aid since he was aware of the flood situation in Tamil Nadu.

20-01-2006

(5580) Hyderabad : Union Labour Minister and Telangana Rashtra Samithi (TRS) president K. Chandrasekhar Rao announced on Thursday a series of programmes which, he said, were aimed at paving way for the party to quit the UPA Government. "We need to get cracking in the next couple of months, creating ground to come out of UPA," he told a meeting of TRS workers from four Telangana districts here.

(5581) Hyderabad : Former Madhya Pradesh Chief Minister Uma Bharti has said that she would "re-establish" Bhartiya Janata Party and accused those heading the organisation of deviating from the ideology. She told press persons here on Thursday that the party had gone off the track and the ideology of Pandit Deendayal Upadhyaya, A.B. Vajpayee and L.K. Advani ignored. There were "millions" like her who felt the BJP had to be re-established.

(5582) Kurnool : The CPI(M) launched its month-long district-wide "padayatra" here on Thursday setting the tone for development of the district. Leaders of other political parties too had gathered there to bid farewell to the teams. The opinion was unanimous - that development should be placed above politics.

(5583) Miryalaguda (Nalgonda) : Secretary of the Communist Party of India (Marxist), B.V.Raghavulu has warned of launching a mass movement if the Y.S. Rajasekhara Reddy Government slashes allocations for welfare sector in the forthcoming budget.

(5584) Bangalore : Karnataka Governor T.N. Chaturvedi on Thursday directed Chief Minister N. Dharam Singh to seek a vote of confidence in the Assembly on or before January 27. The beleaguered Congress-Janata Dal (Secular) Government thus got an eight-day reprieve. Earlier in the day, he addressed the joint session of the legislature. The BJP and the Kumaraswamy group of the JD (S) boycotted it.

(5585) New Delhi : BJP spokesman Arun Jaitley told reporters that Mr. Chaturvedi's decision to give more than a week to the "minority" Dharam Singh Government to prove its majority was a "grave constitutional error."

(5586) New Delhi : The Congress on Thursday denied that it offered the post of Karnataka Chief Minister to H.D. Kumaraswamy, leader of the group of 44 MLAs who broke away from the Janata Dal (Secular), to save its government in the State. According to the Congress, it would rather sit in the opposition than surrender to Mr. Kumaraswamy's demands.

(5587) Bangalore : Governor T.N. Chaturvedi on Thursday categorically said that Deputy Chief Minister M.P. Prakash is the leader of the Janata Dal (Secular) Legislature Party and that he has gone by the recognition given to him by the Speaker of Legislative Assembly Krishna. The decision of the Governor has thus has put to rest the claim made by rebel Janata Dal (Secular) leader H.D. Kumaraswamy that he is the new leader of the legislature party.

(5588) Bangalore : Former Deputy Chief Minister Siddaramaiah on Thursday alleged that the Janata Dal (S) Working President H.D. Kumaraswamy withdrew support to the coalition government on "at the behest of Mr. Deve Gowda" who is the "director, producer, distributor and script writer of the entire political drama."

(5589) Bangalore : Opposing his brother H.D. Kumaraswamy's revolt, Minister for Public Works H.D. Revanna on Thursday said: "I will quit politics, but not oppose my father and Janata Dal (S) President H.D. Deve Gowda."

(5590) Bangalore :KPCC President M. Mallikarjun Kharge said Mr. Deve Gowda must sack Mr. Kumaraswamy and State JD (S) President N. Thippanna for indulging in anti-party activities. "If Mr. Deve Gowda is making sincere efforts to save the secular Dharam Singh Government, then he should sack both leaders." So far Mr. Deve Gowda displayed his sincerity in extending the support to the Government headed by the Congress. The Government would win the vote of confidence on January 27 if the Mr. Deve Gowda extended support to the Government, he said.

(5591) Bangalore : The Janata Dal (Secular) group led by H.D. Kumaraswamy on Thursday appealed to Legislative Assembly Speaker Krishna to recognise it as the official party group in the House. In a letter to Mr. Krishna, Janata Dal (S) State unit President N. Thippanna, who has rallied behind Mr. Kumaraswamy, has said the JD(S) Legislature Party on Wednesday elected a new leader (Mr. Kumaraswamy) in place of Deputy Chief Minister M. P. Prakash. The latter was replaced following a demand for a change, Mr. Thippanna said.

(5592) Panaji : A resolution was passed at the three-day national council meeting of the Communist Party of India (CPI) here on Thursday criticising the UPA Government for failing to make any significant attempt to break away with the past to reverse the previous Government's economic policies.

(5593) Alappuzha : CPI general secretary A.B. Bardhan's statement that there was differences of opinion in the CPI(M) regarding the entry of DIC(K) into the LDF was uncalled for and not expected from a leader of his stature, said CPI(M) State secretary Pinarayi Vijayan on Thursday.

(5594) Kozhikode : Bharatiya Janata Party (BJP) State president P.S. Sreedharan Pillai has said that there are no areas of conflicts between his party and the Rashtriya Swayamsevak Sangh (RSS) in the State.

(5595) Thiruvananthapuram : Leader of the Opposition V. S. Achuthanandan has sought action against five teachers of the Architecture Department of the TKM College of Engineering in Kollam "for victimising students."

(5596) Kochi : Youth Congress State president K.P. Anilkumar has asked the bishops and the leaders of caste-based organisations to keep off politics and Government.

(5597) Thrissur : Janata Dal (Secular) Parliamentary Party leader and Kerala unit president M.P. Veerendrakumar has condemned the decision of a rebel faction led by H.D. Kumaraswamy to form a Ministry in Karnataka with the support of the Bharatiya Janata Party (BJP).

(5598) Miryalaguda (Nalgonda) : The people of West Bengal will not tolerate any attempt to postpone the Assembly elections or "any conspiracy" to impose President's rule in the State, Brinda Karat, CPI(M) Polit Bureau member, said on Thursday.

(5599) New Delhi : National Democratic Alliance convenor George Fernandes has written to United Progressive Alliance Chairperson Sonia Gandhi asking her to prevail upon Italian businessman Ottavio Quattrocchi "to face trial" in the Bofors case in India and "get himself exonerated if he is innocent."

(5600) New Delhi : As the countdown begins for the show of strength in the Karnataka Assembly on January 27, the Congress central leadership has made it clear that it is for the coalition partner in the State, the Janata Dal (Secular), to set its house in order and keep its flock together.

(5601) New Delhi : The Polit Bureau of the Communist Party of India (Marxist) on Thursday demanded that the Government immediately make public the proposals submitted to the United States on separation of civilian and military nuclear facilities.

(5602) New Delhi : The Communist Party of India (Marxist) and the All-India Forward Bloc on Thursday came down on the move by Janata Dal (Secular) rebels in Karnataka to join hands with the Bharatiya Janata Party for forming an alternative Government.

(5603) New Delhi : Union Minister and Lok Janshakti Party (LJP) chief Ram Vilas Paswan on Thursday said his party would launch an agitation if there were no job reservations for Dalit Muslims and Christians in the public and private sectors.

(5604) New Delhi : With Chief Minister Sheila Dikshit deciding to stay away from the executive committee meeting of the Delhi Pradesh Congress Committee, the intra-party struggle is likely to reach the doorstep of the party high command. The meeting deliberated on the issue of demolitions and what could be done to get the matter resolved amicably. It also decided to approach the High Court on behalf of the party during the next hearing.

(5605) Chennai : Chief Minister Jayalalithaa is targeting the PMK because she has not been able to wean away the party from the Democratic Progressive Alliance, PMK founder S.Ramadoss said on Thursday.

(5606) Chennai : Chief Minister Jayalalithaa on Thursday said that defamation proceedings would be initiated against Dravida Munnetra Kazhagam (DMK) president M.Karunanidhi on her and the State Government's behalf, for making remarks to "tarnish" her image and that of persons close to her.

(5607) Salem : A verbal confrontation between Congress and PMK cadres, at a public meeting on Wednesday, has resulted in sharp differences within the Democratic Progressive Alliance (DPA) here.

21-01-2006

(5608) Hyderabad : The State Congress leadership heaved a sigh of relief on Friday after the Madiga Reservation Porata Samiti (MRPS) and the Mala Mahanadu called off their proposed protests on Saturday coinciding with the commencement of the Congress plenary.Representatives of the two groups, which met Chief Minister Y.S. Rajasekhara Reddy separately, expressed satisfaction over the positive response from Dr. Reddy and announced that they were calling off their protests.

(5609) Hyderabad : Expelled BJP leader Uma Bharti has said that the backward Telangana region will witness all-round development only when a separate State was carved out of Andhra Pradesh.

(5610) Chennai : A contingent of 68 BJP MLAs from Karnataka was flown in here on Friday just before 10 p.m. and taken to hotels in the city. K.S. Eswarappa, one of them, told The Hindu on arrival at the airport that they would stay here to await the day of the vote of confidence in the Karnataka Assembly. If Chief Minister Dharam Singh resigns on his own, they would return earlier. Asked why they had chosen to leave Bangalore and come here, Mr. Eswarappa said: "Simply... they are disturbing the MLAs." Asked who was causing disturbance, he replied: "Congress." The decision to come to Chennai was taken in the afternoon. He added: "We are together. We will win."

(5611) Bangalore : Chief Minister N. Dharam Singh, who has been given time to prove his Government's majority in the Legislative Assembly till January 27, has offered to resign if the All India Congress Committee President asks him to.Speaking to presspersons here on Friday, Mr. Dharam Singh said that he is "tired of the latest political developments and running the coalition Government."

(5612) Bangalore : A third consecutive day of political commotion in Karnataka on Friday found the H.D. Kumaraswamy group of the Janata Dal (S) and the Bharatiya Janata Party spiriting away their MLAs to havens outside the State to prevent any poaching during the run-up to the scheduled voting in the Assembly by January 27. A large group of the BJP legislators reached Chennai by a chartered flight a little after 10 p.m. The day also witnessed feverish attempts by the H.D. Deve Gowda group and members of the family of the former Prime Minister to persuade Mr. Kumaraswamy to retrace his steps and terminate his alliance-in-the-making with the BJP. But on Friday it seemed that Mr. Kumaraswamy retracing his steps was a highly unlikely prospect.

(5613) Pathanamthitta : Communist Party of India-Marxist (CPI-M) State secretary Pinarayi Vijayan has alleged that the United Democratic Front Government has been consciously delaying the action-taken report (ATR) on the Narendran Commission recommendations.

(5614) New Delhi : The former Prime Minister, Atal Bihari Vajpayee, said on Friday that the Bharatiya Janata Party was making a "new beginning." "The weather has changed ... ice is melting in the mountains ... the sun has changed direction and we have decided to make a new beginning," he said, congratulating Rajnath Singh for his new "challenging" assignment as party president. Speaking at the conclusion of the BJP's one-day National Council session here, he used metaphors to drive home the point that "change (`parivartan')" was the new flavour, and this "change" would be "beneficial to the party."

(5615) New Delhi : The CPI (M) has condemned what it called the renewed 'repression' by the King's regime in Nepal.

(5616) New Delhi : The Bharatiya Janata Party-led National Democratic Alliance (NDA) on Friday sought President A.P.J. Abdul Kalam's intervention to ensure that Law Minister H.R. Bhardwaj resigns over the Quattrocchi issue.

(5617) New Delhi : The National Council of the Bharatiya Janata Party on Friday endorsed a suggestion that the highest decision making body of the party, the parliamentary board, be expanded to take in 11 members by amending the party constitution. Since the party was founded in 1980, the board has comprised the party president and eight members. Now the party president, who chairs the board, will be able to appoint 10 members.

(5618) New Delhi : Bharatiya Janata Party president Rajnath Singh indicated here on Friday that he wanted the party to return to its Hindutva roots. He said he wanted to lead a party that followed the principle of "integral humanism" expounded by Deen Dayal Upadhyaya, that did not forget the sacrifice of Shyama Prasad Mukherjee and that drew its inspiration from "Guruji" M.S. Golwalkar.

(5619) New Delhi : Describing the resignations of the four Congress MLAs from the Public Accounts Committee of the Delhi Assembly as a "political drama", the Bharatiya Janata Party MLA from Saket, Vijay Jolly, on Friday said it was a frustrated attempt by some of the members of Chief Minister Sheila Dikshit's group "to cover up corruption that took place during privatisation of the power sector in the Capital during 2002".

(5620) New Delhi : Stating that he respected the Delhi High Court's directive to the Municipal Corporation of Delhi to demolish illegal constructions by politicians and other high-profile personalities, Delhi Pradesh Congress Committee president Ram Babu Sharma on Friday said there should be no discrimination between the high and mighty and the poor and demanded that demolition action should also be taken immediately against influential unauthorised colonies like Sainik Farms and Anant Ram Dairy.

(5621) Dehra Dun : The Uttarakhand Kranti Dal's call for a "Dehra Dun bandh" on Friday evoked a partial response. The police detained about 20 Dal workers as they tried to forcibly close the main branch of the State Bank of India. No other major incident was reported. Educational institutions remained closed as a precautionary measure.

(5622) Chennai : The main Opposition parties in the Assembly, Dravida Munnetra Kazhagam (DMK), Congress and Pattali Makkal Katchi (PMK), on Friday accused the Government of inaction on many promises it had made over the years. The PMK staged a walkout protesting the 'Speaker's refusal to allow its leader to conclude" his speech.

(5623) Chennai : The Opposition leaders on Friday dubbed the budget as "repetitive" and said it had "nothing new" for the people. The Dravida Munnetra Kazhagam principal secretary, Durai Murugan, described it as an eyewash.The Congress leader, S.R. Balasubramoniyan, said there were no provisions in the budget for the various announcements made by the Chief Minister, Jayalalithaa.

(5624) Chennai: The State Government's decision to lift the ban on recruitment in government departments is a personal victory for the Pattali Makkal Katchi, claimed its founder-leader S. Ramadoss here on Thursday.

22-01-2006

(5625) Hyderabad : The details of the debate inside the extended Congress Working Committee were not revealed but it led Congressmen and the media to speculate that it centred around coalition politics and Rahul Gandhi. The more tight-lipped the AICC general secretary, Ambika Soni, remained when these issues were raised, the more permutations and combinations the media tried in phrasing questions.

(5626) Hyderabad : Over two dozen BJP leaders and members including office-bearers of the legal cell, Ramchander Rao and Anthony Reddy, were picked up by police outside the State party office here on Saturday as they were about to stage a protest against de-freezing assets of arms dealer Quattrocchi's.

(5627) Hyderabad : The first thing that UPA chairperson Sonia Gandhi did after flying into the State capital for the 82nd AICC plenary was to unveil a pylon installed at Nanal Nagar crossroads in memory of freedom fighters, as Prime Minister Manmohan Singh watched.

(5628) Hyderabad : UPA chairperson Sonia Gandhi on Saturday inaugurated a photo exhibition depicting the history of the over 100-year-old Congress party at the imposing Gachibowli stadium, the venue of the 82nd AICC plenary.

(5629) Visakhapatnam : The Telugu Desam Party is the first to announce its candidate for the byelection to the Visakha-I Assembly constituency by fielding former MLA S.A. Rehaman, while the Congress is yet to decide the nomination of City Congress Committee chief Dronamraju Srinivasa Rao.The Bharatiya Janata Party, a former ally of TDP, announced it was in the fray but yet to decide on its candidate.

(5630) Warangal : If political leaders launched a united fight, separate Telangana could be achieved in no time, said the expelled BJP leader Uma Bharti. Addressing a meeting organised by the Telangana Kranthi Sena floated by another expelled BJP leader N. Venugopal Reddy here on Saturday, Ms Bharti wondered why Telangana was not formed even after five decades of struggle.

(5631) Hyderabad : The Congress Working Committee on Saturday witnessed a sharp debate on the country's foreign policy, even as it did discuss the political and economic resolutions. On the eve of the All-India Congress Committee's 82nd Plenary here, the CWC at its extended meeting discussed four resolutions - political, economic, international and agriculture and rural development. The meeting was attended by all the CWC members, including Prime Minister Manmohan Singh, Congress president Sonia Gandhi, special invitees, permanent invitees and CLP/PCC chiefs. Prominent among those who were not present were Uttaranchal Chief Minister N.D. Tiwari, Himachal Pradesh Chief Minister Veerbhadra Singh and Karnataka Chief Minister Dharam Singh With the Congress firmly in the saddle heading the coalition arrangement at the Centre, the thrust of the political resolution was to determine a path to expand the party's base.On the economic resolution, the party expressed its determination to push ahead with the reforms while ensuring that the vulnerable sections were not affected.

(5632) Bangalore : Chief Minister N. Dharam Singh on Saturday said that he is against the Jammu and Kashmir model of sharing power with the Janata Dal (Secular) to resolve the political impasse in the State.

(5633) Bangalore : The political imbroglio in Karnataka continued for the fourth day on Saturday with no sign of a resolution, although there were clear signs of much behind-the-scenes activity. The Janata Dal(Secular) group and the Bharatiya Janata Party seemed to be trying to pile pressure on Chief Minister Dharam Singh to quit ahead of the trial of strength on the floor of the legislature on January 27.

(5634) Bangalore : Leader of the Opposition in the Legislative Assembly B.S. Yediyurappa on Saturday asked Chief Minister N. Dharam Singh to resign immediately and allow the Bharatiya Janata Party and the Janata Dal (S) to form a coalition government headed by H.D. Kumarawamy, Working President of the State unit of the JD(S).

(5635) Bangalore : KPCC President M. Mallikarjun Kharge has barred partymen from issuing statements to the press on the political situation in the State.

(5636) Gulbarga : Members of the Communist Party of India (Marxist) on Saturday staged a demonstration here and burnt an effigy of the Bharatiya Janata Party (BJP) protesting against what they called a "blatant attempt of the BJP to break the Janata Dal (Secular)" in an bid to form the Government in the State with the help of the breakaway Janata Dal (S) legislators.

(5637) Kollam : Communist Party of India (Marxist) State secretary Pinarayi Vijayan has urged the State Government to come out with a White Paper on the State's financial position.

(5638) Pathanamthitta : Communist Party of India (Marxist) State secretary Pinarayi Vijayan has alleged that the Congress-led United Democratic Front (UDF) is strengthening its "unholy ties" with the Sangh Parivar and the BJP, foreseeing another pathetic defeat in the forthcoming Assembly elections to the State Assembly.

(5639) Panaji : Forty-seven Karnataka MLAs under the leadership of Janata Dal (S) rebel leader Kumaraswamy and JD (S) Karnataka president N. Thipanna arrived in Goa on Saturday afternoon for a three-day sojourn ahead of the crucial voting in the Assembly scheduled for January 27.

(5640) Srinagar : Amid police claims that the recently arrested municipal councillor from Zakura was involved in a conspiracy to assassinate former Chief Minister Mufti Mohammad Sayeed, his daughter and People's Democratic Party (PDP) president Mehbooba Mufti is in controversy over the issue.Councillor Abdul Waheed Dar was arrested by Srinagar police along with three others and all of them allegedly confessed involvement. However, before the arrest Abdul Waheed Dar had reportedly gone to Delhi and met Ms. Mufti. A media report said he was 'given shelter' in her Delhi house. Ms. Mufti refuted the charge and said "the report is just a figment of the imagination." "This is rubbish. He never stayed in my house but certainly met me on January 10 and told me that the police were looking for him," Ms. Mufti told The Hindu here. "I spoke to the SSP Srinagar and sought details and soon asked him to leave."

(5641) Hyderabad : Assamese will have to choose between the performance of the Congress Government and the non-performance of the erstwhile Asom Gana Parishad regime in the Assembly elections later this year, Chief Minister Tarun Gogoi said on Saturday. He brushed aside the suggestion that the anti-incumbency factor might work against the Congress. "It is bound to be there, no doubt. But people still have to make a choice between the beneficial rule of ours and the misrule of the AGP." There was no sense of insecurity among the people and investments were on the rise, he told The Hindu .

(5642) Hyderabad : KeralaChief Minister Oommen Chandy on Saturday said the presence of the nascent Democratic Indira Congress (Karunakaran) would not undermine the prospects of the Congress in the coming Assembly elections.

(5643) Hyderabad : Jumping on the bandwagon of those seeking the induction of Rahul Gandhi into the Congress Working Committee, a group of young MPs wants him to take a "broader responsibility" in national politics. The parliamentarians, here to attend the AICC plenary, say it is time for the charismatic MP to play a decisive role in party affairs rather than confining himself to Amethi or Rae Bareili. "Given his charisma, ability, ideas and vision, every young person across the country is eagerly waiting for him to play a major role in national politics," said Jyotiraditya Scindia, Guna MP. "It is not just our voice, it is a chorus," he told The Hindu.

(5644) New Delhi : The Leader of the Opposition in the Standing Committee of the Municipal Corporation of Delhi, Vijender Kumar Gupta, has alleged that Chief Minister Sheila Dikshit is openly misusing her political power in matters of promotion, demotion and punishment for high-ranking officials.

(5645) Chennai : The Chief Minister's announcements in the Assembly on Friday have drawn a mixed response from the Pattali Makkal Katchi and Dravidar Kazhagam. While the PMK has said that the announcements have been made with an eye on the coming Assembly elections, the DK has argued that when the proposed measures will eventually benefit the people, is it not appropriate for unbiased persons to welcome them.

23-01-2006

(5646) Hyderabad : Former Chhattisgarh Chief Minister Ajit Jogi has cautioned the Congress high- command over the growing influence of the

Rashtriya Swayamsevak Sangh (RSS) in the tribal areas of Central India and underlined the need to check it.

(5647) Hyderabad : APCC president K. Keshava Rao on Sunday welcomed the delegates at the 82nd AICC plenary, saying that the message from the meeting should not only to set a direction but an agenda for the nation.

(5648) Hyderabad : The presence of Congress MP from Amethi Rahul Gandhi on the second day of the 82nd AICC plenary here on Sunday sent thousands of assembled Congressmen into raptures. The discussion on draft resolution was overshadowed by the demand for greater responsibility for Mr. Rahul Gandhi. The meeting was held up for a brief period twice as the delegates were pitching strongly for his elevation in the party hierarchy. The 34-year-old leader was the star attraction and his presence had an electrifying affect on the gathering at the plenary.

(5649) Hyderabad : In a virtual rebuff to the Telangana Rashtra Samithi's demand that the UPA Government announce its stand on Telangana within two months, the chairman of the UPA sub-committee on Telangana, Pranab Mukherjee, said that he was not bound by such deadlines. "I told them it is not simple. This is not a new issue and the matter has been hanging fire since 1956. I don't think an issue which has been pending for half-a-century will be solved immediately," he said.

(5650) Hyderabad : Taking time off from the deliberations at the Congress' 82nd plenary session on Sunday, the high command heard the views of senior party leaders from Karnataka, where its coalition Government is facing a threat. A majority of them said they preferred the present arrangement to continue and wanted to prevent the BJP from assuming power. However, a section of the leaders felt that the State should go in for fresh elections. Party sources said a high power committee that included Pranab Mukherjee, A.K. Antony and Ahmed Patel heard the views.

(5651) Hyderabad : The Congress said on Sunday that while it remained committed to the politics of coalition it was also determined to increase its strength to seek a return to power on its own at the Centre.This was the message it sought to send as it began deliberations at the 82nd plenary session of the All-India Congress Committee at Gachibowli, renamed as Rajiv Gandhi Nagar for the occasion here.Even as the party began serious debate on the four resolutions placed before the assembly, there were persistent demands from vociferous party members and a few senior leaders for a "greater organisational role for Amethi MP, Rahul Gandhi.'' Mr. Gandhi himself had to intervene twice to keep the deliberations on track and not to be sidetracked by personal loyalties. The Hyderabad plenary is the first such exercise after the Congress returned to power at the Centre via the coalition route. It saw a measured response from the party to contemporary issues and an attempt to fine-tune some policies, which have been under attack from the Left parties.In her brief remarks, Congress president Sonia Gandhi touched upon the various resolutions taken up for deliberations and preferred to hear the views of the participants. She said the sentiments expressed by the participants would be taken note of by Prime Minister Manmohan Singh and his colleagues in the Government.

(5652) Gulbarga : The All-India Progressive Janata Dal (AIPJD) on Sunday threatened to abstain from voting in the Assembly to decide the fate of the coalition Government headed by N. Dharam Singh, and said that unless former Deputy Chief Minister Siddaramaiah and two others who were dropped from the Ministry were taken back into it, the party would not support the motion of the Government.

(5653) Panaji : The Nationalist Congress Party (NCP) leadership has decided to act tough against its Minister Micky Pacheco for his public outburst against Chief Minister Pratapsinh Rane.Explaining the background of a show-cause notice issued to Mr. Pacheco on Friday by party general secretary Surendra Furtado, Deputy Chief Minister and party's Goa unit president Wilfred de Souza said on Saturday that the party high command has decided that Mr. Pacheco's outbursts against the Chief Minister should stop before they cause serious damage to the coalition. The Congress can continue to rule even if NCP snaps its ties in the State.

(5654) Thiruvananthapuram : State secretary of the Revolutionary Socialist Party (RSP) T. J. Chandrachoodan has asked Chief Minister Oommen Chandy what he had achieved by rushing in the anti-goonda law through an ordinance.

(5655) Hyderabad : The AICC plenary has suggested a comprehensive re-examination of the agricultural strategy to overcome problems plaguing the compounded agricultural economy growth. A draft resolution on

"Agriculture, employment & poverty alleviation through panchayati raj" stated that the Government should opt for beneficial intervention in favour of farmers, farm labour and the rural poor in general through participatory development and self-governance. Public investment in agriculture, irrigation and rural infrastructure should be enhanced to reflect the State's role. The action plan suggested by the plenary covers land reforms, including computerisation of records at the village level, guaranteed maintenance, inspection and updating of land records and complete elimination of any residual traces of the zamindari system. The plenary sought full implementation of legislation relating to wages and social security for agri-labour from State funding.

(5656) Hyderabad : The All India Congress Committee on Sunday agreed to pursue a twin-pronged political strategy for the party to come to power on its own while retaining the current approach on coalition politicsThis was the thrust of the political resolution adopted by the party after three hours of debate here. The party ruled out any compromise or understanding with the Left parties in West Bengal, Kerala and Tripura and promised to "confront and fight" the four parties supporting the United Progressive Alliance from outside. The resolution, however, did not say how the party would respond in the States where its allies are dominant. The closest it came was a formulation, suggesting that even in a coalition, political parties do not have to give up the expectation or aspiration of securing a larger political space.

(5657) Siliguri : Gorkha National Liberation Front (GNLF) has banned the worship of Saraswati idols in the Darjeeling hills during Vasant panchami next month, a step aimed at "preserving its tribal character".This follows the diktat of the GNLF supremo and administrator of the caretaker Darjeeling Gorkha Hill Council, Subash Ghising, who had disallowed worship of Viswakarma and Durga idols to strengthen his demand for recognition of the council under the sixth schedule of the Constitution.

(5658) Guwahati : Senior Bharatiya Janata Party (BJP) leader Sushma Swaraj on Sunday sought to link Congress president Sonia Gandhi's Italian origin to defreezing of Ottavio Quattrocchi's bank accounts.She alleged that it was Ms. Gandhi who had a link with Mr. Quattrocchi and there was no point blaming others as neither Prime Minister Manmohan Singh nor Law Minister Hansraj Bharadwaj nor the CBI had any relation with the

Italian businessman, Ms. Swaraj said while addressing an women's rally organised by the women's wing of her party in Assam.

(5659) Jaipur : The nomination of senior leader and former Minister Ramnarain Choudhary as the new leader of the Congress Legislature Party (CLP) by party president Sonia Gandhi is being looked upon here as a well thought out strategy to woo the Jats back to the party. The nomination, announced well in time before the ongoing Hyderabad convention of the Congress, has been welcomed by most the senior partymen.

(5660) Chennai : Speakers including DMK president M. Karunanidhi and Union Minister for Communications and Information Technology Dayanidhi Maran paid glowing tributes to film personality, the late A.V. Meiyappan, for his great contributions to the world of cinema. Mr.Karunanidhi released a commemorative postage stamp on the late Meiyappan, while film producer and Meiyappan's son M. Saravanan received the first album.

(5661) Tiruchi : Ruling out the possibility of a third front in the State, Communist Party of India leader R. Nallakannu on Sunday said the Dravida Munnetra Kazhagam (DMK) - led Democratic Progressive Alliance in Tamil Nadu was intact.

24-01-2006

(5662) Hyderabad : The Bharatiya Janata Party(BJP) has declared that it did not recognise the UPA sub-committee on Telangana, headed by Defence Minister Pranabh Mukherjee, and demanded that the Centre convene an all-party meeting to discuss the issue.Referring to Mr. Mukherjee's statement that BJP's opinion was yet to be received by the sub-committee at a press conference here on Monday, BJP State president N. Indrasena Reddy and vice-president S.V. Seshagiri Rao categorically stated that the party would not reply to it.

(5663) Hyderabad : Rahul Gandhi seemed to have bowled over the young and alike with his "inspiring speech, straight from the heart." A majority of the delegates, young MPs in particular, appeared to have received his message well - recognise the importance of hard work and reach out to the grassroots to strengthen the party. Mr. Rahul Gandhi, Amethi MP, was the third speaker on the political resolution. Restless delegates wanted him to speak earlier but AICC president Sonia Gandhi sent a message that his turn would come after the resolution was supported by Home Minister Shivraj Patil and seconded by Jammu and Kashmir leader Saifuddin Soz. A roar went up when Mr. Rahul Gandhi walked towards the dais and began reading out his prepared speech. Although a bit disappointed over the uncertainty on their demand for his inclusion in the CWC, the MPs, however, said they drew strength from the `direction' he had given to build the party, especially in regions where it was weak.

(5664) Hyderabad : The Telugu Desam Party on Monday said that the plenary was held in the city to show to the delegates the immense development achieved in the State under the Chief Ministership of N. Chandrababu Naidu.

(5665) Hyderabad : Chief Minister Y.S. Rajasekhara Reddy told the 82nd AICC plenary on Monday that the initiatives taken by the Government had helped farmers substantially and in spite of a 25 per cent rainfall deficit the gross cropped areas and net area sown increased by two per cent.The State eventually recorded two per cent less food grain production, but it was more than adequately compensated by an increase of 100 per cent in maize and 40 per cent in oilseeds production. As a consequence the overall agricultural activity remained buoyant.

(5666) Khammam : CPI(M) State secretary B.V. Raghavulu said the Congress party, which leads the UPA, should first abide by the code of coalition. Addressing the plenum of the party Khammam district unit here on Monday, he took strong exception to the caution sounded by the Congress party to its coalition partners in a political resolution adopted at its plenary session, against crossing the limits of constructive criticism.

(5667) Bangalore : Janata Dal (Secular) leader H.D. Deve Gowda and his son H.D. Kumaraswamy met here on Monday after the son flew down from Goa. Justifying the action of his son over the past week that led to the political crisis in Karnataka , Mr. Gowda said he would place before Congress president Sonia Gandhi all the unsavoury happenings between the two coalition partners over the past 19 months. "Let us first discuss and a decision on continuing with the relationship or saying good-bye would be taken thereafter."

(5668) Bangalore : Already dubbed "Deputy Chief Minister-in-waiting," Bharatiya Janata Party leader B.S Yediyurappa remains unfazed by the fast-changing political drama witnessed in the State.Mr. Yediyurappa told The Hindu on Monday that he expects Chief Minister N. Dharam Singh to resign by Tuesday and the Janata Dal (Secular)-BJP coalition will be invited to form the government soon after. The 18 BJP Ministers and 16 Janata Dal (Secular) Ministers would be sworn in by January 28.

(5669) Mumbai : The former Shiv Sena leader, Raj Thackeray, on Monday met his uncle and party supremo Bal Thackeray to wish him on his 79th birthday. On December 18, Mr. Raj quit the Sena and announced his decision to float a new party. - PTI

(5670) Hyderabad : In spite of the "difficulties and unnecessary hurdles" created by its opponents, the United Progressive Alliance Government has made an enviable start, Prime Minister Manmohan Singh said on Monday. The important thing was to keep to this course."We need to be in power long enough to be able to make a visible impact," Dr. Singh said in his address on the final day of the 82nd plenary of the All-India Congress Committee here.Spelling out some of the tasks before the party and the Government, he said the country must be rid of chronic poverty and steps taken to ensure that farmers, workers, weavers, minorities and the weaker sections had a bright future. Striking an optimistic note, he said, "With hard work, determination, selflessness and commitment, we are on the verge of creating a new India."

(5671) New Delhi : With the coalition Government in Karnataka tottering, senior Janata Dal (Secular) leader Kunwar Danish Ali on Monday met General Secretary of the Communist Party of India (Marxist) Prakash Karat and reviewed the volatile political situation in the State. Both the leaders held discussions for over half an hour at the CPI (M) headquarters here within hours of a meeting between Janata Dal (S) President H.D. Deve Gowda and his rebel son H.D. Kumaraswamy and amid speculation of a patch-up between the two.

(5672) Thiruvananthapuram : CPI State secretary Veliyam Bhargavan has asked the Kerala Pradesh Congress Committee to come clean on the party's links with the BJP in Kerala in the light of the AICC resolution stating that there would be no such tie-up anywhere in the country.

(5673) Bangalore : In meeting H.D. Deve Gowda here on Monday, H.D. Kumaraswamy gave up his stand that he would not meet his father until January 27. The meeting was described as a "courtesy call" by Janata Dal (S) leaders, after members of the Deve Gowda family conveyed to Mr. Kumaraswamy on Sunday night news that Mr. Deve Gowda had had a setback in his health.

(5674) New Delhi : Samajwadi Party leader Amar Singh on Monday moved the Supreme Court seeking a judicial inquiry into the alleged tapping of his telephone by the Delhi police.

(5675) New Delhi : The Bharatiya Janata Party on Monday attacked the Congress for its "Mission Help Quattrocchi" and "display of hypocrisy, sycophancy and duplicity" at its plenary in Hyderabad. BJP spokesperson Prakash Javadekar said that instead of thinking about solutions to the country's problems, Congressmen were busy chanting "Rahul lao" (bring Rahul) slogan. This only showed that it could not exist outside the framework of the Nehru-Gandhi "dynasty."

(5676) Mumbai : Shiv Sena chief Bal Thackeray has forbidden his nephew, Raj Thackeray from displaying his [Bal Thackeray] portrait in public hoardings. "Do not put my pictures on your banners and confuse the Shiv Sena members," he said at a function held here on Monday to celebrate his 79th birthday.

(5677) Hyderabad : Congress president Sonia Gandhi on Monday asked the party to fight the Left parties as "opponents" in the coming Assembly elections in Kerala and West Bengal and saw no contradiction in taking on the parties supporting the United Progressive Alliance at the Centre.

(5678) Hyderabad : The three-day Congress plenary that concluded here on Monday called upon the United Progressive Alliance Government to make the minorities partners in progress by enhancing their opportunities for education and employment. There could be no development when a considerable portion of the population remained backward due to social, economical and political reasons, it said.

(5679) Srinagar : The People's Democratic Party (PDP) on Monday reportedly endorsed "self rule" as the viable solution to the Kashmir problem, but called for a national consensus, besides a free mind to discuss the options for resolution of the dispute. It also called upon militants to shun violence and present a peaceful agenda. The much-talked about proposal of demilitarisation has also found favour, but with a difference - greater role for Jammu and Kashmir Police in internal security. At a two-day special session of its central working committee, which began in Jammu on Monday,the party mentioned that ideas floated by different quarters to solve the Kashmir issue need to be examined in a resolution circulated to the Press. However, sources said "self- rule" as a viable solution to the problem was unanimously endorsed by the working committee. The former Chief Minister, Mufti Mohammad Sayeed, presided over the meeting, which was also attended by party rebel and former Minister Ghulam Hassan Mir.

(5680) Hyderabad : Amethi MP Rahul Gandhi is not convinced with the diagnosis that the emergence of parties, which practised caste or religion-based politics, eroded the Congress base in the north. "I am not in agreement. I think we are not successful in these areas because we have stopped working for the people, [we] could not match their aspirations," he said speaking at the AICC plenary here on Monday.

(5681) Patna : Union Steel Minister and LJP chief Ram Vilas Paswan on Monday demanded a CBI enquiry into the murder of his party leader and former MP Rajesh Kumar during the Bihar Assembly elections in February last year.Mr. Paswan charged that the name of senior JD (U) leader and Bihar Assembly Speaker, Udai Narain Chaudhary, figured in the police case diary and there was a need for an impartial enquiry into the murder to nail the guilty and do justice to the departed leader.

(5682) Shimla : The Himachal unit of the CPI (M) has questioned the procedure for selecting the panchayats under the Mid-Himalaya Watershed Project by the State Government. The Central Committee member and State party secretary, Rakesh Singha, said that some 545 panchayats from about 10 districts had been chosen at random for the watershed project without specifying any criteria.

(5683) Chennai : Tamil Nadu Congress Committee president G.K.Vasan on Monday met Andhra Pradesh Chief Minister Y.S.Rajasekara Reddy in Hyderabad and urged him to give up his Government's proposal to build a dam across the Palar near Kuppam.

(5684) Chennai : Dravida Munnetra Kazhagam president M. Karunanidhi on Monday welcomed the intention of the State Government to take over Cable TV network, and said that he had "complete faith" in the process of nationalisation of any activity as long as it was "not discriminatory."

(5685) Chennai : The Pattali Makkal Katchi on Monday asked the State Government why it did not apply the yardstick of public welfare with regard to private self-financing colleges and deemed universities. Referring to the Government's move to take over cable television network citing the principle, S. Ramadoss, party founder, contended that several colleges and deemed universities were "law unto themselves." They were collecting the fee exorbitantly. "Can it be said that no complaints have been received? Can it be argued that there is no public interest involved in this issue?" Dr. Ramadoss asked.

(5686) Chennai : DMK president M. Karunanidhi has said that he was confident that the official language review committee, included in the common minimum programme of the United Progressive Alliance Government at the Centre, would be set up soon and its first recommendation would be making Tamil as an official language.

(5687) Chennai : Marumalarchi Dravida Munnetra Kazhagam general secretary Vaiko has requested Prime Minister Manmohan Singh to modify the National Calamity and Contingency Relief Fund (NCCRF) and release the funds sought by the Tamil Nadu Government in the wake of the rains and floods in the State in 2005.

(5688) Madurai : The All India Forward Bloc has appealed to the Government to take steps to observe the birth anniversary of the supreme commander of the Indian National Army, Netaji Subhash Chandra Bose, as Nationalistic Day.The AIFB leaders and party workers paid tributes to Netaji on the occasion of the latter's 109th birth anniversary here on Monday.

(5689) Vellore: The Marumalarchi Dravida Munnetra Kazhagam will, for the first time, enter the Assembly under the leadership of its general secretary Vaiko in the forthcoming Assembly elections, according to MDMK presidium chairman and Member of Parliament L. Ganesan.

25-01-2006

(5690) Hyderabad : The Telugu Desam Party has asked the Congress party at the Centre to own up the moral responsibility for the Supreme

Court's indictment of Bihar Governor Buta Singh for dissolving the Assembly in an unconstitutional manner and take immediate remedial measures.

(5691) Hyderabad : The Bharatiya Janata Party State unit has said that the just-concluded plenary of the Congress and the recent Pravas Bharatiya Divas has served no purpose for the State. While the Government, which conducted the Pravas Bharatiya Divas amidst much hype, failed to secure any commitment for investments in the State, the plenary session turned out to be a flattery session aimed at promoting Rahul Gandhi, the BJP said.

(5692) Rajahmundry : Samajwadi Party MP and film Actress Jayaprada on Tuesday advocated major irrigation project Polavaram, which, she said, would give new life to lakhs of farmers along the river Godavari. Addressing a mammoth gathering from the dais of Godavari Utsav inauguration here tonight, she said she was supporting the project firmly and asked all political parties to extend cooperation in making the dream a reality.

(5693) New Delhi : The Bharatiya Janata Party-led National Democratic Alliance on Tuesday demanded resignations of Prime Minister Manmohan Singh and Bihar Governor Buta Singh following the Supreme Court's indictment of the United Progressive Alliance Government at the Centre for recommending dissolution of the Bihar Assembly in May last year. NDA Convenor and Janata Dal (United) president George Fernandes said not just Mr. Buta Singh but the Prime Minister, along with the Union Council of Ministers, should also resign.BJP leader L.K. Advani said the judgment had a "far-reaching and meaningful impact".

(5694) New Delhi : Efforts to find a solution to the Karnataka imbroglio continued here with Congress president Sonia Gandhi meeting Janata Dal (Secular) president H.D. Deve Gowda at her 10 Janpath residence on Tuesday evening. "Talks are inconclusive and there is a likelihood of another meeting," JD(S) spokesperson Danish Ali told correspondents after the meeting. In any case, the JD(S) would not allow communal forces to take over in Karnataka, he said. During the 30-minute meeting, the JD(S) president apprised Ms. Gandhi of the developments of the past few months. He said Mr. Gowda did not offer any new formula to resolve the crisis. Sources in the Congress said Mr. Gowda had emphasised the need to implement the Maharashtra model of power-sharing in toto.The Congress, however, does not appear to be enthusiastic about the Maharashra model.

(5695) Bangalore : Chief Minister N. Dharam Singh has reiterated that he will abide by the decision of the Congress high command with regard to the political crisis in the State.He told presspersons at his official residence "Anugraha" that he is awaiting the outcome of talks between Congress President Sonia Gandhi and her Janata Dal (Secular) counterpart H.D. Deve Gowda in New Delhi. "Politics is a waiting game... we have to wait," he said.

(5696) Patna : Bihar Chief Minister Nitish Kumar on Tuesday declined to comment on the Supreme Court order indicting Bihar Governor Buta Singh. He said it was against constitutional dignity. He, however, said the court order vindicated his stand that the dissolution of the State Assembly was illegal. I have received justice from the people on this count. They were the first to vindicate my stand." Railway Minister and Rashtriya Janata Dal chief Lalu Prasad said there was no need to react, as the apex court had delivered its verdict earlier. One should desist from commenting on its orders.Steel Minister and Lok Jan Shakti Party chief Ram Vilas Paswan said it was for the Centre to handle the technical aspect of the court order.There was little option other than dissolving the House though he was personally against it.

(5697) Murudeshwar (Karnataka) : Janata Dal (Secular) rebel leader H.D. Kumaraswamy asserted on Tuesday there was no going back on his decision to form an alternate government in Karnataka with the support of his followers and the Bharatiya Janata Party. Talking to newspersons here, he said he would not change his decision even if Congress president Sonia Gandhi offered him Chief Ministership as a patch-up measure to save the coalition Government in the State.

(5698) Bangalore : Sources close to H.D. Deve Gowda told The Hindu tonight that he had a cordial meeting with the Congress president. Earlier in the day, during discussions with Pranab Mukherjee, Ahmed Patel and A.K. Antony, he had stated that what precipitated the crisis was a recent attempt to divide the JD(S). It was obvious that Mr. Deve Gowda wanted certain corrective steps if the coalition arrangement were to continue. Earlier, Mr. Gowda called on Communist Party of India (Marxist) general secretary Prakash Karat at his home. Mr. Karat told correspondents that the JD(S) chief briefed him on his discussions with the Congress leaders. Asked whether the secular formation would continue in Karnataka, Mr. Karat said that would depend on both the coalition partners.

(5699) Bangalore : The former Minister M. Rajasekhara Murthy, who joined the Janata Dal (Secular) recently, has said that what the Bharatiya Janata Party-Janata Dal (S) combine in the State needs to do is to prevent the Congress from creating a situation that would lead to the dissolution of the Legislative Assembly.

(5700) Bangalore : The Rashtriya Swayamsevak Sangh (RSS) has "blessed" the Bharatiya Janata Party (BJP), which is on the verge of forming a coalition government with the Janata Dal (Secular) in the State. At a meeting with BJP leaders B.S. Yediyurappa, Jagadish Shettar and D.H. Shankaramurthy here on Tuesday, RSS leaders M.C. Jayadev and K. Narahari are stated to have told them to provide "good and clean administration."

(5701) Belgaum : It was the Janata Dal (Secular) faction led by H.D. Kumaraswamy that approached the BJP and not vice-versa, Lok Sabha MP from Belgaum Suresh C. Angadi has said. He was talking to presspersons here on Tuesday. The faction led by Mr. Kumaraswamy must have realised that BJP is a secular party.

(5702) Kollur (Udupi District) : Working President of the State unit of the Janata Dal (Secular) H.D. Kumaraswamy on Tuesday said that there is no change in the stand of the party MLAs with regard to forming a coalition government with the Bharatiya Janata Party. Addressing presspersons here, Mr. Kumaraswamy said that the results of the talks between the former Prime Minister H.D. Deve Gowda and the All India Congress Committee President Sonia Gandhi will make no difference in the prevailing situation. The Congress cannot be trusted. The Janata Dal (Secular) MLAs backing him will convince Deve Gowda about their stand, he said.

(5703) Kattakkada : CPI(M) State secretary Pinarayi Vijayan has said that the apathetic attitude of the State Government has spelt doom for more than 7 lakh families employed in the traditional sector in Kerala.

(5704) Jaipur : The Bharatiya Janata Party on Tuesday demanded the resignation of Prime Minister Manmohan Singh in the wake of Supreme

Court's adverse comments on the Bihar Assembly dissolution last year.Bihar Governor Buta Singh alone could not be made the fall guy as the Prime Minister and the Union Cabinet should also own up "the political, constitutional and moral responsibility of the act," BJP general secretary Arun Jaitley said here on Tuesday.

(5705) New Delhi : Two Left parties on Tuesday said Bihar Governor Buta Singh ought to go in the wake of the Supreme Court judgment indicting him in the State Assembly dissolution case. While the Communist Party of India (Marxist) said it would be appropriate for Mr. Singh to step down, the Communist Party of India urged the Government to recall him.

(5706) Chennai : Janata Party president Subramanian Swamy on Tuesday sought the resignation of Prime Minister Manmohan Singh and Bihar Governor Buta Singh following the Supreme Court judgment on the dissolution of the Bihar Assembly. "There is no democratic alternative to the Governor and the Prime Minister submitting their resignation," he said in a statement.

(5707) Mumbai : Three Shiv Sena legislators, who quit the party and the Maharashtra Assembly, romped home on Congress tickets in byelections, proving that their leader Revenue Minister Narayan Rane called the shots in the Konkan region.Mr. Rane reclaimed his Malvan seat last November. His feat was nearly repeated by his supporter Shanker Kambli in the neighbouring Vengurla seat when he defeated Shiv Sena's Ramesh Naik by a massive margin of 52,503 votes and made his rival lose his deposit. In Rajapur, Rane-supporter and now Congressman Ganpat Kadam reclaimed his seat by defeating the Shiv Sena's Rajan Salvi by 3,502 votes.

(5708) New Delhi : Delhi Pradesh Congress Committee president Ram Babu Sharma has once again got the better of Chief Minister Sheila Dikshit, bagging a major share of appointments cleared by the party high command for its districts and blocks here in the Capital. Not only have Ms. Dikshit's supporters been totally ignored, Mr. Sharma has also dropped 11 of the 12 districts presidents in the latest reshuffle.

(5709) Chandigarh : Activists of Chandigarh Vikas Manch (CVM) led by its president and former Union Minister Harmohan Dhawan on Tuesday burnt an effigy of the local Congress MP, Pawan Kumar Bansal, here and demanded his resignation on moral grounds for alleged "misuse" of MP Local Area Development Fund.

(5710) Chennai : The Pattali Makkal Katchi on Tuesday urged the State Government to adopt the bus rapid transit (BRT) system to solve Chennai's public and mass transportation problem. The BRT system, which ensures use of high quality and high capacity buses for public transport, was cheaper than the monorail system and more suited to Chennai," said PMK founder S.Ramadoss, while leading a demonstration near Memorial Hall here.

26-01-2006

(5711) Anantapur : Senior leader of the Communist Party of India and Nalgonda MP Suravaram Sudhakar Reddy has sought to avoid a confrontation between the executive and judiciary arising from issuance of notice to the Lok Sabha Speaker by the Supreme Court on the disqualification of 11 MPs in the case of cash for query scam.

(5712) Hyderabad : Bharatiya Janata Party has accused the Congress of having misused official machinery at the AICC plenary "which had not benefited the country or the State in any manner." At a press conference here on Wednesday, BJP floor leader in the Assembly G. Kishan Reddy alleged that crores of rupees had been spent by the Municipal, Transport, Revenue, Roads and Buildings departments. The demarcation between the party and the Government had been removed. He said that nothing had been achieved at the plenary except that Congressmen "displayed their sycophancy" towards party president Sonia Gandhi and Amethi MP Rahul Gandhi.

(5713) Karimnagar : Communist Party of India floor leader in the Assembly Chada Venkat Reddy has launched 'praja chaitanya yatra' from Alugunur village in the outskirts of Karimnagar town for the overall development of the district.

(5714) Nellore : Vice-President of Pradesh Congress Committee C.V. Sesha Reddy has dismissed the criticism of Opposition parties that the just concluded AICC plenary session at Hyderabad has given much importance to Rahul Gandhi. He maintained that the presence of Mr. Gandhi, was only in accordance with the aspirations of the youth.

(5715) Hyderabad : The Communist Party of India State council has ridiculed the Congress leaders for concentrating more on promoting "hereditary rule" during the party's 82nd plenary rather than taking up important social and economic issues facing the country.

(5716) Thiruvananthapuram : The Left parties would launch a major struggle against the UPA Government decision to allow foreign direct investment in the retail sector beginning with single brands, CPI(M) general secretary Prakash Karat said here on Wednesday. Inaugurating the valedictory rally of the 25-day 'Kerala March' led by party State secretary Pinarayi Vijayan here, Mr. Karat said the Left would strive to rally all political forces and small traders in the fight against the UPA Government's decision.

(5717) Bangalore : All-India Progressive Janata Dal leader A. K. Subbaiah has demanded an inquiry by the Central Bureau of Investigation into the "sanctity and accountability" of the huge expenditure being incurred by legislators of the Bharatiya Janata Party and the Janata Dal (Secular) on trips to other States.

(5718) Bangalore : Though the working president of the State unit of the Janata Dal (S), H.D. Kumaraswamy, has reiterated that he would "convince his father", and persuade him to bless the new coalition in the making, State BJP president Jagadish Shettar and deputy chief minister-designate B.S. Yediyurappa, party leader in the Upper House D.H. Shankaramurthy and others are prepared to step in and do their bit by talking to Mr. Deve Gowda, if the need arises, party sources said. Meanwhile, there are indications that Deputy Chief Minister M.P. Prakash and three other Janata Dal (S) Ministers, excluding P.G.R. Sindhia are toying with the idea of swimming with the tide, and may agree to join the Kumaraswamy faction.

(5719) Kollur (Udupi district) : Working President of the Janata Dal (Secular) State unit H.D. Kumaraswamy said on Wednesday that there is no chance of a rapprochement between his party and the Congress. Addressing presspersons after participating in "Chandika Yaga" at Sri Mookambika Temple here, he said the Janata Dal (S) is not after power, and it only wanted respect from its coalition partner. Since the Congress degraded Janata Dal (S) MLAs, they opted to break up the coalition. The

Congress has not done justice to Janata Dal (S) workers, and "there is no question of going back," he added.

(5720) Bangalore : Former Deputy Chief Minister and All-India Progressive Janata Dal leader Siddaramaiah met leaders of Left parties and the Nationalist Congress Party (NCP) and told them that Janata Dal (Secular) president H.D. Deve Gowda was behind the political turmoil in Karnataka. Speaking to The Hindu from New Delhi, Mr. Siddaramaiah said Mr. Deve Gowda had exposed himself as an unreliable coalition partner and his commitment to secularism was under a cloud. Everyone in the State knew about "the drama." With the withdrawal of support to the coalition government, the Left parties had no sympathy for Mr. Deve Gowda or his son, H.D. Kumaraswamy, he said.

(5721) Thiruvananthapuram : The Indian Union Muslim League on Wednesday maintained that the provisions relating to direct recruitment of backward class applicants, proposed in the fulfilment of the implementation of the Narendran Commission's recommendations, was in effect special recruitment that various Muslim organisations had demanded. Addressing a press conference, IUML general secretary P. K. Kunhalikutty, Education Minister E. T. Mohammed Basheer, Public Works Minister M. K. Muneer, Industry Minister E. K. Ebrahimkunju and leaders of the Youth League and the Muslim Students' Federation, said the decision to amend the Kerala Service and Subordinate Service Rules was a landmark decision. Asked whether the IUML had backtracked on the issue of clearing the backlog in backward class representation, Mr. Kunhalikutty said the new amendments would address the issue of backlog in the long term. The question of clearing the backlog in representation should be viewed in its entirety in relation to its impracticability. Besides, clearing backlog in representation would be only a one-time solution.

(5722) Thiruvananthapuram : General secretary of the CPI(M) Prakash Karat has said that his party will confidently take up the challenge thrown at it by the All India Congress Committee (AICC) plenary session and party president Sonia Gandhi for a no-holds-barred fight in Kerala, West Bengal and Tripura in the upcoming Assembly elections.

(5723) New Delhi : Veteran CPI (M) leader Harkishan Singh Surjeet on Wednesday said Bihar Governor Buta Singh should step down following the Supreme Court judgment on dissolution of the Bihar Assembly.

(5724) Chennai : Janata Party president Subramanian Swamy on Wednesday welcomed the possibility of a Janata Dal (Secular)-Bharatiya Janata Party coalition government headed by H.D. Kumaraswamy as a "healthy development for democracy in the country."

(5725) Jaipur : The Rashtriya Swayamsevak Sangh has asked the Governments in the Bharatiya Janata Party-ruled States to address the Sangh concerns on image and ideology. There was a need for better coordination among the party, the Sangh and the Governments as well as increased involvement of the people in governance, leaders of the Sangh who participated in a joint Chintan baitak (introspection camp) of the BJP and the RSS which ended here on Wednesday, observed. The two-day brain storming session, held at an ethnic five star resort some 25 kms away from the Rajasthan Capital, and marked by the presence of the RSS chief K.S.Sudershan and the BJP president Rajnath Singh, besides senior leaders and functionaries, remained an internal matter of the Sangh Parivar without any formal interaction with the media.

(5726) Chennai : In the wake of the Supreme Court judgment in the Bihar Assembly dissolution case, Governor Buta Singh must resign, Marumalarchi Dravida Munnetra Kazhagam leader Vaiko said here on Wednesday.

(5727) Chennai : Chief Minister Jayalalithaa has no locus standi to criticise the Congress on corruption when she is facing "corruption cases" in Bangalore, Tamil Nadu Congress Committee president G.K.Vasan said on Wednesday.

(5728) Chennai : Pointing to the near three-fold growth of revenues between 1996-97 and the last financial year, the Dravida Munnetra Kazhagam deputy leader in the Assembly, Durai Murugan, faulted the Government for constantly charging the previous government for all current shortcomings.

(5729) Chennai : Senior Congress leader M. Veerappa Moily on Wednesday said the party would not hesitate to take action against those indulging in "anti-party" activities.Party leaders and workers might have grievances. But they should discuss them in the party forum and not in public. If anybody crossed the "Lakshman reka" it would not be tolerated, Mr. Moily, Congress Working Committee member in-charge of Tamil Nadu, told presspersons here.

(5730) Chennai : The Marumalarchi Dravida Munnetra Kazhagam is at the service of everyone, party general secretary Vaiko said on Wednesday night. Addressing a public meeting at T. Nagar, here, to mark the anti-Hindi agitation, he referred to his speech at the first anniversary of the blood donors' network recently, and reiterated that the MDMK was like O+ve, the universal donor group. "It can affiliate with anybody, just as O+ve can be administered to anyone who badly needs blood," he said.

27-01-2006

(5731) New Delhi : Congress Lok Sabha member from Chandigarh, Pawan Kumar Bansal, has resigned as Chairman of the Special Committee of the House set up to probe the allegations of misuse of Member of Parliament's Local Area Development (MPLAD) funds. The resignation came a day after allegations were levelled against him by a private news channel that he himself had spent a part of his MPLAD fund on the Chandigarh Golf Club.Mr. Bansal headed the Lok Sabha Committee that recommended the expulsion of 10 MPs for their involvement in the cash-for-query scam.

(5732) Thiruvananthapuram : The Opposition Left Democratic Front (LDF) has described the Government decisions relating to the Narendran Commission report insincere and meant only to hoodwink the backward communities. Briefing reporters about the deliberations at the LDF State committee meeting here on Thursday, Front convener Paloli Mohammed Kutty said the Cabinet decisions were nothing other than an 'election stunt.' There was no clear estimate of the actual number of posts that the backward communities had lost. In the absence of such figures, it was difficult to see how the backward communities would be compensated, he pointed out.

(5733) Bangalore : Chief Minister N. Dharam Singh continued to remain unruffled on Thursday and is depending on the Janata Dal (Secular) leader H.D. Deve Gowda to stand by him and save the day in the trial of strength in the Legislative Assembly on Friday. Mr. Dharam Singh, who participated in the Republic Day celebrations at the Field Marshal Manekshaw Parade Ground here, told presspersons that "the crisis will blow over and the uncertainty will clear tomorrow."

(5734) Bangalore : The conscience vote of the Janata Dal (Secular) MLAs to be cast on Friday will decide the fate of the Dharam Singh

Government on the floor of the Vidhana Soudha. The party has not issued a whip to its members in the Assembly.Mr. Kumaraswamy told The Hindu that there was no question of any change in the MLAs' stand, irrespective of the "attempts" by the Congress to continue with the present arrangement. "All the legislators in our group are now anti-Congress and totally committed to forming a government with the BJP. We will stand by our commitment given to the BJP. I am confident." Interestingly, all the senior Ministers of the JD (S), including Deputy Chief Minister M.P. Prakash were kept out of the discussions which Mr. Deve Gowda held with Mr. Kumaraswamy and the legislators.A. K. Antony, AICC general secretary in charge of the party affairs in the State, who rushed to the city described the situation as "50:50 touch and go for the Congress."

(5735) Chennai : Marumalarchi Dravida Munnetra Kazhagam general secretary Vaiko called on the Dravida Munnetra Kazhagam president M.Karunanidhi at his residence this morning here in the backdrop of reports of fissures in the Democratic Progressive AllianceMr.Vaiko's comparison of his party to an 'O' positive donor forced the head of the seven- party DPA, Mr.Karunanidhi, to seek a clarification from the MDMK leader. "I asked him about it," Mr.Karunanidhi told The Hindu , when he was asked about the meeting. Mr.Vaiko explained that he has been using the universal donor analogy for "at least two-three years," Mr.Karunanidhi said.

(5736) Bangalore : Bharatiya Janata Party (BJP) legislators, who were moved out of Bangalore last week, returned to Attibele on the city's outskirts on Thursday. The legislators, who arrived at a hotel in two buses, were given a rousing welcome. MLAs Katta Subramanya Naidu and R. Ashok and MLC Aravind Limbavali told presspersons that a whip has been issued to all party legislators.

(5737) Hassan : Minister for Public Works and Energy H.D. Revanna on Thursday appealed to Janata Dal (Secular) MLAs not to go against the wishes of party President H.D. Deve Gowda. Addressing presspersons here, he reiterated his stand that he will not support his brother and party's State unit Working President H.D. Kumaraswamy, who has withdrawn support to the coalition government led by N. Dharam Singh. Under no circumstances will he join a new coalition headed by Mr. Kumaraswamy, he added.However, Mr. Revanna said Mr. Kumaraswamy is only fighting against those who were trying to split the Janata Dal (S). "I am not making accusations against Mr. Dharam Singh. But a few Congress leaders, including a former Chief Minister, tried to divide the Janata Dal (S)."

(5738) Mysore : Minister for Labour and Haj Tanvir Sait said on Thursday regretted the Congress' alliance with the All-India Progressive Janata Dal (AIPJD) in a few zilla panchayats, and said the political crisis could have been averted had the party aligned with the Janata Dal (Secular) in panchayats.

(5739) Thiruvananthapuram : Democratic Indira Congress (Karunakaran) president K. Muraleedharan has said that the Congress was opposing secular democratic forces instead of fighting communalism and by doing this the party was burying Gandhian values.

(5740) New Delhi : The core committee of the United Progressive Alliance on Thursday discussed Bihar Governor Buta Singh's resignation and the political developments in Karnataka, it is learnt. Home Minister Shivraj Patil and Defence Minister Pranab Mukherjee were among those who attended the meeting held at the residence of Prime Minister Manmohan Singh here. The Congress said the resignation of Mr. Buta Singh was in keeping with democratic traditions and conventions. Party spokesperson Abhishek Singhvi said it was the height of irresponsibility on the part of political parties to pick holes.

(5741) New Delhi : Apprehensive that direct foreign investment in the retail trade sector would destroy the country's retail sector, the Delhi Bharatiya Janata Party said on Wednesday that the move by the United Progressive Alliance Government mighty render up to 25 lakh people unemployed in the Capital itself. In a statement, Delhi BJP president Harsh Vardhan called upon the traders and those connected with the industries to oppose the decision of the Government to allow FDI in retail because this step would make the country economically subservient to foreigners.

(5742) Madurai : The Congress will get a "respectable place and proportion of seats" among the Democratic Progressive Alliance partners in the forthcoming elections, assured M. Veerappa Moiley, senior Congress leader who is in charge of party affairs in Tamil Nadu.

(5743) Ramanathapuram : The Bharatiya Janata Party (BJP) has reiterated that it will contest the Assembly elections on its own and field candidates in all 234 constituencies. Speaking to reporters here on Thursday,

BJP State vice-president V.Vaidyalingam said the All Indian Anna Dravida Munnetra Kazhagam and the Dravida Munnetra Kazhagam had ruined the State due to mutual animosity. This had also affected the growth of the State to a great extent. His party would use this election to prove that the BJP was a force to reckon with and an alternative to the two main Dravidian parties.

(5744) Gudiyatham : Bharatiya Janata Party activists on Thursday embarked on a four-day padayatra, led by State president C.P. Radhakrishnan, towards the Andhra Pradesh border, to urge the Centre and the Tamil Nadu Government to prevent the neighbouring State from constructing a dam across the Palar at Kuppam.

(5745) Villupuram : Pattali Makkal Katchi founder S. Ramadoss has called for empowering political parties to appoint their nominees in place of rebel MLAs and those who defect. He called for a national debate on the modalities to be worked out to arrest the trend of MLAs shifting loyalty. If need be, constitutional amendments should be made, and Lok Sabha Speaker Somnath Chatterjee could initiate action, said at a press conference in Thailapuram near here on Thursday.

(5746) Madurai : Former Tamil Nadu Congress Committee president, Tindivanam K. Ramamurthy, on Thursday announced formation of the Annai Indira Gandhi Peravai to "preserve the self respect" of the Congress party in the State.

28-01-2006

(5747) Anantapur : President of Andhra Pradesh Congress Committee (APCC) K. Keshava Rao on Friday said that mere legislation would not solve problems but success in their intended objectives purely depended on implementation. The credit of ensuring right to work to the poor, however, would go to the Congress Government, he claimed.

(5748) Eluru : Communist Party of India State secretary K. Narayana on Friday criticised the Congress for preparing the ground for Rahul Gandhi, son of the party president Sonia Gandhi, to take centre-stage in the party affairs.

(5749) Hyderabad : G. Venkataswamy, member of the Congress Working Committee, has pushed the Telangana Statehood issue further away from the Congress agenda by arguing that it could think of it only when it had absolute majority in the Parliament. Addressing a press conference here on Friday, Mr. Venkataswamy said as long as the Congress was dependent on others in running the Government, there could be little that the party could do. His party needed either the consensus of every one to sanction separate Statehood or an absolute majority to go ahead on its own.

(5750) Kadapa : CPI State Secretariat member T. Lakshminarayana on Friday demanded that the State Government bring out a white paper on unfilled vacant posts and quantum of those filled in accordance with the Congress' electoral promise.

(5751) Kautala (Adilabad) : Ahead of the 480-km Godavari Jala Sadhana Yatra by its Telangana-based leaders from Mancherial, 110 km from here, the Telugu Desam, Party performed a pooja at Pranahita, a tributary of the Godavari on Friday night.

(5752) Thiruvananthapuram : State secretary of the CPI(M) Pinarayi Vijayan has said that the CPI(M) is no longer opposed to the urban local bodies in the State accepting loans from the Asian Development Bank (ADB).

(5753) Bangalore : After a protracted debate and amidst noisy protests by Congress members, Legislative Assembly Speaker Krishna on Friday declared that H.D. Kumaraswamy had been recognised as the leader of the Janata Dal (Secular) Legislature Party. The Speaker's attempts to announce his decision on the basis of a letter dated January 19 from Janata Dal (S) State unit President N. Thippanna seeking the recognition of Mr. Kumaraswamy as the legislature party leader were repeatedly stalled by the Congress members.

(5754) Bangalore : Bharatiya Janata Party leader M. Venkaiah Naidu has expressed happiness that the Janata Dal (Secular) legislators under the leadership of H.D. Kumaraswamy kept their word not to allow relations between the two parties to be affected. He was speaking to presspersons after Legislative Assembly Speaker Krishna recognised Mr. Kumaraswamy as leader of the Janata Dal (S) Legislature Party.

(5755) Panaji : Agriculture Minister Micky Pacheco demanded on Friday that State unit president of Nationalist Congress Party (NCP) and

Deputy Chief Minister Wilfred D' Souza should step down from one of the posts, keeping in line with the party's "one individual, one post" policy. At a press conference on Friday, Mr. D' Souza said the demand is an affront to NCP President Sharad Pawar too.

(5756) Thiruvananthapuram : State secretary of the CPI(M) Pinarayi Vijayan has said that a close evaluation of the decisions taken by the State Cabinet in relation to the Narendran Commission report will show that it will actually prove harmful to the Backward Communities.

(5757) Kolkata : Veteran Marxist leader Jyoti Basu has denied allotment of land in the Salt Lake area here under any quota to his son Chandan. "Chandan has not got the plot [he holds] from any such quota," Mr. Basu said on Friday. "He [Chandan] inherited it through a will made by a relative on his maternal side," he said. The Supreme Court on Monday issued notice to Mr. Basu, Chief Minister Buddhadeb Bhattacharjee, and six others on a petition seeking cancellation of land allotments made in the area.Petitioner Jaideep Mukherjee, seeking a probe into the modalities adopted in land allotment, had submitted a list of several beneficiaries. He had also submitted that a discretionary quota for land allotment had been created illegally and arbitrarily during the tenure of Mr. Basu as Chief Minister.

(5758) Allahabad : Charging the Congress with "deliberately messing up" the issue of Aligarh Muslim University's minority status, the Samajwadi Party on Friday said it was "exploiting Muslim sentiments in its pursuit of vote bank politics." "The Congress had deliberately left loopholes... while provision was being made for 50 per cent reservation for Muslims at the AMU," the party's national secretary and AMU's executive council member, Hafiz Mohammad Usman, told reporters here.

(5759) New Delhi : The Samajwadi Party will initiate moves to convene a meeting of non-Congress, non-BJP parties to discuss a common strategy against "Congress attempts to destabilise non-Congress State governments." The proposal, mooted by Vice-president Janeshwar Mishra, was unanimously accepted at a Parliamentary Board meeting here on Friday. The meeting was chaired by party president, Mulayam Singh Yadav and attended by members of Parliament from both Houses. Briefing mediapersons, party leader Amar Singh said the strategy would be to avoid a recurrence of the situations witnessed in Bihar, Jharkhand and Goa recently. Asked whether the Left parties, which support the United Progressive Alliance Government at the Centre would be invited, he said: "There cannot be anything without them, including the third front." Any criticism of the U.S. imperialism was also not possible without the Left parties. "Ideologically we are very close to Left parties." Despite differences, the SP would not withdraw `outside' support to the UPA Government. "Our support to them here is just like their support to us in Uttar Pradesh."

(5760) New Delhi : Expelled BJP leader Uma Bharti on Friday said she would float a new party based on the principles and ideology of the "real Bharatiya Janata Party" after a 90-day "Janadesh yatra" beginning February 6. Her party would "expose" the "gang of 50" now leading "the pseudo-BJP."

(5761) Jaipur : Congress general secretary Ashok Gehlot said on Friday that the party would concentrate on regaining its popularity in North India, especially in the most populous States of Uttar Pradesh and Bihar. The just concluded plenary session of the All-India Congress Committee was candid enough to admit that the party was weak in the North, he said.

(5762) Chennai : Welcoming the Bill on common entrance tests for students from streams other than the State Board examinations, the Opposition on Friday asked the Government to consider possible problems it could encounter, before going ahead with the enactment.Dravida Munnetra Kazhagam whip E. Pugazhendi said that if the shortcomings were not rectified, it would prove that the Government was not serious about the Bill. An Act with flaws could be questioned in court. The Government should redraft the Bill before bringing it for the consideration of the House. C. Gnanasekaran (Congress) wanted to know whether the Government had considered a scenario where two or more students scored equal marks. He suggested that in such a case, a student who had studied Tamil as one of the subjects should be given preference. Creating additional seats might be a way out. The two streams of students need not be compared. Pattali Makkal Katchi president G. K. Mani said in case of similar marks, three or four yardsticks could be applied. The marks obtained in Tamil could be compared; a student from Tamil medium school could be given weightage; the total marks could be considered and weightage given to students from rural areas.

29-01-2006

(5763) Anantapur : Heated exchanges were witnessed between the Andhra Pradesh Congress Committee President K. Keshava Rao and leaders of Backward Classes forum (93 BC Kulala Aikya Vedika) over the welfare of BCs in the State. The BC Forum leaders led by State general secretary of Aikya Vedika G. Nagaraju went to the APCC president with a memorandum incorporated with their 11 demands.

(5764) Hyderabad : CPI (M) Polit Bureau member and MP Sitaram Yechury has cautioned the student community against the forces that are trying to divide the country by misusing the traditional issues. Participating as chief guest in the inaugural of Sanskriti - 2006, a cultural event organised by Bharat Institutions to commemorate the centenary of Vandemataram here on Saturday, he called upon students to foster unity amidst diversity to meet the challenges. He said intellectuals were those who were not like "a vegetable liked by the cook who can use it any way he likes."

(5765) SIRPUR Kagaznagar (Adilabad) : The Congress launched an all-out offensive against the Telugu Desam here on Saturday for the latter's 'sustained propaganda against the irrigation projects'. Addressing a well-attended public meeting at Kautala mandal headquarters, 50 km away from here, Congress leaders asked the Telugu Desam to clarify its stand on projects. Congress MP G. Venkataswamy, Ministers — P. Lakshmaiah and G. Vinod - MLAs — A. Indrakaran Reddy, Koneru Konappa, G. Chinna Reddy, C. Ramachandra Reddy, N. Divakar Rao and K. Venkat Reddy — said TD leaders were misleading people regarding the projects.

(5766) Mancherial (Adilabad Dt.) : Almost the entire top brass of the Telugu Desam Party belonging to Telangana hit the road marking commencement of a 24-day-long padayatra from this coal town here on Saturday demanding priority for the region in the implementation of irrigation projects.Party president N. Chandrababu Naidu, now in Switzerland, will address a rally when the padayatra terminates in Hyderabad on February 20.

(5767) Koutala (Adilabad Dt.) : Peddapalli MP and Congress Deputy Leader in the Lok Sabha G. Venkatswamy on Saturday thanked Chief

Minister Y.S. Rajasekhara Reddy for taking up the Pranahita-Chevella project which would give life to Telangana area.

(5768) Bangalore : Chief Minister N. Dharam Singh, who resigned on Saturday after a section of Janata Dal (Secular) legislators withdrew support to his government, said he had successfully led the coalition government for 20 months and was satisfied with his performance. Addressing presspersons here after submitting his resignation to the Governor, Mr. Dharam Singh described as meaningless the Janata Dal (S) legislators' decision to join hands with what he called the "communal BJP" and said the Congress had upheld its secular ideology once again and it was a historic day in Indian politics. The BJP will not remain in power for long and the BJP-Janata Dal (S) alliance does not bring dignity to the State, he said.

(5769) Kozhikode : Janata Dal (S) Parliamentary Party Leader M.P. Veerendra Kumar said on Saturday that Mr. D. H Kumaraswamy and the "other rebels" who are about to form a government in alliance with the BJP in Karnataka would be expelled from the party. He expected such a decision at the JD (S) national working committee, which is scheduled to meet on February 3 in New Delhi.

(5770) Bangalore : In a parting shot at the Janata Dal (Secular) leader H.D. Deve Gowda, the Congress on Saturday accused him of a hatching a political conspiracy to anoint his son H.D. Kumaraswamy as the Chief Minister.Addressing presspersons here, Karnataka Pradesh Congress Committee President M. Mallikarjun Kharge blamed Mr. Deve Gowda for "the political drama" aimed at making Mr. Kumaraswamy the Chief Minister. He has now succeeded, he said.

(5771) Angalore : The political crisis in Karnataka has finally blown over with Chief Minister Dharam Singh putting in his papers. Governor T.N. Chaturvedi on Saturday invited the leader of the joint Legislature Party of the Janata Dal (Secular) and the Bharatiya Janata Party, H.D. Kumaraswamy, to form a new government. The Speaker on Friday recognised Mr. Kumaraswamy as the leader of the Legislature party.

(5772) Kozhikode : Janata Dal (Secular) State unit president M.P. Veerendrakumar has said that there will be no dilution of the party's commitment to secularism in the State because of the happenings in

Karnataka, where a group of party MLAs has decided to form a Government in alliance with the Bharatiya Janata Party (BJP). A meeting of the State working committee of the party here on Saturday unanimously decided not to support the alliance with the BJP in Karnataka. Presidents of the district units of the party and office-bearers of its feeder organisations attended the meeting.

(5773) New Delhi : Bharatiya Janata Party president Rajnath Singh on Saturday gave the assurance that his party would give Karnataka a "strong and stable government" in coalition with the Janata Dal (Secular). The BJP State leader, B.S. Yediyurappa would be Deputy Chief Minister for the first 20 months, during which JD (S) leader H.D. Kumaraswamy would be Chief Minister, Mr. Singh said. He indicated that Mr. Yediyurappa would take over from Mr. Kumaraswamy during the next 20 months. Over the next few days, a common agenda for governance would be worked out. He said the BJP always worked cohesively with coalition partners.

(5774) Hyderabad : The Communist Party of India (Marxist) has described the developments in Karnataka as "unfortunate" and said it should serve as a lesson for all the secular forces. "It is unfortunate that the Janata Dal (S) which carries the secular tag in its name has joined hands with communal forces for the sake of power," the CPI (M) MP and Polit Bureau member, Sitaram Yechury, has said. Secular forces in the country should understand that any rift between them would only strengthen the communal elements.

(5775) New Delhi : Upping the ante in view of the Congress-led Municipal Corporation of Delhi serving a notice, the Leader of the Opposition in the MCD, Subhash Arya, and the Leader of the Opposition in the MCD Standing Committee, Vijender Gupta, on Saturday demanded resignation of Chief Minister Sheila Dikshit for "misusing her post to avoiding demolition action".

(5776) Chandigarh : Haryana Chief Minister Bhupinder Singh Hooda said on Saturday that after the Congress came to power in Haryana last year, the people living in South Haryana have been given 35 per cent more water for irrigation and drinking purposes thanks to the steps taken to ensure equitable distribution of water.

(5777) Pondicherry : Pattali Makkal Katchi Parliamentary party leader M. Ramadoss has criticised the Pondicherry Government for what he said "undue publicity on construction of fishing harbour in Karaikal even when no preliminary work has been started" so far.

(5778) Pondicherry: AICC general secretary B K Hariprasad MP, (who is also in charge of affairs of the Congress in Pondicherry) has called upon his party workers to avoid groupism, as their sole aim must be to promote team spirit and ensure that the party regained power in the forthcoming Assembly polls. Addressing a party workers meeting organised by the Pradesh Congress Committee (PCC) here on Friday, Mr. Hariprasad said that the workers should propagate the achievements of the Congress-led UPA rule at the Centre and also theperformance of its Government in Pondicherry for the next three months as the election was round the corner.

(5779) Chandigarh : The Chandigarh unit of the Bharatiya Janata Party on Saturday demanded that the allegations levelled against the Member of Parliament from the city, Pawan Kumar Bansal, about alleged misuse of MP Local Area Development funds should be referred to the Parliamentary Committee for investigation and if the charges are proved the same action should be taken against him as has been taken against or is being contemplated against other MPs already under the scanner.

(5780) Chennai : DMK president M. Karunanidhi on Saturday virtually kick-started his campaign for the ensuing Assembly elections, due by May, terming the Supreme Court indicting the AIADMK Government in the M.G.R., Nagar stampede case as the "first victory" of his party and its allies.

(5781) Chennai : "Selective takeover" of cable television networks by the State Government exposed the "sadist mentality" of Chief Minister Jayalalithaa, charged Dravida Munnetra Kazhagam president M. Karunanidhi here on Saturday. Replying to a question on takeover of cable TV network, Mr. Karunanidhi said the DMK was not against the Government's decision. But its present move was partial as it had decided to takeover control of only 10 networks out of 500 multi-system operators, including Sumangali Cable Vision (SCV) owned by Sun TV, in the State.

(5782) Panaji : Shantaram Naik, Member of Parliament and AICC Secretary in charge of Tamil Nadu, has said that the Supreme Court's remarks on Friday holding Tamil Nadu officers responsible for the death of 42 innocent persons in the stampede caused during the distribution of relief funds on December 18, is an indirect verdict against Chief Minister Jayalalithaa and hence, she should express a public apology before the people of Tamil Nadu.

30-01-2006

(5783) Hyderabad : A brain-storming session of BJP leaders will be held here in March to formulate an action plan on Telangana, keeping in view the party's stand favouring smaller States, State BJP vice-president S.V. Seshagiri Rao and general secretary K. Laxman told reporters here on Sunday. They said BJP had to set aside the Telangana issue during the NDA regime, as it was not part of the common agenda. The party would discuss ways of taking it forward in the wake of changed political situation in the State.

(5784) Karimnagar : Government Whip D Sridhar Babu has demanded that the TDP deputy leader in the Assembly T Devender Goud apologise to the people of Telangana for misleading them on the irrigation projects in the region. Addressing a press conference here on Sunday, Mr. Sridhar said, "The TDP leaders are shedding crocodile tears for the cause of Telangana." He flayed the TDP leaders for organising the padayatra demanding completion of projects when there was good progress. He alleged that the TDP had neglected the projects of the region by just spending Rs 3,851 crores during their nine-years of administration. Within one year, the Congress had spent Rs 13,000 crores for the completion the projects in the region, he said.

(5785) Nellore : Senior vice-president of BJP M. Venkaiah Naidu has said that the party's success in dislodging the Dharam Singh Ministry in Karnataka provides the party gateway to enter the political scene in South India.

(5786) Vijayawada : The Y. S. Rajasekhara Reddy Government is neglecting every sector other than power and irrigation, Communist Party of India (CPI) State Secretary K. Narayana said here on Sunday.

(5787) New Delhi : The United Progressive Alliance Government on Sunday effected its first major expansion of the Council of Ministers, inducting 18 new faces, elevating three to Cabinet rank and re-inducting Shibu Soren.All the new entrants are from the Congress while the only one re-induction and elevation apiece are drawn from the allies. Prime Minister

Manmohan Singh will continue to look after the Foreign Affairs portfolio while four new Ministers have not been given any charge. The swearing-in ceremony at noon at the Rashtrapati Bhavan saw 10 new Cabinet Ministers, one Minister of State with Independent charge and 11 more Ministers of State. Among the Cabinet Ministers are three senior Congress leaders from Maharashtra - Sushil Kumar Shinde, A. R. Antulay and Murli Deora. Mani Shankar Aiyar has been relieved of the Petroleum portfolio, which has been allocated to Mr. Deora. Mr. Shinde is the new Power Minister in place of P.M. Sayeed who passed away, while Mr. Antulay is the Cabinet Minister for Minority Affairs, a newly created portfolio.

(5788) Erode : The Pattali Makkal Katchi has decided not to seek a share in power if the Democratic Progressive Alliance formed the next government in Tamil Nadu, Union Health Minister R. Anbumani said on Sunday. The party would support Dravida Munnetra Kazhagam president M. Karunanidhi for the post of Chief Minister.

(5789) Mysore : The former Prime Minister, H.D. Deve Gowda, deserves an award for staging a "classic political drama" that paved the way for his son H.D. Kumaraswamy to become Chief Minister of the State, the former Deputy Chief Minister, Siddaramaiah, has said.Speaking to presspersons after releasing the Year Planner 2006, brought out by the Mysore Reporters' Guild here on Sunday, Mr. Siddaramaiah said Mr. Deve Gowda's unmatchable political histrionics should bring him the Dada Saheb Phalke award, which is the most prestigious award given by the Government to film personalities.

(5790) Mysore : The Communist party of India (CPI) took out a rally in the city on Sunday to mark its 80th anniversary. Addressing the rally, CPI State Secretary Siddanagowda Patil expressed his displeasure over the recent political developments in the State. He said it has exposed politicians' "lust for power". He accused the Congress, the Bharatiya Janata Party and other political parties of compromising their ideals for the sake of power. He said the CPI, whose leaders were hanged and put behind bars during the freedom struggle, has continued its movement for the welfare of the common man even after Independence. The party is waging a struggle against the threat posed to the country's economy, society and culture by the entry of multinational companies.

(5791) Mysore : The Bharatiya Janata Party (BJP) leader and Deputy Chief Minister designate B.S. Yediyurappa ruled out the possibility of the party deviating from its Hindutva ideology but said efforts will be made to bring minorities into the mainstream of society. Speaking to presspersons here on Sunday, Mr. Yediyurappa said that Hindutva is a way of life and the party will not deviate from its ideology. "However, unlike the Congress, which treats minorities as a `vote bank', the party will strive to bring them into the mainstream," he said.

(5792) Thiruvananthapuram : Leader of the Opposition V.S. Achuthanandan has said that, as in all sectors of the Kerala economy, the power sector had gone through a phase of zero-growth during the last nearly five years of the UDF Government in the State.

(5793) Lucknow : Samajwadi Party president and Uttar Pradesh Chief Minister Mulayam Singh on Sunday criticised the UPA Government for "using Governors as tools to destabilise State Governments." "Today, what we are witnessing is not politics of principles, but vendetta," he told a rally of the SP youth wing here.

(5794) Kolkata : Formation of a "mahajot" (grand alliance) to prevent a division in the anti-Left Front vote in the West Bengal Assembly elections dissipated after a meeting between Defence Minister Pranab Mukherjee and Trinamool Congress leader Mamata Banerjee, late on Saturday night. The two stood firm in their resolve not to make concessions. Their uncompromising stand notwithstanding, both, however, fell short of calling off the move to forge an alliance of sorts. Both put up a brave front at the end of the meeting and insisted that there was still room for discussions to fight united the Left Front. Echoing the decision of the All-India Congress Committee at its recent plenary in Hyderabad against any electoral alliance which involved the Bharatiya Janata Party, Mr. Mukherjee, who is also president of the West Bengal Pradesh Congress Committee, reportedly reiterated at the meeting that his party would welcome an anti-Left alliance, provided Ms. Banerjee disassociated herself from the National Democratic Alliance led by the BJP.

(5795) Nedumbassery : Senior Bharatiya Janata Party leader Murli Manohar Joshi on Sunday defended the party's alliance with the Janata Dal (S) in Karnataka, saying it was the responsibility of every party to fulfil people's aspiration for a stable government.

(5796) New Delhi : The Janata Dal (United), a major component of the opposition National Democratic Alliance (NDA), on Sunday described the

Cabinet expansion as "spurious wine in an old bottle" and warned that it would raise the issue of the presence of charge-sheeted Ministers facing charges at the Budget Session of Parliament beginning next month. The party said Prime Minister Manmohan Singh brought back and retained two such Ministers. He had also 'failed' to drop Law Minister H.R. Bhardwaj though he was "instrumental" in defreezing the bank accounts of Bofors accused Octavio Quattrochi.

(5797) New Delhi : Congress president Sonia Gandhi said on Sunday that inductions in the party organisation at the Centre had become inevitable because of the entry of some office-bearers in the Union Cabinet.However, young aspirants had to "wait a bit" and "work a little bit more" for getting accommodation in the party or the Government.

(5798) New Delhi : Delhi BJP president Harsh Vardhan has charged that it was due to the connivance with land and builder mafia that the Delhi Government and the Municipal Corporation of Delhi were not properly presenting the case before the High Court for protecting the properties of the people from being demolished.In a statement on Saturday, Dr. Vardhan said since 80 per cent of the illegal constructions had taken place in the knowledge of the Delhi Government and so it would be wrong to say that only the public was responsible for the same.

(5799) Chennai : Puducherry Munnetra Congress (PMC) founder P. Kannan called on All-India Anna Dravida Munnetra Kazhagam (AIADMK) general secretary and Chief Minister Jayalalithaa at her residence on Sunday. They held talks on forging a PMC-AIADMK tie-up in the Union Territory for the coming Assembly elections.

(5800) Chennai : The Pattali Makkal Katchi, which often attracted adverse publicity for its agitations, is in the process of an image makeover and plans to publish a newspaper.Though conscious of sending out the message that it remains a "virulent critic" of the All-India Anna Dravida Munnetra Kazhagam Government, the party has come up with its schemes, be it on admission to professional colleges or monorail. So far, it has prepared three alternative budgets, focussing on the State economy. For the last couple of years, the party has been organising the birth anniversary of the late Chief Minister K. Kamaraj and "Tamil Isai" (Tamil music) festivals. "The daily we plan to bring out will not be a party organ. It has been my desire to publish a newspaper conforming to the dharma of the Press," says S. Ramadoss, PMK founder.

31-01-2006

(5801) Eluru : Congress MP from Eluru Kavuri Sambhasiva Rao on Monday commented that party president Sonia Gandhi had drifted into the grip of a band of 'power-brokers.' "As far as our leader Soniaji is concerned, she is a spotless and plain-speaking leader. But she is getting carried away by a handful of mediocre persons," he observed at a press conference while expressing strong dissent against the manner in which the Union Cabinet was expanded. He said he would shortly meet the party chief and register his protest against the handpicking of 'turncoats' who crossed over to the Congress from the TDP and the other opposition parties for induction into the Cabinet at the expense of scores of party senior loyalists.

(5802) Hyderabad : Telugu Desam Party president N. Chandrababu Naidu slammed the Congress for giving a go-by to social justice in Sunday's Cabinet expansion and for continuing to treat Raj Bhavans across the nation as Pradesh Congress offices. Addressing a press conference after a meeting of the TDP Politburo here on Monday, he said there was no semblance of justice to the weaker sections when the Council of Ministers was expanded. Andhra Pradesh may have been given the maximum number of ministerial berths but it got only Ministers of State.

(5803) Hyderabad : APCC president K.Keshava Rao asked the Telugu Desam Party "to mind its own business" and stop commenting on the UPA Government's Cabinet expansion. Addressing a press conference here on Monday, Dr. Keshava Rao said neither the TDP president, N.Chandrababu Naidu, nor his colleagues had any national perspective to comment on the expansion. The TDP president would do well to get the political agenda of his party right before commenting on the Congress.

(5804) Hyderabad : The Telugu Desam Legislature Party has criticised the Congress for making disparagin remarks about the party's 'Pranahita - Chevella padayatra.' At a press conference here on Monday, TDLP Deputy Leader N. Janardhan Reddy and Uma Madhava Reddy said the Congress Legislature Party had no moral right to "sling mud" at the TDP for a drive by its leaders, as it was intended to increase people's awareness and bring pressure on the Government to take up the Pranahita-Chevella project in the interest of the region.

(5805) Mahábubnagar : State BJP president N. Indrasena Reddy has asked cadre to brace up to launch a movement for division of Andhra Pradesh, apparently indicating that the party is keen on reviving the demand for separate Telangana. Addressing the BJP State executive here on Monday, he recalled the party stand favouring smaller States for administrative convenience.

(5806) Chennai : Dravida Munnetra Kazhagam president M. Karunanidhi on Monday hoped that seats sharing talks with Democratic Progressive Alliance allies would be completed before the party's Tiruchi conference in early March.

(5807) Kozhikode : Enthused by the positive response to the Government's decision to ensure reservation norms in its services, the Indian Union Muslim League (IUML) leadership on Monday asked the Communist Party of India (Marxist) to spell out its stand on the Narendran Commission's report instead of criticising the report "in vague terms." Speaking at a press conference here, IUML State general secretary P. K. Kunhalikutty accused the CPI(M) of deliberately speaking in ambiguous terms while criticising the United Democratic Front (UDF) Government's decision. The CPI(M) should spell out its stand vis-a-vis the points raised in the Narendan panel report.

(5808) Bangalore : Karnataka Pradesh Congress Committee President M. Mallikarjun Kharge on Monday made it clear that Chief Minister N. Dharam Singh will function as Leader of the Opposition in the Legislative Assembly as he is the leader of the Congress Legislature Party.

(5809) Alappuzha : Youth Congress State president K.P. Anilkumar has demanded a CBI inquiry into the death of Sivagiri Dharmasanghom Trust's former president Swami Saswatikananda. Addressing pressperson here on Monday, Mr. Anilkumar said he would submit a memorandum to Chief Minister Oommen Chandy in this regard.

(5810) Dadri (U.P.) : The Bharatiya Janata Party on Monday declared Kalyan Singh as its chief ministerial candidate in the Uttar Pradesh Assembly elections due next year. "Kalyan Singh has been the best Chief

Minister of Uttar Pradesh. He will address all your problems, if he is brought back to power... ," BJP president Rajnath Singh said at a rally here.

(5811) Kolkata : The Communist Party of India (Marxist) will organise countrywide protests and mobilise the support of other political forces against the Centre's decision to allow 51 per cent foreign direct investment (FDI) in the retail sector, beginning with single brands, its general secretary, Prakash Karat, said here on Monday. "We have opposed the Centre's decision and are talking to other political parties [to mobilise support against the move]," Mr. Karat said.

(5812) New Delhi : The BJP has refused to comment on the likely visit of senior party leader Jaswant Singh to the mausoleum of Mohammad Ali Jinnah. Mr. Singh left for Pakistan on Monday along with a hundred "pilgrims." "The question is not whether the party approves of Mr. Jaswant Singh's itinerary or not. He will be a state guest in Pakistan, and not visiting Jinnah's 'mazhar' would be akin to a guest in India refusing to visit the Gandhi 'samadhi'," party spokesperson Ravi Shankar Prasad said. "Mr. Singh's is a private visit and he himself had made this clear. Let us leave it at that." Mr. Prasad did not agree with suggestions from reporters that a public figure's visit abroad along with 100 others cannot be a "private one" and "it was open to public scrutiny."

(5813) New Delhi : Angry Bharatiya Janata Party councillors on Monday gheraoed Mayor Satbir Singh at the Special House meeting of the Municipal Corporation of Delhi after he refused to table the "action taken report" on unauthorised constructions carried out by prominent politicians including Chief Minister Sheila Dikshit, Delhi Congress chief Ram Babu Sharma and some Delhi Ministers, MLAs and Councillors.

(5814) CHANDIGARH : The Communist Party of India (Marxist) will have no truck with the Congress for the forthcoming elections to the Punjab Assembly, which are due in a year's time. Instead it will seek to form an alliance of like-minded parties and work to ensure defeat of "communal forces represented in the State by the Akali-BJP combine". Talking to reporters here, the Secretary of the Punjab unit of the CPI (M), Balwant Singh, said that efforts were on to bring the Left and democratic parties like the CPI, a section of the Bahujan Samaj Party, Lok Bhalai Party and others on a common platform.

(5815) Chennai : Union Minister of State for Project Implementation G.K. Vasan has said the Central projects, meant for the welfare of Tamil Nadu, will be implemented within a time frame, and he will remove all hurdles in implementation. Talking to presspersons at the party headquarters, Satyamurthi Bhavan, here on Monday, he said both Congress president Sonia Gandhi and Prime Minister Manmohan Singh were keen on the fruits of the projects reaching the people, especially the weaker sections and the Dalits. Asked whether there would be any change in the State leadership of the party as he had become a Central Minister, Mr. Vasan said it was the high command which took such decisions, and he would abide by its decision.

(5816) Tiruchi : The Desiya Murpokku Dravida Kazhagam has an alliance with the people and not with any political party, its founder and cine actor Vijaykanth said here on Sunday. Seeking votes for his newly floated party at a meeting held at Thiruverambur near here, he claimed that he had entered politics with the objective of serving the people and doing good for them and not with any personal interest or motive.

(5817) Pondicherry : The Pondicherry Congress has urged a two-member delegation of the All-India Congress Committee to ensure that the party got at least 20 seats in the coming elections to the Union Territory. The AICC team, comprising P. Sudhakar Reddy, secretary, and B.K Hariprasad, general secretary and in-charge of Pondicherry, declined to say whether there was any specific claim by party functionaries on the number of seats the Congress must contest. However, local leaders on Monday said that they appealed to the delegation to ensure that the party got at least 20 seats. They said that while the alliance formed in the last Lok Sabha polls continued, there should be no compromise on the fact that the Congress was a major partner in the combine in the Union Territory.

01-02-2006

(5818) Hyderabad : The State Committee of CPI(M) has appealed to the Government not to force farmers to install capacitors to agricultural pumpsets.

(5819) Hyderabad : The Telugu Desam party on Tuesday asserted that the latest decision by the State BJP to take up the issue of separate Telangana and come closer to the Telangana Rashtra Samithi would not have any impact on it.

(5820) Visakhapatnam : The Communist Party of India (CPI) has charged the World Bank with mounting pressure on Chief Minister Y.S. Rajasekhara Reddy to dilute free power scheme meant for farming community.

(5821) Mahabubnagar : The two senior leaders of the Bharatiya Janata Party, who addressed the concluding session of the party State executive meeting here on Tuesday, expressed different views on the movement proposed to take up for separate Telangana. State BJP former national president Bangaru Laxman said there was no hurry for taking up movement for Telangana. The party should wait till the time when both Congress and TRS express their inability on the issue. Bal Apte, national Vice-President of the party, advised the State party unit to take up a movement on the Kakinada resolution (one vote - two States as the party now was free from obligations after serving ties with Telugu Desam).

(5822) New Delhi : The brewing resentment over representation from Andhra Pradesh in the Union Cabinet was conveyed to the party leadership with several State leaders expressing their candid views over their claim being ignored. Guntur MP Rayapati Sambasiva Rao met Congress president Sonia Gandhi on Tuesday and expressed disappointment that party workers who had struggled and fought the Telugu Desam Party were ignored in the expansion.

(5823) Kadapa : Senior Telugu Desam Party (TDP) leaders on Tuesday charged the State Government with perpetrating murder of TDP leaders and activists to snub political adversaries.

(5824) Bangalore : Janata Dal (Secular) leader H.D. Deve Gowda told The Hindu on Tuesday that he was confident that his son and rebel party leader, H.D. Kumaraswamy, and the JD (S) MLAs supporting him would pull out of the understanding with the Bharatiya Janata Party to form a government in Karnataka. Saying that his son had been "tricked into associating himself with the BJP," he warned that if his group went ahead, he would fight to revive the JD (S), treating both the BJP and the Kumaraswamy group as "the party's rival."

(5825) Mysore : Chief Minister-designate H.D. Kumaraswamy on Tuesday said he is facing a dilemma over leading the coalition of the Janata Dal (Secular) and the Bharatiya Janata Party in the wake of widespread aspersions cast on the secular credentials of his father, former Prime Minister H.D. Deve Gowda.

(5826) Chennai : More than 1,000 members of the Dravida Munnetra Kazhagam were arrested on Tuesday when they staged a demonstration demanding the resignation of Chief Minister Jayalalithaa in the light of the Supreme Court's adverse remarks on the handling of the MGR Nagar stampede issue.

(5827) Islamabad : Leading an 86-member delegation, the former Foreign Minister and senior BJP leader Jaswant Singh visited the ancient temple of Hinglaj in Balochistan on Tuesday.

(5828) Mangalore : Deputy Chief Minister-designate B.S. Yediyurappa is confident of the success of the new Bharatiya Janata Party-Janata Dal (Secular) coalition as both the parties are on the same wavelength and have accepted that the Government should focus on the development of the State.

(5829) Thiruvananthapuram : Kerala Pradesh Congress Committee president Ramesh Chennithala on Tuesday said that the CPI (M) stand on the recent Cabinet decision on backward class representation in Government services is "intriguing."

(5830) Kochi : United Democratic Front (UDF) convener P.P. Thankachan has said that the Advocate General's report on the Lavalin deal will be presented in the next Assembly session, which will open on Friday.

(5831) Olkata : Leaders of the two major Left trade unions - the Centre of Indian Trade Unions (CITU) and the All India Trade Union Congress (AITUC) - have threatened a "larger movement including strikes" if the Centre continues "going ahead with its plans of privatisation of airports." Other central trade unions, they expect, will join the movement.

(5832) New Delhi : Janata Party president Subramanian Swamy on Wednesday challenged the decision of the Election Commission to defreeze the "farmer with a plough" symbol, which his party had been allotted since 1977.

(5833) New Delhi : The Rashtriya Lok Dal (RLD) has demanded restoration of minority status for the Aligarh Muslim University through a

Constitutional amendment.An RLD delegation led by Ajit Singh that met Union Human Resources Development Minister (HRD) Minister Arjun Singh here on Monday said the court's decision was "regrettable" and asked the Government to take steps to restore minority character of the institution.

(5834) Chennai : The appointment of L. Ganesan as a vice-president of the Bharatiya Janata Party is seen by party circles here as part of the central leadership's strategy of strengthening the State unit. He was a national secretary for the last four years. The sixty-year-old Ganesan is the only person from the south in the new set of vice-presidents, after Rajnath Singh became the national president. Till now, M. Venkaiah Naidu was one of the vice-presidents.

(5835) Chennai : The Dravida Munnetra Kazhagam treasurer, Arcot N.Veerasamy, on Tuesday flayed the State Government for getting the Tamil Nadu Acquisition, Transfer and Taking Over of the Administration of Cable Television Network (including Multiple Service Optical Transport System) Bill, 2006 passed in the Assembly.

02-02-2006

(5836) Anantapur : The district unit of Telugu Desam Party on Wednesday has written an open letter to UPA Chairperson Sonia Gandhi alleging that the Congress-led Government in the State and at the Centre were deceiving the farming community by not fulfilling their pre-poll promises.

(5837) Bangalore : Chief Minister-designate H.D. Kumaraswamy did not leave for New Delhi on Wednesday to meet national leaders of the Bharatiya Janata Party as announced earlier. He, however, asserted that despite opposition from his father, H.D. Deve Gowda, the Janata Dal (Secular) group led by him will form the next government with the BJP. The cancellation of his trip to Delhi, while State BJP leaders left to meet their leaders there, led to more suspense and speculation.

(5838) Chennai : The All-India Anna Dravida Munnetra Kazhagam is open to poll alliance and talks in this respect are on, party general secretary and Chief Minister Jayalalithaa said here on Wednesday.

(5839) Bangalore : B.R. Patil, MLA and State unit Working President of the All India Progressive Janata Dal, on Wednesday appealed to members of the national executive of the Janata Dal (Secular) to expel former Prime Minister H.D. Deve Gowda from the party for "supporting" an alliance with the Bharatiya Janata Party.

(5840) Bangalore : Minister for Industries and Finance P.G.R. Sindhia said on Wednesday that he does not want the Janata Dal (Secular) to align itself with the Bharatiya Janata Party. Addressing presspersons here, he said he will stand by former Prime Minister H.D. Deve Gowda.

(5841) Bangalore : All India Congress Committee General Secretary B.K. Hariprasad on Wednesday described the coalition of the Janata Dal (Secular) and the Bharatiya Janata Party as "an unholy alliance" and said Friday, when H.D. Kumaraswamy and B.S. Yediyurappa are to be sworn in as Chief Minister and Deputy Chief Minister, respectively, will be a "Black Day".

(5842) Hubli: Basavaraj Horatti has appealed to Janata Dal (Secular) president and former Prime Minister H.D. Deve Gowda to withdraw his resignation as party president.

(5843) Mysore : Former Deputy Chief Minister and All India Progressive Janata Dal leader Siddaramaiah on Wednesday appealed to Chief Minister-designate H.D. Kumaraswamy and the "rebel" group of Janata Dal (Secular) MLAs to opt for mid-term polls instead of entering into an "unholy alliance" with the Bharatiya Janata Party.

(5844) Kannur : CPI(M) Legislature Party deputy leader Kodiyeri Balakrishnan has accused the State Government of 'plundering' the State with corruption and wasteful spending.

(5845) Kollam : More than 50 people were injured as violence broke out during a Communist Party of India-Marxist (CPI-M) siege of the civil station here on Wednesday. Party cadres, policemen and press photographers were among those injured in the stone throwing and police lathi-charge.

(5846) Kottayam: Kerala Congress(Joseph) chairman P.J. Joseph has said that the agenda for the comprehensive development of agriculture prepared on the basis of the brainstorming and interactive sessions at the Karshika Mela at Thodupuzha will be presented to President A.P.J. Abdul Kalam in March. The document is expected to form part of the Vision 2020 programme envisaged by the President for the comprehensive development of the State, he said.

(5847) Thiruvananthapuram : The United Democratic Front (UDF) Government is destroying the professionalism of the Kerala police to save those involved in criminal cases, CPI (M) State secretary Pinarayi Vijayan has said. He was inaugurating the Secretariat siege here on Wednesday.

(5848) Thrissur : A Collectorate blockade here by Communist Party of India-Marxist (CPI-M) activists, part of a State-wide agitation organised by the party on Wednesday, was peaceful. The CPI(M) central committee member E.P. Jayarajan inaugurated the blockade. The party leaders P.R. Rajan and C.O. Paulose spoke.

(5849) New Delhi : The Karnataka Chief Minister-designate, H.D. Kumaraswamy, failed to keep his date with Bharatiya Janata Party leaders here on Wednesday. However, a late afternoon phone call from Mr. Kumaraswamy to Mr. Rajnath Singh, Mr. Naidu and general secretary Ananth Kumar indicated that the coalition project was very much on track. Mr. Naidu told reporters that although H.D. Deve Gowda, former Prime Minister and Mr. Kumaraswamy's father, was opposed to the alliance with the BJP, "we would like Mr. Kumaraswamy to get his father's blessings" for the arrangement. There was no direct communication with Mr. Kumaraswamy throughout the morning and afternoon - till that call came. Meanwhile, the out-going Karnataka Chief Minister, Dharam Singh, who had come here to apprise the central Congress leaders of the political developments in the State, did not rule out the possibility for the coalition arrangement between Congress and JD (S) to continue. "Anything is possible in the present uncertain political situation in the State," he said and referred to the reported statement of Kumaraswamy that he was faced with a dilemma over leading a coalition with BJP in the wake of aspersions cast on the secular credentials of his father.

(5850) Chennai : "The United States should recall its Ambassador, David Mulford, for his statement linking the India-U.S. nuclear deal to India's vote on Iran," Tamil Nadu Chief Minister Jayalalithaa said here on Wednesday.

(5851) New Delhi : The first day of the strike called by airport employees across the country passed off without any major hiccups at

Delhi airport on Wednesday. Apart from loud protests by employees, operations of and for most passengers it seemed to be a "normal" day.

(5852) Madurai : The Communist Party of India (Marxist) has categorically stated that it was not bothered about forming a coalition government in the aftermath of the Assembly elections. Speaking to presspersons here on Wednesday, the State secretary of the party, N. Varadarajan, said coalition government was definitely not an issue. However, any such move would be the exclusive prerogative of the Dravida Munnetra Kazhagam (DMK), which led the Democratic Progressive Alliance (DPA) in the State. His party's top agenda was to oust the ruling All India Anna Dravida Munnetra Kazhagam (AIDMK) Government from power.

(5853) Chennai : The Pattali Makkal Katchi has moved the Madras High Court to restrain the State Government from implementing its "flawed decision" to introduce monorail in Chennai.

03-02-2006

(5854) Hyderabad : State BJP president N. Indrasena Reddy has strongly objected to Prime Minister Manmohan Singh's statement that efforts were on to evolve a consensus on Telangana

(5855) Nalgonda : Secretary of the Communist Party of India (Marxist) B.V. Raghavulu, has charged the Government with lacking a comprehensive water policy.

(5856) Srikakulam : A meeting of the Telugu Desam Party's BC cell demanded withdrawal of the GO. No. 23, which was aimed at deleting some castes from the BCs' list.

(5857) Sangareddy : CPI (M) central committee member and Member of Rajya Sabha P Madhu has warned the State Government of struggles akin to the anti power hike protest at Basheerbagh if it failed to address drinking and irrigation water problem of Medak district.

(5858) Bangalore : The Janata Dal (Secular) is keen on addressing regional issues in its new coalition Government with the BJP that will come into existence from Friday, according to the party's State unit president N. Thippanna.

(5859) Hassan : The outgoing Minister for Public Works and Energy, H.D. Revanna, has said he regrets his brother, H.D. Kumaraswamy's decision to join hands with the Bharatiya Janata Party (BJP), which he termed an "anti-secular party," to form a coalition government in the State.

(5860) Chikmagalur : Janata Dal (Secular) leader and Chief Minister-designate H.D. Kumaraswamy has said that he will consider any harsh decision taken by his father, H.D. Deve Gowda, as a blessing. But he has to discharge the responsibility entrusted with him by Janata Dal (Secular) and Bharatiya Janata Party legislators, he said.

(5861) Thiruvananthapuram : Addressing a news conference, convened here on Thursday to release the party's document on Kerala's development, CPI State secretary Veliyam Bhargavan said the answers to Kerala's problems must be found here and not from elsewhere or through fancy schemes such as the Expressway.

(5862) Thiruvananthapuram : The CPI(M) will oppose the Union Government's decision to privatise the Delhi and Mumbai airports, CPI(M) State secretary Pinarayi Vijayan has said. Addressing the striking employees of the airport on Thursday, Mr.Vijayan said the decision to privatise airports, which will have a bearing on national security, is totally unjustified

(5863) New Delhi : The Left Parties on Thursday demanded that the Manmohan Singh Government hold talks with the employees of the Airports Authority of India and decided to meet the Prime Minister on Friday morning on the issueThey asked the Government to immediately call the representatives of the joint forum of the AAI employees and officers for talks.At a meeting here, leaders of the four Left parties said the Government should also take up the alternative proposal of the AAI for the modernisation of the airports in New Delhi and Mumbai.CPI (M) General Secretary Prakash Karat, CPI leaders Mr. Bardhan and D. Raja, All India Forward Bloc leaders Debabrata Biswas and G. Devarajan and Revolutionary Socialist Party central committee member Abani Roy attended the meeting.

(5864) New Delhi : The Left parties discussed with Union Finance Minister P. Chidambaram their proposals on resource mobilisation here on Thursday. Communist Party of India (Marxist) general secretary Prakash Karat, CPI general secretary A.B. Bardhan, national secretary D. Raja, All-India Forward Bloc general secretary Debabrata Biswas and Revolutionary Socialist Party central committee member Abani Roy attended the meeting.

(5865) New Delhi : Will Leader of the Opposition L.K. Advani be the Bharatiya Janata Party's prime ministerial candidate as he himself has claimed? All that party president Rajnath Singh would say to this question on Thursday was: "The elections are far away. We will take a decision when the elections are just ahead." On the future of Mr. Advani as Leader of the Opposition, Mr. Singh was equally careful not to be precise. How long would he and Jaswant Singh continue as leaders of the Opposition in the Lok Sabha and the Rajya Sabha? This question was asked in the context of the senior leader, Yashwant Sinha's statement earlier that Mr. A dvani's continuance in the post became "untenable" given the manner he was forced to resign his party position and of reports that the Rashtriya Swayamsevak Sangh was unhappy with Mr. Jaswant Singh visiting the Jinnah mausoleum in Karachi. Mr. Rajnath Singh said: "They are in those positions and they will remain." He was addressing a press conference here after the first meeting of the newly constituted office-bearers. The former Prime Minister, Atal Bihari Vajpayee, and Mr. Advani attended the meeting.

(5866) New Delhi : Delhi Bharatiya Janata Party president Harsh Vardhan has charged that by bowing down before Capital's parking mafia the Municipal Corporation of Delhi would be victimising 45 lakh vehicle owners in the city. As such he has demanded that the Corporation immediately withdraw its decision to raise parking charges and provide relief to the vehicle owners by fixing Rs. 5 as the rate for four-wheeler owners and Rs. 2 for two-wheelers for the first four hours of parking.

(5867) Jaipur : The Rajasthan Pradesh Congress Committee proposes to meet State Governor Pratibha Patil to request her to rein in "communal elements" in the Cabinet headed by Chief Minister Vasundhara Raje. The party is demanding dismissal of the Minister for Social Welfare Madan Dilwar for "objectionable" contents in his Republic Day address in Kota.

(5868) Chennai : Dravida Munnetra Kazhagam president, M.Karunanidhi, on Thursday requested parties in the Democratic Progressive Alliance not to give space to outsiders who were trying to create a rift in the alliance.

(5869) Chennai : Prime Minister Manmohan Singh should direct the Neyveli Lignite Corporation to address the grievances of those who had given their land to the NLC, according to Pattali Makkal Katchi deputy leader in Parliament E. Ponnuswamy.

(5870) Villupuram : Only when the Dravida Munnetra Kazhagam-led Democratic Progressive Alliance wins the Tamil Nadu Assembly elections and comes to power, cordial relations could be established with the Centre. According to Dr. S. Ramadoss, founder of Pattali Makkal Katchi, cordial relations will enable the State to get many development schemes from the Centre so as to launch it on the trajectory of growth.

(5871) Chennai : Tamil Nadu Congress Committee president and Union Minister of State for Project Implementation, G. Vasan MP, has suspected "ulterior motive" behind the Tamil Nadu Government's move to opt for monorail system to meet the growing traffic requirements of the city.

04-02-2006

(5872) Hyderabad : Andhra Pradesh Congress Committee president K. Keshava Rao has announced a nine-member committee to monitor the implementation of the National Rural Employment Guarantee Programme (NREGP) renamed as APREGP here.

(5873) Hyderabad : The Congress Legislature Party (CLP) has ridiculed the TDP's claim that the Gachibowli stadium was damaged due to the AICC plenary held at the venue recently. In a statement here on Friday, Government Chief Whip N. Kiran Kumar Reddy and whips — D. Sridhar Babu and S. Udaya Bhanu — said the TDP was drifting listlessly without any constructive political agenda. Its problems seemed to have compounded after the recently drubbing in the civic elections.

(5874) Tirumala : Union Minister of State for Human Resources Development Daggubati Purandareswari on Friday said it was high time for the true followers of the late N.T. Rama Rao, founder president of the Telugu Desam Party (TDP) and who were still with the party, to go in for self-introspection whether or not to continue in the party. ' Continuing her tirade against former Chief Minister and TDP president N. Chandrababu Naidu, she said the ideology for which the party had been established was not being fulfilled. The commitment was not being felt at all and it was the only reason that she was rather forced her to join the Congress. Further substantiating her reason for joining the Congress against which her father had fought and floated the TDP, she said that the Congress was more committed for the uplift of the poor and the downtrodden and women.

(5875) **Bangalore :** The new Janata Dal (Secular)-Bharatiya Janata Party (BJP) Government in the State will shortly come out with a Common Minimum Programme (CMP). It has also decided to continue with several of the pro-people programmes enunciated by the previous coalition Government. Chief Minister H.D. Kumaraswamy soon after assuming office here on Friday held a brief Cabinet meeting with Deputy Chief Minister B.S. Yediyurappa. He said the CMP will be prepared by the two parties.

(5876) **Bangalore :** Janata Dal (S) leader H.D. Kumaraswamy and Bharatiya Janata Party (BJP) leader B.S. Yediyurappa were on Friday sworn in Chief Minister and Deputy Chief Minister of Karnataka by Governor T.N. Chaturvedi. This ended the fortnight-long political uncertainty in the State. The swearing-in took place on the flight of stairs of the Vidhana Soudha here.

(5877) **Bangalore :** President of the Bharatiya Janata Party Rajnath Singh said on Friday that the Congress "harassed" its erstwhile coalition partner, the Janata Dal (Secular), and lost its confidence in the State.

(5878) **Thiruvananthapuram :** The Opposition Left Democratic Front (LDF) has termed the Governor's Address to the Assembly on Friday the most insipid and uninspiring policy address in recent times. Leader of the Opposition V.S. Achuthanandan wondered why the Governor was silent about the fiscal situation in his Address and pointed out that the speech delivered in July, 2001 had 10 pages dedicated exclusively to the subject.

(5879) **New Delhi :** Prof. Bhim Singh, chairman of the National Panthers Party, on Friday urged Prime Minister Manmohan Singh to intervene to ensure that the Aligarh Muslim University (AMU) remained a minority institution.

(5880) **Kolkata :** Whatever might be the outcome of the talks between Prime Minister Manmohan Singh and leaders of the striking employees of the Airports Authority of India (AAI), the Centre was firm on privatising airports,senior Polit Bureau member of the Communist Party of India (Marxist) Jyoti Basu told the media here on Friday.

(5881) **New Delhi :** "While the resolution correctly points out that it will be dangerous to be lulled into a false sense of security, the priority to be given to the fight against the communal forces is not adequately reflected," CPI (M) general secretary Prakash Karat said, commenting on the resolutions adopted by the All India Congress Committee at its Hyderabad plenary. Analysing the resolutions in the latest issue of the party organ People's Democracy, Mr. Karat said the BJP/RSS combine was actively working to overcome the setbacks it suffered and to rally other forces. In a span of three months, the BJP had joined coalition governments in two States - Bihar and Karnataka - where it had never been in government.

(5882) New Delhi : The Congress on Friday suggested that it was time for the Janata Dal (Secular) of H.D. Deve Gowda to drop the suffix 'secular' and said that its coalition partner in Karnataka was offered the Maharashtra model power sharing arrangement."We addressed the issue, had a detailed meeting at the highest level and offered Maharashtra model of power sharing," party spokesperson Abhishek Singhvi said at a regular briefing.

(5883) New Delhi : It is now almost certain that Bharatiya Janata Party president Rajnath Singh will hold office till 2010, even after the next Lok Sabha elections. Mr. Singh on Thursday said a drive to increase membership from 2.2 crore to nearly 3 crore would be undertaken from April and by the year-end the BJP would complete organisational elections.

(5884) New Delhi : Former Delhi Chief Minister Madan Lal Khurana on Friday said he had written to Prime Minister Manmohan Singh urging him to bring in an Ordinance in order to put an end to the ongoing demolition drive across the Capital.

(5885) New Delhi : Stating that the Delhi Government had been thrown into a Constitutional crisis, Leader of the Opposition in the Delhi Assembly Jagdish Mukhi on Friday said Chief Minister Sheila Dikshit should step down immediately following rejection of two successive Bills by the Select Committees of the Assembly.

(5886) Patna : Railway Minister and RJD Supremo Lalu Prasad today said the NDA government in Bihar, led by Nitish Kumar had "miserably failed" in preparing its own schemes and was busy implementing the Centre's programmes.

(5887) Lucknow : Replicating the BSP's efforts to woo the Brahmin community, Ministers from the ruling Samajwadi Party will attend a 'Viraat

Brahmin Mahakumbh' in the neighbouring Sitapur district. The February 5 'Mahakumbh' will thank Chief Minister and SP chief Mulayam Singh Yadav for declaring a holiday on the birth anniversary of Lord Parshuram and launching the 'Kanya Vidyadhan' scheme, which the event's organisers claimed, "helped girls from the upper castes as well." The proposed 'Mahakumbh' was a reaction to the BSP's plans to attract Brahmin electorate.

(5888) Chennai : Leaders of various Dravidian parties, including Chief Minister Jayalalithaa, Dravida Munnetra Kazhagam president M. Karunanidhi and Marumalarchi Dravida Munnetra Kazhagam general secretary Vaiko, led their party cadres in paying homage to the late Chief Minister C.N. Annadurai on his 37th death anniversary.

(5889) Chennai : Dravida Munnetra Kazhagam president M. Karunanidhi asked why Chief Minister Jayalalithaa did not take back the road mazdoors earlier, though the government had a huge outlay for roads and highways.

05-02-2006

(5890) Eluru : Communist Party of India (CPI) State secretary K. Narayana on Saturday said the welfare of poor fishermen in Kolleru was as important as the lake's protection as a wildlife sanctuary for his party.

(5891) Hyderabad : The Chief Minister's Office expressed surprise over the announcement made on Friday by leaders of the Sarpanches Association that Y.S. Rajasekhara Reddy had agreed to their demand on restoring cheque power. Meanwhile, Telugu Desam Party president N. Chandrababu Naidu criticised Dr. Rajasekhara Reddy for going back on the assurance.

(5892) Tirumala : Senior BJP leader and former party president M. Venkaiah Naidu said that the coalition government of the BJP-JD(S) combine in Karnataka would augur well for the party in its run-up to the elections due shortly to the two State assemblies in the south - Tamil Nadu and Kerala.

(5893) Tirumala : APCC president K. Keshava Rao on Saturday sought to downplay the discontent among senior party leaders over their exclusion from the Union Cabinet during the recent reshuffle. It is quite normal during any Cabinet expansion or reshuffle, especially in a huge national party like the Congress, he said, but struck a note of optimism that everything would soon fall in place.

(5894) Sangareddy : Union Minister and TRS leader A.Narendra set another 45-day 'deadline' for the UPA Government to declare statehood for Telangana and warned the Government that the agitation would begin from the "doorsteps of UPA chairperson Sonia Gandhi." Mr. Narendra was addressing a meeting after inaugurating the new TNGO building in Medak on Saturday.

(5895) Bangalore : The disciplinary action proposed against those Janata Dal (Secular) legislators who violated the party line and forged an alliance with the Bharatiya Janata Party (BJP) to form a coalition Government in the State has been put off by at least a fortnight. The national Executive Committee of the Janata Dal (S) will meet on February 20 and take stock of the developments.

(5896) Kochi : Democratic Indira Congress (Karunakaran) leader K. Karunakaran has criticised Communist Party of India leader Veliyam Bhargavan for his outburst against the DIC(K) in the interests of relations within the LDF.

(5897) New Delhi : The CPI (M) and the CPI commended AAI employees on their united and determined struggle. In a statement, the CPI (M) Polit Bureau condemned the Government's 'brazen' policy of privatisation of a strategic sector. It told the employees that "the battle against privatisation and for their rights is not over." It would discuss the issue at its meeting next week.In a similar statement, the CPI said, "If this is a precursor to further privatisation moves in profit-making public sector undertakings, the Left parties will have to fight against them at all levels."

(5898) New Delhi : Hitting back at the Prime Minister for his sharp remarks against him, Bharatiya Janata Party leader L. K. Advani has charged Manmohan Singh with "compromising day after day only to stick on to office," while he gave up his job to stand by his views on Pakistan founder Mohammad Ali Jinnah.Mr. Advani said on Saturday it was a "mistake" on the part of President A. P. J. Abdul Kalam to have accepted the Cabinet recommendation for dissolution of the Bihar Assembly. The Leader of the Opposition in the Lok Sabha appeared to hint, in an interview to Karan

Thapar in the CNN-IBN's `Devil Advocate' programme, that he would be the BJP candidate for Prime Minister in the next elections.

(5899) Dindigul : Responding to a plea made by Marumalarchi Dravida Munnetra Kazhagam general secretary Vaiko to link rivers, with priority to linking of peninsular rivers to find a solution to the problems of Tamil Nadu farmers, the Prime Minister Manmohan Singh said: "We have not forgotten this important project." Dr. Singh was laying the foundation for four-laning of Krishnagiri-Salem-Madurai stretch of National Highway 7 at Chinnalapatti near here. Mr. Vaiko said though the country could take pride in the giant strides it had made in several fields, migration of people from rural to urban areas was a cause for concern.Rural unemployment would be adequately addressed by guaranteeing water for irrigation through linking of rivers, he said. Mr. Vaiko suggested that all inter-State rivers be declared `national rivers.'

(5900) Chennai : Dravida Munnetra Kazhagam president M. Karunanidhi has alleged that the ruling party, with the connivance of police and bureaucrats, was making all out efforts to break the Democratic Progressive Alliance in the State led by the DMK.

(5901) Pondicherry : President of the Puduchery Munnetra Congress (PMC) P. Kannan has announced at a meeting of party office bearers and also its special invitees that the party will have an electoral alliance with All India Anna Dravida Munnetra Kazhagam (AIADMK) in the forthcoming Assembly polls here.

(5902) Tiruchi : The Dravida Munnetra Kazhagam should not remain a silent spectator to the rumours on the fissures in the Democratic Progressive Alliance, State secretary of the Communist Party of India (Marxist) N. Varadarajan said on Friday.

(5903) Chennai : All India Anna Dravida Munnetra Kazhagam general secretary and Chief Minister Jayalalithaa on Saturday appealed to party activists to work for its victory in the coming Assembly polls without bothering about electoral alliances.

06-02-2006

(5904) Hyderabad : The Telugu Desam Party has lashed out at Congress leaders, saying they have no right to criticise a party which is only doing its duty as the Opposition and organising a 'padayatra' to realise the 'Pranahita-Chevella link project'. Addressing a press conference here on Sunday, R. Chandrasekhar Reddy, MP, and N. Janardhan Reddy, Telugu Desam Legislature Party Deputy Floor Leader, urged the Congress to stop mudslinging at TDP and introspect where it was going wrong.

(5905) Hyderabad : The State CPI (M) committee has suggested that Chief Minister Y.S. Rajasekhara Reddy hold a special discussion in the ensuing Assembly session on recognising Telugu as a classical language.

(5906) Nellore : Former Chief Minister and **Visakhapatnam** Member of Parliament N. Janardhana Reddy has said that in accordance with the wishes of AICC President Sonia Gandhi at the recently concluded party plenary at Hyderabad, the party has decided to give more emphasis on agriculture, rural economy and allied sectors.

(5907) Tirupati : The Andhra Pradesh Congress Committee (PCC) president K. Keshava Rao has given a warm pat on the Congress Government's back for discharging its duties in a proper manner, adding that the policy decisions are announced only after due legal consultations. At a media conference here on Sunday, Mr. Rao pooh-poohed the BJP's ambition of emerging strong in the South saying that the party has every right to 'day dream'.

(5908) Tirupati : BJP national leader M. Venkaiah Naidu on Sunday lashed out at Left parities saying they failed to put their coalition partner Congress under check even on the issues which were very close to their heart.

(5909) Visakhapatnam : The Congress is pursuing vote bank politics without any commitment for uplift of minorities, Telugu Desam Party leader and MP Lal Jan Basha has said. "Chief Minister Y.S. Rajasekhara Reddy announced 5 per cent reservation for Muslims keeping an eye on municipal elections. He did not implement three per cent quota finalised by the TDP Government knowing very well that the decision on five per cent would lead to legal complications," Mr. Basha told reporters on Sunday.

(5910) Visakhapatnam : "It is a black spot on the face of democracy. It brings back the dark memories of emergency that was imposed by the then Congress Prime Minister Indira Gandhi in 1975." That was how Telugu Desam Parliamentary Party Leader Yerran Naidu reacted to the State

Government's late night slapping of an ordinance on Visakha Dairy and seven other dairies in the State at a press meet here on Sunday.

(5911) Kasaragod : Communist Party of India (CPI) State secretary Veliyam Bhargavan on Sunday said the Democratic Indira Congress (Karunakaran) has no right to meddle in the affairs of the Left Democratic Front (LDF).

(5912) New Delhi : The Left parties on Sunday said India's vote against Iran in reporting the nuclear issue to the United Nations Security Council was "not in conformity" with the pursuit of an independent foreign policy and maintaining good relations with Teheran. It demanded a full debate in Parliament on the issue.

(5913) Bangalore : Mir Bahadur Hussain, President of the Bharatiya Janata Party Minorities Morcha, has said that the party which has come to power for the first time in the State must ensure adequate representation for legislators from minority communities in the Government.

(5914) Bangalore : Chief Minister H.D. Kumaraswamy, meets senior leaders of other political parties, including those from the Janata Parivar to consolidate his support base. He has met the former Chief Minister S.R. Bommai seeking his guidance in running the administration. As a step towards consolidating the support enjoyed by the new coalition, Mr. Kumaraswamy has sought the support of the five-member Janata Dal (United) group in the State Assembly. He has even sought the merger of that party with the Janata Dal (S).

(5915) New Delhi : The Bharatiya Janata Party has criticised the Manmohan Singh Government's decision to import wheat saying it is the direct result of mismanagement of stocks and failure to procure adequate quantities to maintain a buffer. In a statement here on Sunday, party spokesperson Prakash Javadekar charged the Government with having deliberately reduced procurement of wheat to cut down on the subsidy bill. Now, it would pay more for the five lakh tonnes of wheat it would import.

(5916) Kolkata : Chairman of West Bengal's ruling Left Front Biman Bose has charged the Union Government with "throwing away the Common Minimum Programme (CMP) into the bin as if it were waste paper."

(5917) Kolkata : "There will be no formal mahajot [grand alliance of non-Left parties] in the polls but we are ready to take on any clandestine mahajot [that might be cobbled]," chairman of the Left Front committee and Polit Bureau member of the Communist Party of India, Biman Bose, said here on Sunday. Defence Minister and Congress leader Pranab Mukherjee appeared reconciled to the fact that the formation of the "mahajot" is most unlikely, given the party's differences with the other main Opposition party - the Trinamool Congress.

(5918) New Delhi : The Janata Dal (United) on Sunday warned the United Progressive Alliance (UPA) Government of a prolonged nationwide campaign to oppose what it called the "Government's surrender to the U.S. designs" in voting against Iran.Addressing a press conference here, JD (U) president George Fernandes said that India's vote for taking Iran's `nuclear issues' to the Security Council was another "shameful chapter" in the continuing saga of the Manmohan Singh Government's "surrender" to the dictates of the Bush administration.

(5919) Lucknow : Terming India's vote for referring Iran to the Security Council "unacceptable," Uttar Pradesh Chief Minister and Samajwadi Party president Mulayam Singh Yadav on Sunday condemned the decision.

(5920) New Delhi : Accusing the Bharatiya Janata Party of being responsible for the present mess over regularisation of unauthorised colonies and illegal constructions, newly appointed Union Minister of State for Urban Development Ajay Maken has asserted that the Congress will win the next Assembly polls on the issue of demolitions and regularisation that has created chaos and confusion in the minds of people in the Capital.

(5921) Jalandhar : The Punjab Chief Minister Capt. Amarinder Singh today said the ruling Congress was all prepared to go for Assembly polls in the State any day. Elections are due to be held in February next year.

(5922) Chennai : Dravida Munnetra Kazhagam (DMK) president M. Karunanidhi on Sunday appealed to party activists to fearlessly carry out election work as per their plan and without bothering about what was happening in the All-India Anna Dravida Munnetra Kazhagam (AIADMK) camp.

(5923) Dharampuri : Pattali Makkal Katchi (PMK) founder S. Ramadoss said that Ms. Jayalalithaa's talk on forging electoral ties "exposed her fear" of facing the Assembly polls.

(5924) Madurai : The Bharatiya Janata Party has decided to maintain equidistance from both the ruling All-India Anna Dravida Munnetra Kazhagam and the Dravida Munnetra Kazhagam in the Assembly elections. The party will go it alone as it wants to emerge as a party "acceptable to all sections, including the minorities," BJP national secretary Bandaru Dattatreya said here on Sunday.

07-02-2006

(5925) Hyderabad : The APSRTC bus fare hike came in for severe criticism from the Opposition parties. The Telugu Desam has opposed the move saying it was irrational and lacked an effort to take the consensus of the stakeholders.B.V. Raghavulu, CPI (M) State secretary, demanded withdrawal of the decision, saying it would benefit private bus operators. He said the party opposed the burden of Rs. 200 crores placed on people by Government while failing to bring down the MV Tax and checking illegal operation of private operators. CPI State Secretary K. Narayana condemned the hike and said it would surely lead to a steep fall in occupancy ratio. He said the party would launch a sustained agitation to pressurise Government into reversing its decision.

(5926) Bhubaneswar : The Opposition on Monday demanded resignation of Chief Minister Naveen Patnaik over the Kalinga Nagar police firing in which 12 tribal men and women were killed on January 2. Initiating a debate discussion on the controversy surrounding the firing incident in the State Assembly, the Congress Deputy Leader Narasingha Mishra also demanded criminal proceedings against Mr. Patnaik and administration officials holding them responsible for the killing.

(5927) Bangalore : Chief Minister H.D. Kumaraswamy said on Monday that the former Prime Minister and Janata Dal (S) President, H.D. Deve Gowda, and national office-bearers of the party will decide on whether or not to have an alliance with the Bharatiya Janata Party (BJP) for the next Legislative Assembly elections in the State.

(5928) Bangalore : The Janata Dal (Secular) leadership is in a dilemma on whether to issue a whip to party legislators to vote in favour of the confidence motion to be tabled by Chief Minister H.D. Kumaraswamy in the Legislative Assembly on Wednesday. The BJP has decided to issue a whip to its legislators to vote in favour of the Government. In the 224-member Assembly, the JD(S) has a strength of 59, the BJP 79, the Congress 64 and the JD(U) five. Some independents are associated with the three major parties. In case of a division, the Government has to obtain 113 votes to carry the motion.

(5929) Panaji : Chandrakant Tripathi, Nationalist Congress Party's special envoy to the State, who arrived here on Sunday to resolve the differences between State unit President and Deputy Chief Minister Wilfred de Souza and Agriculture Minister Micky Pacheco, continued his efforts on Monday. After meeting Mr. de Souza, he held a meeting with Mr. Pacheco, who is reportedly upset with Mr. de Souza's style of functioning. Playing down the trouble, Mr. Tripathi said there are bound to be differences in political parties and this is not unique to his party. Responding to the demands of Mr. Pacheco that Mr. de Souza should quit either the post of the Deputy Chief Minister or of party presidentship, Mr. Tripathi said the party's constitution does not speak of the "One man, one post" concept.

(5930) Thiruvananthapuram : Even as the Democratic Indira Congress (Karunakaran) led by K. Karunakaran is faced with problems in striking a direct alliance with the Left Democratic Front (LDF) in Kerala, the fledgling party appears to have found a new friend in the All India Anna Dravida Munnetra Kazhagam (AIADMK) ruling neighbouring Tamil Nadu. Tamil Nadu Chief Minister Jayalalithaa recently sent an emissary to Mr. Karunakaran to explore the possibility of forming an alliance, said DIC(K) president K. Muraleedharan on Monday.

(5931) New Delhi : The Bharatiya Janata Party has demanded that Election Commissioner Navin Chawla "step down" from his office or "face action" by the party. It would do "whatever was necessary" to "get him out" of that job. The provocation for the demand was the "expose" by a television channel that has reported that Mr. Chawla has accepted money from several Congress MPs for trusts run by him and his family members. The money was given by the MPs from their Member of Parliament Local Area Development Scheme. BJP general secretary Arun Jaitley said he did not want to get into the question whether giving of that money from

MPLADS was within the rules or not. He also said it was not material whether those funds were given after or before Mr. Chawla took the job of Election Commissioner. He stressed that for the moment his party wanted to make an issue of the "closeness" of Mr. Chawla to 10 Janpath.

(5932) New Delhi : A day after demanding that the Iran nuclear issue and India's vote be discussed in Parliament, the Left parties continued informal consultations on Monday. The Central Secretariat of the Communist Party of India met here and discussed the economic policies of the United Progressive Alliance Government and reviewed its performance on the front. "The discussions were inconclusive and we decided to carry on with them at our National Executive meeting to be held here from February 25-26," party's national secretary D. Raja said. The Left parties on Sunday decided that each constituent - the CPI, the CPI (M), the All-India Forward Bloc and the Revolutionary Socialist Party - hold discussions within the party on the direction of the economic policies of the coalition government. CPI (M) general secretary Prakash Karat went to the CPI office and met that party's general secretary A.B. Bardhan and other leaders.

(5933) New Delhi : The Congress on Monday said it respected the allies and supporting parties' views but "no single group can or should have a veto of any kind" especially on the foreign policy.Responding to questions on the Left stand, Congress spokesperson Abhishek Singhvi said here the foreign policy reflected continuity and stability and ``no responsible party should seek to undermine it.'' Without commenting directly on the Left stand vis-...-vis Iran, he said the Government had taken a holistic and balanced approach, guided by the national interest, to the foreign policy.

(5934) New Delhi : Indian Justice Party president Udit Raj on Monday said the Dalit Mukti-Yatra launched by his party in Uttar Pradesh on February 2 was aimed at exposing Dalit leaders who were exploiting members of their own community for political gains.

(5935) New Delhi : In a move indicating intensification of the struggle within the Delhi Congress and the Congress Legislature Party (CLP), the party's senior legislator from Ghonda Bhisham Sharma on Monday moved a "breach of privilege and contempt motion" against Chief Minister Sheila Dikshit for attributing motives to the working of the Delhi Assembly's Select Committee and the conduct of its members.

(5936) Pondicherry : All India Congress Committee general secretary V. Narayanasamy MP has said that utmost caution would be exercised when sharing of seats with alliance parties was decided in the context of the forthcoming Assembly polls in Pondicherry.

(5937) Chennai : Tamil Nadu Congress Committee president and Union Minister of State for Statistics and Project Implementation, G.K.Vasan, is confident that the Congress will get its due share of seats to contest the Assembly elections.

(5938) Madurai : The Bharatiya Janata Party has termed as "danger to democracy' the formation of the Ministry for Minority Affairs by the United Progressive Alliance Government."The Congress party will pay a heavy price for attempting to divide the nation and for not treating all the citizens as equals," said the former Union Minister and national secretary of the BJP, Bandaru Dattatreya.

(5939) Chennai : The Bharatiya Janata Party on Monday complained that Tamil Nadu had also started experiencing the problem of illegal Bangladeshi immigrants.L. Ganesan, newly appointed BJP national vice-president, told a press conference here that according to his information, there were about 30,000 such persons in Coimbatore. The problem had the potential of posing a "grave danger" to the State.

(5940) Chennai : State Government employees will not be carried away by various benefits and incentives offered by Chief Minister Jayalalithaa, DMK president M. Karunanidhi said here on Monday. He told reporters that the employees knew that the Chief Minister had made these announcements on the eve of Assembly elections. They would not forget the "various repressive measures," including arrest of thousands of their colleagues, initiated by the Chief Minister during their strike. The employees were fighting for their rights and had announced an agitation to secure their demands.

(5941) Karaikudi : Union Minister of State for Social Justice and Empowerment, Subbulakshmi Jagadeesan claimed on Monday that it was DMK chief M. Karunanidhi, who started self-help group movement in Tamil Nadu. Presiding over a session on SHG held here as a part of five-day Info Expo to showcase the achievements of United Progressive Government, he said the concept was started in 1989 at Dharmapuri when the DMK was power. The concept spread to other areas in Tamil Nadu following its success.

08-02-2006

(5942) Hyderabad : The BJP has demanded village-level all-party committees to oversee the implementation of the National Rural Employment Guarantee Programme and 'Indiramma' scheme and expressed apprehension that the Congress might misuse them.Party general secretary K. Laxman at a press conference here on Tuesday alleged that the 'Indiramma' scheme was being utilised by Chief Minister Y.S. Rajasekhara Reddy for the panchayat poll campaign by "promising the moon to people."

(5943) Hyderabad : Telugu Desam president N. Chandrababu Naidu on Tuesday said he would henceforth focus his attention on promoting agriculture besides seeing that the benefits of reforms reach the poor and result in the welfare of artisans.

(5944) Visakhapatnam : The CPI (M) will protest against the visit of the US President George W. Bush to Hyderabad in March, to oppose the US stance on Iran's nuclear facilities. The party's State secretary and Polit Bureau member B.V. Raghavulu also criticised India for siding with the US on the vote in International Atomic Energy Agency (IAEA) undermining its friendly relations with Iran, which had committed to building a gas pipeline to India via Pakistan. Mr. Raghavulu said the US dictating terms on atomic facilities of a country was an insult to its sovereignty. Stating that India's commitment were an open secret in the US, he demanded at a party meeting here on Tuesday that the UPA Government should discuss in Parliament its agreements with the US on nuclear facilities.

(5945) Mahabubnagar : CPI National Secretariat Member and MP Suravaram Sudhakar Reddy has charged the State Government with failing to solve the naxalite problem.

(5946) Thiruvananthapuram : The Congress has urged the Election Commission to deploy paramilitary forces near sensitive polling booths, particularly in Kannur and Kasaragod districts, during the upcoming Assembly elections in the State.

(5947) Bangalore : Speaking to presspersons after a meeting of the Bharatiya Janata Party Legislature Party, Deputy Chief Minister B.S.

Yediyurappa exuded confidence that Mr. Kumaraswamy will get more than the required support from the BJP and the JD (S) members as also some others. Meanwhile, the Janata Dal (S) has decided to allow its members, numbering 46, and some independents to cast their conscience vote. The BJP has 79 members. An independent member Rajasekhara Sindhoor has joined the party as an associate member and will also vote for the motion.

(5948) New Delhi : The Samajwadi Party on Tuesday suspended its two-time member of Parliament from Agra, Raj Babbar, from the Parliamentary Party on charges of "indiscipline" for his recent public statements against party general secretary Amar Singh.

(5949) Gulbarga : Dalit Sangharsh Samiti will organise taluk-wise agitations against Deputy Chief Minister B.S. Yediyurappa for his alleged attempt to remove the portrait of Ambedkar from his chamber, across the State from Wednesday. The DSS State convenor D.G. Sagar and the Communist Party of India Marxist general secretary Maruti Manpade told presspersons here on Tuesday that they would not stop till Mr. Yediyurappa resigned from his post.Dalit leaders in the BJP have asked Dalit organisations to drop the agitation being carried out against Mr. Yediyurappa. He has clarified that he had not removed the portrait. It had been done by the earlier occupant of the chamber, M. Mallikarjun Kharge, while vacating it. Therefore, no insult has been caused to Dr. Ambedkar, they said. Dalit organisations should realise this and take a mature stand, MLA and BJP Scheduled Caste Morcha State President Rajendra Verma said.

(5950) Hubli: All India Progressive Janata Dal (AIPJD) Working President B.R. Patil has alleged that Deputy Chief Minister B.S. Yediyurappa will be the next victim of the game plan of Janata Dal (Secular) President and former Prime Minister H.D. Deve Gowda to suppress Lingayat leadership in the State. Mr. Patil appealed to Lingayat leaders here on Tuesday not to believe Mr. Deve Gowda. "Mr. Deve Gowda is not only anti-Dalit but is also anti-Lingayat," he said.Mr. Patil alleged that Mr. Deve Gowda made M.P. Prakash Deputy Chief Minister only to ditch him midway and make his son Chief Minister.

(5951) Panaji : The infighting in the Nationalist Congress Party (NCP) State unit is set to escalate even as Agriculture Minister Micky Pacheco on Tuesday contradicted the leadership's emissary to reiterate that the differences in the State party continued. Contradicting the statement made by Chandrakant Tripathi on Tuesday morning that there were no differences in the State unit of the party, Mr. Pacheco said there were differences in the party. Mr. Pacheco told presspersons that he was not going to work under party State unit president and Deputy Chief Minister Wilfred de Souza.

(5952) Kannur : Communist Party of India (CPI) assistant secretary K.E. Ismail has said that the United Democratic Front (UDF) Government has made Kerala bankrupt by pursuing policies aimed at reversing the State's achievements.

(5953) Thiruvananthapuram : The youths who returned to the Congress from the Democratic Indira Congress (Karunakaran) (DIC(K) have complained to the party leadership against the move to exclude two persons under whose leadership they returned to the parent party from leadership positions. In complaints submitted to Congress Working Committee member A.K.Antony, KPCC(I) president Ramesh Chennithala and Chief Minister, Oommen Chandy on Tuesday they said that the leaders who were being sidelined were A.K. Shihab, who had been State general secretary of the Youth Congress(Indira) and Wandannoor Santhosh, who had been a close confidant of K.Muralidharan.

(5954) New Delhi : The Bharatiya Janata Party will petition Chief Election Commissioner B.B. Tandon to use his powers under Article 324 (5) of the Constitution and "recommend" to President A.P.J. Abdul Kalam that Election Commissioner Navin Chawla be dismissed. Party general secretary and spokesperson Arun Jaitley said on Tuesday they would look for support from other Opposition parties in the issue.

(5955) New Delhi : Bharatiya Janata Party general secretary Pramod Mahajan will take care of the coming Assembly elections in Assam, and Arun Jaitley, also a general secretary, has been asked to take charge of the elections in West Bengal. Party president Rajnath Singh made the announcement late on Tuesday evening.Assembly elections are scheduled in five States this year. Rajiv Pratap Rudy has been asked to take charge of Tamil Nadu and L. Ganesan will be in-charge of the elections in Kerala. Thirunavukkarsar will take care of the elections in Pondicherry. The overall charge for the three southern States goes to Venkaiah Naidu.

(5956) New Delhi : The Delhi Bharatiya Janata Party has been thrown into turmoil with former Minister and Madan Lal Khurana loyalist Harsharan Singh Balli accusing both Delhi BJP president Harsh Vardhan and Leader of the Opposition in Delhi Assembly Jagdish Mukhi of playing into the hands of Chief Minister Sheila Dikshit and acting as "loyal Opposition" to the Congress Government.

(5957) Chennai : Vijayakumar, who has excelled in many roles on the screen including a loving husband, affectionate father, majestic village head, honest police officer and passionate freedom fighter, is all set to play a new role in real life.The actor, who heads a family of film artists including wife Manjula, daughters Preetha, Sridevi and Vanitha and son Arunkumar, formally joined the All India Anna Dravida Munnetra Kazhagam (AIADMK) as one of its primary members on Tuesday. He called on AIADMK general secretary and Chief Minister Jayalalithaa at her residence and received the membership card from her after completing the formalities.

(5958) Chennai : The gateway to the South has been opened for the Bharatiya Janata Party with the party coming to power in Karnataka, senior leader M. Venkaiah Naidu said on Tuesday."The Cauvery flows from Karnataka to Tamil Nadu. The BJP too will flow from Karnataka to Tamil Nadu," Mr Naidu told a public meeting at Mudichur, about 30 km from Chennai, to launch the programme of "Makkal Darisanam" (meet the people) to be undertaken by the party vice-president L. Ganesan, in northern parts of the State in the next one month. In the past, the BJP was branded as a "north-Indian" party, he added.

(5959) Chennai : Party offices are coming to life with preparations under way for the Assembly elections. The All-India Anna Dravida Munnetra Kazhagam and the Dravida Munnetra Kazhagam have pressed ahead with the distribution of applications. While the AIADMK began the distribution a week ago, the DMK started the process four days back.

(5960) Pollachi : Calling upon the student community to concentrate on their studies and their task in the respective fields in the future, the Marumalarchi Dravida Munnetra Kazhagam general secretary, Vaiko, on Tuesday said overcoming the weaknesses was also a sacrifice.

(5961) Theni : "Alliance partners in DMK-led Democratic Progressive Alliance could come out of it to protect their parties and for survival. It is the right time for them to exit," AIADMK presidium chairman K. Kalimuthu has said.

(5962) Chennai : The State units of the Communist Party of India (Marxist) and the Communist Party of India appear to have independently decided to adopt a two-pronged strategy for the Assembly elections: get due share for the Left camp and evolve an alternative programme for the new Government.The State Committee of the CPI (M) and the Executive Committee of the CPI met in Chennai on Tuesday to discuss election-related issues.

09-02-2006

(5963) Warangal : TRS rebel legislator Mandadi Satyaranayana Reddy urged party leader A Narendra to restrain from making unwarranted statements that were only confusing people.

(5964) Kadapa : The Telugu Desam Party Government grossly neglected irrigation projects during its nine-year rule, but was undertaking padayatra with regard to Pranahitha project now for political gains, Minister for Social Welfare D.S. Redya Naik alleged on Wednesday. Addressing a gram sabha for Indiramma scheme at Hasanapuram in Ramapuram mandal, Mr. Naik alleged that Congress MLAs were suspended from Assembly in large number whenever they demanded that Chandrababu Naidu Government execute irrigation projects. The Then Irrigation Minister Kadiyam Srihari never spoke about Pranahitha project while in power, but was now demanding its completion and water release up to Chevella, he alleged.

(5965) Chukkapur (Nizamabad Dt.) : The Telugu Desam Party's Godavari Jala Sadhana padayatra led by party's Polit Bureau member T. Devender Goud commenced without any pomp or fanfare at this village in Machareddy mandal in the district on Wednesday.

(5966) Bangalore : The Bharatiya Janata Party-Janata Dal (Secular) Government in Karnataka won a vote of confidence in the Assembly in the early hours of Thursday, the seventh day of the Chief Minister and the Deputy Chief Minister assuming office.The Legislative Assembly adopted the motion of confidence moved by Chief Minister H.D. Kumaraswamy after a marathon 14-hour debate. The motion was supported by 138 members, while 66 opposed it. The Chief Minister defended his father, the former Prime Minister, H.D. Deve Gowda, and said that till the end he opposed the alliance on ideological grounds and his commitment to secularism. He would win over his father through his commitment to development of the State. Mr. Kumaraswamy said he was not doctrinaire in his approach and declared development of the State would be his credo. His father and he were committed to the uplift of the poor. Mr. Kumaraswamy revealed that the BJP had sought an alliance with him ever since the 2004 Assembly elections. At that time BJP leader Arun Jaitley had offered to help him become the Chief Minister and adopt the "Orissa model" of governance. But he spurned the offer as he was not after power. It is the Congress that had pushed him towards an alliance with the BJP. At that, senior Congress member Mallikarjun Kharge said the revelation proved wrong the claim made by the JD(S) of "harassment from the Congress."

(5967) Thiruvananthapuram : The Opposition Left Democratic Front staged a walk-out at the fag end of the three-day debate on the motion of thanks to the Governor's Address in protest against Speaker Therambil Ramakrishnan's refusal to permit Democratic Indira Congress (Karunakaran) leader T. M. Jacob make a mention about the police action against his party workers in the city on Wednesday. DIC(K) leader K. Muraleedharan in a statement demanded a judicial inquiry into the police action against the DIC(K) workers. He said the police action was unprovoked and unwarranted. The action was the outcome of a conspiracy hatched by the "Oommen Congress" and the police, going by the huge posse that had been deployed in view of the march, he said.

(5968) Bangalore : Former Deputy Chief Minister M.P. Prakash said in the Legislative Assembly on Wednesday that he could technically have issued a whip to the Janata Dal (S) MLAs to vote in favour of the Dharam Singh government, but he did not do so as he did not have the moral authority since they were supporting H.D. Kumaraswamy.

(5969) Bangalore : Janata Dal (Secular) leader P.G.R. Sindhia said on Wednesday that his conscience does not permit him to acknowledge Chief Minister H.D. Kumaraswamy as the JD(S) Legislature Party leader.

(5970) Bangalore : In his new role as Leader of the Opposition in the Legislative Assembly, former Chief Minister N. Dharam Singh chastised

Chief Minister H.D. Kumaraswamy for "entering into an unholy alliance with the Bharatiya Janata Party without understanding the dangerous portents of going with a party with anti-secular credentials".

(5971) Bijapur : The Bharatiya Janata Party (BJP) has alleged that the Congress is responsible for the row over the alleged removal of Ambedkar's portrait from the chamber of Deputy Chief Minister B.S. Yediyurappa.

(5972) Gulbarga : Members of the Dalit Sangharsh Samiti and the Communist Party of India (Marxist) staged a protest in Gulbarga on Wednesday against the alleged removal of Ambedkar's portrait from the chamber of Deputy Chief Minister B.S. Yediyurappa.

(5973) Kollam : Union Minister for Overseas Indian Affairs Vayalar Ravi has said that the Congress is least bothered about the snowballing showdown between the Communist Party of India (Marxist) and the Communist Party of India.

(5974) Thiruvananthapuram : The CPI(M) State secretariat has demanded an all-party meeting to discuss the 'serious misgivings' expressed by experts about the health insurance scheme proposed to be implemented in the State.

(5975) Thiruvananthapuram : Congress Working Committee (CWC) member Veerappa Moily on Wednesday termed CPI(M) State secretary Pinarayi Vijayan as one of the "biggest opportunists."

(5976) Thiruvananthapuram : Indian Union Muslim League (IUML) leader P.K. Kunhalikutty on Wednesday said the biggest hurdle to the State's development was the "penchant for duplicity" of the Left Democratic Front (LDF). "In Thiruvananthapuram, you gherao Asian Development Bank (ADB) officials. In Kochi, you receive them with bouquets," he said in the State Assembly, while participating in the discussion on the motion of thanks to the Governor's Address.

(5977) New Delhi : The Samajwadi Party on Wednesday suspended its Agra member of Parliament Raj Babbar from the primary membership of the party charging him with indulging in "anti-party" activities. On Tuesday, the two-time MP was suspended from the Parliamentary Party for his public statements against party general secretary Amar Singh. The actor-turned-politician reportedly questioned the "utility" of Mr. Singh in the party and accused him of having brought a "broker culture" into the party.The leader of the Parliamentary Party and general secretary, Ramgopal Yadav, said Mr. Babbar had also been suspended from the primary membership because of "indiscipline".

(5978) New Delhi : Angry Bharatiya Janata Party Councillors on Wednesday walked out of the Municipal Corporation of Delhi House proceedings after the ruling Congress refused to bring in a resolution asking the Centre to approach the High Court to end the demolition drive till the high-power committee formed by Prime Minister Manmohan Singh submitted its report.

(5979) New Delhi : Traffic movement in large parts of East Delhi came to a standstill for several hours on Wednesday as a large number of Delhi Bharatiya Janata Party workers took to the streets and imposed a "chakka jam" (traffic blockade) protesting against the demolition drive being carried out in the Capital by the Municipal Corporation of Delhi and the Delhi Government's inability to stop it.

(5980) Chandigarh : Senior BJP leader and former Chandigarh MP, Satya Pal Jain, on Wednesday expressed concern over the deteriorating law and order situation in the City Beautiful. Criticising the brutal murder of retired Air Force officer, T.P. Singh, his wife and sister in their house in Sector 34 here, he said that the incidents of theft, murder and dacoity were becoming a daily occurrence.

(5981) Jaipur : The long race for the post of Bharatiya Janata Party chief in Rajasthan has ended with the party leadership settling for RSS ideologue and former Rajya Sabha member Mahesh Sharma. The new incumbent, who originally hails from Churu in the State, has been the vice-president in the party executive headed by the outgoing president Lalit Kishore Chaturvedi.

(5982) Chennai : The DMK was willing to make sacrifices, Mr. Karunanidhi said, while addressing a meeting of the alliance party leaders at the DMK headquarters here on Wednesday. The allies too should be willing to do so. Mr. Karunanidhi made it clear that the DMK would also talk to other parties in the alliance, apart from the six major ones. On the inclusion of the Dalit Panthers of India, he said the issue did not come up for discussion. When it was pointed out that the Pattali Makkal Katchi leader S. Ramadoss had refuted all reports of fissures in the alliance while the Marumalarchi Dravida Munnetra Kazhagam had chosen to remain silent, he said this was a result of the long-standing, close relations between him and the MDMK leadership.

(5983) Chennai : Dravida Munnetra Kazhagam president M. Karunanidhi on Wednesday urged Prime Minister Manmohan Singh to ensure that an appropriate Bill was introduced in the Lok Sabha in the ensuing budget session to provide reservation for Dalit Christians and Muslims. In a letter to the Prime Minister, he said the quantum of reservation could be left to the State Governments to decide.

(5984) Madurai : The State unit of the All-India Forward Bloc has recommended the expulsion of party MLA L. Santhanam, representing the Usilampatti constituency in Madurai district, for alleged anti-party activities.

10-02-2006

(5985) Hyderabad : The BJP has asked the Government to publish a white paper on Jalayagnam, detailing funds mobilised for projects as also water allocation. Senior party leader Ch. Vidyasagar Rao and general secretary K. Naresh on Thursday wanted clarification as to how the Government planned to mobilise funds for irrigation projects.

(5986) Hyderabad : K.S. Menayya, general secretary of the Andhra Pradesh unit of Bahujan Samaj Party (BSP), on Thursday took over as president from P. Lalaiah who was made member of the National Executive.

(5987) Vijayawada : The Communist Party of India, along with other Left parties, will stage dharna to register their protest during the visit of George W.Bush, President of the United States, to Hyderabad in March. CPI State secretary K.Narayana said here on Thursday that Mr Bush had made the toppling of democracies the primary preoccupation of the USA. Afghanistan was followed by Iraq and now the guns were trained at Iran. Left parties would launch a three-day State-wide campaign to educate people on the "ills" of the Bush Administration on March 1.

(5988) Vijayawada : The Telugu Desam Party (TDP) is behaving like the TRS, trying to provoke regional feelings on the Pothireddypadu issue, according to State secretary of the Communist Party of India (CPI) K. Narayana. TDP men in Rayalaseema are demanding that the capacity of the Pothireddypadu head-regulator be increased. But senior TDP leaders are taking out padayatra in Krishna delta opposing the proposal. "They are behaving like coastal Telugu Desam Party," he says.

(5989) Bangalore : Bharatiya Janata Party (BJP) is well-versed in the art of following the coalition dharma. It has no intention to inflict its Hindutva ideology on Janata Dal (Secular), coalition partner in the State, party leader M. Venkaiah Naidu has said.

(5990) Thiruvananthapuram : The Congress Working Committee member Veerappa Moily has ruled out any question of seeking the Democratic Indira Congress (Karunakaran) leader K. Karunakaran's return to the party as he is negotiating with the Left Democratic Front (LDF) for a slot in the Opposition alliance.

(5991) Lucknow : Accusing the United Progressive Alliance Government of lacking a clear-cut view on policy matters, including Iran, BJP president Rajnath Singh on Thursday sought an all-party meeting on the Iran issue."The foreign policy of the country is no longer independent... Neither Parliament nor the Opposition parties were taken into confidence on the Iran issue," he told reporters here.

(5992) Bangalore : The Bharatiya Janata Party (BJP) is thankful to the Congress for "ill-treating" its former coalition partner, the Janata Dal (Secular), for over 19 months, which has now enabled the formation of the new coalition, the former BJP President M. Venkaiah Naidu said here on Thursday. The mandate of the people is being honoured belatedly with the new coalition coming to power, Mr. Naidu told presspersons here after a meeting of the BJP Legislature PartyChief Minister H.D. Kumaraswamy was keen on going with the BJP in 2004, but the Congress played up the bogey of secularism and persuaded Janata Dal (S) national President H.D. Deve Gowda to go into partnership with it. "The 2004 mandate was truly honoured yesterday," he said on Mr. Kumaraswamy winning the confidence motion in the Legislative Assembly.

(5993) Panaji : The Nationalist Congress Party (NCP) has brought to the notice of the Chief Electoral Officer alleged discrepancies and irregularities in the ongoing interim revision of the electoral rolls.

Addressing presspersons here on Thursday, NCP Goa unit President and Deputy Chief Minister Wilfred de Souza pointed out several instances of alleged discrepancies in the work undertaken by the Election Commission staff.

(5994) Kochi : Ending indecision over the Rs. 183-crore Asian Development Bank (ADB) aid for infrastructure projects in Kochi, the Communist Party of India-Marxist (CPI-M) district committee, on Thursday, gave the green signal to its parliamentary party in the Kochi Corporation to accept the financial assistance. Barring Kochi, all the four corporations in the State had earlier decided to accept the aid.

(5995) Thiruvananthapuram : The Democratic Indira Congress (Karunakaran), which is seeking an entry into the LDF, scored a major political point by forcing the Opposition to join its protest against the alleged police action on DIC(K) workers and announce a walkout in the Assembly on Wednesday.

(5996) Kochi : The Indian Union Muslim League (IUML) has gone back on the promise made in the UDF's election manifesto that special recruitment will be held to fill vacancies in Government jobs, says C.H. Secular Forum State general secretary K.T. Jaleel.

(5997) New Delhi : The Bharatiya Janata Party on Thursday made a number of charges against the United Progressive Alliance government: it was getting ready to increase the prices of petroleum products once again; it was not interested in stopping the lottery business; and it was planning to cut the quota for small investors in the capital market instead of getting to the bottom of the demat account scandal. In the 20 months of UPA rule, petroleum product prices had been revised upwards six times leading to a 35 per cent increase, party spokesperson Prakash Javadekar said while expressing fears that it was getting ready for another hike. Rubbishing the UPA excuse that the hike was necessitated by the high international price of crude, he pointed out that 65 per cent of the price in India was on account of taxes and there was room to play with that to keep the prices down to a reasonable level for consumers.

(5998) Kolkata : The "tactical line" to be adopted by the Communist Party of India (Marxist) for the upcoming Assembly elections in four States and one Union Territory, keeping in mind the recent contentious decisions by the Congress-led United Progressive Alliance Government, was the focus of discussions on the first day of the two-day meeting of the CPI (M)'s Polit Bureau here on Thursday.Most members of the party's Polit Bureau were present. The former party general secretary, Harkishen Singh Surjeet, was unable to attend due to ill health.CPI (M) general secretary Prakash Karat also had talks with his counterpart in the Forward Bloc, Debabrata Biswas, on the sidelines of the meeting. They discussed how the Left should prepare for the coordination committee meeting. The party had not received any proposal from the Samajwadi Party to bring a no-confidence motion against the UPA Government, said Polit Bureau member Sitaram Yechury.

(5999) Guwahati : Bharatiya Janata Party general secretary Pramod Mahajan on Thursday urged Chief Election Commissioner B.B. Tandon not to allot any work to Election Commissioner Navin B. Chawla. Mr. Mahajan also demanded that Prime Minister Manmohan Singh request President Abdul Kalam to withdraw his pleasure in the appointment of Mr. Chawla.

(6000) New Delhi : The suspended Samajwadi Party Member of Parliament, Raj Babbar, on Thursday said he was forming a Samajwadi Manch against "criminalisation of politics".

(6001) Guwahati: Bharatiya Janata Party general secretary Pramod Mahajan on Thursday said that a non-Congress government in Assam was not possible without the support of his party.

(6002) New Delhi : Alleging that Congress leaders in the civic body were trying to shield their party members including Chief Minister Sheila Dikshit, Delhi Congress president Ram Babu Sharma and some Delhi Ministers, BJP councillor Vijender Gupta said since he "exposed" Ms. Dikshit and her MP son Sandeep Dikshit regarding unauthorised constructions in their properties, he had been asking the Congress to reveal all details in the MCD House, but to no avail.

(6003) New Delhi : Delhi Pradesh Congress Committee president Ram Babu Sharma on Thursday asked the Delhi Government to file a review petition in the Delhi High Court seeking revision of its order asking hospitals which have got land at discounted rates to provide free treatment to patients whose income is less than Rs. 2,000 per month.

(6004) New Delhi : Accusing the Delhi Government of failure to protect the interests of lakhs of villagers living in the rural "Lal Dora" areas of the Capital, Nationalist Congress Party MLA Ramvir Singh Bidhuri on Thursday demanded an apology from Chief Minister Sheila Dikshit and compensation for those whose properties were recently demolished in the Lal Dora areas due to failure of the Government to present a correct picture before the High Court.

(6005) Alllahabad : BJP national vice-president Mukhtar Abbas Naqvi on Thursday said his party would make no electoral alliance with any party in the next Uttar Pradesh Assembly elections and contest alone on all seats.

(6006) Chennai : Just as the seat sharing talks in the Democratic Progressive Alliance (DPA) has entered the crucial stage, the Communist Party of India (Marxist) and the Communist Party of India want the leader of the front, Dravida Munnetra Kazhagam (DMK), to view the issue de novo instead of citing the formulae adopted for the previous elections. Leaders of the two communist parties, who met here on Wednesday and discussed the issue in detail, had taken a firm stand that they would not compromise on getting a just share of the Assembly seats. They had also agreed to ensure that there was no clash of interest between the two parties while presenting their wish list.

(6007) Chennai : Metro rail is preferable to monorail for major urban centres, Bharatiya Janata Party national secretary in-charge of Tamil Nadu, Bandaru Dattatreya, said here on Tuesday.

(6008) Chennai : All-India Lakshya Dravida Munnetra Kazhagam general secretary Vijaya T. Rajendhar met All-India Anna Dravida Munnetra Kazhagam general secretary Jayalalithaa at her residence on Thursday. A press release said Mr. Rajendhar promised his support to the AIADMK in the Assembly elections.

11-02-2006

(6009) Hyderabad : Andhra Pradesh Government mood was upbeat a day after SemIndia announced the setting up of $ 3 billion Fab facility at Hyderabad and the ruling Congress began looking at ways to reap political benefits from the initiative.Finance Minister K. Rosaiah was the first among its leaders to attempt scoring political points over the Telugu Desam Party.

He said the TDP was soon going to be a 'forgotten chapter' in the State and it would be better if it stopped its malicious campaign against the Government. It would do better to appreciate the development mode that the State had been launched into by the Congress Government, he said.

(6010) Ramayampet (Medak dt) **:** Telugu Desam leaders, who have been on the 'Godavari Jala Sadhana' walkathon for the last 20 days, on Friday asserted that their mission was for a cause — getting Pranahita-Yellampalli- Chevella link project for Telangana and not for securing posts for themselves.

(6011) New Delhi : Aghast at the public warfare and turmoil within the Delhi unit of the Congress over the past few weeks and months, party president Sonia Gandhi is understood to have issued a "stern warning" on Friday to Chief Minister Sheila Dikshit and DPCC president Ram Babu Sharma to mend their ways or face the wrath of the leadership.Ms. Dikshit was also directed to summon a meeting of the Congress Legislature Party to discuss the pressing issues of power, water and demolition of illegal and unauthorised properties in the Capital. Both Ms. Dikshit and Mr. Sharma were summoned by Ms. Gandhi on Friday morning and reportedly "reprimanded" in the presence of her political secretary Ahmed Patel and the party general secretary in charge of Delhi affairs, Ashok Gehlot, for indulging in a public spat hurting the image of the party as well as the Government.

(6012) Kolkata : The United Progressive Alliance Government will face problems if it continues with its stand on Iran's nuclear programme, which has been referred to the United Nations Security Council, according to Communist Party of India (Marxist) general secretary Prakash Karat.

(6013) Bangalore : The Congress has taken serious note of the absence of some of its MLAs from the Legislative Assembly on February 8, when the new Government won the trust vote. It has decided to seek a report from the leader of its legislature party and Leader of the Opposition, N. Dharam Singh, about those of its members who were not present in the House at the time of voting on the motion of confidence.Speaking to presspersons here on Friday, Karnataka Pradesh Congress Committee President M. Mallikarjun Kharge said 12 party MLAs were absent when the voting took place. The legislature party leader would be asked to issue notice to tem for being absent without permission.

(6014) Mangalore : There is a need to extend the scope of democracy and strengthen it before talking of ushering in socialism, State general secretary of the Communist Party of India (Marxist) G.N. Nagaraj has said.He claimed that the brand of "scientific socialism" practised by Marxists in India has yielded desired results. This has helped relax the hold of caste system in CPI(M)-ruled States, he said.

(6015) Palakkad : Pannian Raveendran, MP and Communist Party of India leader, has said that policies of the United Progressive Alliance (UPA) Government at the Centre is to attack the organised sectors by taking away the gains they have achieved through decades-long struggles.

(6016) Thiruvananthapuram : The Budget is the United Democratic Front's campaign manifesto for the coming Assembly elections, said BJP State general secretary P. K. Krishnadas here on Friday.

(6017) Thiruvananthapuram : Leader of the Opposition V. S. Achuthanandan has sought a white paper on the 'messy' State finances. RSP State secretary T. J. Chandrachoodan said the Budget was intended only to hoodwink the people as it contained no proposal for resource mobilisation to finance the benefits and concessions announced by the Finance Minister.

(6018) Malappuram : The Indian Union Muslim League (IUML) on Friday launched a 'padayatra' pre-election campaign to mobilise votes for the ensuing Assembly elections. IUML State general secretary P.K. Kunhalikutty inaugurated the campaign by handing over the party flag to Mr. Majeed, at Veliyankode,. near Ponnani, on Friday.

(6019) New Delhi : The Bharatiya Janata Party on Friday expressed its apprehension that the Government would bring back "through the backdoor" the Illegal Migrants (Determination by Tribunal) Act, which was quashed by the Supreme Court.Its spokesman, Ravi Shankar Prasad, referring to the announcement that the Foreigners Act would be amended, said the Government would change the relevant clause to put the onus of proof of illegal entry on the Government instead of on the suspected foreigner. This, the BJP said, would make it difficult for the Government to identify and deport those who might have entered the country illegally.

(6020) Kolkata : The Polit Bureau of the Communist Party of India (Marxist), in the course of its two-day deliberations here on the coming

Assembly elections in four States and one Union Territory, has concluded that "the Congress party is willing to enter into a covert understanding with the communal forces" where polls are to be held. "The CPI (M) is out to expose such covert, unofficial understandings of the Congress with the Bharatiya Janata Party," party general secretary Prakash Karat said, at the conclusion of the Polit Bureau meeting on Friday. "In West Bengal there is talk of [the Congress] having unofficial adjustments with the Trinamool Congress-BJP alliance," Mr. Karat said.

(6021) New Delhi : The Congress on Friday said the latest suggestion from the Rashtriya Swayamsevak Sangh to the Bharatiya Janata Party to 'cosy up' to the Samajwadi Party exposed the nature of relations between the SP and the BJP. Congress spokesperson Abhishek Singhvi, reacting to an article that appeared in the Organiser, the official organ of the RSS, said there have been several instances in the past to show that both the SP and the BJP enjoyed good equations. The RSS advice now proved that the organisation had the "remote control" on both the parties.

(6022) New Delhi : Stating that it was imperative to regularise all unauthorised colonies in Delhi and build low-cost housing for residents of slum clusters, the newly-appointed Union Minister of State for Urban Development, Ajay Maken, on Friday said these sections had always supported the Congress party and now that it was in power at the Centre, in Delhi, and in the Municipal Corporation of Delhi it was time to give them a stable future.

(6023) New Delhi : The intra-party struggle within the Delhi Congress intensified further on Friday with the senior Congress legislator from Ghonda, Bhisham Sharma, accusing Chief Minister Sheila Dikshit of joining hands with Reliance Energy chairman Anil Ambani and his Samajwadi Party friend Amar Singh to tarnish the image of the Congress party by overlooking discrepancies committed on the power front by the Ambani-owned power distribution company BSES inhere the Capital.

(6024) Jaipur : The Rajasthan Assembly Speaker, Sumitra Singh, has earned the wrath of Union Railway Minister and Rashtriya Janata Dal supremo Lalu Prasad for referring to his wife Rabri Devi, former Bihar Chief Minister, as "kam parhi-likhi" (less educated) in Patna on Tuesday. An unwitting comment, made rather as a word of appreciation at an orientation programme for newly elected MLAs, left Mr. Prasad — who was not in the audience — fuming for the sake of Rabri Devi. The irrepressible Bihar politician, who never spares anyone when it comes to taking pot-shots, termed the comments from the Rajasthan Speaker as uncalled for and against the decorum of parliamentary democracy at a Press conference he addressed in Patna on Wednesday. He accused Ms. Singh of "misusing the platform" meant to educate freshers in parliamentary functioning. Mr. Prasad also talked about taking up the issue with the Lok Sabha Speaker, Somnath Chatterjee.Back now in the Rajasthan Capital, Ms.Singh, a veteran of many elections and governments, said she never meant any disrespect to Ms.Rabri Devi. "I was appreciating the democratic system in the country and Ms. Devi herself when I said a less educated woman like her could administer the State as Chief Minister for nine long years," Ms. Singh said talking to The Hindu on Friday.

(6025) Jaipur : The chief whip of the Bharatiya Janata Party in the Maharashtra Assembly, Raj K. Purohit, has demanded that the Bandra Terminal in Mumbai be named after the legendary Mewar ruler Maharana Pratap.

(6026) Kolkata : The Communist Party of India (Marxist) has reiterated its demand that New Delhi advise the United States to recall David Mulford, U.S. Ambassador to India. Prakash Karat, general secretary of the party, said here on Friday that "it appears that he [Mr. Mulford] does not understand how to behave as an Ambassador in this country. Any Ambassador has to behave in accordance with certain norms... we expect a response [on the demand] from the Government," he added.

12-02-2006

(6027) Hyderabad : Continuing its attack against the Government, alleging irregularities in irrigation projects, the Telugu Desam has levelled a fresh allegation that there was a cost escalation of Rs. 391 crores in the Sripada Sagar lift irrigation scheme in just two days at the conceptual stage of the project in March last year.The estimated cost of the project was fixed at Rs. 1,366 crores and posted on the website. Within two days, an agreement was entered into with the contracting firm for Rs. 1,757 crores, senior TDP leaders M.V. Mysoora Reddy and S. Maruthi told a news conference here on Saturday.

(6028) Karimnagar : Former BJP national president and senior leader, Bangaru Laxman has said the party is committed to forming separate Telangana State.

(6029) Tirupati : The State secretariat of the Communist Party of India (Marxist) began its two-day convention here on Saturday on a cautious note to wait and watch the overtures of the Congress party both at the Centre and in the State in the context of the controversial and hasty steps it was taking in recent times in 'utter disregard' of the 'coalition dharma' and the Common Minimum Programme.

(6030) Vijayawada : The 'jalayagnam' of the Congress would make Andhra Pradesh rich and prosperous and wipe out the Telugu Desam Party, said leaders and elected representatives who participated in a 'padayatra' in Krishna district on Saturday.

(6031) Visakhapatnam : Nationalist Congress Party (NCP) candidate for **Visakhapatnam**-I Assembly bypoll Natti Kumar on Saturday said that he would meet Chief Minister Y.S. Rajasekhara Reddy and complain to him about the huge rally taken out on T. Subbarami Reddy's maiden visit to the city after being inducted into the Union Cabinet.

(6032) Chennai : Before the Election Commission announces the schedule for Assembly election in Tamil Nadu, two major political parties , the All-India Anna Dravida Munnetra Kazhagam and the Dravida Munnetra Kazhagam will complete the exercise of receiving applications from prospective candidates for all constituencies.While the AIADMK has sold over 9,000 application forms, priced at Rs 10,000 each, the DMK has sold nearly 4,000 forms.

(6033) Bangalore : Leader of Opposition in the Legislative Assembly N. Dharam Singh on Saturday assured the Government that the Congress will extend cooperation to its efforts to persuade SemIndia to implement its Fab City project in Bangalore and prevail upon Siemens Ltd. to continue its expansion programme in the State.

(6034) New Delhi : Initiating steps to broad-base the campaign on the Iran nuclear issue and increase pressure on the Manmohan Singh Government, ahead of the March 6 meeting of the International Atomic Energy Agency, the Communist Party of India (Marxist) held discussions with the Samajwadi Party here on Saturday. The SP, which like the Left supports the United Progressive Alliance Government from outside, has backed the Left stand on Iran. The SP chief and Uttar Pradesh Chief Minister Mulayam Singh Yadav on arrival from Lucknow drove down to the CPI (M) party office for a 30-minute meeting with its general secretary Prakash Karat.

(6035) Ahmedabad : Former BJP president L.K. Advani on Saturday said that the President of the country could have avoided the Bihar controversy relating to former Governor Buta Singh if he had not signed the document and returned it.

(6036) New Delhi : The Left parties have given a notice for a debate in Parliament on Iran's nuclear issue under Rule 193, which does not require voting. The notice has been given by members of the CPI and CPI (M), M.K. Pandhe and Shamim Faizi told UNI on Saturday. The Left parties will also give a notice for debate on the Government's 'attempt' to privatise airports and profit-making PSUs.

(6037) Thiruvananthapuram : BJP State president P.S. Sreedharan Pillai said Left Democratic Front (LDF) convener Paloli Mohammed Kutty had confessed some time back that the BJP had the strength to emerge victorious in certain constituencies such as Kasaragod and Manjeswaram. "Even in central Kerala we have the strength to garner 30,000 to 40,000 votes in some constituencies. We believe it is possible to turn this into election victories," he said.

(6038) Lucknow : The Telegu Desam Party declared on Saturday its support to the Samajwadi Party's proposed no confidence motion against the UPA Government on the Iran issue, even as Uttar Pradesh Chief Minister and Samajwadi Party chiefMulayam Singh Yadav ruled out going back on the decision.Joining the Opposition attack against the Government for opposing Iran's nuclear programme at the recent IAEA meeting, TDP leader and the former Andhra Pradesh Chief Minister, Chandrababu Naidu, said the UPA Government had acted against the spirit of non-alignment.

(6039) Bangalore : General Secretary of the Communist Party of India (CPI) A.B. Bardhan on Saturday charged that attempts for disinvestment in public sector banks and their subsequent privatisation was the plan of capitalists and warned that nationalised banks were under the constant threat of being privatised.

(6040) Bangalore : Though the N. Dharam Singh-led coalition government fell without completing its term, Karnataka Pradesh Congress Committee President M. Mallikarjun Kharge is confident that he can reinvigorate the party. Chief Minister H.D. Kumaraswamy's statement that the Bharatiya Janata Party approached him for an alliance soon after the 2004 Assembly election results were announced will come in handy for the purpose, according to Mr. Kharge.

(6041) Bidar : All-India Congress Committee general secretary Praveen Dawar has asked party workers to be prepared for Assembly election in two or three months.

(6042) Hubli: President of the State unit of the Bharatiya Janata Party Jagadish Shettar has said that there is no competition among MLAs and MLCs of his party for ministerial posts.

(6043) Kottayam : Kerala Congress (Joseph) chairman P.J. Joseph on Saturday demanded that the Government publish a White Paper on State finances. He alleged that the annual budget presented by the Finance Minister on Friday was aimed at covering up the real financial condition of the State.

(6044) Kozhikode : State secretary of the Communist Party of India (CPI) Veliyam Bhargavan has ruled out the possibility of the formation of a new coalition in the State with the inclusion of the Democratic Indira Congress(Karunakaran) in the Left Democratic Front (LDF) and the CPI pulling out of the Front.

(6045) Kochi : KPCC president Ramesh Chennithala has accused the CPI(M) leadership of trying to make political capital out of the controversies over implementing the Narendran Commission Report.The CPI(M) has not taken a stand or expressed its opinion clearly on the issue.

(6046) New Delhi : The Left parties on Saturday suggested that the United Progressive Alliance Government increase this year budget outlay by Rs. 52,800 crore to meet the commitments made in the National Common Minimum Programme (NCMP).In a 10-point note to Finance Minister P. Chidambaram, the parties said the total budgetary support for the plan must be increased to Rs. 1,96,296 crore for the next financial year, against Rs. 1,43,496.78 crore for 2005-06. Agriculture, rural credit, rural development, education, health, social security schemes and revival of sick public enterprises need additional allocation.

(6047) Tezpur : Congress president Sonia Gandhi said on Saturday that she had asked Defence Minister Pranab Mukherjee to take action against "guilty security personnel" behind the alleged custodial death of a person at Kakopathar in upper Assam's Tinsukia district.

(6048) New Delhi : The Bharatiya Janata Party on Saturday ruled out any alliance with the Samajwadi Party or the Bahujan Samaj Party for the Uttar Pradesh Assembly elections. However, it did not rule out the possibility of some kind of understanding with the Asom Gana Parishad in Assam. "We cannot think of an alliance with the SP even in our dreams," BJP president Rajnath Singh said replying to questions from mediapersons here. As for Mayawati's BSP, it was a different time when the BJP tried an experiment with her party as its coalition partner. At the most, the BJP could tie up with its National Democratic Alliance partners in Uttar Pradesh. The Rashtriya Swayamsevak Sangh mouthpiece, Organiser, suggested that the BJP go for an alliance given the SP's running battle with the Congress. Asked about Chief Minister Mulayam Singh Yadav's statement that he would bring a no-confidence motion against the Manmohan Singh Government and whether the BJP would support it, Mr. Singh said he should first withdraw support to the United Progressive Alliance regime.

(6049) Coimbatore : The United Progressive Alliance will face a stormy budget session if the Opposition is not allowed to discuss key issues, Bharatiya Janata Party leader M. Venkiah Naidu told reporters on Saturday.

(6050) New Delhi : Delhi Bharatiya Janata Party workers burnt an effigy of Delhi Chief Minister Sheila Dikshit on Mehrauli-Gurgaon Road on Saturday to protest against the ongoing demolitions in the rural "Lal Dora" areas across the Capital and the failure of the Delhi Government and the Centre to stop it. Addressing the demonstrators in front of MG-1 Mall, Delhi BJP president Harsh Vardhan accused the Delhi Government of sending bulldozers into the Lal Dora areas.

(6051) Chennai : Dipankar Mukherjee, Deputy leader of the Communist Party of India (Marxist) in the Rajya Sabha, on Saturday stressed the need for launching a campaign to sensitise the people to the issues relating to foreign direct investment, especially in the retail sector.

Inaugurating the Chennai unit of People for India, he said a systematic attempt was being made by vested interests to "corner, malign and trivialise" the Left because of its opposition to the foreign direct investment in some sectors and the United States' policies towards Afghanistan, Iraq and Iran. Mr. Mukherjee said the Left parties would not stand in the way of FDI for technology upgrade, assets creation and enhancement of employment. But permitting it in the public and retail sectors would result in unproductive assets and lay-offs.

13-02-2006

(6052) Hyderabad : Besides the demand of statehood for Telangana, separate Andhra too is on the agenda of the BJP.The party will give a call for the twin movements on an even keel. It was contemplating an action plan in this regard, BJP leader in Assembly G. Kishan Reddy said. Speaking to reporters here on Sunday, Mr. Reddy said the party was in favour of splitting the State on administrative grounds. For the purpose, it would mobilise people of both regions.

(6053) Hyderabad : The Congress Legislature Party has accused the Telugu Desam Party of levelling false allegations and making a determined bid to derail irrigation project works. Government Chief Whip N. Kiran Kumar Reddy and Government Whips — D. Sridhar Babu and S. Udayabhanu — in a statement on Sunday found fault with TDP leader M.V. Mysoora Reddy for levelling 'baseless' allegations on irrigation projects and attributing motive of corrupt practices in the implementation of works.

(6054) Hyderabad : The Telugu Desam Party has demanded a white paper on suicide/hunger deaths of farmers and weavers, along with details of compensation paid to their families, since the Congress came to power. At a press conference here on Sunday, TDP vice-president J.R. Pushparaj and BC cell president and former MP R. Ramachandraiah regretted the state of affairs with variation in figures given by different people.

(6055) Karimnagar : Bharatiya Janata Party State leaders have clarified that they will not forge any alliance with the Telangana Rashtra Samithi or TDP and contest the ensuing local bodies elections independently. Addressing a press conference here on Sunday, senior party leader and former Union Minister, Bandaru Dattatreya said that "the TRS is on the decline. It is now the party of anti-Telangana stand taken up by the Congress."

(6056) Visakhapatnam : Former Union Minister and Telugu Desam MP K. Yerrannaidu said the President's Fleet Review (PFR) organised by the Indian Navy and Eastern Naval command failed to put up an impressive show.

(6057) Bhadrachalam : Jarkhand Mukti Morcha leader and Union Minister for Coal Shibu Soren said on

(6058) Khammam : Sunday that construction of the Polavaram project would be opposed by making it an issue at the national level. Addressing the Polavaram Garjhana rally organized by the Telangana Rastra Samiti, he wished all success to the resistance building up in the State against the large-scale displacement of tribals by the project in Khammam district.TRS chief and Union Minister K. Chandrasekhara Rao said that Khammam would bear the brunt of the displacement to be caused by the Polavaram project.

(6059) Kozhikode : As part of garnering support of communities, Kerala Pradesh Congress Committee (KPCC) president Ramesh Chennithala held parleys with Samasta Kerala Jemyathul Ulama general secretary Kanthapuram Aboobacker Musaliyar here on Sunday.

(6060) New Delhi : The Left parties plan some plainspeaking at the Coordination Committee meeting with the United Progressive Alliance on Monday. The meeting takes place in the backdrop of their disagreement with the Manmohan Singh Government over its approach to economic policies and on the Iran nuclear issue. "We will tell them there is no point in taking up issues at the Coordination Committee if the Government does what it wants to. There is no agenda [for Monday's meeting]," Communist Party of India (Marxist) general secretary Prakash Karat told The Hindu .

(6061) Bangalore : The Communist Party of India will stick to its decision to protest against the visit of U.S. President George Bush in March, as "he represents the ugly face of aggressive U.S. imperialism," party General Secretary A.B. Bardhan has said. Speaking at the 80th anniversary of the founding of CPI, organised by the Karnataka State Council, Mr. Bardhan said the CPI, which was part of the United Progressive Alliance and supported the Manmohan Singh Government from outside, preferred to follow the policy of "support and struggle" because it knew that the Congress, a bourgeois "capitalist" party, needed the help of the Left parties after the indifferent verdict of the 2004 general elections, to keep the communal Bharatiya Janata Party out.

(6062) Hubli: B.S. Yediyurappa, Deputy Chief Minister, has said that Hindutva will not come in the way of the functioning of the Government.

(6063) Mysore : Just like how the former Prime Minister H.D. Deve Gowda remote-controlled the N. Dharam Singh-led coalition Government in the State, the BJP will influence the decisions of the H.D. Kumaraswamy-led Government, the former Deputy Chief Minister and All India Progressive Janata Dal (AIPJD) leader Siddaramaiah has said.

(6064) Kozhikode : Kerala Pradesh Congress Committee (KPCC) president Ramesh Chennithala has called upon bank managements to be constructive in their approach to serving the needs of society.

(6065) Thrissur : Communist Party of India (CPI) State secretary Veliyam Bhargavan has said that his party and the Communist Party of India (Marxist) will join hands when the need arises.He said that despite differences of opinion on some issues, both the CPI and the CPI(M) were acutely aware of the paramount importance of Communist unity.

(6066) New Delhi : Former Defence Minister and Janata Dal (United) leader George Fernandes on Sunday accused the UPA Government of "weakening the Indian Armed Forces and lowering their morale" by conducting a survey on religion among Army personnel.

(6067) Alappuzha : Bharatiya Janata Party leader Venkaiah Naidu has said the party stands by its ideals of the Common Civil Code, the abrogation of Article 370 and opposition to job reservation based on religion. He called for a pro-active policy to ensure the implementation of family planning in the larger interests of the nation.

(6068) Ranchi : CPI (M) Polit Bureau member Brinda Karat said on Sunday the issues she had raised against Baba Ramadev still stood and asked the media not to "trivialise and sensationalise" such issues. "Violation of Drug and Cosmetic Act and protection of labour rights were first raised in May last, and even today our party supports the labour force in Haridwar. Nobody is above law," she said.

(6069) Guwahati : The Communist Party of India (Marxist) has begun the process of forming a third alternative to the Congress and the Bharatiya Janata Party that would be based on broad principles of pro-people policies and an independent foreign policy, said CPI (M) general secretary Prakash Karat here on Sunday. It has sent proposals in this regard to other Left, secular and democratic parties. Mr. Karat was addressing a State-level rally organised by the CPI (M).

(6070) Kolkata : The Revolutionary Socialist Party, one of the four Left parties supporting the Congress-led United Progressive Alliance [UPA] Government from the outside, will be "underlining the need for the Left to reconsider the conditions of its support." This stand will be made clear at a meeting of Left parties in Delhi on Monday, prior to the UPA-Left coordination committee meeting the same day. . This is necessitated by the manner in which the Government, even after a year since then, has been going ahead with its policies with which we are not in agreement," Abani Roy, central secretariat member of the RSP, who will be representing the party at the coordination committee meeting, told The Hindu from Burdwan in West Bengal on Sunday.

(6071) New Delhi : Shiv Sena's Action Committee for Essential Commodities has protested the import of five lakh tonnes of wheat saying that by the time the commodity reached Indian ports, the new rabi crop would be ready. It said "wrong government policies in the public distribution system" had caused panic in the market, resulting in wheat prices skyrocketing by nearly Rs. 300 a quintal in the last two months. In similar letters written to Prime Minister Manmohan Singh, Food and Agriculture Minister Sharad Pawar and Finance Minister P. Chidambaram, K. Gidwani of the Shiv Sena criticised a new government policy wherein an MNC could hold as much stocks as it desired, while the Food Corporation of India was unable to hold stocks in the required quantities.

(6072) New Delhi : The Telugu Desam Party will join ranks with those extending outside support to the United Progressive Alliance - if only at the dinner meeting being hosted by Lok Sabha Speaker Somnath Chatterjee this week. The TDP representative would join the leaders of the four Left parties, the Samajwadi Party, and the Bahujan Samajwadi Party at the pre-Budget session exercise of Mr. Chatterjee, sources in the Lok Sabha secretariat said.

(6073) New Delhi : Accusing the Congress of failing to solve the civic problems of the people of Delhi, Bharatiya Janata Party president Rajnath Singh on Sunday said instead of providing homes and shops to citizens, the Delhi Government and the Municipal Corporation of Delhi were now busy in carrying out demolitions across the city creating panic among residents.

(6074) Jammu : The Kashmiri Pandits, who have been living in exile here and in other parts of country since 1989, have blamed "the Indian State for betrayal of the nationalists" and termed it as "the invisible enemy that is more dangerous than the Pakistan-sponsored terrorism". During a convention organised here on Saturday, Janata Party chief Subramaniam Swamy and former BJP leader K.N. Govindacharya supported the demand of Kashmiri Pandits for their homeland and adopted a resolution against the peace process. Mr. Govindacharya warned that no talks on Kashmir were possible without the involvement of Kashmiri Pandits and no compromise on Kashmir would be acceptable as "it is the crown of India". While strongly supporting the homeland demand of Kashmir Pandits, he said this would be a first step in fighting the disintegrating menace by Pakistan.

(6075) Lucknow : In an oblique reference to suspended party MP Raj Babbar, Samajwadi Party president and Uttar Pradesh Chief Minister Mulayam Singh Yadav today alleged that the Congress was behind an SP leader's "abusive" tirade against him and Amar Singh.

(6076) Chennai : "The All-India Anna Dravida Munnetra Kazhagam is afraid of facing the Assembly election on its own and that is why the party general secretary and Chief Minister Jayalalitha has said that the party's doors were open to political parties for an alliance," the Union Minister of State for Project Implementation and State Congress Committee president G.K.Vasan said here on Sunday.

14-02-2006

(6077) Hyderabad : The Congress Legislature Party (CLP) will seek to penalise parties wasting time in the Assembly in the next Business Advisory Committee (BAC) meet later this week. It is also planning to reiterate its demand for taking up the adjournment motions only after completion of the question hour. These two decisions were taken at the executive meeting of the CLP here on Monday. Chief Minister Y.S. Rajasekhara Reddy advised members to highlight the Government's performance with specific emphasis on Indiramma, Jalayagnam, housing and ration card distribution to spurn any criticism of the opposition.

(6078) Khammam : Sambhani Chandra Sekhar, Palair MLA and former Minister, and Chandra Lingaiah, Khammam Zilla Parishad Chairman, on Monday said that there was no need for any political party to oppose the Polavaram project. Addressing a news conference here, they said Union Minister for Coal and Jharkhand Mukti Morcha (JMM) leader Shibu Soren was misguided by the Telangana Rashtra Samithi (TRS) on the issue. The Congress leaders said that construction of any major project would certainly result in some measure of displacement and it was so with Polavaram too.

(6079) Visakhapatnam : In a dramatic shift in its stand, State BJP president N. Indrasena Reddy on Monday said that his party was getting ready to support formation of separate Andhra and Telangana in deference to growing public opinion for smaller states.

(6080) Alappuzha : The Bharatiya Janata Party (BJP) will face the coming Assembly polls on the plank of social justice based on Hindutva ideology, party State president P.S. Sreedharan Pillai has said.

(6081) Thiruvananthapuram : The Communist Party of India made it clear in the Assembly on Monday that it was opposed to foreign loans from funding agencies, such as the Asian Development Bank, that would impose a burden on the common man.Participating in a three-day general debate on the budget, CPI legislature party leader K.P. Rajendran said that his party was opposed to funding from agencies such as the ADB in key sectors, such as drinking water supply.

(6082) Thiruvananthapuram : The Janata Dal(S) took out a march to the Raj Bhavan on Monday to protest against the decisions of the World Trade Organisation's ministerial meeting held at Hong Kong.

(6083) Thrissur : The former Chief Minister K. Karunakaran has said that his Democratic Indira Congress-Karunakaran (DIC-K) will not go back on its basic objective of unity of Left and secular forces in the State in spite of the recent decision of the Communist Party of India (Marxist) not to include it in the Left Democratic Front (LDF).

(6084) Bhubaneswar : The proceedings in the Orissa Assembly were disrupted on Monday for a strange reason - a bagful of coins. Opposition Congress members surprised Speaker Maheswar Mohanty and treasury bench members when they produced several bags of coins on the table. They said the coins amounted to Rs. 60, 000 which they were paying towards the fine imposed on three party members for having damaged microphones in the House during the monsoon session.

(6085) New Delhi : The Congress on Monday night assured full cooperation to Speaker Somnath Chatterjee in conducting the proceedings of the Lok Sabha in the Budget Session of Parliament beginning on February 16. At a dinner meeting hosted by Mr. Chatterjee, the Prime Minister Manmohan Singh and UPA chairperson Sonia Gandhi said that the Government was willing to discuss all issues that would be raised in the House.

(6086) New Delhi : The Communist Party of India (Marxist) will raise in Parliament the Iran nuclear issue, the nuclear agreement with the United States, foreign direct investment in the retail trade and privatisation of the Delhi and Mumbai airports. At a meeting of the CPI(M) Parliamentary Party here on Monday, these issues were identified as requiring priority during the budget session. Party MPs have already submitted to the Lok Sabha Secretariat notices under Rule 193, which does not entail voting, for discussing these issues except privatisation of the airports.

(6087) Panaji : Goa Governor S.C. Jamir, who addressed members of the Legislative Assembly on the first day of the five-day winter session that began here on Monday, announced the Government's plans to formulate a blueprint to introduce e-governance in the State by adopting the public-private partnership model, and provide broadband connectivity in all villages. Earlier, the Opposition Bharatiya Janata Party (BJP) staged a silent walkout from the House when the Governor rose to deliver the speech. Later, Leader of the Opposition Manohar Parrikar said at a press conference that the party did not find it appropriate to listen to the Governor's address as he had "lowered the dignity of the Assembly last year when he dismissed the BJP-led coalition Government in the midst of a political crisis even without waiting for the report of the confidence motion from the Speaker."

(6088) New Delhi : The Left parties on Monday conveyed "deep concern" at the manner in which the Manmohan Singh Government had gone ahead with important policy decisions, and said that they would insist on a debate in Parliament on the Iran nuclear issue."People should know how Parliament looks at the Iran nuclear issue. The Government should heed the voice of Parliament at the March 6 meeting [of the International Atomic Energy Agency]. What the Government does, we would take stock after that," Communist Party of India (Marxist) general secretary Prakash Karat said. He was addressing mediapersons at a briefing by the Left parties after the coordination committee meeting with the United Progressive Alliance. During the meeting, Prime Minister Manmohan Singh and Defence Minister Pranab Mukherjee explained the Government stand vis-...-vis Iran and sought to know the nature of discussion sought by the Left parties in Parliament.

(6089) Visakhapatnam : Bharatiya Janata Party general secretary Vinay Katiyar on Monday said the former Prime Minister, P.V. Narasimha Rao, had promised to allow construction of a Ram temple at Ayodhya."We had three rounds of discussions with Rao when he was Prime Minister. He was very secular unlike other Congress leaders. But the plan went haywire because of resistance by Arjun Singh, now Minister for Human Resource Development," Mr. Katiyar told reporters here.

(6090) Chennai : Janata Party president Subramanian Swamy has welcomed the Kumaraswamy Government's decision to seek to constitute special courts to try Liberation Tigers of Tamil Eelam activists who are in prisons in Bangalore.

(6091) Bhopal : The opposition Congress Party in Madhya Pradesh is ready to confront the ruling Bharatiya Janata Party with its arsenal of charges in the Budget session of the State Assembly beginning on Tuesday. The Leader of the Opposition in the State Assembly, Jamuna Devi, addressing newspersons here on Monday said that her party was to corner the Shivraj Singh Chauhan Government inside the House on every issue.She said the BJP-led Government had failed on all fronts. The Opposition leader particularly accused the Government of failing to guarantee protection for the minorities. She said there had been many attacks on members of the Christian community by some Hindu organisations and there was a feeling of insecurity among them.

(6092) Jaipur : Breaking a long spell of passivity in India's politically most significant State Uttar Pradesh, the Congress will launch its agitational programme there from Tuesday to "expose the misrules" the State had for the past one decade and half under various non-Congress Governments. "The Congress party is ready for the elections. Let it come immediately or a year later," Congress general secretary in charge for Uttar Pradesh, Ashok Gehlot said here before leaving for Lucknow on Monday. "This is will mark the beginning of the Congress party's agitational programme in U.P.," he said. "Years of experimentation with non-Congress Governments in U.P. has failed. The State cannot go on like this anymore," Mr.Gehlot said.

(6093) Pondicherry : The General Council of the Pondicherry State unit of the Pattali Makkal Katchi (PMK) adopted a resolution here on Sunday thanking the Union Health and Family Welfare Minister Dr. Anbumani Ramadoss for his attention towards the development of the JIPMER.

(6094) Jaipur : Uttar Pradesh Chief Minister and Samajwadi Party president Mulaym Singh Yadav should have appreciated Raj Babbar for "speaking out the truth" about senior leader Amar Singh instead of suspending him from the party, Congress general secretary Ashok Gehlot said here on Monday.

(6095) Chennai : Efforts are on to induct the Dalit Panthers of India, led by Thol. Thirumavalavan, into the seven-party Democratic Progressive Alliance, said Pattali Makkal Katchi leader S.Ramadoss here on Monday.

(6096) New Delhi : Prime Minister Manmohan Singh on Monday assured Marumalarchi Dravida Munnetra Kazhagam general secretary Vaiko that the Centre would not resort to disinvestment in the Neyveli Lignite Corporation.Mr. Vaiko told The Hindu that Mr. Singh gave this assurance when he presented a memorandum on the issue.

15-02-2006

(6097) Hyderabad : Political parties, barring CPI (M) and Telangana Rashtra Samithi, endorsed the present design of the Polavaram dam with a height of 150 ft at the third and final all-party meeting held here on Tuesday. The CPI (M) and the TRS announced boycott of the meeting midway after airing their views and staged a walkout, the former seeking appointment of yet another experts committee to suggest alterative designs to avoid submersion of tribal areas and the latter a blanket GO specifying project-specific allocations to the Telangana region out of the Godavari.

(6098) Hyderabad : State Secretary of Communist Party of India K. Narayana has slammed the Government for 'arbitrarily' scrapping 5,000 milk cooperative societies and bringing activity to a halt in eight milk-processing factories.

(6099) Hyderabad : Telangana Rashtra Samiti president and Union Labour Minister K. Chandrasekhara Rao is expected to meet Bharatiya Janata Party chief Rajnath Singh in New Delhi on February 19 to seek support for separate Telangana.Mr. Rao along with his Cabinet colleague A. Narendra is likely to meet Mr. Singh and BJP general secretary Arun Jaitely to solicit support for the struggle to achieve a separate State. The TRS chief announced this at a meeting of the party executive and the TRS Legislature Party on Tuesday. Only 16 of the 26 party MLAs attended the meeting.

(6100) Nizamabad : The Bharatiya Janata Party has blamed the Congress and Telugu Desam Party, which ruled the State for 50 long years between them, for the backwardness of Telangana and demanded that they owe an explanation to the people. At a press conference on Tuesday, BJP State Vice-President and former MLA G. Ramakrishna Reddy expressed wonder at the TDP's padayatra saying that the party is equally to be blamed for injustice to the region as it ruled the State for 17 years 6 months, and the Congress for 32 years 6 months.

(6101) New Delhi : The Bharatiya Janata Party on Tuesday said it did not think a nuclear Iran was in India's interest. It, however, criticised the "gross mismanagement" of India's vote at the International Atomic Energy Agency against Teheran and the "unacceptable unilateralism" being pushed in the region by the United States. The party did not oppose the India-U.S. nuclear deal of July 18, 2005 per se, but said the "flexibility" needed for "maintaining a minimum credible deterrent" must be retained to deal with "contingent situations" and the "changing threat scenario." India should not accept any curb or cap on production of fissile material, but this could be "re-examined" when the Geneva-based Conference on Disarmament evolves a fissile material cut-off treaty, and all nuclear weapon states agree to adhere to it.The signals from Washington, it said, indicated that the U.S. wanted to cap India's fissile material production. Leader of the BJP in the Rajya Sabha Jaswant Singh issued separate statements, clarifying the party's views on the two issues. The statements were critical of the Government on the handling of the Iran issue.On Monday, after the Rashtriya Swayamsevak Sangh made its position clear, it became obvious that the BJP would fall in line. The only problems that the RSS and the BJP seem to have with the United Progressive Alliance is that they perceive India's vote followed the U.S. pressure and India's fissile material production will be capped.The statements followed a meeting of the executive of the party's parliamentary wing on Tuesday. There was a 90-minute meeting of senior leaders on Monday at the residence of the former Prime Minister, Atal Bihari Vajpayee. Leader of the Opposition in the Lok Sabha L.K. Advani and Mr. Jaswant Singh were present at both meetings. Party president Rajnath Singh was present at the Monday meeting and Deputy Leaders in both Houses of Parliament V.K. Malhotra and Sushma Swaraj attended the Tuesday meeting.

(6102) Thiruvananthapuram : The CPI(M) State secretariat has said the party is ready to face any inquiry into the deal with SNC Lavalin for the renovation of the Pallivasal, Sengulam and Panniar hydroelectric projects.

(6103) Kochi : Communist Party of India general secretary A.B. Bardhan on Tuesday warned the UPA Government not to take the Left for granted. "We are continuing with our support, but things can't go on like this," he told a press conference here. Mr. Bardhan said the UPA Government was notheeding most suggestions by the Left. "We had submitted 19 notes [written proposals] on various issues. This shows how serious we are." He said the Left's deep concern and frustration over economic and foreign policies were conveyed at the UPA-Left coordination committee meeting held in New Delhi on Monday.On whether this was the beginning of the end of the UPA-Left alliance, he said: "We don't think the end is in sight." Hinting at a united forum to take up various issues, he said that "we are approaching other parties except the BJP." He mentioned the Samajwadi Party, the Telugu Desam Party, the Janata Dal (Secular) and the Janata Dal (United) led by Sharad Yadav.

(6104) New Delhi : The Left parties on Tuesday stayed away from the dinner meeting hosted by Prime Minister Manmohan Singh for the constituents of the United Progressive Alliance and supporting parties, ahead of the budget session. A day after the Coordination Committee meeting with the UPA, the Left leaders present in the capital, Abani Roy of the Revolutionary Socialist Party and D. Raja of the Communist Party of India opted to keep away from the meeting citing preoccupation with official work .CPI (M) general secretary Prakash Karat, his CPI counterpart A.B. Bardhan and All-India Forward Bloc general secretary Debabrata Biswas are away on party work.

(6105) New Delhi : The National Democratic Alliance on Tuesday sought President A.P.J. Abdul Kalam's intervention to "stop" a survey on Muslims in the defence forces by a government-appointed panel. The move was fraught with "dangerous consequences," it said.The Opposition also urged Mr. Kalam to use his "good offices" to prevail upon the government for the resignation of Election Commissioner Navin Chawla and prevent a "constitutional embarrassment." Speaking to newspersons after submitting a memorandum to the President, NDA convener George Fernandes and BJP leader L.K. Advani said: "Both are serious issues."

(6106) Kolkata : West Bengal Chief Minister Buddhadeb Bhattacharjee said here on Tuesday that the "mahajot" being talked of by the Trinamool Congress and the Congress would "be blown off like hay by the wind of popular opinion" in the coming polls. Both parties were "sinking and crying out to be saved."

(6107) New Delhi : Congress members on Tuesday urged Union Finance Minister P. Chidambaram to provide reliefs in the coming budget to the common man, farmers and weavers and resist the temptation to reduce subsidy on domestic cooking gas. Mr. Chidambaram went to the party headquarters here to take inputs from his colleagues, an exercise he conducted last year too in the budget-making process.

(6108) Chennai : The proposed India-U.S. nuclear agreement contains conditions for separating the civil and military facilities, which will be "disadvantageous" to the country. Hence, India should not sign it "in haste," Janata Party president Subramanian Swamy told the media here on Tuesday. Dr. Swamy said that if India signed the agreement then it could not carry out nuclear tests. However, he supported the United Progressive Alliance Government for its decision to vote along with the U.S. against Iran for violating the non-proliferation treaty.

(6109) New Delhi : Charging the Sheila Dikshit Government with being anti-rural, the Nationalist Congress Party MLA and working committee member, Ramvir Singh Bidhuri on Tuesday said he had met Union Urban Development Minister Jaipal Reddy and demanded an end to the ongoing demolition drive in the Capital's rural Lal Dora areas and extended abadi of the villages with immediate effect.

(6110) New Delhi: In a reprieve of sorts to Delhi Chief Minister Sheila Dikshit and avoiding a possible crisis within the Congress Legislature Party (CLP), the party high command is understood to have asked the senior Congress MLA from Ghonda, Bhisham Sharma, to withdraw his "privilege motion and contempt of House" notice against the Chief Minister. However, the other notice by BJP legislator Vijay Jolly continues to stand.Following the directions of the party leadership, Mr. Sharma on Tuesday petitioned the Assembly Speaker submitting that his notice against the Chief Minister stood withdrawn.

(6111) Pondicherry : Secretary of Pondicherry State committee of All India Anna Dravida Munnetra Kazhagam (AIADMK) A. Anbalagan MLA has charged the Union Health Minister Anbumani Ramadoss with adopting an anti people attitude by his efforts to convert the Centrally administered JIPMER here into an autonomous institution.

(6112) Jaipur : Uttar Pradesh Chief Minister Mulayam Singh Yadav has come under attack from the Congress for the meeting he had with the Israeli Ambassador to India, David Danieli, at his official residence in Luknow on Monday. The meeting, between the Ambassador and the Chief Minister, preceded by an interaction between Mr.Danieli and Samajwadi Party leader Amar Singh on Sunday, was kept a secret till the media got to know about it, the Congress leaders point out. "Mr.Yadav owes an explanation on the agenda of the meeting which was a hush affair," Congress leader Mohan Prakash said in a statement here on Tuesday. "The meeting was planned in advance. Yet there was no prior information about the visit to the public," he said wondering as to what have transpired between the two. "Mr.Yadav should make the topic of their discussion public," he said.

(6113) Chennai : The Eelam Tamils' Protection Conference held by the Dalit Panthers here on Tuesday appealed to the Government of India and the world democratic forces to recognise Tamil Eelam, to ensure rehabilitation of Sri Lankan Tamils.

(6114) Chennai : "The Congress party will take severe action against former Tamil Nadu Congress Committee president Tindivanam K.

Ramamurthy for meeting All India Anna Dravida Munnetra Kazhagam general secretary and Chief Minister Jayalalithaa, as it is against the interest of the party," said G.K. Vasan, TNCC president and Union Minister of State for Project Implementation, here on Monday.

(6115) New Delhi : The Congress on Tuesday dismissed as "rumour" reports that MDMK chief Vaiko was quitting the DMK-led Democratic Progressive Alliance (DPA) for the coming election to the Tamil Nadu Assembly, asserting that the tie-up was "quite intact and gaining strength by the day."""Till today, he (Vaiko) is with DPA. There is no such thing. All this talk is rumour. The DPA is quiet intact," CWC member Veerappa Moily told reporters. He said a show cause notice was issued to Ramamurthy when party leader Ambika Soni was in charge of the state and after that there was no action.-PTI

(6116) Pudukottai : : Making it clear that its main task was to unseat the ruling AIADMK Government in Tamil Nadu, the State unit of the Communist Party of India said on Sunday that it expected a fair and reasonable number of seats in the Democratic Progressive Alliance for the coming Assembly elections.Addressing the media at Alangudi after the conclusion of the two-day CPI State Council meet, State Secretary D. Pandian categorically stated that the party had decided not to go with the AIADMK

16-02-2006

(6117) Hyderabad : The Telangana Regional Congress Coordination Committee (TRCCC) has reiterated its commitment to the Telangana cause but preferred development to separate Statehood "for the time being" as the issue is pending with the Centre. Talking to the media, TRCCC leaders - G. Chinna Reddy and A. Indrakaran Reddy - both MLAs, said here on Wednesday that the Congress remained committed to the Telangana cause but was helpless in the face of opposition from some parties.

(6118) Hyderabad : The Congress Legislature Party (CLP) has accused TDP leaders of attempting to mislead people of Telangana in the name of Jala Sadhana yatra and has termed it a political yatra. Addressing a press conference here on Wednesday, CLP members - G. Chinna Reddy, A. Indrakaran Reddy, K. Konappa, G. Gurunath Reddy and Swarna Sudhakar - said that deputy leader of the TDLP T. Devender Goud had embarked on the yatra to safeguard his own interests.

(6119) Hyderabad : Rebel activity in Telangana Rashtra Samithi (TRS), which appeared to have got a respite after the leadership decided to ignore three dissident MLAs, found its echo again at the legislature party meeting here on Wednesday.The three MLAs - T. Jayaprakash Reddy, D. Srinivas Rao and B. Shara Rani - and two of their colleagues - G. Mukund Reddy and Narayan Rao Patel - did not attend the meeting. Mr. Mukund Reddy and Mr. Patel were closely identified with the three legislators but the leadership had not passed any strictures against them.

(6120) Visakhapatnam : Telugu Desam president N. Chandrababu Naidu held a road show in the old city area on Wednesday evening to garner support for his party candidate S.A. Rehman in the February 19 by-election to the Visakha-I Assembly constituency.Mr. Naidu lambasted the Congress Government calling it anti-poor, anti-BC and never showed any concern for the welfare of the people in the last 21 months.

(6121) Visakhapatnam : Telugu Desam Party president N. Chandrababu Naidu on Wednesday said the State Government was shielding IAS officer Praveen Prakash despite strictures passed on him by the Election Commission (EC) for ignoring its recommendation on appointment of returning officer for Visakha-I Assembly poll.

(6122) New Delhi / Chennai : Ahead of the Assembly elections in Tamil Nadu, Congress president Sonia Gandhi on Wednesday appointed M. Krishnaswamy Pradesh Congress Committee (PCC) president in place of G. K. Vasan, who was inducted into the Union Council of Ministers last month. She has constituted a 16-member Election Committee for the State with Mr. Vasan as the chairman and a 53-member Coordination Committee, which the PCC president will chair.

(6123) Hyderabad : TDP president N. Chandrababu Naidu has said his party will launch a Statewide agitation against the Government's move to identify the creamy layer. He contended that all BC castes should be encouraged to prosper, and said his party would oppose "lock, stock and barrel" the attempts to prune the number of beneficiaries. The BJP wanted an all-party meeting to discuss the issue as the Government was trying to deny the benefit of reservation to those categorised as creamy layer without any scientific study. CPI secretary K. Narayana welcomed the creamy layer concept but sought an in-depth study of the issue before any decision was taken.

(6124) New Delhi : There was no consensus among major political parties at the all-party meeting convened by the Election Commission here on Wednesday on State funding of elections. As the parties expressed divergent views there was no imminent solution to the issue, the Commission said. Congress spokesman Abhishek Singhvi said his party, while welcoming the Government's initiative, was of the view that the funding should be through political parties and not directly to candidates. The Congress also advocated that the funding to candidates should be based on the vote percentage of the parties in the previous three years. BJP leader V.K. Malhotra said his party demanded that the model code of conduct be given legal sanction. There should be strict monitoring of election funding. This was in contrast to the view taken by the Congress. The BJP leader said no expenditure should be allowed other than the prescribed limit. His party also urged the Election Commission to frame rules and guidelines for exit polls, opinion polls and poll surveys. CPI (M) Parliamentary Party leader in the Rajya Sabha Nilotpal Basu said his party did not accept the proposal on State funding in the present form as it did not capture the spirit of the recommendations of the Indrajit Gupta Committee. The present form did not help in containing the role of money and muscle power as the committee had clearly underlined that arrangements should be made in such a way that there should be full State funding, no loopholes left to be exploited by the parties and a level playing field ensured for all candidates.On the contrary, CPI National Secretary D. Raja said his party appreciated the United Progressive Alliance Government's initiative. "We are of the strong view that State funding must be in kind and not in cash. " AIADMK leader P.G. Narayanan opposed the proposal, saying government money should not be wasted. However, DMK leader C. Kuppuswami said the proposal was not comprehensive. "What about State funding of elections to local bodies? We must examine the experience of other countries before embarking on State funding." Trinamool Congress leader Mamata Banerjee suggested the creation of a corpus fund with contributions from each MP under the MP Local Area Development scheme.

(6125) New Delhi : The United Progressive Alliance Government on Wednesday declared that it had the "inbuilt efficiency" to face any confrontation, amid growing pressure from the supporting Left parties and the Samajwadi Party ahead of the budget session of Parliament.

(6126) Bangalore : The eight-member core committee of the State unit of the Bharatiya Janata Party, headed by V.S. Acharya, is giving shape to the "Agenda for governance", the document articulating the party's commitment to deliver on the promise of "social justice for the underprivileged and equitable development".

(6127) Bangalore : Janata Party President Subramanian Swamy has welcomed the formation of the Government led by H.D. Kumaraswamy and said the change will serve as a "dress rehearsal" for forming a new government at the Centre.

(6128) Mysore : The All-India Progressive Janata Dal (AIPJD) has appealed to the Janata Dal (Secular) not to include MLA and former Minister D.T. Jayakumar in the Ministry in view of the non-bailable warrant against him in a criminal case.

(6129) Palakkad : Communist Party of India (CPI) State assistant secretary K.E. Ismail has said his party will discuss the report of the Comptroller and Auditor General (CAG) of India on the SNC Lavalin deal and make its stand on the issue public shortly.

(6130) Thiruvananthapuram : Leader of the Opposition and Communist Party of India (Marxist) Polit Bureau member V.S. Achuthanandan has said his party is ready for an impartial inquiry that would bring out the truth in all the cases of irregularities pointed out by the Comptroller and Auditor General (CAG) of India in his latest report tabled in the Assembly on Monday.

(6131) New Delhi : Now that a feeler has been sent to the former Chief Minister K. Karunakaran to return to the party by his "bete noire" A.K. Antony, the Congress on Wednesday kept its cards close to its chest refusing to disclose whether the invitation had the sanction of the party's central leadership.All that party in-charge of Kerala Veerappa Moily was willing to state on the subject was: "Mr. Karunakaran is a senior leader and it is for him to take a decision." At the same time, he did say every effort would be made to strengthen the party ahead of the forthcoming Assembly elections. "We have a war ahead and we will do everything to strengthen the party," he said without elaborating on what "everything" meant. Mr. Moily was speaking to the media after a discussion with Mr. Antony here. Both leaders maintained that the Karunakaran issue did not come up at Wednesday's meeting. On Tuesday, Mr. Antony had issued an open invitation to Mr. Karunakaran to accept Congress president Sònia Gandhi's leadership and return to the party fold.

(6132) New Delhi : The Communist Party of India (Marxist) said it was not surprised at the decision of the Bharatiya Janata Party to support the United Progressive Alliance Government's stand on the Iran nuclear issue and sought to know whether the ruling coalition wanted to be on the same wavelength as the BJP. Reacting to the BJP stand, the CPI (M) Polit Bureau said the Vajpayee regime was the most "pro-American government" India had seen since independence. It was the BJP-led government, which forged a strategic alliance with Israel that acted as the gendarme for United States' imperialism in West Asia, the party said.The Polit Bureau said the BJP did not object to the fact that Israel had 200 nuclear warheads in its arsenal with the blessings of the U.S. and the West. Instead, they were raising the bogey of Iran acquiring nuclear weapons.

(6133) Mumbai : Suspended Samajwadi Party MP from Agra Raj Babbar levels serious political charges against the party chief and Uttar Pradesh Chief Minister Mulayam Singh Yadav but the latter continues to be his leader "at least as of today." Mr. Babbar alleged at a press conference on Wednesday that Mr. Yadav had entertained Israeli Ambassador David Daniel at the official residence of the Chief Minister in Lucknow. He had met RSS chief K. Sudarshan when a communal clash was on at Mahu near Varanasi, and advised the BJP to have an alliance with the SP. He did not mantion Mr. Yadav's name but said `the UP Chief Minister' was weakening the secular forces in the country instead of fighting the communal forces.

(6134) New Delhi : Taking strong objection to U.S. Ambassador David Mulford writing a letter to him as also its tone and tenor, West Bengal Chief Minister Buddhadeb Bhattarcharjee has urged Prime Minister Manmohan Singh to take up the matter at an appropriate level.

(6135) New Delhi : The Samajwadi Party on Wednesday threatened to move a no-confidence motion against the United Progressive Alliance Government if it did not reverse its stand on Iran at the March 6 meeting of the Governing Board of the International Atomic Energy Agency of which India is a member. Asked whether a no-confidence motion against the government could be construed as the SP withdrawing its "outside" support to the Manmohan Singh Government, the party's parliamentary party leader, Ramgopal Yadav, said: "Yes, it should be construed as a final warning to the Government." The party has 38 MPs in the Lok Sabha. The decision was taken at the parliamentary board meeting chaired by party president Mulayam Singh Yadav. The SP would raise the issues of Foreign Direct Investment in retail trade, spiralling prices of commodities, phone-tapping, Quattrochi bank accounts, Volcker oil-for-food report and Election Commissioner Navin Chawla..

(6136) Chandigarh : Indian National Lok Dal (INLD) activists staged "Chetawani Pradarshans" (warning demonstrations) at all the district headquarters in Haryana on Wednesday in protest against the State Government's move to remove the name of the late Deputy Prime Minister Devi Lal from the `Tau Devi Lal Thermal Power Station, Panipat'.The INLD workers demanded immediate withdrawal of this "narrow- minded and short-sighted step" of the Government. They submitted memorandums to Deputy Commissioners.

(6137) Bhopal : The issue of massive losses suffered by farmers due to Bt cotton seeds was raised in the Madhya Pradesh Assembly on Wednesday. It was alleged, through a calling attention notice moved by Opposition MLAs Govind Singh, Arif Aqueel and Sunilam, that the farmers of the Malwa-Nimad area of western Madhya Pradesh had been misled by Monsento and Maharashtra Hybrid Seeds Company (MAHYCO) and suffered huge losses by using the Bt cotton seeds.

(6138) Chennai : Dravida Munnetra Kazhagam president M. Karunanidhi wants the Election Commission to take cognisance of the plethora of election-eve announcements by Chief Minister Jayalalithaa. In a statement here, he said usually governments make a few announcements before elections depending on the necessity. But no other government had made so many announcements like "winged white ants." And in no other government had the announcements met with the fate of the wings of the white ants.

(6139) Cuddalore : The former Tamil Nadu Congress Committee president, Tindivanam K. Ramamurthy, has insisted that his party have alliance with only that front which would offer not less than 60 seats and agree to a power-sharing arrangement or a coalition government

17-02-2006

(6140) Hyderabad : The Telangana Rashtra Samithi (TRS) has declared that it will wage an "uncompromising fight" till the work on Polavaram dam is halted. It has also accused the Government of conspiring to divert waters of Telangana to the Andhra region. Addressing a press conference on Wednesday, TRS Floor leader Vijayarama Rao and other party MLAs declared that the Congress could not bulldoze its way just because it had majority. They said that pressure would be mounted on Prime Minister Manmohan Singh by mobilising all tribal MPs since two lakh tribals would be displaced by the project.

(6141) Hyderabad : The State Assembly was adjourned without taking up its regular agenda on Thursday after members of Telangana Rashtra Samithi (TRS) stalled proceedings to protest against implementation of the Polavaram project.

(6142) Hyderabad : In a succinct response to TDP president N. Chandrababu Naidu' statement that prestigious projects like the Fab City were coming to Andhra Pradesh because of the infrastructure developed by him, Chief Minister Y.S. Rajasekhara Reddy quipped here on Thursday: "I thank him for it."He made a similar comment at a press conference after signing of an MoU for the proposed Fab City with SemIndia Inc.Asked to react to Karnataka Chief Minister H.D. Kumaraswamy's statement that he (Dr. Reddy) had played "a pro-active role" in clinching the project, he remarked pithily: "I am thankful to him." He, however, gave the entire credit to Prime Minister Manmohan Singh, UPA chairperson Sonia Gandhi and Union Minister for IT Dayanidhi Maran.

(6143) Hyderabad : The Congress Legislature Party (CLP) criticised the Telangana Rashtra Samithi (TRS) for stalling the business of the House over Polavaram issue on Thursday. Dubbing the TRS stand as "irrational and illogical," Government Chief Whip N. Kiran Kumar Reddy said the former was holding the House to ransom on a non-issue. The Government had included Polavaram project in the Jalayagnam in the larger interest of the State and benefits had been explained to people and political parties a number of times.

(6144) Visakhapatnam : Telugu Desam president N. Chandrababu Naidu is going all out to please Muslims, who sailed with the Congress in the 2004 elections when the Bharatiya Janata Party was his electoral ally, in a bid to win the Visakha-I Assembly constituency by-election.

(6145) Visakhapatnam : Thousands of men, women and children participated in a rally taken out by the Congress on Thursday evening to seek the support of voters to elect party nominee Dronamraju Srinivas for the Visakhapatnam-I bypoll.Party activists and supporters, who came from different directions, converged at the Jagadamba junction to join the main rally from there. Dronamraju Srinivas greeted the people with folded hands as AP Congress Committee president K. Keshava Rao waved to them from the open top jeep. AP Mahila Congress president Ganga Bhavani appealed to the people to vote for the Congress and strengthen the hand of Chief Minister Y.S. Rajasekhara Reddy.

(6146) Visakhapatnam : Three Congress Ministers on Thursday accused Telugu Desam Party president N. Chandrababu Naidu of shedding crocodile tears for the cause of BCs. "When Mr. Naidu was the Chief Minister, he did nothing for their welfare. Now when we are trying to remove the creamy layer from the list as per the directive of the Supreme Court, he is trying to attribute motives," Ministers Jakkampudi Rammohana Rao (Roads and Buildings), Konathala Ramakrishna (Commercial Taxes) and Botsa Satyanarayana (Marketing) told reporters here.

(6147) Visakhapatnam : Telugu Desam president N. Chandrababu Naidu took exception to the Chief Minister Y.S. Rajasekhara Reddy not participating in the campaign for by-elections."He is expected to come out. There are issues and questions he has to answer (as the Chief Minister). I believe in democracy and in people and finally abide by the people's decision," Mr. Naidu said at a press conference here on Thursday after concluding his campaign for the Visakha-I Assembly constituency by-election.

(6148) Kolkata : Eight Ministers of the West Bengal Government - seven belonging to the Communist Party of India (Marxist) and one to the All India Forward Bloc - have been denied ticket for the upcoming Assembly polls in the State. In all 64 sitting MLAs belonging to the Left Front have not be renominated. There are 130 new faces in the list of candidates belonging to the Front, which has nominated 33 women candidates - the highest ever. The total of number of seats up for grabs in the elections is 294.

(6149) Chikmagalur : Former minister D.B. Chandre Gowda has said that infighting in the State unit of the BJP between followers of H.N. Ananth Kumar and B.S. Yediyurappa will lead to the downfall of the coalition government. Mr. Chandre Gowda said the former BJP leader Uma Bharati is waiting to win over disgruntled legislators who have not been accommodated in the Ministry. Allowing the BJP to form a government in South India was a dangerous development, he added.

(6150) Kochi : The biggest achievement of the Indian Union Muslim League (IUML) is the implementation of the Narendran Commission report by the United Democratic Front (UDF) Government, P.K. Kunhalikutty, general secretary of the IUML, has said.Mr. Kunhalikutty said that all Muslim organisations except Jama-at-Islami had supported the implementation of the report.

(6151) Kochi : The Kerala Pradesh Congress Committee (KPCC) will pursue the SNC Lavalin case seriously. The party is in favour of a thorough discussion on the deal and wanted to go to the roots of the controversial deal. Addressing a press conference here on Thursday, KPCC president Ramesh Chennithala termed the SNC Lavalin deal as the biggest scam in the history of Kerala and urged Leader of the Opposition V.S. Achuthanandan to ask his cadres to cooperate with the KPCC's efforts to bring out the truth.

(6152) Kozhikode : The Bharatiya Janata Party (BJP) State leadership has said that "since evidence pointing to payment of Rs.90 crores as commission in the SNC Lavalin contract is available," there should be an inquiry by the Central Bureau of Investigation (CBI) into the controversial deal. Addressing a press conference here on Thursday, BJP State president P.S. Sreedharan Pillai claimed that his party's public image had brightened since both the United Democratic Front (UDF) and the Left Democratic Front (LDF) were involved in the Lavalin case, in which the Comptroller and Auditor General (CAG) of India had pointed out serious financial irregularities.

(6153) New Delhi : The Bharatiya Janata Party gave notice on Thursday to the Speaker's office that it would like to take up the issue of the "survey" of Muslims employed in the armed forces during zero hour in Lok Sabha on Friday.Disclosing this, BJP deputy leader in the Lok Sabha V.K. Malhotra said a meeting of leaders of the National Democratic Alliance had identified various issues that the Opposition would like to take up this parliamentary session. Mr. Malhotra listed the dissolution of the Bihar Assembly and the related Supreme Court judgment, alleged irregularities in the electoral rolls in West Bengal, the de-freezing of the London accounts of Bofors case accused Ottavio Quattrocchi and the rise of prices of essential commodities and petroleum products as among the subjects that were on the priority list of the Opposition.

(6154) Visakhapatnam : The Left parties too will be approached for forming a third alternative, Telugu Desam Party president and the former Andhra Pradesh Chief Minister, N. Chandrababu Naidu, told the media here on Thursday. The third alternative, not a front, was being proposed with the help of regional parties. "We are not in a hurry or mad after power." A third alternative was being planned to form a secular government and help the poor, who should also enjoy the benefits of technological advances.

(6155) New Delhi : Bharatiya Janata Party general secretary Arun Jaitley on Thursday charged Election Commissioner Navin Chawla's wife Rupika Chawla with showing income from her business as a donation to a trust to claim tax exemption. He denied that his wife, Sangeeta Jaitley, had made any "donation" to trusts run by Mrs. Chawla, but, yes, she had bought some furniture from her.

(6156) New Delhi : The Congress on Thursday said Uttar Pradesh Chief Minister Mulayam Singh Yadav has "no moral right to continue" in office following a television exposure that one of his Ministers agreed to carry narcotics in his official car for a consideration. Describing the report by a channel in which Minister Mehboob Ali was shown allegedly agreeing to transport narcotics across the State, the Congress said it had "shocked the conscious of the nation and what is more shocking is that there had been no reaction from the Samajwadi Party." Congress spokesperson Jayanti Natarajan said: "Nothing can be more shocking to the soul of democracy that a Minister in the State Government has been shown agreeing to accept money to transport drugs in his official car."

(6157) Raipur : The Congress staged a walkout in the Chhattisgarh Assembly on Thursday, alleging that the BJP Government was ignoring elected representatives of Panchayati Raj institutions in development work under the Sarva Shiksha Abhiyan.Raising the issue during question hour, Leader of the Opposition Mahendra Karma alleged that the Government had nominated committees at panchayat level to look after development initiatives.

(6158) Pondicherry : Former legislator and also former chairman of Pondicherry Khadi and Village Industries Board S. Manohar announced at a press conference here on Thursday that he would join the ruling Congress. He said he called on the Pondicherry Pradesh Congress committee president P. Shanmugham a few days ago to convey his intention.

(6159) Chennai : With the Marumalarchi Dravida Munnetra Kazhagam (MDMK) leader Vaiko going to New Delhi for a couple of days, rumour mills are working overtime. It was left to Congress leader Veerappa Moily to deny rumours and clarify that the MDMK was still a part of the Democratic Progressive Alliance (DPA). Till Mr. Vaiko makes a statement to the contrary, the alliance will continue to presume that he is a part of it.

(6160) Villupuram : Pattali Makkal Katchi president G.K.Mani handed over the party's wish list containing the names of Assembly constituencies it wants to contest to Democratic Progressive Alliance leader M. Karunanidhi on Monday.The party has geared up its functionaries and cadres to face the elections and remove the All India Anna Dravida Munnetra Kazhagam from power, PMK founder S. Ramadoss told a press conference at Thailapuram near here on Thursday.

(6161) New Delhi : The Congress on Thursday expelled Tindivanam K. Ramamurthy from its primary membership for six years, with immediate effect, on grounds of indiscipline. The party said Mr. Ramamurthy had been making statements in the print and visual media against the interests of the party and its leaders and also against the Democratic Progressive Alliance and its leaders. The AICC general secretary in-charge of the Tamil Nadu unit had issued Mr. Ramamurthy a show-cause notice asking why he should not be suspended for indiscipline.Responding to the expulsion, Mr. K.Ramamurthy said that he would shortly launch a new political outfit in consultation with "party workers and second line leaders." He told The Hindu here that the new party would have a flag different from that of the Congress and seek ties with the All India Anna Dravida Munnetra Kazhagam (AIADMK).

18-02-2006

(6162) Hyderabad : Eleven TRS members were suspended from the Assembly for two days on Friday when they staged a sit-in near the podium demanding stoppage of Polavaram project and protecting the interests of tribals.

(6163) Hyderabad : Leader of Opposition N. Chandrababu Naidu has decried the claims of the Government about development of the State and contended that it is reaping the fruits of his hard labour for nine long years. In a scathing attack on the ruling party while speaking on the Governor's address on Friday, Mr. Naidu said investors were thronging the State because they were impressed by the great strides made in infrastructure by the Telugu Desam Party during his rule.

(6164) Hyderabad : Telangana Rashtra Samithi member Dugyala Srinivas Rao made the most of the opportunity given to him in the Assembly on Friday to launch a tirade against his party leaders Participating in the debate on the Governor's address after 11 of his follow party members were suspended, the dissident MLA regretted the developments in his party and heaped praises on Chief Minister Y.S. Rajasekhara Reddy, Congress Government and its policies.

(6165) Hyderabad : The Telangana Rashtra Samiti (TRS) has threatened to hold a 'girijana garjana' in the city and lay siege to the Assembly in protest against construction of Polavaram project next month. Talking to reporters, TRS Floor Leader G. Vijayarama Rao and party MLA N. Narasimha Reddy said the party would mobilise tribals for the 'garjana' from all Telangana districts.

(6166) Thiruvananthapuram : What has been in the air for the last several days has been officially confirmed: the CPI(M) and the LDF will not have any truck with the Democratic Indira Congress (Karunakaran) in the upcoming Assembly election in Kerala. "Our State committee is for strengthening the unity of the LDF. We do not propose to have any alliance or understanding with any other party," CPI(M) general secretary Prakash Karat told a news conference here on Friday. Asked whether the decision meant a setback for the section in the party led by State secretary Pinarayi Vijayan who had strongly argued for a tie-up with the DIC(K), the CPI(M) general secretary said it was a collective decision of the Polit Bureau and Mr. Vijayan was also a party to it . Asked why the LDF had sought the support of the DIC(K) in the Thiruvananthapuram Lok Sabha byelection, he said the LDF saw no reason to say `no' if anybody offered it support

(6167) Bangalore : In the first expansion of the two-week old Janata Dal (Secular)-Bharatiya Janata Party (BJP) Government, Chief Minister H.D.

Kumaraswamy on Friday inducted 20 Ministers - 11 from the BJP and nine from the Janata Dal (S). All the 20 are Cabinet Ministers.

(6168) Thiruvananthapuram : Democratic Indira Congress (Karunakaran) leader K. Karunakaran on Friday asserted that the Left Democratic Front (LDF) would not be able to come to power given the current political situation in the State. Addressing a press conference here, Mr. Karunakaran said there was nothing explosive in CPI(M) general secretary Prakash Karat's announcement that there would be no electoral alliance or understanding with any party outside the LDF. He said the LDF was in for a setback as its optimism was based on its electoral success in recent years. Some people in the LDF acted as if they were already in power and even Ministers, according to him, had been decided.He had not approached the LDF with an application for a slot. He had proposed a larger Left-secular-democratic alliance to fight communal forces and the corrupt United Democratic Front (UDF) Government.

(6169) Raichur : Karnataka Pradesh Congress Committee (KPCC) President M. Mallikarjun Kharge has called upon the party workers to create awareness about the National Rural Employment Guarantee Scheme (NREGS) among rural people.Mr. Kharge said it was the responsibility of the party workers to study the details of the scheme and give publicity to it in rural areas.

(6170) Kollam : CPI(M) general secretary Prakash Karat has called upon the United Progressive Alliance (UPA) Government at the Centre to fulfil the basic responsibilities of providing education and health care facilities to the people.Addressing a gathering here on Friday, he said India ranks among the lowest among the countries of the world regarding public expenditure on health. In the year 2006, India spent only 0.9 per cent of the GDP on public health. It is the same as far as education is concerned. Education and health, which are the basic right of the people, are the most neglected sectors in the country. "I am unable to understand how in a democracy Governments get elected and govern without addressing this basis question in society," he said.

(6171) Thiruvananthapuram : The Opposition LDF and DIC(K) members staged a walkout from the Assembly on Friday on rejection of their demand for a judicial inquiry into 'widespread corruption' in the irrigation wing of the Water Resources Department as evidenced by the 'graft-on-camera' episode on Thursday and suspension of Chief Engineer and Kerala's main negotiator in Kerala-Tamil Nadu inter-State river water disputes T. K. Sasi.

(6172) New Delhi : For the Congress leaders from the State, the CPI (M) decision to have no truck with Mr. Karunakaran has not come as a surprise. "The Marxists have a long record in betrayal," was the refrain of former Chief Minister A. K. Antony, Union Minister for Overseas Indian Affairs Vayalar Ravi and Kerala Pradesh Congress Committee president Ramesh Chennithala. Similar sentiments were echoed by Congress in-charge of Kerala Veerappa Moily.

(6173) Chennai : Democratic Indira Congress (Karunakaran) president K. Muraleedharan met All India Anna Dravida Munnetra Kazhagam general secretary and Tamil nadu Chief Minister Jayalalithaa at her residence on Friday. An AIADMK release said the party and the DIC(K) would fight the Kerala Assembly elections as alliance partners. A decision on seat-sharing will be taken soon, the release added.

(6174) New Delhi : The Bharatiya Janata Party on Friday threatened to launch a nationwide agitation on the Sachar Committee that was asked to submit a report on the educational, social and economic status of Muslims. BJP deputy leader in the Lok Sabha V.K. Malhotra said even though the party was especially concerned about the "survey" of Muslims in the armed forces, on the issue of collecting data from universities and government departments, the BJP "would not cooperate with the Sachar Committee." The party had conveyed to the Chief Ministers in the BJP-ruled States "not to provide any data" to the Committee, he said.However, the party appeared to be satisfied with the Prime Minister's statement on the Iran vote. "We do not want to quarrel with the Prime Minister on the statement given by him on the Iran nuclear issue," Mr. Malhotra said.

(6175) Chennai : Janata Party president Subramanian Swamy has described as "hypocritical" the Congress demand for resignation of the Mulayam Singh Government in Uttar Pradesh following the "expose" of a Minister's alleged involvement in drug trafficking. He said the Congress should, instead, ask the United Progressive Alliance Government to resign in the wake of revelations in the Mitrokhin papers and the Volcker Report and the Quattrocchi scandal.

(6176) New Delhi : The Left parties on Friday demanded that the discussion on the Iran nuclear issue be held immediately. They said Prime Minister Manmohan Singh should remember that it was a coalition government and not one of the Congress. "We are the supporting parties, and the Prime Minister is aware of the serious differences [on the Iran issue]. It should be discussed immediately," Communist Party of India leader Gurudas Dasgupta said in the Lok Sabha even as Dr. Singh rose to make a suo motu statement. CPI (M) leader Basudeb Acharia too echoed the demand. All political parties were keen that their views be heard, he said.

(6177) New Delhi : The Government on Friday informed the Lok Sabha that there was no question of compromising with the professional, apolitical and secular character of India's armed forces as was being made out by the Opposition which wanted the uniformed services to be kept out of the survey being undertaken for a report on the social, economic and educational status of Muslims in the country. In the absence of a positive reply from Leader of the House and Defence Minister Pranab Mukherjee to his demand for exempting the armed forces from the survey, Leader of the Opposition L. K. Advani led the National Democratic Alliance (NDA) in a walk-out after accusing the Government of indulging in "vote-bank politics." Describing the survey as a "communal headcount," Mr. Advani urged the Government not to stand on prestige. Poverty and backwardness are non-sectarian issues and should not be seen through the prism of faith, he said.Questioning the purpose of the survey when the report of a similar exercise carried out in 1980 had not been implemented, Mohammad Salim (Communist Party of India-Marxist) took a dig at the Government, citing "an old saying which states that where there is a will, there is a way and where this no will there is a survey." However, Mr. Salim said the Government should not allow the criticism to push it away from its chosen path of uplifting the downtrodden. Similar views were expressed by Gurudas Dasgupta (CPI) who said while the cause was noble, the method adopted was wrong.

(6178) New Delhi : Blaming the Congress leaders in the Municipal Corporation of Delhi and the Delhi Government for the present woes of the people, the Opposition Bharatiya Janata Party in the civic body on Friday said it was because of the inaction and inefficiency on part of the Congress that implementation of the Master Plan 2021 has been delayed.

(6179) Bhopal : The Congress members on Friday protested in the Madhya Pradesh Assembly over the Government's "failure" to give a proper reply to many of their queries and staged a walk-out. The agitated Opposition members were on their feet during the question hour in the morning protesting against the Government's reply, "Information is being collected", in response to queries relating to several departments.

(6180) Pondicherry : Founder of the Puduchery Munnetra Congress (PMC) P. Kannan, called upon the Centre to intervene immediately and dismiss the Rangasamy-led Congress government here, as the "some private hotels" holding objectionable dance shows had been exposed by a privately managed television company. But the hotels were functionng with impunity and there was total absence of intervention by the Government.

19-02-2006

(6181) Hyderabad : Two BJP members — G. Kishan Reddy and Dora Babu — were suspended from the Assembly for a day on Saturday for disrupting proceedings over their demand for a discussion on Friday's violence in Old City during the protest against Prophet Mohammed's caricatures published in a Danish newspaper. TDP members also stalled proceedings for two hours demanding dismissal of two Ministers over their allegation of poll code violation in the byelection to the **Visakhapatnam** I Assembly byelection.

(6182) Hyderabad : The Telangana Rashtra Samithi has accused some Congress leaders of distorting the recommendations of the Girglani Commission on 610 GO and asked the Government to implement them immediately without effecting any changes. Addressing a press conference here on Saturday, TRS floor leader in the Assembly, G. Vijayarama Rao and T. Harish Rao, said there should not be any second thoughts in implementing the complete recommendations and warned that the TRS would react strongly if the Government failed to do so.

(6183) Hyderabad : The Congress party has accused the Telugu Desam Party of violating the election code by raising the Visakhapatnam by-election issue in the Assembly on Saturday and said it would complain to the Election Commission against it. Denying that the Congress Ministers had violated the code, they said it was up to the Election Commission to judge the matter. They said several TD leaders, including former Ministers, were caught red-handed resorting to malpractices in the past but the Congress never demanded their resignations. Meanwhile, Mr. Chandrababu Naidu demanded the dismissal of as many as ten Ministers for allegedly distributing money to voters in the by-poll.

(6184) Hyderabad : "Creation of the separate State of Telangana is not in my hands.The Congress and the Telangana Rashtra Samithi have both left the issue to UPA chairperson Sonia Gandhi," Chief Minister Y.S. Rajasekhara Reddy has said.

(6185) Hyderabad : Telugu Desam president N. Chandrababu Naidu has sought Prime Minister Manmohan Singh' intervention to enable the return to Mahabubnagar of some tribals allegedly being prevented by a construction company in Meghalaya.In a letter to Dr. Singh, he referred to a report in a Telugu daily that some 600 tribal men, women and 150 children were taken by the company to work in its power project site in Meghalaya.

(6186) Visakhapatnam : On the eve of Sunday's polling in the by-election to the Visakha-I Assembly constituency, Telugu Desam Parliamentary Party leader K. Yerrannaidu met election observer Harish Goud on Saturday and complained that irregularities were being committed by the Congress.

(6187) New Delhi : The Janata Dal (Secular) headed by former Prime Minister H.D. Deve Gowda on Saturday suspended Karnataka Chief Minister H.D. Kumaraswamy and 39 other MLAs from the party. The suspension would take immediate effect. Danish Ali, JD (S) secretary general and spokesman, told reporters here that the action was taken as the decision taken by the MLAs [to topple the Dharam Singh Government] was against the "accepted principles of the party." The matter will be placed before the party national executive committee, which meets in the capital on Monday.

(6188) Chennai : Dravida Munnetra Kazhagam (DMK) president M. Karunanidhi made it clear on Saturday, "The ball is in his [Vaiko's] court" in deciding whether the Marumalarchi Dravida Munnetra Kazhagam remains in the Democratic Progressive Alliance (DPA). "I invited him home on Republic Day [January 26] and discussed seat adjustments for one-and-a-half hours. We almost agreed on the numbers; I only asked him to reduce his demand by one or two seats," Mr. Karunanidhi told a press conference at DMK headquarters this morning.

(6189) Bangalore : JD (S) President H.D. Deve Gowda on Saturday held a meeting with presidents of the party's district units. This gains significance in the wake of N. Thippanna's resigning from the post of president of the State unit.

(6190) Gulbarga : Karnataka Pradesh Congress Committee President M. Mallikarjun Kharge on Saturday termed the Cabinet expansion that took place on Friday as a "total disappointment" and "gross injustice" done to the Hyderabad-Karnataka region.

(6191) Mysore : BJP leader and Minister for Water Resources K.S. Eshwarappa has said that his party had to compromise on its anti-Janata Dal (Secular) stand to come to power in the State.Responding to queries on whether the BJP made any such compromises, Mr Eshwarappa said: "Maybe, we have". The BJP considers the Congress its enemy number one. The party was always open to the idea of forming a non-Congress Government. But, most parties considered it a political untouchable, he said.

(6192) Palakkad : Leader of the Opposition in the Kerala Assembly V.S. Achuthanandan on Saturday dismissed DIC (K) leader K Karunakaran's anti-Left Democratic Front (LDF) remarks on Friday as not worth taking seriously. "This statement is a reflection of Mr. Karunakaran's mental state as he is in a state of shock after the CPI(M) decision yesterday not to have any truck with the DIC(K) in the assembly polls," Mr. Achuthanandan said.

(6193) Thiruvananthapuram : The Communist Marxist Party (CMP) favours return of the Democratic Indira Congress (Karunakaran) leader K. Karunakaran into the Congress or UDF fold, Minister for Cooperation and Ports M. V. Raghavan said here on Saturday.

(6194) Madurai : The Communist Party of India (Marxist) would demand the recall of the United States Ambassador to India, David C. Mulford, during the ongoing session of Parliament. The party was unhappy with the Ambassador for writing a letter to the Chief Minister of West Bengal, Buddhadeb Bhattacharya, against the latter's comments opposing the U.S. President, George W. Bush. Addressing a public meeting following a special political conference here on Saturday, the CPI (M) general secretary, Prakash Karat, said the U.S. Ambassador has no right to interfere in the internal affairs of the country and "we are not going to tolerate this kind of arrogance by America."

(6195) New Delhi : The Karunakaran factor is again a subject of discussion within the Congress leadership. Since the State Committee of the Communist Party of India (Marxist) announced on Friday that it would have no truck with the Democratic Indira Congress (Karunakaran), the Congress has been monitoring his statements. On Saturday Pradesh Congress Committee president Ramesh Chennithala apprised party president Sonia Gandhi of the developments in Kerala. However, he refused to divulge details of the meeting here, maintaining that he had called on her primarily to finalise her programme in the State on March 4. Earlier, briefing mediapersons, Mr. Chennithala reiterated that it was for Mr. Karunakaran to decide whether he wanted to return to the Congress. "We never expelled him; he chose to go," was his answer to questionswhether the Congress would take Mr. Karunakaran back or make him a partner in the United Democratic Front.

(6196) Chennai : Janata Party president Subramanian Swamy has demanded the sacking of Uttar Pradesh Haj and Minority Welfare Minister Haji Mohammed Yaqoob for offering a reward of Rs. 51 crore to anyone killing the Danish cartoonist who had caricatured Prophet Muhammed.

(6197) New Delhi : Senior Bharatiya Janata Party leader and former Union Minister Murli Manohar Joshi has described the civilian nuclear agreement of 2005 between India and United States as "prejudicial to national interests." In a letter to Prime Minister Manmohan Singh, he has demanded "a free and full debate" in the current Parliament session on the proposed deal. According to Dr. Joshi, the agreement "puts onerous restrictions on India without any countervailing restrictions or restraints on the other high contracting party." This, he argues, is "designed to emasculate Indian nuclear options - both in the military and civil sectors - and make India perpetually dependent on the United States for all initiatives in application of nuclear energy."

(6198) New Delhi : Communist Party of India (Marxist) Polit Bureau member Sitaram Yechury said that Left support to the UPA Government was dependent on the government sticking to the "Laxman Rekha" of the common minimum programme. If it violated the CMP, it would have to pay for the consequences.

(6199) Hyderabad : The Telugu Desam and the Samajwadi Party have decided to work for a 'third alternative' comprising regional parties to mount pressure on the Centre to ensure autonomy to the States and at the same time focus on national development, TDP president N. Chandrababu Naidu said on Saturday.The exercise was towards "a national cooperative federation" of parties aimed at working together. It was yet to take shape, Mr. Naidu said here before leaving for Bangalore, where he is expected to meet leaders of some outfits.

(6200) New Delhi : A large number of Delhi traders under the leadership of former Union Minister Vijay Goel met the Leader of the Opposition in the Lok Sabha, L. K. Advani, on Saturday and apprised him that following the court orders for demolition, a large number of people would be rendered jobless as the shops in residential areas face imminent closure.

(6201) New Delhi : Stating that the Union Government welcomed the Supreme Court order directing the "big fish'' running commercial ventures in residential areas of the Capital to down their shutters, the Union Minister of State for Urban Development, Ajay Maken, on Saturday said the Government would seek relief for the small traders and business by taking up the matter in court shortly. Talking to newsmen after a meeting of the sitting Congress Members of Parliament from Delhi convened by DPCC president Ram Babu Sharma to discuss the issues arising out of the latest court orders, Mr. Maken said the Congress and its Government had always stood for implementation of the law of the land.

(6202) Bhopal : Four ruling Bharatiya Janata Party MLAs, all known supporters of former Madhya Pradesh Chief Minister and expelled BJP leader Uma Bharti, were suspended from the party on Saturday. The four — Sunil Nayak, Jalam Singh Patel, Rasal Singh and Hakam Singh Chadhar — have been suspended under various sub-clauses of section 25 of the party Constitution. They had backed Ms. Bharti and supported her campaign for leadership change that eventually led to Shivraj Singh Chauhan replacing Babulal Gaur as Chief Minister of Madhya Pradesh.

The suspended MLAs — Mr. Nayak (Jatara in Tikamgarh district), Mr. Patel (Narsinghpur), Mr. Chadhar (Gotegaon in Narsinghpur district) and Mr. Singh (Ron in Bhind district) — have been given 10 days to explain why disciplinary action should not be taken against them.

(6203) Chennai : An announcement saying that any qualified person can become priests in temples in the State is only a few months away, DMK president M. Karunanidhi said on Saturday. Presiding over a function here to release commemorative postage stamps on Kirubananda Variar, Devaneya Pavanar, U.V. Swaminatha Iyer and Tamilavel Umamaheswarar here, he said there was still a big grievance that not all qualified persons could become priests. When the DMK was in power in the State, a government order was issued to redress the grievance. However, it got enmeshed in a legal tangle and could not be implemented till now.

(6204) Chennai : Within an hour of Dravida Munnetra Kazhagam's chief M. Karunanidhi's press conference on Saturday, the Marumalarchi Dravida Munnetra Kazhagam (MDMK) general secretary Vaiko issued a statement expressing regret over his party functionary's speech. "I am sorry for the views that have hurt Doctor Kalaignar. Nanjil Sampath will be asked to explain," he said in a brief release. Mr. Vaiko distanced himself from some of the views expressed by party functionaries as published in a weekly and clarified they were not the official views of the MDMK.

(6205) Chennai : The new Tamil Nadu Congress president, M. Krishnasswamy, has appealed to party cadres to remain united and work for the victory of the Democratic Progressive Alliance led by Dravida Munnetra Kazhagam (DMK) president M. Karunanidhi in the coming Assembly election. Mr. Krishnasswamy, who addressed party workers on Thursday after assuming office, charged that Chief Minister Jayalalithaa, who is also general secretary of the All-India Anna Dravida Munnetra Kazhagam, was making all out efforts to break the Congress party. It was time to retrieve the State from the "clutches" of Ms. Jayalalithaa. She was under the impression that the State was her fiefdom and she could succeed by using money power, he said.

(6206) Madurai : Yet another split in the Tamil Nadu unit of the All-India Forward Bloc (AIFB) became imminent on Thursday, with the suspended general secretary L. Santhanam convening a 'State committee' meeting here, claiming to be the "real AIFB."The decision of the Central

Committee to place the Usilampatti MLA under suspension was taken at a meeting in Kolkata. The meeting took a "unanimous decision" to "seize his membership," according to the party general secretary Debabrata Biswas. This follows a reply to the showcause notice served on Mr. Santhanam "which was not satisfactory."

(6207) Madurai : The Communist Party of India (Marxist) on Saturday called for a "proper representation" to Left parties in seats allocation. The party has also appealed to people to unseat the "anti-people and anti-democratic" All India Anna Dravida Munnetra Kazhagam Government.

20-02-2006

(6208) Guntur : The Communist Party of India (Marxist) will launch political struggles in association with all anti-BJP parties against the alleged anti-people's policies of the Congress-led UPA Government.The Manmohan Singh Government has failed to implement the agreed policies under the Common Minimum Programme, the CPI(M) Polit Bureau member Brinda Karat said here on Sunday. The party would fight for people's cause as they had not been on the political agenda of the country for the past 10 years.

(6209) Hyderabad : The Congress Legislature Party has challenged the Telugu Desam to deny the election manifesto report prepared by the then senior Congress leader and now TDP spokesman M. V. Mysoora Reddy that irrigation sector was neglected by the earlier TDP regime.

(6210) Hyderabad : The State unit of the Bharatiya Janata Party has demanded that the Government desist from its moves to take control of Lord Balaji temple at Chilkur on the city outskirts. The party has also demanded that the Government take steps to amend Act 30 of 1987, which it said was the main cause of the poor conditions in a majority of temples in the State.

(6211) Nellore : Bharatiya Janata Party leader M. Venkaiah Naidu has opposed the Central Government's move to appoint a committee to seek information for preparing a report on the number of Muslims in the armed forces. He told reporters here on Sunday that such a move was highly dangerous and if allowed to continue might even pave the way for yet another division of the country. He contended that in a disciplined force like army, there was no place for any religion, except fitness and devotion for duty.

(6212) New Delhi : The former Lok Sabha Speaker, Purno A. Sangma, of the NCP on Sunday won the Tura Lok Sabha seat for the ninth consecutive time. The Congress, the BJP and the Shiv Sena won one Assembly seats each in the byelections in Maharashtra and Uttar Pradesh. - UNI

(6213) Bangalore : The arrival of the former party President L.K. Advani here to attend the silver jubilee celebrations of the Art of Living Foundation provided an opportunity for the disgruntled BJP legislators to complain about being ignored in the February 17 Ministry expansion. Their grouse was that most of the 11 who made it to the Ministry belonged to Deputy Chief Minister B.S.Yediyurappa's camp. Only three Ministers, Jagadish Shettar, R. Ashok and Katta Subramanya Naidu are not identified as his supporters.

(6214) Gulbarga : The All India Progressive Janata Dal (AIPJD) on Sunday demanded the Janata Dal (Secular) to expel the former Prime Minister H.D. Deve Gowda from the primary membership of the party for his alleged anti-party activity of allowing his son H.D. Kumaraswamy to align with the communal forces to form the Government in the State and allowing the Bharatiya Janata Party (BJP) to get a foothold in south India. Referring to the action taken by Mr. Deve Gowda in suspending Mr. Kumaraswamy and 39 MLAs supporting him from the party, senior AIPJD functionary and MLA B.R. Patil told presspersons here that this is yet another part of the dubious drama enacted by the Janata Dal (S) President to ensure that his son, Mr. Kumaraswamy, remains in the saddle of the Government.He said the belated action of Mr. Deve Gowda was intended to pre-empt any disciplinary action by the party National Executive, which is meeting in New Delhi on Monday.

(6215) Gulbarga : President of the Karnataka Pradesh Congress Committee (KPCC) M. Mallikarjun Kharge on Sunday hinted that the party would urge Governor T.N. Chaturvedi to issue directions to Speaker of the Assembly Krishna to disqualify 40 MLAs of the Janata Dal (S), including Chief Minister H.D. Kumaraswamy, who have been suspended from the party, under the anti-defection law.

(6216) Mysore : Congress activists made a fervent plea to Maharashtra Governor S.M. Krishna to return to active politics in Karnataka, during his private visit to Mysore on Sunday. Several party leaders and activists gathered at the Toll Gate on the outskirts of Mysore with bouquets and garlands to welcome Mr. Krishna, who was visiting the city to attend a wedding. Soon after he alighted from the car, activists raised slogans seeking his return to active politics in Karnataka."Please return to Karnataka politics if you want our survival," an activist shouted drawing the attention of the former Chief Minister. . When reporters sought Mr. Krishna's reaction to the demand from party activists for his return to active politics, the Maharashtra Governor merely expressed gratitude for the faith the party workers have placed in him. "I have come here on a private visit. Friends and party workers have hopes on me because they like me. I am grateful to them", he said.

(6217) Shirva (Udupi Dt.) : Union Minister Oscar Fernandes said on Sunday that the Congress and the United Progressive Alliance (UPA) Government was committed to protecting national interests. He was responding to a question on India's current stance on the Iran nuclear issue.Addressing presspersons here, Mr. Fernandes said that any differences between the Government and the Left parties would be resolved through discussions. Prime Minister Manmohan Singh had made it clear that the Government was ready for a discussion on the floor of the House and in the meetings with alliance partners. Each party has a point of view, but the Congress idea is to find a common find.

(6218) Kochi : Leader of the Opposition V.S. Achuthanandan on Sunday launched Stree Sakthi, an organisation to help women in distress here. Speaking on the occasion, he exhorted people to expose those accused in committing crimes against women and to help rehabilitate the victims. "Of late, accused in sex scandals and those charged with harassing women have been alleging that the media is levelling unfounded accusations against them. This is contrary to facts," he said.

(6219) Kozhikode : Democratic Indira Congress(Karunakaran) president K. Muraleedharan has said that the party has the strength to go it alone in the coming Assembly elections. Mr. Muraleedharan also said that his party was not one that would be finished if any Front refused to take veteran leader K. Karunakaran to its fold. According to Mr.

Muraleedharan, the present LDF comprises those who had earlier ditched the CPI(M). "It is better for the CPI(M) to scrutinise them before scrutinising anybody from outside," he said. To a question, Mr. Muraleedharan said that his party had not submitted any application requesting to take it back to the Congress, nor would it submit any such application.

(6220) Thiruvananthapuram : The Bharatiya Janata Party will reckon the Left Democratic Front (LDF) and the United Democratic Front (UDF) as rivals of equal footing in the coming elections, party State president P.S. Sreedharan Pillai said here on Sunday.

(6221) Alappuzha : The Congress State unit is at present working coherently and it should not become a federation of groups again, Union Minister for Non-Resident Indians Vayalar Ravi said here on Sunday.

(6222) Guwahati: Bharatiya Janata Party (BJP) president Rajnath Singh said on Sunday that he had asked the Chief Ministers of all BJP-ruled states to stop 'conversion attempts' by Christian missionaries at any cost. Kicking off the party's election campaign in Assam, Mr. Singh demanded the United Progressive Alliance (UPA) government to frame legislation to prevent Christian missionaries from 'proselytisation.' He said the BJP had no objection to missionaries implementing welfare measures for people. "However, in the name of welfare missions, they have been luring people, particularly the tribals and Adivasis, to convert to Christianity. This needs to be checked," he added.

(6223) New Delhi : The Communist Party of India (Marxist) MPs demanded the recall of U.S. Ambassador David Mulford on Monday in protest against his letter to West Bengal Chief Minister Buddhadeb Bhattacharjee. Confirming this, CPI (M) Parliamentary Party leader Basudeb Acharia told The Hindu on Sunday that he would give notice to raise the matter during zero hour in the Lok Sabha on Monday. The West Bengal Chief Minister had written a letter to Prime Minister Manmohan Singh earlier this month, taking exception to the tone and tenor of Mulford's letter. Mr. Bhattacharjee said that the U.S. Ambassador had not only exceeded his brief but also overstepped the limits of diplomatic propriety. He said expressions used in the communication were "totally unacceptable."

(6224) Lucknow : Bahujan Samaj Party supremo Mayawati on Sunday supported the reported survey of Muslims in armed forces. "We have to support Prime Minister Manmohan Singh's effort to go in for a survey of Muslims to assess their social representation so that the country knows about their status," she told mediapersons here.

(6225) Guntur : Alienating large tracts of tribal land without consulting the tribals, in the name of development, was a clear violation of the rights vested in the Fifth Schedule of the Constitution, said Communist Party of India (Marxist) Polit Bureau member Brinda Karat.

(6226) Mumbai : The Shiv Sena retained the Shrivardhan Assembly constituency in the Konkan, but lost the prestigious Naigaum seat in by-elections necessitated by the defection of supporters of Narayan Rane from the Shiv Sena to the Congress. Kalidas Kolambkar, who sought re-election on the Congress ticket in Naigaum, defeated Shiv Sena candidate Shradhdha Jadhav by 22,411 votes. Mr. Kolambkar polled 44,694 votes and Ms. Jadhav only 22,283 votes. In Shrivardhan, Sena nominee Tukaram Surve secured 61,984 votes, against 46,232 polled by Congress candidate Shyam Sawant.

(6227) Ghazipur : Uttar Pradesh, says the BJP has retained the Mohammadabad Assembly seat. Alka Rai, wife of slain party MLA Krishnanand Rai, defeated her nearest Samajwadi Party rival Sri Krishna by a margin of over 33,000 votes.

(6228) Puri : The Vishwa Hindu Parshad has decided to maintain a distance from the Bharatiya Janata Party, its international general secretary, Pravin Togadia, announced here on Sunday. "So far, the BJP was reaping the benefit of the work done by the VHP. This resulted in other parties not taking up the cause of the Hindus," Mr. Togadia told a press conference at the end of the 11th Dharma Sansad here. The VHP would now create a vote bank of 15 crore Hindus, and extend support to those parties who agreed to its demands. "This will help us in politicising the Hindu cause at all levels."

(6229) New Delhi : The Janata Dal (United) declared on Saturday its intention to go along with the Samajwadi Party if it moved a no-confidence motion against the Government on the Iran issue. Striking a different note from the line taken by the Bhartiya Janata Party, the National Democratic Alliance (NDA) constituent said it had taken an independent view even in the matter of the "cash-for-question" MPs being referred to the Privileges

Committee . "The sharing of agenda is on a common minimum programme of governance. For the rest we have our independent ideology," JD (U) sources said. JD (U) general secretary Shambhu Srivastava told media persons here that "Prime Minister Manmohan Singh's statement on the [Iran] issue in Parliament is nothing but a jugglery of words and has no content. The logic given is hypocritical." "If we can live with China and Pakistan bombs what's wrong with Iran. Moreover, India is not a signatory to the NPT, unlike China, Pakistan and Iran. Why is India bothered about NPT violations and indirectly bring the provisions of NPT in the country," he asked.

(6230) Pondicherry : All India Congress Committee general secretary B K Hariprasad MP, who is in charge of Pondicherry, has called upon the party workers to be wary of those who had betrayed the party after growing out of it politically. Such persons, who had eaten the salt of the party and had gone out of it, should be taught an effective lesson at the forthcoming Assembly polls here, he said adding that the Congress had really no threat of opposition at the hustings.

(6231) Lucknow : The Congress is working out an action plan for winning back Dalits into the party fold, the newly- appointed chairman of the AICC Scheduled Castes Cell, Yogendra Makvana, said on Sunday. An action plan has been prepared and handed over to Congress President Sonia Gandhi, he told reporters here. Efforts would be made to ensure that past mistakes, which led to the parting of ways by Dalits, were not repeated, Mr. Makvana said.

(6232) Lucknow : Charging Uttar Pradesh Chief Minister Mulayam Singh Yadav with politicising the Iran issue the Bahujan Samaj Party supremo Mayawti on Sunday termed ruling Samajwadi Party's threat of a no confidence vote against the UPA Government as an "eyewash." "Can Mr Yadav reply about his hobnobbing with former US president Bill Clinton and recent visit of Israeli ambassador to the State capital," she questioned at a press conference here. The former UP CM said that on one hand the SP government was honouring a US leader and Isreali ambassador while on the other side it was trying to stage a "mock" fight for the Muslims in the state in the name of Iran. "SP has no policy for the Muslims and it only aimed to garner votes by shedding crocodile tears," she claimed.Demanding the immediate dismissal of the U.P.Minister Haji Yakoob Qureshi following his alleged announcement to reward with Rs 51 crores the assassin of the Danish cartoonist who lampooned the Prophet Mohammed, she said that the State Governor and Union Home Ministry should take swift cognizance of the remarks.

(6233) Coimbatore : Peace and progress of every section of society must be a part of any exercise to protect human rights, the president of the All India Congress Committee Human Rights Department, Muralidhar C. Bhandare, said here on Sunday. "We have guaranteed fundamental rights and the Supreme Court enforces them. Even education for children in the 6-14 age group has been made a basic right," he said while inaugurating the West Zone Conference of the Tamil Nadu Congress Human Right Department. Exhorting party cadre to work for equal rights to all, he said poverty alleviation was vital to achieving it. Poverty stood at 26 per cent and it needed to be brought down to below 10 per cent over the next 10 years.

(6234) Coimbatore : The confusion in the Democratic Progressive Alliance (DPA) over the Marumalarchi Dravida Munnetra Kazhagam keeping off the seat sharing process may end soon, Union Minister of State for Textilcs E.V.K.S. Elangovan said here on Sunday.He told reporters that the Congress hoped for an early end to the confusion. Certain issues would always crop up in an alliance but would be resolved.Mr. Elangovan said his party had not been approached to mediate, but would do so if its intervention was sought. On the exit of former Tamil Nadu Congress Committee president Tindivanam K. Ramamurthy, he said it had enthused the youth in the party. "There are one or two more left," he remarked.

(6235) Karur : Internment under the POTA could prove to be a stumbling block for MDMK leader Vaiko from aligning with the AIADMK, Bharatiya Janata Party State general secretary H. Raja has said. Addressing reporters here on Saturday night, he felt the pressure of not having even a single MLA, after 13 years of running a party, would tell on Mr. Vaiko. He would have to be part of an alliance this time round. Mr. Vaiko would try to enter the Assembly, "just like any other prudent politician." Mr. Raja refused to be drawn into considering the possibility of aligning with Mr. Vaiko in the event of his not joining any other alliance.

21-02-2006

(6236) Hyderabad : The Communist Party of India (CPI) has said that the proposed creamy layer norm for reservations among backward classes be applicable to jobs and educational institutions. Briefing reporters on the deliberations of the State executive committee here on Monday, K. Narayana, Secretary CPI State Council, endorsed the move of the Government to fix Rs. 4 lakhs as income ceiling to implement creamy layer norm saying it would enable the poorer sections to avail reservations. The CPI also urged the Government to implement G.O. 610 in toto without entertaining any re-thinking on the issue.

(6237) Hyderabad : Speakers at a convention organised by the Left parties here on Monday said that it was time the United Progressive Alliance (UPA) Government resisted pressure from an imperialist "Big Brother" and take appropriate steps. The Left parties are gearing up for an anti-US protest with the slogan "Bush Go Back" in every district headquarters on March 2 and specifically on March 3 when US President George W. Bush will be here. Until then, cadres will strive to increase awareness among people. A signature campaign towards the end of February is also on. Senior leaders of the CPI, CPI (M) and CPI-ML (Liberation) said that India had no time for imperialists trying to rob the nation of its sovereignty. How could the US ask India to go against Iran, a friendly nation which was now getting ready to provide natural gas at stable prices for a period of five years?

(6238) Hyderabad : The Opposition picked holes in the budget pointing out that the grey areas left unattended to by Finance Minister K. Rosaiah might lead to disadvantage to several sections here on Monday. Telugu Desam president N. Chandrababu Naidu said it threatened to cripple the economy in the long run. Talking to reporters, Mr. Naidu said it was neither integrated nor comprehensive since it left out welfare, law and order and several other key sectors without specific allocations. There was no truth in the claim of the Government about a surplus budget of Rs. 286 crore for 2004-05 as the fourth quarter releases in that year were highly restricted, particularly for welfare. While welcoming the provision of Rs. 10,000 crores for irrigation in the coming year, he expressed dismay that there was no reference to effective family planning measures initiated by his Government without which the 7.55 per cent growth rate in the Gross State Domestic Product (GSDP) for 2005-06 was impossible.

(6239) Hyderabad : The 24-day padayatra by a host of Telugu Desam Party leaders from Telangana demanding utilisation of Godavari waters for the development of the region culminated in a public meeting at the Nizam College grounds here on Monday evening. Party president N. Chandrababu Naidu who was away in Switzerland when the yatra commenced from Mancherial in Adilabad district on January 28, received the leaders who footed out the 456 km journey through seven districts.

(6240) Hyderabad : Telangana Rashtra Samithi members staged a walkout in the Assembly on Monday protesting against the Government's discriminatory attitude towards Telangana in sanction of new universities.Strangely, the walkout was announced by TRS member T. Harish Rao who raised the issue during question hour and not the floor leader of the party G. Vijayarama Rao. Mr. Harish Rao said Telangana region with ten backward districts, 42 percent of State's population and 1200 affiliated colleges had two regional universities, Osmania and Kakatiya. In contrast, Rayalaseema with four districts, 17 percent population and 100 colleges also has two. The University Grants Commission norms say there should be one university for every 100 affiliated colleges.

(6241) Visakhapatnam : A host of TDP leaders have expressed doubts over the illness suffered by Congress MLA and DCC president Gandi Babji and demanded that a panel of doctors from corporate hospitals be formed to examine him. Mr. Babji was alleged to have brandished a revolver at TDP leaders near the Old Post Office on Sunday evening and the TDP has been demanding his arrest since then.

(6242) Thiruvananthapuram : The Democratic Indira Congress(K) has decided to maintain its identity at all costs, but dropped very broad hints that it was amenable to some kind of arrangement within the UDF setup in Kerala's bipolar coalition politics. At the same time, it took care not to hurt the official leadership of the CPI (M) while hitting out at the LDF partners, CPI and RSP and Opposition leader V. S. Achuthanandan. President of the DIC(K) K. Muraleedharan, addressing a press conference at the end of the party's leadership meeting on Monday, said his party looked forward to a brand of coalition politics that would keep its identity. However, his party would not hesitate to contest in all the 140 Assembly constituencies if necessary.

(6243) New Delhi : The Janata Dal (Secular) is all set to expel H.D. Kumaraswamy and other MLAs who have formed a government in alliance with the Bharatiya Janata Party in Karnataka "in violation of party's basic principle of secularism". The stage for their expulsion was set here on Monday when the national executive of the party ratified the decision of party President and former Prime Minister H.D. Deve Gowda to suspend Mr. Kumaraswamy and others. It resolved to refer the matter to the party's disciplinary action committee. Condemning the move of Mr. Kumaraswamy and others, a resolution adopted at a meeting of the panel said: "The party reiterates that it will continue to uphold secular values." At the meeting, party leader Surendra Mohan caused a furore when he demanded that Mr. Deve Gowda resign as party President for "delaying action" against Mr. Kumaraswamy and others. The other members of the national executive rejected the demand and reiterated their faith in Mr. Deve Gowda's leadership. Addressing a press conference, Mr. Deve Gowda said the meeting discussed whether he should continue as party President. "I wanted to resign. The issue was discussed threadbare and, ultimately, everyone persuaded me to continue." He denied that he deliberately delayed action against Mr. Kumaraswamy.

(6244) Chennai : The Marumalarchi Dravida Munnetra Kazhagam has decided to stay in the Dravida Munnetra Kazhagam-led Democratic Progressive Alliance. In a three-page statement, MDMK general secretary Vaiko said that his party was committed to ensuring the victory of the DPA in the Assembly elections. "The MDMK had done nothing to bring down the esteem of the alliance," he said.

(6245) New Delhi : The Congress found itself isolated in Parliament on Monday as its allies and supporting parties joined hands with the Opposition to demand the recall of American ambassador to India David Mulford for his statements on the Iran vote and letter to West Bengal Chief Minister Buddhadeb Bhattacharjee. While the Left parties and the Samajwadi Party staged a walkout in both Houses to register their dissatisfaction with the Government's response, the Rashtriya Janata Dal joined them in the Lok Sabha. However, the Bharatiya Janata Party-led National Democratic Alliance - which echoed the sentiments aired by the Left parties - did not join the walkout. Earlier, Parliamentary Affairs Minister Priyaranjan Dasmunsi said the views of the members would be conveyed to the Prime Minister. "The Government has never [compromised] and will not compromise with the nation's dignity, and the honour and authority of Parliament," he said. In the Lok Sabha, the issue was raised by Basudeb Acharia (Communist Party of India-Marxist) who first mentioned Mr.

Mulford writing to Mr. Bhattacharjee on his comments against U.S. President George Bush. Stating that it was improper for the ambassador to have written to the Chief Minister, Vijay Kumar Malhotra (BJP) said more objectionable was the manner in which the Government had succumbed to U.S. pressure as was evident from India's vote at the IAEA. Questioning the Government's silence, Ram Gopal Yadav (SP) said it should demand his recall and summon the ambassador to communicate its displeasure. Devendra Prasad Yadav (RJD) and A. Krishnaswamy (Dravida Munnetra Kazhagam) expressed similar views.In the Rajya Sabha, Leader of the Opposition Jaswant Singh described the ambassador's statement and letter as a gross impropriety and violation of existing diplomatic norms. "Hegemony of power is not necessarily hegemony of wisdom. Such a statement could have been made on the spur of a moment. But a letter is a deliberate act which the entire House condemns." Sharad Yadav (Janata Dal-United) said it was a serious matter. "A country of 100 crore population cannot be insulted in this manner." Describing the issue as "shameful", Nilotpal Basu (CPI-M) said while the country's self-respect was at stake, the UPA Government was "pussyfooting" with the ambassador. Sitaram Yechury (CPI-M) said it was an "unprecedented" situation involving the self-respect of the country.

(6246) Thiruvananthapuram : Opposition LDF members staged a walkout from the Assembly on Monday to protest against what it termed the Government's refusal to initiate stern action to check RSS-sponsored violence in Thrissur district. Significantly, the two-member Democratic Indira Congress (Karunakaran) did not join the LDF in the walkout.

(6247) New Delhi : Rashtriya Lok Dal (RLD) president Ajit Singh on Monday called for an all-party meeting to evolve a consensus on the need for a bill to tackle communal violence in the country. He made this suggestion at a seminar organised here. Mr. Singh's Private Member's Bill, the Communal Violence (Prevention, Control and Rehabilitation of Victims) Act, which was introduced in the Lok Sabha on March 14, 2005, is listed for discussion during the ongoing session of Parliament. The Bill, which has exactly the same title as the Union Home Ministry's Bill on communal violence introduced in Parliament in the winter session, seeks to establish a 'National Commission on Inter Community Peace and Justice' headed by a retired Supreme Court judge or a retired Chief Justice of a High Court.

(6248) New Delhi : The Janata Dal (Secular) has criticised the Centre for pursuing "anti-people policies" and "yielding to the wishes of global capital, including allowing of privatisation of airports, FDI in retail sector and privatisation of forest land."A resolution adopted at a meeting of the party's national executive here on Monday said: "The Union Government [had] at the WTO Ministerial meet from December 13 to 18 submitted to the pressure of the U.S. and the European Union and agreed to open up the entire agricultural and service sectors in response to a paltry cut in export subsidies in 2013." By another resolution, the JD (S) criticised the Centre for signing an agreement with the U.S. on the civilian nuclear programme. It said the July 18 pact was a threat to the country's security and sovereignty.

(6249) New Delhi : Terming the publication of cartoons about Prophet Muhammed "insensitive," Congress president Sonia Gandhi has said she shared the sense of outrage of the Muslim community. The Congress had the greatest regard and respect for all faiths and was committed to protecting their rights and beliefs, for preserving and strengthening the secular nature of our society, she said in reply to a letter written Shahi Imam of Delhi's Jama Masjid.

(6250) New Delhi : Led by the Janata Dal (United), the Opposition in the Lok Sabha on Monday demanded Prime Minister Manmohan Singh's resignation in the light of the Supreme Court judgment holding the dissolution of the Bihar Assembly as "unconstitutional and illegal." Initiating the short impromptu discussion, Prabhunath Singh (JD-U) said while the Congress had a tradition of "murdering the Constitution," this was not expected of a Government headed by someone of the reputation of Dr. Singh. More so, since this Government is being supported by the Communist Party of India (Marxist). The BJP deputy leader, Vijay Kumar Malhotra, said the Centre was as guilty as the Governor. "Since Buta Singh has resigned, the Central Government should also resign." Of the view that the Government could not escape responsibility, Ramji Lal Suman (Samajwadi Party) sought to point out that it had the option of rejecting the Governor's recommendations.

(6251) Pondicherry : The All India Congress Committee general secretary B. K. Hariprasad said that the Congress "is a major partner in the Democratic Progressive Alliance in Pondicherry." The Congress president

Sonia Gandhi would take into consideration the "inputs and recommendations" of PCC leader P. Shanmugham and Chief Minister N. Rangasamy for finalising the poll strategy.

(6252) Pondicherry : Though the Election Commission is yet to announce poll schedule for the Pondicherry Assembly, parties - though yet to announce their plans on the seat sharing have started holding meetings with their workers. The ruling Congress has been holding a 'district level' workers meeting. AICC general secretary B.K. Hariprasad, who is in-charge of party affairs in Pondicherry addressed party workers.

(6253) Lucknow : Bahujan Samaj Sangharsh Samiti (BS-4) on Monday demanded reservation for Dalits in private sector, armed forces and judiciary to maintain "social balance in Indian society." Addressing the "diversity rally," Uttar Pradesh Sports Minister and BS-4 leader R K Chaudhury said India should adopt the 'diversity pattern' on the lines of the United States to provide "social uplift for Blacks or African Americans." He said without social diversity, India could not achieve overall development as only 15 per cent of people were ruling the remaining 85 per cent. "This is gross injustice as the makers of India's democratic system had dreamt for justice and equality to all."

(6254) Chennai : The expelled Congress leader, Tindivanam K.Ramamurthy, on Monday announced the formation of a new party, the Tamil Nadu Indira Congress, at a meeting here. He said that the party would seek to redeem the Congress and appealed to all true Congressmen to support the new party. Mr. Ramamurthy also unveiled the party flag - the Tricolour with the face of Kamaraj at the centre.

(6255) Coimbatore : The Congress will focus on the achievements of the United Progressive Alliance Government at the Centre in its Assembly election campaign. Congress Working Committee member in-charge of Tamil Nadu, Veerappa Moily, made this announcement while speaking to reporters here on Monday. Earlier, he flagged off a padayatra by Congress Seva Dal workers, highlighting the achievements of the UPA Government, to Chennai. Asked if the Congress would seek to be a part of the State Government after elections, Mr. Moily said the objective was to ensure the victory of the Democratic Progressive Alliance. Issues relating to power sharing could be considered after the polls.

22-02-2006

(6256) Hyderabad : K. Ramulu, president of the State BJP Dalit Morcha, resigned from the party and joined Telugu Desam Party (TDP) here on Tuesday. TDP president N. Chandrababu Naidu welcomed him at the party office. G. Sayanna, TDP MLA from Secunderabad Cantonment, and others were present.

(6257) Hyderabad : APCC president K. Keshava Rao dismissed the Opposition ire against the Government's Budget as 'unfounded and irrational' here on Tuesday. The Congress Legislature Party (CLP) too welcomed the budget on similar lines at a separate press conference.

(6258) Mahabubnagar : Communist party of India (Marxist) State secretary B.V. Raghavulu has expressed apprehensions over the continuation of free power to the farm sector and poor families.

(6259) Adilabad : The TDP has criticised the State budget calling it "anti-people". The party leaders charged that though the Government claimed to be pro-farmer there were no signs of it in the budget.

(6260) Pathanamthitta : Revolutionary Socialist Party (RSP) State secretary T.J. Chandrachoodan has said that his party is of the view that the Left parties should to stick to political morality and ethics. What differentiate the Left from the Right are the differences in their words and deeds, he said. According to him, the Left Front stands for the working class, the poor and the needy. It will not align with those forces bereft of the ideals.

(6261) New Delhi : The Left parties on Tuesday continued with their offensive against the policies of the Manmohan Singh Government charging that "economic growth does not mean economic development." The debate also witnessed brief skirmishes between the Left and the Congress.Participating in the resumed discussion in the Lok Sabha on the motion of thanks to the President's address, C.K. Chandrappan of the Communist Party of India, said despite the claims of the Government, India has slipped in the human development index. He said even now some 233 million people in the country remain hungry; four million were unemployed and 16 crore families had a wage lower than Rs. 3 a day. Though not comparable, a cow in the United States gets feed worth a minimum of $ 2, he said.

(6262) New Delhi : The Left parties on Tuesday joined the Bharatiya Janata Party (BJP) in demanding that the Parliamentary Joint Committee on 'The Scheduled Tribes (Recognition of Forest Rights) Bill, 2005' table its report in the Budget session itself. The demand was made in the Lok Sabha after Chairman of the Committee V. Kishore Chandra S. Deo sought the permission of the House to extend the deadline to the first day of the Monsoon Session. Questioning Mr. Deo's request, Vijay Kumar Malhotra (BJP) said the report should be tabled in the post-recess part of the Budget session while wondering whether the Government was trying to delay the Bill. Mr. Malhotra found support from Basudeb Acharia (CPI-M) and Gurudas Dasgupta (CPI), forcing an intervention from the Leader of the House, Pranab Mukherjee.

(6263) Srinagar : Visibly upset over the "timing" and "handling" of the February 25 round table conference on Kashmir, former Jammu and Kashmir Chief Minister Farooq Abdullah on Tuesday said he was disappointed and felt sad with regard to the "agenda-less conference" convened by Prime Minister Manmohan Singh. Expressing inability to attend the conference due to "personal engagements," he said that the National Conference president Omar Abdullah would be attending. Referring to his and Omar Abdullah's meeting with Union Home Minister Shivraj Patil, he said that the latter had told them that the proposal of autonomy will be considered. Mr Patil, he said, even asked them to suggest names for a high level committee. But nothing has moved forward even after our president reminded him repeatedly, he said. Dr. Abdullah said that autonomy was within the Constitution and "we do not know anything about General Musharraf's proposal on demilitarisation and self rule."

(6264) New Delhi : Congress president Sonia Gandhi on Tuesday asked party leaders and workers to actively propagate and monitor the implementation of social welfare measures being implemented by the United Progressive Alliance Government and also counter the "misleading propaganda" of some State Governments. Referring to the National Rural Employment Guarantee Act, Ms. Gandhi said she was aware that some party workers were agitated that the programme was being propagated as an initiative of the State Government while in reality 90 per cent of the funding was coming from the Centre. "Had we not been in power, the Act would not be in place. I know the Prime Minister is looking into this but at the same time our party leaders and workers must be very active in countering this misleading propaganda," she told the general body of the Congress Party in Parliament. Ms. Gandhi said the All-India Congress Committee had already activated the State and district units to get involved in the 200 districts where registration of job seekers under the Act had begun. By the middle of the next month, the party would have a convention of 200 district units. Similarly, while the Government had achieved much in just 20 months, there was a need to place over-riding emphasis on the actual execution of major programmes like the Bharat Nirman, the Rural Employment Guarantee or the National Rural Health Mission. "The full effect of these schemes must begin to be felt at the village level well before the year is out. This is where our party MPs, MLAs and workers must play a major role by raising public awareness, by ensuring social mobilisation and by keeping watch as implementation unfolds," she said.

(6265) New Delhi : The Bharatiya Janata Party threatened to stall Parliament over the issue of large-scale demolition of illegal and unauthorised buildings in Delhi. It may do so next week, possibly after the Union Budget is presented on February 28. The party's deputy leader in the Lok Sabha, V.K. Malhotra, told reporters here on Tuesday that the BJP expects the Urban Development Minister or someone else responsible to take Parliament into confidence on what the Centre proposes to do to deal with the sword of demolition hanging over the heads of thousands, if not lakhs, of owners of unauthorised structures.

(6266) Pondicherry : The Pondicherry Bharatiya Janata Party unit president R. Kesavalu said though there was a possibility of aligning with the All India Anna Dravida Munnetra Kazhagam (AIADMK) for the Assembly elections here, the State unit was awaiting the decision of the high command.

(6267) Chennai : Kamarajar Deseeya Congress has claimed that it has registered with the Election Commission its flag that bore the image of the former Chief Minister Kamaraj. "No one else could use its name or the flag," M. S. Rajendran, general secretary, said in a statement issued on Tuesday.

(6268) Tiruchi : The Dravida Munnetra Kazhagam will press for a Constitutional amendment to provide for reservation to Muslims, party president Karunanidhi has said. "We have already written to the Centre. The demand will be reiterated in the party's election manifesto and we will strive to implement the same. The party's Union Ministers and Members of Parliament will also impress upon the Centre," Mr. Karunanidhi told reporters here on Tuesday.The party will also seek an enquiry by the Centre into its recent allegations of irregularities in the disbursement of tsunami relief in Tamil Nadu. Commenting on the emerging situation in Sri Lanka, especially in wake of the arrival of refugees, Mr. Karunanidhi said though the DMK backed the Centre's foreign policy, it had drawn attention to the sufferings of the Sri Lankan Tamils. "The interests of Eelam Tamils are dear to our heart and their plight is a matter of concern."

23-02-2006

(6269) Tirupati : Vinod Pandey, national president of the Bharatiya Kisan Morcha, the farmers'wing of the BJP, on Wednesday lashed out at the UPA government for 'reversing and undoing' all pro-farmer policies and programmes launched by the Vajpayee government.

(6270) Visakhapatnam : Accusing the Congress and the Telugu Desam Party of trying to woo voters with inducements, the Bharatiya Janata Party has demanded countermanding of the Visakha-I bypoll.

(6271) Hyderabad : Congress MLAs presented a divided picture on Wednesday over the issue of implementing the Girglani Commission's report on repatriation of non-local employees of the Government to their native zones. A section of Congress MLAs from coastal Andhra made no secret of their discontent over the Cabinet's recent decision to implement in toto the commission's report. On the other hand, ruling party MLAs from Telangana opposed any move to dilute this decision. A similar predicament faced the Telugu Desam Party on this issue. The party's whip in the Assembly, P. Keshav, who belongs to Rayalaseema, wanted people of all regions to be represented in Hyderabad whereas E. Dayakar Rao, MLA from Warangal district, favoured implementation of the six-point formula and the Girglani Commission's report.

(6272) New Delhi : Chief Minister H.D. Kumaraswamy said here on Wednesday that he is still a part of the Janata Dal (Secular) and expressed confidence that he will be able to convince the party National Executive that his decision to form a Government with the Bharatiya Janata Party was in the interest of the party.

(6273) New Delhi : Prime Minister Manmohan Singh on Wednesday ruled out recall of the U.S. Ambassador David Mulford for writing a letter to West Bengal Chief Minister Buddhadeb Bhattacharjee.Dr. Singh, however, described the envoy's action as "unwarranted" and at variance with diplomatic practice. The Government had taken note of the issue and the action taken so far would suffice, he said.The Left parties had demanded Mr. Mulford's recall for writing to Mr. Bhattacharjee following the Chief Minister's criticism of the U.S. President George W. Bush. "I share the sentiments [of Left members]. But my own feeling is that the action we have taken would suffice for the time being," Dr. Singh said at the end of a 50-minute speech in the Rajya Sabha. He was winding up the debate on the President's address to Parliament.The response followed queries from Nilotpal Basu and Brinda Karat of the Communist Party of India (Marxist). They wanted to know whether the Government would consider recalling Mr. Mulford. Mr. Basu said the Government should deliver a strong message as it was a matter of national pride and self-respect.

(6274) Bangalore : Even as the new government is making arrangements for Governor T.N. Chaturvedi's second address of the year to the joint session of the legislature on Friday, the main Opposition party, the Congress, has appealed to him against doing so on the ground that he will be committing a "constitutional impropriety". A delegation of Congress leaders, comprising Leader of the Opposition in the Legislative Assembly N. Dharam Singh, President of the Karnataka Pradesh Congress Committee M. Mallikarjun Kharge and others, called on Mr. Chaturvedi at the Raj Bhavan and presented a brief memorandum.

(6275) Bangalore : Deputy Chief Minister B.S. Yediyurappa must apologise for his reported comment that "money for ministerial berth is a culture of the Congress and not the Bharatiya Janata Party", V.S. Ugrappa, spokesman of the Karnataka Pradesh Congress Committee, said here on Wednesday. He told presspersons that the "power-hungry" BJP and its coalition partner, the Janata Dal (Secular), are "given to pecuniary considerations in granting Cabinet berths".

(6276) New Delhi : Seeking to renew a link between the fight against globalisation/imperialism and caste and class oppression, the Communist Party of India (Marxist) will launch a struggle and convert it into a movement. "It is not enough to pass a general resolution. We have to make a concrete study on the form of caste and class oppression in different areas, mobilise the people and link different sections of the society. Only then will we be able to generate a movement," general secretary Prakash Karat said at a CPI (M)-organised, all-India convention on the problems of Dalits here on

(6277) Panaji : Stating that after many years the Central Government had made huge allocations for poverty alleviation programmes, Congress president Sonia Gandhi said the challenge was to ensure that these allocations reach the actual beneficiaries. She appealed to the party workers across the country to take the help of activists and NGOs to follow up these programmes to grassroot levels, ascertain the weaknesses in the implementation and to correct them.She was addressing a workers' convention on Wednesday as part of her two-day visit to the State. Ms. Gandhi emphasised the need for the Congress governments whether in the Centre or in the States to be true to promises made in the election manifesto and be committed to implementing the promises made to the people as "we have been found wanting on this front."

(6278) Ahmedabad : A local leader in Gujarat has given a call for the "eyes" of painter M. F. Husain, in return for a "reward" of 1 kg of gold. Jashubhai Patel, a former Mehsana district unit president of the BJP, announced on Wednesday the "reward" to anyone who would "gouge" out the eyes of the painter and cut out the thumb of his right hand so that he cannot draw "perverted" paintings of Hindu gods and goddesses and of Bharat Mata. Mr. Patel, however, said his party had nothing to do with his announcement and that "it is the voice of my own inner self."

(6279) Chandigarh : The proceedings of the Punjab Assembly had to be suspended for an hour when a noisy Opposition, led by former Chief Minister Parkash Singh Badal, demanded an adjournment motion to discuss the situation arising out of recent revelations by the State police chief, S.S. Virk, about rehabilitation of terrorists. Earlier, Mr. Badal said that the revelations by Mr. Virk about sparing the life of an Area Commander of the Khalistan Liberation Force (KLF), Amritpal Singh alias Sukhvinderpal Singh alias Sukhi, after closing all cases and granting him an assumed identity of Harjit Singh Kahlon, smacked of a larger conspiracy. He said that Mr. Virk had also admitted before journalists that another 300 terrorists had been rehabilitated secretly. Mr. Badal demanded that the names of all the terrorists who had been clandestinely rehabilitated be made public. He demanded a thorough probe to ascertain the identity of those who were killed in place of these terrorists. He also sought a status report about officers who claimed major amounts as reward for eliminating these terrorists, who were described by Mr. Virk as the "unsung heroes."

(6280) Chennai : Marumalarchi Dravida Munnetra Kazhagam general secretary Vaiko on Wednesday met Dravida Munnetra Kazhagam president M.Karunanidhi to present the MDMK wish list. The meeting lasted about an hour and a half. Mr.Vaiko said the talks would continue. "I cannot say anything more. I cannot divulge anything," he said and denied there was no confusion in the alliance. "I have already clearly stated that I am part of the alliance. What more do you want?" Mr. Karunanidhi said that the MDMK would be given "honourable" number of seats.

24-02-2006

(6281) Hyderabad : Coastal Andhra Congress MLAs belonging to Scheduled Castes have opposed the categorisation of SCs for reservation and urged withdrawal of the move. Addressing a press conference on Thursday MLAs — N. Subramanyam, D. Sambaiah, P. Viswaroop, Vamsi Krishna, K. Narayana Swamy and G.V. Prasad — said though they initially agreed for the categorisation among Malas and Madigas, their community was mounting pressure on them to maintain status quo. All these MLAs belong to the Mala sub-caste.

(6282) Hyderabad : The entire Opposition staged a walkout in the Assembly protesting against the 'unsatisfactory reply' of the Government on sick industries during the question hour on Thursday. Leader of the Opposition N. Chandrababu Naidu charged the Government with failing to revive a single industry in the last two years.

(6283) New Delhi : Raising the pitch against the Indirasagar (Polavaram) project, a multi-party round table on Thursday decided to appeal to the Centre to intervene and appoint an expert committee to study the alternative proposals to avoid subversion. Organised by CPI(M) MP P. Madhu, the round table saw as many as 18 MPs from the CPI, the TDP, the TRS, the Janata Dal (United) and the Republican Party of India attending it.

(6284) New Delhi : Parliament was adjourned on Thursday amid pandemonium over a news report claiming that the United Progressive Alliance Government interfered with the functioning of the Central Bureau of Investigation in the Babri Masjid case against Bharatiya Janata Party leader L.K. Advani.In the Lok Sabha, BJP members did not allow the House to function, leading to four adjournments in the afternoon. Prime Minister Manmohan Singh's reply to the motion of thanks to the President's address was lost in the din as the slogan-shouting BJP members sought his resignation.

(6285) New Delhi : Prime Minister Manmohan Singh on Thursday said in the Lok Sabha that it was not the Congress culture to allow "shadowy organisations to interfere in the work of elected governments." Replying to the motion of thanks to the President's address amid slogan-shouting by the Opposition, he said the Opposition was raising inconsequential issues in the vital debate. "Time and again a question is raised about prime ministerial authority. It resembles some totalitarian system in a fascist State, where authority has to be visibly asserted to command compliance." Referring to comments of BJP leader V.K. Malhotra on the United Programme Alliance leadership, Dr. Singh said: "That may be the culture of those who keep raising this issue of authority."

(6286) New Delhi : Samajwadi Party leader Amar Singh on Thursday moved the Supreme Court, seeking a judicial inquiry into circulation of CDs containing conversations tapped from his telephone. - PTI

(6287) Mysore : Members of the Communist Party of India staged a demonstration in the city on Wednesday condemning the "anti-labour" and "anti-people" policies of the Government.

(6288) Panaji : Though elections to the Goa Assembly are "still a little away," Congress President Sonia Gandhi, nevertheless, advised local party workers to be "active and in a state of preparedness." In her address to the party convention here on Wednesday evening, Ms. Gandhi recalled the events leading to the last change in Government in the State and expressed happiness that the people of Goa had once again reposed faith in a secular Government. The Congress President asked party activists to work together to ensure that Goa is not subjected again to "communal politics, communal government and communal administration." Ms. Gandhi repeatedly hailed Goa's pluralistic tradition and its communal harmony, which she described as "a true reflection of the ethos of the country". The Congress President accused the Bharatiya Janata Party (BJP) of "trying to distort the centuries-old communal harmony when it was in power in the State"."To my mind this is a grave affront to the peace-loving people of Goa. I cannot simply conceive of Goa as a place of communal tension," she said. The Congress President asked the State Government "not to be complacent and take people for granted but implement the agenda to ensure quality of life for all Goans".

(6289) Kannur : The two-day district conference of the Indian Union Muslim League (IUML) began here on Thursday. Inaugurating the delegates' session in the morning, IUML leader Panakkad Hyderali Shihab Thangal said that the implementation of the Narendran Commission report through consensus was a great achievement of the United Democratic Front (UDF) Government and the IUML.He said that the Communist Party of India (Marxist), which had raised issues when the report was implemented, was yet to clarify its stand on the commission's recommendations, he said.

(6290) Thiruvananthapuram : The CPI(M) State secretariat on Thursday said the party was united on the decision to keep the Democratic Indira Congress (Karunakaran) out of the LDF. In a statement here, the CPI(M) secretariat said there was no confusion in the party on the issue and all party members would join hands to implement the party decision. It accused the anti-Communist media of trying to create the impression that the party was divided on the issue. The decision to use the break-up in the Congress to the advantage of the working class was taken by the party after discussions at various levels, including the Polit Bureau.The secretariat said the decision to have local-level adjustments with the DIC(K) for the local body elections was also taken collectively.

(6291) New Delhi : Communist Party of India (CPI) is planning to bring a privilege motion against Minister of State for External Affairs E. Ahamed for misleading the Lok Sabha on Wednesday on the question of whether the United States had asked India to reconsider its purchase of an oilfield in Syria. This was announced by CPI leader Gurudas Dasgupta at a briefing here on Thursday, shortly after the Government gave an entirely different answer to a similar question in the Rajya Sabha. While the Government had answered in the negative in its written reply in the Lok

Sabha, its response to a similar question in the Rajya Sabha by Congressman Motilal Vora was that the matter had been "raised informally by the U.S." Mr. Ahamed is learnt to have written to the Lok Sabha Secretary-General stating that a correct picture was not presented on the issue because of an inadvertent lapse in handling of papers in the External Affairs Ministry. As a result, an uncorrected version of the answer was sent to the Secretariat. The Ministry has submitted a corrected version for the records of the House. Seeking the indulgence of the Chair, Mr. Ahamed also sought permission to apprise members of the House in person of the correct position.

(6292) New Delhi : The Communist Party of India (CPI) on Thursday said the Government had quietly begun downsizing the banking business. This charge was made against the Government on the basis of a circular issued by the Reserve Bank of India (RBI) to all banks asking them to offload a large part of retail banking services to outsiders, including corporate entities. Disclosing this at a press conference, CPI leader Gurudas Dasgupta said he had wanted to raise the matter in the Lok Sabha on Thursday but was unable to do so because of disruption of proceedings. Circulating copies of the circular, he said that the work that the RBI wanted to be offloaded included identification of borrowers, preliminary processing and submission of loan applications to banks, post-sanction monitoring for recovery.

(6293) New Delhi : Communist Party of India (Marxist) came out in support of the demand of journalists and employees of the print media for constitution of a wage board. In a statement, the Polit Bureau said the Government should without delay announce the setting up of a wage board. The Government should also set up a media commission to look into the entire gamut of the media from print to electronic. "This is necessary in view of the entry of foreign media and the conditions of journalists and workers and the various issues which have been thrown up by the expansion of the media. The commission should also look into the condition of journalists and employees" the statement said.

(6294) Panaji : The Centre's initiative to make available software, aimed at enabling all Indians to be equal partners in the information technology revolution, would soon cover all major languages, Congress president Sonia Gandhi said on Thursday. Laying the foundation stone for the Rajiv Gandhi IT Habitat of the Goa Government at Dona Paula near here, she described information technology as a major instrument of social transformation. The Centre was planning to use IT to monitor the implementation of the National Rural Employment Guarantee Programme. Coupled with the Right to Information Act, IT could be a major tool to ensure transparency in the functioning of the Government.

(6295) New Delhi : The Delhi Assembly Deputy Speaker, Shoaib Iqbal, on Thursday condemned the publication of Prophet Mohammad cartoons in a Danish newspaper. He also criticised the British artist who reportedly depicted Lord Rama and Sita on tissue papers of a company. The Janata Dal (S) leader said the Union Government should intervene in the matter so that such things do not occur again.

(6296) New Delhi : Describing the state of affairs in all urbanised and rural villages of Delhi as very pathetic and employment resources of the villagers being destroyed by the Municipal Corporation of Delhi without any consideration for human aspects, Delhi BJP president Harsh Vardhan has demanded that the Delhi Villages Protection and Development Act be enforced for all-round development of villages in the Capital.

(6297) Pondicherry : Secretary of Pondicherry State committee of All India Anna Dravida Munnetra Kazhagam (AIADMK) and legislator A Anbalagan has said that the Lt Governor M M. Lakhera's address to the Assembly delivered earlier in the day contained nothing and caused disappointment to the people of the Union Territory. Contents of Lt Governor's address carried only the policy decisions of the government.

(6298) Pondicherry : Pondicherry State Janata Dal (Secular) president E. Ganesan said here on Wednesday that his party would have alliance with the front formed by the All India Anna Dravida Munnetra Kazhagam (AIADMK) and Puduchery Munnetra Congress (PMC) in the forthcoming Assembly polls here.

(6299) Chennai : The Bharatiya Janata Party will work out a strategy to ensure that it emerges as a key player in Tamil Nadu, party general secretary Rajiv Pratap Rudy said here on Thursday. The BJP national executive member said the party was aware of its strength in the State. It would work hard to strengthen its roots. The current political situation in the State was conducive for national parties such as the BJP to make their presence felt. During his tour of interior villages, he found that the conditions were similar to those that prevailed in Bihar before the Assembly elections. People in remote areas were fed up with the Dravidian parties and yearning for a change. The phase of domination by the DMK and the AIADMK was over. In the absence of any alternative to these parties, the BJP could fill the void. Reiterating the party's stand to go it alone in the coming Assembly elections, Mr. Rudy said the State executive meeting in the first week of March would review the political situation and take a final decision.

(6300) Chennai : Irked at DMK president Karunanidhi's attitude, the Dalit Panthers of India (DPI) on Thursday appealed to the Pattali Makkal Katchi (PMK) to come out of the Democratic Progressive Alliance (DPA) to lead an "alternative front" in the Assembly elections."If the PMK stays with the DPA, the DPI will work for the victory of its candidates and refrain from contesting the polls in other places," DPI general secretary Thol. Thirumavalavan told a news conference here. "We will continue to preserve the relationship between the DPI and the PMK." The DPI's main goal was to get "due recognition" from the Election Commission ."

25-02-2006

(6301) Hyderabad : The State Assembly was adjourned for half an hour on Friday after a furore over the change in design of the Pulichintala project. As soon as the House met, Telugu Desam members, holding placards, raised the Pulichintala issue by seeking an adjournment motion. They said the sudden change of design from cement concrete to earthen dam, symbolised the corruption in irrigation projects.

(6302) Hyderabad : Telugu Desam president N. Chandrababu Naidu has said that the State received a raw deal in the railway budget in spite of being represented by ten Union Ministers. The fact that only four new trains were sanctioned bore testimony to the injustice meted out to the State, Mr. Naidu told reporters here while reacting to the budget proposals presented to Parliament by Railway Minister Lalu Prasad. He said this was the third consecutive railway budget of the UPA Government to ditch the State. It got 'peanuts' as it was allotted only 3 to 6 per cent of the funds under various heads. The State was not only neglected in the sanctioning of new trains but new lines and gauge conversion as well.This was notwithstanding the contribution of Rs. 4,000 crores to the revenue of the Railways by the South Central Railway (SCR) last year.

(6303) Bangalore : The Janata Dal (Secular)-Bharatiya Janata Party (BJP) Government on Friday sought to drive home the point that its focus is on development at a faster pace. It was the second address by Governor T.N. Chaturvedi to the Legislature in a month. At the beginning, Mr. Chaturvedi said he was addressing the joint session under the provisions of Article 175 (1) of the Constitution. The Congress appealed to the Governor to refrain from going ahead with his address since in its view it was unconstitutional. When the Governor ignored its plea, Leader of the Opposition in the Legislative Assembly N. Dharam Singh led a walkout accompanied by all Congress members.

(6304) Bangalore : The Congress, which is the principal Opposition in the Legislative Assembly, is considering petitioning President A.P.J. Abdul Kalam against what it regards as a violation of the Constitution by Governor T.N. Chaturvedi in addressing a joint session of the legislature for the second time in the same session. The party has alleged that the Governor acted as an agent of the ruling parties - the Janata Dal (Secular) and the Bharatiya Janata Party.Leader of the Opposition in the Assembly N. Dharam Singh and the Karnataka Pradesh Congress Committee President M. Mallikarjun Kharge told presspersons that it is a black day in the history of the Karnataka legislature and added that they would continue their agitation against what they called "the unconstitutional act of the Governor."

(6305) Alappuzha : The difference of opinion between the CPI and the CPI(M) over certain issues will be sorted out amicably, CPI State assistant secretary K.E. Ismail has said. At a press conference here on Friday, Mr. Ismail said that both the parties had different views on certain issues, including Asian Development Bank loan and relations with the Democratic Indira Congress (Karunakaran). The DIC(K) issue had been sorted out, he said. Mr. Ismail arrived here as a part of his Janakeeya Yatra. He said the CPI had no reason to be apologetic about their opposition to the LDF entering into an alliance with the DIC(K). The stand of the CPI in the Thiruvanamthapuram byelection was that the DIC(K) should contest independently. But the DIC(K) refused to stand independently and supported CPI candidate, Mr. Ismail said.

(6306) Kochi : Preliminary discussions are on with like-minded parties in forming an alliance with the Democratic Indira Congress (Karunakaran) and nothing concrete has emerged so far, K. Muraleedharan, State president of DIC(K) has said. He was speaking to presspersons after inaugurating the State convention of the Kerala Students Union (Indira) here on Friday. At present, the decision was to go it alone in the Assembly election, but alliances without compromising the identity of the party would be welcome, he said. After the organisational elections on March 27, district-level activities would be taken up to prepare the party to contest in all the 140 Assembly constituencies, he said. Refusing to attack the CPI(M) for its decision, Mr. Muraleedharan criticised the CPI saying the party "is on the verge of extinction ."

(6307) New Delhi : Ahead of the Assembly polls, Left MPs from Kerala on Friday targeted the Congress over the Union Railway Budget, accusing the party-led coalition of "neglecting" the State totally and decided to take up the issue with Prime Minister Manmohan Singh."The Budget had meted out severe injustice to the State. While the Railway Minister proposed a 32 per cent increase in the overall financial allocation for infrastructure development, the share for the State has come down drastically," CPI(M) Lok Sabha member N. N. Krishnadas said. He said that last year, the Centre had allocated around Rs.240 crores for the infrastructure development for the State, while this year the allocation had been slashed to just Rs.129 crores. Mr. Krishnadas gave a veiled threat to the Centre that the Budget could not be passed without the support of the Left parties.

(6308) New Delhi : The BJP could move a privilege motion against Prime Minister Manmohan Singh and Leader of the House in the Lok Sabha, Pranab Mukherjee. Deputy leader of the Bharatiya Janata Party V.K. Malhotra said here on Friday that the party would be going through the text of what Dr. Singh and Mr. Mukherjee had said in Parliament on the issue of "non-interference" in the functioning of the Central Bureau of Investigation when the question of defreezing of the London bank accounts of Bofors·accused Ottavio Quattrocchi was raised. "Now it had become clear" that the Government had asked the CBI to give it details of its decision in the Babri Masjid demolition case against Leader of Opposition L.K. Advani.

(6309) New Delhi : Commenting on the Railway Budget presented by Mr. Prasad here on Friday, BJP deputy leader V.K. Malhotra focussed on the "transformed" Minister who had left behind the "kulhar," the "matha" and the "khadi" uniforms for employees. Mr. Malhotra said the emphasis on privatisation and "Western ideas" would mean loss of jobs, and that was not a good idea..Some reporters asked the BJP leader whether the party was against better facilities for passengers and were only worried that small vendors at railway stations would lose business. Mr. Malhotra said, "Creating jobs is more important." He pointed out that by its own admission the Railways had cut back 300,000 jobs over the past 16 years. The BJP was silent on the profits shown by the Railways in the current financial year, nor did it comment on the reduced fares for air-conditioned travel. "We will make a detailed comment after reading the Railway Budget carefully," the party spokesperson said. But it found fault with the budget for "lack of adequate provision for gauge conversion, new lines and doubling of tracks." The Congress described the budget as a "sensitive, comprehensive and balanced exercise." Party spokesperson Abhishek Singhvi said the Railway Minister has not touched passenger fares and provided relief to farmers and others. He said the exercise was difficult since different regions had different demands and there could never be a perfect budget in this context.

(6310) New Delhi : The Left Parties said on Friday that the apparent move towards "privatisation" in the railway budget was "unacceptable." They cautioned against ignoring the supporting parties, especially on the shifting of the east-west freight corridor stops. At a press conference, MPs of the Communist Party of India (Marxist) and the Communist Party of India said they disagreed with proposals on setting up of food plazas and cyber cafes, and slashing the rates of upper class train travel as they would make no difference to the common man. In a statement, the CPI (M) Polit Bureau welcomed the 50 per cent concession for farmers and dairy product producers, and the fact that no further burden had been imposed on the people by way of higher fares. But it was unfortunate that despite the financial health of the Railways and the projections of higher passenger and freight traffic, there was no provision for the acquisition of rolling stock, particularly locomotives and coaches.

(6311) New Delhi : Samajwadi Party members in the Rajya Sabha on Friday attempted to raise the issue of compact discs containing phone conversations of Amar Singh reaching some television channels. Deputy Chairman K. Rahman Khan, however, disallowed it, as there was no prior notice. Jaya Bachchan and Shahid Siddiqui interrupted the zero hour proceedings to draw the Chair's attention to their demand.

(6312) Srinagar : The General Officer Commanding (GOC) of the Srinagar-based 15 Corps, Lt. Gen. S. S. Dhillon, sought to clarify that the Army did not target the civilians in Handwara on Wednesday and that they were killed in the crossfire. In New Delhi , Congress president Sonia Gandhi on Friday expressed deep anguish over the death of four civilians. "On learning of the tragedy, I spoke with Defence Minister and the Chief Minister as well. The Indian Army is confronted with daunting challenges as it fights terrorism and militancy in the State. Even so, I want to urge all concerned to ensure that such events do not recur in future. I extend my feelings of empathy and support to the families who lost their dear ones," Ms. Gandhi said in a message. The Communist Party of India (Marxist) condemning the killing has demanded setting up of a time-bound judicial enquiry.

(6313) Neemuch (MP) : Expelled BJP leader and former Madhya Pradesh chief minister Uma Bharti has said she would form a party on April 30 and also demand the Election Commission of India to allot the lotus as her election symbol. "If the EC rejects the demand, an alternative will be sought," the firebrand sadhvi, who is undertaking a Janadesh Yatra, told mediapersons on Thursday night after addressing a mammoth rally here. Pointing out that, in principle, her organisation would be the "real BJP," she added it was her desire that the BJP office be handed over to her outfit. "However, if that fails to happen, we will construct an office building. It's not a crucial issue," Ms Bharti added.

(6314) Jaipur : Congress leaders here have demanded immediate arrest of the Bharatiya Janata Party legislator from Makrana against whom a local court had found prima facie case of rape charge. They have also sought his dismissal from the State Assembly. Former Rajasthan Minister Harendra Mirdha and president of State Mahila Congress Mamta Sharma, who presented the victim of alleged rape before media persons here on Thursday, said it was a matter of serious concern that in a State where the Governor, the Chief Minister and the Speaker of the Assembly were women even legislators were charged with rape. "This is the real face of BJP.

which claims to be a party with a difference. Mr. Rajpurohit has a past history of such offences. There have been 22 cases registered against him in Nagaur district's Parbatsar, Rupangarh and Makrana police stations from 1952 onward," charged Mr. Mirdha, a former MLA from Nagaur. Mr. Rajpurohit was the main accused in the Makrana communal riots following which he was jailed for a month, he added.

(6315) Lucknow : Protesting against the circulation in TV news channels of CDs said to contain conversations of Amar Singh, Uttar Pradesh Chief Minister Mulayam Singh Yadav on Friday claimed the CDs were aimed at creating an atmosphere against the State Government ahead of the court decision in connection with BSP MLAs' defection issue. The circulation of CDs in the electronic media was a part of the "sponsored conspiracy" to build an atmosphere before the vital court decision on February 28 on the defection of 40 BSP MLAs to the SP, he said while addressing a rally here. Taking a dig at the Congress, Mr. Yadav said the freedom struggle was not fought just by one political party but all sections of society. He claimed to be a champion of the Dalits and Backward Classes and accused the Congress of "undermining the Constitution to strengthen the forces responsible for their exploitation". PTI

(6316) Chennai : The State committee of the All India Forward Bloc, at its executive meeting on Friday, resolved that L. Santhanam, Member of Legislative Assembly, be expelled from the party. Those members who did not take part in the meeting in support of Mr. Santhanam should be suspended, the committee decided.A resolution was adopted at the meeting. It was also decided to authorise M. Karthik, chairman and general secretary of the State unit, to finalise the poll strategy of the party.

26-02-2006

(6317) Hyderabad : Former CLP leader and Khairatabad MLA, P. Janardhan Reddy has asked Chief Minister Y.S. Rajasekhara Reddy to clarify his stand on G.O. 610 to silence those who were trying to create confusion by claiming that Hyderabad is a 'free zone'. He said the TRS and the CPI(M) had alleged that the Congress was enacting a drama by raking up the issue of 'free zone'. He said Presidential Order had clearly mentioned that there was no free zone and pointed out that GO 610 was issued only when the Presidential Order was violated.

(6318) Hyderabad : The Telugu Desam Party Polit Bureau has asserted that it will support the Government in any steps taken to implement the recommendations made by the Girglani Commission provided there is no deviation from the six-point formula and Presidential order governing the recruitments in Telangana region.

(6319) Hyderabad : The Telugu Desam Party is getting ready to launch "palle palle ki TDP," a programme to take party leaders to the villages to educate the people about the "anti-people" policies of the Government from March 1. It will last till April 15. The members of the party's constituency coordination committees along with district leaders will undertake tours to interact with people and in a bid to endear the party to them. The State-level leaders would join them at important places. This decision was taken by the TDP Polit Bureau which met here on Saturday.

(6320) Dhobipet (Ranga Reddy Dist.) : A week-long programme "Palle Pilupu" was launched by the State BJP here on Saturday with leaders accusing the Congress Governments both at the Centre and in the State of neglecting the common man. They urged people to pressure the ruling party to fulfil its election promises. Launching the programme from this village in Chevella constituency, the BJP vice-president M. Venkaiah Naidu described Palle Pilupu as "melukolupu" (wake-up call) for both Governments.

(6321) Sangareddy : Union Minister A. Narendra has announced that the TRS will come out of the UPA Government at the Centre if the bill for separate Telangana is not introduced in the current budget session of Parliament. He said that TRS had sought the support of the BJP for separate Telangana but not decided on a formal tie-up with that party. He brushed aside reports on the growing bonhomie with the BJP.

(6322) Jaipur : The Bharatiya Janata Party-led Government in Rajasthan is planning to introduce a Bill during the budget session of the Assembly starting February 28 outlawing religious conversions. The proposed Bill is expected to target Christian missionaries even as some radical organisations have launched a major offensive against Christian organisations across the State. At a press conference here on Saturday Home Minister Gulab Chand Kataria said the draft Bill was being given final touches. "We are trying to table it in the Assembly's Budget session and get it passed into legislation as soon as possible."

(6323) Alappuzha : Bharatiya Janata Party (BJP) State president P.S. Sreedharan Pillai has said that the Railway Budget for the year 2006-07 has humiliated the State, and the MPs from the State who support the UPA Government has conceded their inability to work for protecting the interests of the State. While Vajpayee Government's Railway Budget for the year 2002-03 had earmarked Rs.444 crores for the development of railways in the State, the amount earmarked in the present budget for the State was less than Rs.100 crores, Mr. Pillai said.

(6324) Kannur : Leaders of the Communist Party of India-Marxist (CPI-M) has come out strongly against the attacks on its offices on Friday night, while the Indian Union Muslim League (IUML) has denied having any role in them.

(6325) Kochi : United Democratic Front (UDF) convener P.P. Thankachan asserts that the Front has not entrusted anyone to hold talks with the Democratic Indira Congress (Karunakaran). Mr. Thankachan said the issue K. Karunakaran's party returning to the UDF had not come up before the Front liaison committee so far. Any decision on inducting new members into the Front will be taken only after the UDF leadership discusses the issue. Regarding reports of talks between the DIC(K) and the Indian Union Muslim League (IUML) in this direction, Mr. Thankachan said the IUML might be holding talks on its own. The UDF leadership is not aware of any such talks, he said.

(6326) Kozhikode : Janata Dal (S) State president M.P. Veerendrakumar, MP, has warned the proposal to allow more private participation in Railways would have an adverse effect. The moves as indicated by Lalu Prasad's budget introduced in Lok Sabha on Friday appeared to be to implement the proposals of the Rakesh Mohan Committee, which were in favour of total privatisation of Railways, he remarked.

(6327) Thiruvananthapuram : The Opposition Left Democratic Front (LDF) has alleged a raw deal to the State in the Railway Budget for 2006-07 presented in Parliament on Friday. Briefing presspersons after the front's State committee meeting here on Saturday, its convener, Paloli Mohammed Kutty, said the Railway Ministry had done gross injustice to the State by cutting back on its allocation from around Rs.240 crores last year to Rs. 130 crores. This, he said, had happened despite MPs from Kerala taking up the State's demands for railway development strongly with the Centre. CPI(M) Polit Bureau member and Leader of the Opposition V.S. Achuthanandan; Revolutionary Socialist Party (RSP) general secretary K. Pankajakshan; CPI State secretary Veliyam Bhargavan; and RSP State secretary T.J. Chandrachoodan also came out strongly against the Railway Budget which, they said, fell far short of the expectations of the State. Several other organisations had also come out against what they termed injustice meted out to Kerala by the Railway Ministry.

(6328) Thiruvananthapuram : Constituents of the Opposition Left Democratic Front (LDF) have decided not to go public with their differences over the Democratic Indira Congress (Karunakaran) and acceptance of the Asian Development Bank (ADB) loans by LDF-controlled local bodies. This follows a detailed discussion on these issues at the LDF State committee meeting here on Saturday. Leaders of the CPI(M), CPI and the RSP had made mutually critical observations about their respective stand on both the issues. Briefing the media after the LDF State panel meeting, Front convener Paloli Mohammed Kutty said the meeting had concluded that the exchanges between alliance leaders were unfortunate and should be avoided in future. Asked whether this applied to him as well (as he had also made some unsavoury remarks about the CPI), Mr. Mohammed Kutty replied that since he also belonged to one of the Left parties, it would apply to him too.

(6329) Lucknow : Uttar Pradesh Congress on Saturday demanded the arrest of Samajwadi Party general secretary Amar Singh under the Prevention of Corruption Act for "demanding a cut in a business transaction." Quoting the SP leader's interview to NDTV on phone tapping CDs available with the channel, Uttar Pradesh Congress Committee president Salman Khurshid said that since Mr. Singh enjoyed the status of a Cabinet Minister, a case be registered against him for demanding monetary benefits in a business transaction. He claimed that since one of Mr. Singh's reported conversations with Chief Minister Mulayam Singh Yadav pertained to a High Court judge, the Union Home Ministry commenced a discussion on imposition of Article 356 in the State.

(6330) Chennai : Janata Party president Subramaniam Swamy has welcomed U.S. President George Bush's statement that patience is required to finalise the proposed India-U.S. civilian nuclear deal. In a statement issued here, Mr. Swamy said the proposed deal was a "manifestation of the worst of both alternatives - the difficulties of continuing on our own as before, and the restrictions to adhere to if India were a signatory to the NPT [Non-proliferation Treaty]."

(6331) New Delhi : A delegation of Delhi Bharatiya Janata Party legislators and leaders led by the Leader of the Opposition in the Delhi Assembly, Jagdish Mukhi, called on Lieutenant-Governor B. L. Joshi over the weekend and demanded immediate dissolution of the Assembly and the Congress-ruled Municipal Corporation of Delhi stating that there was a complete breakdown of constitutional machinery as the Sheila Dikshit Government had failed to discharge its responsibilities in an effective and efficient manner.

(6332) New Delhi : Delhi Pradesh Congress Committee president Ram Babu Sharma on Saturday constituted a 17-member high-power committee to gather suggestions from party workers on the issue of unauthorised constructions and demolitions and place them before the five-member high-power committee headed by former Lieutenant-Governor Tejinder Khanna.

(6333) Pondicherry : CPI (M) Pondicherry unit Secretary V. Perumal said here on Saturday that the budget presented by Chief Minister N. Rangasamy was "disappointing".

(6334) Chennai : Railway Minister Lalu Prasad received kudos from Dravida Munnetra Kazhagam president M. Karunanidhi. In a statement here, Mr. Karunanidhi welcomed the introduction of three new routes in Tamil Nadu and fare concession to farmers for attending farmers' meets, milk producers, the handicapped and the unemployed.

(6335) Chennai : "Congress is confident of getting a respectable number of seats in seat-sharing talks with the Democratic Progressive Alliance led by Dravida Munnetra Kazhagam," said senior party leader M.Veerappa Moily here on Saturday.The first phase of negotiations began when Mr. Moily met the DMK president M.Karunanidhi in the evening. It was too early to disclose the number of seats the party wanted to contest, Mr.Moily said.

27-02-2006

(6336) Hyderabad : Ridiculing the talk of the Third Front at the national level, which was reportedly discussed by the Telugu Desam Polit

Bureau on Saturday, the Congress Legislature Party has asked TDP president N. Chandrababu Naidu to enter the Rajya Sabha and lead the front. "Only Mr. Naidu is capable of leading the third alternative at the national level as he has earlier played a key role in national politics," Government Chief Whip N. Kiran Kumar Reddy said. Addressing a press conference here on Sunday, he alleged that Mr. Naidu was behaving as if he had lost his balance every time he saw the Chief Minister's seat in the Assembly. Hence, the claims that every achievement in the State was because of his (Mr. Naidu's) policies. "We can understand his agony of losing power after enjoying it," he said.

(6337) Nalgonda : The BJP MLA G. Kishan Reddy has said that the TDP president N. Chandrababu Naidu is talking about the formation of a Third Front since "he has realised that there is no future for his party." He was speaking to reporters after launching "Palle Pilupu" programme at Maadaram of Kanagal mandal on Sunday.

(6338) Kozhikode : Moves to induct the Democratic Indira Congress (Karunakaran) (DIC-K) into the United Democratic Front (UDF) at the initiative of the Indian Union Muslim League (IUML) have gained momentum. "Moves have begun to condition the workers of the Congress and the DIC(K) to prepare for the latter's entry into the UDF," said an IUML manager, speaking on condition of anonymity. A DIC(K) leader said "IUML leaders had begun talks with us on an alliance for the Assembly polls even before the CPI(M) took a decision not to have any truck with us." With IUML State general secretary P.K. Kunhalikutty openly declaring that he had already held talks with Chief Minister Oommen Chandy and DIC(K) president K Muraleedharan in this regard, the IUML initiatives are out in the open.

(6339) Varanasi : Over 350 Shiv Sena activists were arrested from different parts of the city on Sunday as they proceeded towards the Kashi Vishwanath temple to offer 'jalabhishek' en masse on the occasion of Shivratri, police said. The arrests were made from Luxa, Sigra, Ansphatak, Ram Nagar and Mugasarai police circle areas. The district administration had banned en masse 'jalabhishek' and prayers at the temple and Shringar Gauri adjacent to the Gyanvapi mosque.

(6340) Bangalore : The Congress, which had announced that it will complain to President A.P.J. Abdul Kalam against Governor T.N. Chaturvedi for addressing two joint sittings of the State Legislature in the current session, seems to have second thoughts about it. According to party sources, the issue will not be stretched to the extent of taking it to the Rashtrapati Bhavan.

(6341) Bidar : The coalition government in the State will last as long as the Bharatiya Janata Party (BJP) can tolerate Janata Dal (Secular), former Deputy Chief Minister Siddharamaiah has said.

(6342) Kollam : Democratic Indira Congress (Karunakaran) president K. Muraleedharan has said his party had already taken up the issue of releasing People's Democratic Party leader Abdul Nasir Maudany with the All India Anna Dravida Munnetra Kazhagam (AIADMK) leadership during the first round of talks with the party in Chennai. Taking to presspersons here on Sunday, he said the DIC(K) would follow up the issue with Tamil Nadu Chief Minister Jayalalithaa during the second round of talks to be held next month on a possible political alliance in Kerala. He reiterated that his party was preparing to fight the elections on its own.

(6343) Pathanamthitta : The assistant State secretary of the Communist Party of India (CPI), K.E. Ismail, has said that the Left Democratic Front (LDF), if elected to power, was bound to implement the recommendations in the Narendran Commission Report in letter and spirit.

(6344) Thiruvananthapuram : Kerala Pradesh Congress Committee (KPCC) president Ramesh Chennithala on Sunday said there was no pressure on the Congress to accommodate the Democratic Indira Congress (Karunakaran) as a partner in the ruling UDF. Replying to questions at a news conference here, Mr. Chennithala said though individual UDF constituents such as the Indian Union Muslim League (IUML) may have their views on the subject, nobody has so far approached the Congress with any such suggestion and neither the Congress nor the UDF leadership has so far taken up the issue for discussion. The aim of the Pradesh Congress leadership was to bring back the Congressmen who had left the party. As for Mr. K.Karunakaran, it is for him to decide whether he wants to return to the party or the UDF, the KPCC president said.

(6345) Thrissur : Leader of the Opposition V.S. Achuthanandan, a Polit Bureau member of the Communist Party of India (Marxist), has said that the Congress appears to be often forgetting that it is leading a coalition

Government at the Centre with the support of the Left parties. At the Kerala State Karshaka Thozhilali Union (KSKTU) State convention here on Sunday, Mr. Achuthanandan said the total neglect of States such as Kerala in the just-presented Railway Budget was due to this overconfident attitude of the Congress-led United Progressive Alliance (UPA) Government.

(6346) New Delhi : Admitting that the gap between the Government and the Left parties had "widened" over the past few months, the Communist Party of India (CPI) general secretary A. B. Bardhan on Sunday said, the "stability and longevity" of the present dispensation would depend on its "strict adherence to the National Common Minimum Programme (NCMP)." Further, he accused the Government of taking unilateral decisions - particularly on issues relating to the economy and foreign policy - and said the United Progressive Alliance (UPA)-Left coordination committee meetings had been turned into an exercise akin to a "post-mortem." On the foreign policy front, the CPI charge is that the Government was toeing the line taken by the Bharatiya Janata Party-led National Democratic Alliance (NDA). "The NDA foreign policy was not only tilting towards the U.S. but also surrendering to it." Briefing mediapersons after a daylong meeting of the CPI national executive - called specifically to review the performance of the Government over the past 20 months - Mr. Bardhan said, "we want to stay in [this arrangement] but it is not our job alone to keep the UPA in power."

(6347) New Delhi : The Communist Party of India on Sunday said the Narendra Modi Government in Gujarat had lost the moral right to continue in office after its indictment by a Mumbai Sessions Court in the Best Bakery case. A resolution to this effect was passed by the national executive of the party which met here.

(6348) New Delhi : The Bharatiya Janata Party (BJP) on Sunday said Prime Minister Manmohan Singh should have "dismissed outright" the idea of self-rule and autonomy for Jammu and Kashmir instead of trying to evolve a "common understanding" on these issues. A statement to this effect was made by BJP president Rajnath Singh after the party's central leadership met at former Prime Minister Atal Behari Vajpayee's residence here in the evening to discuss the first ever round-table conference on the State, on Saturday.

(6349) New Delhi : Delhi Bharatiya Janata Party president Harsh Vardhan has asked the Municipal Corporation of Delhi to stop its ongoing demolition drive for three months till the technical committee formed by the Centre on the issue submits its report to the Union Government.

(6350) Chennai : Dravida Munnetra Kazhagam president M. Karunanidhi on Sunday contested Chief Minister Jayalalithaa's claim that there was nothing for the common people in the Railway Budget. In a statement here, he pointed out the 50 per cent fare concession given to farmers and asked whether a farmer was a common man or not.Contesting the claim that Tamil Nadu's needs were not taken care of, he said 11 new trains had been sanctioned. Of the 104 over bridges cleared, 40 were under Southern Railway. Of this, 33 were in Tamil Nadu. Did Ms. Jayalalithaa not realise this, he asked. Also, Rs. 85 crore has been sanctioned for doubling work in Tamil Nadu. Pattali Makkal Katchi founder S. Ramadoss said the budget had received widespread acclaim.

(6351) Chennai : Marumalarchi Dravida Munnetra Kazhagam general secretary Vaiko on Sunday held discussions with district secretaries, the parliamentary committee and the political affairs committee of the party on the Assembly elections.

(6352) Salem : Union Minister of State for Textiles E.V.K.S. Elangovan on Sunday said the exit of senior Congress leader Tindivanam K. Ramamurthy and his supporters from the party would have "very little impact" on the Assembly elections in Tamil Nadu and Pondicherry. It was an "insignificant" political happening which the Congress did not take seriously. Mr. Elangovan said the first phase of negotiations with Dravida Munnetra Kazhagam leader M. Karunanidhi on seat sharing was "highly satisfactory." He was optimistic that the Congress would get its due share of seats. The status quo would also be maintained in Pondicherry .

28-02-2006

(6353) Hyderabad : Telugu Desam Legislature Party deputy leader N. Janardhana Reddy on Monday said the nearly two-year-old Congress Government was a saga of failed promises. Participating in the debate on budget in the Assembly, Dr. Reddy said the ruling party could not keep up any of its pre-poll promises. Free power to farm sector was diluted with the Government imposing restrictions.

(6354) Hyderabad : Congress MLA P. Janardhan Reddy on Monday demanded a fresh investigation by a new team of officials into the multi-crore fake stamp paper scam in light of some recent revelations. Raising the issue during question hour in the Assembly, he alleged that a retired police officer and several other serving police officials, all holding senior positions, were involved in the scam in which kingpin A. R. Telgi had been convicted. He, therefore, urged Chief Minister Y. S. Rajasekhara Reddy to order a fresh probe.

(6355) Hyderabad : Taking strong objection to the criticism of BJP leadership by the TDP polit bureau, the Bharatiya Janata Party State unit has said the comments made by TDP president N. Chandrababu Naidu reflected his party's 'ideological bankruptcy' and increasing frustration after being thrown out of power. The TDP president is feeling "like a fish out of water" ever since the people outright rejected him in the last elections and is trying to cover up his failures by criticising the BJP, party State president N. Indrasena Reddy has said.

(6356) Hyderabad : The Telangana Rashtra Samithi (TRS) staged a walkout from the Assembly on Monday protesting against the 'reckless manner' in which two Government Orders relating to the welfare of Scheduled Castes and Scheduled Tribes were issued within a span of one month. These orders are in conflict with each other.

(6357) Visakhapatnam : Leader of CPI (M) in Rajya Sabha Deepankar Mukherjee and MPs Chittabrata Mazumdar and P. Madhu assured a delegation of representatives of various VSP trade unions in New Delhi on Monday that their demand would be pursued with the Government, according to information received by the CITU-affiliated Steel Plant Employees Union.

(6358) New Delhi : The Government said in the Rajya Sabha on Monday that it was considering amendments to the Criminal Procedure Code (Cr.P.C.) to provide protection to witnesses as the existing law had lacuna. Speaking after members expressed concern over the tardy investigation and threats to witnesses in the Jessica Lal murder case leading to the acquittal of all the accused, Union Home Minister Shivraj Patil admitted that the Cr.P.C. did not have enough provisions to protect witnesses. Raising the issue during zero hour, Sitaram Yechury (CPI-M) wondered about the fate of common citizens when sloppy investigation and hostile witnesses marked cases involving Page 3 celebrities. Calling upon the Government to restore the people's faith in the delivery of justice, Mr. Yechury said the Jessica case was unacceptable in a civil and democratic society. The Leader of the Opposition, Jaswant Singh, supported the Government in anything it wished to do in this regard and regretted that the "disease" had become widespread. Brinda Karat (CPI-M) described the case as a "symbol of huge injustice" and called for strong action against the Delhi Police officials for contamination of investigation as well as the Central Forensic Laboratory, if the need arose.

(6359) New Delhi : The Committee against the visit of U.S. President George Bush on Monday declared that he "was certainly not welcome in India." "We emphatically oppose the forthcoming visit... President Bush is the topmost official of U.S. imperialism, leading enemy of the sovereignty of nations and the peoples of the world today. He is the leader of the imperialist quest at neo-colonial world domination. He is certainly not welcome in India... " the Committee consisting of the Left, the Samajwadi Party, the Janata Dal (Secular) and the Indian Justice Party said in a joint statement.

(6360) New Delhi : The CBI on Monday arrested the former Samata Party treasurer, R.K. Jain, for his alleged role in procuring hand-held thermal imagers for the armed forces. - PTI

(6361) Kochi : Kerala Pradesh Congress Committee (KPCC) president Ramesh Chennithala said the Left Democratic Front (LDF) was in the grip of a crisis and the Front partners were fighting against one another, while the United Democratic Front (UDF) was surging ahead with increased confidence and cohesion. Talking to mediapersons at the venue of the proposed Congress meeting here, on Monday, Mr. Chennithala said neither the Front nor the party had so far discussed the issue of including the Democratic Indira Congress (Karunakaran) as UDF partner. He said there was no difference of opinion among the Front partners in this regard. A large number of DIC(K) party workers was returning to the Congress fold, he added.

(6362) Thiruvananthapuram : The Indian Union Muslim League (IUML) will not exert pressure on the United Democratic Front (UDF) to induct the Democratic Indira Congress-Karunakaran (DIC-K) into the front, IUML State general secretary P.K. Kunhalikutty has said.

(6363) Thiruvananthapuram : Leader of the Opposition in Kerala Assembly V.S. Achuthanandan on Monday described the permission given by the Supreme Court to raise the water level in the Mullaperiyar Dam from 136 feet to 142 feet as 'unilateral and suicidal' and asked the State Government to take steps to get the case referred to a Constitution Bench of the apex court.

(6364) Thiruvananthapuram : K. Muraleedharan has been unanimously elected president of the Democratic Indira Congress-Karunakaran (DIC-K) at the conclusion of the party's organisational elections on Wednesday.

(6365) New Delhi : A compact disc (CD) containing alleged conversation transcripts of Samajwadi Party leader Amar Singh led to tumultuous scenes in Parliament, with the Government maintaining that the Union Home Ministry was examining its authenticity. "The Home Ministry is examining the authenticity of the CD and if any action is called for as per law, it will be taken,'' Leader of the Lok Sabha Pranab Mukherjee said. Mr. Mukherjee responded after Bahujan Samaj Party MPs, led by Brajesh Pathak, raised the issue and waved a photocopy of a newspaper report.

(6366) New Delhi : With the possibility of an Indo-U.S. deal being inked during the visit of President George W. Bush, the Bharatiya Janata Party has said that while the Government must keep in mind the energy security of the country, there should be no compromise on the "dynamics of a credible and effective nuclear deterrence as determined by us." On Monday BJP president Rajnath Singh wrote him a letter on what the party (BJP) expects from President Bush's coming visit.

(6367) Guwahati : The Bharatiya Janata Party will explore legal options to scrap the Foreigners (Tribunals for Assam) Order, 2006, notified by the Centre on February 10. This was stated by party general secretary Pramod Mahajan here on Monday while releasing a "charge sheet" against the Tarun Gogoi-led Congress Government. The charge sheet accused the Government of "ignoring the threat perception of the ISI and the Al Qaeda, non-performance, misgovernance, minority appeasement and going back on the poll promises."

(6368) Chandigarh : The fourth anniversary of the present Congress government in Punjab led by Chief Minister Amarinder Singh was marked by a symbolic dharna on Monday by the Bharatiya Janata Party which claimed that the State was in economic, social and political disarray.

(6369) Chennai : Tamil Nadu Indira Congress president Tindivanam K. Ramamurthee on Monday said "self-respecting Congress members" were agitated over the way the Dravida Munnetra Kazhagam was treating their party on the seat-sharing issue. Talking to reporters after inaugurating his party head office at Royapettah, he said many of them were disgusted with the treatment and had joined his organisation. There was mutual suspicion among the constituents of the Democratic Progressive Alliance. They would work in such a manner that would ensure the defeat of one another. Mr. Ramamurthee said his party would fight the polls with the All-India Anna Dravida Munnetra Kazhagam. Asked how many seats it would seek, he said the executive and general body of the party would meet here on Friday or Sunday and decide it. "We will make a demand that will reflect our strength."

(6370) Chennai : The Pattali Makkal Katchi has demanded the resignation of Chief Minister Jayalalithaa in the light of the Madras High Court order, scrapping the law on Common Entrance Test.In a statement, S. Ramadoss, founder of the party, said the Court's observation that the purpose for which the law had been brought in would not be achieved had unmasked the face of the Chief Minister. Ms Jayalalithaa should own full responsibility.

(6371) Chennai : The All-India Anna Dravida Munnetra Kazhagam on Monday decided to face the Assembly elections jointly with the Dalit Pathers of India, allotting it nine seats.The agreement signed by AIADMK general secretary Jayalalithaa and DPI general secretary Thol. Thirumavalavan, said the parties decided to form an electoral front for Tamil Nadu and Pondicherry.

(6372) Chennai : Senior leader of Bharatiya Janata Party M. Venkaiah Naidu on Monday lambasted Prime Minister Manmohan Singh for seeking a common understanding on self-rule in Jammu and Kashmir. Describing Dr. Singh's observation as "very dangerous and divisive," Mr. Naidu told a media conference here that this was disturbing, particularly on the eve of the U.S. President's visit.

(6373) Chennai : The People's Party (PP), which was formally launched here on Monday, decided to strive for achieving "fiscal federation at Centre and fiscal autonomy in State." The party, at its first general council meeting, adopted a resolution saying that the new strategy became necessary as the slogan of "federal governance at the Centre and autonomy in the States" could not make any headway. The general council elected the party's office-bearers with Dheeran as president, R. Viswanathan and Vijayalakshmi as general secretaries and N.V. Ganesan as propaganda secretary.

01-03-2006

(6374) Hyderabad : Telugu Desam president N. Chandrababu Naidu has condemned the foreign policy of US President George Bush, which he said, was promoting religious hatred. Talking to reporters here on Tuesday, he said the party was not opposed to his visit to India but to the US policy to curb Iran's nuclear weapons while blinking at Pakistan's N-programme. He said India should not take sides and maintain its non-aligned stand. "We need not get identified with Bush policies," he added.

(6375) Hyderabad: Contradictions within the Telangana Rashtra Samithi again came to the fore in the Assembly on Tucsday when senior party legislator, S. Santosh Reddy, spoke in support of the Government embarrassing his party that has been highly critical of the ruling party of late. Participating in the debate on the budget, Mr. Reddy made two specific points that were at variance with his party's stand — seven hour power supply was enough and there was nothing wrong in going ahead with Polavaram project but work on Inchampalli should be taken up with equal interest.

(6376) Hyderabad: Describing the Election Commission's decision on cancelling byelection to **Visakhapatnam** I constituency as a "slap on the face of Government", Telugu Desam Party president N. Chandrababu Naidu has demanded its resignation.

(6377) Vijayawada: The Communist Party of India (Marxist) is not interested in forming 'fronts' that collapse after a short duration, but has no objection to working together with parties with "correct policies," State secretary and party Polit Bureau member B.V.Raghavulu said.

(6378) New Delhi: The Mulayam Singh Yadav-led Uttar Pradesh Government on Tuesday sought and won a trust vote in the Assembly within minutes of the Allahabad High Court's verdict in a case seeking disqualification of 40 Bahujan Samaj Party rebels, who joined the Samajwadi Party in 2003. Delivering the judgment on a BSP petition, the Lucknow Bench by a 2:1 majority held the merger invalid. It, however, did not decide on the question of the MLAs' disqualification. The court remanded the matter back to the Speaker, asking him decide on it. Even as the BSP, the Bharatiya Janata Party and the Congress demanded the resignation of Chief Minister Mulayam Singh Yadav, the Government moved and won the confidence vote with 207 votes to nil in a House with a strength of 402. Apparently the 40 rebel MLAs voted with the Government, defying a BSP whip. The entire Opposition, including the BJP and the BSP staged a walkout.

(6379) Alappuzha: The alleged attack on Mahila Congress State president Shanimol Usman at the Alappuzha Medical College on February has raked up a controversy with the Congress accusing the CPI(M) of involvement in the attack. CPI (M) Alappuzha district secretary G. Sudhakaran has refuted the allegation. Kerala Pradesh Congress Committee (KPCC) president Ramesh Chennithala and DCC president C.R. Jayaprakash had alleged that the CPI(M) was behind the attack.

(6380) Palakkad: Leader of the Opposition V.S. Achuthanandan has demanded a judicial inquiry into the way the Mullaperiyar dam case was conducted by the State Government and its officials.

(6381) Thrissur: CPI(M) Central Committee member M.A. Baby said here on Tuesday that he was of the opinion that higher education should not be given free to all sections of society. "Primary education should be universally free, but higher education should be free only for the poorer sections of society. The rich should pay for higher education, or some cess should be imposed on them," Mr. Baby said, participating in a discussion on 'Asian Development Bank (ADB) loan and the Sustainable Urban Development Project,' organised by the COSTFORD.

(6382) Thiruvananthapuram: Senior Congress leader V.M. Sudheeran has sought UPA chairperson Sonia Gandhi's intervention to obtain political clearance from the Centre for the proposal to develop an international container terminal project at Vizhinjam.

(6383) New Delhi: Describing the Union budget as "outstanding," Prime Minister Manmohan Singh has said the challenge is the economy has to grow at between 8 and 10 per cent from 7.5 per cent. The Congress said the budget was "balanced and growth-oriented." Since the advent of the United Progressive Alliance Government, nation building had been continuing and tremendous growth had been witnessed in all sectors.

(6384) New Delhi: The Bharatiya Janata Party on Tuesday reiterated its decision to raise in Parliament defreezing of the London bank accounts of the Bofors payoffs case accused Ottavio Quattrocchi; the Volcker Report on oil vouchers given by the Saddam Hussein regime in Iraq, and the Scorpene deal. There was corruption in these issues, the party alleged.At the weekly meeting of the BJP Parliamentary Party here, it was also decided to raise issues of the United Progressive Alliance Government's "minorityism." The party opposes the idea of a round table on self-rule and autonomy for Jammu and Kashmir. "A notice for a discussion on the Kashmir round table conference has already been given to the Speaker," said the party deputy leader in the Lok Sabha, V.K. Malhotra.

(6385) New Delhi: The Left parties on Tuesday lambasted various aspects of the Union budget, with the Communist Party of India (Marxist) saying that it failed to address many vital problems faced by the common man, particularly the peasantry and the unemployed. "While the Finance Minister has increased outlays for the Plan by 20.4 per cent, the proposed outlay for agriculture, health, education and employment generation are inadequate to meet the goals outlined in the National Common Minimum Programme," a party statement said. The All-India Forward Bloc said it was a "lacklustre" budget; a more realistic approach could have been accepted. Party general secretary Debabrata Biswas said the proposals did not meet the commitments made in the CMP. The CPI (ML) said Mr. Chidambaram's budget was a "gift to U.S. President George Bush" and the proposals were meant to speed up neo-liberal policies. In a statement, party secretary K.N. Ramachandran and Central Executive Member Subodh Mitra said the budget would lead to further withdrawal of States from socio-economic spheres and welfare policies. CPI National Secretary D. Raja described the Union budget as "disappointing." Party Lok Sabha leader Gurudas Dasgupta said the budget was "distressing," made the tax system regressive, ignored Left parties' proposals on resource mobilisation and made no effort to recover tax arrears and non-performing assets in public sector banks.

(6386) New Delhi: The Rajya Sabha Ethics Committee has recommended the expulsion of Samajwadi Party member Swami Sakshiji Maharaj but gave the benefit of doubt to Bahujan Samaj Party member Isam Singh who featured in the "Operation Chakravyuh" on misuse of MP Local Area Development (MPLAD) funds aired on television on December 19.

(6387) New Delhi: The Opposition parties on Tuesday said they found nothing in the Union budget for farmers and little for aam aadmi, the common man. The former Finance Minister, Yashwant Sinha, who presented five budgets for the National Democratic Alliance Government, said the NDA regime lowered interest rates for short-term credit to farmers to nine per cent in 2004. Finance Minister P. Chidambaram should have brought it down to six per cent. "We are disappointed." It was reduced to seven per cent. Bharatiya Janata Party president Rajnath Singh expressed a similar view. " Mehngai aur badegi (prices will rise), said the former Prime Minister Atal Bihari Vajpayee. Leader of the Opposition L.K. Advani said the budget "punishes farmers, ignores the middle classes and gladdens the affluent." Janata Dal (United) leader Sharad Yadav described the budget as an "eyewash," saying there was nothing in it for unemployed youth, farmers or the rural population. Samajwadi Party leader Amar Singh found the budget negative. "The growth projection and economic development are artificial. Unless there is prosperity with equality the budget will remain meaningless." Akali Dal leader Sukhbir Singh Badal said: "There is no proposal to ensure that farmers' produce is bought at the right price. No proposal to compensate farmers for crop loss. The reduction in interest rates is for a limited section, up to a limited amount. The interest for buying farm equipment and for Kisan Card loans is 12 per cent."

(6388) New Delhi: Congress president Sonia Gandhi has expressed anguish at the killing of a large number of people in Dantewara district of Chhattisgarh. It was "yet another wanton act of violence" by naxalites, she said. The incident was unfortunate, as the victims were participating in peace marches designed to restore normality in the State. "There can be no compromise with such deliberate and heinous acts," she said in a statement. Prime Minister Manmohan Singh condemned the attack and expressed sorrow at the loss of innocent lives, according to his media adviser Sanjaya Baru.

(6389) New Delhi: Levelling a serious allegation of wrongdoing by vested interests that has led to the present mess on the demolition issue in the Capital, the Leader of the Opposition in the Delhi Assembly, Jagdish Mukhi, on Tuesday charged the Delhi Government with being hand in glove with the shopping mall lobby and not taking any steps to get relief for lakhs of people affected by the recent High Court and Supreme Court directions.

(6390) Shimla: The Himachal Pradesh State Committee of the Communist Party of India (Marxist) has decided to organise month-long protests "to oppose imperialism and the visit of U.S. President George Bush to India". The party would mobilise more than 1,000 activists for the protest in Delhi and organise seminars, talks and street plays all over the State. On March 23, the martyrdom day of Shaheed Bhagat Singh, Rajguru and Sukhdev, the party will observe "anti-imperialist" day.

(6391) Pondicherry: Yogendra Makwana, chairman of the Scheduled Caste Welfare cell in the AICC, has said the Scheduled Castes (SCs) had always remained with the Congress and that no other party, including the Bahujan Samaj Party and Bharatiya Janata Party, has real concern for the poor and downtrodden.

(6392) Jaipur: The Union Budget presented on Tuesday evoked mixed reaction in the political circles in Rajasthan with the Congress leaders welcoming it and Chief Minister Vasundhara Raje terming its provisions an "encroachment" on the finances of the States. The Communist Party of India's state unit found the Budget "disappointing" as it did not offer any solutions to the problems of the farmers and the unemployed.

(6393) Dehra Dun: Uttaranchal Chief Minister Narayan Dutt Tiwari on Tuesday described the Union Budget presented by Finance Minister P. Chidambaram as an instrument aimed at accelerating the pace of India's development into a powerful nation. . Former Uttaranchal Finance Minister and Bharatiya Janata Party general secretary Ramesh Pokhriyal Nishank, however, felt that the Budget had failed to fulfil even a part of the hill people's aspirations.

(6394) Chennai: Constituents of the Democratic Progressive Alliance on Tuesday welcomed the "farmer-friendly and taxless" Union budget. DMK president Karunanidhi commended the Finance Minister for coming out with a package of welfare measures M. Krishnasswamy, president of the Tamil Nadu Congress Committee, said the budget would benefit all sections of society. Marumalarchi Dravida Munnetra Kazhagam general secretary Vaiko welcomed several features of the budget but appealed to Mr. Chidambaram to withdraw the move to levy service tax on ATM operations. The interest rate for farmers should have been reduced further. PMK founder S. Ramadoss appreciated the increase in levy on cigarettes.

(6395) Chennai: It is because of sustained efforts of the Janata Party leader Subramanian Swamy that Tamil Nadu won the Mullaperiyar case in Supreme Court, the president of the State unit of the party V.S. Chandralekha said on Tuesday. In a statement, Ms. Chandralekha said while Dr. Swamy had maintained dignity now, the Dravidian parties should not seek to claim the credit.

(6396) Chennai: Describing the Union budget as a "tepid, colourless exercise," Chief Minister Jayalalithaa on Tuesday said Finance Minister P. Chidambaram had lost a "golden opportunity" to take the country's growth process on to a new trajectory.

(6397) Chennai: General secretary of the Dalit Panthers of India (DPI) Thol.Thirumavalavan on Tuesday appealed to the Pattali Makkal Katchi (PMK) to quit the Democratic Progressive Alliance (DPA) and join the electoral alliance led by the All India Anna Dravida Munnetra Kazhagam to maintain unity and social harmony among Tamils.

02-03-2006

(6398) Hyderabad: Even as the State Government is making hectic arrangements to welcome U.S. President George W. Bush, the Left parties have questioned the propriety of Chief Minister Y.S. Rajasekhara Reddy in holding discussions with the "imperialist" on key issues such as agriculture. CPI(M) State secretary B. V. Raghavulu and CPI State secretary K. Narayana told reporters here on Wednesday that Mr. Bush had no right to visit India because of his 'anti-India acts.' The visit was only to pressure India to sign certain agreements which were not in the interest of the country.

(6399) Hyderabad: Soon after they were suspended and removed from the House, slogan-shouting Telugu Desam legislators staged an impromptu "dharna" in front of the Mahatma Gandhi's statue on Assembly premises. They were led by leader of the Opposition N. Chandrababu Naidu, who was spared of the suspension.

(6400) Visakhapatnam: The Bharatiya Janata Party, which was the only party which demanded countermanding of the **Visakhapatnam**-I bypoll, on Wednesday appealed to the Election Commission to advance the polling date. "Holding election on March 25 will give a wide scope to the cash-rich Congress and the Telugu Desam Party to further indulge in malpractices by offering inducements to the voters," BJP city president Bandaru Rangamohan Rao and candidate for the bypoll Kasi Viswanadha Raju told reporters.

(6401) Visakhapatnam: A day after countermanding of the **Visakhapatnam**-I bypoll held on February 19 by the Election Commission, the Congress and its arch-rival Telugu Desam Party indulged blame game. While TDP claimed that the State Government forced the local police to foist false cases against TDP activists, the Congress said none of their leaders was caught with money or liquor.

(6402) Sangareddy: Countermanding of the **Visakhapatnam** byelection has been termed as a drastic action by CPI (M) State secretary B.V. Raghavulu. Addressing the press here on Wednesday, Mr. Raghavulu said there were large-scale violations of the model code during the general election also. "Does it mean countermanding those elections also?" he questioned. He pointed out that the Election Commission should look into preventive measures available under the legal and constitutional framework.

(6403) Kadapa: The UPA and State Governments should accord priority to rural development for hastening the country's progress, but they are adopting anti-poor policies, former BJP National President M. Venkaiah Naidu alleged on Wednesday.

(6404) Kadapa: The UPA Government's survey of Muslims working in various jobs including defence forces and gauging their population Assembly and Parliament constituency-wise with a view to extending reservations is unconstitutional, former BJP national President M. Venkaiah Naidu asserted on Wednesday.

(6405) Lucknow: Four MLAs, including two Ministers, resigned from the ruling Samajwadi Party in Uttar Pradesh on Wednesday and rejoined the Bahujan Samaj Party. - UNI

(6406) Hyderabad: Chief Minister Y. S. Rajasekhara Reddy has rejected Telugu Desam president N. Chandrababu Naidu's demand for his resignation in the wake of the Election Commission's decision to countermand the Assembly byelection in **Visakhapatnam**-I Assembly constituency. He has described it as a case of the pot calling the kettle black since the Election Commission has stated that those huge amounts of money have been seized from persons belonging to the Telugu Desam Party. Yet, Mr. Naidu is demanding his resignation. The Government has no plans of challenging the EC's decision in a court, he has added. Meanwhile, the Congress Legislature Party (CLP) too objected to the TDP's demand for the Chief Minister's resignation on the ground that the commission had not indicted the Government in any way.

(6407) Bidar: The Congress will launch a campaign to create awareness among the rural poor about the National Rural Employment Guarantee Scheme. Karnataka Pradesh Congress Committee (KPCC) Secretary C.R. Narayanappa told presspersons here on Wednesday that the success of the programme depends on its implementation. "The panchayat raj institutions are responsible for its implementation. These bodies are under the control of the State Government. It is finally the responsibility of the State Government to make the programme a success," Mr. Narayanappa said.

(6408) Gulbarga: Former Chief Minister and Leader of the Opposition in the Legislative Assembly N. Dharam Singh rebuked Janata Dal (Secular) President H.D. Deve Gowda on Wednesday on his "silence" over the statements made by Mr. Gowda's son, Chief Minister H.D. Kumaraswamy, on the Bangalore metro rail project. Asked whether he felt Mr. Deve Gowda was responsible for the fall of his government, Mr. Dharam Singh said this is for the people to judge. "When Janata Dal (S) legislators went to the Governor declaring their withdrawal of support to the Congress-JD(S) government, Mr. Deve Gowda spoke to Governor T.N. Chaturvedi. In a letter he said Mr. Kumaraswamy was not the leader of the Janata Dal (S) Legislature Party, and M.P. Prakash continued to head the legislature group. However, Mr. Deve Gowda preferred not to write to the Speaker of the Legislative Assembly, he added.

(6409) Kochi: Leader of the Opposition and CPI(M) Polit Bureau member V.S. Achuthanandan has called for a people's agitation across party lines against the 'cruel and merciless neglect' of Kerala by the Union Finance and Railway Ministers.

(6410) Pathanamthitta: Congress leader G. Karthikeyan has said that the opportunistic face of the Communist Party of India (Marxist) will be exposed in the coming elections to the State Assembly. Mr. Karthikeyan said the CPI(M) had no right to talk about development as it had been trying to scuttle each and every development project introduced by the UDF Government during the past four-and-a-half years. A party with an opportunistic political stand like the CPI(M), especially towards development, could hardly survive in a State like Kerala, he said.

(6411) Thiruvananthapuram: The month-long 'Janakeeya Yatra' of the CPI from Kasaragod to Thiruvananthapuram concluded here on Wednesday evening with CPI Lok Sabha leader Gurudas Dasgupta calling upon party cadres to work for the ouster of the UDF Government.

(6412) New Delhi: Leaders of several political parties on Wednesday joined hands with various Muslim organisations to oppose the visit of U.S. President George Bush at a massive rally held at Ramlila Grounds here. The rally, which witnessed the participation of nearly a lakh people, denounced American policies and criticised the publication of cartoons on Prophet Muhammed. Addressing the rally, organised by the Jamiat Ulema-I-Hind, CPI general secretary A.B. Bardhan said Mr. Bush cannot be welcomed in India as he was an "imperialist aggressor" who has also "incited a war of civilisations" by bullying Iran over its nuclear programme. Former Prime Minister V.P. Singh also criticised the United States for its "double standard" on the nuclear policy saying it measures Iran and Israel with different yardsticks. Mr Singh also denounced India's policy of supporting the U.S. on the Iran nuclear issue in the International Atomic Energy Agency The spokesman of the Jamiat Ulama-I-Hind, Abdul Hameed Naumani, termed President Bush as the "biggest terrorist of the world." The rally, in which anti-Bush and anti-American slogans were raised every now and then and a large number of protestors waved black flags to show their feelings, was also addressed by Indian National Lok Dal leader Ajit Singh, suspended Samajwadi Party leader Raj Babbar and social activist Medha Patkar.

(6413) Guwahati: The ruling and Opposition parties in Assam have welcomed the announcement of election dates for the State (April 3 and

10). The CPI (M), however, wants the polls to be held in more phases. The Pradesh Congress Committee (PCC) president, Bhubaneswar Kalita, said the Congress had requested Chief Election Commissioner (CEC) B. B. Tandon that elections be held before Bihu as the onset of monsoon after the festival might hamper the poll process. The party was fully prepared and selection of candidates was on. The Asom Gana Parishad (AGP) was fully prepared and started poll related exercises, its spokesman Apurba Kumar Bhattacharyya said. The Bharatiya Janata Party said it was in an upbeat mood and confident of winning the elections. The CPI (M), however, said that in view of the "deteriorating law and order situation," particularly in Karbi Anglong hill district and upper Assam, polls should be held at least in three phases so that adequate security forces could be made available for all the constituencies.

(6414) Bangalore: The former Prime Minister, H.D. Deve Gowda, on Wednesday led a demonstration by the Janata Dal (Secular) here against the visit of U.S. President George Bush and the United Progressive Alliance Government's "subservience" to Washington. Addressing a large gathering at the party headquarters, Mr. Gowda referred to the U.S. attempts to "dictate our foreign and economic policies". Mr. Gowda said the JD (S), which maintains equidistance from both the Congress and the Bharatiya Janata Party, was one with the Left parties in the anti-U.S. protest.

(6415) New Delhi: The Communist Party of India (Marxist) on Wednesday demanded that the Manmohan Singh Government inform the people and Parliament about the terms and conditions of the Indo-U.S. Science and Technology Umbrella Agreement signed last year before any agreement on knowledge initiative was signed. Among the many agreements being signed during the visit of U.S. President George Bush, two agreements have a vital bearing on more than 60 per cent of the Indian population, namely the "Indo-U.S. Knowledge Initiative on Agricultural Research and Education" and a Biotechnology Agreement. This is a follow-up to the understanding reached during Dr. Singh's U.S. visit and subsequently, the Umbrella Agreement signed in October last year. Under the agricultural initiative, Monsanto and Wal Mart are set to decide the Indian agriculture research agenda, as they are on the governing board of this initiative, the party Polit Bureau said in its statement.

(6416) New Delhi: As U.S. President George Bush arrived on Wednesday night on his State visit, the Left parties announced a programme of protest for Thursday both inside and outside Parliament. "President George Bush's visit to India is an affront to Indian Parliament which passed a resolution calling for the withdrawal of occupation forces led by the United States from Iraq," Communist Party of India (Marxist) Rajya Sabha leader Nilotpal Basu and Lok Sabha leader Basudeb Acharia said here.

(6417) New Delhi: The naxal attack on civilians in Chhattisgarh led to frayed tempers in both Houses of Parliament with the ruling coalition demanding the resignation/dismissal of the Bharatiya Janata Party-led State Government, accusing it of "criminal negligence" in failing to provide security to innocent tribals. The verbal exchanges in the Lok Sabha, led to a brief adjournment after the members insisted that each party be provided a chance to express its views. The issue was raised during zero hour. Ramjilal Suman (SP) demanded the resignation of the Chhattisgarh Chief Minister owning moral responsibility. Ajit Jogi (Congress) demanded dismissal of the State Government and an immediate halt to the Salva Judum anti-naxalite campaign. Devendra Prasad Yadav (RJD) said the State Government pitted the unarmed tribals against the naxalites with the police taking a backseat. Karuna Shukla (BJP) countered this and charged that the situation had deteriorated in Chhattisgarh under the previous Congress rule. She claimed the Salva Judum was a peaceful movement. Her party leader, Vijay Kumar Malhotra objected to the tendency of politicising an issue that required national response. Responding to the concern of the members, Home Minister Shivraj Patil said the Centre had given prior information to the State Government. In the Rajya Sabha, BJP members sought to counter the charges against the Chhattisgarh Government. Nilotpal Basu (CPI-M), Digvijay Singh and Motilal Vora (Congress) sought adequate compensation by both the Centre and the State to the families of those killed.

(6418) New Delhi: The BJP on Wednesday distanced itself from the critical statement of its vice-president Mukhtar Abbas Naqvi on Prime Minister Manmohan Singh receiving U.S. President George Bush at the Delhi Airport. Shortly after Mr. Naqvi told reporters that Dr. Singh's action "compromised on national security," BJP parliamentary party spokesman Vijay Kumar Malhotra told PTI: "It is Mr. Naqvi's personal view." At the party's daily press briefing, Mr. Malhotra had welcomed Mr. Bush's visit to India and expressed the hope that the Government would convey to him

New Delhi's concerns on a wide range of issues, including the nuclear deal, Jammu and Kashmir and relations with Pakistan. - PTI

(6419) New Delhi: After at least four MLAs, including two Ministers in the Mulayam Singh Government in Uttar Pradesh, quit the Samajwadi Party on Wednesday, the Rashtriya Lok Dal chief Ajit Singh, a key ally of the ruling alliance, said he was assessing the "serious political situation."

(6420) Kolkata: Protests have begun here though the city does not figure in U S President George W Bush's itinerary. "Beware of the Bush - bird flu!" is the slogan. Students, teachers, trade union activists, belonging to different Leftist youth and workers' federations and women organisations congregated in large numbers at the Saheed Minar in central Kolkata on Wednesday afternoon in protest against President Bush's visit to the country. Carrying banners and shouting slogans against U.S. imperialism, they wound their way in a procession to outside the American Center where demonstrations were held later in the day. Representatives of the Student Federation of India and leaders of Central trade unions affiliated to the Left parties addressed the gathering.

(6421) Kolkata: The election schedule for West Bengal was unprecedented, Senior Polit Bureau member of the Communist Party of India (Marxist) Anil Biswas said here on Wednesday.Though the party feels it "unnecessary... .we have no difficulty [with the decision]," he said. Trinamool Congress leader, Mamata Banerjee, said: "We welcome the announcement and we shall abide by the guidelines and directives issued by the Commission." She appealed to the Commission to ensure `a clean voters' list.' "The polls begin two days after the Bengali New Year and I am hopeful that the new year will usher in a change of Government," she said. The State Congress leadership feels that the Election Commission might have decided on a phased polling owing to "the deplorable law and order situation and the need for time for the deployment of paramilitary forces."

(6422) Bhopal: The president of the Madhya Pradesh unit of the Bharatiya Janata Party, Satyanarayan Jatiya, said here on Wednesday that the Union Budget proposal to lower the short-term interest rate for farmers to 7 per cent was "no big deal".Dr. Jatiya said that instead of accepting the Swaminathan Committee's recommendation that the interest rate for short-term farm loans be brought down to 4 per cent, the Union Budget only proposed the lowering of short term interest on farm sector loans to 7 per cent. "This does not amount to doing any justice to the farmers."

(6423) Jaipur: An ambiguous stand of the Bharatiya Janata Party-led Government in Rajasthan on the abolition of house tax, which it had promised in its election manifesto, led to noisy scenes in the State Assembly on Wednesday. The Opposition Congress accused the BJP of having misled the people to come to power.

(6424) Chennai: The Janata Party is keen on an alliance with the Bharatiya Janata Party for the Assembly elections in Tamil Nadu and Kerala. Party president Subramanian Swamy told reporters here on Wednesday that he welcomed a BJP leader's statement that the party would like to have a tie-up with the Janata Party.

(6425) Tiruchi: The Tamil Nadu Congress Committee president M. Krishnaswamy on Tuesday said Congress president Sonia Gandhi would participate in the final day of the DMK conference at Tiruchi on March 5. Mr. Krishnaswamy said Prime Minister Manmohan Singh and Ms. Gandhi would campaign for the Democratic Progressive Alliance (DPA) in the State during the run up to the Assembly elections. The party's main election plank, he said, would be to remove the "corrupt, arrogant and undemocratic" AIADMK Government. He made it clear that the DMK-led DPA formed during the Parliamentary polls was intact. To a query on seat sharing, he said the party high command would discuss the issue with the DMK. The Congress high command would obtain inputs from the party's State unit and analyse everything before taking a decision on this issue, he said. The exit of Congress leader Tindivanam K. Ramamurthee would not have any impact on the party, he said. The party would seek an explanation from those Congressmen who had joined hands with Mr. Ramamurthee.

03-03-2006

(6426) Guntur: The Government has failed to protect interests of people by not ensuring enough allocation of funds or projects in the Union Budget for the State, with the implementation of irrigation projects facing some uncertainty, said Communist Party of India (Marxist) State general secretary B.V. Raghavulu.

(6427) Karimnagar: Bharatiya Janata Party (BJP) former national president Bangaru Laxman has asked Chief Minister Y. S. Rajashekhar

Reddy to meet the Maharashtra Chief Minister and stop the illegal Babli project on the river Godavari in the neighbouring State.

(6428) Hindupur: The State Government has completely failed in protecting the interests of the people in utilisation of Krishna and Godavari waters, State unit president of Bharatiya Janata Party (BJP) N. Indrasena Reddy has alleged.

(6429) Hyderabad: Despite determined efforts by the Asom Gana Parishad (AGP), Telugu Desam Party president N. Chandrababu Naidu appeared reluctant to accept the leadership of the fledgling forum of regional parties. Addressing a joint press conference with his AGP counterpart Brindavan Goswamy, he said that more than leadership, the intention of the forum was to bring together all regional parties, widen the base and make it a strong force. Moreover, there were many capable leaders in several regions. "We will have to sit and decide," he said. Mr. Naidu was responding to a question on the appeal made by the AGP to accept the leadership and its efforts to project him as Prime Ministerial candidate. "We are not for power. Nor are we ambitious. We want to strengthen regional parties." But Mr. Goswamy made it clear that he would continue to convince Mr. Naidu. To a question, the TDP president said that he would campaign for AGP in the ensuing elections. Asked if he thought regional parties could form a Government at the Centre, Mr. Naidu shot back: "Anything is possible."

(6430) New Delhi: The Election Commission has served notice on the Telugu Desam MP K. Yerran Naidu for alleged violation of moral code of conduct in the Vishakapatnam bypoll.

(6431) Bangalore: Speakers at a rally on Thursday to oppose the visit of U.S. President George W. Bush said that Mr. Bush symbolised colonialism. They called for keeping aside political and ideological differences in fighting colonialism being forced through globalisation. The Samajwadi Party, the Communist Party of India (Marxist) (CPI-M), the Sarvodaya Karnataka Party, the All India Progressive Janata Dal (AIPJD), several Dalit and Muslim outfits participated in the rally, which started from Chikkalalbagh and concluded at Jakkarayanakere grounds here on Thursday.

(6432) Panaji: Congress MP Shantaram Naik on Wednesday demanded in the Rajya Sabha that devotees be allowed to celebrate two annual religious feasts on the Anjediva Islands by the Indian Navy according to the commitment made while the islands were handed over to the Navy.

(6433) Kozhikode: Kalathingal Mohiyuddin has been elected State president of the Janata Dal(U) at a meeting held in Kozhikode to discuss the political climate in the State in the context of the coming elections to the State Assembly.

(6434) New Delhi: Breakaway Bahujan Samaj Party (BSP) MLA Rajindra Singh Rana on Thursday challenged the verdict of the Allahabad High Court which on Tuesday by a majority of 2:1 held invalid the merger of 40 Bahujan Samaj Party MLAs who defected from the parent party and merged with the Samajwadi Party led by the Chief Minister, Mulayam Singh Yadav. The court, however, did not decide on the question of disqualification of the defected MLAs, but left it for the Assembly Speaker to take a decision on the issue.While the Chief Justice, Ajoy Nath Ray, in a separate verdict dismissed the petition, two other Judges, Justice Pradeep Kant and Justice Jagdish Bhalla, held the merger invalid. While remitting the matter to be put before the Speaker, these two Judges said that in the meantime the group of 40 rebel legislators would be known as Loktantrik Bahujan Dal. The court refused to accept the argument of the BSP counsel, Satish Chandra Mishra, who claimed that the rebels should be considered as part of the BSP, their parent party.

(6435) New Delhi: Shouting slogans and carrying placards denouncing American policies, thousands of people, led by senior Left and Samajwadi Party leaders, took out a protest march here on Thursday from Ramlila Grounds to Jantar Mantar. The leaders warned the United Progressive Alliance (UPA) Government against ignoring popular sentiment and aligning with the United States. Addressing the gathering at Parliament Street, Communist Party of India (Marxist) general secretary Prakash Karat demanded prosecution of President Bush blaming him for the deaths of 1.5 lakh people in Iraq. "He should be treated like a war criminal," he said, adding that protests across the country had proved that President Bush was not welcome here. He asked the Government to pursue an independent foreign policy and not follow the dictates of the U.S. Communist Party of India general secretary A.B. Bardhan said that by aligning itself with the U.S., India had severed its relationship with a large number of developing countries across the globe. "In a bid to forge new allies, India should not abandon her old and traditional partners," he said. CPI (M) Polit Bureau member Sitaram Yechury said it was because of widespread protests that President Bush was not called upon to address a joint session of Parliament. As for the nuclear deal, he said the Government would be asked to reveal details of the pact. Uttar Pradesh Chief Minister Mulayam Singh Yadav criticised the imperialist policies of the U.S. and said the Indian people would not succumb to any kind of pressure. Others who participated in the rally included CPI (M) Polit Bureau member Brinda Karat, CPI leader D. Raja, son of U.P. Chief Minister Mulayam Singh Yadav Akhilesh Yadav, Forward Bloc leader Debabrata Biswas, Samajwadi Party general secretary Amar Singh and MP Jaya Prada. Booker Prize winner Arundhati Roy was also present.

(6436) New Delhi: Protests against the visit of U.S. President George Bush raged both inside and outside Parliament with the Left and Samajwadi Party members holding a demonstration in front of the main gate of the building and then stalling proceedings of the House leading to an adjournment. Members of the four Left parties, the CPI, CPI (M), RSP and AIFB, along with those from the SP held placards and staged a demonstration for nearly an hour in the porch leading the main gate of Parliament House and carried it inside both the Houses just as the proceedings began for the day.Raising slogans "Bush Go Back," the MPs carried placards that read "War Criminal Go Back," "Killer Bush" and "UPA Government stop surrender to U. S. Imperialism." While some held a poster reading: "B-Barbaric U-Uncivilised S-Sadist H-Horrendous." Parliamentary Affairs Minister Priyaranjan Dasmunsi in the Lok Sabha and Suresh Pachauri in the Rajya Sabha gave an assurance to this effect in both the Houses on Thursday after members sought details on the Indo-US agreement.

(6437) New Delhi: The Rajya Sabha on Wednesday passed by voice vote a Bill to amend the National Commission for Minority Educational Institutions Act, 2004 for giving more teeth to the Commission set up under the Act. The Bhartiya Janata Party opposed the Bill saying it was against the secular character of the country, and piloted with an eye on the "minority vote bank." Seeking more clarity on the definition of minorities other than linguistic minorities, BJP leader Murli Manohar Joshi urged the government to withdraw the Bill and come back to the House with comprehensive legislation.

(6438) New Delhi: The Left parties on Thursday said there was no satisfactory explanation for declaring a five-phase polling in West Bengal and a three-phase polling in Kerala. The CPI (M), CPI, AIFB and the RSP said there was no reason for having extended polling in the two States. Kerala has had only single day elections and West Bengal not more than two phases. "There is no satisfactory explanation for this unprecedented decision, especially when the Commission has decided on a one-phase polling in Tamil Nadu," a statement issued by the parties said.

(6439) Kolkata: Chairman of the ruling Left Front committee in West Bengal Biman Bose said the election schedule for the State was "discriminatory." "It is unwarranted and unprecedented," Mr. Bose said.

(6440) New Delhi: Accusing the Delhi Government of failing to prevent demolitions in the Capital, particularly in the rural areas, Nationalist Congress Party MLA Ramvir Singh Bidhuri on Thursday charged Chief Minister Sheila Dikshit with "sleeping" while Delhi was burning and reacting only when her own residence and that of her son were declared unauthorised and faced demolition by the Municipal Corporation of Delhi.

(6441) Patna: The Opposition forced four adjournments in the Bihar Assembly on Thursday, protesting U.S. President George Bush's visit to India and the police firing on students in Gaya on Wednesday. The RJD, under the leadership of Rabri Devi, staged a protest against the police firing. The Left and the Samajwadi Party also voiced their opposition to Mr. Bush's visit.

(6442) Mumbai: Over a lakh Muslims participated in a rally at the Azad Maidan in Mumbai to protest the three-day visit of U.S. President George Bush. The rally also drew the support of the Left parties and the Samajwadi Party, with leaders like Ahilya Rangnekar and Abu Asim Azmi sharing the dais with imams from across the country.

(6443) Ayodhya: BJP on Thursday demanded President's Rule in Uttar Pradesh in the wake of the Allahabad High Court disqualifying the defection of 40 BSP MLAs on whose support the Mulayam Singh Yadav government came into existence. It was imperative for the Chief Minister to resign and pave way for imposition of Central rule, BJP vice president Kalyan Singh said adding under no circumstances should the present government be allowed to hold the election, as it would be against democratic traditions and moral grounds.

(6444) Lucknow: In a show of strength after being jolted by desertion in its ranks in the wake of the Allahabad High Court verdict on rebel Bahujan Samaj Party MLAs, Uttar Pradesh's ruling Samajwadi Party on Thursday paraded 29 ministers, who along with 13 others had defected in 2003, before the media and sought

(6445) New Dehli : Disqualification of those who quit its fold. On the other hand, BSP supremo Mayawati, upping the ante against Mulayam Singh Yadav government, met the Governor, T V Rajeshwar, and demanded its dismissal following the High Court judgment derecognising the split in her party.

(6446) Chennai: The Dalit Panthers of India, which has forged an electoral tie-up with the All India Anna Dravida Munnetra Kazhagam, will independently field its candidates in 10 Assembly constituencies in Pondicherry, according to party general secretary Thol.Thirumavalavan. He told reporters here on Thursday that the AIADMK-DPI alliance in Tamil Nadu would not suffer any setback, as the decision to go it alone in Pondicherry was taken with a view to consolidating the party's vote bank in the Union Territory.

(6447) Chennai: "No political party in the State has extended an official invitation to the Puthiya Tamizhagam to forge an electoral pact for the ensuing Assembly polls," party president K. Krishnasamy said here on Thursday.

(6448) Vellore: The Dalit Christians and Muslims Reservation Conference organised by the Dalit Panthers of India (DPI) here on Tuesday has urged the Tamil Nadu government to bring in an Ordinance to provide for reservation in government jobs and educational institutions for the Muslims in order to ensure the social protection of the minority Muslims in the State. The conference pleaded for the immediate release of all Muslims arrested in connection with the Coimbatore bomb blasts eight years ago.

Panthers of India, had taken a hasty decision to align with the All-India Anna Dravida Munnetra Kazhagam.

04-03-2006

(6450) Guntur: The Telugu Desam Party (TDP) has found fault with the State Government headed by Chief Minister Y.S. Rajasekhara Reddy for its alleged inefficiency in effectively presenting its points before the Brajesh Kumar Tribunal on the distribution of river waters.

(6451) Hyderabad: The Left parties — CPI(M), CPI, CPI (ML) committee and CPI (ML-Liberation) — took out a rally here on Friday to protest against the visit of George W. Bush who according to them, was the symbol of "U.S. imperialism." Addressing the gathering, CPI(M) State secretary B.V. Raghavulu, CPI Central Secretariat member Suravaram Sudhakar Reddy, PUCL leader, K.G. Kannabiran and others cautioned the Government against succumbing to US pressures to take control over India in the name of bilateral agreements in the economic, defence and nuclear research areas.

(6452) New Delhi: A Congress delegation from Andhra Pradesh on Friday urged the Centre to intervene and ask the Maharashtra Government to stop construction of the Babli barrage on the Godvari, which it said was against a decision taken at inter-state meetings. "The mater of resumption of the construction of the barrage, contrary to the decision taken during the inter-state meetings, has raised commotion among people of Andhra Pradesh and the matter has come up for discussion in the Legislative Assembly and Parliament," the delegation said in a letter to Water Resources Minister Saifuddin Soz.

(6453) Bangalore: The senior Congress member M. Mallikarjun Kharge said in the Legislative Assembly on Friday that the Government should restrict itself to routine administrative matters and should not take any decisions involving major policies and programmes in view of the petition pending in the Karnataka High Court seeking the disqualification of Chief Minister H.D. Kumaraswamy and 39 Janata Dal (S) MLAs.

(6454) Mysore: State Samajwadi Party President S. Bangarappa, MP, has said there is a possibility of a third front assuming power at the Centre in the wake of growing differences between the Congress-led United Progressive Alliance (UPA) and the Left parties. Mr. Bangarappa told presspersons here on Friday that the visit of U.S. President George W. Bush could well turn out to be the last straw in the strained relationship between the Congress and the Left parties, which are extending outside support to the UPA. "It is quite possible that the CPI(M) and the CPI, which are propping up the UPA, could withdraw support, paving the way for the third front to assume power at the Centre," Mr. Bangarappa said. Criticising the nuclear deal between India and the U.S., Mr. Bangarappa said it is a threat to India's "sovereignty and freedom."

(6455) Kochi: The political situation in the 'changed context' of the electoral announcement came in for discussion at the KPCC executive meeting held here on Friday morning as part of the ongoing KPCC Plenary Session. One of the topics for discussion is said to be the possibility of a tie-up with the Karunakaran-led DIC(K). Addressing a news conference, KPCC president Ramesh Chennithala said no decision on a tie-up had been taken.

(6456) Malappuram: People's Democratic Party (PDP) working chairman Poonthura Siraj has said that Indian Union Muslim League (IUML) is not his party's chief enemy. Addressing a news conference here on Friday, Mr. Siraj said that the PDP differed with the policies of the IUML. C.K. Abdul Azeez, former acting president of the PDP, had called the IUML the enemy number-one a few weeks ago. Mr. Siraj said that "right-wing fascists" were the main enemy of the PDP.

(6457) Ahmedabad: The Sangh Parivar in Gujarat has described the U.C. Banerjee Commission's final report on the Godhra train carnage as "mere eye-wash and an attempt to please the political bosses," while human rights activists claimed it to be the "final outcome of the whole truth." The Narendra Modi Government, which has appointed the G.T. Nanavati and K.G. Shah judicial inquiry commission to probe the incident, refused to make any comment on the Bannerjee Commission report. Bharatiya Janata Party spokesman Purshottam Rupala, dismissed the report as "meaningless" and said it was meant to provide "political mileage" to the non-BJP parties in the coming elections in five States. The BJP member of the State Assembly from Godhra, Haresh Bhatt, described it as a "most foolish report and a mockery of justice." The Leader of the Opposition in the State Assembly, Arjun Modhvadia, said the Commission had proved that if there was any "conspiracy" it was by the Modi Government.

(6458) New Delhi: The issue of Indian cricket coach Greg Chappell's controversial remarks against former captain Sourav Ganguly in a foreign journal was raised in the Lok Sabha during zero hour on Friday. CPI(M) member Minoti Sen from West Bengal demanded an apology from Mr. Chappell.

(6459) New Delhi: The Congress on Friday hailed the "historic agreement" signed between India and the U.S. in civilian nuclear energy cooperation and congratulated Prime Minister Manmohan Singh on his "courage, determination and vision" in clinching the deal. The party said this agreement should be seen as part of the larger objectives of meeting the requirements for development and the growing demand for energy. "It's part of the larger process of energy co-operation and energy security. The Congress party is proud that an Indian initiative was accepted by the U.S.," party spokesperson Abhishek Singhvi said. "Left to itself, the U.S. would have wanted much, much more. But what they got is an equilibrium India desired in its national interest," he added. In a separate statement, the party praised Dr. Singh for having "assiduously" kept his commitment made in Parliament to protect India's strategic interests, and his vision in clinching a far-reaching deal. "We hope the U.S. administration will speedily obtain the approval of the U.S. Congress and the Nuclear Suppliers Group to fully operationalise the deal," the statement said.

(6460) New Delhi : A day after India and the United States signed agreements on nuclear energy cooperation and other areas, the Left parties, the Samajwadi Party, the Telugu Desam and the Biju Janata Dal asked in the Lok Sabha how the accords served the national interest. "When lakhs of people were demonstrating against the visit of U.S. President George Bush, nuclear and other agreements were finalised keeping Parliament and the country in the dark. ... How is it historic," CPI (M) leader Basudeb Acharia asked on Friday.

(6461) New Delhi: Congress and the Bharatiya Janata Party (BJP) members clashed in the Rajya Sabha on Friday over allegations of disrespect to Mahatma Gandhi. They said sniffer dogs were taken to Rajghat, Gandhi's samadhi, before the visit of U.S. President George Bush. However, Dipankar Mukherjee (CPI-M) had the last word when he pointed out there was much sparring over dogs, but none had a word to say about Mr. Bush's visit. Raising the issue during zero hour, Kripal Parmar (BJP) referred to reports that American sniffer dogs had desecrated Rajghat where people were allowed to enter only barefoot. Amid the din, Minister of State for Parliamentary Affairs Suresh Pachouri said a standard security drill was followed at Rajghat since an attempt was made on the life of former Prime Minister Rajiv Gandhi.

(6462) New Delhi: Stating that mishandling of the bureaucracy was responsible for the defeat of the Ashok Gehlot-led Congress Government in Rajasthan in the last elections, Delhi Chief Minister Sheila Dikshit on Friday asserted that any leadership change in Delhi would take place only at the instance of Congress president Sonia Gandhi and her political secretary Ahmed Patel.

(6463) New Delhi: The Delhi Assembly was thrown into a turmoil on Friday as the Opposition BJP stalled the proceedings forcing adjournment of the House, demanding resignation of Chief Minister Sheila Dikshit for the "strong indictment" by the Public Accounts Committee (PAC) report that probed the controversial privatisation of power distribution in the Capital three years ago. Later in the day all BJP members were expelled from the House for trying to disrupt the proceedings.

(6464) Bhopal: The Congress members led by Opposition leader Jamuna Devi staged a walkout in the Madhya Pradesh Assembly on Friday over a February 20 incident of loot in Tikamgarh district that came up for discussion through a calling attention notice.

(6465) Lucknow: Joining the tirade against the Mulayam Singh Yadav Government in Uttar Pradesh, BJP President Rajnath Singh on Friday demanded immediate imposition of President's rule in the State. Mr Singh said U.P. had plunged into "political crisis" after the Allahabad High Court's verdict in the 40 rebel BSP MLAs case.

(6466) Tiruchi: Dravida Munnetra Kazhagam (DMK) president M. Karunanidhi on Friday said that his party had offered the Marumalarchi Dravida Munnetra Kazhagam (MDMK) 22 seats, as part of the seat sharing among the Democratic Progressive Alliance constituents for the Assembly elections. The offer was made on Thursday. This was the maximum the DMK could offer the MDMK, which had demanded 25 seats.

(6467) Nellikuppam: The people of Tamil Nadu should support the Bharatiya Janata Party to usher in a healthy political culture in the State, BJP national vice-president L.Ganesan has said.

05-03-2006

(6468) Hyderabad: Criticising the Government for what it called "half-hearted efforts", the Telugu Desam Party has demanded that the Chief Minister Y. S. Rajasekhara Reddy consult all parties and irrigation experts to strengthen the State's case before the Krishna Water Tribunal.

(6469) Vizianagaram: Telugu Desam Party Polit Bureau Member P. Ashok Gajapathiraju said at the Telugu Mahila district committee meeting here on Saturday that atrocities on women had increased after the Congress came to power. Mr. Gajapathiraju said that 12 rape cases and 7 dowry deaths were registered during the last two months against 5 rape cases and 4 dowry deaths during 2003 in the district. This shows that women lack security, he said and added that the number of murders too had increased from 28 in 2003 to 42 so far this year.

(6470) Sangareddy : Union Minister and TRS leader A. Narendra has reiterated his party's claim for the Rajya Sabha seat. Addressing a press conference here on Saturday, Mr. Narendra pointed out that it was Chief Minister Y.S. Rajasekhara Reddy who made unilateral decision to hand over the seat to the CPI, but the Congress high-command had not yet ratified his decision. He alleged that the Chief Minister had purposefully done this to belittle the TRS which had far better strength in the Assembly when compared to the CPI. He cautioned the Congress that TRS would be forced to contest for the seat if its legitimate demand was not conceded.

(6471) Chennai: "I endorse her view," said Marumalarchi Dravida Munnetra Kazhagam (MDMK) general secretary Vaiko, when All India Anna Dravida Munnetra Kazhagam (AIADMK) general secretary and Chief Minister Jayalalithaa referred to the oft-repeated dictum that there were "no permanent friends or foes in politics." The one time bete noire of Ms.Jayalaithaa described the signing of the seat sharing agreement as "the finest moment" in the State's political history. Activists of the two parties would jointly take a plunge in the election battle with utmost confidence that the AIADMK would return to power, he said. Ms.Jayalalithaa on her part said, "It feels great to be friends," when asked repeatedly on how could she share the election platform with the former Prevention of Terrorism Act (POTA) detenue. Just as Mr.Vaiko's white Mercedes Benz van, followed by as many as 20 cars carrying MDMK's top functionaries including party chairman L.Ganesan, zoomed into Poes Garden, activists raised slogans hailing the decision. Slogans such as "Long live Puratchi Puyal Vaiko!," "Thanmana Singam Vaazhga!" Later, at a press conference, Mr.Vaiko said though the MDMK initially wanted to contest 35 seats to give representation to all its district units, it finally agreed to settle for 25. But Dravida Munnetra Kahagam president M.Karunanidhi wanted him to reduce the number by one or two more seats. But when the MDMK stuck to its claim, the DMK chief agreed to consider the demand, Mr. Vaiko said. Activists of the MDMK overwhelmingly wanted to have ties with the AIADMK, Mr.Vaiko said. Experience showed that parties never compromised on their ideologies by forging poll alliances. The MDMK would not deflect from its 1994 position on the Eelam Tamils' issue.

(6472) Dehradun: Uttaranchal Chief Minister Narayan Dutt Tiwari sprang a surprise at a public function on Saturday when he announced that he had urged the Congress high command to relieve him of the responsibility within a month. "I am too old and have no desire to continue as Chief Minister or hold any other assignment and would like to be relieved after a rather illustrious innings in Indian politics," Mr. Tiwari said. Coming two days after he completed four years as Chief Minister, the announcement puts the onus on the high command for allowing him to bow out gracefully.

(6473) Kochi: Congress president Sonia Gandhi has called to reject the politics of obstruction, violence and false propaganda. Addressing a mammoth public rally organised by the Kerala Pradesh Congress Committee (KPCC) here on Saturday, kick-starting the election campaign of the party in the State, Ms. Gandhi said the political opponents of the United Democratic Front (UDF) Government in the State were "obstructing the Government at all stages." The Government, she said, was working hard to fulfil all its promises. She said that some of the parties with which the Congress was working at the Centre were its opponents in Kerala, West Bengal and Tripura. She said many parties were attempting to claim the credit for the initiatives of the United Progressive Alliance (UPA) Government at the Centre. However, the initiatives of the UPA Government were there in the Congress manifesto released in 2004, she said. "We reject our political opponents' politics of restriction, violence, gherao and false propaganda," she said, taking a dig at the CPI(M).

(6474) Bangalore: Leader of the Opposition in the Legislative Assembly N. Dharam Singh on Saturday said the party is exploring the possibility of taking legal recourse against the ruling given by the Speaker, Krishna, allowing a discussion on the motion of thanks to the Governor for his February 24 "speech" to the joint session of the legislature.Addressing a press conference, Mr. Singh and Karnataka Pradesh Congress Committee President M. Mallikarjun Kharge said the Speaker was wrong in allowing the discussion on the motion as it was unconstitutional.

(6475) Kochi: KPCC president Ramesh Chennithala has accused the CPI(M) of playing "blackmail politics" against the United Progressive Alliance (UPA) Government at the Centre. Speaking at a massive Congress rally taken out in the city in connection with the KPCC plenary session, Mr. Chennithala said unlike in Kerala, the CPI(M) had a different face in New Delhi. "In Kerala, the party is resorting to violence and fascism especially in Kannur and Kasaragod districts," he said. "The CPI(M) is also allying with the BJP in Kerala to defeat the Congress. The party is immersed in corruption in the State and the CPI(M) State secretary is the first accused in the SNC Lavlin case," charged Mr. Chennithala. In his address, Chief Minister Oommen Chandy said that the State would go to the polls with the question whether to select the UDF, which brings in development or the CPI(M), which opposes everything.

(6476) Kochi: A leadership meeting of the ruling United Democratic Front (UDF) here Saturday left it to the Congress leadership to decide whether K. Karunakaran and his party, the Democratic Indira Congress (Karunakaran), should be accommodated in the coalition. Pending a decision, the coalition leaders also decided to initiate bilateral discussions on sharing of seats on March 8 and 9. Kerala Pradesh Congress Committee (KPCC) president Ramesh Chennithala told a press conference here on Saturday that the UDF leaders wanted the Congress leadership to consult the party high command at the earliest and take a decision.

(6477) Kochi: The United Democratic Front (UDF) partners, led by the Indian Union Muslim League, have smoothened the road for entry of Democratic Indira Congress-Karunakaran (DIC-K) to the front by forcing the Congress leadership to agree to a tie-up with that party despite strong opposition by a majority of its top-and middle-rung leaders. The UDF leaders, at a meeting held here mainly to formulate a common approach to be presented before the Congress High Command, sought to convey the message that the ruling coalition was prepared to accept the DIC(K), but the modalities of the arrangement would have to be worked out after sounding out Congress president Sonia Gandhi, who arrived here on the proposal. Kerala Pradesh Congress Committee president Ramesh Chennithala told The Hindu that his party would come out with a clear-cut view on the DIC(K) issue at the end of the plenary session. The matter would be deliberated at all levels during the grand conference, which would also witness the KPCC's general body meeting, he said.

(6478) Thiruvananthapuram : The BJP has demanded a Central Bureau of Investigation (CBI) probe into the bomb blasts. Addressing a press conference here on Saturday, party spokesman B. K. Shekhar said the State police could not be depended upon to expose and bring to book the men behind these bomb explosions.

(6479) Madurai: The Marumalarchi Dravida Munnetra Kazhagam joining the All India Anna Dravida Munnetra Kazhagam will have its consequences at the Centre, according to Bharatiya Janata Party leader M. Venkaiah Naidu.He attributed the exit of the MDMK from the Democratic Progressive Alliance to the strained relationship with the DMK. "The MDMK has taken a new path as it was unhappy with the DMK," he told reporters here on Saturday.

(6480) Bangalore: Communist Party of India (Marxist) Polit Bureau member Sitaram Yechury has said the India-United States nuclear agreement was not a serious issue to "rock" the United Progressive Alliance Government. But he warned the Centre against voting against Iran at the International Atomic Energy Agency (IAEA) meeting. He told reporters here on Saturday that "if the Centre does not address four apprehensions raised by the CPI (M), then it will have to think over it (continuing in the UPA)."

(6481) Bhopal: Madhya Pradesh Chief Minister Shivraj Singh Chauhan on Saturday said expelled BJP leader Uma Bharti didn't pose a challenge to the BJP or the State Government. "I am not feeling any pressure. The only challenge before me is to place Madhya Pradesh in the league of developed States," Mr Chauhan told UNI in an interview here. "Politics of mud-slinging is not good for democracy and public will not spare political leaders obstructing development," he said, referring to "baseless" allegations being levelled by Congress leaders mainly to gain media mileage.

(6482) Guwahati: The State unit of the Bhartiya Janata Party(BJP) on Saturday flayed the Asom Gana Parishad(AGP) for the latter's effort to reach an understanding with the Left parties for the ensuing Assembly polls. Expressing doubts over the sincerity of the AGP to give a fight to the Congress in Assam, State BJP leader Indramoni Bora said: "How will the AGP fight the Congress in Assam after reaching an alliance with the Left parties? The Left parties have been supporting the Congress at the Centre and are just B-teams of the Congress." Mr. Bora said that the BJP has been holding parleys with several groups and organisations but declined to name them.

(6483) Pondicherry: After a meeting with district level functionaries in Pondicherryto elicit their viewson strategies to be adopted in the forthcoming Assembly polls, PCC president P Shanmugham left for Karaikal, (his home town), to carry out a similar exercise.

(6484) Lucknow: Uttar Pradesh Chief Minister Mulayam Singh Yadav today ruled out early Assembly elections in the state "despite a disinformation campaign mounted by the Congress". He alleged that whenever the Congress came to power at the Centre, it tried to destabilise non-Congress governments in states.The Samajwadi Party Chief claimed his party was not afraid of polls and was ready to take on any political rival. Referring to a book authored by a former Intelligence Bureau joint director, Mr Yadav said efforts were on to project him as an ISI agent. - UNI

(6485) Tiruchi : The Dravida Munnetra Kazhagam general secretary, K. Anbazhagan, on Saturday expressed confidence that the people of the State would put an end to the "misrule" of Chief Minister Jayalalithaa in the Assembly elections.

(6486) Tiruchi: Dravida Munnetra Kazhagam has opposed the opening up of the retail sector for Foreign Direct Investment. In a resolution adopted at its ninth State Conference here on Saturday, its organising secretary, T.K.S. Elangovan, said the move will affect the livelihood of lakhs of small and medium retailers. Many retailers were self-employed and if FDI was allowed in this sector, it would lead to financial difficulties for all those involved in the trade now, the resolution pointed out. The DMK also opposed mindless FDI across sectors and wanted the Government not to allow foreign investment in the Press, defence and other sectors of strategic importance. As many as 41 resolutions were adopted on the second-day of the conference.

(6487) Tiruchi: The Dravida Munnetra Kazhagam and its alliance partners appeared unfazed by the sudden decision of the Marumalarchi Dravida Munnetra Kazhagam to leave the DMK-led Democratic Progressive Alliance. In fact, a few senior leaders said MDMK's departure gave the coalition the vital breathing space it required. It also means that the DMK could contest close to 140 seats instead of the earlier 130. But the leaders hastened to point out that the DMK leadership had tried "till the very last moment" to accommodate the MDMK. It was the MDMK's intransigence that led to his leaving the alliance.

(6488) Tiruchi: Dravida Munnetra Kazhagam president M. Karunanidhi on Saturday said that the Marumalarchi Dravida Munnetra Kazhagam had decided to leave the Democratic Progressive Alliance "before January 18. Only the official announcement is being made now." The DMK will not accept MDMK's continuance in the United Progressive Alliance, he said in response to a question. And it was not because of the fewer seats allocated to the MDMK. It was notable that on January 18, the day on which the DPA had organised meetings condemning the AIADMK government across the State, Mr. Vaiko had not spoken against the AIADMK or the Chief Minister, though he had addressed a public meeting in Virudhunagar.

(6489) Chennai : The former Finance Minister, Yashwant Sinha, on Friday said the Union budget for 2006-07 has missed out on pushing forward the reform agenda and does not address the underlying concerns of the economy, particularly inflation. Though the inflation was not yet out of control, there were underlying factors, especially the rising international crude oil prices that could push it up he said, delivering a lecture organised at the Indian Institute of Technology here.

06-03-2006

(6490) Hyderabad: The CPI (M) would mobilise tribals from all the nine Agency areas for a 'chalo Hyderabad' programme on Thursday to focus their problems that had been neglected by the Government. Party's Polit Bureau member and State secretary, B.V. Raghavulu, told reporters on Sunday that the legislature party would meet Chief Minister Y.S. Rajasekhara Reddy on Monday with the demands. They would await the Government's response and if it were not satisfactory, the future course of agitation would be announced at the rally near the Indira Park. He said foremost among the demands was an alternative for the Polavaram project. More recently, the Government cheated in the issue by not incorporating in the minutes of the Tribal Advisory Council meeting the contents of a letter submitted by 11 out of 15 MLAs who attended.

(6491) Hyderabad : The BJP, the TRS and the CPI (M) have taken strong exception to Panchyat Raj Minister J.C. Diwakar Reddy's remarks writing off the zonal system in the State as of no use. BJP State president N. Indrasena Reddy told newsmen that Mr. Reddy was free to make such controversial statements after resigning from the Cabinet. At a separate news conference, Telangana Rashtra Samithi (TRS) MLA Nayani Narasimha Reddy asked Dr. Reddy to sack the Minister. By making such remarks, the Minister did not appear to have held the Cabinet or the Chief Minister in high esteem.CPI (M) State secretary B.V. Raghavulu said the remarks of the Minister reflected the typical Congress culture. There was no need to be surprised over them as no one was sure how Congress leaders would react to a situation.

(6492) Visakhapatnam: A team of MPs of the CPI(M) met Prime Minister Manmohan Singh recently and asked him to stop privatisation of thermal power and air separation plants as part of expansion project of the **Visakhapatnam** Steel Plant (VSP).

(6493) Kolkata: Chances of an anti-Left Front mahajot (grand alliance) for the upcoming Assembly elections in West Bengal were virtually ruled out on Sunday with the State Congress forming an alliance with eight political parties without the State's main Opposition party, the Trinamool Congress. The seat adjustment between the Trinamool and its National Democratic Alliance (NDA) partner, the Bharatiya Janata Party, would be finalised within "two or three days," after BJP leader Arun Jaitley holds final talks with Trinamool leader Mamata Banerjee, senior BJP MP, Murli Manohar Joshi said. Defence Minister and president of the West Bengal Pradesh Congress Committee Pranab Mukherjee said. "We have launched the UDA on the lines of the United Progressive Alliance at the Centre and will fight the coming elections jointly," he said. Among the constituents of the alliance are the Party for Democratic Socialism, a breakaway group of the CPI(M), the Lok Janashakti Party and the Jharkhand Mukti Morcha.

(6494) Tiruchi: Making a fervent plea to the electorate to free Tamil Nadu from the "clutches" of All India Anna Dravida Munnetra Kazhagam (AIADMK), the Congress president and United Progressive Alliance chairperson, Sonia Gandhi, on Sunday asserted that only the Democratic Progressive Alliance (DPA) under the leadership of Dravida Munnetra Kazhagam president, M. Karunanidhi, could create a prosperous future for Tamil Nadu. "Ensure that people are freed from the misrule of AIADMK," Ms. Sonia Gandhi told a mammoth gathering of cadres at DMK's ninth State conference, here today.

(6495) Thiruvananthapuram: CPI(M) State secretary Pinarayi Vijayan has said that the people will reject Congress president Sonia Gandhi's call to return the United Democratic Front (UDF) to power, given the failure of the Government to fulfil the UDF's election promises, including that to provide jobs to 15 lakh youth in five years, and the neglect of the State in the Union and Railway Budgets.

(6496) Kochi: The Indian Union Muslim League (IUML) and other United Democratic Front (UDF) partners have pitched for the Democratic Indira Congress (Karunakaran) as a coalition partner and might consider other options if the Congress rejects a compromise formula. All the UDF partners adopted a common line when they met Congress president Sonia Gandhi late Saturday night. The common line was adopted after a few rounds of discussion among themselves. The IUML leader P.K. Kunhalikutty, in his 15-minute discussion with Mrs. Gandhi, said his party had traditionally stood by whatever decisions the Congress leadership took from time to time. But in this matter, the IUML has formulated its own opinion, he reportedly told her. Kerala Pradesh Congress Committee (KPCC) president Ramesh Chennithala on Sunday said that his party would examine all aspects relating to the inclusion of the DIC(K) before announcing its stand.

(6497) Gulbarga: Former Chief Minister and Leader of the Opposition Party in the Legislative Assembly N. Dharam Singh on Sunday

(6498) Shimoga: Samajwadi Party State unit President and Shimoga MP S. Bangarappa said here on Saturday that his party will contest independently in the forthcoming elections to the municipal corporations, city municipal councils, town municipal councils and town panchayats.

(6499) Panaji: Leader of the Opposition and former Chief Minister Manohar Parrikar has advocated the need to keep a check on migrants coming to the State from Bhatkal, Karnataka. He said this in reference to the violence that has gripped Curchorem-Sanvordem following damage of a disputed structure on Wednesday. Mr. Parrikar said on Saturday that it is cause for concern when migrants start threatening the interests of local people. He alleged that there is a big influx of people of a particular minority community into Goa from Bhatkal.

(6500) Kannur: Communist Party of India-Marxist (CPI)M) State secretary Pinarayi Vijayan has said that the United Progresssive Alliance (UPA) Government headed by the Congress is changing the country's independent foreign policy under pressure from the United States. Delivering the Pamban Madhavan memorial speech at a function organised by the Congress (S) here on Sunday, Mr. Vijayan said that Congress president and UPA chairperson Sonia Gandhi had not held discussions with UPA partners or with the Left parties on the visit of U.S. President George Bush.

(6501) Kochi: The Democratic Indira Congress-Karunakaran (DIC-K) leader K. Karunakaran on Sunday predicted a hung Assembly if his party were to be kept away from mainstream coalition politics. The United Democratic Front (UDF) and the Left Democratic Front (LDF) would not win a ruling majority without his party's support, he said. Reacting to the Congress deliberations on its ties with the DIC(K), Mr. Karunakaran told The Hindu that the Communist Party of India (Marxist) leadership was not confident of victory owing to internal squabbles.

(6502) Kochi: Representatives of the mass organisations of the Congress met the All India Committee (AICC) president and United Progressive Alliance (UPA) chairperson Sonia Gandhi at the venue of the State conference of the Congress being held here at the Ambedkar Stadium on Sunday. Representatives of the Mahila Congress, Kerala Students Union (KSU), State Employees and Teachers Organisation (SETO), Kerala NGO

Association and Kerala Pradesh Karshaka Congress submitted memoranda to the Congress president raising various demands.

(6503) Kochi: A new power struggle seems to be emerging in the Congress centered on the inclusion of the DIC(K) and the selection of candidates for the Assembly elections, with the former Speaker V.M. Sudheeran becoming the rallying point. Mr. Sudheeran, who has been constantly sidelined by the present leadership, had his say before Congress president Sonia Gandhi on Sunday morning. Mr. Sudheeran's name did not figure in any of the programme committees for the Congress plenary session and the grand conference as such. Even though Mr. Sudheeran did not make an issue out it, the party president apparently took note of this, sources said. According to sources, Mr. Sudheeran was allowed separate time by the Congress president who had inquired about him. Mr. Sudheeran reportedly told the Congress president that Congress would have to bring in fresh faces if it wants to capitalise on the present favourable political climate. He also favoured the inclusion of the Democratic Indira Congress (Karunakaran) in the UDF scheme of things if only to gain an edge over the CPI(M)-led LDF.

(6504) Kochi: Congress president Sonia Gandhi on Sunday said it was up to the party's Kerala unit to take a decision on whether or not to have any tie-up with the K. Karunakaran-led Democratic Indira Congress (Karunakaran). Ms. Gandhi said this to editors of four Malayalam newspapers and a television channel who met her informally for 35 minutes in the morning, Congress secretary Tom Vadakkan told presspersons here.

(6505) Kottayam: The Kerala Congress (M) set the ball rolling for the pre-election wrangling in the ruling United Democratic Front (UDF) staking claim for more number of seats in the coming elections. Last time the party had contested 11 seats and won nine. Senior leaders who attended the party steering committee meeting here on Sunday said the party had never been treated on a par with its real strength and it always had to give in to accommodate the larger interests of the UDF. Under the changed climate, the party would seek to get its legitimate share in the UDF seat allocation process, they said.

(6506) Thiruvananthapuram: Even as the Opposition Left Democratic Front (LDF) is getting ready to discuss seat sharing for the upcoming Assembly elections, the CPI has struck a combative posture and demanded more than the 24 seats it had contested in 2001. Party State secretary Veliyam Bhargavan told a news conference here on Sunday that the party wanted the seats to be taken from the minor allies to be put in a common pool and shared proportionately among the others.

(6507) New Delhi: The Bharatiya Janata Party (BJP) on Sunday welcomed the India-U.S. joint statement on strategic partnership. It said the statement was a confirmation by the UPA Government of the continuing validity of the previous BJP-led NDA Government's strategic initiative of deepening, broadening and strengthening relations with the U.S. In a statement here, Leader of the Opposition in the Rajya Sabha Jaswant Singh said the joint statement also covered issues of economic prosperity; trade; innovation and knowledge economy; global safety and security; democracy and international challenges. "The BJP, as the initiator of this process of strategic cooperation with the U.S. whom the then Prime Minister A.B. Vajpayee had termed India's `natural ally,' is gratified by this development," he said. This is the direction in which the BJP-NDA Government had set the entire policy; the March 2 joint announcement reaffirms the centrality of that policy, Mr. Singh said.

(6508) Patna: Former External Affairs Minister Yashwant Sinha on Sunday took strong exception to Prime Minister Manmohan Singh's reported decision to invite Muslim scholars and intellectuals to a meeting with him to explain the nuclear deal clinched with the U.S.. "The decision is highly objectionable. Today he has convened a meeting of Muslims, tomorrow he will call the Christians and Parsis to explain if another agreement is signed," Mr. Sinha told reporters here. He said the deal was "tilted in favour of America" and the "agreement will not be complete unless it is ratified by the American Congress, International Atomic Energy Agency and the Nuclear Suppliers Group."

(6509) New Delhi: The Left parties on Sunday said the "bad bargain" by India with the U.S. in economic, defence, agriculture and other crucial fields dealt during President George W. Bush's visit was detrimental to the country's commercial and strategic interests. The four Left parties supporting the UPA government - CPI(M), CPI, Forward Bloc and RSP - will analyse and review Bush's visit in a day or two. Left leaders also took a serious view of the U.S. President "advising" India to open up FDI in all sectors, including agriculture and services, and join the fight with the U.S.

for "freedom and democracy," especially in Iran, Cuba, North Korea and Zimbabwe. Communist Party of India general secretary A. B. Bardhan said: "We believe that Mr. Bush has struck a deal with the Manmohan Singh government which will benefit the American corporates and boost the U.S. arms indsutry." CPI(M) Parliamentary group leader in the Lok Sabha, Basudeb Acharia, demanded that the Prime Minister make a detailed statement on all aspects of the agreements. CPI National Secretary Shamim Faizi said Mr. Bush came "hawking" and in his Purana Qila speech, named certain MNCs, which he wanted to see in India. "For that, he advised the Congress-led government to open up FDI in all sectors." CPI(M) Polit Bureau member Brinda Karat said: "The UPA government by agreeing to the pre-determined framework of the U.S. is pushing India into a relationship which will not serve the interests of the Indian people." - UNI

(6510) Mumbai: Former Shiv Sena leader-turned Congressman Narayan ne on Sunday charged Sena executive president Uddhav Thackeray with keeping the latter's father and Sena chief Bal Thackeray under "house arrest." "Uddhav has kept Balasaheb under house arrest, as can be seen from the latter's absence at all party functions these days," said Mr. Rane who was expelled from the Sena last year and is now a minister in the State Government.

(6511) New Delhi: Union Information and Broadcasting Minister Priyaranjan Dasmunshi has said that the launch of the National Rural Employment Guarantee Scheme (NREGA) was a challenge to the Youth Congress and that it should oversee its implementation.Addressing delegates at the convention of 200 district presidents under the purview of the National Rural Employment Guarantee Scheme here on Friday, he said while urban India was witnessing development and unprecedented economic growth, the NREGA and Bharat Nirman programmes offered a major thrust for development in the rural pockets of the country. The schemes were a big opportunity, especially for the unemployed youth, for whom it would be a means to start earning a livelihood. The role of the Youth Congress, Mr. Dasmunshi said, was not limited to politics, but to social service in the real sense of the term. The Youth Congress should not hesitate to crack the whip and even launch agitations against errant State Government officials and programme officers if they are found not to be implementing the scheme in letter and spirit, he added.

(6512) Guwahati: Senior Bharatiya Janata Party leader Arun Shourie on Sunday urged the Asom Gana Parishad to come out of the "illusion of getting Muslim votes by forging [an] opportunistic alliance with the communists." Mr. Shourie, who was here to release the "Asom Vision 2020" brought out by the State unit of the party, took strong exception to AGP chief Brindaban Goswami calling the BJP a communal party. "Communists parties are more communal than any party," he said.

(6513) Dehra Dun: Senior Congress leader Moti Lal Vora, after a meeting with Chief Minister N.D. Tiwari who had announced his desire to be relieved, said party President Sonia Gandhi would take a decision. Emerging from the hour-long meeting with Mr. Tiwari at his official residence here, Mr. Vora told reporters that the Chief Minister would meet Ms. Gandhi soon and a decision would be taken. Mr. Vora said he would appraise the party high command of the political situation in the State that goes to Assembly polls next year. However, he refused to comment when asked whether the Assembly elections would be held under Mr. Tiwari's leadership.

(6514) Tiruchi: Constituents of the Democratic Progressive Alliance (DPA) on Sunday resolved to dislodge "the anti-people and anti-democratic" Jayalalithaa government.At the ninth State conference of the Dravida Munnetra Kazhagam here, Paatali Makkal Katchi founder-president S. Ramadoss said the Assembly elections would bring about a big political change. Tamil Nadu Congress Committee president M. Krishnassamy appealed to the cadres of the DPA allies to sink their differences and work together for the front's victory. DPA leader and DMK president M. Karunanidhi was capable of sorting out any difference through talks. The Congress workers would work shoulder to shoulder to make him the next Chief Minister.CPI (M) State secretary N. Varadarajan said Mr. Karunanidhi should finalise the seat-sharing arrangement at the earliest and lead the front to victory.The "autocratic government" of the AIADMK should be removed and the DPA should take up the cause of farmers, labourers and the common man. CPI State secretary D. Pandian said the people should vote for the DPA to restore democratic norms. IUML president Khader Mohideen said the "anti-people Jayalalithaa government" should be dislodged to ensure good governance. Tamizhnadu Muslim Munnetra Kazhagam president M. H. Jawahirullah appealed to Congress president

Sonia Gandhi to consider Mr. Karunanidhi's plea for a constitutional amendment to ensure reservation for Muslims.

(6515) Tirupur: The Bharatiya Janata Party (BJP) will contest all the 234 seats in the State and try to emerge as an alternative to the DMK and the AIADMK, its national secretary in charge of Tamil Nadu, Bandaru Dattatreya, has said.

(6516) Chennai: The Desiya Murpokku Dravida Kazhagam (DMDK) president, Vijayakanth, has criticised the State Government for poor planning in the Common Entrance Test (CET) issue. Blaming the Government and authorities for the uncertainty, he said students and parents were not even sure of holding the CET in the coming academic year.

(6517) Ramanathapuram: Though the All India Anna Dravida Munnetra Kazhagam has kept its door open for more alliance partners, the Bharatiya Janata Party has not received any invitation, according to Venkaiah Naidu, BJP's national vice-president.

(6518) Tiruchi: Buoyed by the success of the youth wing conference here on Friday, Dravida Munnetra Kazhagam deputy general secretary M.K. Stalin says he will continue to build the youth movement.

(6519) Pondicherry: All India Congress Committee (AICC) general secretary V. Narayanasamy MP has said that the alliance between the Marumalarchi Dravida Munnetra Kazhagam (MDMK) and the All India Anna Dravida Munnetra Kazhagam (AIADMK) "is not surprising." Addressing reporters here on Sunday, he said Mr. Vaiko had been endeavouring to align with the AIADMK and had sent emissaries to strike a deal for the Assembly elections. Mr. Vaiko's decision would leave a "black mark" on him and he would regret it.

07-03-2006

(6520) Hyderabad: Opposition members, who were suspended from the Assembly, called it a 'black day' in the history of democracy and accused the ruling party of shielding the guilty in the alleged Rs.400-crore scam relating to the Sripadasagar project. Leader of the Opposition N. Chandrababu Naidu staged a dharna on the steps leading to the Assembly, raising slogans against the Government.

(6521) Warangal: Separate Telangana cannot be achieved by TRS, rebel MLA Dugyala Srinivasa Rao said on Monday. Addressing a press conference, Mr. Rao said only the Congress or BJP could bring a separate Telangana. "K. Chandrasekhar Rao and A. Narendra are trying to demand Rajya Sabha ticket for K. Jayashankar only to deceive the intellectual community. Had they felt the necessity of intellectuals in the Upper House, they would have accommodated him in the last Lok Sabha elections. They are out to grab power," he commented.

(6522) Mahabubnagar: Former national president of Bharatiya Janata Party (BJP) Bangaru Laxman has said Chief Minister Y.S. Rajasekhara Reddy should convene a meeting of District Collectors and SPs to discuss the report submitted by the Justice Punnaiah Commission. Mr. Laxman said that the commission in its 600-page report has described in detail how untouchability is still prevailing in Hindu society and how several welfare programmes aimed at ameliorating the lives of Dalits have not benefited them.

(6523) Adilabad: Communist Party of India (Marxist) Polit Bureau member B.V. Raghavulu on Monday asked the Government to complete giving compensation to oustees of various projects before taking up projects such as Polavaram. He cited the example of the oustees under the Rallivagu and Gollavagu projects in Adilabad district where the farmers, whose lands are being submerged, were yet to get compensation.

(6524) New Delhi: One with the Opposition in expressing concern over the situation arising out of the demolition drive here in the Capital, the Government on Monday informed the Lok Sabha that "legislation was inescapable". However, dissatisfied with the response of Union Minister for Urban Development S. Jaipal Reddy to a calling-attention motion on the issue moved by Vijay Kumar Malhotra (Bharatiya Janata Party), the Opposition staged a walkout. While the Government joined the Opposition in voicing concern over the demolitions, Mr. Reddy urged the BJP not to play to the gallery and create false fears among the people.

(6525) Dehra Dun: After causing a stir by sending his resignation to Congress president Sonia Gandhi, Uttaranchal Chief Minister N.D. Tiwari on Monday said he would abide by the high command's decision on his political future.

(6526) Hassan: The former Union Minister V. Srinivas Prasad, who has distanced himself from the Janata Dal (Secular), has said that he is under pressure from senior leaders and close friends to join the Congress.However, he has decided to take a decision after carefully studying the situation, he said.

(6527) Hospet (Bellary District)**:** Sitaram Yechury, CPI (M) leader, has ruled out any threat to the UPA Government from parties supporting it "from outside".

(6528) Panaji: The Congress on Monday sought a judicial inquiry into the Curchorem-Sanvordem riots. Addressing presspersons here after a meeting of the Goa Pradesh Congress Committee (GPCC) to take stock of the situation, Ravi Naik, President of the GPCC said the role of some politicians and other leaders in the violence should be probed. Those found guilty should be punished within a month.

(6529) Kochi: All India Congress Committee general secretary Margaret Alva on Monday made a fervent appeal to the Kerala Pradesh Congress Committee to give a larger role to women in the State's electoral politics. Inaugurating the KPCC general body here, Mrs. Alva said, "it is unfortunate that in a State like Kerala, with a high level of literacy, women are not visible. Women constitute more than 60 per cent of India's electorate, but they are hardly represented in the organisation and legislatures. Women are needed to catch votes through door-to-door campaigns. They are either too old or too young to be in politics. Political establishments come with all kinds of excuses to keep women out," Mrs. Alva said. In this context, she pointed out that women headed five political parties in the country.

(6530) Kochi: The Kerala Pradesh Congress Committee general body on Monday endorsed the stand of senior leaders that the party is willing to welcome the Democratic Indira Congress (Karunakaran) if its leaders and workers recognised the leadership of Sonia Gandhi. The party has set the acceptance of Ms. Gandhi's leadership as a pre-condition for such a move and it was left to the leaders

(6531) Kochi: The draft economic resolution of the KPCC general body condemned the CPI (M) and the Left parties for their blind opposition to all kinds of privatisation. Its blind opposition to the WTO regime was against all economic logic reasoning. The only way towards economic progress was to become competitive in the international market. The resolution said that the Indian Communist parties had not yet learnt from their counterpart from else where in the world and that it was time to shelve political opportunism, the resolution said.

(6532) Kollam: Democratic Indira Congress (Karunakaran) vice-president M.A. John has said that any understanding for an alliance between the DIC(K) and the United Democratic Front (UDF) will lead to a split in the party. Speaking at a meet-the-press programme here on Monday, he said many in the DIC(K) were not happy with the move to go back to the UDF fold.

(6533) Kollam: The Kerala Congress(B) leader R. Balakrishna Pillai, MLA, has denied reports that his party is going to merge with the Congress.

(6534) Palakkad: Communist Party of India (Marxist) State secretary Pinarayi Vijayan has demanded that the Central and State Governments create a permanent corpus fund for providing support price to farmers affected by the crash in prices of agriculture produce.

(6535) New Delhi: The Bharatiya Janata Party on Monday criticised the United Progressive Alliance constituents for disrupting Parliamentary proceedings vis-…-vis the Banerjee Committee report on burning coaches of the Sabarmati Express at Godhra in Gujarat in 2002. The BJP deputy leader in Lok Sabha, V. K. Malhotra charged that the leak of the report just before Assembly polls in five States was a UPA bid to "garner minority votes." "A similar move to leak the interim report of the Banerjee Committee ahead of the Bihar polls backfired on the Congress and its allies. They lost in Bihar and local body elections in Gujarat as well," Mr. Malhotra said. Stating that the Nanavati Commission report was yet to be tabled, the BJP said the Banerjee Committee's findings were "not the last word" on the subject.

(6536) New. Delhi : The Communist Party of India on Monday expressed outrage at the way U.S. President George Bush used "Indian soil" to criticise countries, which have longstanding friendly relations with the country and said it would "oppose" any move by the Centre to be part of U.S. strategies. The party central secretariat in a statement said: "It shows once again the imperialist arrogance and is a direct call to the Indian

Government to join U.S. imperialist strategies the world over in the name of promotion of global democracy."

(6537) New Delhi: The Manmohan Singh-led United Progressive Alliance Government's approach to foreign policy is contrary to the National Common Minimum Programme and against the country's security interests, the Communist Party of India (Marxist) said on Monday. The party said it would work to reverse "this course," harmful to India and its people. The CPI (M) would announce its stand on the Indo-U.S. nuclear deal after the Prime Minister set out the details of the accord in Parliament. The concern was not just over the nuances of the deal but also at the "unacceptable price India will have to pay in terms of its independent foreign policy and strategic autonomy," the Polit Bureau said in a statement.

(6538) New Delhi: The Congress on Monday described as "personal views," the suggestion made by the Dravida Munnetra Kazhagam chief M. Karunanidhi that the Marumalarchi Dravida Munnetra Kazhagam (MDMK) could no longer remain in the United Progressive Alliance following its alliance with the AIADMK. Asked about the party's response, Congress spokesperson Abhishek Singhvi said that the move of the MDMK in the State would not affect the Centre.

(6539) Guwahati: Opposition parties in Assam complained to the Election Commission on Monday that the Congress was violating the model code of conduct. The Asom Gana Parishad, the Bharatiya Janata Party, the Communist Party of India, the CPI (M) and the Nationalist Congress Party called on Chief Election Commissioner B.B. Tandon and the other two members, Navin B. Chawla and N. Gopalswamy, separately here to draw their attention to media reports on backdated appointments and distribution of cash, cheques and yarn under government schemes even after the election dates were announced. The Congress denied the Opposition allegations and said the EC could take action if there was any violation of the code.

(6540) Bhopal: The main Opposition Congress on Monday staged a walk-out in the Madhya Pradesh Assembly in support of a demand for withdrawing power theft-linked cases against farmers and also alleging that the treasury benches did not furnish a satisfactory reply on the problem. Raising the matter during question hour, former minister Ramniwas Rawat (Congress) accused the government of straightaway incarcerating such peasants and, as a result, fear prevailed in cultivators' families.

(6541) Bhubaneswar: The Justice Banerjee Commission finding that the Godhra train fire was an accident is "politically biased." It "supports the minority appeasement policy of the Congress," Bharatiya Janata Party general secretary Vinay Katiyar said here on Monday. "If the Godhra carnage is called a mishap, can the Congress accept the assassination of Rajiv Gandhi and Indira Gandhi as accidents?"

(6542) Jaipur: Many fresh faces figure in the new State executive committee of the Bharatiya Janata Party announced here over the weekend. The choice of the team has been a balancing act of castes and region on the part of the new party chief Mahesh Sharma but what is obvious is the say Chief Minister Vasundhara Raje has had in the selection. The 18-strong team of office-bearers and the 69-member executive have not many from the groups in the party represented by the outgoing president Lalit Kishore Chaturvedi or for that matter the other party stalwarts. The representation to Muslims is nominal while women account for 10 per cent of the members. There is no Muslim among the office- bearers while executive and the 73-member strong special invitees team have one Muslim each.

(6543) Lucknow: Uttar Pradesh Chief Minister and Samajwadi Party chief Mulayam Singh Yadav on Monday charged that the Congress was behind the move for disqualification of Jaya Bachchan as the party's Rajya Sabha member. "People know who is behind this drama and how the Congress is bent upon targeting Samajwadi Party to finish it off. The SP would give a befitting reply to such forces," Mr. Yadav told reporters here. Mr. Yadav sought to dismiss charges levelled by party MP Raj Babbar against Amar Singh and the Chief Minister and said history is replete with instances of people revolting and bringing "unfounded and baseless" charges against their leaders.

(6544) Chennai: Seat-sharing talks among the constituents of the Democratic Progressive Alliance (DPA) will be over soon, said Dravida Munnetra Kazhagam president M. Karunanidhi here on Monday. Talking to reporters after holding talks with the Communist Party of India, Mr. Karunanidhi said the discussions were progressing smoothly and an agreement would be reached shortly. State CPI secretary D. Pandian said the party's three-member committee held discussions with the DMK and the negotiations were proceeding smoothly. Leaders of the Communist Party of India (Marxist) led by the State secretary N.Varadarajan met Mr. Karunanidhi later in the evening and held seat-sharing talks.

(6545) Chennai : The Marumalarchi Dravida Munnetra Kazhagam will contest two Assembly constituencies in Pondicherry. This follows an agreement signed between the All India Anna Dravida Munnetra Kazhagam and the MDMK on Monday, according to a party release.

(6546) Chennai : A new party, the Pattali Munnetra Kazhagam (Pa.Mu.Ka), was launched on Monday to protect the rights of Dalits and backward and most backward classes, besides defending social justice. The party's general secretary, P.D. Elangovan, told reporters here that it would finalise strategy for the Assembly elections shortly. It would hold seat-sharing talks with the All-India Anna Dravida Munnetra Kazhagam if invited. The party had moved the Election Commission for recognition. Mr. Elangovan, who was a leader of the Pattali Makkal Katchi (PMK) till his expulsion in 2004, charged PMK founder S. Ramadoss with "systematically sidelining" those who made great contributions to the growth the Vanniyar Sangam and the party.

08-03-2006

(6547) Anantapur : Telugu Desam leaders have urged people to end the 'corrupt' rule of the Congress by teaching a fitting lesson to it the forthcoming sarpanch and mandal elections. Participating in NTR Jana Chaitanya Yatra at Gooty, Pedda Vaduguru, Pamidi, Kalluru and Garladinne on Monday TDP Polit Bureau member K. Srinivasulu alleged that Congress leaders had forgotten the promises made before the Assembly elections after assuming power.

(6548) Anantapur : CPI State secretary K. Narayana has observed that the State Government's arguments before the tribunal on Krishna waters are lopsided and harming the interests of the State.

(6549) Hyderabad: Continuing their tirade against the Government's refusal to table records pertaining to the Rs. 400-crore cost escalation in the Sripadasagar project, Opposition MLAs took to the streets by marching in a procession from the Assembly to Ambedkar's statue on Tank Bund here on Tuesday. The coordination they showed on the floor on Monday was, however, missing and opposition parties took out rallies separately. While the CPI (M), CPI and the MIM organised a silent rally together, with some MLAs wearing black bands across their mouths, Telangana Rashtra Samithi and the main opposition, Telugu Desam took out separate processions.

(6550) Hyderabad: Accusing the opposition Telugu Desam of trying to hold the House to ransom, Chief Minister Y.S. Rajasekhara Reddy has said the TDP is creating obstacles in the construction of irrigation projects, as it is afraid of its survival if the projects are completed. Speaking to reporters here on Tuesday, Dr. Reddy charged the TDP with "living under a false prestige that it is still ruling the State." "The way TDP president N. Chandrababu Naidu indulged in personalised remarks against the Speaker is not in the interest of democracy," he said.

(6551) Hyderabad: The Telangana Rashtra Samiti has demanded that GO 72 be kept in abeyance, on the grounds that it is against the spirit of the Girglani Commission report. TRS floor leader G. Vijayarama Rao told a press conference here on Tuesday that the order was aimed at 'hurting the sentiments of the people of Telangana.' "The GO is nothing but a clear attempt to harm the interest of the people of the region and is against the spirit of the Six-Point Formula."

(6552) Nalgonda: Former Union Minister and Bharatiya Janata Party national secretary Sayyad Shahnawaz Hussain has alleged that the Congress Government led by Y.S. Rajasekhara Reddy has failed to come to the rescue of weavers as promised by him as an opposition leader.

(6553) Visakhapatnam: The TDP owes an apology to people since the welfare programmes came to standstill because of the repoll caused by its conduct, Dronamraju Srinivas, Congress nominee for the **Visakhapatnam** One Assembly byelection, has said.

(6554) New Delhi: An echo of the controversy over the suspension of 62 Opposition members from the Andhra Pradesh Assembly on Monday was heard in Parliament on Tuesday with Telugu Desam Party members forcing two adjournments of the Rajya Sabha and one in the Lok Sabha. Though efforts by TDP leader K. Yerrannaidu to raise the issue before question hour in the Lok Sabha came to naught, Speaker Somnath Chatterjee adjourned the House for 15 minutes during zero hour following a war of words between TDP and Congress members.

(6555) Thiruvananthapuram: As expected, the Opposition LDF State committee could not make much of a headway in its efforts to evolve an amicable formula for sharing of seats for the coming Assembly election despite that being the single important item on the agenda at its meeting here on Tuesday. The talks between the LDF constituents got stuck in claims and counter-claims about the eligibility of each partner and the impossibility of accommodating conflicting claims within the alliance parameters.

(6556) Kochi: The KPCC plenary session has authorised a four-member committee comprising Congress Working Committee member A. K. Antony, Chief Minister Oommen Chandy, KPCC president Ramesh Chennithala and Union Minister Vayalar Ravi to work out the party's election strategies, including the relation with the DIC(K).

(6557) Bidar: The former Minister Basavaraj Patil Humnabad has accused the Janata Dal (Secular)-Bharatiya Janata Party (BJP) Coalition Government of trying to hijack development programmes initiated by the previous Congress Government.

(6558) New Delhi : Leader of the Opposition in the Lok Sabha L.K. Advani accused the Congress of indulging in "competitive minority appeasement." This was "good neither for the country nor for the community." "A little while ago I got the news of blasts in Varanasi. Then I realised that my apprehensions are correct in the light of recent developments. The former Prime Minister, Atal Bihari Vajpayee, has condemned the blasts and appealed to people to maintain peace. The Rashtriya Swayamsevak Sangh has termed as "shocking and disturbing" the bomb blasts and accused both the Central and State Governments of being "incapable" to deal with the menace of terrorism.

(6559) New Delhi: The Bharatiya Janata Party will seek legal advice on whether the positions of Chairperson, National Advisory Board, and Chairperson of the Rajiv Gandhi Foundation held by Congress president Sonia Gandhi are offices of profit under Article 103 of the Constitution and could attract disqualification for membership of Parliament. BJP deputy leader in the Lok Sabha V.K. Malhotra told reporters on Tuesday that after getting legal advice the party could move the Election Commission to consider disqualifying Ms. Gandhi in the manner it had recommended disqualifying Samajwadi Party MP from the Rajya Sabha, Jaya Bachchan, for holding an "office of profit." Her position as Chairperson of the Uttar Pradesh Film Development Council was held by the Commission to come under the category "office of profit."

(6560) New Delhi: Stating that the Indo-U.S. nuclear deal was part of a wider strategic partnership into which the U.S. sought to drag India, the Communist Party of India (Marxist) warned the Government not to accept external conditions in pursuit of the deal. "On the issue of foreign policy and Indo-U.S. strategic cooperation, differences between the Left parties and the United Progressive Alliance have come to the fore and the central committee at its meeting this week would discuss it," party general secretary Prakash Karat said here. In a separate statement, the party's Polit Bureau said it must be ensured that India's future energy programme did not become dependent on imported nuclear reactors and imported fuel. The deal must take into account the techno-economics of nuclear energy to determine its quantum in India's energy basket.

(6561) New Delhi: Bharatiya Janata Party president Rajnath Singh is leaving for Varanasi, where 12 persons were killed and 20 injured in blasts at the Sankat Mochan temple and the cantonment railway station on Tuesday evening. Emerging from a meeting of party leaders here, he blamed the blasts on the "soft policies" of the United Progressive Alliance Government towards terrorist activities. Talking to reporters, he said he could not rule out any possibility including the involvement of the ruling Samajwadi Party. He said the SP had a track record for spreading communal tension.

(6562) Chennai: The Communist Party of India will contest 10 seats, as a part of the Democratic Progressive Alliance led by the Dravida Munnetra Kazhagam, in the Assembly elections The agreement was arrived at following talks between CPI State secretary D. Pandian and DMK president M. Karunanidhi on Tuesday.

(6563) Chennai: The Bharatiya Janata Party has reiterated that it will face the Assembly elections without the support of the Dravida Munnetra Kazhagam and the All India Anna Dravida Munnetra Kazhagam. Briefing mediapersons here on Tuesday after a two-day meeting of district presidents and other office-bearers, senior leader M. Venkaiah Naidu, who is overseeing the party's electoral strategy for the south, said, "Our aim is to contest independently and get a good presence in legislature." Asked whether any discussion had taken place with Desiya Morpokku Dravida Kazhagam founder Vijayakanth, Mr Naidu replied in the negative. (In the past, several BJP leaders expressed their inclination to a tie-up with Mr Vijayakanth).

(6564) Eluru: CPI (M) State secretary B.V. Raghavulu on Wednesday stated that his party would stall the "Operation Kolleru" undertaken by the State Government as part of enforcing the GO 120 and the High Court directive.

(6565) Hyderabad: Thirtythree Telugu Desam members were suspended once again from the Assembly on Wednesday when they created an uproar demanding a debate on the irregularities in escalating the cost of the Sripadasagar project. However, the period of suspension was limited to question hour and the members participated in the proceedings later. Majlis Ittehadul Muslimeen (MIM) members staged a walkout in protest against the suspension.

(6566) Hyderabad: Telugu Desam deputy leader T. Devender Goud has specified five pieces of evidence to substantiate his party's charge that the Government had escalated the cost of the Sripadasagar Project by Rs. 381 crores to benefit the contractor.

(6567) Hyderabad: The Telangana Rashtra Samithi (TRS) staged a walkout in the Assembly on Wednesday in protest against the Government failing to assert itself in the running of the Begumpet branch of the Hyderabad Public School (HPS) in spite of owning the land of the institution.

(6568) Thiruvananthapuram: Leader of the Opposition V.S. Achuthanandan has said that the Supreme Court verdict against Zahira Sheikh for perjury must be a warning for the accused and witnesses in the Kozhikode ice-cream parlour sex scandal case.

(6569) Thiruvananthapuram: Leader of the Opposition V.S. Achuthanandan and Communist Party of India-Marxist (CPI-M) State secretary Pinarayi Vijayan have demanded a comprehensive inquiry into the alleged lax manner in which SSLC question papers were transported, resulting in loss of secrecy needed for the proper conduct of the examination, which is written by lakhs of students.

(6570) Varanasi: Bharatiya Janata Party president Rajnath Singh, who visited this city on Wednesday to take stock of the situation following the bomb attacks at the Sankat Mochan temple and the Cantonment railway station, alleged that the "soft policies" of the Central and State Governments helped the emergence of disruptive elements. He wanted the probe into the blasts to be handed over to the CBI. Bahujan Samaj Party president Mayawati said the Uttar Pradesh Government had not learnt any lesson from the terror attack in Ayodhya and the riots in Mau. She alleged that the law and order situation in the State worsened whenever there was a Samajwadi Party-led Government in Lucknow. She demanded the dismissal of the Mulayam Singh Government and the imposition of President's rule in the State. BJP leaders Kalyan Singh, Kalraj Mishra and Kesri Nath Tripathi also visited the city. Congress president Sonia Gandhi, accompanied by Union Home Minister Shivraj Patil visited the injured late on Tuesday. Both she and Mr. Patil said the Centre would not allow the atmosphere of communal harmony and peace to be disturbed in the city and the State.

(6571) New Delhi: The Leader of the Opposition, L.K. Advani, and Bharatiya Janata Party president Rajnath Singh are to embark on simultaneous 'rath yatras' to cover the country to mobilise support for the party's "anti-minority" and "anti-Muslim vote-bank politics" plank ahead of the Assembly polls in five States. Mr. Advani announced the yatra plan here on Wednesday: the party would speak up against the attempt by the Congress to give reservations to Muslims in Andhra Pradesh; it was against the Aligarh Muslim University being declared a minority institution; it was apprehensive that the Congress would bring the quashed Illegal Migrants (Determination by Tribunal) Act through the backdoor by amending the Foreigners Act; it was not in favour of the Sachar Committee trying to establish the status of Muslims in employment and education through "surveys"; it had already rubbished the Banerjee Committee report on the Godhra carnage and had described it as politically motivated and finally, the BJP would attack what it described as the Government's "soft approach" to terrorism. In response to a question, Mr. Advani confirmed that the 'yatras' would be part of political mobilisation. "The BJP is a political party. We cannot keep politics out." Party managers have been told to ensure that the route of the 'yatras' covered the five States going to the polls.

(6572) New Delhi: Parliamentary Affairs Minister Priyaranjan Dasmunsi charged the Bharatiya Janata Party with playing politics with the tragic blasts in Varanasi, and condemned the "behaviour" of its leaders who disrupted both Houses on Wednesday.

(6573) New Delhi: The Congress and the Left parties on Wednesday condemned the bomb blasts in Varanasi and regretted that the Bharatiya Janata Party was seeking to draw political mileage from the incident. Expressing its deep shock and strong condemnation, the Communist Party of India (Marxist) said the fact that the blasts took place at a temple and in the railway station in Varanasi shows the "diabolical motive" behind this terrorist attack, which is to create communal tensions and a backlash. "Recognising the nature of this provocation, all sections of the people must rebuff this heinous attempt," the party Polit Bureau said in a statement. The party said while it is time for people to be united and determined to counter such terrorist violence, it was unfortunate that the BJP was resorting to mean politics by attributing the terrorist outrage to so-called minority appeasement by the Government and the secular parties. Demanding that the perpetrators of such a crime should not go scot-free, the CPI said the Union and the State Governments should make all efforts to pin down the culprits. The Congress said that when it was in the Opposition it did not disrupt proceedings during terrorist attacks on temples like Akshardham in Gandhinagar and Raghunath in Jammu, the Red Fort and Parliament. Did the BJP not celebrate Holi then, asked party spokesperson Rajiv Shukla, reacting to the BJP suggestion that the party would not participate in the Holi festival next week. The party flayed the BJP decision to take out twin yatras and dubbed them as "riot yatras". The CPI (ML) Liberation too strongly condemned the blasts and called for speedy and credible probe to identify the guilty and ensure swift punishment. The party also condemned the Mulayam Singh Government for not taking pre-emptive steps to stop any recurrence of such incidents, especially in the backdrop of the Mau riots and tension in Lucknow following recent anti-Bush protests. The party cautioned that vested political interests in Uttar Pradesh could use the blasts to trigger communal polarisation.

(6574) New Delhi: Rajya Sabha Deputy Chairman K. Rahman Khan has condemned Tuesday's bomb blasts in Varanasi and expressed his sympathies to the bereaved families and those who were injured. The Nationalist Congress Party echoed similar views and said that in such a situation political parties should ensure that communal harmony was not disturbed. "It is also the responsibility of political parties that they do not take any step which would endanger peace and amity in the country," said Jafar Akhtar, national president of the party's Minority Department. Lok Jan Shakti Party president and Union Minister Ram Vilas Paswan described the incident as "unfortunate and against humanity." The Telugu Desam Parliamentary Party demanded that the Centre and the Uttar Pradesh Government take stringent measures to prevent any recurrence. In a statement, the party leaders, K. Yerrannaidu, M. Jagannath and R. Chandrasekar Reddy demanded immediate action to arrest the culprits.

(6575) New Delhi: Agitated over the explosions in Varanasi, the Bharatiya Janata Party and Shiv Sena on Wednesday forced the adjournment of both Houses of Parliament. Barring a statement by Union Home Minister Shivraj Patil on the blasts, very little business was transacted in either House as the Opposition - shouting 'Har Har Mahadev' slogans - held the Centre responsible for the explosions.

(6576) New Delhi: The Bharatiya Janata Party legislators were expelled for three days from the Delhi Assembly after a condolence session in memory of the victims of the Varanasi blasts was turned into a war of words between the ruling Congress and the Opposition party on Wednesday. While the BJP tried to give a communal colour to the situation, the Congress too was not behind to capitalise on the tragedy.

(6577) Bhopal: Amid loud protests Congress members walked out of the Madhya Pradesh Assembly on Wednesday after Finance Minister Raghoji refused to treat Bharatiya Janata party's election manifesto as an official document and told the House that the State Government was not ready to offer the Central dearness allowance (D.A.) to its employees.

(6578) Shimla: Congress Ministers, who have been named by the BJP for corruption in the recent charge- sheet given to the Governor, have started giving their explanations on the properties they own in the media. After the IPH Minister Kaul Singh Thakur and Transport Minister G.S. Bali's press conference on Tuesday, it was the turn of Forest Minister Ram

Lal on Wednesday. The Minister while talking to the reporters in the Vidhan Sabha premises admitted that his son was a transporter who also owned a petrol pump.

(6579) Lucknow: The twin blasts in Varanasi have given the Opposition parties in Uttar Pradesh an opportunity to intensify its campaign against the Samajwadi Party Government accusing it of failing in all fronts including law and order situation. The 'Oust Mulayam' chorus gained momentum as separate delegations of the BJP, the BSP, the Congress and the JD(U) met Governor T V Rajeswar on Wednesday and demanded the dismissal of the Mulayam Singh Yadav Government. Led by Leader of Opposition in the Vidhan Sabha Lalji Tandon, the BJP delegation apprised the Governor about recent incidents including the twin blasts to highlight "total failure" of the Government on the law and order front. The Congress delegation, led by its legislature party leader Pramod Tewari, also apprised the Governor of the situation arising out of Varanasi blasts and urged him to "take necessary" action in this regard. Before commencing the march, BSP MLAs also held a demonstration at the gates of the Legislature building to criticise the interim order of Speaker Mata Prasad Pandey allowing rebel BSP MLAs to share seats with treasury benches.

(6580) Pondicherry: A. Anbalagan, MLA and AIADMK Pondicherry State committee secretary, has alleged that the Pondicherry Government was violating the model code of conduct, which came into force on March 1. Addressing reporters here on Wednesday, Mr. Anbalagan said it was shocking to see that the Government was distributing rice to ration cardholders under the free rice scheme in bags carrying the picture of the AICC leader Sonia Gandhi. He was not against distribution of rice.

10-03-2006

(6581) Hyderabad : BJP national vice-president Bandaru Dattatreya advised political parties and religious organisations to learn from Ghulam Mustafa - father of ISI activist Ghulam Yazdani - who disowned his son for his anti-national activities and put the nation before religion.

(6582) Hyderabad: Charging the Government with adopting a unilateral stand on Polavaram project and bauxite mining in Visakhaptnam district, the CPI (M) has asserted that it would oppose any moves by the Government to harm tribals. The party has given a call for a bandh in the agency areas on March 24 in protest against the Government's moves.

(6583) Hyderabad: The Congress Legislature Party (CLP) has termed the uproar over the estimates of Sripada Sagar Project an "engineered controversy" aimed at stalling the project work.

(6584) Hyderabad: Telugu Desam president N. Chandrababu Naidu has said that he will place on the Floor of the Assembly on Friday fresh evidence about involvement of the State Government in scandalous implementation of irrigation projects, particularly Sripadasagar lift-irrigation scheme.

(6585) Visakhapatnam: The Congress-led UPA Government at the Centre should own responsibility for explosions in Varanasi as it failed to take proper steps to curb Pak-sponsored terrorism, State BJP president N. Indrasena Reddy said here on Thursday.

(6586) Chennai: The Dravida Munnetra Kazhagam on Thursday signed seat-sharing agreements for the Assembly elections with the Congress, the Communist Party of India (Marxist) and the Indian Union Muslim League. The Congress will contest 48 seats, the CPI(M) 13 and the IUML 3. All the three candidates of the IUML will contest on the DMK symbol. The DMK had earlier inked an agreement with the Communist Party of India, allotting it 10 seats.The only major party in the alliance that is yet to clinch an agreement is the Pattali Makkal Katchi. "The PMK will come tomorrow for talks," DMK president M. Karunanidhi said, after clinching the deals with the three parties. PMK leader S. Ramadoss had said that his party would conclude an agreement latest by Friday.

(6587) Thiruvananthapuram: The Indian Union Muslim League on Thursday officiated as the mediator to bring the Democratic Indira Congress(Karunakaran) into the UDF fold. General secretary of the IUML P. K. Kunhalikutty and IUML Minister E. T. Mohammed Basheer met the veteran DIC(K) leader K. Karunakaran and held discussions with him for more than two hours. President of the DIC(K) K. Muraleedharan was also present at the meeting.

(6588) Mumbai: Former Shiv Sainik Raj Thackeray on Thursday launched his new party, the Maharashtra Navnirman Sena, at a packed hall in South Mumbai. He did not reveal anything about his party's ideology or structure, saying that he would do so at a public rally at Shivaji Park on March 19.

(6589) Kozhikode: Bharatiya Janata Party (BJP) State president P.S. Sreedharan Pillai has alleged that the police probe into the twin blasts in Kozhikode on Friday is being scuttled.

(6590) Thiruvananthapuram: The bilateral discussions between the CPI(M) and its allies, CPI and RSP, on sharing of seats for the coming Assembly elections ended in a stalemate here on Thursday with neither side yielding even an inch from their stated positions. The talks between the CPI(M) and the Kerala Congress (Joseph) and the Janata Dal on Wednesday also did not make much headway. The talks would now resume on March 13 .

(6591) New Delhi: The Centre on Thursday came in for all-round criticism by the BJP-led Opposition as well as the UPA coalition partners, including the Left parties, in both the Houses of Parliament.In the Rajya Sabha, the BJP slammed the budget for its lack of initiative in economic reforms and infrastructure development, while its allies in the Lok Sabha rapped the Government for not providing enough in the budget to help farmers.Participating in the ongoing debate on the budget in the Lok Sabha, P. Satheedevi (CPI-M) urged the Finance Minister, P. Chidambaram, to take steps to tax the corporate sector and announce steps for internal resource mobilisation. Echoing similar concerns, Avinash Rai Khanna (BJP) pleaded for a halt to wheat imports to ensure that farmers got appropriate remuneration for their produce. Noting that the budget was "modest towards corporates and immodest towards the working people," S. Sudhakar Reddy (CPI) said that while no steps were being taken to tap black money, the growth rate of taxes on corporates was low. Raghunath Jha (RJD) favoured a further reduction in the interest rate on farm loans from 7 per cent while M. Ramadoss (PMK) pointed out that the GDP growth of 8.1 per cent was not an indication of the socio-economic development of the people.E.G. Sugavanam (DMK) proposed that the Centre take up a scheme to convert seawater into drinking water in Tamil Nadu. In the Rajya Sabha, Yashwant Sinha said that while neglecting reforms and infrastructural growth, the budget provided sops only for "pasta and ice cream eaters." Brinda Karat (CPI-M) said the budget had belied the expectations of the people especially when "many crucial and important spheres of the budget directly affect the livelihood of the people."

(6592) New Delhi: The Bharatiya Janata Party has demanded that the book Haqeeqat be banned and withdrawn immediately. It also demanded that the Padma Shri given to its publisher three years ago by the Vajpayee Government be "taken back." Parliamentary party spokesperson V.K. Malhotra criticised the Left parties for defending the publication when the matter was raised in the Lok Sabha on Thursday, leading to an adjournment for an hour.

(6593) New Delhi: Bharatiya Janata Party and Shiv Sena members disrupted proceedings in the Lok Sabha on Thursday over the alleged denigration of Hindu deities in a publication brought out by a Rajasthan-based Christian organisation. Raising the issue, Srichand Kriplani said Hindu deities were shown in a poor light in Hakeekat brought out by the Emmanuel Mission. He demanded a ban on the book and action against the author.

(6594) New Delhi: Making a strong pitch for quality education to everyone, Congress member of Parliament Rahul Gandhi on Thursday emphasised the need to develop India as a global educational hub. Participating in a discussion on the Union budget, the Amethi MP made his maiden speech that was heard with rapt attention by members on the Treasury benches, ruling coalition members and an appreciative Opposition. Congress president Sonia Gandhi was present in the House while sister Priyanka, her husband Robert Vadra were in the Speaker's gallery.

(6595) Kolkata: West Bengal's ruling Left Front on Thursday announced the names of four candidates to fill Rajya Sabha seats from the State. They include three from the Communist Party of India (Marxist) and one from the Forward Bloc. The CPI (M) candidates are Mainul Hasan, a former MP; Tapan Sen, a leader of the Centre for Indian Trade Unions, and Suman Pathak from the Darjeeling hills. The Forward Bloc nominee is Barun Mukherjee, according to the chairman of the Left Front committee and member of the CPI (M) Polit Bureau, Biman Bose.

(6596) Chennai: The Janata Party president, Subramanian Swamy, on Thursday said there was a need for unity among Hindus and for the creation of a Hindu platform. Addressing a press conference here, he said the serial blasts in Varanasi on Tuesday was a further confirmation that Hinduism was under siege from nefarious foreign forces.

(6597) Patna: BJP president Rajnath Singh and Leader of Opposition L.K. Advani would launch their separate National Integration yatras from April 6 targeting the alleged "appeasement policies of the Congress and the Left that had encouraged the rise of terrorism in the country." Claiming that the BJP alone was secular, the BJP chief charged that the Congress was sowing the seeds of partition once again through its "minorityism and appeasement of the minorities." He alleged that both the Congress and the Left were out to rip the social fabric of the country to shreds.

(6598) New Delhi: In a confrontation that could throw the ruling party in the Capital into turmoil, Congress Chief Whip Ramakant Goswami on Thursday evening issued a three-line whip asking the party MLAs to vote against the Public Accounts Committee report on the Rs. 150-crore smart card scam that had recommended a CBI probe into the whole deal.

(6599) Chandigarh: The Indian National Lok Dal demanded resignations of Haryana Education Minister Phool Chand Mullana and Mr.Venod Sharma. Addressing a press conference here, Mr. Chautala said the entire State had been shocked by the incidents of alleged rape of schoolgirls by the teachers. The Education Minister should resign immediately over the failure of the Government to check such heinous crimes. Mr.Chautala also demanded that Mr.Venod Sharma resign as a hue and cry had been raised against the court verdict acquitting his son Manu Sharma in the Jessica Lal murder case. He charged that the law and order situation had deteriorated during the one-year tenure of the Hooda Government, adding that it was being ruled by "classmates" of the Chief Minister.Mr.Chautala said the Congress regime in the State was "politically maligning" his family.

(6600) Dehra Dun: Uttaranchal Bharatiya Janata Party State unit president Bhagat Singh Koshiary has suspended three party leaders for openly canvassing support for the "Janadesh Yatra" of Uma Bharati which enters the region on April 13. The three are Anand Singh Rawat of Chamoli, Usha Bhardwaj of Hardwar and Rajesh Dhyani of Lansedowne. Reports indicate that a good number of BJP, Vishwa Hindu Parishad, Bajrang Dal and Rashtriya Swayam Sewak Sangh cadres are holding meetings and going round the villages in all districts urging the people to participate in Ms. Bharati's Yatra in a big way.

(6601) Chennai: The secretary of the Communist Party of India (Marxist) in Kerala, Pinarayi Vijayan, on Thursday said that the Kerala Government should tap Malayalees outside the State for its development.

(6602) Chennai: The All India Anna Dravida Munnetra Kazhagam (AIADMK) has moved the Election Commission (EC), seeking action against four Union Ministers for "violating the model code of conduct." An AIADMK release here on Thursday said that the party's election wing secretary O. Paneerselvam submitted a complaint to the Commission on Wednesday, alleging that Union Finance Minister P. Chidambaram, Minister for Communications and Information Technology Dayanidhi Maran, Union Minister of State for Statistics and Programme Implementation G.K. Vasan and Minister of State for Textiles E.V.K.S. Elangovan had "consciously violated" the code that came into force on March 1.

(6603) Chennai: The State unit of the Congress suffered a setback on Thursday, when its trade union wing, the Indian National Trade Union Congress (INTUC), dissociated itself from the party and entered into an alliance with the All-India Anna Dravida Munnetra Kazhagam for the Assembly elections. The INTUC will contest in two constituencies on the AIADMK symbol, Two Leaves. The agreement was signed between the AIADMK and the INTUC in the presence of Chief Minister Jayalalithaa, INTUC president P.L. Subbiah and its general secretary G. Kalan.

(6604) Pondicherry: A. M. Krishnamoorthy, lone legislator of the Bharatiya Janata party, resigned from the Pondicherry Assembly on Thursday.

11-03-2006

(6605) Hyderabad: The Telugu Desam Party on Friday dared the Government to order a probe or direct a forensic expert to examine the files pertaining to Sripadasagar project in its possession to prove whether they were genuine or not.

(6606) Hyderabad: Telangana Rashtra Samithi members staged a walkout in the Assembly on Friday protesting against the neglect of minor irrigation tanks in Telangana. "Funds are being allotted only for major irrigation projects that too in other regions," G. Vijayarama Rao alleged while leading the walkout.

(6607) Nizamabad : Vice-president, political affairs committee of the Telangana Rashtra Samithi, A.S. Posetty has maintained that the desertions by some leaders from TRS will not affect its future. Only a few leaders from Armoor who are non-entities deserted the party with a selfish motive keeping an on the coming local body elections. All important leaders in the constituency still are sailing with the party.

(6608) Hyderabad: The election of Telugu Desam legislator Rajendra Pratap Bhanj Deo from Salur (ST) Assembly constituency in Vizianagaram district was set aside by the Andhra Pradesh High Court on Friday and it was declared that P. Rajanna Dora would be the MLA. Mr. Rajanna Dora of the Congress had lost to Mr. Bhanj Deo in the 2004 Assembly elections by a margin of 2,493 votes. Mr. Bhanj Deo secured 48,580 votes against Mr. Dora's 46,087.

(6609) New Delhi: The Election Commission on Friday slapped a notice on Samajwadi Party general secretary Amar Singh on a complaint - referred to it by President A.P.J. Abdul Kalam - seeking his disqualification from the Rajya Sabha on the ground that he is holding an office of profit. He is the Chairman of the Uttar Pradesh Development Council.

(6610) Islamabad : National Conference leader Omar Abdullah on Friday said the time has come for India to respond to Pakistan President Pervez Musharraf's proposals to resolve the Kashmir issue. "Gen. Musharraf has taken Pakistan away from the maximalist position on Kashmir. New Delhi should meet him somewhere if not at least half way," Mr. Farooq, who is here in connection with the conference organised by Pugwash, told The Hindu after an hour-long session with the General. "Kashmir is a political dispute, though it has military and economic dimension. It requires a political solution."

(6611) New Delhi: The Communist Party of India (Marxist) on Friday warned the United Progressive Alliance Government that the consequences of its stand on the Iran nuclear issue would be serious. Due to "capitulation to the United States," India now stood with the "bellicose, illegal stand" of the Bush administration, it said. On the decision of the International Atomic Energy Agency board meeting to shift the Iran issue to the U.N. Security Council, the Polit Bureau said the matter was now outside the IAEA's ambit.

(6612) Chennai: The Pattali Makkal Katchi will contest in 31 constituencies in the Assembly elections as part of the Democratic Progressive Alliance.The agreement was signed by Dravida Munnetra Kazhagam president M. Karunanidhi and PMK founder S. Ramadoss at the DMK headquarters here on Friday.

(6613) Chennai: Marumalarchi Dravida Munnetra Kazhagam (MDMK) general secretary Vaiko's decision to join the All India Anna Dravida Munnetra Kazhagam alliance was an "act of treachery," senior Congress leader M. Veerappa Moily said here on Friday.

12-03-2006

(6614) Hyderabad: The Telugu Desam Party has claimed that the State Government has lined up proposals to handover 70,000 acres of urban land, mostly in Hyderabad, to private parties against the spirit of Government Orders issued during its tenure keeping in view suggestions of the High Court.

(6615) Hyderabad: The Congress Legislature Party (CLP) has accused the Telugu Desam of attempting to stall the development of Telangana region on the basis of fake documents of the Sripadasagar Project tenders in the Assembly.

(6616) Kottayam: Senior Congress leader and Union Minister for Overseas Indian Affairs Vayalar Ravi said on Saturday that only those parties which respected the Congress leadership would be allowed to have a trek with the UDF.

(6617) Thiruvananthapuram: The Democratic Indira Congress (Karunakaran) on Saturday maintained that it would retain its identity and contest the Assembly polls under the symbol allotted to it by the Election Commission. The party set March 20 as deadline for the wrapping up the formula being worked out by the Indian Union Muslim League as an intermediary. The party has in effect rejected the suggestion that it contest the election under the Congress party's election symbol. President of the DIC K. Muraleedharan, however, was categorical about his party retaining its identity. He appreciated the IUML leaders' mediatory efforts and did not want to discourage them, but made it clear that the dialogues could not go on endlessly.

(6618) Guwahati: The Asom Gana Parishad (AGP) on Saturday reached an understanding on sharing of seats with the two Left parties - the Communist Party of India (Marxist) and the Communist Party of India. T he Opposition parties failed to forge any alliance. The AGP has agreed not to put up candidates in seven seats where the CPI(M) will be contesting but the two parties would contest each other in nine seats. The CPI(M) will release the list of candidates for all 16 seats on Sunday. The AGP has agreed with the CPI not to put up candidates in seven seats to be contested by that party. However, there would be friendly contests in two seats. The AGP has agreed to back Autonomous State Demand Committee candidates in all five seats in the two hill districts - Karbi Anglong and North Cachar Hills - in return for support in other seats.

(6619) Lucknow: Describing BSP as a "pariah" in the contemporary politics, the Uttar Pradesh Chief Minister, Mulayam Singh Yadav, on Saturday admitted that his Samajwadi Party's alliance with it in 1993 was a big "political mistake". "SP's alliance was the flashpoint in the emergence of BSP in the Indian politics, which in hindsight looks like a blunder," he said in the State Assembly during discussion on the budget.

(6620) New Delhi: The India-U.S. nuclear deal came in for sharp criticism in Parliament on Saturday with the Left parties accusing the Government of bartering the country's independent foreign policy for an unequal treaty, while the Bharatiya Janata Party (BJP) said India had emerged a junior partner of the U.S. Both the parties pressed for evolving a political consensus on the nuclear and other agreements reached with the U.S.. They wanted the Agriculture Knowledge Initiative and the CEO's Agreements to be tabled. In Rajya Sabha, CPI-Marxist member Nilotpal Basu described Prime Minister Manmohan Singh's reply to the clarifications as "disappointing" adding that it did not address "serious concerns."

(6621) New Delhi: Exuding confidence that the CPI(M)-led Left Front would return to power in the State, West Bengal Chief Minister Buddhadeb Bhattacharjee on Saturday described the Opposition as "a confused arrangement." Without referring to any party, Mr. Bhattacharjee said unlike the United Progressive Alliance or the National Democratic Front, the Left Front was a product of years of struggle of anti-Congress forces that came to power for the first time in 1977 and have stayed since then.

(6622) New Delhi: The Lok Jan Shakti Party on Friday decided to field Ranjan Prasad Yadav for the biennial elections to the Rajya Sabha from Bihar.

(6623) New Delhi: The Nationalist Congress Party's MLA from Badarpur, Ramvir Singh Bidhuri, on Saturday said he had suggested to the Union Urban Development Ministry that private developers be allowed to promote residential and commercial areas to meet the housing and other needs of the Capital. Similarly mixed land use should be permitted under various categories on 60-foot and 80-foot roads in residential areas.

(6624) New Delhi: Warning the government of another "mass suicide" like those of farmers in Andhra Pradesh and Maharashtra if the interests of small shopkeepers in the Capital were overlooked, the BJP on Saturday said rendering 'rehri-patri' owners out of the pavement and sealing of shops in residential areas would lead to "deaths by the dozen" here.

(6625) Pondicherry: The Pondicherry unit of the Bharatiya Janata Party on Saturday requested the Election Commission to set up flying squads in all constituencies to keep vigil on distribution of money and materials to voters in the Union Territory.

(6626) Pondicherry: The general secretary of the All-India Congress Committee, B.K. Hariprasad, MP, has said that Pondicherry had made progress in the last five years because of the unique and unparalleled welfare measures the Congress government had evolved and implemented in the Union Territory.

(6627) Jaipur: Communist Party of India leader and AITUC general secretary Gurudas Dasgupta MP led a delegation here on Thursday to meet Rajasthan Chief Minister Vasundhara Raje. Mr.Dasgupta, who was here to address a State-level rally of AITUC members and workers during the day, discussed the issues of minimum wages, implementation of labour laws in industrial units, rights of the female workforce, equal pay for equal work and privatisation, with Ms.Raje in the Rajasthan Assembly premises.

(6628) Chennai: The need for social reforms should be kept in mind while tackling issues of economic development, Dravida Munnetra Kazhagam president M. Karunanidhi said on Friday. "Without social uplift and self-respect, any amount of economic development is meaningless.

This will not add pride to such an economic development," Mr. Karunanidhi said releasing a publication in Tamil on Indian economy.

(6629) Chennai: The Marumalarchi Dravida Munnetra Kazhagam wants to continue in the Congress-led United Progressive Alliance at the Centre. But if the UPA takes any other decision, the party will take appropriate steps. Addressing a press conference after the party's general council meeting here on Saturday, MDMK general secretary Vaiko said leaders of the Congress and other UPA constituents had expressed different views on his party continuing in the alliance, after it switched over to the All-India Anna Dravida Munnetra Kazhagam front.

(6630) Chennai: Makkal Thamizh Desam founder S. Kannappan has decided to merge his party with the DMK. The merger meeting will be held here on March 14, he said at a press conference here on Saturday. In the rival front, an All-India Forward Bloc delegation, led by its general secretary Biswas and State unit chief and actor Karthik, called on Chief Minister and AIADMK leader Jayalalithaa at her residence this evening. While expressing their support to her alliance, they initiated discussions on a tie-up, an AIADMK release said.

13-03-2006

(6631) Hyderabad: The Congress Legislature Party has hit back at the Telugu Desam by coming out with an 11-page note highlighting the "irregularities" committed by the previous Government in the irrigation sector.

(6632) Hyderabad: The CPI (M) State Committee has demanded amendments to the Act passed last year on private medical colleges in view of the apprehensions expressed by a large number of doctors over use of its provisions. Party secretary B.V. Raghavulu raised this in a letter to Chief Minister Y.S. Rajasekhara Reddy on Sunday.

(6633) Bangalore: Deputy Chief Minister B.S. Yediyurappa and the 11 other Ministers from the Bharatiya Janata Party (BJP) will have to straddle both administration and party cadre's expectations, and remain open to performance audit by the party, the former President of the BJP M. Venkaiah Naidu said on Sunday.

(6634) Bangalore: The United Progressive Alliance (UPA) Government had proved to be a "failure" on all fronts, and was placing itself in an increasingly vulnerable position by pursuing a blatant vote-bank politics, the former BJP President M. Venkaiah Naidu said here on Sunday. He told presspersons after a two-day deliberations with the BJP Ministers and with party office-bearers and cadre that the Congress would badly in three of the five States going to the polls- Assam, Pondicherry and Kerala. The other two States being Tamil Nadu and West Bengal.

(6635) Bidar: Congress President Sonia Gandhi had agreed to all the demands of Janata Dal (S) President H.D. Deve Gowda in order to save the Dharam Singh Government, Karnataka Pradesh Congress Committee President M. Mallikarjun Kharge said here on Saturday. He told party workers that the Mr. Deve Gowda had sought the portfolios of Home and Water Resources. Ms. Gandhi had also agreed to form a coordination committee to settle issues between the coalition partners. The Congress had nominated senior leaders C.K. Jaffer Sharief, Shamanur Shivashankarappa and D.B. Chandre Gowda to the committee.However, the JD (S) did not nominate its leaders to the committee. Mr. Deve Gowda and his son H.D. Kumaraswamy were jealous of the growth of the Congress. They could not stomach its good performance in the zilla and taluk panchayat elections. They brought down the Government deliberately, he alleged.

(6636) Panaji: The Bharatiya Janata Party (BJP) has said that the reluctance on the part of the State Government to order a judicial probe into last week's riots in South Goa's twin towns of Curchorem-Sanvordem was understandable because its outcome will expose the shortcomings of the Government in protecting the people, including the minorities. The former Chief Minister and Leader of the Opposition in the Legislative Assembly Manohar Parrikar has said that the fact that the ruling Congress demanded a judicial probe proves that the administration has failed to tackle the law and order situation.

(6637) Kannur : Senior Congress leader and Union Minister for Overseas Indian Affairs Vayalar Ravi said the question of the Democratic Indira Congress (Karunakaran)'s entry into the United Democratic Front (UDF) would be brought into the agenda of the Congress leadership only if the breakaway party conveyed its wishes and preferences.

(6638) Kozhikode: Senior Congress party leader and Union Minister for Overseas Indian Affairs, Vayalar Ravi, has said that the anti-incumbency factor against the United Democratic Front (UDF) Government would be negligible considering the development activities implemented under the leadership of Chief Minister Oommen Chandy in the State.

(6639) Malappuram: The Indian Union Muslim League (IUML) will step up its efforts to woo the Democratic Indira Congress (Karunakaran) into the United Democratic Front (UDF). The IUML State working committee, which met at party chief Syed Mohammedali Shihab Thangal's house at Panakkad near here on Sunday, decided to continue talks with the DIC(K) more earnestly.

(6640) Kolkata: The CPI (ML-Liberation) will contest 26 seats in the West Bengal Assembly polls, said its general secretary Dipankar Bhattacharjee on Sunday. The alleged failure of the Left Front Government in improving the condition of the poor and containing starvation deaths will be highlighted during its campaign, he said. The party would also contest the coming elections in Tamil Nadu, Kerala, Pondicherry and Assam.

(6641) Lucknow : Simultaneous "yatras" to be led by the Bharatiya Janata Party president Rajnath Singh and Leader of the Opposition L.K. Advani are to begin in different directions across the country from April 6 for nearly five weeks till May 9. Commenting on the political situation in Uttar Pradesh over the last few days since the Varanasi blasts that resulted in both the Congress and the Samajwadi Party leaderships sounding positive about supporting each other in dealing with the situation, Mr. Singh said, "it is good for us [the BJP] if the two parties [Congress and SP] cooperate." He added that the ground situation for the BJP had improved since the last Assembly elections in the State when the BJP's electoral fortunes had dipped sharply.

(6642) Kolkata: Urging the people to ensure the Left Front's victory for the seventh time in a row and better its record of six successive terms, veteran Marxist leader Jyoti Basu said here on Sunday that it would continue to safeguard the workers' right to strike, "which should be invoked, however, only as a last resort." "Unlike [in] other parts of the country, we do not employ the police to break up strikes or hartals; we have granted State employees the right to strike but this should be an alternative only if talks with the Government [on the issues at hand] fail to make any headway," Mr. Basu, senior member of the Polit Bureau of the

Communist Party of India (Marxist) and former West Bengal Chief Minister, said. Chief Minister Buddhadeb Bhattacharjee said the Government did not favour removing hawkers from the streets without providing them alternative means of employment. "Pedestrians as well as hawkers should be allowed to use these public spaces, and the police would ensure that the former are not inconvenienced."

(6643) New Delhi: The Bharatiya Janata Party has charged the Delhi Government and the Municipal Corporation of Delhi with deliberating trying to uproot five lakh shopkeepers in the Capital. If the two administrative wings had the will, a majority of such outlets could be regularised and issued licenses. At a joint press conference here over the weekend, Delhi BJP president Harsh Vardhan, Leader of the Opposition in the Standing Committee Vijender Gupta and Leader of Opposition in the MCD House Subhash Arya said on one hand the Congress leaders by creating an uproar in the Assembly and the MCD wanted to demonstrate that they were the well wishers of small shopkeepers and rehri patri shopkeepers, but on the other hand the civic body was deliberately not going to court on the issue.

(6644) Pondicherry : Chairperson of the all India Mahila Congress Committee Rita Bahuguna Joshi has said that the five years of Congress rule in Pondicherry had seen advances in empowerment of women, enhancement of their literacy and also in implementing unique schemes making Pondicherry a model State.

(6645) Chandigarh: The Shiromani Akali Dal president, Parkash Singh Badal has urged Prime Minister, Manmohan Singh to intervene and put an end to the humiliation and harassment of the November 1984 anti-Sikh riots' victims at the hands of the Punjab Government.In a letter to the Prime Minister, the copy of which was distributed to the media here on Sunday, Mr. Badal said that the affected families have chosen a path of agitation and warned that if timely action was not taken, the situation could take a serious turn. Mr Badal demanded that all those who had applied for the red cards must be compensated immediately as announced by the Union Government. He also demanded that the date for filing claims be extended. In addition, guidelines must be issued for non-red cardholders where some other genuine documents should be accepted.

(6646) Jaipur: A delegation of Members of Parliament belonging to the Communist Party of India (Marxist), which toured Kota in Rajasthan on Saturday on a fact-finding mission in the wake of attacks on Christian institutions in the area by the radical Hindu organisations, has termed the attacks "unprovoked". "The Sangh Parivar elements are using the controversial book as a convenient tool to carry out a systematic campaign against the minority groups," said Suresh Kurup. "We will raise the issue in Parliament and also brief our party and the Central Government on the situation here," he said.

(6647) Lucknow: The BJP on Sunday demanded immediate dismissal of the Mulayam Singh Yadav Government in Uttar Pradesh in the wake of twin bomb blasts in temple town Varanasi, saying it had failed to protect lives of innocent people. "The BJP will support the Centre if it dismisses the Mulayam Government which has failed to protect lives of innocent people," party President Rajnath Singh told a meeting of party workers here. He, however, attacked the Congress charging it with sowing seeds of another division of the country by pursuing "minority appeasement policy".

(6648) Chennai: The Communist Party of India on Sunday scotched rumours that it would turn to the All-India Anna Dravida Munnetra Kazhagam, in view of "non-allocation of seats to match its strength and political influence" by the Dravida Munnetra Kazhagam, which heads the Democratic Progressive Alliance. The DMK has allotted only 10 seats to the CPI for contesting the Assembly elections. A senior CPI leader told The Hindu here that the party was firm in its stand to enter the fray as a DPA constituent.

(6649) Chennai: The Communist Party of India, which supports the UPA Government from outside, has criticised Marumalarchi Dravida Munnetra Kazhagam general secretary Vaiko for forging an alliance with the All India Anna Dravida Munnetra Kazhagam for the Assembly elections. CPI national secretary D. Raja told The Hindu here on Sunday that by his action, Mr. Vaiko had "negated all his political and ethical positions." The CPI criticism comes at a time when Mr. Vaiko has expressed his desire to continue in the Congress-led United Progressive Alliance. While refraining from commenting on the MDMK's stand, Mr. Raja said Mr. Vaiko could not justify his decision to align with the AIADMK.

(6650) Chennai: The alliance between the State branch of the Indian National Trade Union Congress (INTUC) and the All India Anna Dravida

Munnetra Kazhagam for the Assembly election is "against the decision of the working committee and political policy of the INTUC," union president G. Sanjeeva Reddy said. In a letter to Tamil Nadu Congress Committee president M. Krishnasswamy (a copy of which was released to the press), Mr. Reddy said the INTUC's Working Committee decided to support candidates fielded by the Congress in the Assembly election. If any INTUC leader wanted to contest, they should do so only on a Congress ticket. "This decision of the Working Committee applies to INTUC leaders in State branches as well," he said.

(6651) Tirunelveli : The All-India Forward Bloc would contest the forthcoming Tamil Nadu Assembly elections on its own, its general secretary Deva Pratab Biswas has announced. Addressing the party's State conference held here on Sunday, Mr. Biswas said that the AIFB was prepared to contest the elections on its own and State unit president M. Karthik would lead the party in the campaign.

14-03-2006

(6652) Hyderabad: The Communist Party of India (CPI) is in favour of a constitutional amendment to provide for ratification by Parliament of any agreement on India's foreign policy. It is opposed to the recent nuclear deal reached with the US. At a press conference here on Monday, party's national secretary Suravaram Sudhakar Reddy, MP, said the CPI opposed the Government's foreign policy as it was "pro-US" and would be harmful for the country in the long run.

(6653) Tirupati: The CPI(M) has warned the State Government to watch its steps that are going in the same path trodden by the previous Telugu Desam Party (TDP) regime. The party was extremely critical of the Government for its 'indifference' to the pressing needs of the unorganised sector.

(6654) New Delhi: The Bharatiya Janata Party announced on Monday that the simultaneous "yatras" to be taken out by party president Rajnath Singh and Leader of the Opposition L.K. Advani "would not touch the five States going to polls in the next two months." This reverses Mr. Advani's March 8 statement when he announced the decision to go on these "yatras." He had then said that the "yatras" would touch all five States where elections are scheduled. The BJP was a political party and politics would not be kept out, he had added. It seems that the party leadership has concluded that mobilisation for "yatras" in the midst of a hectic poll campaign would be counter-productive.

(6655) Gulbarga: President of the All India Progressive Janata Dal (AIPJD) C.M. Ibrahim, the former Deputy Chief Minister Siddaramaiah and other leaders of the party will begin their State tour from the Hyderabad-Karnataka region in April to strengthen the party at the grassroots. Addressing presspersons here on Monday, Mr. Siddaramaiah and Mr. Ibrahim said that after completing the first-leg of the tour, covering the Hyderabad-Karnataka region and the Mumbai-Karnataka region, they will visit south Karnataka. Mr. Siddaramaiah and Mr. Ibrahim said there is scope for a third force in the State after the Janata Dal (Secular) drifted away from its secular policies and aligned with communal forces led by the Bharatiya Janata Party (BJP). People are now looking towards the AIPJD for an alternative with the Congress becoming weak owing to squabbling and losing power.

(6656) Kollam: F ormer State president of the Bharatiya Janata Party C.K. Padmanabhan has said that a surfeit of coalition politics in Kerala has resulted in the general development of the State suffering heavily.

(6657) New Delhi: The Communist Party of India (Marxist) has condemned the decision of the United Democratic Front (UDF) Government in Kerala to refer the SNC Lavalin case to the Central Bureau of Investigation (CBI) and termed it as a "patently political move." Taking note of the development, the party's Central Committee said on Monday that the decision taken on the eve of the Assembly election was a "patently political move" to implicate CPI(M) State secretary Pinarayi Vijayan, who is also a Polit Bureau member.

(6658) New Delhi: Ahead of the forthcoming Assembly elections in five States, Congress President Sonia Gandhi on Monday reconstituted the party's Central Election Committee (CEC), bringing in four new faces while retaining seven existing members. This is the first reconstitution of the CEC since the Lok Sabha election in 2004. Mrs. Gandhi will head the panel and the new entrants are her political secretary Ahmed Patel, former Union Minister Mohsina Kidwai, Union Minister of State Oscar Fernandes and special invitee to the Congress Working Committee Ashok Ram. Existing members who have been included in the reconstituted set-up are

Defence Minister Pranab Mukherjee, Union Human Resources Development Minister Arjun Singh, former Kerala Chief Minister A. K. Antony, Union Tourism & Culture Minister Ambika Soni, former Union Ministers Margaret Alva and M. L. Fotedar and former Uttar Pradesh Chief Minister Ram Naresh Yadav. The CEC decides on candidatures based on the recommendations made by State Election Committees. The previous CEC was constituted on January 20, 2004. Those dropped from the panel are Union Ministers Mahavir Prasad and Sushil Kumar Shinde, Maharashtra Pradesh Congress Committee president Prabha Rau, former Union Minister L. P. Sahi and former Lok Sabha member Noor Bano.

(6659) New Delhi: The Communist Party of India (Marxist) on Monday said it would make an overall assessment of the political situation after the April-May Assembly elections and chalk out its future course of action. "Whether it is the airport privatisation, foreign direct investment in retail trade or the foreign policy, on a number of issues the Government is going ahead despite the opposition of the Left. The Central Committee decided to make an overall assessment of the political situation after the Assembly elections and to chalk out its future course of action," party general secretary Prakash Karat told a press conference at the end of its three-day Polit Bureau/Central Committee meeting. Endorsing the Polit Bureau stand on the United Progressive Alliance government on various issues, the Central Committee said the party must take them up "more assertively" and work with other parties who agree with it, both inside and outside Parliament.

(6660) Kolkata: Trinamool Congress chief Mamata Banerjee on Monday said her party has kept 53 seats for the Congress for the coming Assembly elections. The Trinamool would contest in 193 out of the 294 seats. Eight seats have been allotted for the smaller constituents of the Trinamool-led Paschim Banga Ganatrantik Front. Surprised by Ms. Banerjee's announcement, State unit president of the Bharatiya Janata Party, which leads the National Democratic Alliance (of which the Trinamool is a constituent) Tathagata Roy told The Hindu : " Her announcement is a unilateral one. It has come at a time when seat-sharing talks between her and our leader Arun Jaitley are still on." Ms. Banerjee's decision to set aside seats for the Congress suggests that the leadership of the two parties have been able to reach an agreement to avoid a split in the anti-Left votes even without the Trinamool breaking away from the NDA - a condition laid down by the Congress earlier for any understanding between the two. The deal between the two parties was clinched during recent talks between Ms. Banerjee and Margaret Alva, AICC general secretary in-charge of West Bengal.

(6661) New Delhi: The Lok Sabha on Monday witnessed turmoil after Communist Party of India (Marxist) members criticised the move of Bharatiya Janata Party leader L.K. Advani to take out a yatra. Describing the proposed yatra as "diabolic," Basudeb Acharia of the CPI (M) said a similar yatra by Mr. Advani in 1990 had created a communal frenzy and there were riots in a number of places. The BJP members were quick to retort with some stating that it was a party programme. Led by Vijay Kumar Malhotra, they raised the pitch leading to turmoil. Suresh Kurup (CPI-M) raised the issue of attacks against a mission. He said a five-member delegation of party MPs had visited Kota where State BJP leaders were subjecting the Emmanuel Mission to harassment. BJP MPs, especially from Rajasthan, were up on their feet and said the CPI (M) MPs were defending a Mission, which had published a controversial book, Haqeeqat. They also charged that the CPI (M) move was with an eye on the Kerala elections. Mr. Kurup said the party was not justifying what had appeared in the book and that action should be taken if it contained anything unlawful. The BJP, he said, was using the book as an excuse to attack the Mission.

(6662) New Delhi: Former Madhya Pradesh Chief Minister and expelled BJP leader Uma Bharti has written to former Delhi Chief Minister Madan Lal Khurana asking him to join her during the "Janadesh Rally" to be held at the Ramlila Grounds here on March 21.

(6663) Pondicherry: The Bharatiya Janata Party (BJP) leader Venkaiah Naidu has said his party is on a comeback trail what with the Congress-led UPA Government losing public support. Addressing newsmen here on Monday, Mr Naidu said the BJP would contest the elections on its own in Tamil Nadu, Pondicherry, Kerala and Assam. The party would work out an alliance with Trinamool Congress in West Bengal. He said all major parties were distancing themselves from the UPA and the continuation of MDMK in the alliance was also in doubt.

(6664) Jaipur: The Communist Party of India (Marxist) has taken umbrage at the comments of Rajasthan Social Welfare Minister Madan Dilawar on the visit of a team of Members of Parliament from the party to

Kota this weekend to enquire into the attack on Christian institutions there. The party on Monday demanded action by the Rajasthan Governor against the Minister for use of "unparliamentary language against the Members of Parliament".

(6665) Jaipur: Congress general secretary Ashok Gehlot has drawn the attention of the Rajasthan Chief Minister to the recent crop damage due to the unseasonal rains and hailstorm in the State as well as the problems faced by the farmers in selling mustard at the minimum support price (MSP).

(6666) Lucknow: Lamenting that party leaders were not taking interest in development of their areas, Samajwadi Party president Mulayam Singh Yadav on Monday exhorted them to gear up for the next Vidhan Sabha elections, which he termed as "very tough" and "important" for the party. "Most of the recommendations of the MPs, MLAs and MLCs pertain to transfers of officials and not about development,"Mr. Yadav said addressing a meeting of the SP districts and city chiefs here. He regretted that these public representatives failed to give the names of 10 villages from their respective areas for the integrated rural development scheme. Only 12 districts had sent the names of the villages.

(6667) Chennai: State secretary of the Communist Party of India (CPI) D. Pandian said here on Monday that the "anger" among cadres over non-allocation of more than 10 seats to the party had subsided and they would work wholeheartedly for the success of the Democratic Progressive Alliance in the Assembly elections.

(6668) New Delhi: The All India Anna Dravida Munnetra Kazhagam (AIADMK) members in the Rajya Sabha staged a walkout on Monday to protest against an all-party decision in Kerala to enact legislation prohibiting raising the water level in the Mullaperiyar dam from 136 to 142 feet by the Tamil Nadu government.

15-03-2006

(6669) Hyderabad: Leader of Opposition N. Chandrababu Naidu has alleged that a 'systematic conspiracy' was hatched to knock away Rs. 400 crores by enhancing the project cost of Sripadasagar (Yellampallly) irrigation project.

(6670) Hyderabad: Telangana Rashtra Samiti (TRS) members staged a walkout in the Assembly on Tuesday accusing the Government of neglecting Telangana in setting up thermal power stations.

(6671) Vijayawada: The Communist Party of India (Marxist) is not opposed to construction of the Polavaram project, but wants alternative proposals to be explored first in order to minimise inundation of large tracts of land and displacement of many people.

(6672) Thiruvananthapuram: The Congress on Tuesday deputed its Working Committee member Veerappa Moily for negotiations with the Democratic Indira Congress (Karunakaran) with the Indian Union Muslim League (IUML) as the mediator. Mr. Moily who arrived here on Monday lost no time in catching up with the latest position by meeting the IUML leaders P.K. Kunhalikutty and E.T. Mohammed Basheer. He later attended a meeting of United Democratic Front (UDF) leaders.

(6673) Bangalore: The Congress will not be fielding a second candidate for the fourth Rajya Sabha seat from the State, for which biennial elections are being held on March 28, the former Chief Minister N. Dharam Singh said here on Tuesday. Since the Congress does not have the required number of votes and it cannot bank on the independents or count on the support of "friendly parties," the party will not field a second candidate.

(6674) New Delhi: The Varanasi blasts were the "trigger" that led the Leader of the Opposition, L.K. Advani, to announce two simultaneous `yatras' to mobilise public opinion against "minorityism," but the "idea" that the party should use the `yatra' mechanism preceded the blasts. "The idea had been at the back of my mind earlier before the Varanasi blasts," Mr. Advani told reporters on Tuesday. Asked why there were terrorist attacks on the Akshardham temple in Gujarat and the Raghunath temple in Jammu when he was the

(6675) New Delhi: The leader of the Opposition and former External Affairs Minister, Jaswant Singh, on Tuesday said there was a "crippling deficiency" in the Government's foreign policy. Initiating a discussion in the Rajya Sabha on the functioning of the Ministry of External Affairs, he said the Government must make a choice between idealism and realism. "India is the only country in the world which still has unsettled borders, and that does shackle India internationally. Launching a scathing attack on the Bharatiya Janata Party for the stand taken by Mr. Singh, Communist Party of India (Marxist) leader Sitaram Yechury said that while criticising the foreign policy, the Leader of the Opposition had not taken a stand and outlined how the policy framework should be. "Realism cannot change with which side of the House you are on. The Left parties engage with the existing reality in order to bring about a change."He said the Government talked of a convergence of interest with the U.S., but one could wonder what kind of interest the country could share with the U.S., which had butchered thousands of people all over the world in the name of regime change. "Surrendering to U.S. hegemony cannot be called realism. After the demise of [the] bi-polar cold war, there ought to be movement of international relations towards multi-polarity, which the U.S. tries to convert to uni-polarity." India must move towards a multi-polar world and not succumb to uni-polarity of the U.S., which was the hallmark of "enlightened national interest."

(6676) New Delhi: Union Home Minister Shivraj Patil on Tuesday urged political parties to think over the decision to take out Rath Yatras that could divide society and left it to the judgment of those who have decided to embark on it. Making an appeal in the Lok Sabha, he said taking out such yatras exerted pressure on the police in maintaining law and order. Everybody got affected if any untoward incident happened. However, Mr. Patil made no reference to the proposed twin yatras Bharatiya Janata Party leader L.K. Advani announced after the Varanasi bomb blasts. The Home Minister's observation came during his response to a calling attention motion by Basudeb Acharia (CPI-M) on the alleged brutal attack and killing of tribal people in Kalinga Nagar in Orissa in January. He said taking out Rath Yatras with the ashes of those killed had to be avoided.

(6677) New Delhi: The Communist Party of India (Marxist) has urged the Government not to take a unilateral decision on the Delhi and Mumbai airports privatisation. It demanded that the management handover be "kept in abeyance," pending the report of the tripartite committee formed following the agitation by Airports Authority of India (AAI) employees.In a letter to Prime Minister Manmohan Singh, CPI (M) general secretary Prakash Karat said the agitation was withdrawn following Dr. Singh's appeal and an assurance from the Civil Aviation Minister. However, no meeting of the committee had been held so far. It has to submit its report in three months.

(6678) Kolkata: Rebuffed by the "unilateral" decision of the Trinamool Congress, its partner in the National Democratic Alliance (NDA), on seat adjustments with the Congress for the coming Assembly elections in West Bengal, the State BJP unit took stock of the sudden turn of eventsat a meetinghere on Tuesday. The meeting was held against the backdrop of signs of strains developing in relations between the two NDA constituents less than five weeks before the first of the five-phase elections in the State begins on April 17. State BJP leaders are peeved over the manner in which Trinamool leader Mamata Banerjee made public on Monday the Trinamool's decision to set aside 23 seats for the BJP when "one-to-one talks are underway between Ms.Banerjee and Arun Jaitley, the BJP's central observer for the State." The Trinamool leader, however, has maintained that the doors are open for further seat adjustments with both the BJP and the Congress. "We have been saying that the Congress would like to have seat adjustments with the Trinamool but this will be difficult for as long as the latter remains aligned to the BJP," working president of the West Bengal Pradesh Committee, Pradip Bhattacharya, said.

(6679) New Delhi: Warning that any attempt by the Delhi Jal Board to raise water charges in the Capital would be opposed tooth and nail, Nationalist Congress Party MLA Ramvir Singh Bidhuri on Tuesday said it would be criminal to indulge in such an exercise when there was a public outcry against severe water shortage in the city.

(6680) New Delhi: Delhi Pradesh Congress Committee president Ram Babu Sharma and Lok Sabha members from Delhi on Tuesday urged Union Minister for Urban Development Jaipal Reddy to initiate steps immediately to regularise unauthorised colonies and expand the "Lal Dora" areas of villages in order to meet the needs of the expanding population.

(6681) Chennai: The Bharatiya Janata Party on Tuesday criticised the Dravida Munnetra Kazhagam for remaining silent on the Mullaperiyar dam issue. Referring to the Kerala move to adopt a law that would overrule the Supreme Court judgment, BJP national secretary in-charge of Tamil Nadu unit, Bandaru Dattatreya, told reporters: "Karunanidhi , should have rushed to New Delhi and met Prime Minister Manmohan Singh instead of remaining here. He should have persuaded the Prime Minister to exert pressure on the Kerala Government."

(6682) Chennai: Makkal Thamizh Desam, floated by former All India Anna Dravida Munnetra Kazhagam Minister S. Kannappan, merged with the Dravida Munnetra Kazhagam at a function here on Tuesday.

16-03-2006

(6683) Hyderabad: The Telugu Desam Party on Wednesday said that the A. Gopal Rao Commission's enquiry report on the killing of Penukonda legislator Paritala Ravi that it was out of "personal enmity" and not "political animosity" was on expected lines. M.V. Mysoora Reddy, TDP spokesman, told a press conference here that the party knew that the enquiry would only be "eyewash" and that justice would not be done to Paritala's family. It believed that the murder was only "political." The Congress and the Government only wanted a certificate terming it otherwise, he stated.

(6684) Khammam: A delegation of the CPI-ML (New Democracy) leaders who visited the Polavaram project site and some of the villages facing the risk of submersion on Wednesday, said the rehabilitation and resettlement package announced by the government for the project-affected families needed a thorough review.

(6685) Tirupati: The TDP's road show, 'Palle Palle ku Desam', believed to have got underway from Wednesday in the home district of party supremo N. Chandrababu Naidu, was a low-key affair.The programme was conceived to breathe fresh life into the otherwise inert rank and file of the party after the severe drubbing it received in the recent municipal elections. The party high command's Statewide call for a 'Palle Palleku Desam' became a damp squib in Naidu's own home ground due to a marked disinterest and indifference among the district top brass for some reason or other.

(6686) Kolkata: Hopes of forging an anti-Left "mahajot" (grand alliance) for the coming Assembly elections in West Bengal have virtually fizzled out with the Congress deciding on Wednesday to contest, along with its allies, all the 294 seats in the State. The Congress leadership, however, is still willing to give the Trinamool Congress "time" - till the filing of nomination papers - to disassociate itself from the Bharatiya Janata Party if there is to be any electoral understanding with it.

(6687) Thiruvananthapuram: The CPI(M) State secretariat has picked Left Democratic Front (LDF) convener Paloli Mohammed Kutty to lead the Opposition LDF's electoral battle.

(6688) Thiruvananthapuram: The meeting between the Congress Working Committee member Veerappa Moily and Democratic Indira Congress (Karunakaran) president K. Muraleedharan on Wednesday brought the two parties a step close towards cooperation, but a two-hour dialogue between the two only exposed the road blocks that remained to be cleared before a working formula could emerge. The first round of discussion characteristically proved to be a no-win affair, even though Mr. Moily and Mr. Muraleedharan waxed eloquent that they all belonged to the Congress and there was no difficulty in communicating with each other. Mr. Moily performed his brief by informing Mr. Muraleedharan about the Congress stand that the DIC(K) should contest under the party's "hand" symbol. The rest of the issues were mere technicalities that could be sorted out through discussions. According to DIC(K) sources, Mr. Muraleedharan made it clear to Mr. Moily that his party could not surrender on the issue of symbol. He was firm about the DIC(K) contesting on its symbol as allotted by the Election Commission.

(6689) New Delhi: Bahujan Samaj Party founder Kanshi Ram, who has been ailing for some time now, made a public appearance on Wednesday. The occasion was his 72nd birthday. A large number of party workers, MPs, MLAs and supporters gathered at the Talkatora Indoor Stadium to celebrate the day. Mr. Kanshi Ram was offered a birthday cake by party president Mayawati. Addressing the gathering, Ms. Mayawati said the Bharatiya Janata Party helped Mulayam Singh Yadav to form a government by splitting her party. "The BJP helped him form a government in an illegal manner by splitting our party to ensure that I am not able to run the party after Kanshi Ram fell ill," she said.

(6690) Chennai: Janata Party president Subramanian Swamy on Wednesday criticised the Union Government for putting on hold the test-firing of Agni III for the last six months.

(6691) Pondicherry: Pattali Makkal Katchi (PMK) Parliamentary party leader M. Ramadoss has said that he had reiterated the demand for B2 status for Pondicherry while participating in a debate on the motion for grant of funds moved by the Union Home Minister in Parliament on Tuesday.

(6692) Kollam: Revolutionary Socialist Party (RSP) State secretary T.J. Chandrachoodan has said that Left coalitions have no tradition of projecting a Chief Minister candidate and contesting the elections.

17-03-2006

(6693) Hyderabad: Is the Telengana Rashtra Samithi (TRS) planning to bid adieu to the United Progressive Alliance (UPA) coalition at Centre? This was what had been indicated to the State Bharatiya Janata Party (BJP) leaders by Union Minister of State for Rural Development and TRS leader A. Narendra when he met them at the BJP office here on Thursday. According to BJP sources, Mr. Narendra wanted the BJP central leadership to come out openly in support of Telangana State at the earliest. He told them that such a move would provide leeway for TRS to quit since the Congress was not coming forward to create a separate State. Besides, it would also strengthen the NDA at the national level. He was also believed to have mentioned about growing Telangana sentiment and criticism that TRS-Congress combine was causing delay in the formation of Telangana.

(6694) Hyderabad: TDP president N. Chandrababu Naidu on Thursday criticised that the Government delayed taking action against Osmania University Inspector and Sub-Inspector who arrested students and professors on the campus on Wednesday while they were celebrating Holi.

(6695) New Delhi: Reacting sharply to his continued neglect by the party and its failure to step in to resolve the various problems faced by the Capital's citizens, former Delhi Chief Minister and senior Bharatiya Janata Party leader Madan Lal Khurana on Thursday accused the party leadership of doing precious little to end the sufferings of lakhs of people affected by the move to seal commercial properties in residential areas across Delhi. Warning that his patience was running out after being ignored by the new BJP leadership in giving him any responsibility, Mr. Khurana told a crowded press conference here that he had written to party president Raj Nath Singh seeking effective steps to retrieve the situation or else allow him to chalk out his own course of action.

(6696) Thiruvananthapuram: Chief Minister Oommen Chandy said here on Thursday that United Democratic Front (UDF) had not considered admission of any new party into the Front.

(6697) Thiruvananthapuram: The Democratic Indira Congress (Karunakaran)'s Parliamentary Board, which met at senior leader K. Karunakaran's residence on Thursday, made it very clear that the party would retain its identity and contest the election on its own symbol. The party indicated that it was at best prepared to consider seat adjustments with the UDF. The Parliamentary Board, headed by Mr. Karunakaran himself, decided to keep in abeyance all discussions on this till its meeting on March 21 soon after the proposed delegates' meeting of the party scheduled to be held on March 20 in Ernakulam.

(6698) New Delhi : The National Democratic Alliance on Thursday presented President A.P.J. Abdul Kalam with a memorandum signed by over 200 MPs for the removal of Election Commissioner Navin Chawla. It questioned his "impartiality" in the light of his alleged links with the Congress.

(6699) New Delhi: Accusing the Delhi Government of taking people, particularly housewives, for a ride, Nationalist Congress Party MLA Ramvir Singh Bidhuri on Thursday said the promised reduction in the prices of Liquid Petroleum Gas (LPG) cylinders had not materialised so far exposing the false claims of the Government. "The Government has failed to allocate funds for important sectors including the welfare of the poor, minorities and Scheduled Castes," he added.

(6700) New Delhi: Bharatiya Janata Party vice-president and former Delhi Chief Minister Sahib Singh Verma on Thursday announced the launch of a weeklong "Dilli Bachao Jansangharsh Yatra" across Outer Delhi to protest against the Delhi Government's "anti-people" policies which have led to demolitions, price-rise, corruption and water and electricity problems in the Capital.

(6701) Jaipur: After a gap of many years, the Rajasthan Pradesh Congress Committee has decided to share the revenue from membership fees with the bloc committees in the State. Nearly 250 hitherto fund-starved bloc committees would be the beneficiaries of the decision. The move is a momentous one as far as the Congress Party's inner democracy and decentralisation of resources are concerned. The amount involved too is no mean sum considering that a 40 per cent share of Rs.1 crore collected as fees for active membership in the party in Rajasthan would mean Rs.40 lakhs to the bloc committees.

(6702) Kolkata: Defence Minister and president of the West Bengal PCC Pranab Mukherjee on Thursday ruled out the possibility of "any secret or covert understanding" with the Trinamool Congress for the coming

Assembly elections. He was reacting to comments by some CPI(M)leaders that even though the "mahajot" (grand alliance) proposal had fallen through, the Congress and the Trinamool had a covert understanding in certain constituencies. "We had wanted seat adjustments or an alignment with the Trinamool Congress but had put before the party the condition that it part ways with the Bharatiya Janata Party [its senior partner in the National Democratic Alliance]. They refused to do this," he said. The All India Congress Committee had a clear policy that it would have no truck with communal parties, Mr. Mukherjee said.

(6703) Chennai: Kerala Irrigation and Water Conservation Bill, 2006, introduced in the Kerala Assembly on Tuesday to nullify the Supreme Court order on Mullaperiyar dam storage level, is not legally binding on Tamil Nadu, according to Janata Party president Subramanian Swamy.

(6704) Chennai: Tamil Nadu should undergo a change so that Tamils can live with self-respect and Tamil language gets pre-eminence, Dravida Munnetra Kazhagam president M.Karunanidhi said here on Thursday. Noting that the State had experienced cultural degeneration in recent times, he said the change should come at least for the sake of reviving the cultural ethos. People should make it a reality, he said, launching the Tamil daily Thamizh Osai, published with the support of the Pattali Makkal Katchi.

(6705) Chennai: The State unit of the Communist Party of India on Thursday urged the Centre to take immediate steps to find a solution to the Mullaperiyar dam issue.

18-03-2006

(6706) Hyderabad : The BJP will extend support if a bill on creation of Telangana was introduced in Parliament by the UPA Government. BJP national secretary Bandaru Dattatreya told a press conference here on Friday that the party was committed to the creation of smaller States for administrative convenience. Referring to TRS leader and Union Minister A. Narendra's visit to the BJP office here, he said "it is a good development. They are seeking the help of BJP." Ruling out the question of a tie-up with the TRS in the local body elections as long as it remained in the UPA, he said the TRS had failed to lobby support for Telangana at national level. He urged the party leaders to change their approach.

(6707) Hyderabad: Leader of the Opposition N. Chandrababu Naidu on Friday handed over to the Assembly Speaker a sealed cover purportedly containing "evidence" on the alleged irregularities in the tendering process of the Sripadasagar project.

(6708) Visakhapatnam: Repolling in the Visakha-I Assembly constituency by-election was postponed due to the total failure of the Government, charged the Telugu Desam party here on Friday.

(6709) New Delhi: The Bharatiya Janata Party has finalised the twin 'yatra' plan. The 'yatra' will see Leader of the Opposition L.K. Advani hurtling through 10 States, covering 5,800 km, over 26 days. Party president Rajnath Singh will cover 12 States over 24 days, logging 5,000 km. While both 'yatras' will start on April 6, Mr. Advani's 'rath' will be flagged off from Dwarka in Gujarat and Mr. Singh's chariot from Puri in Orissa. Details of the 'yatras' - named the Rashtriya Ekatmata Yatra (National Integration Yatra) - were finalised at a meeting of the State unit president, organising secretaries and central office-bearers here on Friday.

(6710) New Delhi: President A.P.J. Abdul Kalam has disqualified Jaya Bachchan of the Samajwadi Party from Rajya Sabha membership with retrospective effect from July 14, 2004 for holding an "office of profit" as Chairperson of the Uttar Pradesh Film Development Council (UPFDC). What makes the issue a political hot potato is that the President has also forwarded to the Election Commission a complaint seeking the disqualification of SP general secretary Amar Singh on the ground that he was holding an "office of profit" while being an MP. The Commission has already sent notice to him.

(6711) Thiruvananthapuram: Terming media reports about a sharp division within the party over candidate selection a deliberate construction by the media, Communist Party of India (Marxist) State secretary Pinarayi Vijayan has said that the party has chosen its final team after due deliberations at various levels. Mr. Vijayan told a news conference here on Thursday that there would be no change in the composition of the team chosen by the State committee and that it was never the practice of the CPI(M) to project any individual as the future Chief Minister when contesting Assembly elections. Asked why V.S. Achuthanandan was kept out of contest after he had performed impressively as Leader of the Opposition, he said it was an undisputed fact that his performance had received widespread approval. He said Mr. Achuthanandan was very much active in the bilateral seat-sharing talks between the CPI(M) and other LDF constituents.

(6712) Bangalore: D.V. Sadananda Gowda, MP for Mangalore, is the new President of the State unit of the Bharatiya Janata Party. He succeeds Jagadish Shettar, who has been appointed Minister for Revenue.

(6713) Palakkad: Several groups of people took out demonstrations and put up banners and posters in support of CPI(M) Polit Bureau member and Leader of the Opposition V.S. Achuthanandan who has been excluded from the list of CPI(M) candidates for the Assembly polls.

(6714) Thiruvananthapuram: The Left Democratic Front (LDF) State committee began a two-day meeting here on Thursday to finalise seat-sharing and campaign formalities. In the absence of any agreement between the coalition partners, the LDF meeting could not get into substantive questions of seat-sharing and had to confine its discussions to poll campaign strategies and finalisation of the manifesto.

(6715) Thiruvananthapuram : The United Democratic Front (UDF) partners on Friday put pressure on the Congress leadership to concede more seats for them during the resumed discussion on seat sharing. Most of the UDF partners appeared to be hedging their positions on the basis of their assessment that the DIC(K) was unlikely to return home.

(6716) New Delhi: The Samajwadi Party on Friday said its disqualified Rajya Sabha member Jaya Bachchan would be re-nominated in the by-election to her seat once it is notified vacant. Party general secretary Amar Singh told mediapersons, "The party is fully behind Ms. Bachchan. She will be re-nominated. She has been disqualified not because of any misdeed but on technical grounds. Only Jaya Bachchan can prevent Jaya Bachchan from entering Parliament."

(6717) New Delhi: The CPI (M) on Friday said the issue of whether a Member of Parliament was holding an office of profit or not should be decided by the legislature and the Election Commission should do so only at the time of polls. The Joint Committee on Offices of Profit, comprising members of both Houses, has notified posts that do not fall in this category, CPI (M) leaders Mohammed Salim and Basudeb Acharia said. He said the

Joint Committee would sort out the matter like how Parliament set up a special panel on the cash-for-query scam or the MPLADS scandal.

(6718) Chennai: Communist Party of India (Marxist) general secretary Prakash Karat has outlined his party's strategy to reach the people of West Bengal ahead of the elections: wear aprons with the party symbol on it!

(6719) New Delhi: Nationalist Congress Party MLA Ramvir Singh Bidhuri on Friday said his party and other like-minded secular parties were ready to join hands with former Delhi Chief Minister Madan Lal Khurana provided he quits the Bharatiya Janata Party and denounces communal politics.

(6720) Chennai: Communist Party of India (Marxist) general secretary Prakash Karat said here on Friday that the party should strive to double its strength in the Tamil Nadu Assembly in the coming elections.

19-03-2006

(6721) Hyderabad: The BJP's offer of support to the Telangana cause was ridiculed by the Congress leadership here on Saturday. Responding to the BJP's latest stand on the issue, Andhra Pradesh Congress Committee president K. Keshava Rao and Telangana Regional Congress Coordination Committee (TRCCC) leader G. Chinna Reddy said on Saturday that the party should first clarify its stand on Telangana. They said the party had not responded to the letter written by the UPA sub-committee. It had kept on the backburner its Kakinada resolution convention extending support to the "one-vote-two-States" concept due the "understanding" between TDP president N. Chandrababu Naidu and former BJP president M. Venkaiah Naidu. If the BJP was honest, it should give its consent to the UPA sub-committee in writing. The AICC was in favour of Telangana and it had formed the sub-committee to explore the options. The Congress leaders said their party had unconditionally supported the formation of Jharkhand, Uttaranchal and Chhattisgarh when the NDA was in power. Asking the Congress to clarify its stand was absurd as it never opposed the concept of smaller States. They accused the BJP of playing politics with the Telangana sentiment.

(6722) Hyderabad: BJP president Rajnath Singh has said the Inter-Services Intelligence modules of Hyderabad were behind all terrorist attacks in the country except Jammu and Kashmir. Addressing a party workers' meeting here on Saturday, Mr. Singh said Hyderabad had emerged as the hub of ISI activities. Unfortunately, the UPA Government at the Centre was soft towards terrorists.

(6723) Khammam : The CPI (ML new Democracy) has asked Maoists to return the weapons snatched away from party dalam members in Bayyaram forests on Thursday.

(6724) Hyderabad: BJP president Rajnath Singh announced here on Saturday that his party's national executive would endorse the eight-year-old resolution adopted by the Andhra Pradesh unit at Kakinada favouring separate Statehood for Telangana.

(6725) Thiruvananthapuram: The Karunakaran-Moily talks on Saturday hit a blind alley over the question of the supporters of Mr. Karunakaran contesting on the Congress election symbol. Even though the Congress Working Committee member Veerappa Moily termed the talks 'cordial,' it was held amidst increasing suspicion among Congress leaders about the designs of the DIC(K) in forging a larger alliance in the event of seat adjustments between the UDF and the former. Addressing mediapersons soon after his talks with Mr. Karunakaran, Mr. Moily said the cloud of misunderstanding was yet to be cleared. He was confident that the differences could be sorted out during the next round of talks to be resumed on Sunday. The comfort level was high and the discussion covered all matters relating to the election, he said. The IUML leader P. K. Kuhalikutty said the talks could not be prolonged indefinitely in view of the elections.

(6726) Mangalore: The President-designate of the State unit of the Bharatiya Janata Party (BJP) D.V. Sadananda Gowda said here on Saturday that the ideology of the Rashtriya Swayamsevak Sangh (RSS) motivated him to work hard in the party.

(6727) Kochi: Bharatiya Janata Party leader Venkaiah Naidu has said the Election Commission should take a pro-active role in initiating action against Parliament members holding offices of profit. Referring to the disqualification of Jaya Bachchan, he said similar action should be taken in the case of Congress president and United Progressive Alliance chairperson, Sonia Gandhi, who was enjoying Cabinet status. About 40 cases have been identified where action could be initiated by the Commission. The BJP would take up the issue, he told a press conference on Saturday.

(6728) Coimbatore: Prakash Karat, general secretary of the Communist Party of India (Marxist), has alleged that "forces within and outside the country" hatched a conspiracy to "weaken and isolate" the Left parties in West Bengal and Kerala, where they were poised to return to power in the coming Assembly elections.

(6729) New Delhi: Buoyed by the open support extended by the BJP to a Bill for the formation of a separate State, the Telangana Rashtra Samiti (TRS) said the declaration almost cleared the way for it. "We wanted the BJP to support it and now party president Rajnath Singh has made his stand clear. With this, almost all political parties in the country have agreed for Telangana and we will move smoothly towards it," TRS chief and Union Minister K. Chandrasekhara Rao told a press conference.

(6730) New Delhi: Delhi Pradesh Congress Committee president Ram Babu Sharma on Saturday held a meeting with Congress Members of Parliament and legislators to deliberate on the ongoing demolitions drive in the Capital, unauthorised constructions and closure of shops in residential areas. Senior Congress legislator and member of the Tejinder Khanna Committee, S. C. Vats, was among those present at the meeting. Mr. Sharma sought a feedback from the elected representatives on what was the best solution that could emerge to resolve the present problems being faced by the people of Delhi.

(6731) Pondicherry: Founder of the Puducherry Munnetra Congress (PMC), P. Kannan, today expressed full satisfaction over the allocation of constituencies to his party in the AIADMK-led front in Pondicherry and Karaikal regions for the coming Assembly elections at the talks he had held with the Tamil Nadu Chief Minister and AIADMK supremo Jayalalithaa in Chennai on Friday.

(6732) Chennai: General secretary of the All India Anna Dravida Munnetra Kazhagam (AIADMK) and Chief Minister Jayalalithaa on Saturday released the list of constituencies earmarked for the constituents of the Democratic People's Front (DPF) in Pondicherry. As per Ms. Jayalalithaa's announcement, the AIADMK will field its candidates in 16 of the 30 constituencies, leaving 10 seats for the Puducherry Munnetra Congress (PMC) and two each for the Marumalarchi Dravida Munnetra Kazhagam (MDMK) and the Dalit Panthers of India.

(6733) Chennai: Marumalarchi Dravida Munnetra Kazhagam (MDMK) leader Vaiko has written to the President, A.P.J. Abdul Kalam, "to take necessary steps to set right the conduct of the Election Commission and the CEC so as to re-establish the prestige of the Commission and to restore the public confidence in the Election Commission." Taking strong exception to what he described as an "inexplicable authoritarian act" - the Election Commission ordering the transfer of Chennai Police Commissioner R. Nataraj - Mr. Vaiko in his letter,appealed to the President to have a "fair and free enquiry into the highly improper and undemocratic action taken by the Chief Election Commissioner."

20-03-2006

(6734) Mahbubnagar : Communist Party of India (Marxist) State secretary B.V. Raghavulu on Sunday came down heavily on the State Government for not paying attention to the recommendations of the Girglani Commission.

(6735) Hyderabad: The commitment to separate Telangana expressed by BJP president Rajnath Singh evoked mixed reactions in political circles on Sunday. Andhra Pradesh Chief Minister Y.S. Rajasekhara Reddy, who was on a tour of Karimnagar, refused to comment as the Congress had left the issue to AICC president Sonia Gandhi. He merely said that the State Government would develop the region on all fronts. The Telugu Desam said its stand on separate Telangana had not changed. It had always held that the development of the region was possible only in a unified State. The party's deputy leader in Assembly, N. Janardhan Reddy, expressed surprise over shifting of stand by the BJP. The Telangana Rashtra Samithi (TRS) welcomed Mr. Singh's statement and said this was an indication for Congress to move a Bill on Statehood for Telangana in Parliament.. The TRS floor leader in Assembly, G. Vijayarama Rao, said they were not perturbed by Mr. Singh's refusal to join hands with them. They were only interested in creation of a separate Telangana. It was immaterial how the objective was achieved. Reiterating the BJP's stand, its spokesman, Prakash Javadekar, who was in city wanted the UPA Government at the

Centre to initiate the Constitutional procedures required for the creation of a separate State. "Once the Bill on Telangana is introduced in the Parliament, the UPA should not have fears of their motion getting defeated."

(6736) New Delhi: Bharatiya Janata Party president Rajnath Singh in consultation with senior party leaders suspended former Delhi Chief Minister Madan Lal Khurana from the primary membership of the party on Sunday.

(6737) Thiruvananthapuram: Talks between Democratic Indira Congress (Karunakaran) leaders and the Congress Working Committee member Veerappa Moily have hit another roadblock over the number of seats that the former would be allotted as part of seat adjustments. Both the parties are, however, willing to compromise on the symbol issue.

(6738) Bangalore: Chief Minister H.D. Kumaraswamy and the Janata Dal (Secular) led by H.D. Deve Gowda have come together to hit out at the candidature of Jnanpith Award winner U.R. Ananthamurthy in the March 28 elections to the Rajya Sabha from the State Assembly. General Secretary of the State unit of the Janata Dal (S) Y.S.V. Datta, who is a confidant of Mr. Deve Gowda, came out with a statement that no intellectual could buy Dr. Ananthamurthy's argument that he has entered the fray to uphold Kannadiga pride. However, he would not question his erudition and standing as a writer.

(6739) Kodaikanal : Desiya Murpokku Dravida Kazhagam (DMDK) leader Vijaykant on Sunday reiterated that his party would not have a tie-up either with the All-India Anna Dravida Munnetra Kazhagam (AIADMK) or the Dravida Munnetra Kazhagam (DMK) for the Assembly elections.

(6740) Thiruvananthapuram: The United Democratic Front (UDF) high power committee meeting has arrived at a general agreement regarding seat-sharing among the coalition partners for the Assembly elections. The Congress will contest 94 seats, Indian Union Muslim League 23, Kerala Congress (Mani) 11, JSS 5, CMP 3 and the RSP factions four. In the event of the Democratic Indira Congress-Karunakaran (DIC-K) joining the coalition, the seats will be allotted from the Congress quota. A final decision on seat-sharing will be taken only on March 22.

(6741) Gulbarga: The State unit of the Communist Party of India (Marxist) has taken exception to what it termed violation of the Supreme

Court direction on observing rituals during the famous urs celebrations at the Bababudangiri shrine in Chikmagalur district this year.

(6742) Mangalore: The Karnataka State Committee of the Indian Union Muslim League (IUML) has urged Chief Minister H.D. Kumaraswamy to take the lead in spreading the message of unity and communal harmony. A delegation from IUML led by C. Ahmad Jamal, secretary, called on Mr. Kumaraswamy during his visit here on Saturday.

(6743) Bangalore: Karnataka Chief Minister H.D. Kumaraswamy and his father and Janata Dal (Secular) president, H.D. Deve Gowda, were to share the dais at the Karnataka Raju Kshatriya Sangha convention. But Mr. Kumaraswamy arrived at the venue only after his father had left. The former Prime Minister spoke sadly of the situation that the father and son found themselves in, after Mr. Kumaraswamy decided to join forces with the Bharatiya Janata Party two months ago. "Everyone says I conspired to make my son Chief Minister. Only he is aware of the pain and agony all this has caused me, and that this is what makes me ill," Mr. Gowda, who has still not completely recovered from his illness, said. "My son promised the BJP that he would join them and form the new coalition, and he kept his promise. Only, I, the father, knows now how he is silently suffering because he has been unable to save his father the agony and the illness that is slowly consuming him [Mr. Gowda]," Mr. Gowda said, stoutly defending his son. "Dynasty building or filial feelings come last with me, and what has happened is God's will. I choose to believe Bhishma's dictum - never blame anyone or hate anyone for what happens." That his son abandoned him to go with the communal BJP is a "vamshada kalanka" (an indelible blot on the family), he said, and he would never come to terms with what has happened.Several minutes after he left, Mr. Kumaraswamy's arrival was announced, and it was his turn to speak in a sentimental vein. "It pains me to see the lion's roar, which was characteristic of my father, now turn into a whimper. I know his ill-health is because of the disappointment over the events of the past two months," Mr. Kumaraswamy said

(6744) Kannur: Communist Party of India (Marxist) leader M.A. Baby has accused a section of the media of

(6745) New Delhi : circulating fabricated stories about the party with a clear motive of portraying the party leadership in a poor light at a time when the State is going to the Assembly polls.

(6746) Erode: Janata Party president Subramanian Swamy has termed a resolution passed by the Kerala Assembly seeking bail for the People's Democratic Party (PDP) leader Abdul Nasir Maudany, currently lodged in Coimbatore central jail, as "heights of minority appeasement."

(6747) Pondicherry: Bharatiya Janata party president Rajnath Singh said here on Sunday that the Congress-led United Progressive Alliance Government at the Centre had "lowered the dignity of constitutional institutions." Mr. Singh, on a day's poll campaign in the Union Territory, said terrorists were gaining ground due to "inability of the Centre to contain terrorism." Apart from political centres, the terrorist forces were attacking cultural and research establishments. The Government had abolished POTA and was "soft" towards terrorism. He said the prices of essential commodities and petroleum products were rising. When the BJP, under the leadership of Atal Bihari Vajpayee, was in power for six years, the prices were under control. Now price hikes had become the rule rather than the exception. The increase in service tax from 10 to 12 per cent should be lowered. If the recommendations of the Rangarajan Committee were implemented, there would be a sharp rise in prices.Mr. Singh charged the Centre with appeasing the minorities for votes. The Government was also misusing the CBI.

(6748) Srinagar: Kashmir is purely a political issue that needs a political solution and Prime Minister Manmohan Singh should reciprocate "positively" to Pakistan President Pervez Musharraf's proposals, National Conference president Omar Abdullah said on Sunday. "I found President Musharraf a forthright person. He doesn't say ten things before coming to the point and is keen to resolve Kashmir issue," he said.

(6749) New Delhi: Leader of the Opposition L.K. Advani on Sunday described the Government's 'appeasement' of minorities as a crime against society. Calling for a campaign against "minorityism," Mr. Advani said such appeasement did not hurt the majority community but annoyed it because secularism meant justice, equality and fair play. "If appeasement caused any serious damage, it was to the minority community itself by isolating it from the mainstream," he said. Mr. Advani was speaking at a seminar on "Minorities and Minority Rights: The Supreme Court and The State" organised by India First Foundation and Chetanya Kasyap Foundation here.

(6750) Mumbai: Maharashtra Navnirman Sena founder Raj Thackeray on Sunday announced his intention to launch a revolution in the State, and show the world how great it can become. Addressing a massive rally at Shivaji Park here, Mr. Thackeray outlined his party's vision. Stating that he believed in nationalism, he said he did not like the double-faced character of the Congress. He said people were anxious about what will happen to Hindutva.

(6751) Chandigarh: Criticising the Congress government on rising budgetary deficit, decline in tax revenue growth and a "faulty" Excise policy, the Opposition Indian National Lok Dal in Harayana on Sunday said the budget reflected its "failure" on fisal management front. "The non-plan expenditure has increased from Rs 9,806 crore in 2003-04 to Rs 11,213 crore and is estimated to touch Rs 11,903 crore in 2006-07. The budgetary deficit, which was Rs 48 crore in 2004-05, has increased to Rs 54 crore in the current fiscal and has been pegged at Rs 65.47 crore in 2006-2007," senior INLD leader and former State Finance Minister Sampat Singh told reporters here.

(6752) Bhopal: Accusing some BJP leaders of making fun of her when she was expelled from the party, firebrand leader Uma Bharti today threatened to teach them a lesson saying their "offence" can never be forgiven.

(6753) Pondicherry : The president of the Bharatiya Janata Party (BJP) Rajnath Singh has said that the BJP was the only party that remained firm and united. Addressing a large meeting of party workers here on Sunday Mr. Singh said that several parties including the Congress had split vertically over the years.

(6754) Ferozepur : Accusing Punjab Chief Minister Amarinder Singh of unleashing "political vendetta", opposition Shiromani Akali Dal chief Parkash Singh Badal on Sunday said his party would hold a probe into the alleged atrocities by his government if voted to power.

(6755) Salem: The Communist Party of India (Marxist) has aligned with the Dravida Munnetra Kazhagam-led Democratic Progressive Alliance to save the lofty principles of parliamentary democracy and remove the "anti-people" All-India Anna Dravida Munnetra Kazhagam government, its Central Committee member T.K. Rengarajan has said.

(6756) Tiruchi : Political democracy, without social and economic equality, will become meaningless and the country's youth should exercise their franchise to ensure that Constitutional guarantees are implemented by rulers, said R. Nallakannu, national executive council member of the Communist Party of India.

21-03-2006

(6757) Hyderabad: Members belonging to Telangana Rashtra Samithi and the CPI(M) staged a walkout in the Assembly on Monday, protesting against the "discrimination against the Telangana region" in allotment of funds to irrigation projects, especially the Srisailam Left Bank Canal (SLBC).

(6758) New Delhi: The Telugu Desam Party on Monday urged the Election Commission to go into the question of disqualifying Congress president Sonia Gandhi, Union Minister, T. Subbirami Reddy, party MP Karan Singh and Kapila Vatsayana on the grounds of holding "offices of profit.'' Submitting a copy of the letter they wrote to the President, TDP parliamentary party leaders — K. Yerrnanidu and R. Chandrasekhar Reddy — brought to the notice of the Election Commission the relevant constitutional provisions.

(6759) New Delhi: Senior Bharatiya Janata Party leaders warned on Monday that "any party members" attending the public rally being organised by Uma Bharti here on Tuesday would face "suspension and expulsion."

(6760) New Delhi: The Communist Party of India (Marxist) on Monday said Prime Minister Manmohan Singh's statement on a movement towards capital account convertibility would be disastrous for the economy. "It is a major decision and he has announced this outside Parliament when it is in session," Rajya Sabha leader Nilotpal Basu said at a press conference here.

(6761) Kochi: Democratic Indira Congress (Karunakaran) leader K. Karunakaran has asserted that he will not return to the Congress fold and that his party will contest the coming Assembly election alone on the symbol to be allotted to it by the Election Commission.

(6762) New Delhi: The National Democratic Alliance (NDA) on Monday demanded the termination of the multi billion-dollar deal to purchase submarines from a French company even as Defence Minister Pranab Mukherjee dismissed allegations of violation of the contractual terms and promised action if there was any. BJP leader L.K. Advani said the Scorpene deal was a bigger scam than Bofors. His party colleague Jaswant Singh maintained that the NDA Government decided not to finalise the deal after it was told that the World Bank had blacklisted the firm. Besides the scrapping of the deal, they demanded a probe into the linkages with the leak of classified documents from the Navy's war room.

(6763) Bangalore: Janata Dal (Secular) President H.D. Deve Gowda on Monday appointed former Deputy Chief minister M.P. Prakash the party's State unit president.Mr. Prakash will also be the joint Leader of the Janata Dal (S) Legislature Party. Chief Minister H.D. Kumaraswamy is leader of the JD(S) Legislature Party. Mr. Prakash succeeds N. Thippanna, who resigned as State unit President following his decision to support the Kumaraswamy group in the party.

(6764) Alappuzha: People's Democratic Party (PDP) State working chairman Poonthura Siraj has said that the resolution passed by the State Assembly for the release of the party leader Abdul Nasir Maudany who is lodged in a Coimbatore jail is a farce.

(6765) Kozhikode: CPI(M) State secretary Pinarayi Vijayan on Monday denied that the seat-sharing exercise among the constituents of the Left Democratic Front (LDF) for the Assembly elections had run into trouble.

(6766) Nedumbassery : The Congress will contest more seats in the forthcoming Assembly elections than it did last time, Kerala Pradesh Congress Committee (KPCC) president Ramesh Chennithala said here on Monday.

(6767) Nedumbassery : The Kerala Congress(J) leader P. C. Thomas has said that there are no major problems in the Communist Party of India (Marxist) and that reports to the contrary are part of a misinformation campaign to cover up the misrule of the United Democratic Front (UDF) Government.

(6768) Chennai: The Bharatiya Janata Party's "yatra" programme was to create greater public awareness on "minority appeasement" of the United Progressive Alliance Government at the Centre and the "upward trend" of activities of terrorists, the party president Rajnath Singh said on Monday.

To a query on whether the programme was to revive the image of the party, the party president told the media that it was not so. "We had organised such yatras earlier. We have a good image."

(6769) New Delhi: In view of the present spate of demolitions in the Capital, Delhi Bharatiya Janata Party president Harsh Vardhan on Monday demanded that the Master Plan for Delhi be amended and the landowners of all the buildings may be allowed to run commercial activities in the basement and ground floors constructed on roads having a width of 40 feet or more. Also, he said, all the markets in the city should be "regularised".

(6770) New Delhi: Continuing with his tirade against senior Bharatiya Janata Party leaders, former Delhi Chief Minister Madan Lal Khurana, on Monday termed his suspension from the party as an unwarranted step and blamed the "influential coterie" in the party close to L. K. Advani for his suspension.

(6771) New Delhi :LOK SABHA members on Monday demanded that the Government stop the move to disinvest the remaining 49 per cent equity in the public sector Bharat Aluminium Company Ltd.. It would result in a loss of Rs.9,000 crore to the exchequer said Ram Gopal Yadav of the Samajwadi Party.

(6772) Bhopal: The Bharatiya Janata Party Madhya Pradesh unit has come down heavily on six prominent party members and suspended them from primary membership for supporting Uma Bharti, the expelled party leader and former Chief Minister of the State. The action comes close on the heels of the suspension of Madan Lal Khurana, a senior party leader, who had announced his intention to join the 'Janadesh Rally' of Ms. Bharti in Delhi on March 21. The six include State Cattle Conservation Board member Rajendra Parsai, former MLA Gajanan Patidar, Suresh Mahajan, Ganapati Gupta and Rajeev Verma. The BJP had earlier suspended four party MLAs — Sunil Nayak, Jalam Singh Patel, Rasal Singh and Hakam Singh Chadar — as they had failed to apologise after being served a show-cause notice and asked to explain their conduct following Ms. Bharti's walkout from the BJP legislature party meeting held here in November 2005. At this meeting, Shivraj Singh Chauhan was elected to succeed Babulal Gaur as Chief Minister.

(6773) Pondicherry: The Ambedkar Republican Party of India will support the All-India Anna Dravida Munnetra Kazhagam and its allies in the Assembly elections in Tamil Nadu and Pondicherry.

(6774) Pondicherry: Leader of the Opposition in the Pondicherry Assembly and convenor of Pondicherry State Dravida Munnetra Kazhagam (DMK) R.V. Janakiraman has urged the election authorities to ensure that political parties faced no hindrances or hiccups in displaying their graffiti in the context of the coming Assembly polls.

(6775) Jaipur: A fact-finding team of the Rajasthan Pradesh Congress Committee which visited Kota a few days ago to enquire into attacks on Christian institutions in the wake of the controversy over the book "Haqeeqat" has termed the developments a "well-planned, well-organised and well-orchestrated conspiracy" by Sangh Parivar outfits. "The attacks on the Christian institutions deserve condemnation from all sections of society," the team has noted.

(6776) Chennai: After failing to get a favourable response from major political fronts in the State, the All-India Forward Bloc has decided to go it alone in the forthcoming Assembly elections in the State. Talking to newsmen here on Monday, party's State president M.Karthik said cadres were in favour of the party contesting on its own and were against aligning with any other party. In deference to the wishes of the workers, the party decided to go it alone. It had already identified 111 constituencies for the party to contest.

(6777) Dindigul: This Assembly election is a war against autocracy and despotism. People should decide whether the democratic power or autocracy should rule the State, said N. Varadarajan, general secretary, Communist Party of India (Marxists). Hitting hard on the MDMK general secretary Vaiko, he said the man (Vaiko) who spoke on honesty and straightforwardness had conspired to get more seats.

(6778) Chennai: Members of Parliament belonging to the Dravida Munnetra Kazhagam on Monday handed over a memorandum to Chief Election Commissioner B. B. Tandon in New Delhi, seeking intervention in cancelling a Government Order appointing temporary employees for poll-related work.

22-03-2006

(6779) Hyderabad: Alleging that there were several irregularities in the works pertaining to the Yellampalli (Sripadasagar) project, TDP deputy leader in the Assembly T. Devender Goud has offered to quit politics if he was not able to prove his claims.

(6780) Hyderabad: The Telugu Desam Party has said that the 'one-sided behaviour' of Speaker K.R. Suresh Reddy was responsible for the failure of its strategy to corner the Government on the Sripadasagar issue. Rejecting the Government's offer to place files before the Irrigation Minister, it vowed to continue its struggle inside and outside the House. Addressing a press conference, TDP president N. Chandrababu Naidu said the Government had taken its own time to tamper with the files before agreeing to place them with the Minister.

(6781) Hyderabad : TRS leader S. Santosh Reddy has said that the statement of BJP national president Rajnath Singh, supporting separate Telangana, although welcome, could not be entirely believed. He said he was unhappy over the conditions listed by the BJP leader for extending his party's support.

(6782) Nellore: The BJP will support categorisation of Scheduled Castes, said M. Venkaiah Naidu, senior party leader on Monday. "The party has already assured Madiga Reservation Porata Samiti (MRPS) that it would support the bill whenever it was introduced in Parliament," he said at a press conference here. The BJP's support to a separate Telangana would bring in a qualitative change in the politics of Andhra Pradesh, he said.

(6783) Bangalore: The new President of the State unit of the Janata Dal (Secular), M.P. Prakash, has said that the Janata Dal (S) has been compelled to accept the status of the legislature party leader accorded to Chief Minister H.D. Kumaraswamy by Speaker Krishna.

(6784) New Delhi: The Polit Bureau of the Communist Party of India (Marxist) on Tuesday took stock of the political situation in Kerala, where certain divergences of opinion within the State party have recently spilled on to the streets, ahead of the April-May Assembly elections. It met here for over six hours to discuss how the party should unitedly face the election so that the Left Democratic Front can be victorious. "The Polit Bureau will meet the Secretariat and the State Committee of Kerala on March 24 to ensure that the party's decisions are fully implemented," party general secretary Prakash Karat told mediapersons.

(6785) Hyderabad: Capping a 16-day-long debate, often marred by pandemonium, Chief Minister Y. S. Rajasekhara Reddy on Tuesday conceded in part a persistent Opposition demand in the Assembly to place the contentious files relating to the Sripadasagar irrigation project tenders with the Irrigation Minister. The main Opposition party, the TDP, ended on the defensive following an admission by its leader N. Chandrababu Naidu that his party had furnished wrong figures in a related question as part of a "deliberate strategy" to extract correct information from the Government. This confession took some of the sting away from the party's criticism since the debate over the past fortnight had centred round the issue of the genuineness of documents.

(6786) Bangalore: The former Prime Minister H.D. Deve Gowda has revealed his true colours by recognising his son, H.D. Kumaraswamy, as the leader of the Janata Dal (Secular) Legislature Party, suspended party leader Siddaramaiah has said. Therefore, Mr. Deve Gowda deserves to be expelled from the party, he said.

(6787) Kollam: Revolutionary Socialist Party (Bolshevik) leader A.V. Thamarakshan has said that Kerala could register development only if the Left Democratic Front (LDF) rules the State for 25 years at a stretch. He said that West Bengal could develop only because the Communist Party of India (Marxist)-led Left Front could rule the State for almost 30 years at a go.

(6788) Kozhikode: Janata Dal (Secular) Parliamentary Party leader M.P. Veerendrakumar has demanded the resignation of H.D. Deva Gowda from the post of party president for recognising his son H.D. Kumaraswamy as party leader in the Karnataka Assembly.

(6789) Guwahati: Assam paid homage to its former Home Minister and senior Asom Gana Parishad (AGP) leader Bhrigu Kumar Phukan who passed away in New Delhi at the All India Institute of Medical Sciences (AIIMS) on Monday night. President of AGP, Brindaban Goswami said: "Phukan, though a soft-spoken man, was uncompromising and gave directions to the Assam agitation as a successful and able student leader."

The AASU described Phukan's demise as "a great loss for Assam and the northeast." "He was selfless, fearless and clean man," the student body said in its condolence statement.

(6790) New Delhi: Bharatiya Janata Party leader from Assam Charn Chandra Deka has filed a writ petition in the Supreme Court challenging the amendment made by the Centre in the Foreigners Order of 1964, party spokesperson Prakash Javadekar said here on Tuesday.He said the BJP wanted a "complete withdrawal" of the Government Order of February 10 that put the onus of proof of citizenship on the complainant or the State as in the case of the now quashed Illegal (Migrants Determination by Tribunal) Act. The BJP views the amendment as a way of bringing back the IMDT "through the backdoor."

(6791) New Delhi: Bharatiya Janata Party president on Tuesday took swift disciplinary action against former all India general secretary and national executive committee member Sangh Priya Gautam for participating in the rally organised by Uma Bharti at the Ramlila grounds here.

(6792) New Delhi: Bharatiya Janata Party Lok Sabha member Mahadeo Rao Shiwankar sought a Central Bureau of Investigation (CBI) inquiry into the Government's purchase of bird flu vaccines in the wake of avian influenza cases reported from Maharashtra.Raising the matter during zero hour, Mr. Shiwankar said though the Government procured vaccines worth Rs. 400 crore, another order for additional vaccines worth Rs. 1,600 crore was placed with multinational companies. At a press conference, the Communist Party of India (Marxist) demanded why the Government placed orders worth 18 million dollars with an international drug manufacturer to purchase Tamiflu earlier this year when a domestic firm made the drug at a much lower price. Party MP Nilotpal Basu said there was a "chilling coincidence" in stockpiling the medicine and outbreak of bird flu in India. He also charged the Western media of blowing up the outbreak of bird flu in small pockets of India out of proportion.

(6793) New Delhi: Former Madhya Pradesh Chief Minister Uma Bharti on Tuesday said the Bharatiya Janata Party had been hijacked by "political managers" while the "real" leaders who worked for the party were being banished. Addressing her "Janadesh Rally" at the Ramlila Grounds here, the expelled BJP leader said she would announce the formation of a new party on April 30. "Hindutva, which believes in respect for all religions, will be the core ideology of the party with aggressive nationalism and a life with dignity as its guiding force," she said.

(6794) Pondicherry: The PMK Parliamentary party leader M. Ramadoss has said that he has requested the Union Finance Minister. P. Chidambaram to abolish Central Sales Tax (CST), as the CST and Value Added Tax (VAT) were incompatible.

(6795) Dehra Dun: A question on the minds of almost every politician, bureaucrat and common man here is whether Narayan Dutt Tiwari will step down as Uttaranchal Chief Minister after the budget session of the State Assembly beginning on Wednesday or was his recent public announcement to quit yet another move to silence his detractors within the ruling Congress party. Senior party leaders in Delhi deny having received any request from the aging leader to be relieved of the post. "He is doing fine and will continue to remain Chief Minister even after the Assembly elections due early next year because we are bound to return to power," Health Minister Tilak Raj Behad told media persons here on Tuesday.

(6796) Madurai: With the slogan of installing the first Dalit Chief Minister in Tamil Nadu, Puthiya Tamizhagam (PT) has decided to go it alone in the Assembly elections and will contest in 150 constituencies.

23-03-2006

6797) Hyderabad: Leader of the Opposition N. Chandrababu Naidu on Wednesday released fresh documents as proof of irregularities in the Sripadasagar project tenders and vowed to present more in the coming days.

(6798) Kadapa: Congress is promoting politics of murder in a planned manner since it regained power, Telugu Desam Party official spokesman and Rajya Sabha member-elect M.V. Mysoora Reddy alleged on Wednesday.

(6799) Kadapa: The Congress Government's Jalayagnam' programme has become a 'money-spinner', TDP leaders alleged on Wednesday. The Government is allegedly resorting to financial irregularities in constructing irrigation projects and for questioning it in Assembly, the TDP was being charged with obstructing' irrigation projects and farmers' interests, TDP official spokesman M. Linga Reddy, alleged at Proddatur.

(6800) Hyderabad: A large number of Congress MLAs belonging to Rayalaseema and coastal Andhra regions have frowned upon the State Cabinet's decision to implement GO 610 on repatriation of non-local Government employees and cautioned against its hasty implementation.

(6801) Thiruvananthapuram: The Congress hardened its stand on the UDF's alliance with the Democratic Indira Congress (Karunakaran) making an issue of the hard speeches of the leaders of that party recently in Kochi. Kerala Pradesh Congress Committee president Ramesh Chennithala said that the speeches of the DIC(K) leaders in Kochi were provocative and had hurt the feelings of the Congress. The hardening stand was quite evident early in the day when the Congress Working Committee member Veerappa Moily said on arrival that there was no proposal to expand the UDF and that there was no political room for two Congress parties The doors on electoral adjustments appeared to be partially open as indicated by IUML leaders P. K. Kunahlikutty and E. T. Mohammed Basheer's hurried visit to Mr. Karunakaran's residence. Mr. Kunhalikutty said that he was making one last attempt to hold the bridge from falling apart.

(6802) Bangalore: Janata Dal (Secular) national President H.D. Deve Gowda has categorically denied having recognised his son, H.D. Kumaraswamy, as leader of the Janata Dal (Secular) Legislature Party. The appointment of M.P. Prakash as President of the State unit of the party is similar to what the Congress has done in the two Houses of Parliament, he told presspersons here on Wednesday. Mr. Gowda said he has not approved of the alliance entered into by his son with the Bharatiya Janata Party.

(6803) Thiruvananthapuram: Breaking his silence over the recent issues in the CPI(M) in Kerala triggered by the party decision to keep him off the electoral fray, the Marxist veteran V.S. Achuthanandan said on

(6804) Wednesday night that he wanted an end to the propaganda that the party in the State was divided over the issue.

(6805) Hyderabad: There was no end in sight to the Sripadasagar controversy in the Assembly with the roller-coaster debate taking a new turn resulting in the suspension of 31 Telugu Desam Party members, including N. Chandrababu Naidu, and walkout by the rest of the Opposition.

(6806) Bangalore: Leader of Opposition N. Dharam Singh challenged Chief Minister H.D. Kumaraswamy and Deputy Chief Minister B.S.

Yediyurappa in the Legislative Assembly on Wednesday to seek a mandate from the people for the coalition of the Janata Dal (Secular) and the Bharatiya Janata Party.

(6807) Kannur: Communist Party of India-Marxist (CPI-M) State secretary Pinarayi Vijayan has said that the Oommen Chandy Government has no moral right to continue as a caretaker Government in the wake of the Central Bureau of Investigation's (CBI) disclosure that question papers of all subjects were leaked in 2005.

(6808) Thiruvananthapuram: The Congress will have an electoral understanding with the Democratic Indira Congress (Karunakaran) only if that party promised to continue support even after the elections, Chief Minister Oommen Chandy has said.

(6809) Thiruvananthapuram: The Indian Union Muslim League (IUML), which has higher stakes in an electoral adjustment with the Democratic Indira Congress (Karunakaran), sounded a cautious note by calling for a conducive atmosphere that would remove the current roadblocks to a negotiated settlement.Talking to mediapersons soon after meeting DIC(K) leader K. Karunakaran, Mr. Kunhalikutty said the dialogues had made good progress till Wednesday, but it received a setback because of the hard hitting statements. Dialogues could be held only if the right atmosphere was set and both sides desisted from making extreme statements, he said. He had briefed Mr. Karunakaran about the strong objection his and K. Muraleedharan's Kochi speeches had evoked. He said that there was still time for working out a formula and, therefore, did not consider the chapter as closed. The IUML had not withdrawn from its mediatory efforts. Mr. Karunakaran, who also spoke to mediapersons, chose to smoothen the ruffled feelings by stating that he respected Congress president Sonia Gandhi as a member of the Nehru family and no one could shake this sentiments.

(6810) New Delhi: The political row on the issue of "office of profit" boiled over on Wednesday when it became known that the two Houses of Parliament were to be adjourned sine die at the end of the day's sitting. The Opposition said the move to adjourn the Houses sine die was to enable the Government to bring in an ordinance designed to "save" Congress president Sonia Gandhi from attracting disqualification for holding the office of chairperson of the National Advisory Council. But Parliamentary

Affairs Minister Priyaranjan Dasmunsi and the Congress asserted that this was a canard spread by the Opposition and that the NAC was "not an office of profit". "Arun Jaitley and Prakash Javadekar [both BJP] have said publicly that the law on office of profit should be changed"Mr. Dasmunsi said. Soon after Parliament was adjourned sine die, NDA leaders led by the former Prime Minister, Atal Bihari Vajpayee, and Janata Dal (United) leader George Fernandes met President Abdul Kalam with a memorandum suggesting that if the Government were to issue an ordinance on the subject of office of profit he should refuse to sign it. What is law for Ms. Bachchan should also be the law for Ms. Gandhi, they said. The memorandum also pointed out that recently the Governor of Uttar Pradesh had refused assent to a Bill exempting certain positions from the purview of offices of profit legislation with retrospective effect. What cannot be done in Uttar Pradesh should not be allowed at the Centre, the NDA said. With the Trinamool Congress complaining that Speaker Somnath Chatterjee was holding a position on the Shantiniketan Development Council, Mr. Chatterjee kept away from the House on grounds of "propriety". Leaders of the Samajwadi Party and the Telugu Desam Party met Mr. Kalam and drew his attention to the abrupt adjournment of the budget session. Urging him to intervene, they said the move was an effort by the Government to promulgate an ordinance to determine "office of profit". SP general secretary Amar Singh and TDP Parliamentary Party leader K. Yerran Naidu met the President after the NDA delegation called on him.

(6811) Guwahati: Asom Gana Parishad (AGP) president Brindaban Goswami on Wednesday stunned the political circle by expressing his desire that the party should relieve him from contesting in the election so that he could campaign.

(6812) New Delhi: Expressing strong opposition to the move to introduce full capital account convertibility, the Communist Party of India (Marxist) on Wednesday demanded that the decision to form the S.S. Tarapore Committee to chalk out a road map for it be rescinded. Reacting to Prime Minister Manmohan Singh's announcement in Mumbai, the CPI (M) termed it as a significant departure from the Common Minimum Programme. It said the CMP, far from advocating capital account convertibility, is committed to reducing the "vulnerability of the financial system to the flow of speculative capital."

(6813) New Delhi: The Congress on Wednesday emphasised that the National Advisory Council (NAC), headed by party president Sonia Gandhi, was a "purely advisory body" and its suggestions were "recommendatory" in nature. Responding to news reports that the body was an "office of profit," the party said that the NAC did not exercise any executive, legislative or judicial powers. It did not have any powers for the allocation/ distribution of funds, allotment of lands, issue of licences, making of appointments, etc., party spokesperson Abhishek Singhvi said.

(6814) New Delhi : Defence Minister Pranab Mukherjee on Wednesday ruled out the presence of middlemen in the multi-billion-dollar Scorpene submarine deal with France.He said the then Defence Minister, George Fernandes, had given a "clean chit" to the company while answering questions in Parliament even as his Government refused to sign integrity pacts for the deal as suggested by the Central Vigilance Commissioner. On the other hand, senior National Democratic Alliance (NDA) leaders claimed "there is a middleman who has received huge amounts said to be on behalf of the Congress." They demanded his arrest, scrapping of the deal and placing of all files before an enquiry commission to clear the air on whether the previous Government had cleared the contract. Deprived of the opportunity to air their views in Parliament, both sides met the media separately to give their versions of the submarine contract with French companies. "We have been disappointed by the response [Tuesday's statement in Parliament by Mr. Mukherjee]. We would like to reiterate that in this particular matter, the agreement has been violated. A comprehensive inquiry should be instituted to fix political responsibility and ascertain all other facts relating to scandal," said the Leader of the Opposition, L. K. Advani. Former Defence Minister Jaswant Singh said Mr. Mukherjee did not touch "some parts" in his statement.

(6815) New Delhi: Senior Bharatiya Janata Party leader and former Delhi Industries Minister Harsharan Singh Balli was on Wednesday suspended from the party for his anti-party activities. He has been charged with discrediting the party by taking arbitrary decisions and continuously disregarding the directions of the party for selfish interests. Delhi BJP president Harsh Vardhan issued the suspension order at the direction of the party leadership.

(6816) New Delhi: A delegation of the Communist Party of India on Wednesday met Union Minister of State for Urban Development Ajay Maken asking him to get demolitions in Delhi's residential areas stopped immediately and hasten the process of regularising of unauthorised colonies. Demanding strict action against land mafia and corrupt officials, the CPI leaders urged him to spare the poor and lower income group people in the ongoing demolitions.

(6817) Shimla: The newly elected Rajya Sabha member from the State, Viplov Thakur, who is also the Himachal Pradesh Congress Committee president, said here on Tuesday that despite strong opposition by Chief Minister Virbhadra Singh to her bid for the Rajya Sabha ticket "there is no division within the rank and file of the party in the State". She claimed that she had very successfully bridged the gap between the two warring factions in the Congress.

(6818) Jaipur: Congress MLA Raghuvir Singh Meena was suspended from the Rajasthan Assembly on Wednesday for the remainder of the Budget session and physically removed from the House for his refusal to tender an apology for his confrontation with a ruling BJP member over recent attacks by radical groups on Christians.

(6819) Lucknow: Uttar Pradesh Assembly Speaker Mata Prasad Pandey on Wednesday adjourned till March 25, the hearing in the case related to defection of 40 BSP MLAs to the ruling Samajwadi Party in 2003, despite strong protest by the BSP counsel — who demanded prompt decision on the legislators' status. Submitting his third application demanding fresh party position of U.P. Assembly after the February 28 Allahabad High Court decision, BSP counsel Satish Chandra Mishra said till the Speaker decided on the issue, there was no question of attending the hearing. Mr. Mishra also objected to the "incomplete" affidavit submitted by 26 rebel MLAs claiming they belonged to the Loktrantrik Bahujan Dal (LBD).

(6820) Chennai: After marathon negotiations spread over two days, the Dravida Munnetra Kazhagam and the Congress completed their seat-sharing exercise on Wednesday morning, identifying 48 constituencies earmarked for the Congress. DMK president M. Karunanidhi and Tamil

Nadu Congress Committee president M. Krishnasswamy signed the agreement at the DMK headquarters Anna Arivalayam here.

24-03-2006

(6821) Hyderabad: In a unique protest, suspended Telugu Desam MLAs held a mock Assembly session at "Media Point" on the Assembly premises to the last detail on Thursday and like the real House, it was adjourned abruptly amid pandemonium.

(6822) Hyderabad: Chief Minister Y.S. Rajasekhara Reddy and Andhra Pradesh Congress Committee president K. Keshava Rao left for Delhi on Thursday evening to call on AICC president Sonia Gandhi in the wake of her resignation as MP and Chairperson of the National Advisory Council. Before leaving, Dr. Reddy told reporters that there was no example of such a gesture in contemporary politics. The entire nation stood in ovation to her. He said Congress strode to power in the last elections solely due to the contribution of Ms. Gandhi. "We are all proud to be in Congress led by her."

(6823) Siddipet (Medak): TRS president and Union Minister K. Chandrasekhar Rao has said that the appeal of coastal Andhra legislators to Chief Minister Y.S. Rajasekhara Reddy against implementing the Girglani Commission's recommendations is proof enough that Telangana region will never flourish under Andhra rulers and bifurcation is the only solution.

(6824) New Delhi: Congress president Sonia Gandhi on Thursday resigned from the 14th Lok Sabha and as chairperson of the National Advisory Council (NAC). She made the announcement at a press conference. After holding talks with senior leaders, Ms. Gandhi stepped out of her study in 10 Janpath and announced that she was anguished over attempts by some persons to create an atmosphere that the Government and Parliament were being used for her benefit.Ms. Gandhi said she did not step into political and public life for personal gains. It was only to serve the country, society and protect secular values. Keeping in view her values of public life, ideals of politics and beliefs, she had tendered her resignationShe, however, expressed the confidence that people of her Rae Bareli constituency and the country would understand her sentiments. To a question, Ms. Gandhi said she decided to resign, as it was "the right thing to do."Asked if she planned to contest again, Ms. Gandhi declared that she would do so from Rae Bareli. Prior to her announcement, Ms. Gandhi informed Prime Minister Manmohan Singh about her decision. Dr. Singh arrived at her residence and left before the announcement. Senior party leaders, including Defence Minister Pranab Mukherjee, Home Minister Shivraj Patil, AICC general secretary Janardhan Dwivedi and her political secretary Ahmed Patel, were present. Rahul Gandhi was around when Ms. Gandhi announced her decision.The development turned the course of political discourse, with the Congress asserting that Ms. Gandhi had proved that she was above considerations of office, and the Bharatiya Janata Party describing it as a step that followed its intense pressure.Later, Ms. Gandhi called on Lok Sabha Speaker Somnath Chatterjee and handed over her resignation letter. It was accepted with immediate effect, the Speaker's office said Dr. Singh had accepted Ms. Gandhi's resignation as National Advisory Council chairperson.

(6825) Lucknow: The Samajwadi Party said here on Thursday that its leader Amar Singh would not resign from the Rajya Sabha.Talking to mediapersons after the party's Parliamentary Board meeting, its Chairman Ram Gopal Yadav said the Union Government planned to bring in an ordinance on the office of profit issue just to save Congress president Sonia Gandhi from disqualification as MP. Mr.Singh, against whom a disqualification petition had been filed and is being heard by the Election Commission, offered to resign last week and expressed the hope that leaders of other parties in a similar condition, would resign. Mr. Yadav alleged that a pre-Emergency like situation prevailed owing to "dictatorial" attitude of Congress.

(6826) Thiruvananthapuram: The Democratic Indira Congress (Karunakaran) and the Congress have succeeded in thrashing out a workable seat adjustment formula under which the former would contest 18 seats. The Congress would allot 17 seats, while the Indian Union Muslim League (IUML) would release Koduvally, considered to be a safe seat, for DIC(K) president K. Muraleedharan. The package took shape only after high voltage drama at the DIC(K) leader K. Karunakaran's residence with his son, Mr. Muraleedharan, walking out in a huff over certain provisions of the agreement. The uncertainty that Mr. Muraleedharan's action caused was cleared only when Congress Working Committee member Veerappa Moily and Mr. Karunakaran addressed a joint press conference late in the night announcing that the DIC(K) and the Congress would work together.

The exact reason for Mr. Muraleedharan's reaction is not known, but it is believed to be over the question of Mala, Mr. Karunakaran's old constituency, which does not figure in the list of constituencies that had been allotted to the DIC(K).

(6827) Chennai: The Dravida Munnetra Kazhagam-led Democratic Progressive Alliance completed the process of constituency identification on Thursday, with the Pattali Makkal Katchi signing an agreement with the DMK.

(6828) New Delhi: Congress Rajya Sabha member Karan Singh on Thursday night resigned from the House, sources in the party said. He had been accused by the Opposition of holding an "office of profit" by being chairman of Indian Council for Cultural Relations (ICCR). The sources said Dr. Singh had sent his resignation letter to Rajya Sabha chairman Bhairon Singh Shekhawat and to Congress president Sonia Gandhi. Dr. Singh is also chairman of the Ethics Committee of the House. - PTI

(6829) New Delhi: The Bharatiya Janata Party on Thursday described the resignation of Sonia Gandhi from the Lok Sabha and chairpersonship of the National Advisory Council as "mere grandstanding that will not do." Just hours before she announced her decision, four BJP leaders met President A.P.J. Abdul Kalam to ask that Ms. Gandhi be disqualified under Article 102 (1) of the Constitution. A similar petition was filed by the Telugu Desam Party nine days ago, and has been forwarded by Mr. Kalam to the Election Commission for inquiry. BJP president Rajnath Singh virtually charged Ms. Gandhi with "lack of courage" to "face Parliament and an inquiry by the Election Commission." He criticised her resignation, and said she was "running away" from the charges levelled against her. "We had not raised the issue of Ms. Gandhi losing the confidence of the people of Rae Bareli. Why did she resign? She should have faced Parliament, and by resigning she is trying to divert the people's attention from the failures of the Government." On the alleged Government plan to bring in an Ordinance with retrospective effect to exempt certain offices from being declared offices of profit, general secretary Arun Jaitley said the BJP objected to the "subverting of the Constitution and Parliament" to "save" one person from disqualification. By resigning, Ms. Gandhi had tried to "save her face.He compared her to a "culprit caught red-handed" but admitted that the "legal and constitutional" aspect whether the NAC was an office of profit was not very clear. On whether the party's deputy leader in the Lok Sabha, V.K. Malhotra, and other MPs and MLAs who might face similar charges would resign, Mr. Jaitley said it would be up to the leaders to take their decisions. Some National Democratic Alliance parties did not see eye-to-eye with the BJP on the issue. Janata Dal (United) spokesperson Shambhu Srivastava "welcomed" Ms. Gandhi's decision to resign. In fact, he added that Lok Sabha Speaker Somnath Chatterjee too should resign. This was also the view of the Trinamool Congress, which was the first to charge the Speaker with holding an office of profit.

(6830) Bangalore: The discontent and division in the Janata Dal (Secular) came into the open in the Legislative Assembly on Thursday when the party's senior member P.G.R. Sindhia attacked the Government for not taking the Opposition into confidence before filing an affidavit in the Supreme Court saying that the Idgah Maidan in Hubli would be converted into a park.

(6831) Hassan: Criticising the statements made by Chief Minister H.D. Kumaraswamy on the decision of Jnanpith Award winner U.R. Ananthamurthy to contest the Rajya Sabha elections to be held on March 28, as an independent, Manjunatha Datta, senior leader of the All India Progressive Janata Dal (AIPJD), has said that the statements of the Chief Minister is a disgrace to democracy.

(6832) Thrissur: The Janata Dal (Secular) State unit has demanded immediate convening of the party's national executive to discuss the controversy triggered off by the reported statement of party national president H.D. Deve Gowda, accepting Karnataka Chief Minister H.D. Kumaraswamy as party leader in that State Assembly.

(6833) New Delhi: Reacting to Congress president Sonia Gandhi's resignation from the Lok Sabha and as chairperson of National Advisory Council, senior Congress leader M.L. Fotedar said on Thursday that she had taken a "very wise step". She proved that she was the true inheritor of the national heritage of the Nehru-Gandhi legacy which epitomises service and sacrifice. "The Congress stands rejuvenated by this bold decision." Haryana Chief Minister Bhupinder Singh Hooda, one of the many party leaders who called on Ms. Gandhi, said the move proved she had maintained the highest moral traditions in public life. "She has listened to her inner voice and this has silenced the din." He reminded that even after the 2004

Lok Sabha polls, she listened to the inner voice and turned down the prime minister's post even though the Congress sought votes in her name. Congress MP V. Hanumantha Rao said the high moral standards set by her was a shining example for all party workers to follow in public life.

(6834) New Delhi : The Telugu Desam Parliamentary Party welcomed the resignation. The party leaders K. Yerran Naidu and K. Rama Mohan Rao said it proved that law was equal for all. However, the party felt that she should have resigned before the Government adjourned Parliament abruptly on Wednesday. "It is a victory for democracy and not of any party," Mr. Naidu said. Communist Party of India national secretary D. Raja said Ms. Gandhi had taken a moral stand since she felt the Opposition was targeting her. Yet, the larger issue on `office of profit' remained unresolved.

(6835) New Delhi: The Communist Party of India (Marxist) on Thursday said Parliament should immediately undertake legislation to put certain offices held by members of Parliament outside the purview of "office of profit" until Parliament comprehensively defines what is an office of profit. In a statement, the party Polit Bureau said under the Constitution, Parliament is empowered to decide on the definition of "office of profit" and to exempt any office from disqualifying its holder under the "office of profit" clause. "It is necessary for Members of Parliament to discharge various responsibilities as part of public service. It will not be proper to bring all such positions under the `office of profit' definition. It is unfortunate that Jaya Bachchan has been disqualified under the existing law because Parliament has so far not unde taken such an exercise," the statement said. Later, party general secretary Prakash Karat said the CPI (M) MPs would not resign.

(6836) Vijayawada: Within hours of Congress president Sonia Gandhi announcing her resignation from the post of chairperson of the National Advisory Council and as member of the Lok Sabha, Union Minister of State for Commerce Jairam Ramesh, also a member of the NAC, said he would "follow the example set by Soniaji".

(6837) New Delhi: The Janata Dal (United) on Thursday "welcomed" Congress president Sonia Gandhi's decision to quit her Lok Sabha seat and her post of Chairperson of the National Advisory Council. The party urged all Congress MPs to emulate the example set by their leader.

(6838) Chennai : The Dravida Munnetra Kazhagam on Thursday came out in defence of the Congress president Sonia Gandhi, who resigned her parliamentary seat and chairpersonship of the National Advisory Council over the office of profit controversy. "Mrs. Sonia Gandhi is an example of the saying that `one who conquers one's self conquers the world'," M. Karunanidhi, DMK president, told mediapersons at his party headquarters after completing the process of constituency identification for the Democratic Progressive Alliance for the Assembly poll. "Just now, I spoke to her and commended her action," he said. On Ms. Gandhi's resignation, the Pattali Makkal Katchi founder S. Ramadoss said, "she has again created history." Janata Party president Subramanian Swamy, in a statement, said Ms. Gandhi had tried to make a virtue of necessity by resigning her posts.

(6839) New Delhi: Mir Khurshid, president of the Jammu and Kashmir Mutahida Mahaz, on Thursday declared the merger of his party with the Janata Dal (United). Speaking to mediapersons at the JD (U) office, Mr. Khurshid said the decision followed a meeting with chairman of the JD (U) Parliamentary Board Sharad Yadav.

(6840) Kolkata: The Trinamool Congress leadership has moved President A.P.J. Abdul Kalam and the Election Commission seeking action against 11 MPs belonging to the Communist Party of India (Marxist) who, it said, hold offices of profit."We did so on March 8," Trinamool leader Mamata Banerjee said here on Thursday. Reacting to Congress president Sonia Gandhi's decision to resign from Parliament, she said that the 11 MPs should follow suit. As for Mrs. Gandhi "there was no other way out for her than resigning," she said. "If Jaya Bachchan can be disqualified from Parliament how can they [the CPI(M) MPs concerned] continue? The law is the same for all," Ms. Banerjee, whose party is a constituent of the National Democratic Alliance, said. Bharatiya Janata Party vice president Baburam Marandi, who is in the city, demanded that Lok Sabha Speaker Somnath Chatterjee should also resign from Parliament as he holds an office of profit.

(6841) Lucknow: The people of Rae Bareli on Thursday came out onto the streets shouting pro-Sonia Gandhi slogans after her resignation was announced. Equating her with former Prime Minister Indira Gandhi, they gathered at the Rae Bareli Congress office and staged a demonstration in her support. "The people of Rae Bareli are not unhappy with the decision...in fact they are happy she has taken the wind out of the Opposition's sails," said Uttar Pradesh Congress chief spokesperson A.P. Singh. The U.P. Congress welcomed her move and claimed it would force the Opposition to rethink its strategy. "After refusing the post of PM, her latest decision proves she is not after posts," it said.

(6842) Hyderabad: Telugu Desam Party president N. Chandrababu Naidu on Thursday said Sonia Gandhi had no option but to resign as Member of Parliament and it was unfortunate that a compulsion was being portrayed as a sacrifice.

(6843) Chennai: Marumalarchi Dravida Munnetra Kazhagam general secretary Vaiko on Thursday called for encouragement of scientific research to preserve and protect Tamil culture and popularise it globally. He made this appeal while participating in the 17th annual celebrations of the Indian Science Monitor (ISM), a non-profit research organisation, established in 1989, aimed at generating awareness in the field of science and technology, social anthropology and archaeology.

25-03-2006

(6844) Hyderabad: An emergency meeting of the Congress Legislature Party (CLP) paid rich tributes to AICC president Sonia Gandhi as a 'tall personality' in contemporary politics in the light of her resignation from Parliament and as chairperson of the National Advisory Council (NAC). Presiding over the meeting during a recess of the Assembly on Friday, CLP leader and Chief Minister Y.S. Rajasekhara Reddy criticised the BJP and other parties for targeting her.

(6845) Hyderabad : Twenty Congress MLAs of Telangana met at the Gandhi Bhavan on Friday in the backdrop of a large number of party legislators from the Andhra region submitting a memorandum to Chief Minister Y.S. Rajasekhara Reddy to keep in abeyance implementation of GO 610.

(6846) Thiruvananthapuram: Bowing to popular sentiment and the demand articulated by a large number of people within and outside the party, the Communist Party of India (Marxist) on Friday decided to field the Leader of the Opposition in the Kerala Legislative Assembly, V.S. Achuthanandan, in the coming Assembly elections. CPI(M) general secretary Prakash Karat told newspersons here late on Friday that the party Polit Bureau had decided to "reopen" the candidature after reviewing the situation following the earlier decision not to field Mr. Achuthanandan and CPI(M) State secretary Pinarayi Vijayan.

(6847) Thiruvananthapuram: BJP State president P. S. Sreedharan Pillai on Wednesday demanded a CBI inquiry into the purchase of land by the kin of Finance Minister Vakkom Purushothaman.

(6848) Thiruvananthapuram: Democratic Indira Congress (Karunakaran) president K. Muraleedharan has decided to opt out of the fray for the Assembly election. The decision has been taken in view of the widespread protest against electoral adjustments struck with the Congress. Mr. Muraleedharan, when contacted, said that he was reluctant to contest in the light of the widespread reservations expressed by party workers. The seat adjustments have led to bitterness in both the DIC(K) and the Congress, though it was slightly more visible in the former.

(6849) Thiruvananthapuram: The Congress State leadership has succeeded in restricting the Democratic Indira Congress (Karunakaran) manoeuvres to a mere electoral understanding in 18 seats. The DIC(K) failed to achieve its target in terms of numbers and in getting accommodation as a partner in the ruling United Democratic Front (UDF). The terms of understanding, confirmed through an unprecedented written agreement signed by Kerala Pradesh Congress Committee president Ramesh Chennithala and DIC (K) president K. Muraleedharan here on Friday, clearly spelt out the contours of the arrangement, stating that the DIC(K) would work for the victory of the UDF. "It has been agreed that only the UDF can provide a clean and stable Government for the benefit of Kerala. Issues of merger of the DIC with the Congress will be discussed and facilitated after the elections. It is felt that those having Congress culture should unite under the leadership of Ms. Gandhi in view of the above. It is agreed that the DIC will contest in 17 seats on their own symbol," the agreement, signed in a white paper, said.

(6850) Srinagar: Four MLAs from the Congress, heading Corporations and Boards in Jammu and Kashmir, have resigned following the controversy over the office of profit issue.

(6851) New Delhi: Congress workers from across the country continued to pour into the capital expressing support to party president

Sonia Gandhi who resigned from her Lok Sabha membership and as Chairperson of the National Advisory Council. Party leaders including general secretaries and office-bearers, legislators, Chief Ministers Vilasrao Deshmukh and Narayan Dutt Tiwari and State unit chiefs called on her. The party said Ms. Gandhi was planning to visit Rai Bareilly on Monday. With the mood in the party on the upswing, the Congress launched a counterattack on the Opposition Bharatiya Janata Party and demanded an apology for carrying on a "campaign of disinformation". Party spokesperson Abhishek Singhvi said the opposition had based its premise on the grounds that the disqualification of Jaya Bachchan was in pursuit of policy of revenge and that the Government was making an attempt to protect Ms. Gandhi who was heading the NAC. He also said the effort by the Opposition was to paint a picture that Ms. Gandhi was desperate to hold on to her office and that an ordinance "which no one had seen" was being promulgated.

(6852) Ranchi: Amidst hurling of chairs and overturning of tables by Opposition United Progressive Alliance (UPA) members, the Jharkhand Assembly on Friday passed a controversial Bill to protect four National Democratic Alliance (NDA) MLAs from possible disqualification on the ground of their holding of offices of profit. The MLAs are Karia Munda, who heads the 20-Point Programme Implementation Committee; Chhatruram Mahto heading the State Agriculture Marketing Board; Saryu Roy, vice-chairman of the State Planning Board; and Khiru Mahto, chairman of the Hazaribag Mines Board.

(6853) New Delhi: The Left parties on Friday asked the United Progressive Alliance Government to speedily resolve the "office of profit" issue in consultation with all parties so that appropriate legislation could be brought in Parliament. They also opposed the move to do so through the ordinance route. The Communist Party of India (Marxist) reiterated its stand that the issue must be clarified and necessary legislative action taken by Parliament "without recourse to the ordinance route." In a statement the party Polit Bureau said Congress president Sonia Gandhi had resigned as member of the Lok Sabha and as chairperson of the National Advisory Council in response to the Bharatiya Janata Party and Opposition charge that she was holding an office of profit. The post of chair of the NAC could not be termed an "office of profit", it said. Terming as "baseless" the demand for the resignation of Lok Sabha Speaker Somnath

Chatterjee, the statement said that as an MP he had been holding the position of chairman of the Sriniketan-Santiniketan Development Authority for the past 17 years. Communist Party of India Lok Sabha leader Gurudas Dasgupta said the party was of the view that Parliament should be called upon to deliberate on the issue and adopt legislation. "No shortcut method should be taken to settle the controversy," he said in a letter to the Prime Minister. Mr. Dasgupta also expressed deep anguish at the way Parliament was adjourned sine die without consulting any party. "We protest against the action of the Government that has led to doing away with the second spell of the budget session," he said. The Revolutionary Socialist Party MP Abani Roy said the move to curtail the budget session was not in the interest of Parliamentary democracy. He said the Government should refrain from promulgating an ordinance to amend the Parliament (Prevention of Disqualification) Act, 1959.

(6854) New Delhi: CPI (Marxist) Rajya Sabha member Brinda Karat, writer Arundhati Roy and national secretary of the CPI, Amarjit Kaur, visited the families displaced by the Narmada dam. The displaced people are on dharna here since a week to protest the decision to raise the height of the dam in Gujarat from 110.64 metres to 121.92 metres.

(6855) New Delhi: A large number of Congress workers and leaders continued to throng Akbar Road for the second day running on Friday in support of Sonia Gandhi who resigned from the Lok Sabha as well as chairpersonship of the National Advisory Council on Thursday. Lauding yet another sacrifice by the Congress president, party workers shouted slogans against the Bharatiya Janata Party and even burnt an effigy of its leader, L.K. Advani, for targeting Ms. Gandhi. The dharna and demonstration that began on Thursday afternoon continued through the night with leaders and party workers, a majority of them belonging to India Youth Congress and National Students Union of India, taking turns to hold fort. Since early on Friday morning, Congress workers had again started pouring in near Ms. Gandhi's residence to express their solidarity with their party chief. They shouted slogans in support of Ms. Gandhi and some even urged her to take her resignation back. Workers, including many women, described Ms. Gandhi as the "epitome of sacrifice" and lambasted the BJP and the Samajwadi Party for pursuing the politics of vendetta against the Congress president. Some section of party workers also appreciated the way in which Ms. Gandhi took the sting out of the

BJP campaign against her by resigning. Carrying party flags, workers from nearby States and also from Rae Bareli and Amethi joined the sit-in on Friday. Congress leaders who joined the workers included MPs, MLAs, senior party leaders and student leaders from Delhi University and Jawaharlal Nehru University. Interestingly, the entire Akbar Road on which the All-India Congress Committee office is situated has been draped with banners and hoardings by various leaders in support of Ms. Gandhi.

(6856) New Delhi: Indicating a softening of stand following his utterances against senior party leaders and "power brokers" in the party, former Delhi Chief Minister and suspended BJP leader Madan Lal Khurana on Friday refused to talk "politics", saying that he had given word to very senior party leader that he would not speak on controversial issues till the end of this month. Mr. Khurana, suspended from the party on March 19 for speaking out against senior party leaders including L.K. Advani, once again indicated that he was seeking a possible return to the saffron party, a repeat of what he had done in September 2005. At that time Mr. Khurana had lashed out at Mr. Advani for his Jinnah remarks and was suspended from the party. He was taken back after he regretted his action and tendered an apology. "Do not ask me political questions. I have given word to a very senior BJP leader that I will not speak anything about politics or party affairs till April 1. Just wait for some more time," he told reporters at a press conference here.

(6857) Chandigarh: Haryana Chief Minister Bhupinder Singh Hooda said here on Friday that no Congress MLA was enjoying any office of profit. Mr. Hooda was talking to media persons shortly after presiding over a meeting of the Congress Legislative Party. The CLP members unanimously passed a resolution dedicating themselves to the leadership of Sonia Gandhi and affirmed that they were committed to her "ideas and ideals."

(6858) Bhopal: Amid noisy scenes the Madhya Pradesh Assembly was adjourned twice on Friday as Congress members cited the example of their party president Sonia Gandhi and demanded resignation of the State Chief Minister and several of his Cabinet colleagues saying that they were heading State-owned autonomous corporations and enjoying offices of profit.

(6859) Pondicherry: Assembly speaker, M. D. R. Ramachandran has expressed shock over the resignation of Sonia Gandhi as Member of Parliament and also the chairperson of National Advisory Council on Thursday. In a telegram sent to her (copy of which was distributed to media persons) the Speaker said that she had however proved once again that she was a unique personality who could relinquish higher positions to enhance the image of the Congress in the country as a whole and to serve the nation.

(6860) Pondicherry: Around 200 volunteers of the Pondicherry State Youth Congress committee were arrested at Pattanikadai junction here on Friday when they held a demonstration condemning the Opposition leader, L. K. Advani. They also burnt an effigy of Mr. Advani.

(6861) Dehra Dun: The Narain Dutt Tiwari Government tabled the Uttaranchal (The Uttar Pradesh State Legislature (Prevention of Disqualification) Act, 1971 (Amendment) Bill, 2006, in the Vidhan Sabha on Friday amid sloganeering for and against it by the Treasury and Opposition benches. To take retrospective effect from November 9, 2000, the day Uttaranchal was born, the Bill aims at declaring the office of chairman, vice-chairman or member whether called director or by any other name of 27 Government boards as honorary office-bearers. The remuneration or salary paid to them will be called "compensatory allowance". The Bharatiya Janata Party and Bahujan Samaj Party members stormed the well of the House and the Uttarakhand Kranti Dal members lent them vocal support from their seats the moment Speaker Yashpal Arya arrived .Former Speaker and BJP member Prakash Pant said that the party had faxed its protest with all relevant details to the CEC. Local Congress leaders burnt effigies of BJP leaders Atal Bihari Vajpayee and L.K. Advani. They also staged a candlelight march in support of Sonia Gandhi.

(6862) Chennai: Congress workers demonstrated throughout the State on Friday condemning the Bharatiya Janata Party for "forcing" Congress president Sonia Gandhi to resign from the Lok Sabha and the National Advisory Council. In some places, including the party State headquarters Sathyamurthi Bhavan here, they burnt the effigy of BJP leader L.K. Advani. Office-bearers of the Tamil Nadu Congress Committee (TNCC), adopted a resolution congratulating Ms. Gandhi for upholding moral and democratic values. Though there was no need for her to quit the posts, she did so in line with the democratic traditions cherished by the Nehru family. They condemned the BJP for adopting "unethical political practices."

(6863) Chennai: One group of the Tamil Nadu unit of the Indian National Trade Union Congress (INTUC) led by general secretary G. Kalan went ahead with its special representatives meeting on Friday despite a warning issued by the central leadership that disciplinary action would be taken against those who participated in the meeting. Mr. Kalan on his part warned that the State unit would sever its ties with the central network if any disciplinary action was initiated against the participants. He said the meeting was held to protect the self-respect of the State unit, which had been "humiliated" by the Congress over the years. For the INTUC, self-respect was more sacrosanct than blindly supporting the Congress. He urged the central leadership to amend its constitution to empower State units to take independent decisions on having alliances.

(6864) Chennai: Tamil Nadu Chief Minister and AIADMK general secretary Jayalalithaa on Friday urged President Abdul Kalam to go into the "entire sordid episode" of the Union Government "shutting down" Parliament to pass an Ordinance on the Office of Profit issue. In a statement, she said Congress president Sonia Gandhi by resigning as Member of Parliament and as chairperson of the National Advisory Council had only tried to make a virtue out of a compelling necessity. "Her usual spiel about sacrifice and nobility cuts no ice," she added.

26-03-2006

(6865) Hyderabad: The Bharatiya Janata Party took the Central and the State Governments to task for what it called the "abject failure" to control rise in prices of almost all essential commodities imposing a heavy burden on the common man. BJP leaders alleged that instead of ensuring that the inflation rates did not go up, the United People's Alliance Government at the Centre was mired in several corruption scandals, including the Scorpene submarine deal.

(6866) Hyderabad : Two TRS MLAs exchanged heated remarks with APSRTC Chairman Gone Prakash Rao in the enclosure earmarked for legislators to speak to the electronic media on the Assembly premises on Saturday. Mr. Prakash Rao was facing the cameras and criticising TRS chief K. Chandrasekhara Rao saying he was an "opportunist and one who had only his own personal interests in mind". As Mr. Prakash Rao went on to criticise the TRS president, party MLA Laxma Reddy intervened and asked Mr. Prakash Rao as to what gave him the right to criticise the party president's actions. Another party MLA Kasipet Lingaiah joined the argument.

(6867) Hyderabad: K. Yerrannaidu, leader of the Telugu Desam Parliamentary Party, described as "high drama," the resignation of Sonia Gandhi as MP.

(6868) Vijayawada: The Bharatiya Janata Party, which considers itself a disciplined cadre-based political organisation, had to witness a strange situation here on Saturday when a section of its leaders from coastal Andhra region openly opposed the party's stand on separate Telangana.

(6869) Rajahmundry: The Telugu Desam Party (TDP) on Saturday alleged that the Bharatiya Janata Party (BJP), which had kept the smaller States issue in cold storage during the Telugu Desam Party regime, was now again raising it to get political mileage. Addressing a press conference here, TDP campaign committee president Ganni Krishna criticised the meeting organised by the BJP in Vijayawada on Saturday to discuss the separate Andhra issue. He recalled that the BJP did not pursue the Kakinada resolution on smaller States till the TDP was in power and now was raising the banner, as there were no other issues for it to go to the public. He also recalled that the BJP had joined hands with the TDP for a united Andhra and was now trying to woo the Telangana Rashtra Samithi (TRS). Mr. Krishna also criticised the TRS 'double standards' in praising Sonia Gandhi after she resigned as MP and on the other hand bargaining with the BJP on the separate Telangana issue.

(6870) New Delhi: Two days after Congress president Sonia Gandhi resigned from the Lok Sabha and as chairperson of the National Advisory Council, following the controversy over the office of profit issue, Congress leaders, MLAs, MPs and workers continued to express their support for her. On Saturday, 25 MLAs from Madhya Pradesh offered to resign. The MLAs, led by Leader of the Opposition Yamuna Devi met Ms. Gandhi, who rejected their offer to resign. Jyotiraditya Scindia, Congress MP from Guna, and Minister of State for Personnel Suresh Pachauri also met Ms. Gandhi. "We are with Soniaji. She is our leader and we have expressed our feelings to her. If she wants and allows, all of the MLAs are ready to resign," Ms.

Yamuna Devi said. The MLAs also submitted a letter to the party president, saying they had full faith in her leadership. The letter was signed by 38 MLAs. Congress workers and volunteers continued to stay put outside her 10 Janpath residence, though their numbers appeared to have dwindled. Cadres of the National Students Union of India (NSUI), the Youth Congress, the Sewa Dal and the Nehru Brigade were sitting on a dharna on Akbar Road, near her residence and the party headquarters.

(6871) Bangalore: The Congress high command is understood to have directed the State unit to extend support to U.R. Ananthamurthy in the biennial elections to the Rajya Sabha scheduled to be held on Tuesday. Sources in the party told The Hindu here on Saturday that Leader of the Opposition in the Legislative Assembly and former Chief Minister N. Dharam Singh and KPCC President M. Mallikarjun Kharge called on Congress President Sonia Gandhi in the evening and apprised her of the situation with regard to the Rajya Sabha elections in the State.

(6872) Bangalore: Devaragunda Venkappa Sadananda Gowda, new President of the Bharatiya Janata Party's State unit, has said there are many challenges before him in the era of coalition politics and he will act as a link between the party and the Government, and address grievances of party workers.

(6873) Alappuzha: The Janata Dal (United) will contest 20 seats in alliance with the BJP in the elections to the State Assembly, party State president A.S. Radhakrishnan has said. Mr. Radhakrishnan said the recent developments in Karnataka where a major group of the Janata Dal (Secular) broke away from the alliance with the Congress had proved that socialist parties could not align with the Congress for long. While the UDF and the LDF MPs supported the UPA Government at the Centre, both had failed to force it to take favourable steps for the development of State.

(6874) Thrissur: Prakash Karat, general secretary of the Communist Party of India-Marxist (CPI-M), has warned secular forces, including Left parties, against a tendency to confine the battle against communal forces to the electoral arena. Delivering the Bishop Paulose Mar Paulose Memorial Lecture on 'Challenges before secular democracy in India' here on Saturday, Mr. Karat said communal forces were systematically active in other fields, such as education and ideological propaganda.

(6875) Thrissur: Democratic Indira Congress (Karunakaran) leader K. Karunakaran on Saturday said that no agreement had been reached so far in regard to the merger of his party with the Indian National Congress after the Assembly elections. Mr. Karunakaran told reporters here that a decision in this regard would be taken only after consulting party workers.

(6876) Lucknow: Seeking a clarification on 'office of profit,' CPI(M) leader Brinda Karat on Saturday said there were a series of resignations on the issue, but most were aimed at gaining political mileage. Reiterating that none of the CPI(M) MPs would resign, as no one was holding 'office of profit,' she said "the Congress president may have resigned, but we do not consider even the National Advisory Council as an office of profit." Opposition parties in Parliament had alleged that CPI(M) MP and Lok Sabha Speaker Somnath Chatterjee had been holding 'office of profit' as Sriniketan-Shantiniketan Development Authority chairman.

(6877) New Delhi: The Bharatiya Janata Party on Saturday continued to demand the scrapping of the Scorpene submarine deal, undaunted by the threat of a criminal defamation suit from Abhishek Verma, the alleged middleman.The party has refused to accept the statement in Parliament of Defence Minister Pranab Mukherjee that there was no scope for a middleman, since an "integrity clause" had been included in the agreement with Thales, the manufacturer of Scorpene, specifying that commissions would not be paid. Violation of that clause would lead to cancellation of the contract. In fact, party spokesperson Prakash Javadekar charged that the Government was "silent" despite serious charges being levelled.When asked whether BJP leaders had given notice of privilege on the Defence Minister's statement, Mr. Javadekar said that this had not yet been done, but would be done.The party claimed that it had provided details of the "money trail" in the deal and insisted that the disclosed e-mails between Thales and Mr. Verma were not fake or fabricated as alleged by Thales and the Government.

(6878) New Delhi: The Loktantrik Bahujan Dal (LBD), the breakaway faction of the Bahujan Samaj Party (BSP) in the Uttar Pradesh Assembly, will choose its new leader shortly. "The present leader, Rajinder Singh Rana, will be replaced ... in a day or two," State Minorities Welfare and Haj Minister, Haji Yaqoob Qureshi, told presspersons here on Saturday. On Friday, the Supreme Court asked 32 of the 37 MLAs, who merged with the

Samajwadi Party, to sit as a separate group under the LBD till the matter was disposed of. In an interim order, the court also allowed five MLAs, who had resigned from the Ministry and the post of chairmen of various boards following the High Court order, to function as BSP MLAs.

(6879) New Delhi: Congress president Sonia Gandhi appealed to her party workers on Saturday to end the sit-in they were staging outside her 10 Janpath residence since her resignation from the Lok Sabha on Thursday. Senior party leaders Ahmed Patel, Motilal Vora and Oscar Fernandes conveyed the Congress president's appeal to the workers and leaders on Saturday evening. AICC secretary P. Sudhakar Reddy said that the leaders conveyed the decision of Ms. Gandhi and the reasons for her quitting the Lok Sabha and as chairperson of the National Advisory Council (NAC). They said the party members should now fan out to various parts of the country to counter the propaganda of the Opposition and convey to the people the sentiments of the party president which prompted led her to take the decision. They said that she at all times was for protecting secular values in the country and politics based on principles.

(6880) New Delhi: Welcoming the decision of the Union Urban Development Ministry to amend the Master Plan for Delhi - 2021 and provide relief to lakhs of people of the Capital, Delhi Pradesh Congress Committee president Ram Babu Sharma on Saturday termed it as a historic step that would go a long way in saving the livelihood and employment of lakhs of shop owners and workers who otherwise would have faced dislocation.

(6881) Pondicherry: Even as the rank and file of the ruling Congress was planning to begin poll-related activities ever since the Election Commission announced the schedule for Pondicherry, the resignation by AICC leader Sonia Gandhi as Member of Parliament and chairperson of the National Advisory Council virtually dampened the partymen's vigour here. All debate on the number of seats the Congress should get and share with the alliance partners virtually took a back seat. One could see volunteers holding busy meetings urging the AICC leader to withdraw her decision. The louder one raised his voice the greater the prominence he gained.

(6882) Pondicherry: The president of the Pondicherry unit of the Bharatiya Janata party (BJP), R. Kesavalu, has condemned the behaviour of the Youth Congress volunteers who had burnt on Friday an effigy of Leader of the opposition in the Lok Sabha L.K. Advani.

(6883) Jaipur: A group of MLAs belonging to the Congress met the Governor, Pratibha Patil, here on Saturday to request her to terminate the Assembly membership of three legislators of the Bharatiya Janata Party in the State on account of their holding posts of profit. The MLAs who are mentioned in the memorandum submitted to the Governor are Arjun Singh Devra, Premsingh Bajor and Vishnu Modi.

(6884) Chennai: Groupism in the State unit of Congress took a "bloody and nasty turn" on Saturday when two groups indulged in violence at the party headquarters at Satyamurthi Bhavan here, resulting in bleeding injuries to 10 workers. It all started when supporters of former Youth Congress president A.S. Chellakumar, who was suspended from the party on Friday for "anti-party activities," came to the Bhavan that morning and tried to barge into the office. However, they were prevented from entering by the party workers there. Soon wordy quarrel ensued between the two groups. When it was about to take a violent turn, party treasurer D. Sudarsanam tried to pacify them by taking one of the Chellakumar supporters to his room for talks. The others squatted in the complex stating that they would go on an indefinite fast till the suspension of Mr. Chellakumar was revoked.

27-03-2006

(6885) Hyderabad: Andhra Pradesh Congress Committee secretary T. Seshnarayan has demanded resignation of T. Subbarami Reddy, Union Minister of State for Mines and TTD Chairman, and G. Vinod, Labour Minister and president of the Hyderabad Cricket Association, "as they are holding office of profit."

(6886) Hyderabad: The BJP has said that it had awakened Congress and saved it from embarrassment by seeking the resignation of AICC president Sonia Gandhi, on the controversy surrounding her over holding dual posts. The proposed ordinance enabling Ms. Gandhi to continue as an MP while holding an office of profit would have spelt doom for the UPA Government, BJP secretary B. Dattatreya told reporters here on Sunday.

(6887) Nellore : The BJP has ruled out the possibility of joining hands with the TRS on statehood for Telangana. "Both parties differ on various aspects pertaining to Telangana and therefore the question of the BJP aligning with the TRS does not arise. Besides, the TRS view is different on the issue while the BJP is in favour of smaller states for administrative convenience," BJP vice-president S.V. Seshagiri Rao told reporters here on Sunday.

(6888) Kadapa : The TRS demand for implementation of the GO No. 610 will be suicidal for the party, according to Andhra Pradesh Congress Committee official spokesman N. Tulasi Reddy. The TRS demand for repatriating non-locals, if implemented, would create chaos and cause injustice to employees of nine districts of Telangana, recruited under V and VI zones, he told a press conference here on Sunday.

(6889) New Delhi : The issue of separate Telangana has created a fissure in the Opposition ranks with a senior Janata Dal (United) leader from Andhra Pradesh distancing himself from the party move on the issue. Upset over the move by the party to set up a separate State committee for Telangana, former Samata party president and JD (U) leader V.V. Krishna Rao has resigned from it. Mr. Rao sent in his resignation both from the national executive and primary membership of the party to JD (U) president George Fernandes. Taking objection to the move of the central party leadership to form a separate state committee for Telangana, Mr. Rao has said this is against the views prevalent in the State unit of the party.

(6890) Hyderabad: Telangana Rashtra Samithi president K. Chandrasekhara Rao has called upon the party cadre to punish rebel MLAs led by Dugyala Srinivasa Rao for "aligning" with anti-Telangana forces and playing down hopes on formation of a separate State. It was unfortunate that some MLAs had fallen into the trap of the Congress and were running a 'vicious campaign,' he said while addressing the executive meeting of the party here on Sunday. This was despite BJP president Rajnath Singh's emphatic support to the cause.

(6891) New Delhi: The Government on Sunday continued consultations on the issue of office of profit, with Parliamentary Affairs Minister Priyaranjan Dasmunsi meeting Janata Dal (United) leader Sharad Yadav and establishing contact with others."The process is almost complete. I have held consultations with all parties, barring three, and will submit my report to the Prime Minister on Monday after speaking to the rest," Mr. Dasmunsi told The Hindu While there was consensus that the law be amended, most parties, barring the Bharatiya Janata Party, felt that an all-party meet should be convened. In New Delhi, Mr. Sharad Yadav suggested that since all parties were for a change in the law, the Government bring forward a Bill. However, the power to determine the office of profit should remain with Parliament, which has a Joint Committee to look into it, he said.The Left parties favoured a comprehensive Bill before Parliament. Abani Roy (RSP) favoured an all-party meet.Mr. Dasmunsi also spoke to Telugu Desam Parliamentary Party leader K. Yerran Naidu, who said the Government should reconvene Parliament. The TDP felt an all-party meeting would be beneficial. Union Minister Prem Chand Gupta of the Rashtriya Janata Dal suggested that a Bill be brought forward. He said the BJP-led Opposition now favoured legislation, since its Governments in the States were affected.Telangana Rashtra Samiti MP B. Vinod Kumar said he had written to the Law Commission to identify laws needing review and those requiring amendments.

(6892) Hubli: Samajwadi Party State unit Vice-President S.R. Khan has alleged that Indian sovereignty has been "mortgaged" through the nuclear treaty with the U.S. He told presspersons here on Sunday that the Samajwadi Party feels that through the treaty is a violation of the principles of Non-Aligned Movement and it is one of the failures of the United Progressive Alliance Government at the Centre.

(6893) Mysore: AIPJD leader and former Deputy Chief Minister Siddaramaiah has reaffirmed his decision to violate the whip issued by the Janata Dal (Secular) to vote for its official nominees for the Rajya Sabha elections thus queering the pitch for a political battle that may see the realignment of forces in the State. Mr. Siddaramaiah, who was elected from the Chamundeshwari Assembly constituency on a Janata Dal (S) ticket, technically continues to be a member of that party though he broke away from it to constitute the AIPJD following differences with former Prime Minister H.D. Deve Gowda.

(6894) Kollam: President of Bahujan Samaj Party (BSP) Mayawati, MP, said here on Sunday that though her party may not be able to open its account in the Kerala Assembly in the coming elections, the Dalits and Backward Classes in the State would ensure that the BSP becomes a formidable force in Kerala. Ms. Mayawati was here to inaugurate the State-level workers convention of the party. Ms. Mayawati announced that her party would contest independently in all 140 constituencies in the State. To applause from BSP cadres, Ms. Mayawati said she would campaign in Kerala for six days.The BSP leader said that while the Constitution granted protection and reservation to Dalits, under the "Manuvadi" rule, the Dalits would continue to be sidelined and oppressed. She called upon the Dalits and the Backward Classes to join the BSP. "Only if we come to power can our problems be addressed," she said. She alleged that the Congress, BJP and Communists would pump in huge amounts of money to manipulate the elections in their favour. She asked the BSP cadres to be vigilant against such moves. She demanded that the reservation provision of the Constitution be extended to Dalit Christians.

(6895) New Delhi: The Left parties on Sunday mourned the death of Anil Biswas, West Bengal State Secretary of the Communist Party of India (Marxist). Lok Sabha Speaker Somnath Chatterjee said Mr. Biswas' death came as a great shock to him and all members of the party. The CPI national secretary D. Raja said Mr. Biswas had grown from being a student activist to an acknowledged political leader of standing. The Revolutionary Socialist Party MP Abani Roy said loss of Mr. Biswas would be felt more because he departed at a time when elections were due in the State.

(6896) Jagiroad: A battery of star campaigners of the Bharatiya Janata Party (BJP) including Gujarat Chief Minister Narendra Modi and L. K. Advani on Sunday appealed to the voters of Assam to give their party a chance. Addressing his first public meeting in Assam, the Gujarat Chief Minister told an election rally at Jagibhakat village here in central Assam's Morigaon district that people have experienced the rule of both the Congress and the Asom Gana Parishad (AGP) and hence they should give the BJP a chance. Mr. Modi also addressed an election rally at Rangiya in Kamrup district.

(6897) Guwahati: Bharatiya Janata Party leader Sushma Swaraj on Sunday said she would not take on the Congress president Sonia Gandhi if she runs for the Lok Sabha from Rae Bareli once again. Addressing presspersons here, Ms. Swaraj said she was not against Ms. Gandhi personally. "I am opposed only to any person of foreign origin becoming the Prime Minister." The country's security would be put into jeopardy if a person of foreign origin was given the reins of power, she said. - UNI

(6898) New Delhi: The Lok Janshakti Party (LJP) will contest in alliance with the Congress in West Bengal but has so far been unable to find allies from major parties in the rest of the States going to the polls from next month. As things stood, the LJP would contest alone in Tamil Nadu, Kerala and Pondicherry party president Ram Vilas Paswan told newspersons on Saturday. In West Bengal, the LJP would put up 10 candidates , he said. His brother Ram Chandra Paswan would be visiting the States going to the polls in an effort to avoid a contest among the UPA allies and supporting parties.

(6899) New Delhi: The former Defence Minister, George Fernandes, said here on Sunday that the National Democratic Alliance would use every forum to "nail the corrupt clique" behind the Scorpene submarine deal.Refusing to apologise as demanded by Abhishek Verma through his lawyer and being threatened with a defamation suit, Mr. Fernandes said in a statement that "those who know me and my public life spanning nearly 50 years, know that George Fernandes has never apologised for raising his voice against the corrupt deeds of the Congress Governments. As far as tendering an apology, the question does not arise . Mr. Fernandes sought to know why the United Progressive Alliance Government was maintaining a "guilty silence" over why it did not act on the alleged money trail between Thales (the French company that makes the submarines) and Mr. Verma.He said both Thales and Mr. Verma have claimed that the e-mails exchanged between them were fabricated but asked why the Government was accepting the claims of the accused at face value instead of probing it.

(6900) Lucknow: Under constant attack by Opposition parties, Uttar Pradesh Chief Minister and Samajwadi Party supremo Mulayam Singh Yadav today mooted 'offensive politics' against rivals. Addressing youth here who had gone to thank him for announcing Unemployment Allowance, Mr Yadav said now his party would not follow the route of defensive politics, but would counter the Opposition onslaught with its own offensive. He also asked the youth not to get bogged down by the Opposition's onslaught.

(6901) Chennai: The Dravida Munnetra Kazhagam (DMK) and the All-India Anna Dravida Munnetra Kazhagam (AIADMK) have not lived up to the expectations of the people of Tamil Nadu although they have been in power for long, the Desiya Murpokku Dravida Kazhagam (DMDK) founder Vijaykant said on Sunday.

28-03-2006

(6902) Hyderabad: Blaming the police, TDP, TRS, CPI (M), CPI, BJP, BSP and MIM on Monday demanded a judicial enquiry and action against the police for the Gangavaram firing. They slammed the Government for mishandling the fishermen's agitation against the private port leading to the firing and death of a person.

(6903) New Delhi: Parliamentary Affairs Minister Priyaranjan Dasmunsi , having almost completed consultations with leaders across the political spectrum, briefed Prime Minister Manmohan Singh on his meetings with them. Emerging from his nearly 30-minute meeting with Dr. Singh, he told reporters that the Samajwadi Party and the Bharatiya Janata Party were not in favour of calling an all-party meeting. (A few days ago BJP leader Jaswant Singh said May 10 was consensus date for the start of the second part of the budget session.) Leaders of the All-India Anna Dravida Munnetra Kazhagam and the Akali Dal had told Mr. Dasmunsi that their parties would give their views in writing. Both the Left parties and the BJP were agreeable to the new legislation. But they wanted the Government to spell out details first. It seems that all major parties favour legislation with retrospective effect as they are affected in one way or another.In a letter to Mr. Dasmunsi on Monday, Janata Dal (United) leader George Fernandes said he learnt "from the media" that the Minister was to visit him on Sunday morning. But "you neither fixed an appointment, nor did you turn up. " Mr. Fernandes said there was a large pool of capable people inside and outside political parties who could competently hold "offices of profit" and such persons should be accommodated. He was in favour of "separation" of all MPs and MLAs from "offices of profit."

(6904) Bangalore: Karnataka Pradesh Congress Committee President M. Mallikarjun Kharge on Monday announced that the party's surplus votes will be cast in favour of the independent candidate and litterateur U.R. Ananthamurthy in the Rajya Sabha elections scheduled for Tuesday.

(6905) Chennai: About 70 per cent of the candidates of the ruling All India Anna Dravida Munnetra Kazahgam in the list of 182 candidates released by the party general secretary and Chief Minister Jayalalithaa on Monday for the May 8 Assembly elections are new faces. Barring Ms.Jayalalithaa and 51other sitting MLAs who have been re-nominated, all the other candidates are new faces. She also announced the names of candidates for 54 Assembly constituencies in Kerala and 16 segments in the Union Territory of Pondicherry.

(6906) Panaji: Aggrieved over the alleged irregularities and lapses in the revision of electoral rolls in the State, the Bharatiya Janata Party (BJP) is all set to approach the Election Commission in New Delhi seeking its intervention to remedy the situation. Addressing presspersons here on Monday, Leader of the Opposition in the Assembly and former Chief Minister Manohar Parrikar alleged that the State Chief Electoral Officer Rajiv Yaduvanshi "cannot be counted on to be fair as he is susceptible to political pressure." His contention was that Mr. Yaduvanshi has held positions such as Secretary to Governor S.C. Jamir and other major posts.

(6907) Pathanamthitta: National vice-president of the Bharatiya Janata Party (BJP) L. Ganesh has alleged that a resolution unanimously passed by the Communist Party of India (Marxist)-led Left Democratic Front (LDF) and the Congress-led United Democratic Front (UDF) seeking the release of Abdul Nasser Maudany from jail exposed the support extended to religious fundamentalism and extremism by both the opposing parties.

(6908) Jaipur: The ruling party MLAs from Jharkhand, led by Chief Minister Arjun Munda, arrived here on Monday on a "pilgrimage," even as the Opposition Congress raised the issue of "herding" of the legislators. The MLAs, numbering 40, checked into a five-star hotel on Jawaharlal Nehru Marg. While the threat to the stability of the Bharatiya Janata Party-led Government in Jharkhand, in the wake of the chances of disqualification of MLAs holding office of profit, has apparently brought the party MLAs once again to Rajasthan, the reasons given for their presence: thanksgiving visit to the Dargah of Kwaja Moinuddin Chisti at Ajmer and invitation to participate in the ongoing Rajasthan Day celebrations.

(6909) Chennai: The Bharatiya Janata Party says it favours the route of legislation to resolve the office of profit issue. "We want legislation, not ordinance. The issue has to be debated thoroughly in Parliament. A broad consensus has to be developed," M. Venkaiah Naidu, former BJP president, told a press conference here. There was a need to define what constituted an office of profit, Mr. Naidu said and referred to reports of a number of complaints being filed against MPs and MLAs. "A chaotic situation is prevailing in the country. We have to set certain standards on this issue. The concept of office of profit has to be defined clearly." Criticising the United Progressive Alliance Government's handling of the issue, he said suspicion arose because the Government adjourned Parliament sine die hoping to bring in an ordinance instead of facing Parliament.

(6910) Patna: Railway Minister and Rashtriya Janata Dal chief Lalu Prasad on Monday renewed his old battle with his Cabinet colleague and Lok Janshakti Party president Ram Vilas Paswan thanks to the Rajya Sabha elections in which the two constituents of the UPA are locked in a tussle. The RJD and the LJP are fighting it out for the sixth seat, with five seats assured: three to the JD (U) and one each to the BJP and the RJD. In the race are LJP vice-president Ranjan Prasad Yadav, a former close aide of Mr. Prasad, and RJD's Rajniti Prasad. The candidate who gets 35 votes will emerge the victor. The RJD has 30 in its kitty and the LJP 18. Mr. Prasad took exception to the CPI and the CPI-ML's support to the LJP, saying the latter's candidature was sponsored by the BJP. The BJP alone had the surplus votes to spare its first preference votes, he pointed out. The stand of the CPI, which has three members and the CPI-ML (five), he said, could blot their secular character, but hoped they would reconsider. He ruled out the possibility of his candidate being defeated and any of his party legislators cross-voting in favour of the LJP nominee. The RJD would issue a whip and openly ensure that each cast his vote in favour of the party nominee. The RJD chief admitted that he had not contacted the Samajwadi Party for its two votes. He also denied any overtures to placate the LJP. Mr. Prasad hailed the sacrifice made by Congress president Sonia Gandhi and ruled out any possibility of a mid-term election. He said the UPA would complete its term. He denied knowledge of any legislation on the office-of-profit issue.

(6911) Kupwara : Congress president Sonia Gandhi is an "immense moral force in Indian polity," Union Minister for Water Resources, Saifuddin Soz, said on Monday. BJP leader L.K. Advani's yatra would only lead to disruption.

(6912) Bhopal: The president of the Madhya Pradesh unit of the Bharatiya Janata Party, Satyanarayan Jatia, said here on Monday that Congress president Sonia Gandhi's resignation from Parliament and as Chairperson of the National Advisory Council was not a sacrifice as it was being propagated but a joke.

(6913) Jaipur: The Rajasthan Assembly witnessed noisy scenes on Monday over the implementation of the policy for promotion of wind power generation with the Opposition Congress accusing the Bharatiya Janata Party-led Government of changing the prices for purchase of electricity to benefit the private players in the field.

(6914) Chennai: The Pattali Makkal Katchi has demanded that the Centre hold talks with the industrialists at the earliest to evolve consensus on providing reservation for Other Backward Classes and Scheduled Castes/ Scheduled Tribes in private sector.

(6915) Chennai: Dalit Panthers of India General Secretary Thol.Thirumavalavan on Monday released the party's manifesto for the May 8 Assembly elections. Mr. Thirumavalavan told reporters here that the DPI, which is part of the All India Anna Dravida Munnetra Kazhagam-led Democratic People's Alliance, would urge the electorate to defeat the Dravida Munnetra Kazhagam (DMK)-led Democratic Progressive Alliance (DPA) which had "shunned the Dalits."

(6916) Madurai : Puthiya Tamizhagam would strive to consolidate Dalits in the ensuing Assembly elections by attempting to rally organisations working for Dalit welfare under one umbrella, said its president K. Krishnasamy here on Monday.

29-03-2006

(6917) Hyderabad : The CPI State council has asked the Government to rehabilitate fishermen in the affected villages before commencing works on the Gangavaram port.

(6918) Hyderabad : The Telugu Desam Legislature Party on Tuesday accused the Government of behaving 'irresponsibly' and making the Assembly session 'most unproductive' while the Left rued the House's ineffectiveness in taking up people's issues.

(6919) Visakhapatnam: "If the authorities think that are successful in quelling the agitation by using brute force they are mistaken. This is just the beginning of a sustained fight by the voiceless. The atrocities committed by the police on the innocent fishermen of Gangavaram on Monday would only fuel the agitation further," observed CPI (M) MP Penumalli Madhu.

(6920) Visakhapatnam: Several leaders made a beeline to Gangavaram village, 30 km from here, to express solidarity with the fishermen in their fight for a suitable relief and rehabilitation package to allow construction of a private port. Leader of Opposition N. Chandrababu Naidu, who called on the family members of Ch. Nookaraju, killed in a clash with the police on Monday, announced financial assistance of Rs. 2 lakhs on behalf of Telugu Desam Party.

(6921) Chandigarh: Bansi Lal, senior Congress leader and former Haryana Chief Minister, died in New Delhi on Tuesday night, family sources said here. He was ailing for some time.Considered the architect of modern Haryana, Mr. Bansi Lal was the Chief Minister for four terms, first in 1968 and the last from 1996 to 1999. He was a controversial figure during the Emergency for his proximity to Sanjay Gandhi. He was the Defence Minister then. He later parted ways with Congress and set up the Haryana Vikas Party before returning to the parent party ahead of last year's Assembly poll. - PTI

(6922) Rae Bareli (U.P.): Launching a scathing attack on her political opponents for targeting her in the office of profit controversy, Congress president Sonia Gandhi on Tuesday said she would continue her fight against injustice. "I will neither lose nor backtrack," she said addressing her voters here. This was her first visit outside the capital after she resigned from the Lok Sabha and as chairperson of the National Advisory Council (NAC) in the wake of the allegations that the United Progressive Alliance (UPA) Government was planning to bring in an ordinance to "protect" her. In an emotional, 20-minute speech in Hindi, Ms. Gandhi said she had always shared her happiness and grief with the people of Rae Bareli and it was her responsibility to tell them the truth behind her resignation. "Every stone is thrown at me, guns are trained at me and every arrow is aimed at me. I am even blamed for natural calamities that hit the country. And, when the office of profit controversy came up, my opponents remembered Sonia Gandhi. I am their enemy number 1," she said evoking a thunderous response from the thousands of people gathered on the Government Inter College ground.

(6923) Chennai: Chief Minister and All India Anna Dravida Munnetra Kazhagam (AIADMK) general secretary Jayalalithaa on Tuesday ruled out the possibility of a coalition government in the State after the May 8

Assembly elections. Her party would return to power with absolute majority, she said. After releasing the AIADMK manifestos for the Assembly elections in Tamil Nadu, Kerala and Pondicherry at the party headquarters, she said, "We will form our Government with independent majority."

(6924) Kozhikode: The election manifesto of the Left Democratic Front (LDF) promises priority to efforts for making the State achieve an economic growth higher than the national average. The manifesto was released by Front convener Paloli Mohammed Kutty by presenting a copy of it to Kozhikode Mayor M. Bhaskaran at the Communist Party of India (Marxist) district committee office here on Tuesday.

(6925) Bangalore: Congress members staged a walkout in the Legislative Council on Tuesday protesting against Chief Minister H.D. Kumaraswamy not agreeing to its demand for a CBI investigation into alleged illegal mining in Bellary district. The Congress based its demand for an investigation on a report submitted by Minister for Forests, Environment and Ecology C. Chennigappa.

(6926) New Delhi: The Bharatiya Janata Party on Tuesday described the 'yatras' to be simultaneously launched by its president Rajnath Singh and Leader of the Opposition L.K. Advani on April 6 as "political pilgrimages." Senior leader and chief coordinator of the 'yatras' M. Venkaiah Naidu said here that these were renamed "Bharat Suraksha Yatra," with emphasis on "security" issues. The earlier plan was to call them "National Integration Yatra" with the focus on unity. Mr. Naidu compared Mr. Advani's proposed journey from Rajkot in Saurashtra (instead of from Dwarka as earlier announced) to Delhi to Adi Sankara's pilgrimage from Kanyakumari to Kashmir centuries earlier. But Mr. Advani's journey would be a "political pilgrimage." While Mr. Advani sets off from Rajkot, Mr. Rajnath Singh will start from Bhubaneswar (after prayers at the Puri temple). Both will criss-cross the country, each covering 5,000-6,000 km, and meet here on May 10. In between, they will take time off to campaign for the Assembly elections. Mr. Naidu said the party rejected the Home Ministry's suggestion that bullet-proof 'raths' be used for the two leaders on the plea that the 'yatras' posed security problems. "That was not possible as it would slow down the speed." Even as Mr. Naidu claimed that the 'yatras' were to "safeguard national security from 'jehadi' terrorism and Left extremism," Vishwa Hindu Parishad leader Ashok Singhal, pooh-poohed the idea, pointing out that "nothing was done" to contain terrorism when the BJP was in power at the Centre. Mr. Advani "has lost the trust of Hindus, who will not turn up for his yatra."

(6927) Guwahati: The Shahi Imam of Delhi's Jama Masjid, Maulana Syed Ahmed Bukhari, on Monday appealed to Muslims in Assam to vote against the Congress in the Assembly polls. Maulana Bukhari, touring the State to campaign for Assam United Democratic Front (AUDF) candidates, alleged that there was no difference between the Congress and the Bharatiya Janata Party. Muslims had become victims of riots when the Congress was in power for 46 years. He pointed out that Nelli, Kokrajhar, Mumbai, Surat and Bhagalpur riots happened during the Congress rule. Describing the recent amendment to the Foreigners (Tribunal) Order 1964 as an "election gimmick" by the Congress, he said any foreigner who came to Assam after the agreed cut-off date of March 25, 1971 must be detected and deported irrespective of whether he was a Hindu or a Muslim.Muslims were observing the formation of the AUDF and would replicate this new model or front if it succeeded in the Assam polls. "The country will get a new direction from the outcome of the Assam Assembly elections and the success of the AUDF, a front not only of Muslims but a common platform of the oppressed sections."

(6928) New Delhi: Senior Bharatiya Janata Party leader and party MLA from Saket in the Capital, Vijay Jolly, on Tuesday filed a complaint with President A. P. J. Abdul Kalam seeking disqualification of 18 Congress MLAs and one Member of Parliament from Delhi "for holding offices of profit and benefiting from their appointments to various boards and corporations".

(6929) Jaipur: The Rajasthan Assembly was plunged into turmoil on Tuesday when a Bahujan Samaj Party MLA, agitated over the State Government's failure to fill up the backlog of reservation in services, tore off his kurta and fainted after storming into the well during zero hour. The BSP MLA, Suresh Meena, along with another party colleague wanted to raise the issue of non-compliance with the norms for reservation for Scheduled Caste and Tribes, but the Speaker, Sumitra Singh, did not allow him to speak. Mr. Meena hurled charges against the BJP-led Government and left his seat to storm into the well.

(6930) Bhopal: Former Union Minister and Congress leader Aslam Sher Khan, has called for a special AICC session immediately after the Assembly elections in five States to provide a definitive direction to the Congress, particularly with respect to its policy vis-a-vis the Muslim community. In an open letter, Mr Khan said "consolidation in voting pattern" had already taken place where Muslims were joined by Dalits, backward classes and communists.

(6931) Chennai: The All India Anna Dravida Munnetra Kazhagam (AIADMK) on Tuesday made it clear that if returned to power, its government would not implement the Value added Tax (VAT) until the Centre brought forward the necessary amendments. The AIADMK manifesto for the Assembly elections released by party general secretary and Chief Minister Jayalalithaa here, urged the Centre to bring a suitable legislative amendment acceptable to traders and producers so as to remove all problems faced by them on account of VAT.

(6932) Chennai: "Providing an alternative to the Dravida Munnetra Kazhagam (DMK) and the All-India Anna Dravida Munnetra Kazhgam (AIADMK)" is a theme that has cropped up several times in State politics. This time round, the Bharatiya Janata Party (BJP) and the Desiya Murpokku Dravida Kazhagam (DMDK) are stressing this point in their campaign. BJP president Rajnath Singh, launching the party's campaign on March 19, said if given a chance, the BJP would put the State on the path of development. The DMK and the AIADMK could not eradicate poverty and unemployment despite remaining in power for long. DMDK founder Vijaykant alleged that the DMK and the AIADMK did not care for the poor.

(6933) Chennai: The State Government's decision to hold common entrance test for professional courses has only betrayed its lack of interest in scrapping the CET, the Pattali Makkal Katchi founder S. Ramadoss said on Tuesday.

(6934) Madurai : The former Pattali Makkal Katchi Vandavasi MLA, S. K. Murugavelrajan, who recently joined the ruling All India Anna Dravida Munnetra Kazhagam, on Tuesday floated a new political party, named People's Liberation Party.

(6935) Chennai: The All India Anna Dravida Munnetra Kazhagam (AIADMK) on Tuesday assured that the party would secure the status of a "Special State" for Pondicherry in order to enable the Union Territory to take its own policy decisions, besides implementing schemes as in other States. The manifesto released by party general secretary and Tamil Nadu Chief Minister Jayalalithaa here for the May 8 Assembly elections in Pondicherry said that a law would be enacted to enable the Union Territory to appoint higher officials, college teachers, doctors, provincial civil service officers and other posts for which recruitment was now done by the Union Public Service Commission.

30-03-2006

(6936) Hyderabad: Telugu Desam stepped into 25th year of its founding on Wednesday with party president N. Chandrababu Naidu calling upon partymen to rededicate themselves to the cause of people and fight against a regime that has the least concern for them.

(6937) Visakhapatnam: Leader of Opposition in the Assembly N. Chandrababu Naidu on Wednesday said Ch. Nookaraju, a fisherman, died of bullet wound in his chest on Monday and demanded a judicial probe into firing at Gangavaram.

(6938) New Delhi: Upbeat over the rousing welcome the Congress president Sonia Gandhi received in Rae Bareli on her first visit to her Lok Sabha constituency after her resignation, the party on Wednesday dared any Opposition leader to contest against Ms. Gandhi. Congress spokesman Abhishek Manu Singhvi threw a challenge to "any leader of any political party of any stature", including rebel Bharatiya Janata Party leader Uma Bharti, to contest against Ms. Gandhi in Rae Bareli. "Those aspiring to contest against Ms. Gandhi will need to keep in mind the political history ranging from Indira Gandhi to Rajiv Gandhi to Sonia Gandhi which spans not only Rae Bareli and Amethi but also Chikmagalur, Medak and Bellary."He said those who seek to 'mislead' the people about Ms. Gandhi were going to be victims of their own vicious propaganda. The Congress spokesman compared Ms. Gandhi's decision to quit the twin positions of MP and National Advisory Council chairperson and the conduct of the Jharkhand MLAs who took shelter in Rajasthan. Turning to the former BJP president L.K. Advani's proposed yatra, Mr. Singhvi described him as an "All India Nowhere Destination Traveller."

(6939) Chennai: Dravida Munnetra Kazhagam president M. Karunanidhi on Wednesday released the party's election manifesto for the Assembly election, promising a world of concessions and goodies to the people, especially farmers and women. Quality rice at Rs. 2 a kg on ration cards, free colour television for every family "for women's recreation and general knowledge," a maternity assistance of Rs. 1,000 a month for six months, wavier of all cooperative loans to farmers and free electricity to weavers in addition to farmers, were some of the highlights. The DMK has promised free gas stove to all poor women, a monthly financial assistance up to Rs. 300 to unemployed youth, assignment of two acres to landless poor families, restoration of all concessions withdrawn to government employees and teachers and reservation for Muslim and Christians.

(6940) Hyderabad: APCC president K.Keshava Rao has begun ironing out his party's differences with the Telangana Rashtra Samithi (TRS) leadership. He had two meetings with TRS president K.Chandrasekhara Rao in the past one week and also met the dissident TRS leaders on Wednesday morning. Although Dr.Keshava Rao described what transpired among them as "purely political talk," it is learnt that he is trying to bridge the gap between the two estranged allies to prevent any damage to the ruling party in the upcoming panchayat elections. Dr. Keshava Rao reportedly reiterated the Congress stand and advised the TRS president not to precipitate matters by hasty decisions. The meeting with the 'dissident' TRS leaders led by Mandadi Satyanarayana Reddy on Wednesday morning was also just "political talk" and in the interest of both the parties, he said.

(6941) Perinthalmanna : CPI(M) State secretary Pinarayi Vijayan has said that the results of the coming Assembly elections will have a bearing on the way the United Progressive Alliance (UPA) Government handles national and international issues that affect the people of the country. He also said that the Indian Union Muslim League (IUML) is not interested in the welfare of the Muslim community. Instead, it is power hungry.

(6942) Bhopal: Senior leader of the Bharatiya Janata Party (BJP) Venkaiah Naidu told a press conference here on Wednesday that the Bharat Suraksha Yatra, to be led by former party president L.K. Advani and his successor Rajnath Singh, was aimed at raising the issue of national security and spreading awareness about the failure of the United Progressive Alliance (UPA) Government on all fronts.

(6943) Patna: Railway Minister and Rashtriya Janata Dal chief Lalu Prasad on Wednesday outwitted Cabinet colleague and Lok Jan Shakti

Party leader Ram Vilas Paswan and Bihar Chief Minister Nitish Kumar in the first major political battle after the Assembly elections.

(6944) Berhampur (Orissa): Communist Party of India (Marxist) leader Brinda Karat on Wednesday criticised the Centre and different State Governments for facilitating transfer of tribal land to various companies in the name of development and industrialisation. "Although there was a very specific provision in the Constitution for protection of tribal land, it is being violated by the authorities in connivance with industrial houses," Ms. Karat said.

(6945) Chennai: The Samajwadi Party has won the Uttar Pradesh Assembly by-election to Karoram (Gorakhpur district) constituency held on Tuesday. This victory, and the consequent defeat of the Congress "reveals how hollow the media hype is about Ms. Sonia Gandhi's popularity," the Janata Party president Subramanian Swamy has said.

(6946) New Delhi: Terming the notification on the mixed land use policy by the Union Urban Development Ministry as a "historic step", Delhi Pradesh Congress Committee president Ram Babu Sharma on Wednesday said the credit for giving relief to lakhs of small traders goes to Congress president Sonia Gandhi and the United Progressive Alliance Government at the Centre.

(6947) Jaipur: The proposed "Bharat Suraksha Yatra" of the BJP leader, L.K. Advani — which is set to criss-cross Rajasthan — was an issue of concern in the State Assembly on Wednesday with the Opposition Congress members expressing anxiety over its potential to instigate trouble and disturb law and order. The House witnessed noisy scenes when the Congress MLAs pointed out that the yatra would cross the regions which had recorded communal violence in the past and could lead to tension again. The treasury members pointed out that the objective of the simultaneous yatras of Mr. Advani and BJP president Rajnath Singh was to strengthen security and national integration.

(6948) Lucknow: The Uttar Pradesh Government on Wednesday passed a Bill in Assembly upgrading U.P. Development Council into an autonomous body with powers like local authority, thus taking another step to save the disqualification process against Rajya Sabha member Amar Singh. Although BJP members protested the passing of bill in a hurry and demanded it be referred to the House's select committee, Chief Minister Mulayam Singh Yadav said the only motive to upgrade UPDC was to give more teeth for development. When passed and approved by the U.P. Governor, UPDC Act-2006 would be implemented with retrospective effect from October 15, 2003, the day when the Council was registered under the Societies Act.

(6949) Chennai: Chief Minister Jayalalithaa is inclined to join the third front and has accepted the views of Samajwadi Party (SP) president Mulayam Singh Yadav, according to the party's chief whip in the Rajya Sabha Uday Pratap Singh. Mr. Singh told reporters after inaugurating the State headquarters of the SP here on Wednesday that he was confident that the AIADMK would be one of the major constituents of the front. The Left parties and Telugu Desam president Chandrababu Naidu were open to the idea floated by the SP. It was in touch with some non-Congress, non-BJP parties, which had also shown interest. People were tired of the United Progressive Alliance led by the Congress and the Bharatiya Janata Party-led National Democratic Alliance. The third front was the only alternative. Mr. Singh said the SP was strengthening its base outside Uttar Pradesh. In Tamil Nadu it would make its effective presence felt in the Assembly elections.

31-03-2006

(6950) Hyderabad: The Communist Party of India (Marxist) has demanded that the Government put an immediate halt to the ongoing works on Indirasagar (Polavaram) project in the non-tribal areas as it amounted to violation of the norms laid down by the Union Ministry of Environment and Forests.

(6951) Hyderabad: Claiming that there was political consensus on separate statehood for Telangana now, Telangana Rashtra Samiti president K. Chandrasekhara Rao asserted that it was just a matter of time before the State would come into existence. Mr. Rao, who had called on APCC president K. Keshava Rao twice in the last few days, met former Congress Legislature Party leader P. Janardhan Reddy at his residence here on Thursday over lunch. Later, Mr. Rao told reporters that major political parties, barring the Telugu Desam Party, had opined that creation of Telangana State was inevitable.

(6952) Pondicherry : Actor and Desiya Murpokku Dravida Kazhagam (DMDK) president Vijaykant on Thursday said his party would not ally with any other outfit.

(6953) Palakkad : Leader of the Opposition V.S. Achuthanandan has said that he had informed the Communist Party of India (Marxist) Polit Bureau about his intention not to contest earlier, but considering protests by people and party workers, it had to retract the decision not to field him.

(6954) New Delhi : Bharatiya Janata Party leader Murli Manohar Joshi on Thursday demanded that the UPA Government take the nation into confidence to dispel the apprehensions over the India-U.S. nuclear deal. Addressing a press conference here, Dr. Joshi said people hardly knew the details of the "Waiver Authority Bill" (WAB) introduced by the Bush Administration in the U.S. Congress on March 16. "After going through the Bill my apprehensions about compromising of our energy security have come true," he said.

(6955) Amethi (U.P.): Congress member of Parliament Rahul Gandhi on Thursday said both his sister Priyanka Vadra and he backed their mother Sonia Gandhi's decision to resign as MP and chairperson of the National Advisory Council in the wake of the Opposition attack on the office of profit issue.

(6956) Tinsukia: Expressing satisfaction over the law and order situation in Assam, Congress president Sonia Gandhi claimed on Thursday that it was her party's Government that was responsible for the "improved situation." Whatever progress had been achieved was during the Congress-led regime at the Centre and in the State, she said at an election rally here. The party had assumed power at a critical juncture, and it had taken a long time to improve the situation. "We have, however, consolidated the situation in Assam and have started the long journey of progress and development, which will continue and be further improvedunder the Congress," Ms. Gandhi, who was attired in a traditional Assamese sari, said.

(6957) New Delhi : Stating that the biggest mistake of his life was to accept the advice of senior BJP leader L.K. Advani to resign as Chief Minister of Delhi in 1995, suspended BJP leader Madan Lal Khurana on Thursday announced that he would embark on a "rath yatra" in the Capital next month to highlight the problems being faced by the people.

(6958) Pondicherry: The Lok Jansakthi party will go it alone in 10 Assembly constituencies in the coming polls in Pondicherry, according to the State unit president of the party C. M. Puratchi Vendhan.

(6959) Lucknow: Announcing to field a woman candidate from Rae Bareli parliamentary constituency against Congress president Sonia Gandhi, expelled BJP leader Uma Bharti said on Thursday that she would be the 'shadow' candidate against Congress leader. Seeking to blast 'sacrificial' image of Ms Sonia Gandhi in her own firebrand manner, the sadhvi-turned-politician disclosed that she wanted to contest from Rae Bareli herself but for the constraint of time in view of the launching of her new party by April 30.

(6960) Chennai : The election promises of the Dravida Munnetra Kazhagam - providing quality rice at Rs.2 a kg and securing more funds from the Centre - are "just empty words," Bharatiya Janata Party `prabhari' (in-charge) for Tamil Nadu, Bandaru Dattatreya, said on Thursday.

